# The Heinemann World Atlas

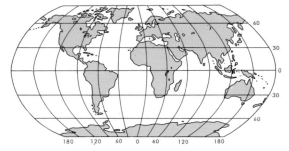

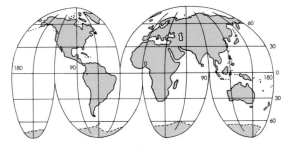

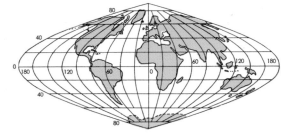

# The Heinemann World Atlas

HEINEMANN : LONDON

# Contents

**Index to Maps**  4

**Legend to Maps**  5

**The World**  6–19
Maps and Map Projections  6
Physical Earth  8
Climatic Regions  10
Natural Vegetation  12
Population Density  14
Predominant Economies  16
Earth Structure  18

**The Oceans**  20–27
Atlantic Ocean Floor  22
Pacific Ocean Floor  24
Indian Ocean Floor  26
Arctic Ocean Floor  27
South Polar Ocean Floor  27

**Planets and Earth-Sun Relations**  28

**North Sea Energy Resources**  29

**Environment Maps**  30–45
Environment Map Legend  30
Europe  32
Northern Asia  34
Southern Asia  36
Africa  38
Australia and New Zealand  40

North America  42
South America  44

**National Flags**  46–47

**Comparative World Time**  48–49

**Political-Physical Maps**  50–103
Europe  50
British Isles  52
Southern England and Wales  54
Central England  56
Northern Scotland  58
Ireland  60
Northern Europe  62
Southern Scandinavia  64
Central Europe  66
France and the Alps  68
Spain and Portugal  70
Italy  72
Southeastern Europe  74
Western and Central Soviet Union  76
Eastern and Central Soviet Union  78
China, Japan and Korea  80
Southeast Asia  82
India, Pakistan and Southwest Asia  84
Western North Africa  86
Eastern North Africa  88
Southern Africa  90
Australia and New Zealand  92

Canada  94
United States  96
Middle America  98
Northern South America  100
Southern South America  102

**World Political Information Table**  104–108

**Largest Metropolitan Areas of the World, 1978**  109

**Index to Political-Physical Maps**  110–128

## Index to Maps

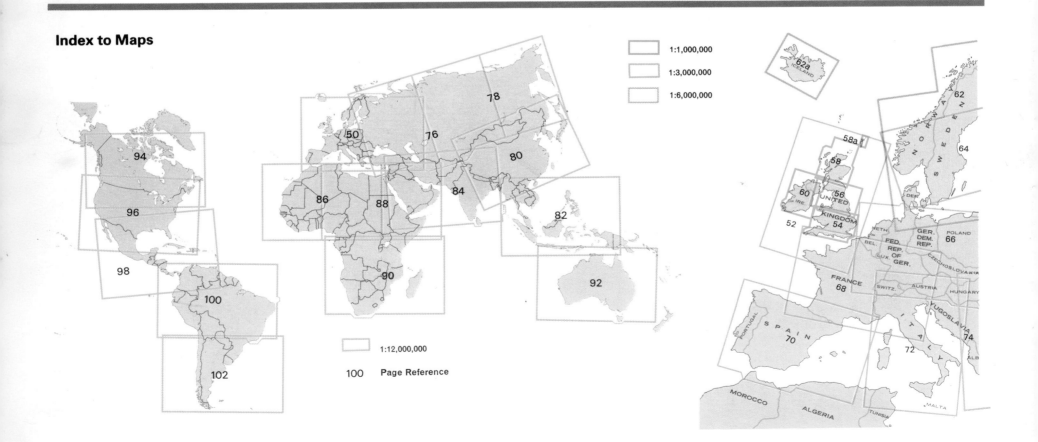

1:1,000,000
1:3,000,000
1:6,000,000
1:12,000,000

100  Page Reference

First published in Great Britain in 1979
by William Heinemann Ltd
15 Queen St., Mayfair, London W1X 8BE

Designed and Edited by
Rand McNally & Company
P.O. Box 7600, Chicago, Illinois 60680

# Legend to Maps

## Inhabited Localities

The symbol represents the number of inhabitants within the locality

| 1:1,000,000 | • 0—10,000 | 1:12,000,000 | · 0—50,000 |
| 1:3,000,000 | ○ 10,000—25,000 | | ⊙ 50,000—100,000 |
| 1:6,000,000 | ⊚ 25,000—100,000 | | ⊡ 100,000—250,000 |
| | ⊡ 100,000—250,000 | | ⊟ 250,000—1,000,000 |
| | ▣ 250,000—1,000,000 | | ■ >1,000,000 |
| | ■ >1,000,000 | | |

▭ **Urban Area** (area of continuous industrial, commercial, and residential development)

The size of type indicates the relative economic and political importance of the locality

| Écommoy | Lisieux | **Rouen** |
| Trouville | **Orléans** | **PARIS** |

Hollywood □  Section of a City, Neighbourhood
Westminster

Bi'r Safājah °  Inhabited Oasis    Kurdwi °  Uninhabited Oasis

### Capitals of Political Units

**BUDAPEST**  Independent Nation

**Cayenne**  Dependency (Colony, protectorate, etc.)

GALAPAGOS (Ecuador)  Administering Country

Villarica  State, Province, etc.

White Plains  County, Oblast, etc.

### Alternate Names

Basel / Bâle   **MOSKVA** / 'MOSCOW  English or second official language names are shown in reduced size lettering

Ventura (San Buenaventura)   Volgograd (Stalingrad)  Historical or other alternates in the local language are shown in parentheses

## Transportation

| 1:12,000,000 | 1:3,000,000 / 1:6,000,000 | 1:1,000,000 | |
|---|---|---|---|
| | | PENNSYLVANIA TURNPIKE | Primary Road |
| | | | Secondary Road |
| | | | Minor Road, Trail |
| | | CANADIAN NATIONAL | Primary Railway |
| | ✈ | CHICAGO-MIDWAY AIRPORT ✈ | Airport |

MACKINAC BRIDGE  Bridge    ··········  Shipping Channel

GREAT ST. BERNARD TUNNEL  Tunnel    Canal du Midi  Navigable Canal

TO CALAIS  Ferry    Intracoastal Waterway

## Metric-English Equivalents

Areas represented by one square centimeter at various map scales

| ▭ | 1:1,000,000 / 100 km² / 39 square miles | ▭ | 1:6,000,000 / 3,600 km² / 1,390 square miles |
| ▭ | 1:3,000,000 / 900 km² / 348 square miles | ▭ | 1:12,000,000 / 14,400 km² / 5,558 square miles |

Meter=3.28 feet    Meter² (m²)=10.76 square feet
Kilometer=0.62 mile    Kilometer² (km²)=0.39 square mile

## Political Boundaries

International (First-order political unit)

1:1,000,000
1:3,000,000
1:6,000,000    1:12,000,000

Demarcated, Undemarcated, and Administrative

Disputed de jure

Indefinite or Undefined

Demarcation Line

Internal

State, Province, etc. (Second-order political unit)

County, Oblast, etc. (Third-order political unit)

*ANDALUCIA*  Historical Region (No boundaries indicated)

## Miscellaneous Cultural Features

PARQUE NACIONAL CANAIMA  National or State Park or Monument

FORT CLATSOP NAT. MEM.  National or State Historic(al) Site, Memorial

BLACKFOOT IND. RES.  Indian Reservation

FORT DIX  Military Installation

TANGLEWOOD  Point of Interest (Battlefield, cave, historical site, etc.)

STEINHAUSEN  Church, Monastery

UXMAL  Ruins

WINDSOR CASTLE  Castle

AMISTAD DAM  Dam

Quarry or Surface Mine

Subsurface Mine

## Hydrographic Features

Shoreline

Undefined or Fluctuating Shoreline

Amur  River, Stream

Intermittent Stream

Rapids, Falls

Irrigation or Drainage Canal

Reef

764 ▽  Depth of Water

The Everglades  Swamp

SEWARD GLACIER  Glacier

L. Victoria  Lake, Reservoir

Tuz Gölü  Salt Lake

Intermittent Lake, Reservoir

Dry Lake Bed

(395)  Lake Surface Elevation

## Topographic Features

Mt. Kenya △ 5199  Elevation Above Sea Level

76 ▽  Elevation Below Sea Level

Mount Cook ▲ 3764  Highest Elevation in Country

Khyber Pass 1067  Mountain Pass

133 ▼  Lowest Elevation in Country

(106)  Elevation of City

Lava

Sand Area

Salt Flat

**A N D E S** / KUNLUNSHANMAI  Mountain Range, Plateau, Valley, etc.

BAFFIN ISLAND / NUNIVAK ISLAND  Island

POLUOSTROV / KAMČATKA / CABO DE HORNOS  Peninsula, Cape, Point, etc.

Elevations and depths are given in meters
Highest Elevation and Lowest Elevation of a continent are underlined

# Maps and Map Projections

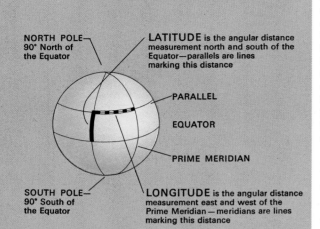

NORTH POLE—
90° North of
the Equator

LATITUDE is the angular distance
measurement north and south of the
Equator—parallels are lines
marking this distance

PARALLEL

EQUATOR

PRIME MERIDIAN

SOUTH POLE—
90° South of
the Equator

LONGITUDE is the angular distance
measurement east and west of the
Prime Meridian—meridians are lines
marking this distance

## CONIC PROJECTIONS

### Simple Conic

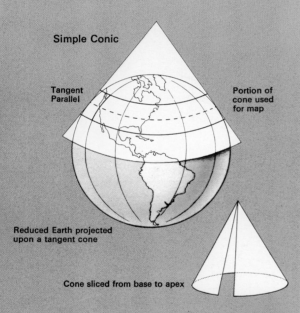

Tangent
Parallel

Portion of
cone used
for map

Reduced Earth projected
upon a tangent cone

Cone sliced from base to apex

Cone developed
onto a flat surface

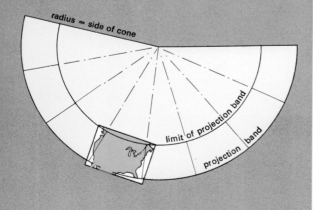

radius = side of cone

limit of projection band

projection band

From the earliest crude drawing to the latest
highly accurate, skilled execution, maps have
played a very important part in man's understanding of the planet upon which he lives. For
only through the map, a reduced representation
of the Earth's surface, can man visualize information about the location of places and things.
Cities, rivers, mountain ranges, and transportation routes take on new meaning when viewed in
relation to one another. Maps expand our con-
ceptions about areas. The following is designed
to point up some significant elements of map
projections which are useful in intelligently inter-
preting maps and the variety of information they
contain.

## Map Projections

The systematic arrangement of parallels and meridians
on a plane or flat surface is the framework upon which a
map is constructed, and this orderly network is called a
map projection. Projections are actually developed
through the use of mathematical formulae. The process
can best be comprehended by visualizing the following
four steps.

1. The earth reduced to a small sphere.

2. Geometric forms—cone, cylinder, plane surface—
placed upon or around this sphere.

3. Transferral of the Earth's imaginary grid of parallels
and meridians to one of these forms.

4. The form flattened, producing the projection.

When projecting the Earth's curved surface to a flat
surface, the *scale* of the map is never consistent
throughout, and there may be some distortion of
*shapes* of landmasses, and of *area* and *direction* representation. By planning the arrangement of the parallels
and meridians some of these important properties can
be preserved undistorted. However, to do so, one or
more of the other properties must be sacrificed, for only
the spherically shaped globe can represent all the
characteristics and properties of the Earth's grid abso-
lutely.

The text and diagrams on these pages treat some of
the projections found in this atlas, their development,
their properties, and characteristics.

## Conic Projections

The Simple Conic or Conic as it is often called, the
Lambert Conformal Conic, and the Polyconic, as their
names imply, are all conically derived. Many of the
maps in the atlas utilize conic projections. Parallels and
meridians are projected onto a cone that is tangent to
the reduced earth. Slicing the cone from its base to
apex and flattening it onto a flat surface results in the
Simple Conic Projection. Along the line that is tangent
to the surface, the scale of the map is true. This line,
usually a parallel, is called a standard parallel. As regions away from this line are mapped, the alterations of
scale, shape, areal size, and direction increase. See
pages 32—33 for example.

The Lambert Conformal Conic Projection is similar to
the Simple Conic, but it is modified so that the cone
intersects the sphere in two places and thus provides
two lines along which scale is true. Unlike the simple
conic, the parallels and meridians are arranged in such
a way as to retain correct shapes of regions throughout
the map. This is conformality. Though the scale does
vary as one moves away from the standard parallels, by
selecting parallels that are closely spaced and by avoid-
ing a region with a great north-south extent, relatively
little distortion occurs. See pages 54—55 for an example.

The Polyconic Projection is formed by combining the
surface of many cones to produce a projection with
many standard parallels, in the fashion illustrated here.
When flattening the surfaces of the cones, there is con-
siderable stretching and consequent distortion toward
the periphery. Again, by utilizing only the central portion of the projection (coloured part of the diagram) the
distorted area can be avoided and a map which
minimizes scale alteration, shape, area, and direction
distortion results. See the illustration to the right for an
example.

## Cylindrical Projections

By projecting the Earth's grid onto a tangent cylinder,
we can achieve a series of parallels and meridians at
right angles to one another, as they are on the Earth.

### Lambert Conformal Conic

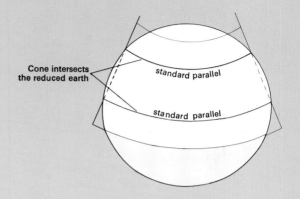

Cone intersects
the reduced earth

standard parallel

standard parallel

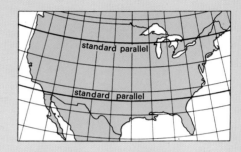

standard parallel

standard parallel

After flattening the cone, minor mathematical
adjustments create the Lambert Conformal
Conic with two standard parallels

### Polyconic Projection

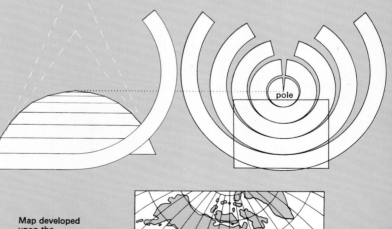

pole

Map developed
upon the
portion of the projection
with least distortion

## CYLINDRICAL PROJECTIONS

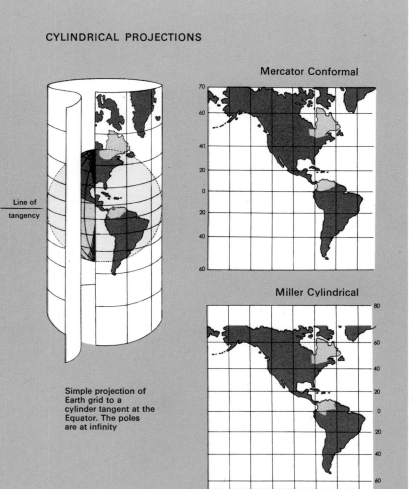

Line of tangency

Simple projection of Earth grid to a cylinder tangent at the Equator. The poles are at infinity

Mercator Conformal

Miller Cylindrical

## PLANE PROJECTIONS

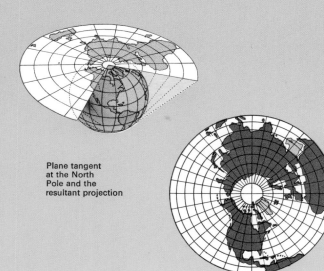

Plane tangent at the North Pole and the resultant projection

Lambert Equal Area Projection

However, sizes of areas and scales are extremely distorted as regions away from the line of tangency are mapped.

The Mercator Conformal Projection is a modification of this method of projecting. On it latitudinal distances are increased in the same proportion as longitudinal distances increase. The chief use of this familiar Mercator Projection has been in navigation because upon it straight lines represent constant compass directions. It shows the correct shapes of limited regions, but exaggerates areas in polar regions.

The Miller Projection was developed for general reference maps showing the entire world. Here, too, the parallels and meridians meet at right angles, but the latitudinal distances are not increased in proportion to the longitudinal distances, and for this reason shapes of landmasses are distorted toward polar regions, as is direction representation. However, exaggeration of area and scale has been reduced.

The three cylindrical projections illustrated here show how the same outlined regions look on all three. Notice that on all the maps there is a difference between the regions' areal extent; however, the difference is minimized by the Miller Projection. Comparison of the shapes of the regions with those on a globe shows the Mercator indicating this property most accurately. Other cylindrical projections enable the areas to be correctly shown while distorting the shapes of the landmasses; the cylinder may be tangent to the reduced earth at a position other than the Equator, thereby shifting the zone of least distortion to that region. There is a Miller Projection used on pages 48–49.

### Plane Projections

Here transformation of the sphere directly to a tangent flat surface is the method of projection. The Lambert Azimuthal Equal Area Projection is one upon which the correct relationships between areas have been maintained. For instance, Greenland and the lower portion of the Arabian Peninsula, which are approximately the same in areal extent, appear to be so on the Lambert Azimuthal Equal Area Projection. Notice, however, that although Africa's area is shown correctly, it has been stretched in one direction and compressed in another, thus altering its shape and the scale of the projection. By arranging the spacing of the parallels and meridians differently on the plane surface, true shape (conformality), consistent scale, or correct directions from the centre in all directions may also be obtained instead of the equal area property. In any case, retention of the one important property of the sphere creates extreme distortion of all the other properties as regions away from the centre of the projection (the point of tangency) are mapped. See pages 42–43 for an example of the Lambert Azimuthal Equal Area projection.

### Equal Area Projections of the World

To show the world in its entirety on a flat surface so that areas may be compared intelligently, is extremely difficult without altering the shapes of areas without recognition. Cylindrical projections do not accomplish this, and plane and conic projections also do not represent the whole world this way. Two projections are frequently used today to accomplish this — the Homolographic and the Sinusoidal. Each retains the equal area property of the sphere, although each sacrifices uniform scale and invites some extreme shape compression and shearing in the polar areas of the projections.

Using the Homolographic from 40° to the poles and the Sinusoidal from the Equator to 40°, J. Paul Goode took advantage of each of these projections to create the Goode's Interrupted Homolosine Projection. This technique of interrupting a projection can be better understood by visualizing the surface of the earth peeled and laid flat. Splitting in the oceanic regions enables the land areas to remain relatively free from shape distortion and allows the land areas to be realistically compared for size. See pages 18–19 for an example.

In summary, where maps cover approximately a hemisphere of the Earth's surface, extreme distortion of some type is evidenced. On most of the maps in the atlas, however, individual choices of projections have been made to present a realistic picture of the Earth. With these maps the user may compare sizes of areas, shapes of landmasses, and measure distances and directions as accurately as necessary.

## EQUAL AREA PROJECTIONS OF THE WORLD

Mollweide Homolographic (Equal Area)

Sinusoidal

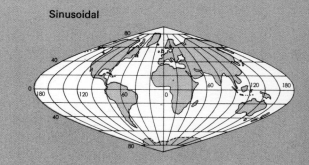

Goode's Interrupted Homolosine

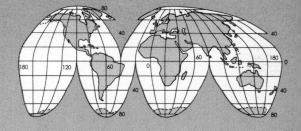

# Physical Earth

One centimeter represents 750 kilometers.
One inch represents approximately 1200 miles.

Robinson Projection

Scale 1:75,000,000

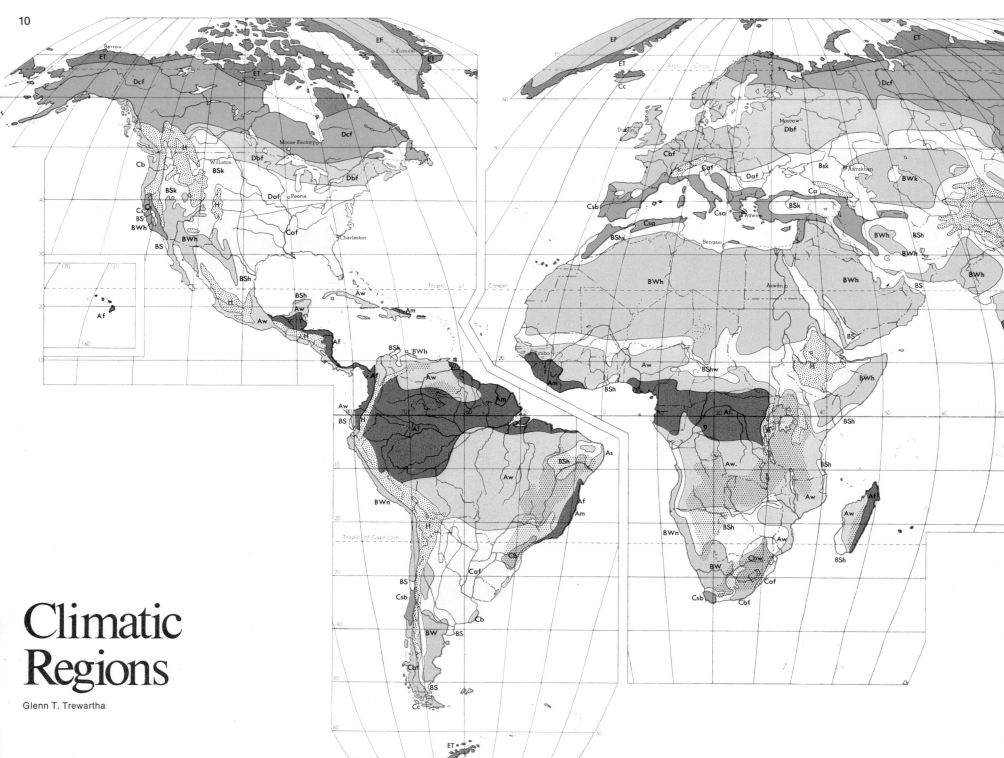

# Climatic Regions

Glenn T. Trewartha

Rupinder Khullar/Van Cleve

Polar Ice Cap (EF) climate in Antarctica has average monthly temperatures that never rise above freezing (0° C.). Snow that falls doesn't melt, but accumulates to form Antarctica's polar ice cap.

Right. Tropical Monsoon (Am) climates have wet and dry seasons. Western India's monsoon (wet) season is a time of heavy rainfall and constantly cloudy skies.

Below. Humid continental (Daf) climates have warm summers, and severe winters and rain through the year. In summer months cumulus clouds may develop into thunderheads that produce violent rainfall.

R. O'Neill

Betty Crowell/Van Cleve

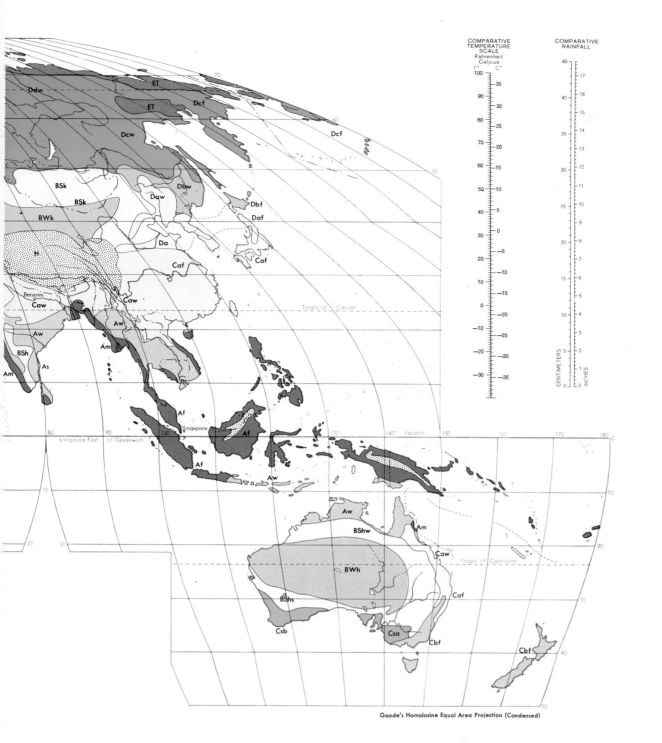

Goode's Homolosine Equal Area Projection (Condensed)

COMPARATIVE TEMPERATURE SCALE
Fahrenheit Celsius
F° C°
100 — 35
90 — 30
80 — 25
70 — 20
60 — 15
50 — 10
40 — 5
30 — 0
20 — -5
— -10
10 — -15
0 — -20
-10 — -25
— -30
-20 —
-30 — -35

COMPARATIVE RAINFALL
45 — 17
— 16
40 — 15
— 14
35 — 13
— 12
30 — 11
— 10
25 —
— 9
20 — 8
— 7
15 — 6
— 5
10 — 4
— 3
5 — 2
— 1
CENTIMETERS   INCHES

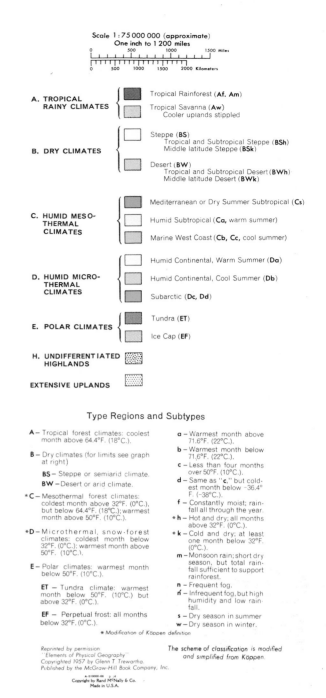

Scale 1:75 000 000 (approximate)
One inch to 1 200 miles
0   500   1000   1500 Miles
0   500   1000   1500   2000 Kilometers

A. TROPICAL RAINY CLIMATES
  Tropical Rainforest (Af, Am)
  Tropical Savanna (Aw)
    Cooler uplands stippled

B. DRY CLIMATES
  Steppe (BS)
    Tropical and Subtropical Steppe (BSh)
    Middle latitude Steppe (BSk)
  Desert (BW)
    Tropical and Subtropical Desert (BWh)
    Middle latitude Desert (BWk)

C. HUMID MESO-THERMAL CLIMATES
  Mediterranean or Dry Summer Subtropical (Cs)
  Humid Subtropical (Ca, warm summer)
  Marine West Coast (Cb, Cc, cool summer)

D. HUMID MICRO-THERMAL CLIMATES
  Humid Continental, Warm Summer (Da)
  Humid Continental, Cool Summer (Db)
  Subarctic (Dc, Dd)

E. POLAR CLIMATES
  Tundra (ET)
  Ice Cap (EF)

H. UNDIFFERENTIATED HIGHLANDS

EXTENSIVE UPLANDS

### Type Regions and Subtypes

A – Tropical forest climates: coolest month above 64.4°F. (18°C.).

B – Dry climates (for limits see graph at right)

  BS – Steppe or semiarid climate.

  BW – Desert or arid climate.

*C – Mesothermal forest climates: coldest month above 32°F. (0°C.), but below 64.4°F. (18°C.); warmest month above 50°F. (10°C.).

*D – Microthermal, snow-forest climates: coldest month below 32°F. (0°C.); warmest month above 50°F. (10°C.).

E – Polar climates: warmest month below 50°F. (10°C.).

  ET – Tundra climate: warmest month below 50°F. (10°C.) but above 32°F. (0°C.).

  EF – Perpetual frost: all months below 32°F. (0°C.).

a – Warmest month above 71.6°F. (22°C.).
b – Warmest month below 71.6°F. (22°C.).
c – Less than four months over 50°F. (10°C.).
d – Same as "c," but coldest month below -36.4°F. (-38°C.).
f – Constantly moist; rainfall all through the year.
*h – Hot and dry; all months above 32°F. (0°C.).
*k – Cold and dry; at least one month below 32°F. (0°C.).
m – Monsoon rain; short dry season, but total rainfall sufficient to support rainforest.
n – Frequent fog.
ñ – Infrequent fog, but high humidity and low rainfall.
s – Dry season in summer.
w – Dry season in winter.

* Modification of Köppen definition

Reprinted by permission
"Elements of Physical Geography"
Copyrighted 1957 by Glenn T. Trewartha.
Published by the McGraw-Hill Book Company, Inc.

The scheme of classification is modified and simplified from Köppen.

A-519000-86
Copyright by Rand McNally & Co.
Made in U.S.A.

R. O'Neill

Left. Tropical Desert (BWh) climates are continuously hot and dry. Saharan skies are almost always clear; the sun's glare is constant during the day.

Lower Left. Tropical Savanna (Aw) climates are hot throughout the year. However alternating wet and dry seasons affect vegetation. During the dry winter season, East Africa's grasses are dormant.

Below. High (H) climates include climate zones by altitude in mountainous areas. North America's Mt. Rainier has a zone of permanent snow.

R. O'Neill

Robert Frerck

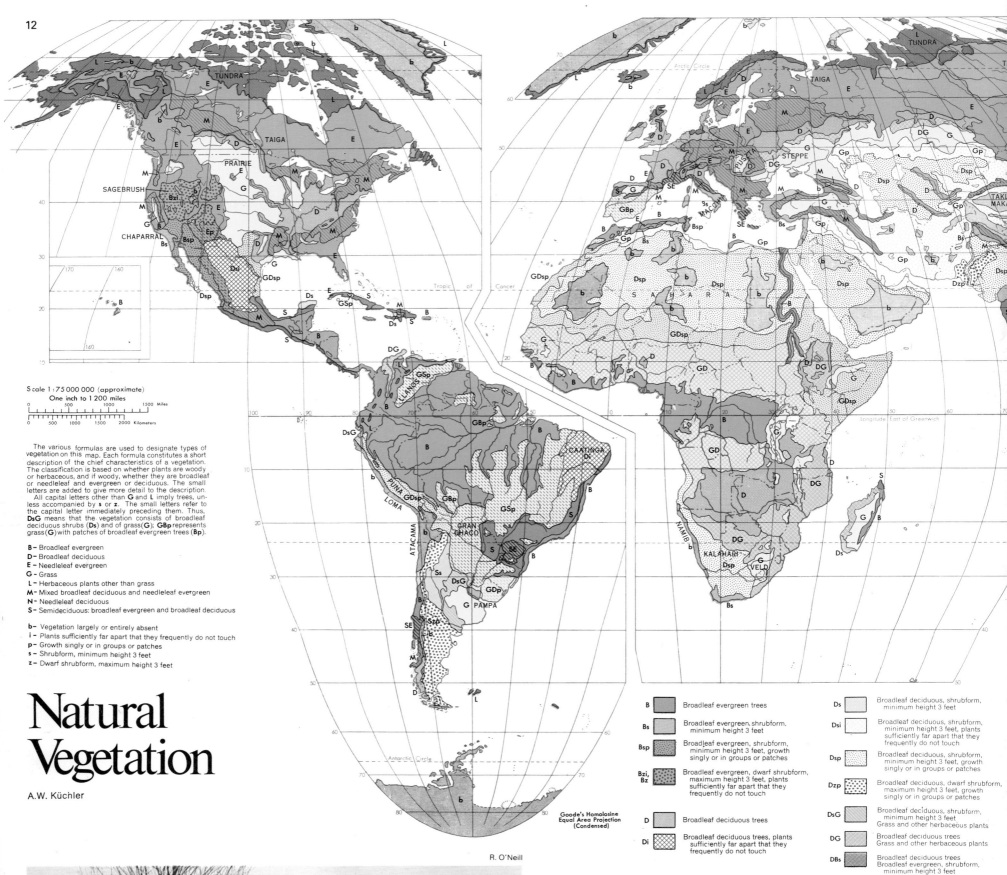

Scale 1:75 000 000 (approximate)
One inch to 1 200 miles

The various formulas are used to designate types of vegetation on this map. Each formula constitutes a short description of the chief characteristics of a vegetation. The classification is based on whether plants are woody or herbaceous, and if woody, whether they are broadleaf or needleleaf and evergreen or deciduous. The small letters are added to give more detail to the description.

All capital letters other than **G** and **L** imply trees, unless accompanied by **s** or **z**. The small letters refer to the capital letter immediately preceding them. Thus, **DsG** means that the vegetation consists of broadleaf deciduous shrubs (**Ds**) and of grass (**G**); **GBp** represents grass (**G**) with patches of broadleaf evergreen trees (**Bp**).

**B** – Broadleaf evergreen
**D** – Broadleaf deciduous
**E** – Needleleaf evergreen
**G** – Grass
**L** – Herbaceous plants other than grass
**M** – Mixed broadleaf deciduous and needleleaf evergreen
**N** – Needleleaf deciduous
**S** – Semideciduous: broadleaf evergreen and broadleaf deciduous

**b** – Vegetation largely or entirely absent
**i** – Plants sufficiently far apart that they frequently do not touch
**p** – Growth singly or in groups or patches
**s** – Shrubform, minimum height 3 feet
**z** – Dwarf shrubform, maximum height 3 feet

# Natural Vegetation

A.W. Küchler

Goode's Homolosine
Equal Area Projection
(Condensed)

R. O'Neill

| | |
|---|---|
| **B** | Broadleaf evergreen trees |
| **Bs** | Broadleaf evergreen, shrubform, minimum height 3 feet |
| **Bsp** | Broadleaf evergreen, shrubform, minimum height 3 feet, growth singly or in groups or patches |
| **Bzi, Bz** | Broadleaf evergreen, dwarf shrubform, maximum height 3 feet, plants sufficiently far apart that they frequently do not touch |
| **D** | Broadleaf deciduous trees |
| **Di** | Broadleaf deciduous trees, plants sufficiently far apart that they frequently do not touch |

| | |
|---|---|
| **Ds** | Broadleaf deciduous, shrubform, minimum height 3 feet |
| **Dsi** | Broadleaf deciduous, shrubform, minimum height 3 feet, plants sufficiently far apart that they frequently do not touch |
| **Dsp** | Broadleaf deciduous, shrubform, minimum height 3 feet, growth singly or in groups or patches |
| **Dzp** | Broadleaf deciduous, dwarf shrubform, maximum height 3 feet, growth singly or in groups or patches |
| **DsG** | Broadleaf deciduous, shrubform, minimum height 3 feet. Grass and other herbaceous plants |
| **DG** | Broadleaf deciduous trees. Grass and other herbaceous plants |
| **DBs** | Broadleaf deciduous trees. Broadleaf evergreen, shrubform, minimum height 3 feet |

Left. Deciduous trees in the middle latitudes lose their leaves during the cold winter months. These broadleaf deciduous trees remain from the forest that once covered this area.

Below. Broadleaf evergreen shrubs growing in the southwestern United States have adapted to the dry climate. The shrubs' hard waxy leaves help preserve the plants' moisture by slowing the evaporation rate.

R. O'Neill

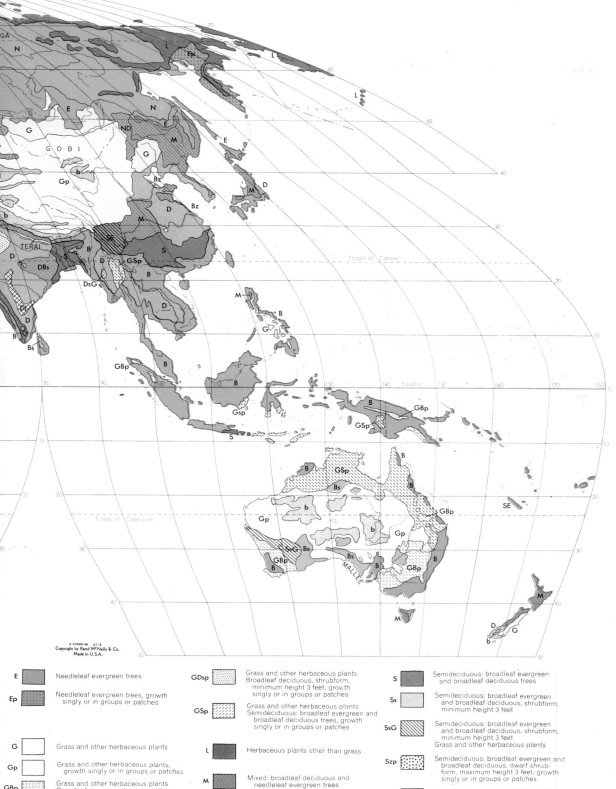

Copyright by Rand McNally & Co.
Made in U.S.A.

|  |  |
|---|---|
| E | Needleleaf evergreen trees |
| Ep | Needleleaf evergreen trees, growth singly or in groups or patches |
| G | Grass and other herbaceous plants |
| Gp | Grass and other herbaceous plants, growth singly or in groups or patches |
| GBp | Grass and other herbaceous plants Broadleaf evergreen trees, growth singly or in groups or patches |
| GD | Grass and other herbaceous plants Broadleaf deciduous trees |
| GDp | Grass and other herbaceous plants Broadleaf deciduous trees, growth singly or in groups or patches |
| GDsp | Grass and other herbaceous plants Broadleaf deciduous, shrubform, minimum height 3 feet, growth singly or in groups or patches |
| GSp | Grass and other herbaceous plants Semideciduous: broadleaf evergreen and broadleaf deciduous trees, growth singly or in groups or patches |
| L | Herbaceous plants other than grass |
| M | Mixed: broadleaf deciduous and needleleaf evergreen trees |
| N | Needleleaf deciduous trees |
| ND | Needleleaf deciduous trees Broadleaf deciduous trees |
| S | Semideciduous: broadleaf evergreen and broadleaf deciduous trees |
| Ss | Semideciduous: broadleaf evergreen and broadleaf deciduous, shrubform, minimum height 3 feet |
| SsG | Semideciduous: broadleaf evergreen and broadleaf deciduous, shrubform, minimum height 3 feet Grass and other herbaceous plants |
| Szp | Semideciduous: broadleaf evergreen and broadleaf deciduous, dwarf shrubform, maximum height 3 feet, growth singly or in groups or patches |
| SE | Semideciduous: broadleaf evergreen and broadleaf deciduous trees Needleleaf evergreen trees |
| b | Vegetation largely or entirely absent |

Lower right. Needleleaf evergreen forests are found in humid areas with cool summers and severe winters. The trees thrive in the infertile acidic soils that hinder deciduous trees' growth.

Below. Parts of deserts may be devoid of vegetation. Not enough moisture is present in the rocky ground to support plant growth.

R. O'Neill

FPG

A natural vegetation area may have several types. Here trees grow on higher ground in a vast slough of grasses and herbaceous plants.

R. O'Neill

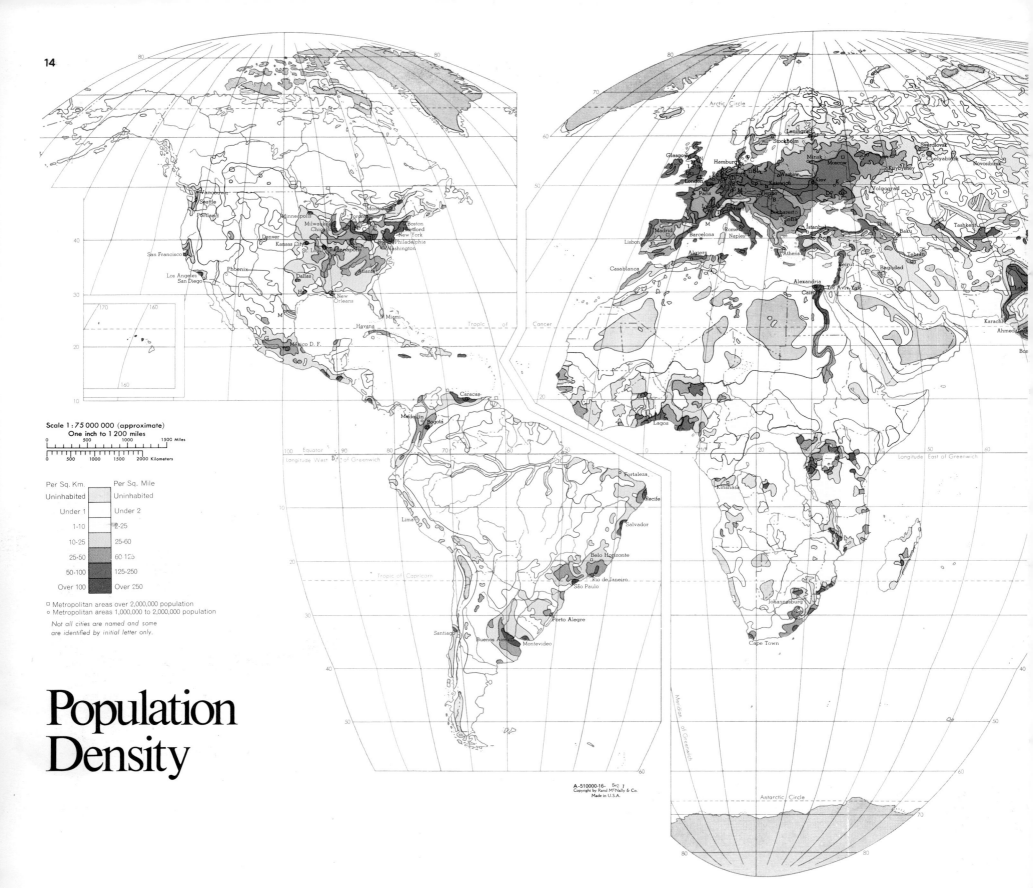

# Population Density

**Scale 1 : 75 000 000 (approximate)**
One inch to 1 200 miles

| Per Sq. Km. | Per Sq. Mile |
|---|---|
| Uninhabited | Uninhabited |
| Under 1 | Under 2 |
| 1-10 | 2-25 |
| 10-25 | 25-60 |
| 25-50 | 60-125 |
| 50-100 | 125-250 |
| Over 100 | Over 250 |

□ Metropolitan areas over 2,000,000 population
○ Metropolitan areas 1,000,000 to 2,000,000 population

*Not all cities are named and some
are identified by initial letter only.*

Central European farm families live in rural villages, a cluster of
houses surrounded by the villagers' fields.

A.E. Schiesel/Van Cleve

In the sparsely settled Arctic aeroplanes often provide Eskimoes
with transportation to schools, hospitals, and fishing grounds.

Ben Strickland/Van Cleve

Goode's Homolosine Equal Area Projection (Condensed)

R. O'Neill

Upper left. Mexico City is densely populated. The people depend on produce markets to supply fresh fruits and vegetables.

Lower left. Rural Egyptian families live in villages of mud brick houses near irrigation channels that provide water.

Lower right. The walled Moroccan town of Moulay Idriss is built on two hills. The 8th century Arab builders chose this location for their settlement because the hills were easy to fortify.

Below. A Bavarian village band marches in Munich's annual Oktoberfest parade. The villagers dress in their traditional attire.

R. O'Neill

R. O'Neill

R. O'Neill

Goode's Homolosine Equal Area Projection (Condensed)

Scale 1 : 75 000 000 (approximate)
One inch to 1 200 miles

# Predominant Economies

Carol Lee/Van Cleve

Lower left. Intensive agriculture supports a dense rural population. Here Indian rice farmers set young plants into the paddies near their village. Rice provides both livelihood and subsistence for the village.

Lower right. European farmers grow several crops and raise livestock on their land. The use of agricultural machinery increases individual productivity. These Hungarian farmers use machinery to make harvesting faster and easier.

Right. Both workers and technology contribute to manufacturing. Workers in an automobile assembly line each perform one specific task on each car body as it moves past them by conveyor.

Rupinder Khullar/Van Cleve

A.E. Schiesel/Van Cleve

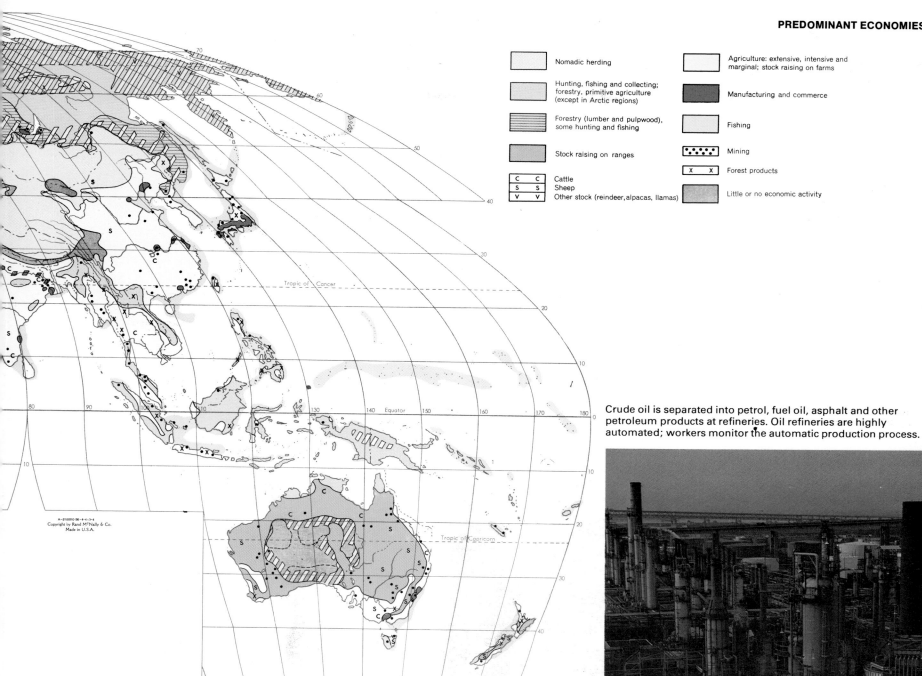

Nomadic herding

Hunting, fishing and collecting; forestry, primitive agriculture (except in Arctic regions)

Forestry (lumber and pulpwood), some hunting and fishing

Stock raising on ranges

C    C    Cattle
S    S    Sheep
V    V    Other stock (reindeer, alpacas, llamas)

Agriculture: extensive, intensive and marginal; stock raising on farms

Manufacturing and commerce

Fishing

Mining

X    X    Forest products

Little or no economic activity

A-310000-98-4-4-3-4
Copyright by Rand McNally & Co.
Made in U.S.A.

O'Neill

R.J. Witkowski/Van Cleve

Crude oil is separated into petrol, fuel oil, asphalt and other petroleum products at refineries. Oil refineries are highly automated; workers monitor the automatic production process.

Left. In handicraft manufacturing the artisan produces goods for sale in his home or shop. This Mexican craftsman is weaving a cotton rug from yarns supplied by his customer.

Lower left. Shipbuilders design and custom-build each ship to meet the specific needs of its purchaser. This highly skilled welder is fitting parts of the hull.

Lower right. Stock raising on open ranges is important in dry regions. Here cowhands round up cattle on the open range in western Canada for shipment to eastern markets.

T. Rhodes/Van Cleve

Barbara Van Cleve/Van Cleve

## Earth Structure and Tectonics

- _ _ _ _  Precambrian stable shield areas
- Exposed Precambrian rock
- Paleozoic and Mesozoic flat-lying sedimentary rocks
- Principal Paleozoic and Mesozoic folded areas
- Cenozoic sedimentary rocks
- Principal Cenozoic folded areas
- Lava plateaus
- Major trends of folding

### Geologic Time Chart

Precambrian—from formation of the earth (at least 4,500 million years ago) to 600 million years ago

Paleozoic—from 600 million to 200 million years ago

Mesozoic—from 200 million to 70 million years ago

Cenozoic—from 70 million years ago to present time

| | | |
|---|---|---|
| Areas of frequent quakes | Mid-ocean rifts | Extinct land volcanoes |
| Areas of intense quakes | Continental rifts | Land volcanoes active within historic time |
| | | Active and extinct submarine volcanoes |

# Earth Structure

Lower left. Soil and organic matter deposited in a shallow coastal lake gradually fills and changes the lake to new land. The trees' roots aid the process by trapping sediments.

Below. Streams erode the land by wearing away the underlying rocks and carrying away soils picked up from their banks.

Right. The Hawaiian islands are volcanic in origin. Several Hawaiian volcanoes including Kilauea are active today. Molten lava from inside the earth can be seen in Kilauea's crater.

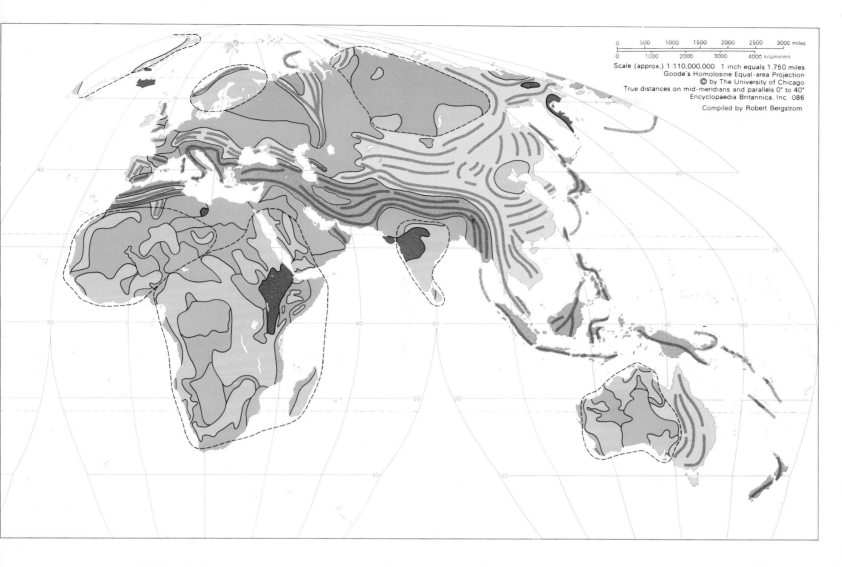

Scale (approx.) 1:110,000,000  1 inch equals 1,750 miles
Goode's Homolosine Equal-area Projection
© by The University of Chicago
True distances on mid-meridians and parallels 0° to 40°
Encyclopaedia Britannica, Inc. 086
Compiled by Robert Bergstrom

## Development of the Earth's Structure

The earth is in process of constant transformation. Movements in the hot, dense interior of the earth result in folding and fracture of the crust and transfer of molten material to the surface. As a result, large structures such as mountain ranges, volcanoes, lava plateaus, and rift valleys are created. The forces that bring about these structural changes are called tectonic forces.

The present continents have developed from stable nuclei, or shields, of ancient (Precambrian) rock. Erosive forces such as water, wind, and ice have worn away particles of the rock,

depositing them at the edges of the shields, where they have accumulated and ultimately become sedimentary rock. Subsequently, in places, these extensive areas of flatlying rock have been elevated, folded, or warped, by the action of tectonic forces, to form mountains. The shape of these mountains has been altered by later erosion. Where the forces of erosion have been at work for a long time, the mountains tend to have a low relief and rounded contours, like the Appalachians. Mountains more recently formed are high and rugged, like the Himalayas.

The map above depicts some of the major geologic structures of the earth and identifies them according to the period of their formation. A geologic time chart is included in the legend. The inset map shows the most important areas of earthquakes, rifts, and volcanic activity. Comparison of all the maps will show the close correlation between present-day mountain systems, recent (Cenozoic) mountain-building, and the areas of frequent earthquakes and active volcanoes.

Below. Tectonic movements may compress and push rock layers up into mountain ranges. Rock layers were compressed and folded to form the Medicine Bow Range in western North America's Rocky Mountains.

Upper right. Waves change the earth's surface by erosion. In southern England the sea cliffs are retreating before the pounding waves.

Lower right. Dead vegetation may accumulate in bogs and form layers of peat. Buried peat layers are a source of energy. In Skye, a Scottish farmer and his sons cut and stack peat for use as fuel.

David Muench/Van Cleve

# The Oceans

Dr. H.W. Menard, Scripps Institution of Oceanography, *Consultant*
The helpful assistance of Dr. Bruce C. Heexen of the Lamont-Doherty Geological Observatory and of the
U.S. Naval Oceanographic Office in the preparation of this section must be gratefully acknowledged

Photographs of earth taken from space dramatize a salient fact: about three-fourths of the planet is covered by water. To be more precise, if all water bodies are counted, 77.2% of the earth's surface is water, with 71.2% being oceans and major seas. Long surrounded by mystery and myth, the oceans have played a vital role in shaping the destiny of man by influencing his settlement patterns, by offering routes of communications, and by providing food. While the impact on man appears most direct at the fringes of the sea, planetary water bodies play a decisive role in producing world climatic realms and thus affect the livelihood of man in virtually every part of the world. By the same token, ocean-influenced climates affect the patterns of growth of flora and fauna.

Despite a centuries-old preoccupation with the seas, man has only recently had the technology to explore the deeps, measure currents and temperatures, and chart the topography of the ocean floor. The vastness of the ocean world is such that despite new scientific tools, man's understanding of the seas still is puny. But every day sees new information added to a rapidly growing store of knowledge, and as a result important new theories have been advanced concerning the characteristics and origins, not only of the oceans, but also of the earth itself. Yet much remains to be done. In a world faced with dwindling resources, man is looking toward the oceans as an important supply of food and minerals. Scientific methods of raising and harvesting crops of fish and other marine life are being perfected. Efficient means for recovering known reserves of oil and mineral resources are being developed. One of the most dramatic results of deep-sea exploration has been the discovery of baseball-size nuggets of high-grade manganese lying on the ocean floor at great depths. It remains to be seen whether economic ways to gather these nodules can be developed. Without question, scientists must develop ways to exploit these resources without harming ecological balances.

Oceanographic research is also directed toward learning more about the seas' influence on climates, the mechanics of tidal movements, and how these and other elements of the sea can be controlled for man's benefit.

The following maps are intended to convey an impression of the physical nature of the world's sea floors, with the graphs and illustrations on the opposite page indicating some characteristics of the water envelope and of the nature of the sea bottom itself. From man's still-sketchy knowledge of the ocean environment some broad patterns of its physical form are emerging. Towering mountain ranges, vast canyons, broad plains, and a variety of physiographic features exceed in magnitude those found on the continents.

Scientific explorations of the last decade have revealed the existence of many distinctive features on the ocean floor, among them being a number of ridges. One of the most pronounced is the Mid-Atlantic Ridge, a lazy-S chain of mountains that bisects the Atlantic Ocean. A remarkable feature of such ridges is a trough that runs along the entire centre, in effect producing twin ridge lines. Away from the centre are a series of parallel and lower crests, while at right angles to them are numerous fracture zones. Measurements of temperatures and magnetism indicate that the troughs are younger in age than the paralleling ridges,

whose ages increase with distance from the centre. It is believed that the central troughs mark a line where molten materials from the earth's interior rise to the ocean floor where they form gigantic plates that move slowly apart. This theory suggests that continents are moving away from each other, having once been a single land mass in ancient times. The matching curves of the Atlantic shorelines of both South America and Africa have long given rise to such conjecture. The map below shows the world-wide distribution of these plates.

Where these subsea plates meet certain continental areas or island chains, they plunge downward to replenish the inner earth materials and form trenches of profound depths. Along the northern and western edge of the Pacific Ocean several lines of such gutters include some of the deepest known spots. Deep trenches also parallel the western coasts of Central and South America, the northern coast of Puerto Rico and the Virgin Islands, and other coastal areas.

Many other unique features have been identified. Great submarine canyons lead from the edges of continents. Seamounts rise miles above the ocean floor. Tablemounts are like seamounts, but culminate in plateau-like summits hundreds of feet below sea level. Continental shelves appear to be underwater extensions of land masses, and vary in shape from narrow fringes to broad plains. The deep floor of the sea itself shows a variety of characteristics. Muddy ooze, piles of rounded rock ("pillow" lava), sand, and coral formations are found in different locations.

With the accumulation of knowledge of the configuration and mechanics of the sea floor, more information about the characteristics of the sea itself is being added. Salinity, pressure, opacity, and temperature are studied to discover how and why they vary spatially and seasonally.

The scales and projections of the maps were selected to show major sea areas in the most optimal way. Thus scales of the Atlantic and Indian oceans are the same, with the Pacific Ocean being somewhat smaller. Coverage for the polar areas is at the same scale. Projections and dimensions maximize the water areas relative to land areas. In general, colours used are those thought to exist on the seafloors. For continental shelves or shallow inland seas, greyish green is used to correspond to terrigenous oozes, sediments washed from continental areas. In deeper parts of the oceans, calcareous oozes derived from the skeletons of marine life appear in various shades of white and the fine mud from land is red. In the Atlantic materials accumulate relatively rapidly, have a high iron content, and thus are a brighter red than elsewhere. Slower sedimentation in the Pacific and Indian oceans result in more manganese and darker colours. Undersea ridges are shown in black to suggest recent upwelling of molten rock. Small salt-and-pepper patches portray areas where manganese nodules are found. Around certain islands, white is used to show coral reefs. Land areas carry a generalized portrayal of continental land forms.

Colours otherwise do not coincide with specific depth zones, and differences in relief are conveyed through the technique of relief shading. The perspective of relief features is from directly above, so that the topmost part of, for example, a seamount corresponds to its actual geographic position.

## World-Wide Distribution of Tectonic Plates

Credit: adapted from a drawing by Scripps Institution of Oceanography

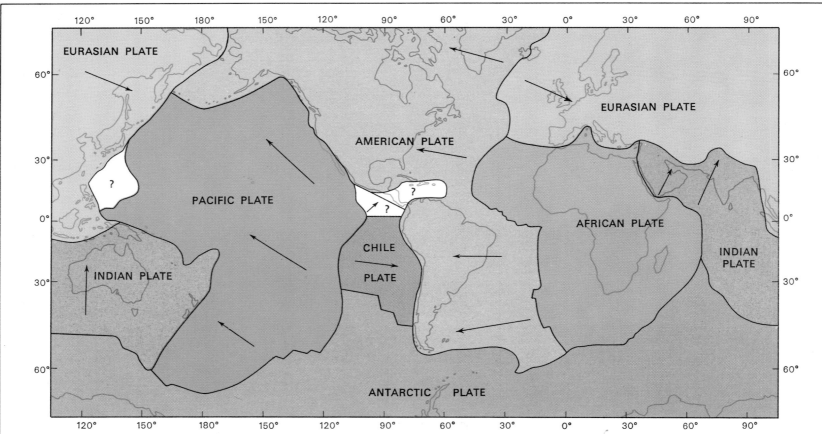

## Sea-Floor Terminology

This glossary should familiarize the reader with some of the important terms associated with undersea features. Because the development of terms describing sea-floor features is so recent, not all of them enjoy universal usage.

**Abyssal Plain:** a nearly flat area of the sea floor, smaller than a basin, and at a greater depth than surrounding features.

**Basin:** a depression of the sea floor usually of moderate or large extent.

**Continental Shelf:** a flat or gently sloping zone surrounding a landmass between its coast and continental slope.

**Continental Slope:** a steep slope at the outer edge of the continental shelf.

**Deep:** the lowest recorded depth in a trench.

**Fault:** a fracture in the sea floor.

**Fracture Zone:** an extensive linear zone of irregular sea floor with parallel faults, seamounts, ridges, and troughs.

**Mid-Ocean Ridge:** an extensive area of roughly parallel ridges and troughs, often crossed by fracture zones, with heights generally well above the surrounding sea floor. Example: Mid-Atlantic Ridge.

**Ridge:** a long narrow elevation of the sea floor with sides.

**Seamount:** an elevation rising 1,000 metres or more from the sea floor, and of limited areal extent at its summit. Several seamounts clustered together may be termed seamount chain, group, province, range, or line.

**Tablemount:** a seamount with a flat top (sometimes called a guyot).

**Trench:** a long, narrow, deep, steep-sided depression of the sea floor.

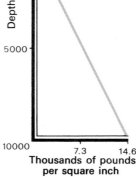

**A.** Pressure increases at a fairly constant rate with depth, although the rate is affected by salinity and temperature variations. At around 10,000 metres, corresponding to the deepest known spot in the ocean, the pressure is nearly 7 tons per square inch, or almost 1,000 times atmospheric pressures at sea level.

**B.** Quantities of dissolved salt, measured in parts per thousands, are shown for open sea areas. At depths below 1,500 metres, measurements indicate similar quantities, but in shallower depths proportions vary.
*Credit:* the salinity graph was adapted from *Descriptive Physical Oceanography*, Dr. G. L. Pickard, Pergamon Press, London, 1963.

**C.** Temperatures in the open ocean show a range of some 17°C (63°F) on the surface, and even more at a depth of 100 metres or so, where, near polar regions, subsurface water can be a few degrees below 0°C (32°F). Because of salt content, ocean water does not freeze until temperatures of −10°C (14°F) are reached.
*Credit:* the temperature graph was adapted from *Descriptive Physical Oceanography*, Dr. G. L. Pickard, Pergamon Press, London, 1963.

**D.** Because of high evaporation rates in the Mediterranean Sea, waters there are more saline than in the Atlantic Ocean. Thus, the denser Mediterranean waters which slip over the sill at the Strait of Gibraltar extend seaward into the Atlantic as a tongue, hundreds of metres below sea level.
*Credit:* the illustration is adapted from *Geographie der Atlantischen Ozeans*, G. Schott, Verlag Boysen, Hamburg, 1942.

**E.** A diagram of the earth's crust including part of South America shows the mechanics of plate tectonics. Molten rock wells up to the centre of mid-ocean ridges, and adds new material to plates that slowly move apart carrying land masses with them. Colliding plates may build volcanic mountains and deep trenches.
*Credit:* adapted from an illustration by Dr. P. Vogt, U.S. Naval Oceanographic Office.

**a.** National Park Service

**b.** Johns Hopkins Press

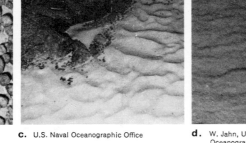

**c.** U.S. Naval Oceanographic Office

**d.** W. Jahn, U.S. Naval Oceanographic Office

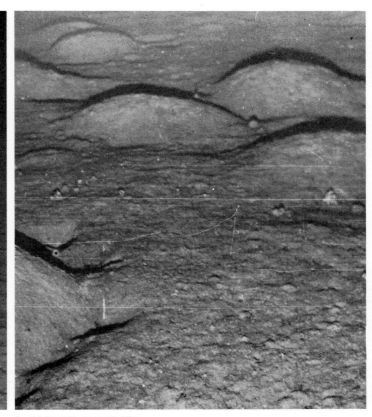

**e.** U.S. Naval Oceanographic Office

**a.** Where seas are shallow, filtering sunlight permits a rich variety of fish, coral, and other animal life. Often showing bright colors, sea life here produces a beautiful ocean world.

**b.** One of the results of deep-sea exploration is the discovery of wide-spread carpets of manganese nodules lying on the sea floor. Despite the high ore content, no economical method for recovery has been devised.

**c.** Molten rock issuing from deep water crevasses cools to form pillow lava. Found on or near underwater mountain chains, pillow lava is associated with activity that causes sea-floor spreading.

**d.** This deep-sea animal is related to living coral and was photographed at a depth of 5,300 metres on the sea bottom west of the African coast. It is approximately one metre in length and with a bulb-like foot imbedded in the soft-mud bottom, its tentacles capture food and pass it to its central mouth.

**e.** These mounds, found at a depth of 3,510 metres in the eastern Atlantic, are thought to be made by a bottom-dwelling animal that has yet to be photographed.

**Atlantic Ocean Floor**

22

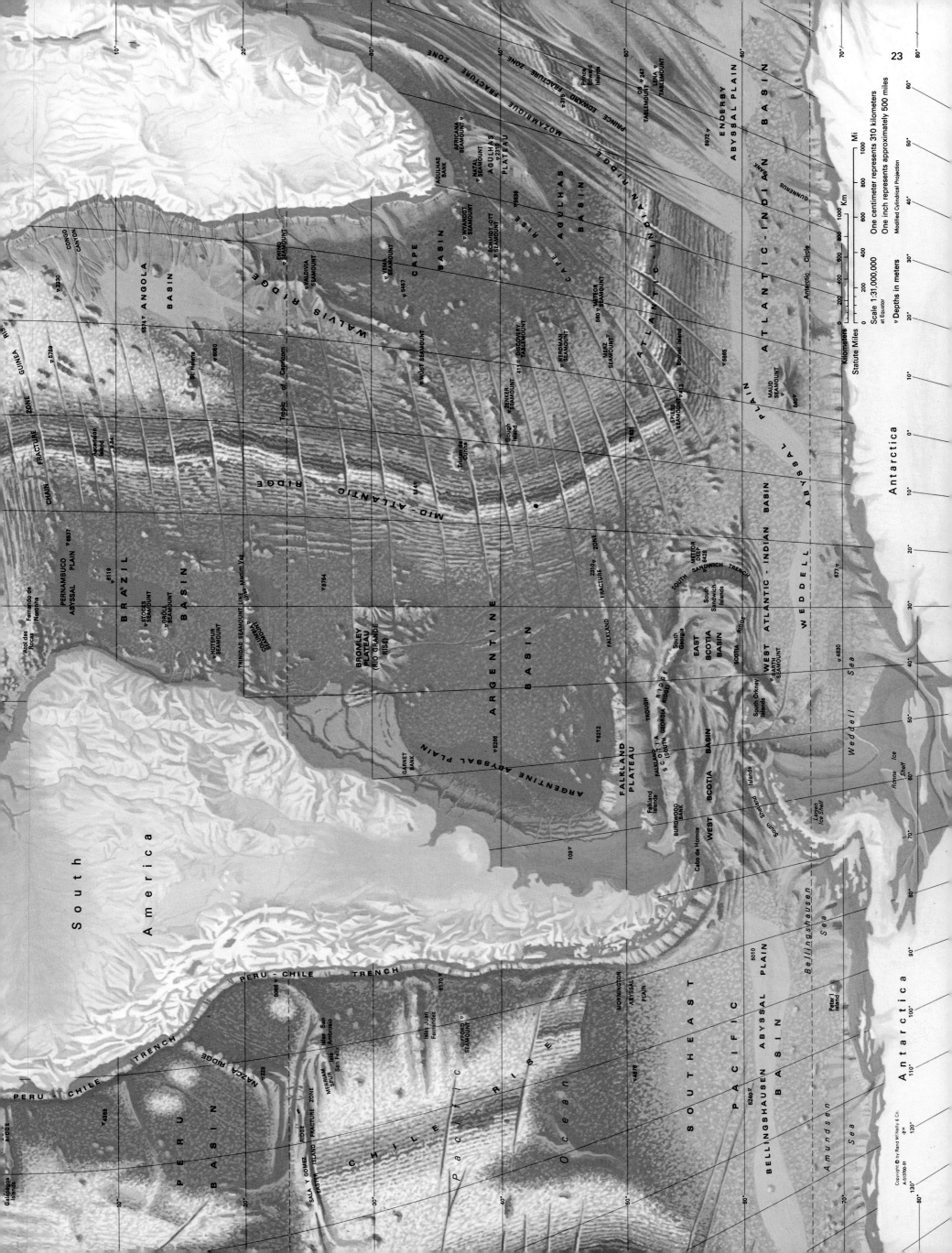

23

South America

Antarctica

Antarctica

**Scale 1:31,000,000**
at Equator

Modified Cylindrical Projection

One centimeter represents 310 kilometers

One inch represents approximately 500 miles

▽ **Depths in meters**

Kilometers

Statute Miles

Km

Mi

Copyright © by Rand McNally & Co.
A-312700-91

24

**Pacific Ocean Floor**

Asia

*Bering Sea*

ALEUTIAN BASIN

Ozero Bajkal

Sea of Okhotsk

BOWERS RIDGE

Aleutian

▽3758
▽4097
▽8109

Ostrov Sachalin

TINRO BASIN

Kamčatka

SHIRSHOV RIDGE

KAMCHATKA TRENCH

KURIL BASIN

KURIL TRENCH

HOKKAIDO RISE

EMPEROR SEAMOUNT CHAIN

EMPEROR TROUGH

CHINOOK TROUGH

AMLIA FRACTURE ZONE

Hokkaido

10542

JAPAN BASIN

NINTOKU SEAMOUNT 949

▽3511

MEN

Korea

Japan

JAPAN TRENCH

SHATSKY RISE

KINMEI SEAMOUNT

HESS RISE

Yellow Sea

SHIKOKU BASIN

BONIN TRENCH

▽10374

SOUTH HONSHU RIDGE

H

East China Sea

7507

RYUKYU TRENCH

8649

MID-PACIFIC MOUNTAINS

MARMAKER SEAMOUNTS

Tropic of Cancer

Taiwan

PHILIPPINE BASIN

Mariana Islands

MARIANA TRENCH

MAGELLAN SEAMOUNTS

HESS TABLEMOUNT

NECKER

South China

MACCLESFIELD BANK ▽

KYUSHU PALAU RIDGE

MARIANA BASIN

▽6674

▽6519

▽859

SOUTH CHINA BASIN

Philippine

DANGEROUS GROUND

SULU

Islands

PHILIPPINE TRENCH

PALAU TRENCH

YAP TRENCH

11034

CHALLENGER DEEP

Marshall Islands

CENTRAL

China Sea

▽10497

8527

Caroline Islands

PACIFIC

SULU BASIN

WEST CAROLINE BASIN

EAURIPIK RIDGE

EAST CAROLINE BASIN

KAPINGAMARANGI (SOLOMON) RISE

Gilbert Islands

BASIN

▽65

CELEBES BASIN

Nauru

▽4462

Equator

Kalimantan (Borneo)

Celebes

New Guinea

Phoenix Islands

Sumatera

Djawa

Java Sea

SOUTH BANDA BASIN

NEW BRITAIN TRENCH 9140

Solomon Islands

New Hebrides Islands

Tuvalu

Tokelau Islands

JAVA TRENCH

Arafura Sea

VITYAZ TRENCH

Samoa Island

7450

CORAL SEA

4176

NEW HEBRIDES TRENCH

FIJI PLATEAU

Christmas Island

18 CORONA SEAMOUNT

BASIN

D'ENTRECASTEAUX FRACTURE ZONE

Cocos Islands

ARGO ABYSSAL PLAIN

Nouvelle Calédonie

▽3580

Indian

EXMOUTH PLATEAU

ROWLEY SHOALS

▽5303

HUNTER FRACTURE ZONE

SOUTH FIJI BASIN

TONGA TRENCH

10882

WHARTON

6658 ▽

CUVIER BASIN

NEW CALEDONIA BASIN

NORFOLK RIDGE

COOK FRACTURE ZONE

LAU RIDGE

BASIN

Australia

Kermadec Islands

Ocean

▽1555

LORD HOWE RISE

Norfolk Island

VENING MEINESZ FRACTURE ZONE

10047

PERTH ABYSSAL PLAIN

1518▽

KERMADEC TRENCH

BROKEN RIDGE

NATURALISTE PLATEAU

GREAT BIGHT ABYSSAL PLAIN

TASMAN ABYSSAL PLAIN

TASMAN

497▽

New

DIAMANTINA FRACTURE ZONE

SOUTH AUSTRALIAN

5670

BASIN

Tasman Sea

▽5267

Zealand

SOUTHEAST

▽2890

INDIAN

3017

RIDGE

SOUTH

TASMANIA RISE

BASIN

CHATHAM RISE

Chatham Island

BOUNTY TROUGH

KERGUELEN PLATEAU

WILKES ABYSSAL PLAIN

Macquarie Island

EMERALD BASIN

Bounty Islands

Antipodes Islands

CAMPBELL PLATEAU

Auckland Islands

Campbell Island

▽4425

▽677

PACIFIC-ANTARCTIC

Kilometers ——— 400  800  1200 Km
Statute Miles ——— 400  800  1200 Mi

Scale 1:41,000,000 at Equator

One centimeter represents 410 kilometers
One inch represents approximately 660 miles

▽ Depths in meters      Modified Cylindrical Projection

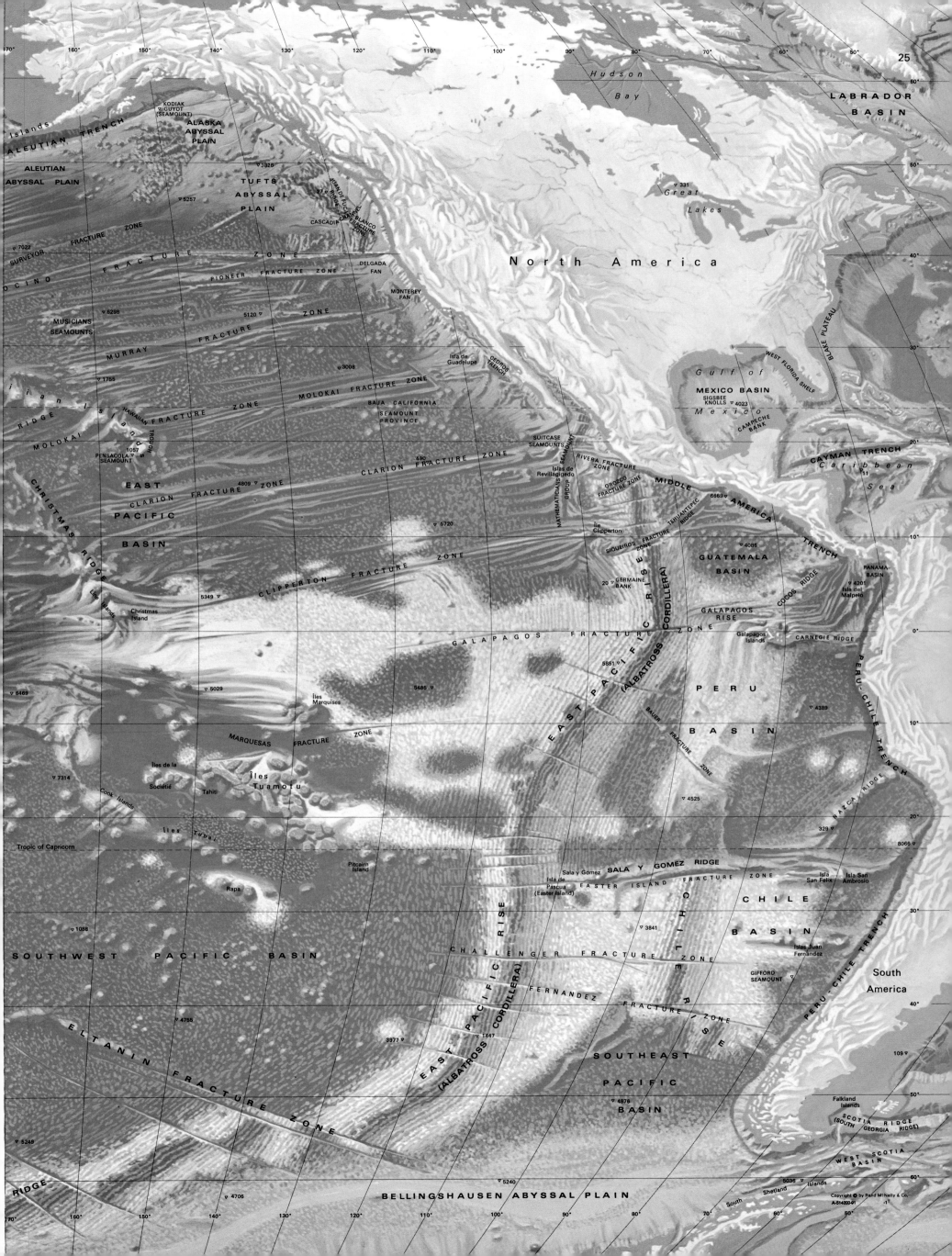

Islands
ALEUTIAN TRENCH
ALEUTIAN
ABYSSAL PLAIN
▽7022
SURVEYOR FRACTURE ZONE
▽5257
KODIAK GUYOT (SEAMOUNT)
ALASKA ABYSSAL PLAIN
ALASKA ABYSSAL PLAIN
▽3828
TUFTS ABYSSAL PLAIN
VAN DE FUCA RIDGE
CHANNEL
CAPE BLANCO FRACTURE ZONE
CASCADIA

Hudson Bay

LABRADOR BASIN

CINO FRACTURE ZONE
PIONEER FRACTURE ZONE
DELGADA FAN
MONTEREY FAN

North America

Great Lakes
▽331

▽8298
MURRAY FRACTURE ZONE
5120 ▽

MUSICIANS SEAMOUNTS

▽1755
MOLOKAI FRACTURE ZONE
▽3008
Isla de Guadelupe
CEDROS TRENCH

Gulf of
MEXICO BASIN
SIGSBEE KNOLLS
▽4023

Mexico

WEST FLORIDA SHELF
BLAKE PLATEAU

i i a n
Islands
RIDGE
MOLOKAI
HAWAIIAN FRACTURE ZONE
TROJ
1057
PENSACOLA SEAMOUNT
EAST
CLARION FRACTURE ZONE
CLARION FRACTURE ZONE
490
BAJA CALIFORNIA SEAMOUNT PROVINCE
SUITCASE SEAMOUNTS
4809 ▽
PACIFIC
BASIN
Islas de Revillagigedo
MATHEMATICIANS SEAMOUNT
GROUP
RIVERA FRACTURE ZONE
OROZCO FRACTURE ZONE
MIDDLE
6663 ▽
CAMPECHE BANK
CAYMAN TRENCH
Caribbean Sea
11

CHRISTMAS RIDGE
▽6720
Îles Islands
Christmas Island
5349 ▽
CLIPPERTON FRACTURE ZONE
Île Clipperton
SIQUEIROS FRACTURE ZONE
20 ▽ GERMAINE BANK
AMERICA TRENCH
▽4086
GUATEMALA BASIN
TEHUANTEPEC RIDGE
COCOS RIDGE
PANAMA BASIN
▽4201
Isla del Malpelo

GALAPAGOS FRACTURE ZONE
GALAPAGOS RISE
Galapagos Islands
CARNEGIE RIDGE

▽6469
▽5029
Îles Marquises
5485 ▽
5851 ▽
EAST PACIFIC RISE (ALBATROSS CORDILLERA)
BAUER FRACTURE ZONE
PERU BASIN
▽4389

MARQUESAS FRACTURE ZONE
▽7314
Îles de la Société
Tahiti
Îles Tuamotu
▽4525

Cook Islands
Îles Tubai
Tropic of Capricorn
Pitcairn Island
Rapa
329 ▽
8066 ▽
NAZCA RIDGE

Sala y Gómez
SALA Y GOMEZ RIDGE
Isla de Pascua (Easter Island)
EASTER ISLAND FRACTURE ZONE
Isla San Felix
Isla San Ambrosio

▽1088
EAST PACIFIC RISE
▽3841
CHILE BASIN

SOUTHWEST PACIFIC BASIN
CHALLENGER FRACTURE ZONE
EAST PACIFIC RISE (ALBATROSS CORDILLERA)
FERNANDEZ FRACTURE ZONE
RISE
Islas Juan Fernández
GIFFORD SEAMOUNT

South America

▽4755
3977 ▽
1447 ▽
SOUTHEAST PACIFIC BASIN
PERU-CHILE TRENCH
109 ▽

ELTANIN FRACTURE ZONE
▽4876
Falkland Islands
SCOTIA RIDGE (SOUTH GEORGIA RIDGE)

▽5249
WEST SCOTIA BASIN

RIDGE
5240 ▽
BELLINGSHAUSEN ABYSSAL PLAIN
4706 ▽
5036 ▽
Shetland Islands
South

**Indian Ocean Floor**

Asia

Arabian Sea

India

Bay of Bengal

South China Sea

Africa

Australia

RED SEA RIFT

Gulf of Aden

Persian Gulf

INDUS CANYON

▽3694

Suqutra

▽6143

INDUS FAN

ARABIAN BASIN

▽3858

INDIA ABYSSAL PLAIN

CARLSBERG RIDGE

CHAIN RIDGE

▽848

▽1752

▽5115

SOMALI ABYSSAL PLAIN

SOMALI BASIN

▽5340

▽5870

Laccadive Islands

Maldive Islands

CHAGOS-LACCADIVE PLATEAU

Ceylon

▽3244

Equator

▽5243

Andaman Islands

ANDAMAN BASIN

Nicobar Islands

▽2095

▽2359

GANGES FAN

GANGES CANYON

Taiwan

MACCLESFIELD BANK

Philippine Islands

DANGEROUS GROUND

SULU BASIN

CELEBES BASIN

Seychelles

Amirante Islands

Coetivy Island

SAYA DE MALHA BANK

Aldabra Islands

Cerf

Farquhar Group

AMIRANTE TRENCH

Agalega Islands

▽1812

NINETY EAST RIDGE

MENTAWEI RIDGE

MENTAWEI TROUGH

Sumatera

▽65

Kalimantan (Borneo)

Java Sea

NIKITIN (AFANASIY) SEAMOUNT

▽1549

CEYLON ABYSSAL PLAIN

MID-INDIAN BASIN

COCOS BASIN

Cocos Islands

▽6335

CHRISTMAS RISE

Christmas Island

KARMA RISE

ROO RISE

Djawa

JAVA TRENCH

▽7450

ARGO ABYSSAL PLAIN

CORONA SEAMOUNT

▽18

ROWLEY SHOALS

Chapos Archipelago

▽5408

VEMA TRENCH

▽6237

Comoro Islands

COMORO RIDGE

MASCARENE BASIN

Tromelin

Cargados Carajos Shoals

NAZARETH BANK

SEYCHELLES-MAURITIUS PLATEAU

Rodriguez

RODRIGUEZ FRACTURE ZONE

▽5347

Mauritius

Réunion

▽6090

WHARTON BASIN

WEST AUSTRALIAN BASIN

EXMOUTH PLATEAU

▽6668

CUVIER BASIN

Madagascar

Bassas da India

Ile Europa

MADAGASCAR BASIN

▽6400

MID-INDIAN RIDGE

▽1706

▽1555

PERTH ABYSSAL PLAIN

BROKEN RIDGE

DIAMANTINA

NATURALISTE PLATEAU

MOZAMBIQUE CHANNEL

NATAL BASIN

▽3840

MOZAMBIQUE RIDGE

MADAGASCAR RIDGE

▽945

▽870

▽2067

NINETY EAST RIDGE

ARGO FAULT

AMSTERDAM FRACTURE ZONE

DIAMANTINA FRACTURE ZONE

▽4472

▽5670

AFRICANA SEAMOUNT

AGULHAS PLATEAU

▽2310

SOUTHWEST INDIAN RIDGE

MOZAMBIQUE FRACTURE ZONE

PRINCE EDWARD FRACTURE ZONE

MALAGASY FRACTURE ZONE

▽315

CROZET RIDGE

CROZET BASIN

Iles Crozet

▽5440

Ile Amsterdam

Ile St Paul

SOUTHEAST INDIAN RIDGE

▽2650

▽2984

Prince Edward Islands

OB TABLEMOUNT

▽247

LENA TABLEMOUNT

Iles de Kerguelen

KERGUELEN PLATEAU

Heard Island

SOUTH WILKES ABYSSAL PLAIN

▽4425

INDIAN BASIN

ATLANTIC-INDIAN RIDGE

MOZAMBIQUE

▽6972

SOUTH INDIAN BASIN

ENDERBY ABYSSAL PLAIN

BANZARE BANK

▽6089

WEDDELL ABYSSAL PLAIN

THIRTY EAST SPUR

▽5124

▽4974

GRIBB BANK

GAUSSBERG ABYSSAL PLAIN

Antarctic Circle

Copyright © by Rand McNally & Co.

A-51460-91

Scale 1:31,000,000 at Equator
One centimeter represents 310 kilometers
One inch represents approximately 500 miles
Modified Cylindrical Projection

Kilometers  0  200  400  600  800  1000  Km
Statute Miles  0  200  400  600  800  1000  Mi

▽ Depths in meters

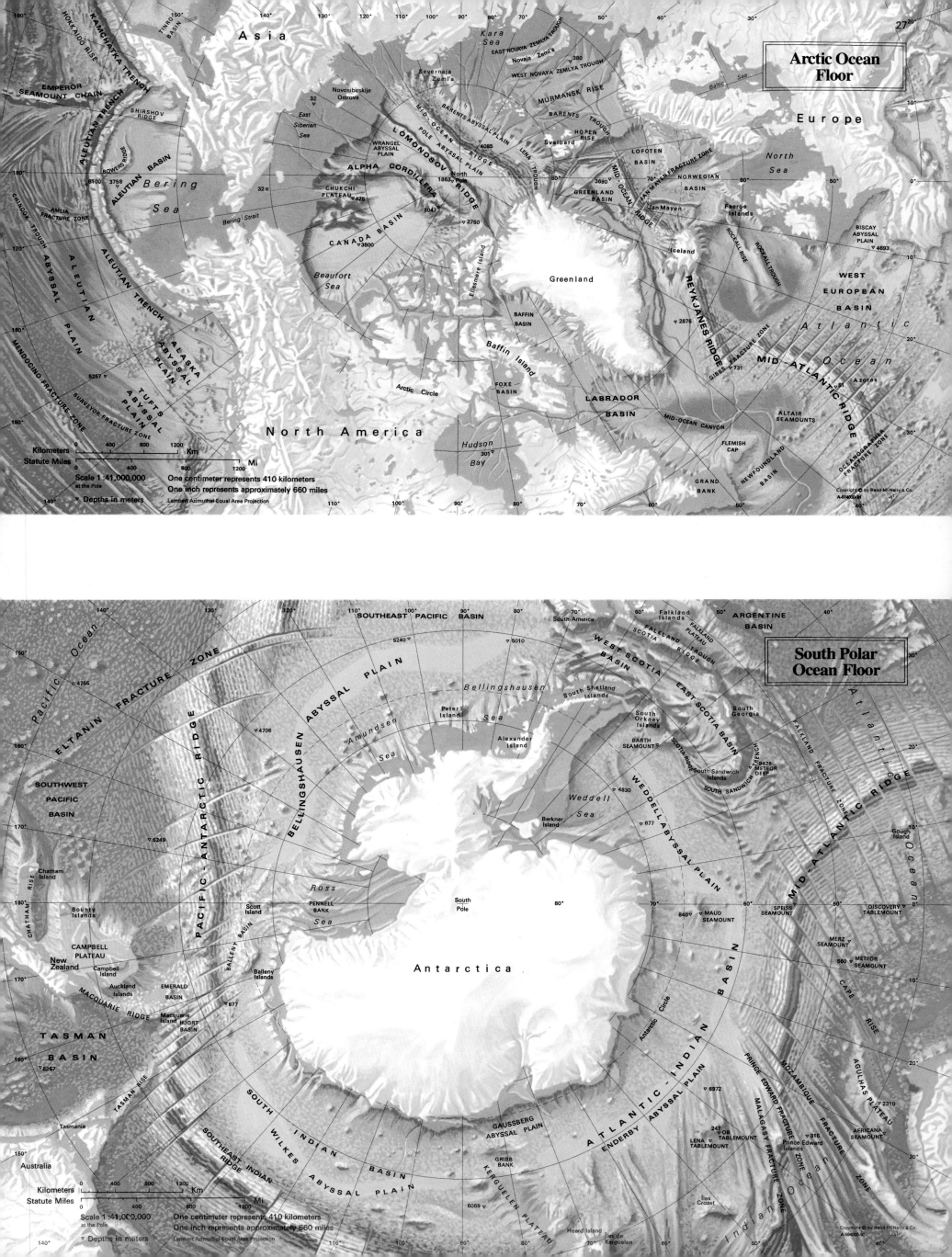

**Arctic Ocean Floor**

Asia · Europe

27

Kamchatka Trench · Emperor Seamount Chain · Shirshov Ridge · Aleutian Trench · Bering Sea · Hokkaido Rise · Tinro Basin · Kara Sea · East Novaya Zemlya Trough · Novaja Zemlja · West Novaya Zemlya Trough · Murmansk Rise · Barents Trough · Hopen Rise · Svalbard · Lofoten Basin · Jan Mayen Fracture Zone · Norwegian Basin · North Sea · Baltic Sea

Severnaja Zeml'a · Novosibirskije Ostrova · East Siberian Sea · Mid-Ocean Ridge · Lomonosov Ridge · Pole Abyssal Plain · Barents Abyssal Plain · Greenland Basin · Jan Mayen · Faeroe Islands · Biscay Abyssal Plain

Wrangel Abyssal Plain · Alpha Cordillera · North Pole · Chukchi Plateau · Canada Basin · Beaufort Sea · Iceland · Reykjanes Ridge · Rockall Rise · Rockall Trough · West European Basin · Mid-Atlantic Ridge · Azores · Atlantic Ocean · Gibbs Fracture Zone · Oceanographer Fracture Zone

Bowers Bank · Aleutian Basin · Amlia Fracture Zone · Chinook Trough · Aleutian Abyssal Plain · Mendocino Fracture Zone · Surveyor Fracture Zone · Alaska Abyssal Plain · Tufts Abyssal Plain

North America · Ellesmere Island · Greenland · Baffin Basin · Baffin Island · Foxe Basin · Arctic Circle · Labrador Basin · Mid-Ocean Canyon · Altair Seamounts · Flemish Cap · Newfoundland Basin · Grand Bank

Hudson Bay

Depths: 5100 · 3758 · 5257 · 4085 · 4475 · 1047 · 1863 · 2750 · 3800 · 380 · 731 · 2875 · 301 · 3690 · 4693

Kilometers 0 400 800 1200 Km
Statute Miles 0 400 800 1200 Mi
Scale 1:41,000,000 at the Pole
One centimeter represents 410 kilometers
One inch represents approximately 660 miles
▽ Depths in meters
Lambert Azimuthal Equal Area Projection
Copyright © by Rand McNally & Co.
A-614000-81

---

**South Polar Ocean Floor**

Pacific Ocean · Eltanin Fracture Zone · Southeast Pacific Basin · South America · Falkland Islands · Falkland Plateau · Scotia Ridge · Argentine Basin

Pacific-Antarctic Ridge · Bellingshausen Abyssal Plain · Bellingshausen Sea · Amundsen Sea · Peter I Island · Alexander Island · South Shetland Islands · West Scotia Basin · East Scotia Basin · South Orkney Islands · South Georgia · Falkland Fracture Zone · Atlantic Ocean

Southwest Pacific Basin · Chatham Rise · Chatham Island · Bounty Islands · Scott Island · Ross Sea · Pennell Bank · South Pole · Weddell Sea · Berkner Island · Barth Seamount · South Sandwich Islands · Scotia Ridge · Weddell Abyssal Plain · Mid-Atlantic Ridge · Gough Island

New Zealand · Campbell Plateau · Campbell Island · Auckland Islands · Emerald Basin · Balleny Basin · Balleny Islands · Antarctica · Maud Seamount · Spiess Seamount · Discovery Tablemount · Meteor Deep

Tasman Basin · Macquarie Ridge · Macquarie Island · Hjort Basin · Tasman Rise · South Indian Basin · Southeast Indian Ridge · Wilkes Abyssal Plain · Gaussberg Abyssal Plain · Gribb Bank · Atlantic-Indian Basin · Enderby Abyssal Plain · Kerguelen Plateau · Antarctic Circle · Prince Edward Fracture Zone · Ob Tablemount · Lena Tablemount · Prince Edward Islands · Africana Seamount · Merz Seamount · Meteor Seamount · Cape Rise · Agulhas Plateau

Australia · Tasmania · Heard Island · Iles de Kerguelen · Iles Crozet · Malagasy Plain · Mozambique Fracture Zone · Indian Ocean

Depths: 4755 · 5240 · 5010 · 4706 · 5249 · 4830 · 677 · 5267 · 677 · 6089 · 840 · 560 · 6972 · 247 · 316 · 2310 · 9428

Kilometers 0 400 800 1200 Km
Statute Miles 0 400 800 1200 Mi
Scale 1:41,000,000 at the Pole
One centimeter represents 410 kilometers
One inch represents approximately 660 miles
▽ Depths in meters
Lambert Azimuthal Equal Area Projection
Copyright © by Rand McNally & Co.
A-594000-81

# Planets and Earth-Sun Relations

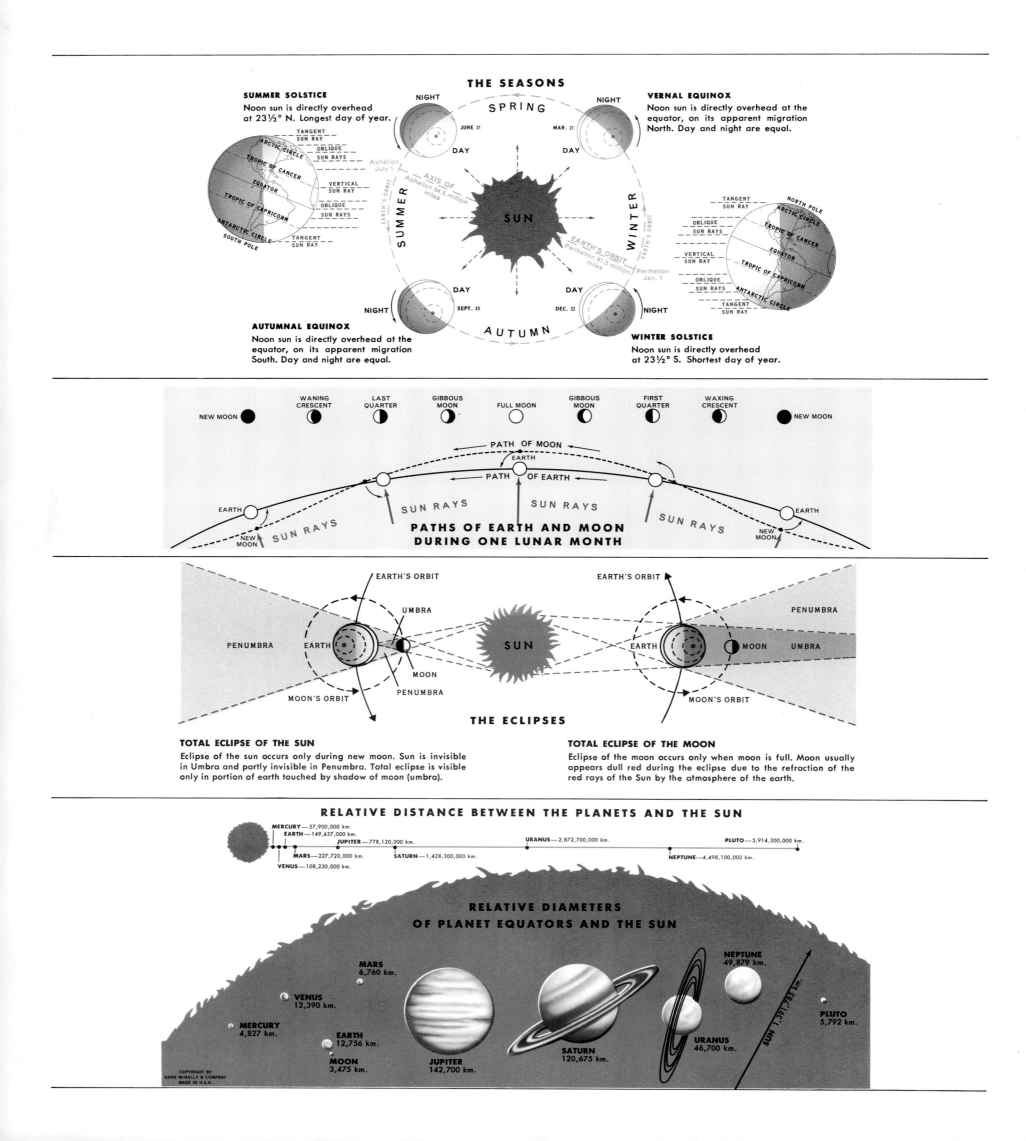

## THE SEASONS

**SUMMER SOLSTICE**
Noon sun is directly overhead at 23½° N. Longest day of year.

**VERNAL EQUINOX**
Noon sun is directly overhead at the equator, on its apparent migration North. Day and night are equal.

**AUTUMNAL EQUINOX**
Noon sun is directly overhead at the equator, on its apparent migration South. Day and night are equal.

**WINTER SOLSTICE**
Noon sun is directly overhead at 23½° S. Shortest day of year.

SPRING — SUMMER — WINTER — AUTUMN

SUN

JUNE 21 — MAR. 21 — SEPT. 23 — DEC. 22

NIGHT / DAY / NIGHT

AXIS OF EARTH'S ORBIT
Aphelion July 1
Aphelion 94.5 million miles

EARTH'S ORBIT
Perihelion 91.5 million miles
Perihelion Jan. 1

TANGENT SUN RAY / ARCTIC CIRCLE / OBLIQUE SUN RAYS / TROPIC OF CANCER / EQUATOR / VERTICAL SUN RAY / TROPIC OF CAPRICORN / OBLIQUE SUN RAYS / ANTARCTIC CIRCLE / TANGENT SUN RAY / SOUTH POLE

NORTH POLE / ARCTIC CIRCLE / TROPIC OF CANCER / EQUATOR / TROPIC OF CAPRICORN / ANTARCTIC CIRCLE

## Moon Phases

NEW MOON — WANING CRESCENT — LAST QUARTER — GIBBOUS MOON — FULL MOON — GIBBOUS MOON — FIRST QUARTER — WAXING CRESCENT — NEW MOON

PATH OF MOON
EARTH
PATH OF EARTH
SUN RAYS — SUN RAYS — SUN RAYS
EARTH — NEW MOON — EARTH — NEW MOON

### PATHS OF EARTH AND MOON DURING ONE LUNAR MONTH

## THE ECLIPSES

EARTH'S ORBIT — UMBRA — MOON — PENUMBRA — MOON'S ORBIT — PENUMBRA — EARTH — SUN — EARTH — EARTH'S ORBIT — PENUMBRA — MOON — UMBRA — MOON'S ORBIT

**TOTAL ECLIPSE OF THE SUN**
Eclipse of the sun occurs only during new moon. Sun is invisible in Umbra and partly invisible in Penumbra. Total eclipse is visible only in portion of earth touched by shadow of moon (umbra).

**TOTAL ECLIPSE OF THE MOON**
Eclipse of the moon occurs only when moon is full. Moon usually appears dull red during the eclipse due to the refraction of the red rays of the Sun by the atmosphere of the earth.

## RELATIVE DISTANCE BETWEEN THE PLANETS AND THE SUN

MERCURY—57,900,000 km.
EARTH—149,637,000 km.
JUPITER—778,120,000 km.
URANUS—2,872,700,000 km.
PLUTO—5,914,300,000 km.
MARS—227,720,000 km.
SATURN—1,428,300,000 km.
NEPTUNE—4,498,100,000 km.
VENUS—108,230,000 km.

## RELATIVE DIAMETERS OF PLANET EQUATORS AND THE SUN

MARS 6,760 km.
VENUS 12,390 km.
MERCURY 4,827 km.
EARTH 12,756 km.
MOON 3,475 km.
JUPITER 142,700 km.
SATURN 120,675 km.
URANUS 46,700 km.
NEPTUNE 49,879 km.
PLUTO 5,792 km.
SUN 1,391,785 km.

# North Sea Energy Resources

A large natural gas field was discovered in The Netherlands' Groningen Province in 1959. Petroleum geologists found the Permian layer containing the gas continued under the North Sea to Yorkshire, where there was also a natural gas field. In the 1960's, additional exploration led to discoveries of more natural gas fields beneath the North Sea, and commercial gas production began.

In 1967, a commercial oil deposit was found in the Danish sector. In 1970, a major oil strike in the Norwegian sector at Ekofisk field was announced. This was followed by the discovery of other major oil fields—Forties, West Ekofisk, Auk, Argyll, Brent, Beryl, Montrose and Statfjord in the British and Norwegian sectors.

Oil production began at Ekofisk field in 1971. At first oil tankers transported the crude oil to shore; in 1975, a pipeline was completed between the field and Teesside. Today, producing North Sea fields may have storage platform facilities, may pump crude oil directly to shore via pipeline, or the wells may produce and load oil tankers directly.

Before oil was discovered under the North Sea, Britain imported almost all the crude oil she needed for fuel and industry. The bill for imported oil contributed to the huge trade deficit that helped slow the nation's economic growth. Since the North Sea wells have been producing oil, British imports of crude oil and petroleum products have been declining steadily. It is hoped that by the 1980's, Great Britain will become self-sufficient in oil and greatly reduce her trade deficit.

**Pipeline Construction**

Pipeline technology has advanced enough in the 1970's so that workers have been able to lay oil and gas pipelines in the southern, western and northern North Sea in spite of bad weather and treacherous underwater currents. To lay pipeline, workers cut a trench into the sea floor, lower pipeline into it and refill it. The North Sea's currents may help finish the job by covering the pipeline and trench with sediments. However, along Norway's coast, the Norwegian Trench's great depth (over 300 metres deep) has prevented construction of proposed pipelines to Norway from Statfjord and Frigg fields.

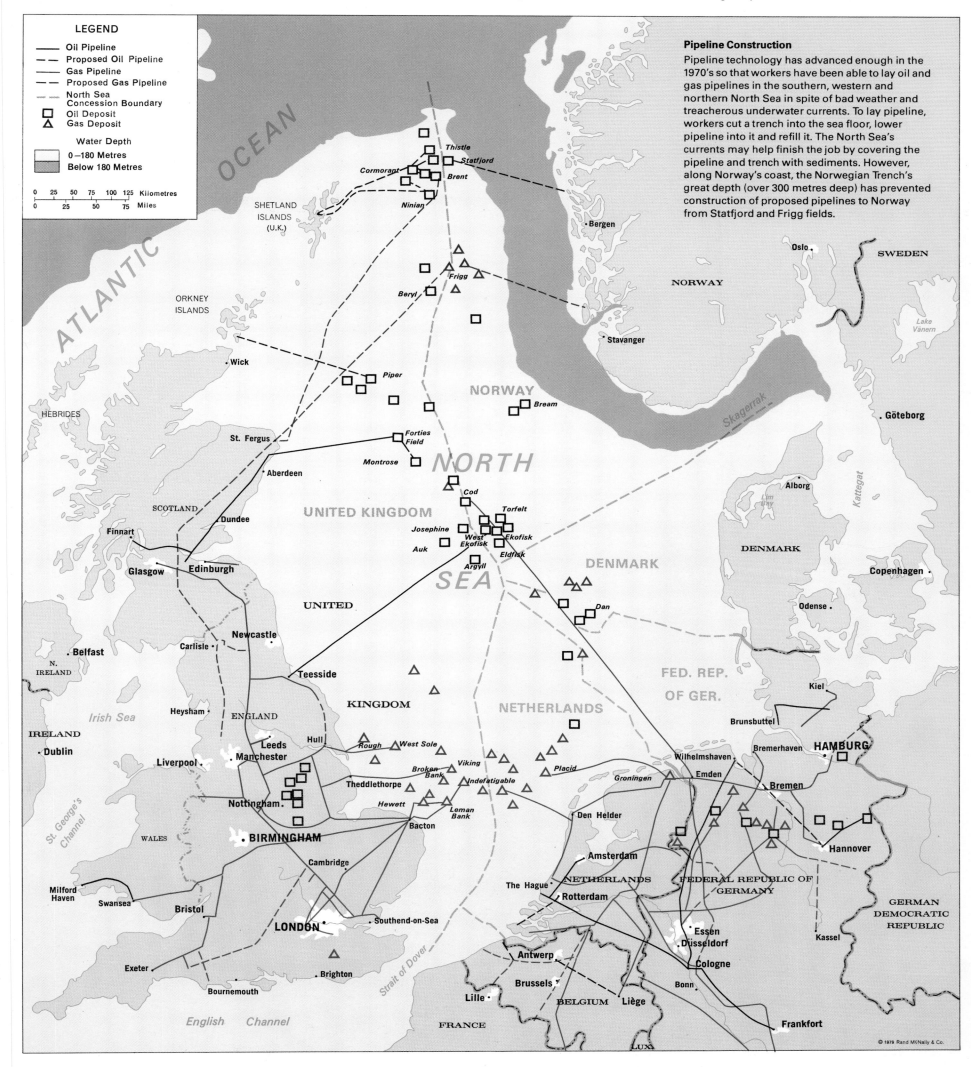

LEGEND

—— Oil Pipeline
- - - Proposed Oil Pipeline
—— Gas Pipeline
- - - Proposed Gas Pipeline
—·—· North Sea Concession Boundary
□ Oil Deposit
△ Gas Deposit

Water Depth
☐ 0−180 Metres
▨ Below 180 Metres

0 25 50 75 100 125 Kilometres
0 25 50 75 Miles

© 1979 Rand McNally & Co.

# Environment Maps

The environment-map series on the following pages shows the general nature of the environment, whether natural or modified by man. The appearance and/or general activity which characterize an area are the conditions for its being classified in one of the map categories. Inclusion in a category is determined largely by the percent of the area covered by urban development, crops (including pasture), trees, or grass. On these small-scale maps, no attempt is made to depict specific crops or an area's productivity.

Ten major environments are depicted and the categories identified and described in the legend below. The colours and patterns for each category are chosen to illustrate the results of man's activity. Hill shading is used to show land configuration. Together, these design elements create a visual impression of the surface environment.

Naturally, when mapping any distribution it is necessary to limit the number of categories. Therefore, some gradations of meaning exist within the limits of the chosen categories. For example, the grassland, grazing-land category identifies the lush pampas of Argentina and the savanna of Africa as well as the steppes of the Soviet Union. Furthermore, in areas of cropland certain enclaves which might not be defined as cropland are included within the

boundary. Tracts such as these, through the process of generalization, were included within the boundary of the dominant environment surrounding them. Finally, it should be pointed out that boundaries on these maps, as on all maps, are never absolute but mark the centre of transitional zones between categories.

Actual urban shapes are shown where metropolitan areas are of a large areal extent. A red dot indicates concentrated urbanized development where actual shapes would be indistinguishable at the map scale. Black dots are used to locate selected places important as locational reference points.

From these maps one may make comprehensive observations about the extent and distribution of the major world environments. For example, the urban areas of the world are limited in extent, although over 40 percent of the world's population lives in these areas. Together, the categories of cropland and cropland associated with woodland or grazing land apply to relatively small portions of the earth's surface. Conversely, vast areas of each continent show man's limited influence on the natural environment. The barren lands, wasteland, and tundra, the sparse grass and steppe land, and the tropical rain forests are notable in this respect.

## Environment Map Legend

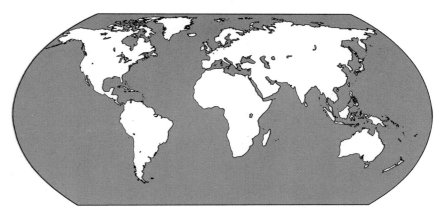

 **URBAN**
Major areas of contiguous residential, commercial, and industrial development.

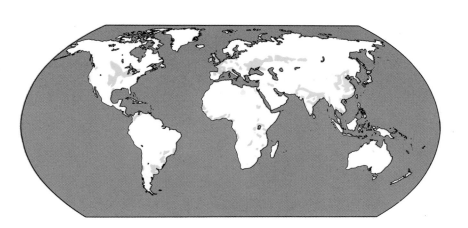

**CROPLAND**
Cultivated land predominates (includes pasture, irrigated land, and land in crop rotation).

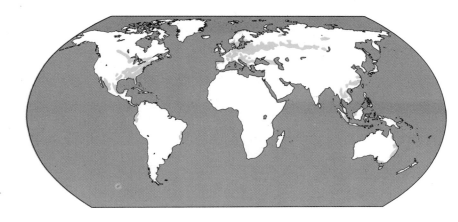

**CROPLAND AND WOODLAND**
Cultivated land interrupted by small wooded areas.

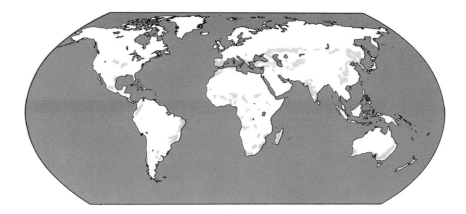

 **CROPLAND AND GRAZING LAND**
Cultivated land with grassland and rangeland.

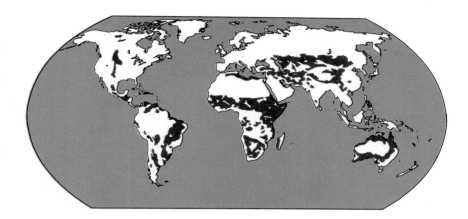

 **GRASSLAND, GRAZING LAND**
Extensive grassland and rangeland
with little or no cropland.

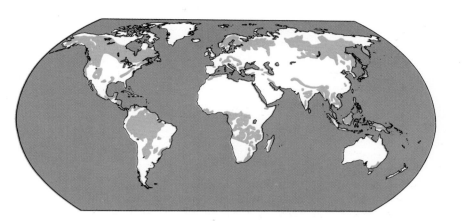

**FOREST, WOODLAND**
Extensive wooded areas
with little or no cropland.

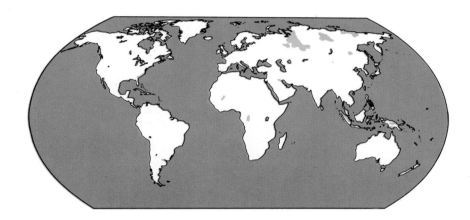

**SWAMP, MARSHLAND**
Extensive wetland areas
(includes mangroves).

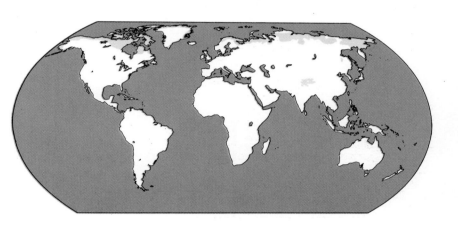

**TUNDRA**
Areas of lichen, shrubs,
small trees, and wetland.

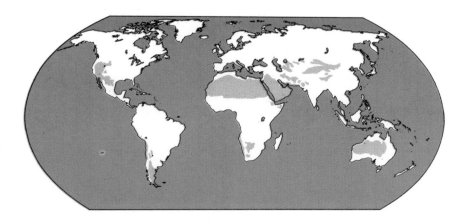

**SHRUB, SPARSE GRASS;
WASTELAND**
Desert shrub and short grass, growing
singly or in patches. Wasteland includes
sand, salt flats, etc. (Extensive
wastelands shown by pattern.)

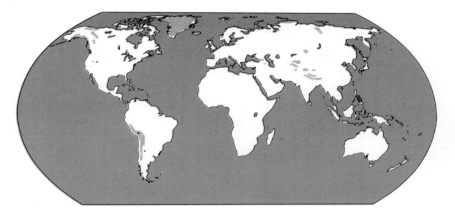

**BARREN LAND**
Icefields, glaciers,
permanent snow, with exposed rock.

 • *Selected cities as points of reference.*

 *OASIS—Important small areas of cultivation
within grassland or wasteland.*

Urban

Cropland

Cropland & Woodland

Cropland & Grazing Land

Grassland, Grazing Land

Forest, Woodland

Swamp, Marshland

Tundra

Shrub, Sparse Grass,
Wasteland (pattern)

Barren Land

Oasis

Longitude West of Greenwich    Longitude East of Greenwich

Conic Projection

| 0 | 50 | 100 | 200 | 300 | 400 | 500 Miles |
| 0 | 100 | 200 | 400 | 600 | 800 Kilometers |

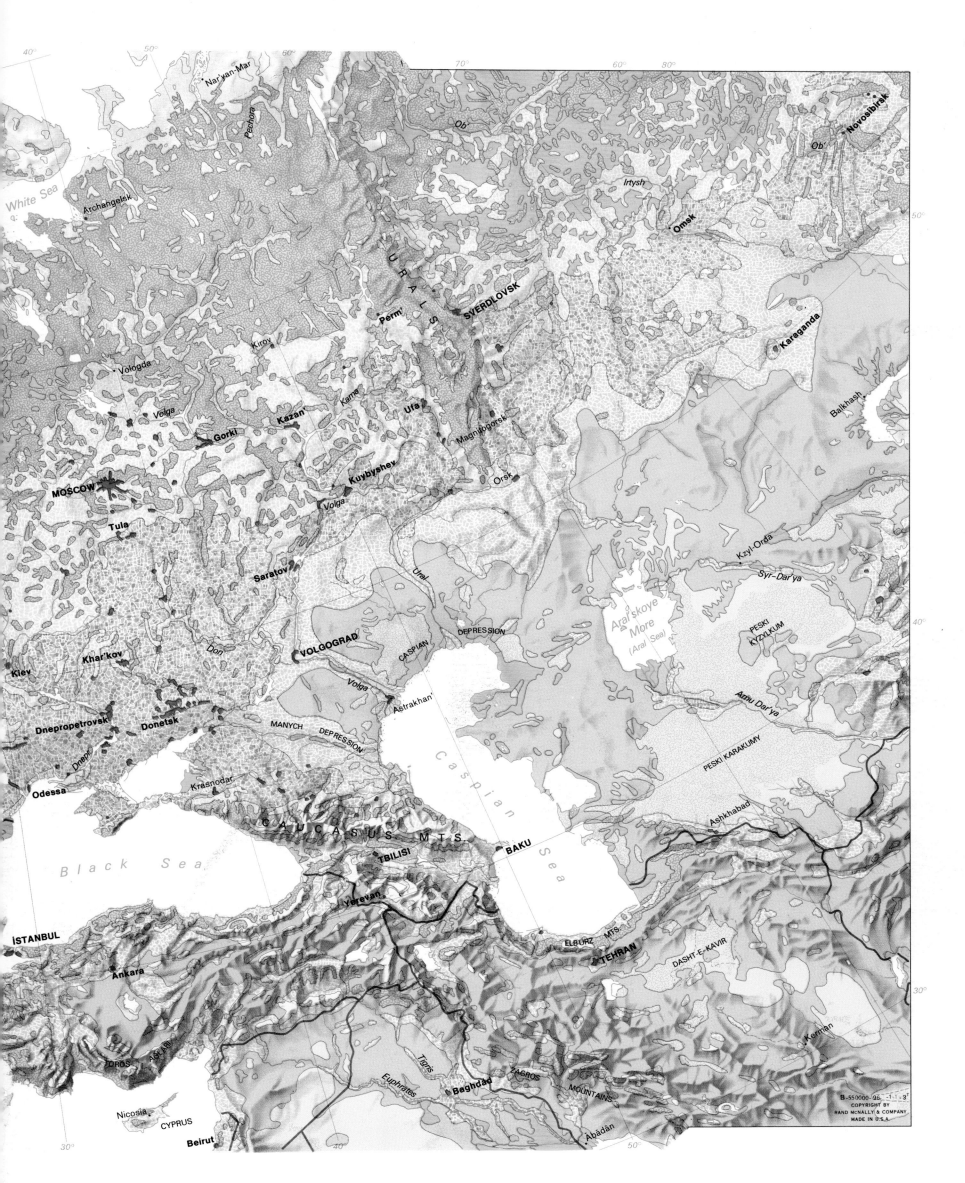

White Sea

Nar'yan-Mar

Pechora

Ob'

Novosibirsk

Ob'

Irtysh

Archangelsk

URALS

Omsk

SVERDLOVSK

Perm'

Karaganda

Kirov

Vologda

Kama

Ufa

Balkhash

Volga

Kazan'

Gorki

Magnitogorsk

Kyzl-Orda

Kuybyshev

Orsk

Syr-Dar'ya

MOSCOW

Volga

Ural

Aral'skoye More (Aral Sea)

Tula

PESKI KYZYLKUM

Saratov

DEPRESSION

Amu Dar'ya

Khar'kov

Don

VOLGOGRAD

CASPIAN

Kiev

Volga

PESKI KARAKUMY

Astrakhan'

Dnepropetrovsk

Donetsk

MANYCH DEPRESSION

Dnepr

Ashkhabad

Odessa

Krasnodar

Caspian Sea

CAUCASUS MTS.

BAKU

Black Sea

TBILISI

Yerevan

İSTANBUL

ELBURZ MTS.

TEHRAN

DASHT-E-KAVIR

Ankara

ZAGROS

Kerman

TOROS AĞLARI

MOUNTAINS

Nicosia

CYPRUS

Tigris

Euphrates

Baghdad

Beirut

Abadan

B-550000-96

COPYRIGHT BY
RAND McNALLY & COMPANY
MADE IN U.S.A.

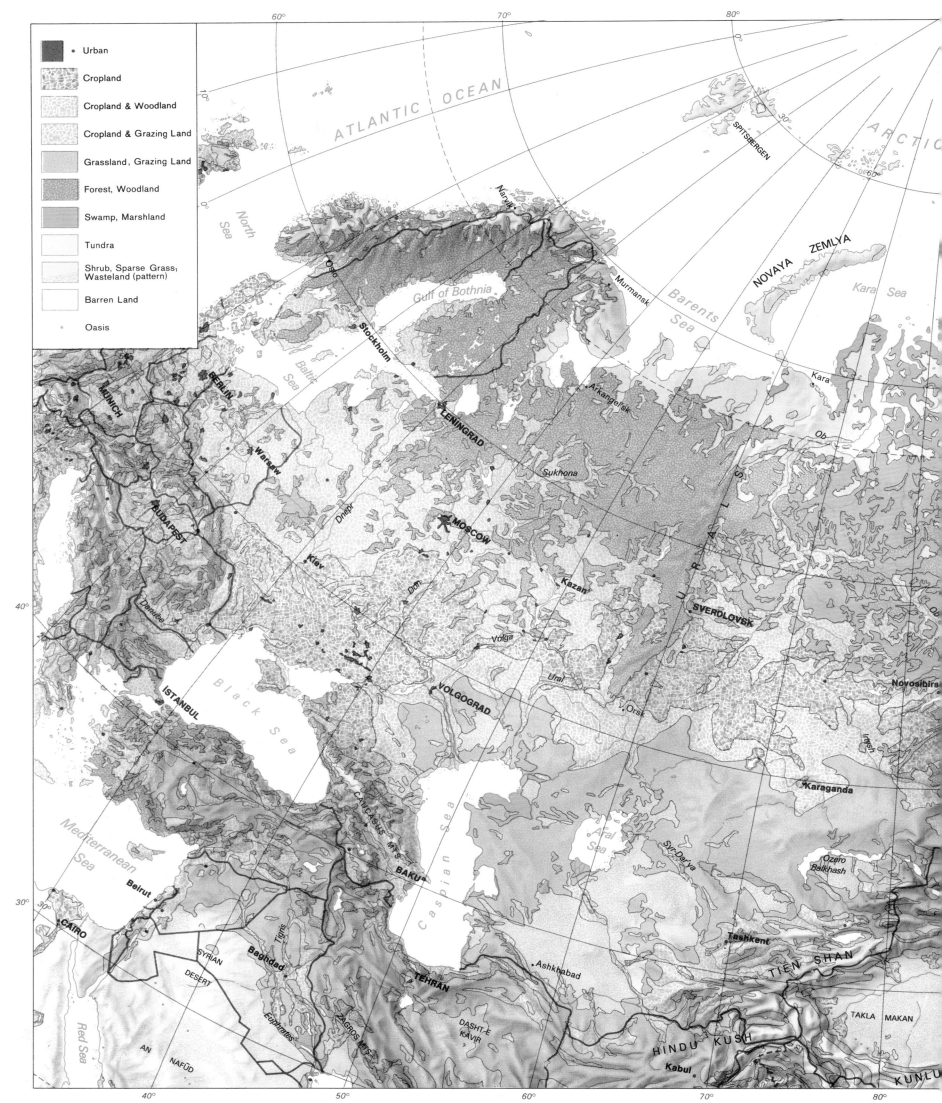

Legend:
- Urban
- Cropland
- Cropland & Woodland
- Cropland & Grazing Land
- Grassland, Grazing Land
- Forest, Woodland
- Swamp, Marshland
- Tundra
- Shrub, Sparse Grass, Wasteland (pattern)
- Barren Land
- Oasis

ATLANTIC OCEAN

ARCTIC

North Sea

Narvik

Murmansk

Barents Sea

NOVAYA ZEMLYA

SPITSBERGEN

Kara Sea

Gulf of Bothnia

Oslo

Stockholm

Baltic Sea

Arkangelsk

Kara

Ob

LENINGRAD

Sukhona

BERLIN

MUNICH

Warsaw

Dnepr

MOSCOW

Kazan

SVERDLOVSK

BUDAPEST

Kiev

Don

Volga

Ural

Danube

Ural

Orsk

Novosibirs

ISTANBUL

Black Sea

VOLGOGRAD

Irtysh

Karaganda

CAUCASUS MTS.

BAKU

Caspian Sea

Aral Sea

Syr-Dar'ya

Ozero Balkhash

Mediterranean Sea

Beirut

Tashkent

30°

CAIRO

SYRIAN DESERT

Baghdad

Tigris

TEHRAN

Ashkhabad

ZAGROS MTS.

DASHT-E KAVIR

TIEN SHAN

Red Sea

AN NAFŪD

Euphrates

HINDU KUSH

TAKLA MAKAN

Kabul

KUNLU

Lambert Azimuthal Equal-Area Projection

OCEAN

East Siberian Sea

Anadyrskiy Zaliv

Bering Sea

Laptev Sea

Ambarchik

Zhigansk

POLUOSTROV KAMCHATKA

Petropavlovsk-Kamchatskiy

Nordvik

KHREBET-GYDAN

Magadan

Sea of Okhotsk

GORY PUTORANA

Olenek

Lena

Yakutsk

SAKHALIN

Tura

Lena

Komsomolsk-na-Amure

Krasnoyarsk

Amur

HOKKAIDŌ

Sapporo

Lake Baikal

MTS.

Amur

GREATER KHINGAN

Irkutsk

Vladivostok

HONSHŪ

Sea of Japan

Ulaan Baatar

Haerhpin

TOKYO

ALTAI

MTS.

MUKDEN

SEOUL

GOBI (DESERT)

Tihua

PEKING

KYŪSHŪ

Yellow Sea

Hwang Ho

East China Sea

Chengchou

PACIFIC OCEAN

SHANGHAI

Yangtze

MOUNTAINS

B-568500-96   -1-1-1ᵀ
COPYRIGHT BY
RAND McNALLY & COMPANY
MADE IN U.S.A.

| 0 | 100 | 200 | 400 | 600 | 800 Miles |

| 0 | 150 | 300 | 600 | 900 | 1200 Kilometers |

Urban

Cropland

Cropland & Woodland

Cropland & Grazing Land

Grassland, Grazing Land

Forest, Woodland

Swamp, Marshland

Tundra

Shrub, Sparse Grass,
Wasteland (pattern)

Barren Land

Oasis

B-568600-96   -1-·1-·5
COPYRIGHT BY
RAND MCNALLY & COMPANY
MADE IN U.S.A.

Lambert Azimuthal Equal-Area Projection

ALTAI MTS.

Ulaan Baatar

GOBI (DESERT)

Tihua

MOUNTAINS

OF TIBET

HIMALAYAS

Ganges

CALCUTTA

Brahmaputra

Mekong

Hwang-Ho

Mandalay

Salween

Rangoon

Bay of Bengal

Andaman Sea

Equator

SUMATRA

Medan

SINGAPORE

JAKARTA

JAVA

Bangkok

Mekong

Hanoi

HO CHI MINH CITY

HAINAN TAO

South China Sea

Kuching

BORNEO

Java Sea

Ujung Pandang

K'unming

CANTON

CHUNGKING

WUHAN

Chengchou

PEKING

SHANGHAI

MUKDEN

Haerhpin

Vladivostok

SEOUL

East China Sea

Yellow Sea

T'aipei

FORMOSA

Tropic of Cancer

Sea of Japan

HONSHŪ

TOKYO

KYŪSHŪ

PACIFIC OCEAN

Philippine Sea

MANILA

Cebu

MINDANAO

Celebes Sea

Kota Kinabalu

Manado

CELEBES

GREATER KHINGAN MTS.

Ulaan Baatar

| 0 | 100 | 200 | 400 | 600 | 800 Miles |
|---|-----|-----|-----|-----|-----------|

| 0 | 150 | 300 | 600 | 900 | 1200 Kilometers |
|---|-----|-----|-----|-----|-----------------|

90°    100°    130°    140°    40°    30°    20°    10°    0°    10°    120°

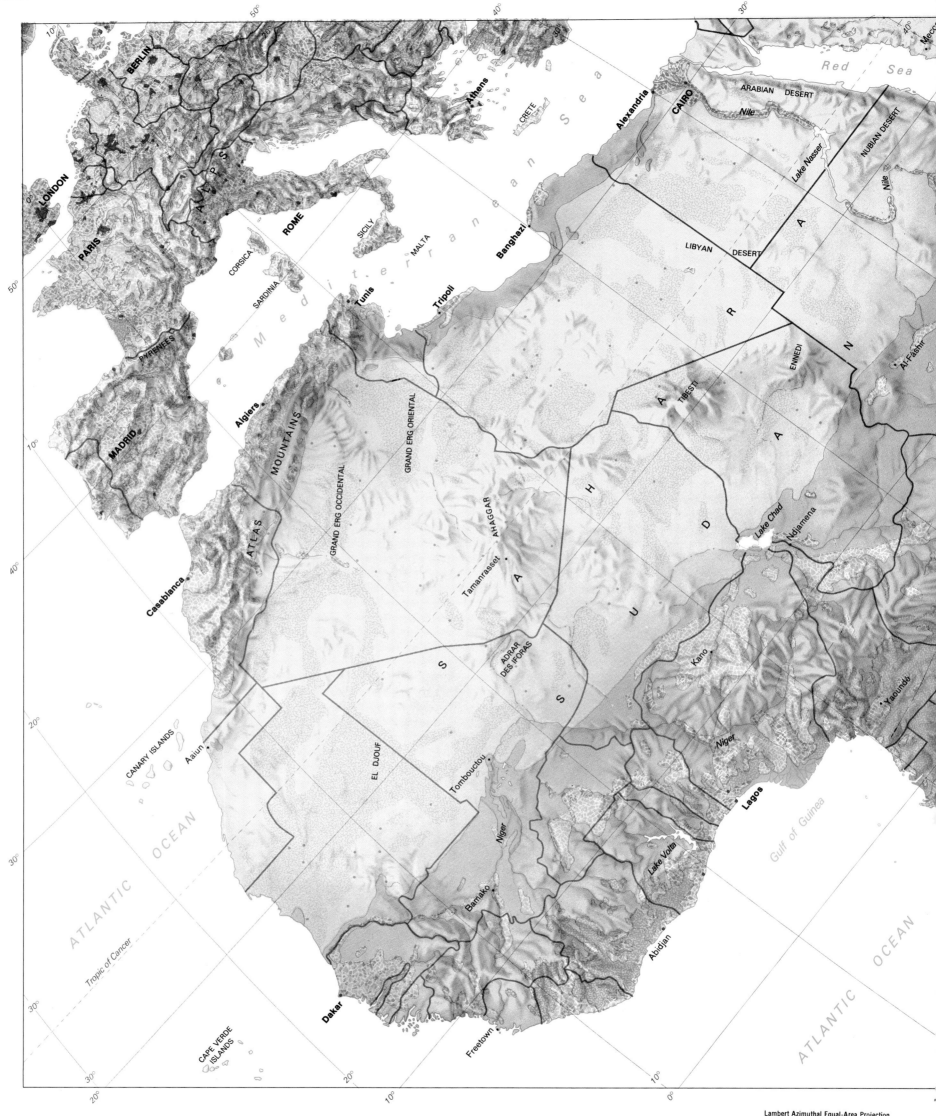

Red Sea

BERLIN

Athens

CRETE

Alexandria · CAIRO · ARABIAN DESERT

Nile

LONDON

Mediterranean Sea

ROME

SICILY

MALTA

Banghazi

LIBYAN DESERT

NUBIAN DESERT

Lake Nasser

Nile

PARIS

CORSICA

SARDINIA

Tunis

Tripoli

Al-Fashir

MADRID

PYRENEES

Algiers

ENNEDI

ATLAS MOUNTAINS

GRAND ERG OCCIDENTAL

GRAND ERG ORIENTAL

AHAGGAR

TIBESTI

Casablanca

Tamanrasset

S A H A R A

Lake Chad

Ndjamena

Kano

ADRAR DES IFORAS

Yaoundé

CANARY ISLANDS

Aaiun

EL DJOUF

Niger

Lagos

Tombouctou

Gulf of Guinea

Niger

Bamako

Lake Volta

ATLANTIC OCEAN

Tropic of Cancer

Abidjan

ATLANTIC OCEAN

Dakar

Freetown

CAPE VERDE ISLANDS

Lambert Azimuthal Equal-Area Projection

Urban
Cropland
Cropland & Woodland
Cropland & Grazing Land
Grassland, Grazing Land
Forest, Woodland
Swamp, Marshland
Shrub, Sparse Grass, Wasteland (pattern)
Barren Land
Oasis

INDIAN OCEAN

SEYCHELLES

COMORO ISLANDS

MADAGASCAR

Antananarivo

Mozambique Channel

Tropic of Capricorn

Gulf of Aden

Aden

Berbera

DANAKIL

Asmera

Khartoum

Blue Nile

Addis Ababa

White Nile

Mountain Nile

Mogadisho

Nairobi

Dar-es-Salaam

Lake Victoria

Lake Tanganyika

Lake Nyasa

Blantyre

Kisangani

Uele

Bangui

Congo (Zaire)

Ubangi

Kasai

Kinshasa

Lubumbashi

Lusaka

Salisbury

Zambezi

Limpopo

Luanda

Johannesburg

Durban

KALAHARI DESERT

Windhoek

Orange

NAMIB DESERT

Orange

Cape Town

Equator

0   100   200   400   600   800 Miles

0   150   300   600   900   1200 Kilometers

BORNEO

CELEBES

SERAM

Jayapur

**Palembang**

Banjarmasin

Ujung Pandang

*Java    Sea*

SUMATRA

**JAKARTA**

**Surabaya**

*Arafura    Sea*

JAVA

SUMBA

TIMOR

*Timor*

*Sea*

Darwin

*Gulf    of*

CAPE
YORK
PENINSUL

*Carpentaria*

*Daly*

I  N  D  I  A  N        O  C  E  A  N

KIMBERLEY
PLATEAU

*Victoria*

Broome

*Fitzroy*

Mount Isa

GREAT SANDY DESERT

Alice Springs

GREAT
ARTESIAN

GIBSON DESERT

SIMPSON

BASIN

DESERT

Tropic of Capricorn

Carnarvon

GREAT VICTORIA DESERT

*Lake
Eyre*

Kalgoorlie

NULLARBOR PLAIN

*Lake
Gairdner*

Broken
Hill

DARLING RA.

*Great Australian Bight*

*Murray*

**Perth**

**Adelaide**

I  N  D  I  A  N    O  C  E  A  N

| | |
|---|---|
| Urban | |
| Cropland | |
| Cropland & Woodland | |
| Cropland & Grazing Land | |
| Grassland, Grazing Land | |
| Forest, Woodland | |
| Swamp, Marshland | |
| Shrub, Sparse Grass, Wasteland (pattern) | |
| Barren Land | |

Lambert Azimuthal Equal-Area Projection

NEW
GUINEA

NEW BRITAIN

Port Moresby

SOLOMON ISLANDS

*Coral Sea*

Cairns

Townsville

GREAT

DIVIDING

RANGE

Rockhampton

Darling

Brisbane

SYDNEY

Canberra

GREAT DIVIDING RANGE

MELBOURNE

*Tasman Sea*

TASMANIA

Hobart

*Equator*

GILBERT
ISLANDS

P A C I F I C        O C E A N

NEW
HEBRIDES

SAMOA ISLANDS

Pago Pago

NEW
CALEDONIA

ÎLES
LOYAUTÉ

Nouméa

FIJI
ISLANDS

Suva

TONGA ISLANDS

P A C I F I C

O C E A N

Auckland

NORTH ISLAND

Wellington

SOUTHERN ALPS

Christchurch

SOUTH ISLAND

STEWART
ISLAND

Dunedin

| 0 | 100 | 200 | 400 | 600 | 800 Miles |
|---|-----|-----|-----|-----|-----------|

| 0 | 150 | 300 | 600 | 900 | 1200 Kilometers |
|---|-----|-----|-----|-----|-----------------|

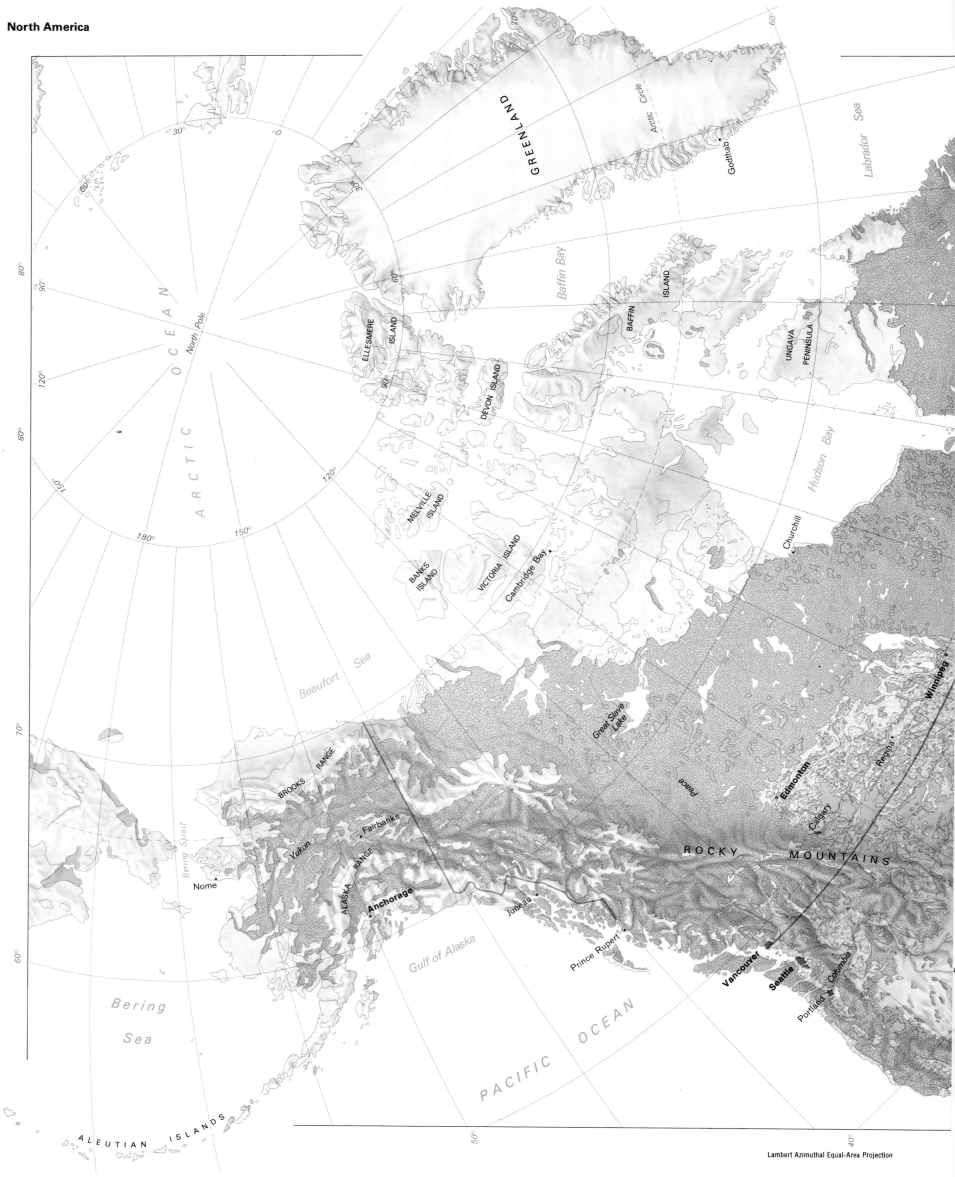

GREENLAND

Arctic Circle

Labrador Sea

Baffin Bay

Godthab

ELLESMERE ISLAND

BAFFIN ISLAND

DEVON ISLAND

UNGAVA PENINSULA

ARCTIC OCEAN

North Pole

MELVILLE ISLAND

BANKS ISLAND

VICTORIA ISLAND

Cambridge Bay

Hudson Bay

Churchill

Beaufort Sea

Great Slave Lake

Winnipeg

BROOKS RANGE

Peace

Edmonton

Regina

Fairbanks

ROCKY    MOUNTAINS

Calgary

Yukon

Bering Strait

ALASKA RANGE

Nome

Anchorage

Juneau

Prince Rupert

Gulf of Alaska

Vancouver

Seattle

British Columbia

Bering

Sea

Portland

PACIFIC    OCEAN

ALEUTIAN    ISLANDS

Lambert Azimuthal Equal-Area Projection

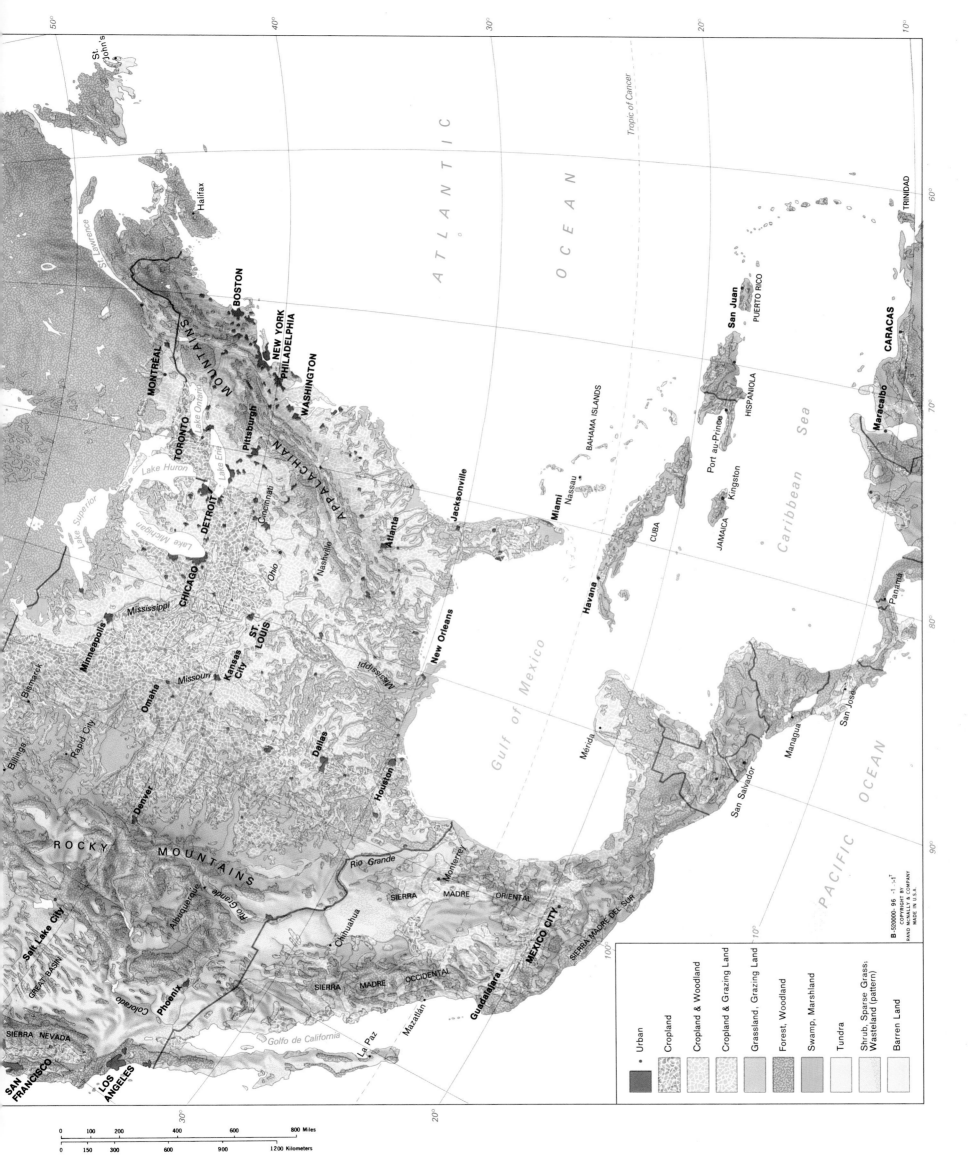

ATLANTIC

OCEAN

*Tropic of Cancer*

St. John's

Halifax

MONTREAL

BOSTON

NEW YORK
PHILADELPHIA
WASHINGTON

TORONTO

Pittsburgh

APPALACHIAN

Cincinnati

DETROIT

Nashville

Lake Superior

Lake Michigan

Lake Huron

Lake Erie

Lake Ontario

St. Lawrence

MOUNTAINS

CHICAGO

Ohio

Atlanta

Jacksonville

Miami

Havana

San Juan

PUERTO RICO

Port au-Prince

HISPANIOLA

Nassau

BAHAMA ISLANDS

CUBA

JAMAICA    Kingston

Caribbean    Sea

CARACAS

Maracaibo

TRINIDAD

60°

Minneapolis

Bismarck

Mississippi

ST. LOUIS

Kansas City

Missouri

Omaha

Rapid City

Billings

Dallas

New Orleans

Houston

Mississippi

Gulf of Mexico

Mérida

Panama

San José

Managua

San Salvador

Denver

ROCKY    MOUNTAINS

Rio Grande

Monterrey

SIERRA    MADRE    ORIENTAL

Chihuahua

SIERRA    MADRE    OCCIDENTAL

Albuquerque

Rio Grande

Salt Lake City

GREAT BASIN

Colorado

Phoenix

SIERRA NEVADA

SAN FRANCISCO

LOS ANGELES

MEXICO CITY

SIERRA MADRE DEL SUR

Guadalajara

Mazatlán

La Paz

Golfo de California

PACIFIC

OCEAN

100°

90°

80°

70°

10°

20°

30°

40°

50°

B-500000-96  -1  -1ᵀ

COPYRIGHT BY
RAND McNALLY & COMPANY
MADE IN U.S.A.

- Urban
- Cropland
- Cropland & Woodland
- Cropland & Grazing Land
- Grassland, Grazing Land
- Forest, Woodland
- Swamp, Marshland
- Tundra
- Shrub, Sparse Grass, Wasteland (pattern)
- Barren Land

0    100    200    400    600    800 Miles

0    150    300    600    900    1200 Kilometers

Lambert Azimuthal Equal-Area Projection

45

Belo Horizonte

RIO DE JANEIRO

SÃO PAULO

Paraná

Porto Alegre

Asunción

Montevideo

San Miguel de Tucumán

Córdoba

BUENOS AIRES

Bahía Blanca

P A M P A S

G R A N   C H A C O

A N D E S

Iquique

SANTIAGO

Puerto Montt

P A T A G O N I A

Punta Arenas

TIERRA
DEL FUEGO

FALKLAND
ISLANDS

SOUTH
GEORGIA

ANTARCTIC PENINSULA

Drake   Passage

A T L A N T I C

O C E A N

P A C I F I C

O C E A N

Tropic of Capricorn

B-540000-96  -1  -2ᵀ
COPYRIGHT BY
RAND McNALLY & COMPANY
MADE IN U.S.A.

• Urban

Cropland

Cropland & Woodland

Cropland & Grazing Land

Grassland, Grazing Land

Forest, Woodland

Swamp, Marshland

Shrub, Sparse Grass,
Wasteland (pattern)

Barren Land

0    100   200        400           600        800 Miles

0    150   300        600           900        1200 Kilometers

# National Flags

| | | | | |
|---|---|---|---|---|
| AFGHANISTAN | ALBANIA | ALGERIA | ANDORRA | ANGOLA |
| ARGENTINA | AUSTRALIA | AUSTRIA | BAHAMAS | BAHRAIN |
| BANGLADESH | BARBADOS | BELGIUM | BENIN | BHUTAN |
| BOLIVIA | BOTSWANA | BRAZIL | BULGARIA | BURMA |
| BURUNDI | CAMBODIA | CAMEROON | CANADA | CAPE VERDE |
| CENTRAL AFRICAN EMPIRE | CHAD | CHILE | CHINA | CHINA (TAIWAN) |
| COLOMBIA | COMORO ISLANDS | CONGO | COSTA RICA | CUBA |
| CYPRUS | CZECHOSLOVAKIA | DENMARK | DJIBOUTI | DOMINICAN REPUBLIC |
| ECUADOR | EGYPT | EL SALVADOR | EQUATORIAL GUINEA | ETHIOPIA |
| FIJI | FINLAND | FRANCE | GABON | GAMBIA |
| GERMAN DEMOCRATIC REPUBLIC | GERMANY, FEDERAL REPUBLIC | GHANA | GREECE | GRENADA |
| GUATEMALA | GUINEA | GUINEA-BISSAU | GUYANA | HAITI |
| HONDURAS | HUNGARY | ICELAND | INDIA | INDONESIA |
| IRAN | IRAQ | IRELAND | ISRAEL | ITALY |
| IVORY COAST | JAMAICA | JAPAN | JORDAN | KENYA |
| KOREA, NORTH | KOREA, SOUTH | KUWAIT | LAOS | LEBANON |

Flags shown are *national* flags in common use and vary slightly from official *state* flags, most particularly by omitting coats of arms in some cases.

LESOTHO LIBERIA LIBYA LIECHTENSTEIN LUXEMBOURG MADAGASCAR MALAWI MALAYSIA MALDIVES MALI

MALTA MAURITANIA MAURITIUS MEXICO MONACO MONGOLIA MOROCCO MOZAMBIQUE NAURU NEPAL

NETHERLANDS NEW ZEALAND NICARAGUA NIGER NIGERIA NORWAY OMAN PAKISTAN PANAMA PAPUA NEW GUINEA

PARAGUAY PERU PHILIPPINES POLAND PORTUGAL QATAR RHODESIA ROMANIA RWANDA SAN MARINO

SAO TOME & PRINCIPE SAUDI ARABIA SENEGAL SEYCHELLES SIERRA LEONE SINGAPORE SOLOMON ISLANDS SOMALIA SOUTH AFRICA SPAIN

SRI LANKA SUDAN SURINAM SWAZILAND SWEDEN SWITZERLAND SYRIA TANZANIA THAILAND TOGO

TONGA TRINIDAD & TOBAGO TUNISIA TURKEY UGANDA U.S.S.R. UNITED ARAB EMIRATES UNITED KINGDOM UNITED STATES UPPER VOLTA

URUGUAY VATICAN CITY VENEZUELA VIETNAM WESTERN SAMOA YEMEN YEMEN, P.D.R. OF YUGOSLAVIA ZAIRE ZAMBIA

# Comparative World Time

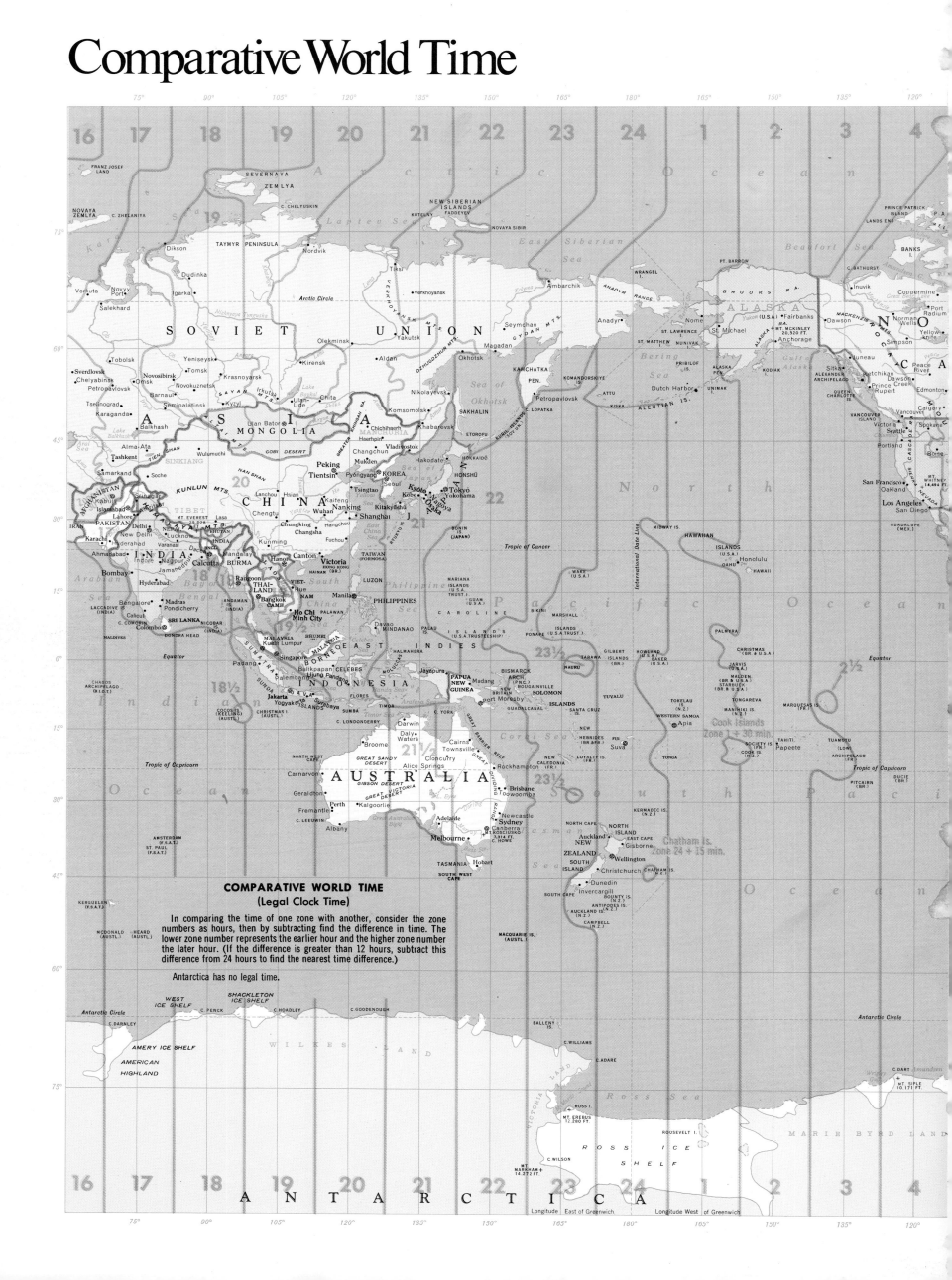

**COMPARATIVE WORLD TIME**
(Legal Clock Time)

In comparing the time of one zone with another, consider the zone numbers as hours, then by subtracting find the difference in time. The lower zone number represents the earlier hour and the higher zone number the later hour. (If the difference is greater than 12 hours, subtract this difference from 24 hours to find the nearest time difference.)

Antarctica has no legal time.

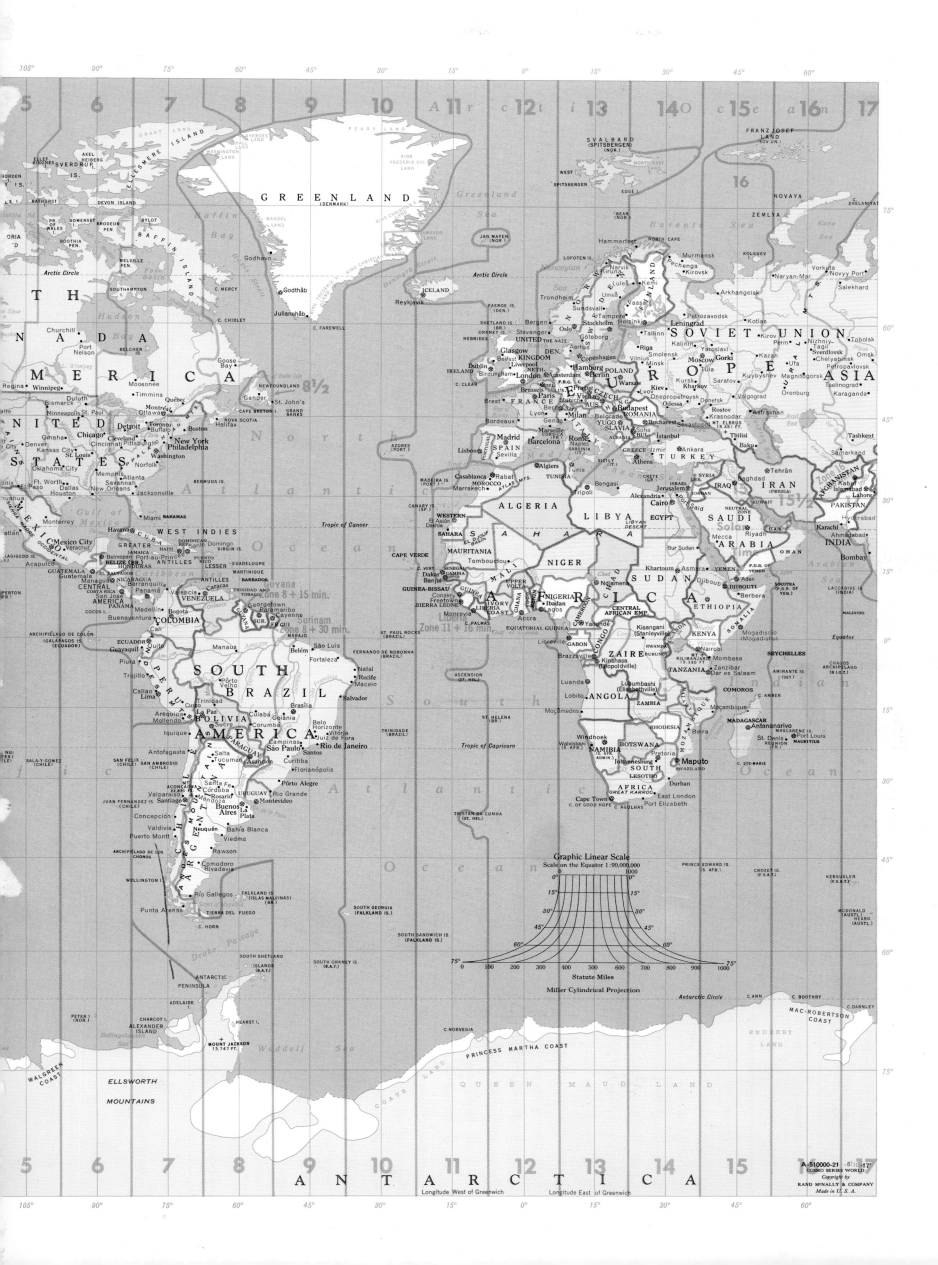

Scale 1:12,000,000

One centimeter represents 120 kilometers.
One inch represents approximately 190 miles.

Miller Oblated Stereographic Projection

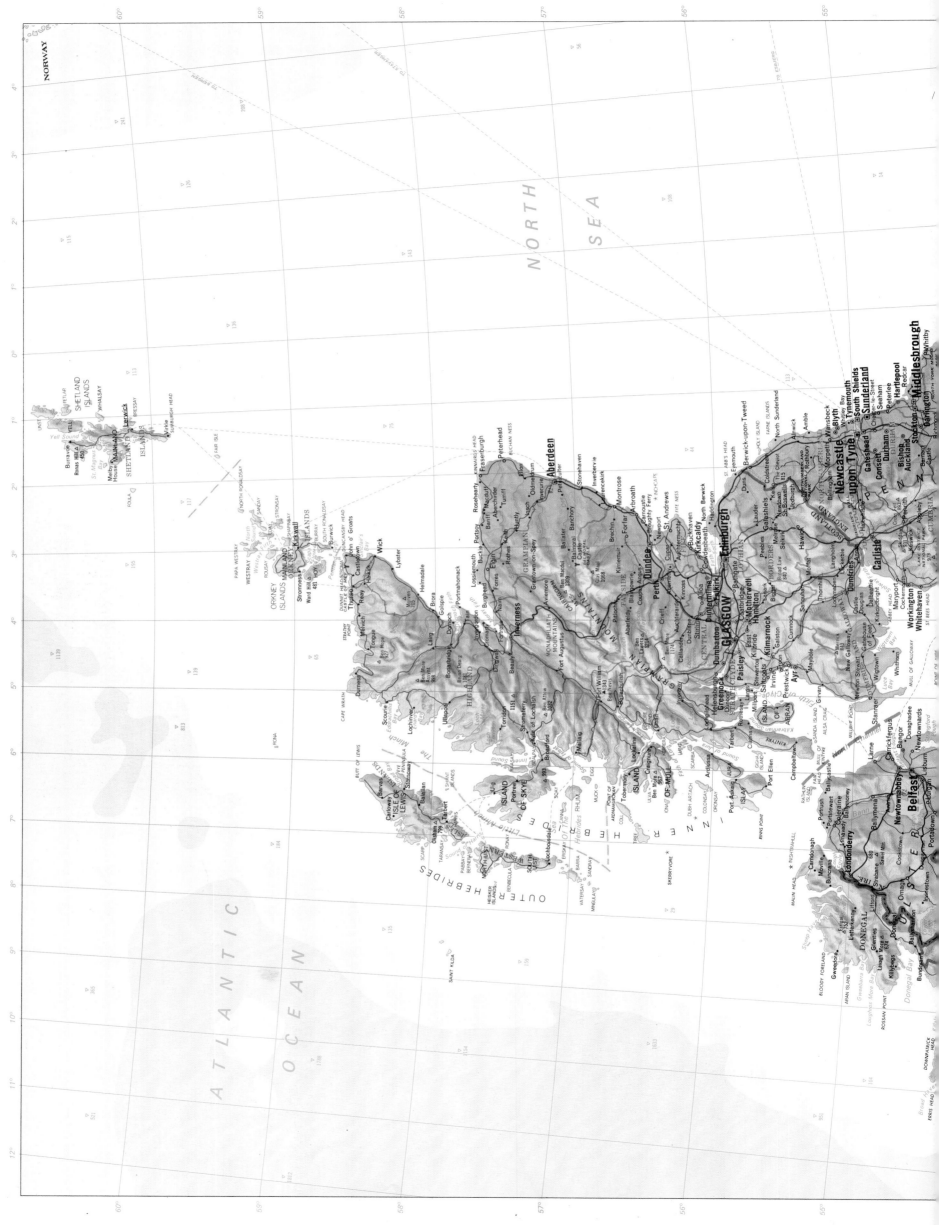

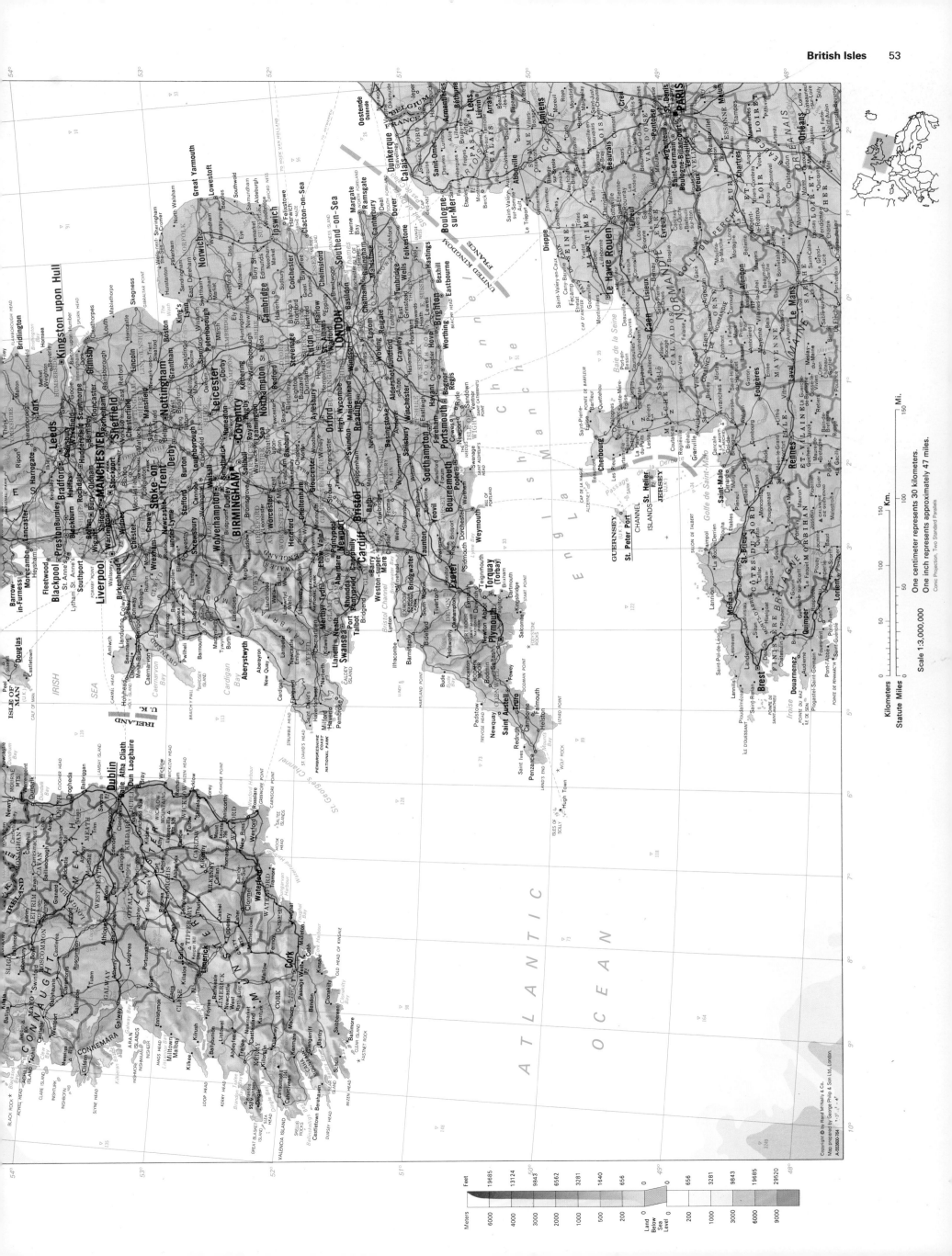

Copyright © by Rand M°Nally & Co.
Map prepared by Rand M°Nally & Co.
A-553292-264

Kilometers  0  10  20  30  40  50  Km.
Statute Miles  0  10  20  30  40  50  Mi.

Scale 1:1,000,000

One centimeter represents 10 kilometers.
One inch represents approximately 16 miles.

Lambert Conformal Conic Projection

Kilometers 0 10 20 30 40 50 Km.
Statute Miles 0 10 20 30 40 50 Mi.

Scale 1:1,000,000

One centimeter represents 10 kilometers.
One inch represents approximately 16 miles.

Lambert Conformal Conic Projection

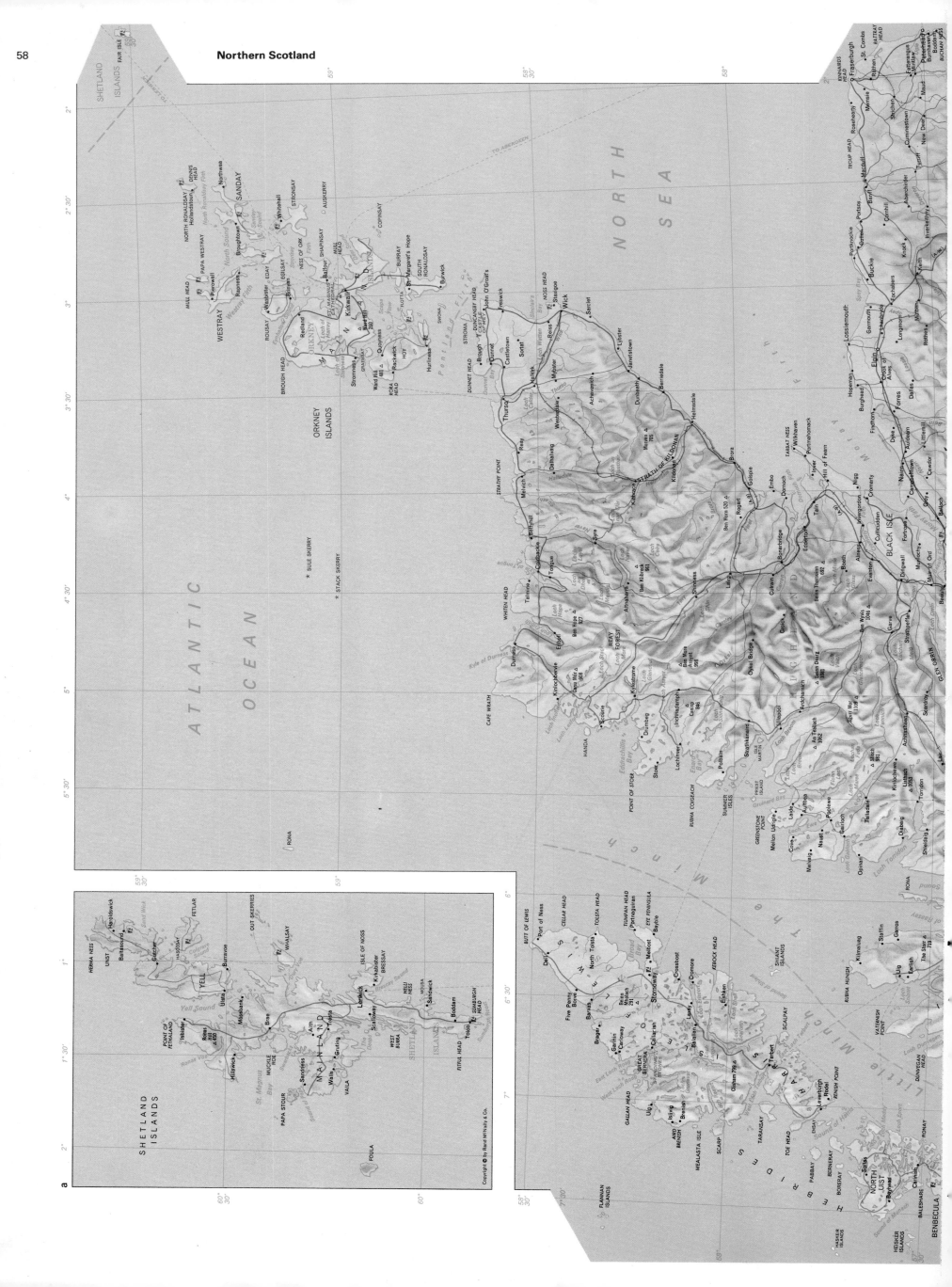

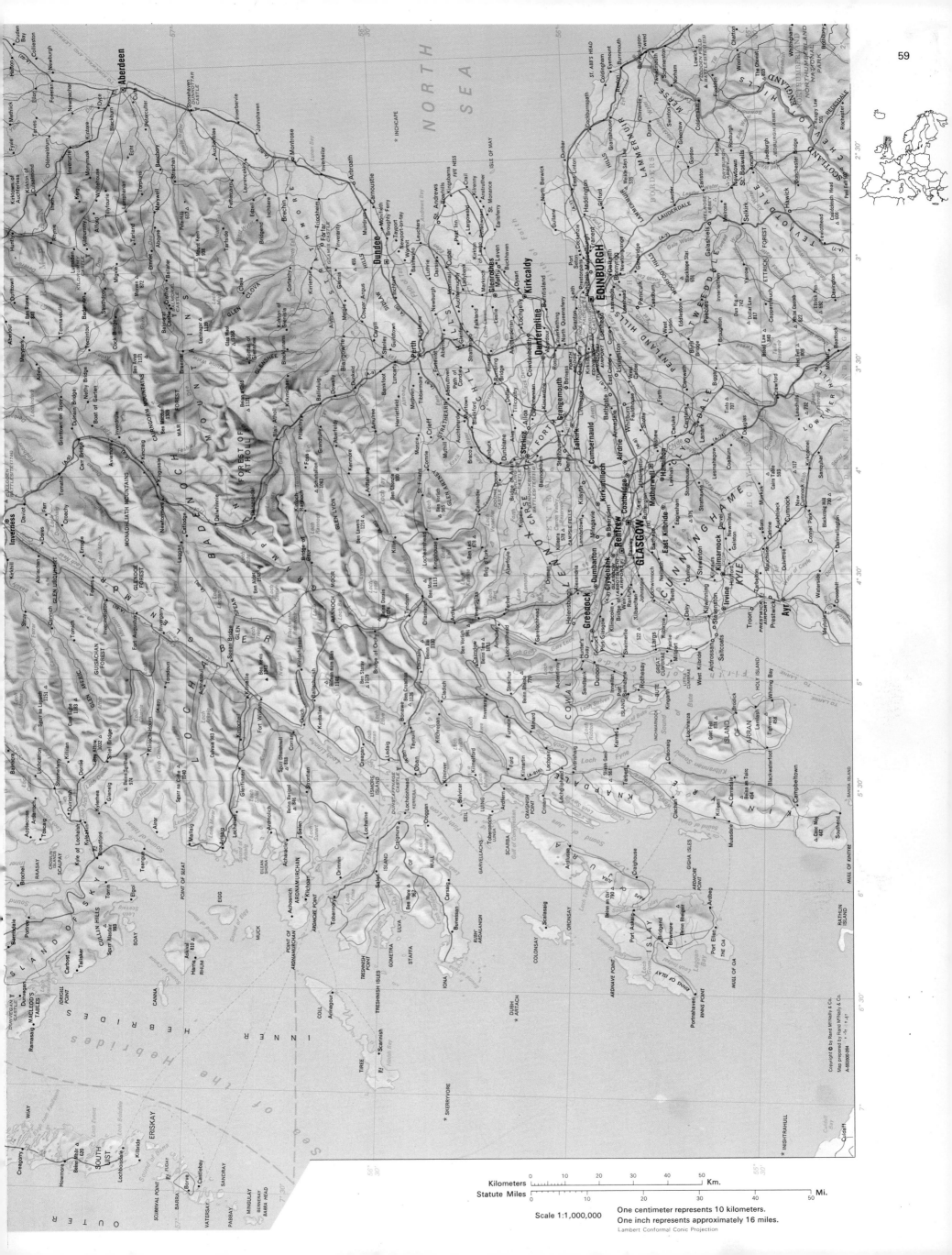

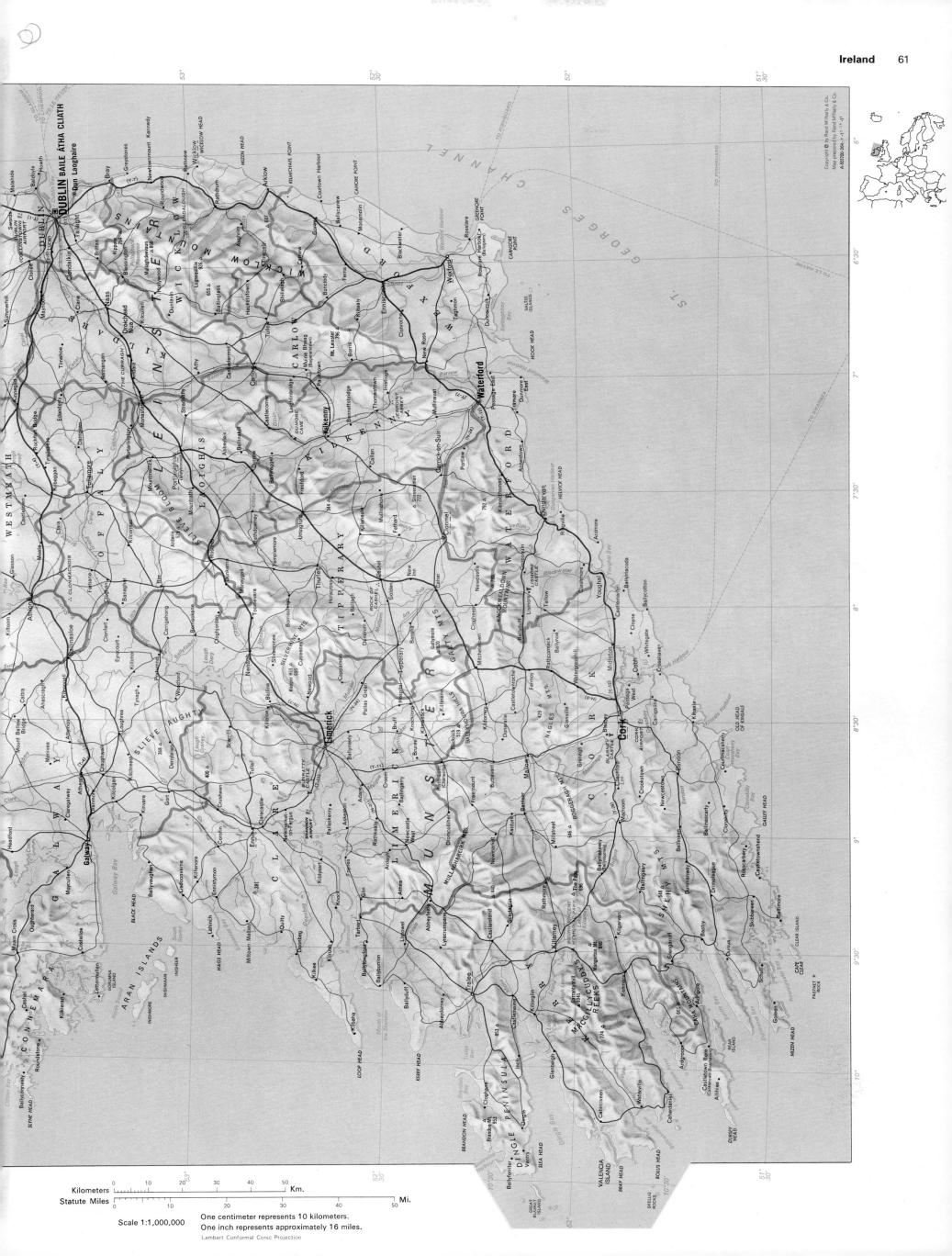

Kilometers
Statute Miles

Scale 1:6,000,000

One centimeter represents 60 kilometers.
One inch represents approximately 95 miles.
Lambert Conformal Conic Projection

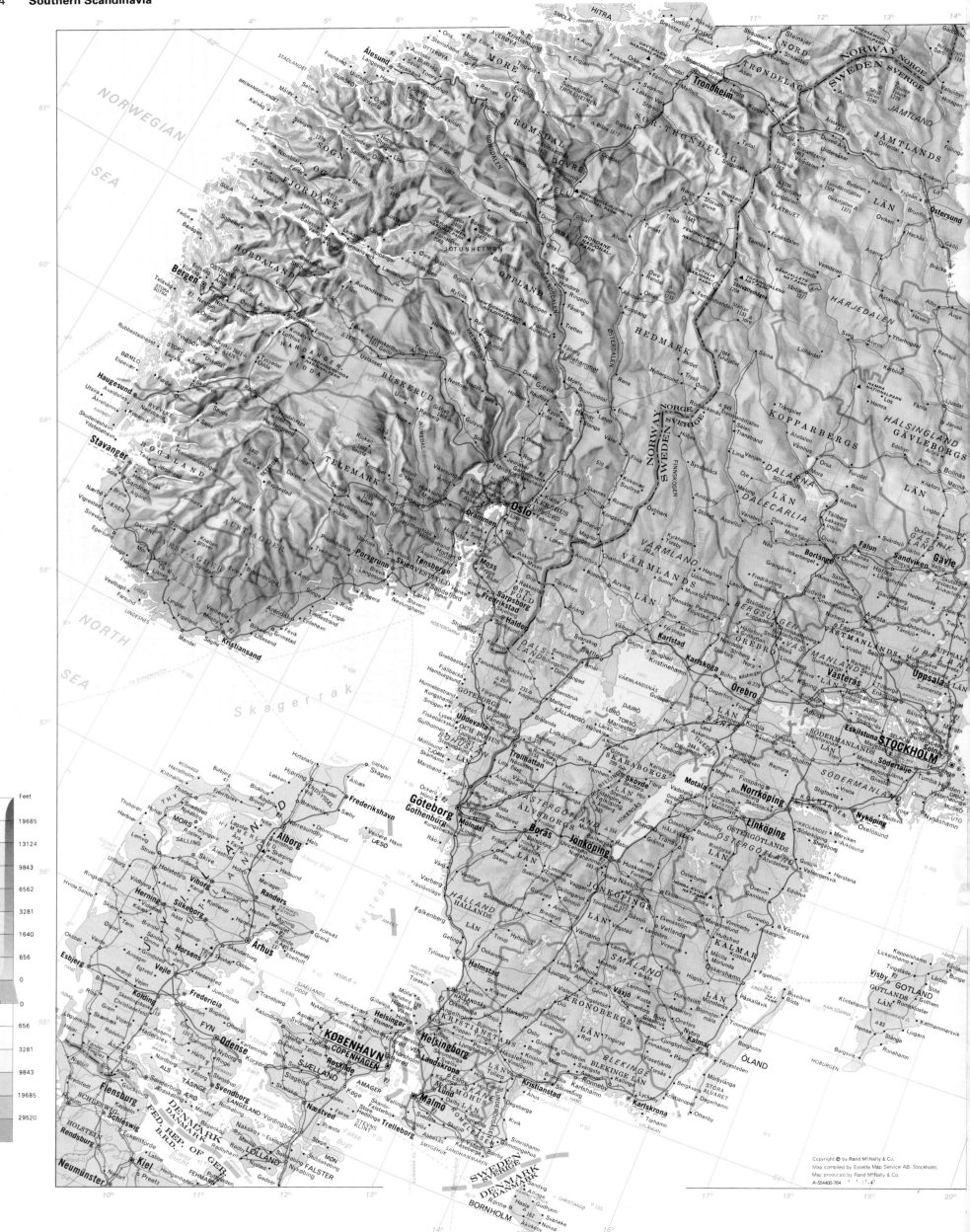

Kilometers
0    50    100    150
|————————————|———————|———————| Km.

Statute Miles
0    50    100    150
|————————————————|——————————————| Mi.

Scale 1:3,000,000

One centimeter represents 30 kilometers.
One inch represents approximately 47 miles.
Conic Projection, Two Standard Parallels

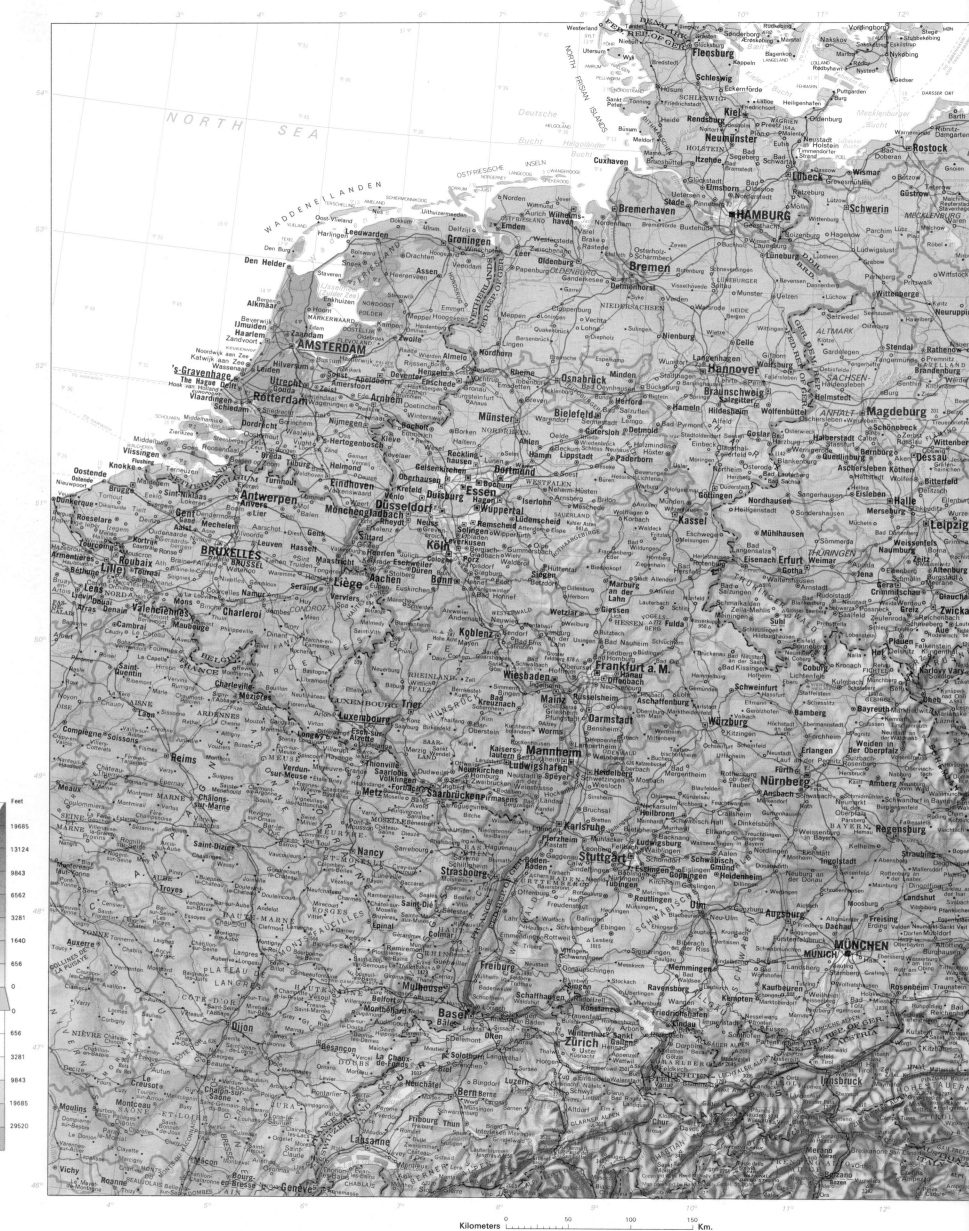

Kilometers

Statute Miles

Scale 1:3,000,000

One centimeter represents 30 kilometers.
One inch represents approximately 47 miles.
Conic Projection, Two Standard Parallels.

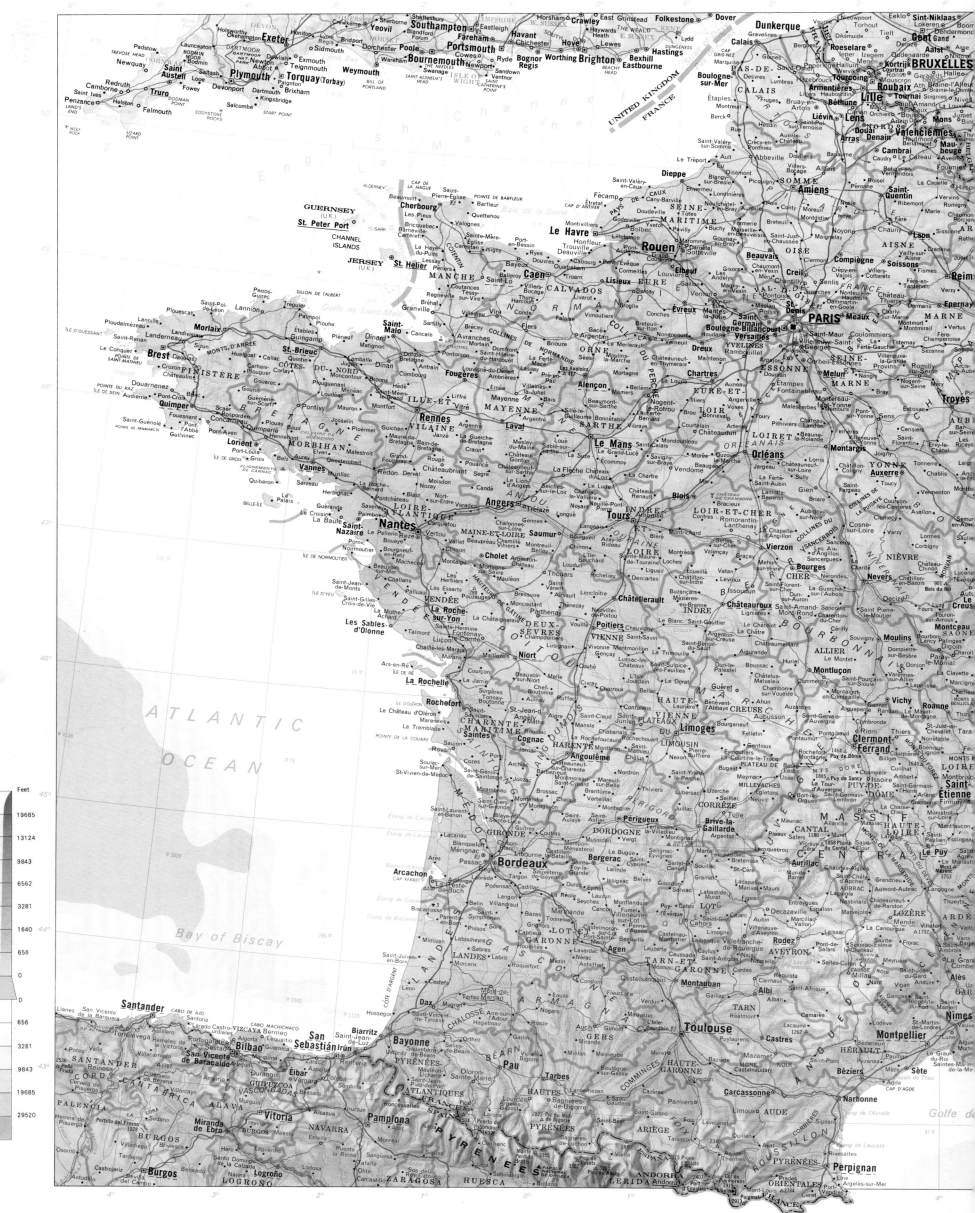

Kilometers

Statute Miles

Scale 1:3,000,000

One centimeter represents 30 kilometers.
One inch represents approximately 47 miles.

Lambert Conformal Conic Projection

Kilometers
Statute Miles

Scale 1:3,000,000

One centimeter represents 30 kilometers.
One inch represents approximately 47 miles.
Conic Projection, Two Standard Parallels

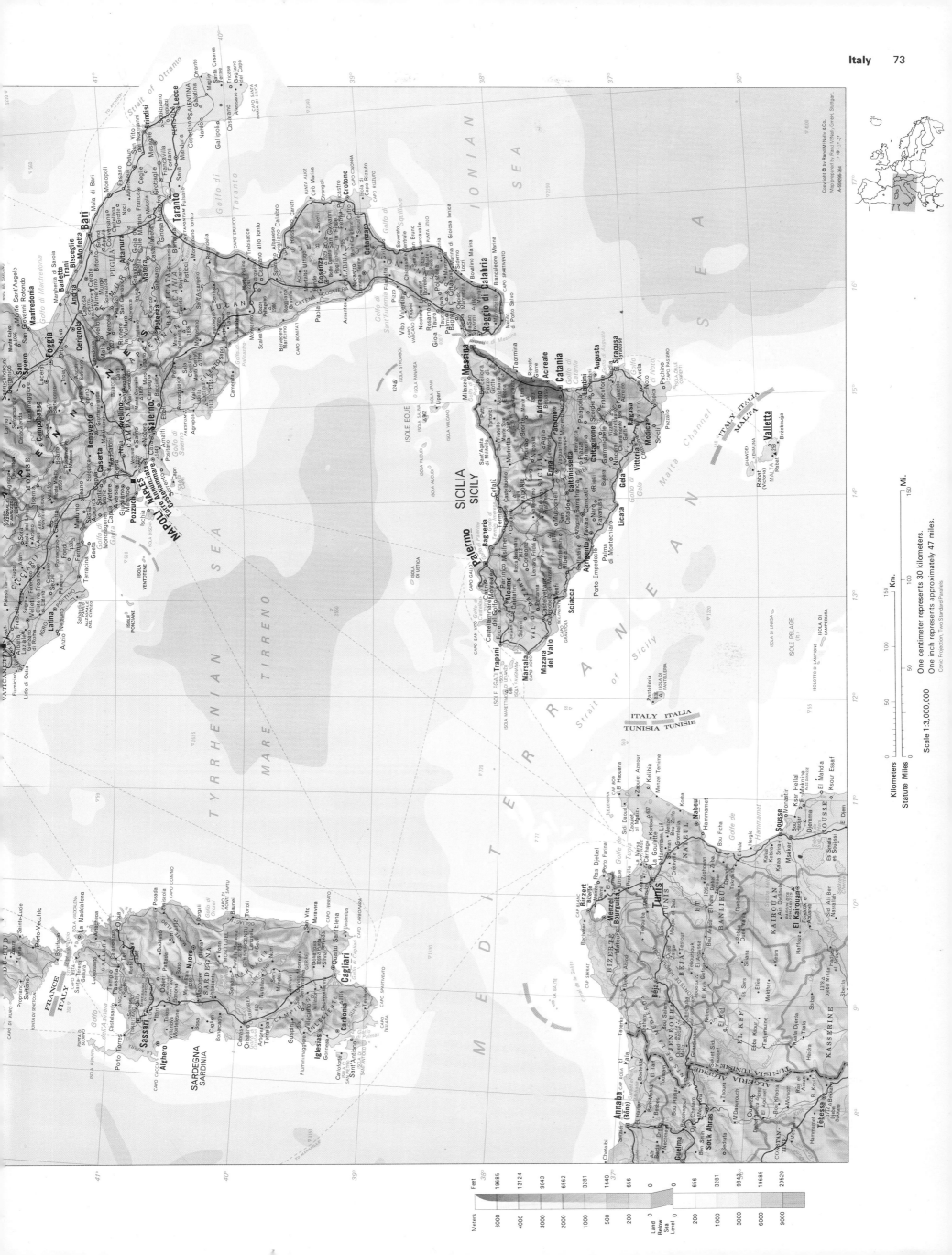

Scale 1:3,000,000

One centimeter represents 30 kilometers.
One inch represents approximately 47 miles.

Conic Projection, Two Standard Parallels

Kilometers
Statute Miles

Mi.
150

Km.
150
100

Scale 1:3,000,000

One centimeter represents 30 kilometers.
One inch represents approximately 47 miles.
Conic Projection. Two Standard Parallels

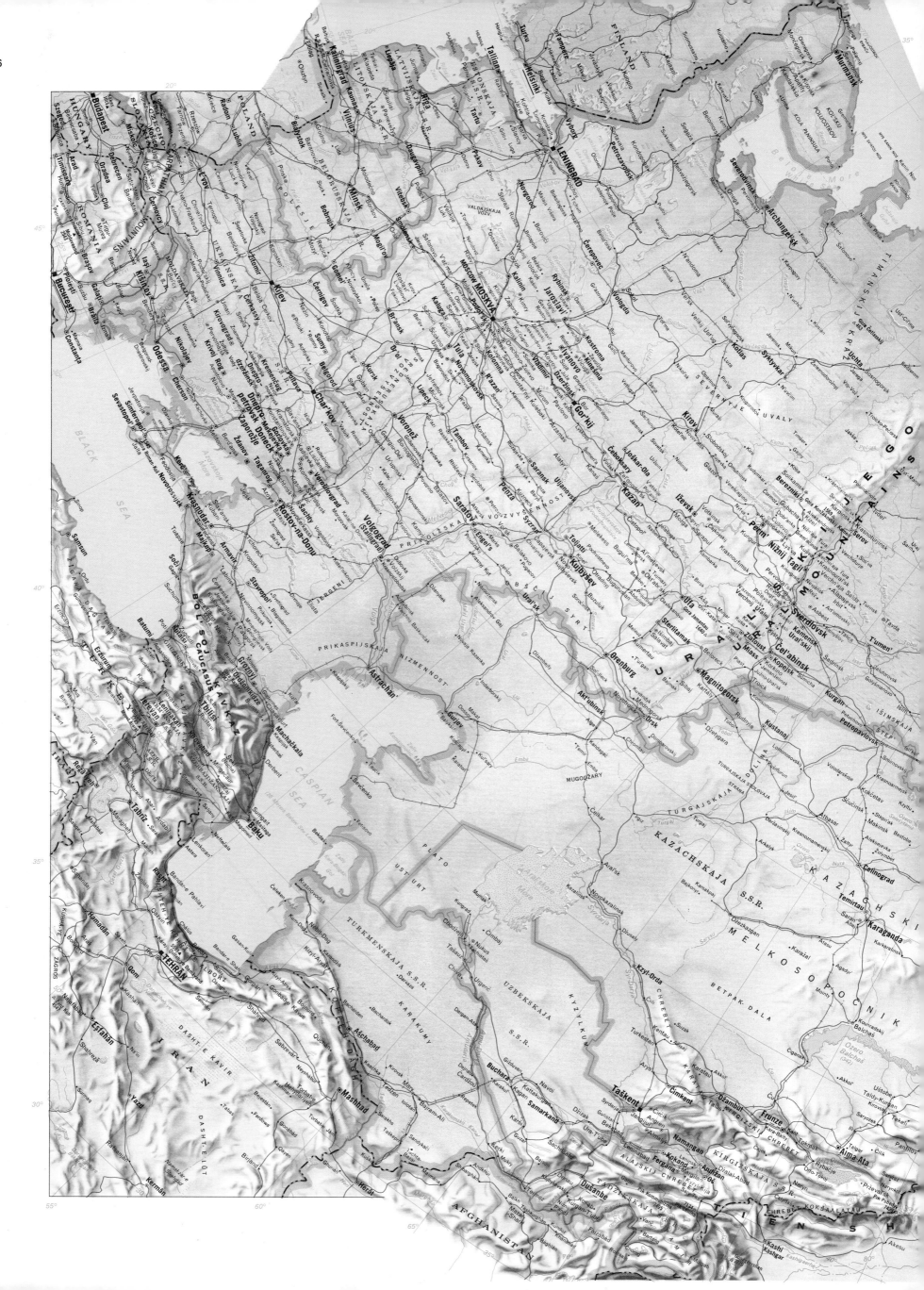

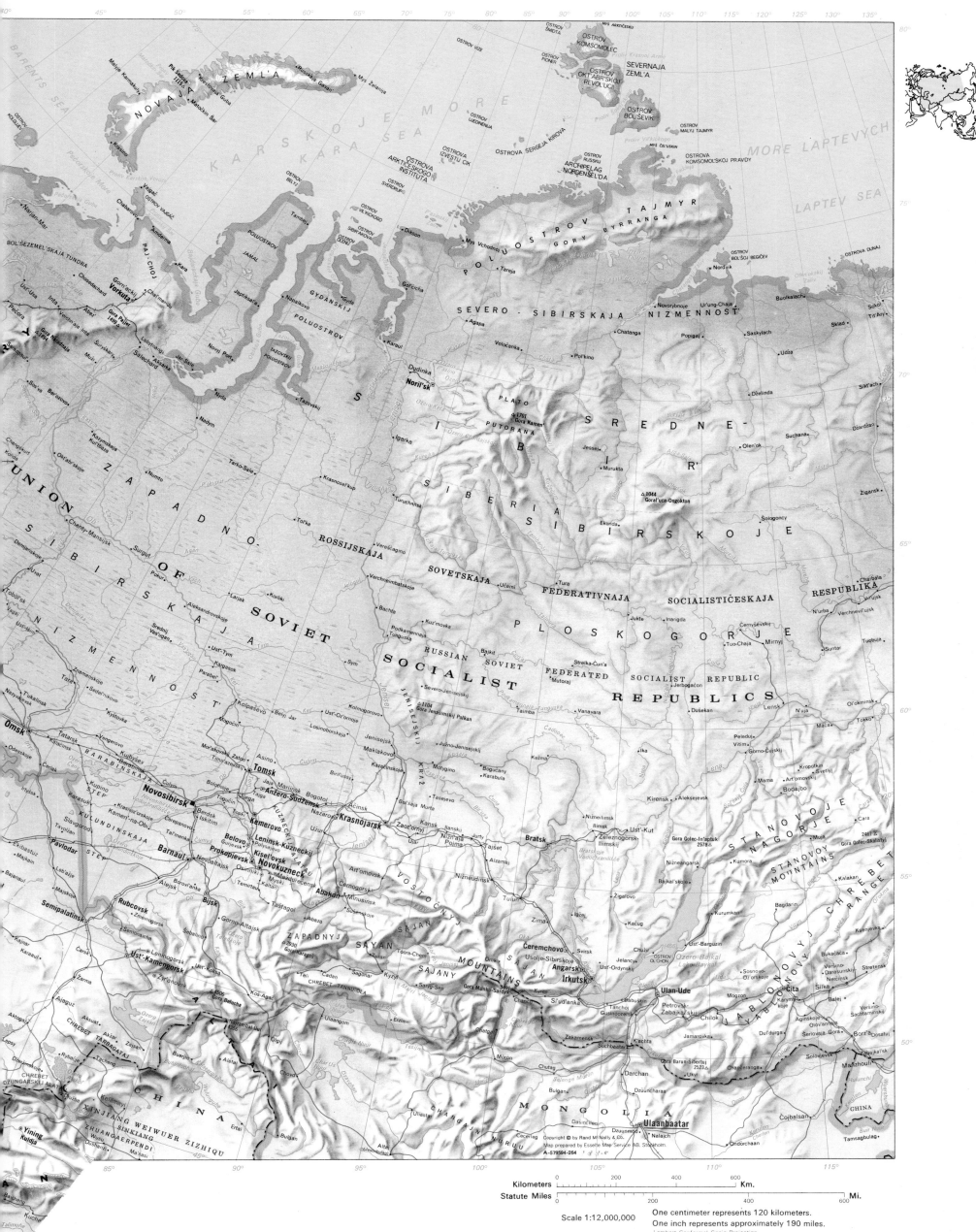

Scale 1:12,000,000

One centimeter represents 120 kilometers.
One inch represents approximately 190 miles.

Lambert Conformal Conic Projection

Kilometers  0    200    400    600   Km.

Statute Miles  0    200    400    600   Mi.

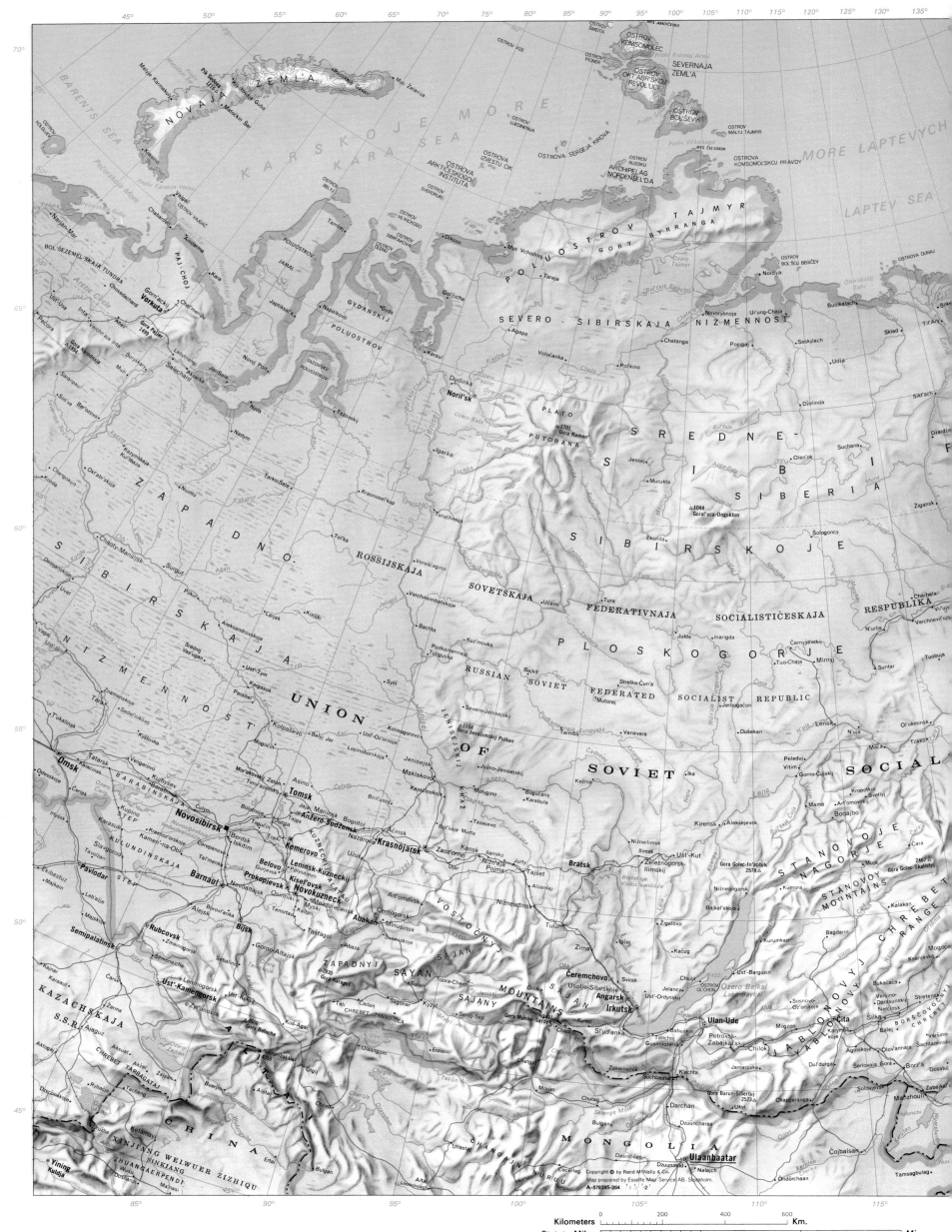

Kilometers

Statute Miles

Scale 1:12,000,000

One centimeter represents 120 kilometers.
One inch represents approximately 190 miles.
Lambert Conformal Conic Projection

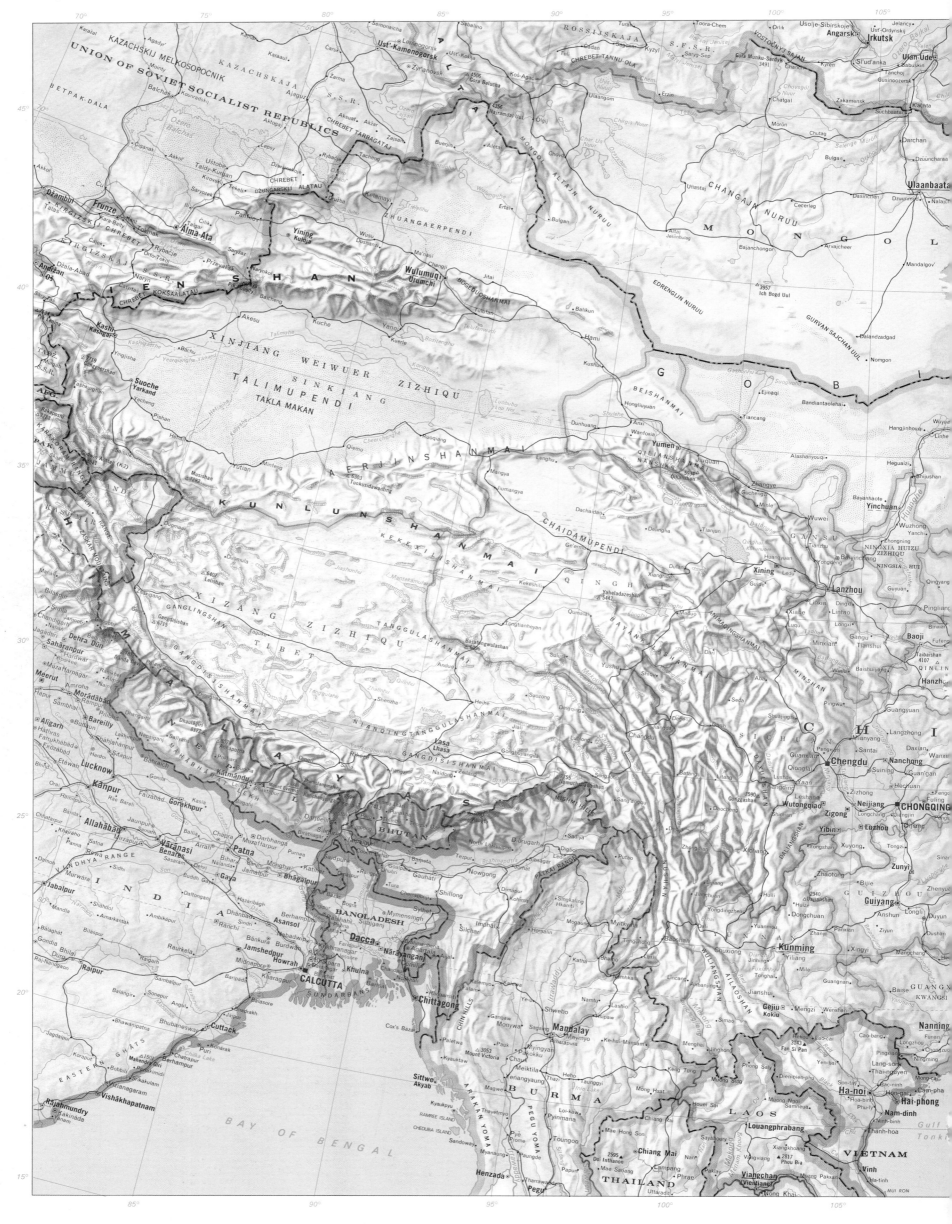

Scale 1:12,000,000

One centimeter represents 120 kilometers.
One inch represents approximately 190 miles.

Lambert Conformal Conic Projection

Scale 1:12,000,000

Kilometers

Statute Miles

One centimeter represents 120 kilometers.
One inch represents approximately 190 miles.

Lambert Conformal Conic Projection

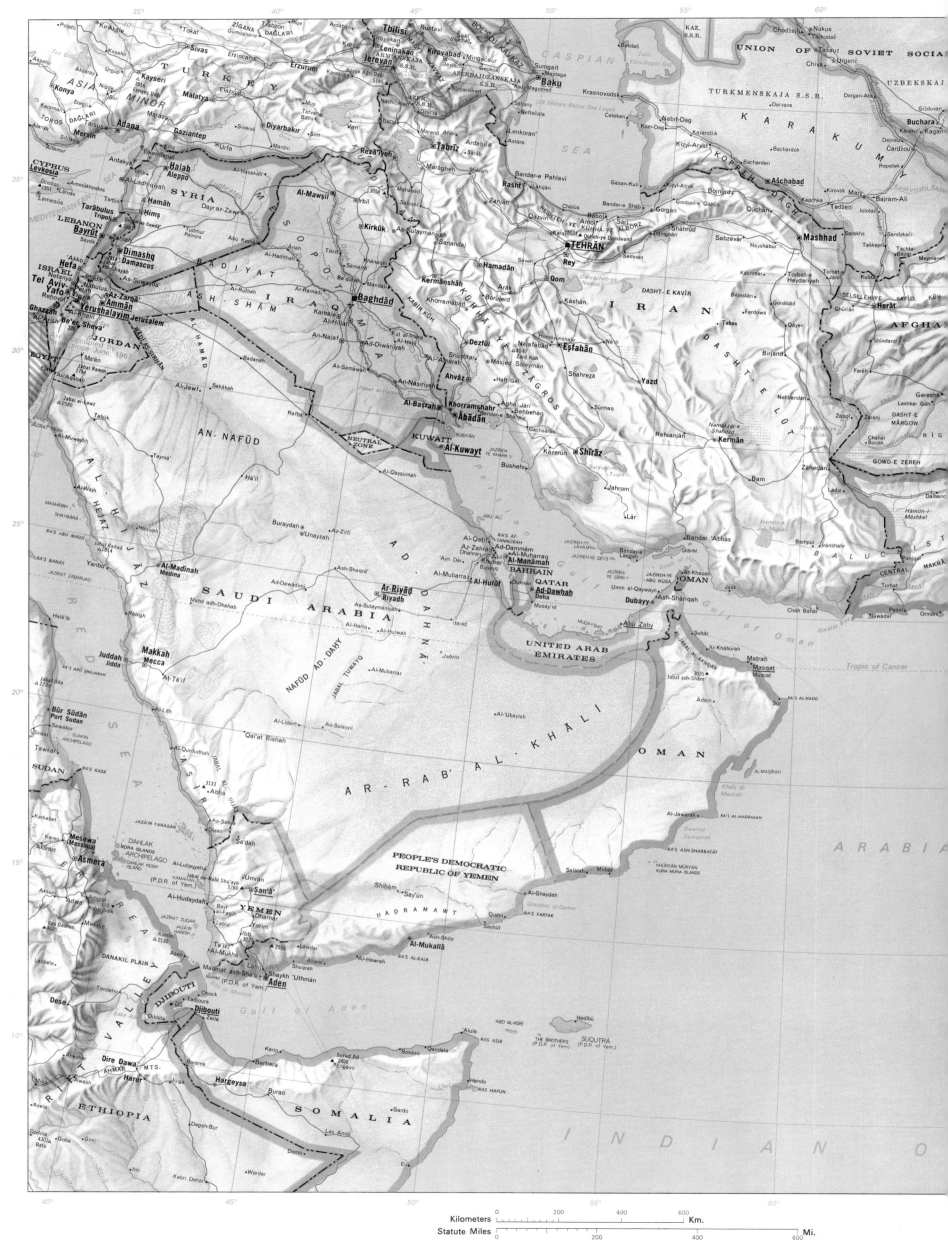

Kilometers |⊢⊢⊢⊢| 200        400        600
Statute Miles |⊢⊢| 0        200        400        600

Scale 1:12,000,000

One centimeter represents 120 kilometers.
One inch represents approximately 190 miles.

Lambert Conformal Conic Projection

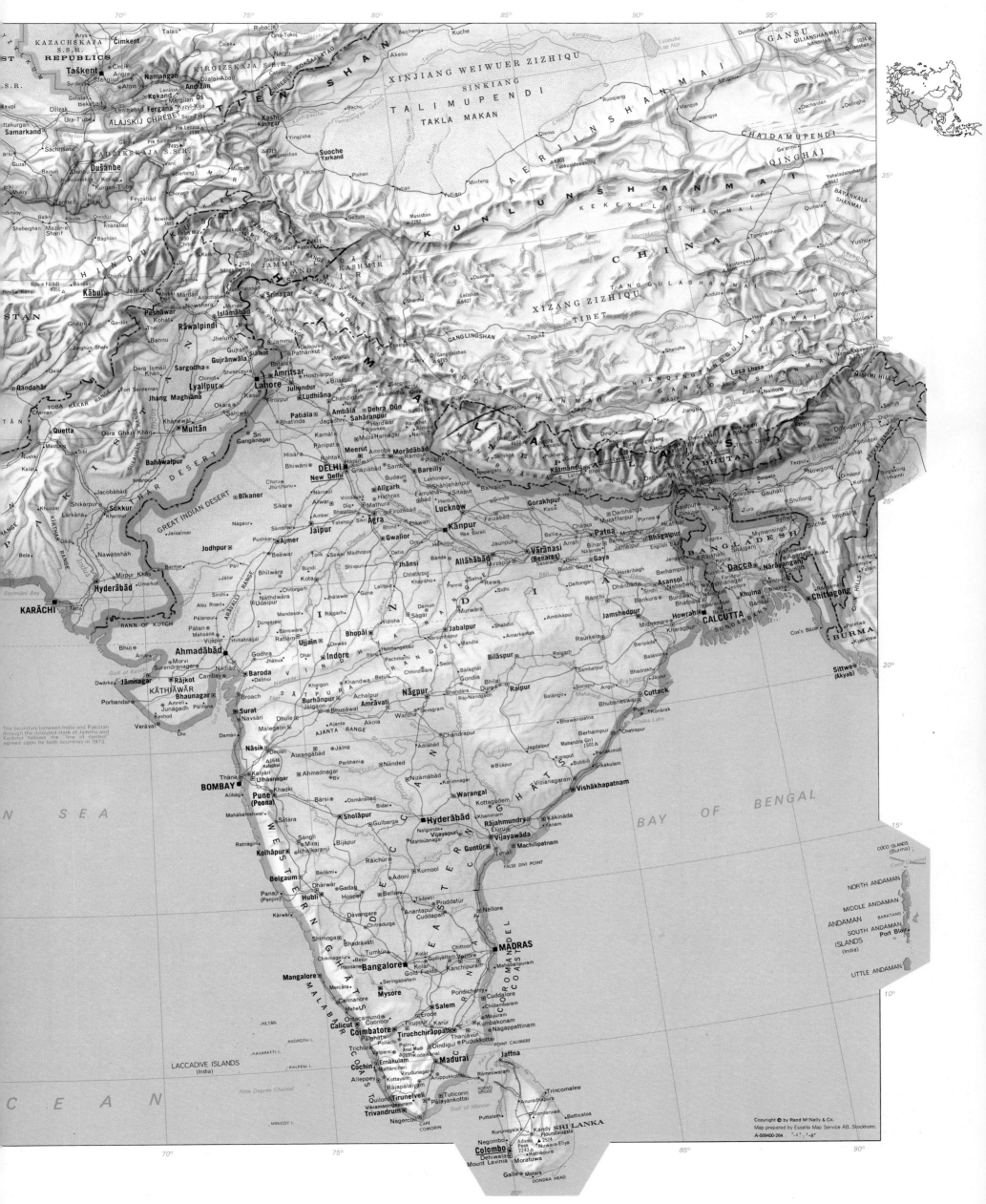

Kilometers |0    200    400    600| Km.

Statute Miles |0    200    400    600| Mi.

Scale 1:12,000,000

One centimeter represents 120 kilometers.
One inch represents approximately 190 miles.
Miller Oblated Stereographic Projection

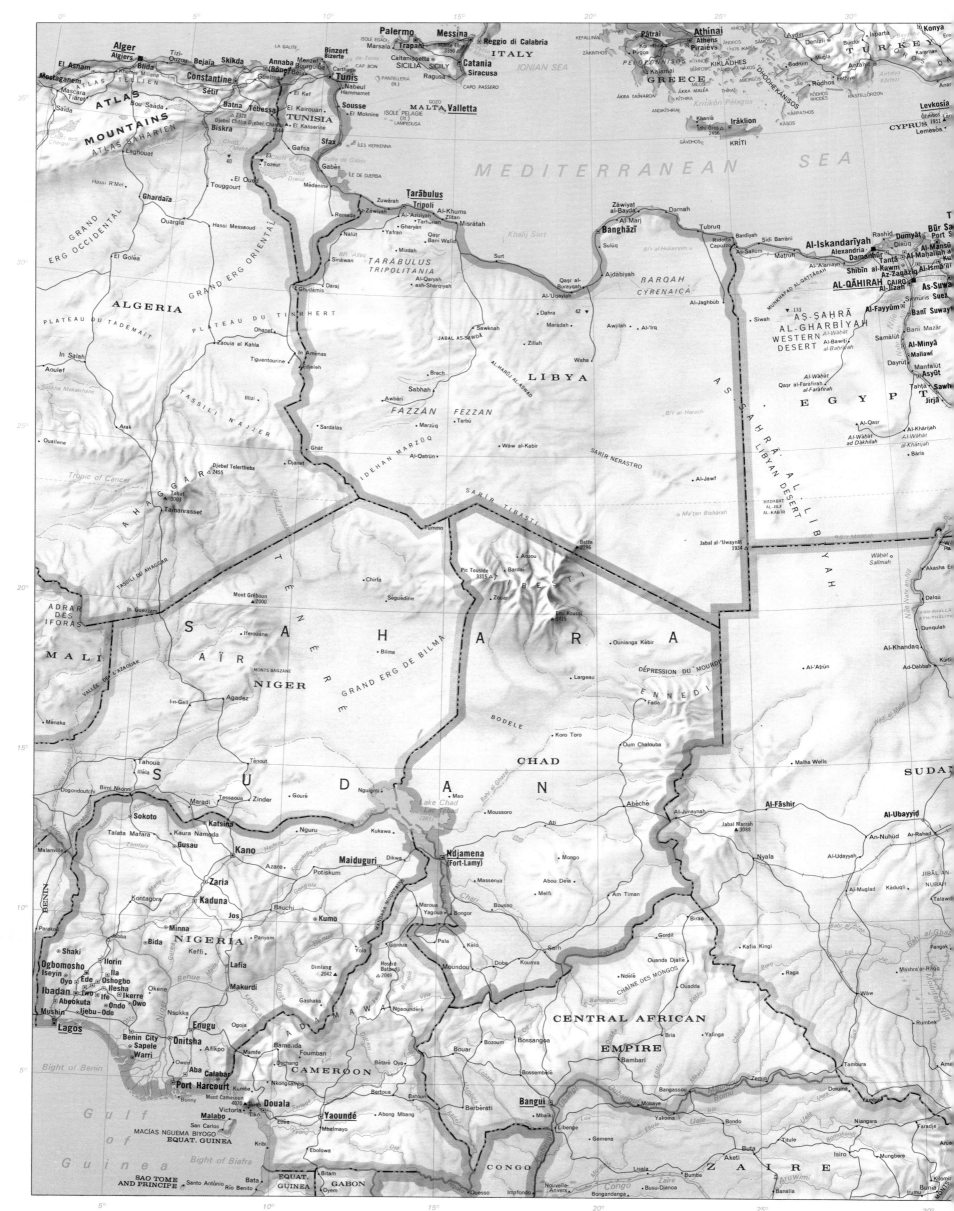

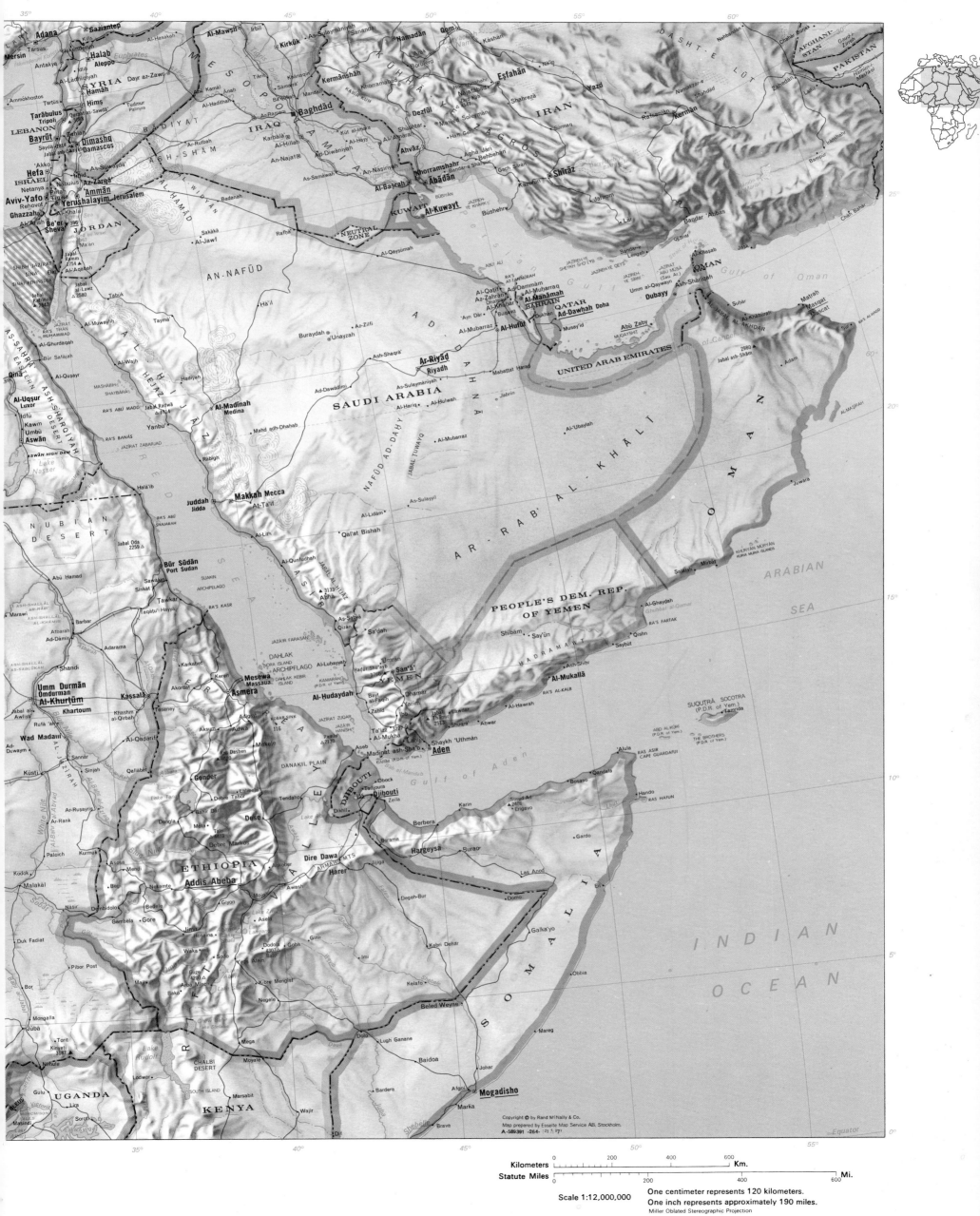

Kilometers |—|—|—|—|—|—|—| Km.
0    200    400    600

Statute Miles |—|—|—|—|—| Mi.
0    200    400    600

Scale 1:12,000,000

One centimeter represents 120 kilometers.
One inch represents approximately 190 miles.

Miller Oblated Stereographic Projection

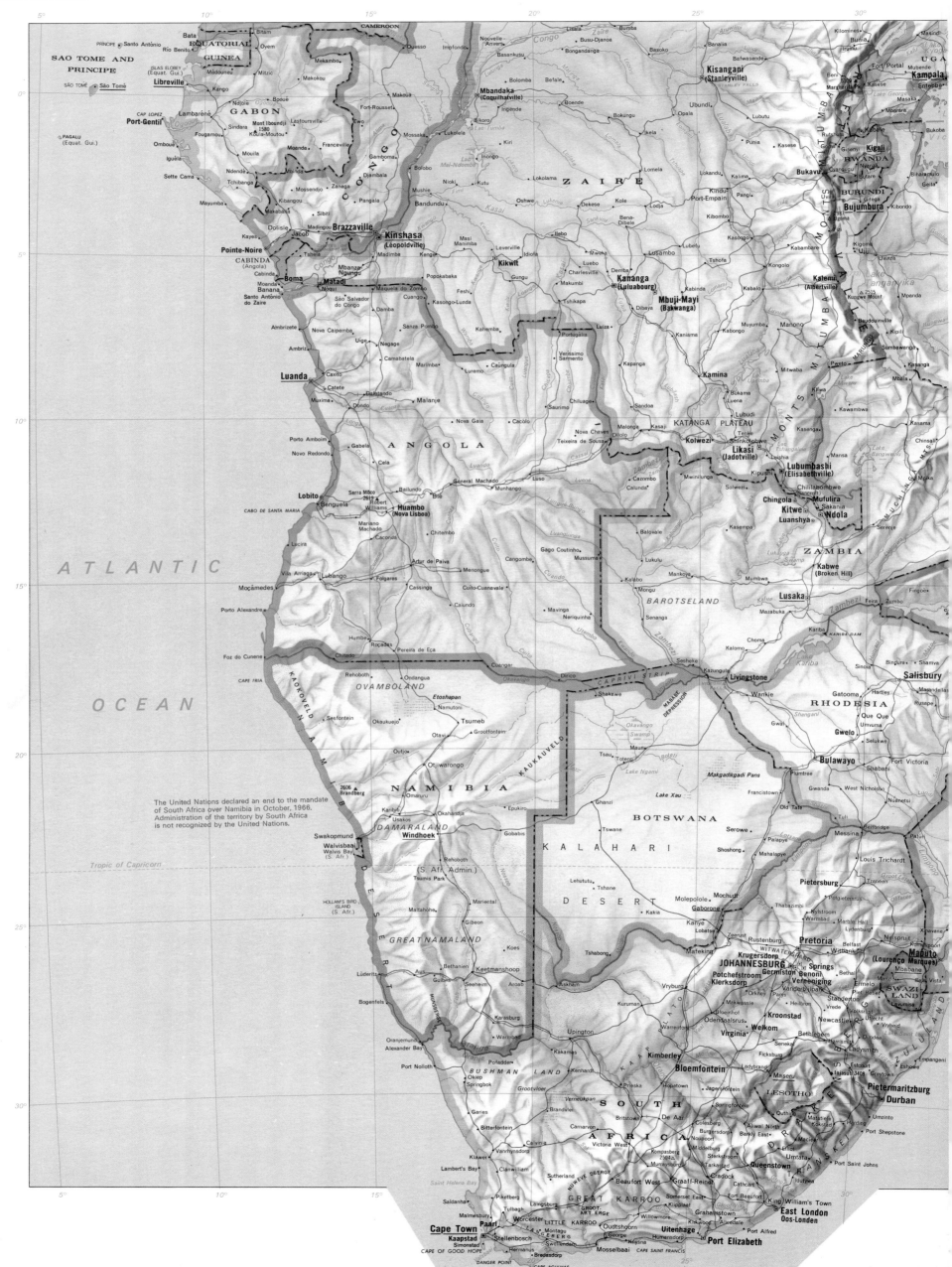

The United Nations declared an end to the mandate of South Africa over Namibia in October, 1966. Administration of the territory by South Africa is not recognized by the United Nations.

INDIAN OCEAN

*Equator*                                                        0°

SOMALIA

Di                    Atinadu Jillib
SOMALIA              Jamame

Brava

Kismayu  Jumbo

Bur Gavo

PATE ISLAND
Lamu

SEYCHELLES

PRASLIN
ISLAND  LA DIGUE
SILHOUETTE   **Victoria**
MAHÉ ISLAND                        5°

KENYA

**Nairobi**  Kitui

Mombasa

MASAI

STEPPE

TANZANIA

Tanga   PEMBA ISLAND
Chake Chake

**Zanzibar**
ZANZIBAR

**Dar-es-Salaam**
ULUGURU
MOUNTAINS

AMIRANTE ISLANDS
(Sey.)   ÎLE DESROCHES
(Sey.)     PLATTE ISLAND (Sey.)

COETIVY ISLAND
(Sey.)

ALPHONSE ISLAND (Sey.)

MAFIA ISLAND
Kilindoni

Kilwa Kivinje
Kilwa Kisiwani

Liwale

Lindi

AGALEGA ISLANDS
(Mauritius)                        10°

PROVIDENCE ISLAND
(Sey.)

Nachingwea

Mikindani
**Mtwara**  CABO DELGADO
Palma

Mocímboa da Praia

MALAWI

Ibo
Quissanga
Porto Amélia

Montepuez

ALDABRA ISLANDS
(Sey.)

ASSUMPTION ISLAND
(Sey.)

COSMOLEDO GROUP
(Sey.)

ASTOVE ISLAND
(Sey.)

SAINT PIERRE ISLAND
(Sey.)

CERF ISLAND
(Sey.)

FARQUHAR GROUP
(Sey.)

GRANDE COMORE
Moroni   **COMOROS**

Fomboni
MOHÉLI   Mutsamudu
ANJOUAN

BANC DU GEYSER

CAP
SAINT-SÉBASTIEN   CAP D'AMBRE

**Diégo-Suarez**

MAYOTTE
(Fr.)   Dzaoudzi

NOSY MITSIO

NOSY BE
**Hell-Ville**   Ambilobe   Vohémar

Ambanja
MASSIF DU
Maromokotro 2876
TSARATANANA

Sambava

NOSY LAVA
Analalava   Bealanana   Andapa   Antalaha

Befandriana

Montepuez

Namapa
Nacala-Velha

Lúrio

**Moçambique**
Namib

MOZAMBIQUE

Mogincual   Quinga

CAP SAINT-ANDRÉ

ÎLE CHESTERFIELD

Port-Bergé   Mandritsara

Mampikony

Maroantsetra   CAP EST
PRESQU'ÎLE
MASOALA

Baie de Narinda

**Majunga**

ÎLE SAINTE-MARIE
Ambodifototra

Marovoay

Antsohihy

Soalala

Tsaratanana

Mananara

Antònio Enes
ILHA ANGOCHE

Nampula

Maua

Nova Freixo   Entre-Rios

Mandimba

**Zomba**
**Blantyre**
Sapitwa 3000
Mulanje

Tete

Namib

Mocuba

Pebane

CAP SAINT-ANDRÉ

Besalampy

ÎLE JUAN DE NOVA
(Fr.)

Maevatanana

Tsaratanana

Andriamena   Fénérive

TROMELIN
(Fr.)                              15°

Ambatondrazaka

**Tamatave**

Tamatave

Tambohorano

ÎLES BARREN

Maintirano

Morafenobe

Ankazobe

Brickaville

**Antananarivo**

MADAGASCAR

Tsiroanomandidy   Anjozorobe

Ankavandra

**Antsirabe**
ÂNKARATRA

Beld

Miandrivazo

Ambatolampy   Vatomandry

Miarinarivo

Mahanoro

Morondava   Mahabo
Malaimbandy

Ambositra   Nosy Varika

Mandabe

Manja

Mananjary

**Fianarantsoa**
Ambalavao
Manakara

Beroroha

A. Pic Boby
2658

Morombe   CAP SAINT-VINCENT

Ankazoabo

Manja

**Port Louis**
Curepipe   Mahébourg
**MAURITIUS**

Le Port
Saint-Paul   **Saint-Denis**
**RÉUNION**
Saint-Pierre
(Fr.)

MASCARENE
ISLANDS                            20°

Farafangana

**Tuléar**
Betroka

Vangaindrano

Betioky

Midongy Sud

*Tropic of Capricorn*

Ampanihy

Bekily

Androka   Tsihombe   Ambovombe   **Fort-Dauphin**

CAP SAINTE-MARIE                   25°

INDIAN OCEAN

Rhodesia unilaterally
declared its independence
from the United Kingdom
on November 11, 1965.

Kilometers   0   200   400   600   Km.

Statute Miles   0   200   400   600   Mi.

Scale 1:12,000,000

One centimeter represents 120 kilometers.
One inch represents approximately 190 miles.
Miller Oblated Stereographic Projection

INDONESIA

JAWA    JAVA

Tasikmalaya  Magelang
Cilacap    Yogyakarta  Surakarta
Stamet 3428    Kediri  Malang  Jember
Madiun  Blitar  Banyuwangi  Singaraja  Sumbawa Besar
Gunung Mahameru  Denpasar  Praya  SUMBAWA  NUSA  TENGGARA
BALI  LOMBOK  Mataram  LESSER  SUNDA  ISLANDS
Waikabubak  Waingapu  SUMBA  Laut Sawu  TIMOR  Soe
Baing    Savu Sea    Kupang
PULAU SEMAU
PULAU SAWU    PULAU ROTI

HIBERNIA REEF

ASHMORE ISLANDS    CARTIER ISLAND
(Austl.)

BROWSE ISLAND

SCOTT REEF

ADÈLE ISLAND    BEAGLE REEF

BUCCANEER ARCHIPELAGO
CAPE LEVEQUE    Yampi Sound
Collier Bay

ROWLEY SHOALS    Derby
CAPE LATOUCHE TREVILLE    Mount Ord  936
La Grange    Fitzroy Crossing  Halls Creek
EIGHTY MILE BEACH    Gordon Downs

INDIAN

OCEAN

Timor    Sea

Arafu

CAPE CROKER    CROKER ISLAND
MELVILLE  GOULBURN ISLANDS
ISLAND    COBOURG PENINSULA
BATHURST  Van Diemen Gulf
ISLAND    Beagle  Darwin
Gulf    POINT BLAZE  Rum Jungle    ARNHEM LAND
CAPE  Pine Creek
LONDONDERRY  Katherine
Joseph    Roper
Bonaparte
Gulf  York Sound    Birdum
BONAPARTE  Wyndham  Kununurra
ARCHIPELAGO    Daly Waters
Victoria
KIMBERLEY PLATEAU    River Downs
KING LEOPOLD RANGES    Wave Hill  Newcastle
KING    DURACK RANGE    Waters
Lake
Woods

NORTHERN

TANAMI

Gregory Lake    DESERT    TERRITORY

GREAT SANDY DESERT    Lake White  Barrow Creek
(Dry)
Lake Wills
MONTEBELLO    Port Hedland  Shay Gap    Lake
ISLANDS    Marble Bar    Lake Dora    Mackay  Mount Zeil
DAMPIER    Dampier  Roebourne    (Dry)    (Dry)    1511
ARCHIPELAGO    Nullagine    Lake Auld    Mount Leisler    Alice
BARROW ISLAND    (Dry)    901    Springs
NORTH WEST CAPE    Onslow  Pannawonica  Wittenoom    Lake
MUIRON ISLANDS    HAMERSLEY RANGE    Lake    Macdonald    MACDONNELL
Mount Brockman    1235    Disappointment    (Dry)
1129    Mount Bruce    (Dry Salt Lake)    Lake Neale  Mount Olga
POINT CLOATES    Tom Price    1069    AUSTR
Paraburdoo  Newman    WESTERN    GIBSON DESERT    Lake Amadeus    Ayers Rock
CAPE CUVIER    1105    Lake    867
Tropic of Capricorn    Lake Macleod    Mount Augustus    906    Mount Aloysius    1439
Geographe Channel    Mount Essendon    1085    Mount Woodroffe
BERNIER ISLAND    Carnarvon  Gascoyne    Peak Hill    Lake Carnegie (Dry)    Lake Gillen
DORRE ISLAND    ROBINSON RANGES    (Dry)
Wooramel    Lake Wells
Naturaliste Channel    Woor    (Dry)
DIRK HARTOG    Wiluna
ISLAND    Meekatharra    Lake Carey  GREAT VICTORIA DESERT
STEEP POINT    Nannine    (Dry Salt Lake)    Lake Maurice
AUSTRALIA    Yeo Lake    (Dry)
Cue    Lake Austin    (Dry)    SOUTH
Sandstone    Agnew    Laverton    Maralinga
Boogardie    Mount Redcliffe  Malcolm    Qoldea
Northampton    Mount Magnet    576    Leonora
HOUTMAN    Mullewa    Lake    Menzies    Lake Carey    Forrest  Deakin
ABROLHOS    Geraldton    Ballard    Kanowna    Penong
Dongara    Barlee    (Dry)    Lake Minigwal    NULLARBOR  PLAIN    Eucla
Three    (Dry Salt    Kalgoorlie    (Dry)    Zanthus  Rawlinna  Haig    CAPE ADIEU
Springs    Lake)    Boulder    SAINT PETER ISLAND
GREEN HEAD    Lake Moore    Kanowna    Penong
Moora    Dalwallinu    (Dry)    Norseman    POINT CULVER    INVESTIGATOR
DARLING RANGE    Bonnie Rock    Coolgardie    Eyre
Bencubbin    Lake Lefroy    Great Australian Bight
Bullfinch    (Dry Salt Lake)
Stirling    Northam  Merredin  Southern Cross
Perth    York  Kellerberrin    Lake Cowan
Fremantle    Beverley    (Dry Salt Lake)    Esperance  CAPE ARID
Pinjarra    Brookton  Hyden    Norseman
Narrogin    Lake Johnston    Ravensthorpe    ARCHIPELAGO
Bunbury    Wagin  Newdegate    (Dry)    Hopetoun    OF THE
Geographe Bay    Collie    Nyabing    RECHERCHE
CAPE NATURALISTE    Busselton  Katanning    HOOD POINT
Bridgetown    Gnowangerup    CAPE KNOB
Augusta    Manjimup    Bluff Knoll  1096    CAPE VANCOUVER
CAPE LEEUWIN    Pemberton  Denmark    Mount Barker
POINT D'ENTRECASTEAUX    Albany
WEST CAPE HOWE    King George Sound

INDIAN    OCEA

Scale 1:12,000,000
One centimeter represents 120 kilometers.
One inch represents approximately 190 miles.
Lambert Conformal Conic Projection

Kilometers |0    200    400    600| Km.

Statute Miles |0    200    400    600| Mi.

Scale 1:12,000 000

One centimeter represents 120 kilometers.
One inch represents approximately 190 miles.
Lambert Conformal Conic Projection

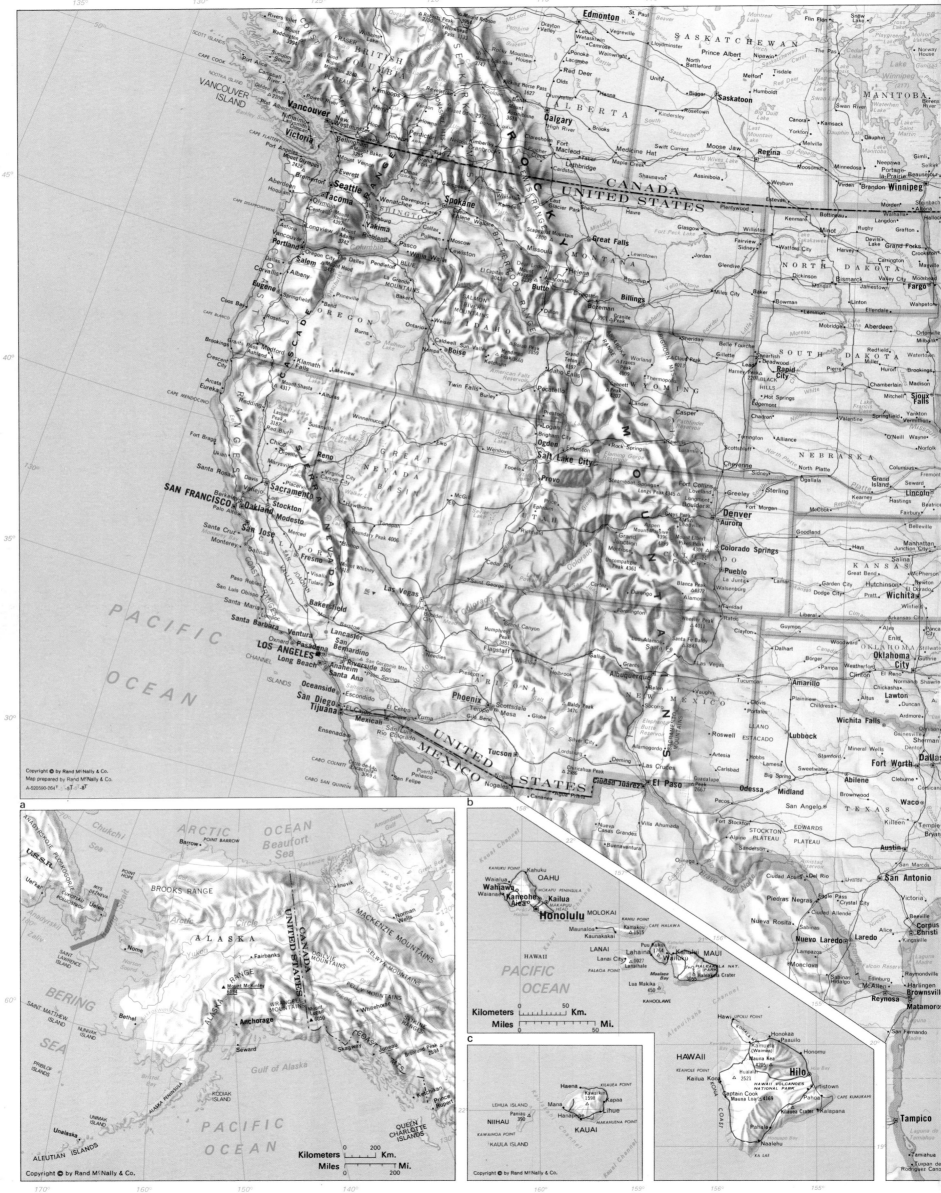

Kilometers
Statute Miles

Scale 1:12,000,000    One centimeter represents 120 kilometers.
One inch represents approximately 190 miles.
Albers Conical Equal-Area Projection

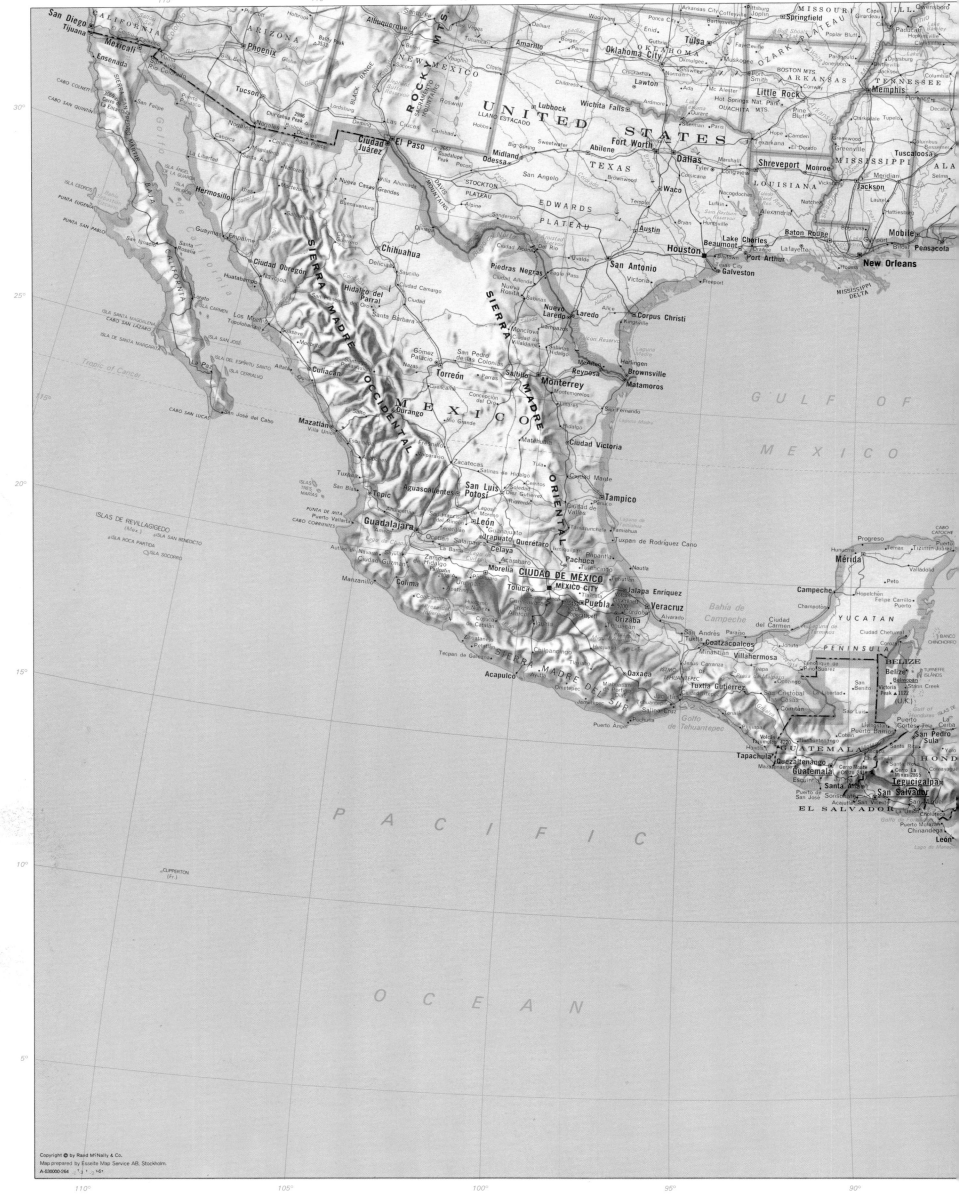

Kilometers |0    200    400    | Km.

Statute Miles |0    200    400    | Mi.

Scale 1:12,000,000

One centimeter represents 120 kilometers.
One inch represents approximately 190 miles.

Oblique Conic Conformal Projection

Kilometers
Statute Miles

Scale 1:12,000,000
One centimeter represents 120 kilometers.
One inch represents approximately 190 miles.
Oblique Conic Conformal Projection

Copyright © by Rand McNally & Co.
Map prepared by Esselte Map Service AB, Stockholm.
A-549100-264

Vista
Poola Pora
Pedro Juan Caballero
Amambái
Dourados
Presidente Epitácio
Pauliceia
Paulicéia
Guaxupé
Lins
Tupã
Ribeirão Prêto
Cachoeiro de Itapemirim
Itapemirim
Araraquara
São João del Rei
Barbacena
Uba
Juiz de Fora
Leopoldina
Itaperuna
Presidente Prudente
Marília
São Carlos
Jau
Varginha
Itajubá
Rio das
Pouso Alegre
Nova Friburgo
São João da Barra
TRINDADE
(Brazil)
ILHAS MARTIN VAZ
(Brazil)

BRAZIL

Campinas
SÃO PAULO
Jundiaí
Mogi das Cruzes
Santos
RIO DE JANEIRO
Niterói
Petrópolis
Teresópolis
Macaé
Campos
CABO DE SÃO TOMÉ
CABO FRIO

Curitiba
Paranaguá

Joinvile
Blumenau
Itajaí
São Francisco do Sul

Florianópolis
ILHA DE SANTA CATARINA

Caxias do Sul

Pôrto Alegre

Pelotas
Rio Grande

Montevideo

Tropic of Capricorn

ATLANTIC

OCEAN

SHAG ROCKS
BLACK ROCK
BIRD ISLAND
SOUTH GEORGIA
(Falkland Is.)
ANNENKOV ISLAND
Mount Paget
CAPE DISAPPOINTMENT
CLERKE ROCKS

Kilometers |          | 200 | 400 | 600 | Km.
Statute Miles |          | 200 | 400 | 600 | Mi.

Scale 1:12,000,000
One centimeter represents 120 kilometers.
One inch represents approximately 190 miles.
Oblique Conic Conformal Projection

# World Political Information Table

This table lists all countries and dependencies in the world, U.S. States, Canadian provinces, and other important regions and political subdivisions. Besides specifying the form of government for all political areas, the table classifies them into six groups according to their political status. Units labeled **A** are independent sovereign nations. Units labeled **B** are independent as regards internal affairs, but for purposes of foreign affairs they are under the protection of another country. Areas under military government are also labeled **B.** Units labeled **C** are colonies, overseas territories, dependencies, etc., of other countries. Together the **A, B,** and **C** areas comprise practically the entire inhabited area of the world. The areas labeled **D** are physically separate units, such as groups of islands, which are *not* separate countries, but form part of a nation or dependency. Units labeled **E** are States, provinces, Soviet Republics, or similar major administrative subdivisions of important countries. Units in the table with no letter designation are regions or other areas that do not constitute separate political units by themselves.

| Region or Political Division | Area in sq. miles | Estimated Population 1/1/78 | Pop. per sq. mi. | Form of Government and Ruling Power | Capital; Largest City (unless same) | Predominant Languages |
|---|---|---|---|---|---|---|
| **Afars & Issas, see Djibouti** | | | | | | |
| **Afghanistan†** | 250,000 | 20,565,000 | 82 | Republic ... A | Kābul | Dari, Pushtu |
| **Africa** | 11,706,727 | 429,400,000 | 37 | | ........; Al-Qāhirah (Cairo) | |
| **Alabama** | 51,609 | 3,725,300 | 72 | State (U.S.) ... E | Montgomery; Birmingham | |
| **Alaska** | 586,412 | 407,500 | 0.7 | State (U.S.) ... E | Juneau; Anchorage | English, Indian, Eskimo |
| **Albania†** | 11,100 | 2,655,000 | 239 | People's Republic ... A | Tiranë | Albanian |
| **Alberta** | 255,285 | 1,889,000 | 7.4 | Province (Canada) ... E | Edmonton | English |
| **Algeria†** | 919,595 | 18,073,000 | 20 | Republic ... A | Alger (Algiers) | Arabic, French, Berber |
| **American Samoa** | 76 | 33,000 | 434 | Unincorporated Territory (U.S.) ... C | Pago Pago | Polynesian, English |
| **Andaman & Nicobar Is.** | 3,202 | 132,000 | 41 | Territory (India) ... D | Port Blair | Andaman, Nicobar Malay |
| **Andorra** | 175 | 28,000 | 160 | Principality ... A | Andorra | Catalan, Spanish, French |
| **Angola†** | 481,353 | 7,214,000 | 15 | People's Republic ... A | Luanda | Bantu languages, Portuguese |
| **Anguilla** | 35 | 6,000 | 171 | Colony (U.K.) ... C | The Valley; South Hill | English |
| **Antarctica** | 5,100,000 | | | | | |
| **Antigua (incl. Barbuda)** | 171 | 75,000 | 439 | Associated State (U.K.) ... B | St. Johns | English |
| **Arabian Peninsula** | 1,142,050 | 19,682,000 | 17 | | .......; Al-Kuwayt | Arabic |
| **Argentina†** | 1,072,162 | 26,075,000 | 24 | Federal Republic ... A | Buenos Aires | Spanish |
| **Arizona** | 113,909 | 2,359,600 | 21 | State (U.S.) ... E | Phoenix | |
| **Arkansas** | 53,104 | 2,143,700 | 40 | State (U.S.) ... E | Little Rock | |
| **Arm'anskaja (Armenia) S.S.R.** | 11,500 | 2,887,000 | 251 | Soviet Socialist Republic (U.S.S.R.) ... E | Jerevan | Armenian, Russian |
| **Aruba** | 69 | 62,000 | 899 | Division of Netherlands Antilles (Neth.) ... D | Oranjestad | Dutch, Spanish, English, Papiamento |
| **Ascension I.** | 34 | 2,000 | 59 | Dependency of St. Helena (U.K.) ... D | Georgetown | English |
| **Asia** | 17,085,000 | 2,432,000,000 | 142 | | .......; Tōkyō | |
| **Australia†** | 2,967,909 | 13,858,000 | 4.7 | Monarchy (Federal) (Comm. of Nations) ... A | Canberra; Sydney | English |
| **Australian Capital Territory** | 939 | 202,000 | 215 | Federal Territory (Australia) ... E | Canberra | English |
| **Austria†** | 32,374 | 7,500,000 | 232 | Federal Republic ... A | Wien (Vienna) | German |
| **Azerbajdžanskaja (Azerbaidzhan) S.S.R.** | 33,450 | 5,801,000 | 173 | Soviet Socialist Republic (U.S.S.R.) ... E | Baku | Turkic languages, Russian, Armenian |
| **Azores Is.** | 905 | 298,000 | 329 | Part of Portugal (3 Districts) ... D | ........; Ponta Delgada | Portuguese |
| **Baden-Württemberg** | 13,803 | 9,088,000 | 658 | State (Germany, Federal Republic of) ... E | Stuttgart | German |
| **Bahamas†** | 5,380 | 222,000 | 41 | Parliamentary State (Comm. of Nations) ... A | Nassau | English |
| **Bahrain†** | 240 | 268,000 | 1,117 | Emirate ... A | Al-Manāmah | Arabic |
| **Balearic Is.** | 1,936 | 577,000 | 298 | Part of Spain (Baleares Province) ... D | Palma | Catalan, Spanish |
| **Baltic Republics** | 67,150 | 7,439,000 | 111 | Union of Soviet Socialist Republics | ........; Rīga | Lithuanian, Latvian, Estonian, Russian |
| **Bangladesh†** | 55,126 | 84,605,000 | 1,535 | Republic (Comm. of Nations) ... A | Dacca | Bangla, English |
| **Barbados†** | 166 | 250,000 | 1,506 | Parliamentary State (Comm. of Nations) ... A | Bridgetown | English |
| **Basutoland, see Lesotho** | | | | | | |
| **Bayern (Bavaria)** | 27,239 | 10,687,000 | 392 | State (Germany, Federal Republic of) ... E | München (Munich) | German |
| **Bechuanaland, see Botswana** | | | | | | |
| **Belgium†** | 11,781 | 10,005,000 | 849 | Monarchy ... A | Bruxelles (Brussels) | Dutch, French |
| **Belize** | 8,867 | 150,000 | 17 | Colony (U.K.) ... C | Belmopan; Belize | English, Spanish, Indian languages |
| **Belorusskaja (Byelorussia) S.S.R.†** | 80,150 | 9,520,000 | 119 | Soviet Socialist Republic (U.S.S.R.) ... E | Minsk | Byelorussian, Polish, Russian |
| **Benelux** | 28,549 | 24,315,000 | 852 | | Bruxelles (Brussels) | Dutch, French, Luxembourgish |
| **Benin (Dahomey)†** | 43,484 | 3,405,000 | 78 | Republic ... A | Porto Novo; Cotonou | French, native languages |
| **Berlin, West** | 185 | 1,991,000 | 10,762 | State (Germany, Federal Republic of) ... E | Berlin (West) | German |
| **Bermuda** | 21 | 59,000 | 2,810 | Colony (U.K.) ... C | Hamilton | English |
| **Bhutan†** | 18,200 | 1,245,000 | 68 | Monarchy (Indian protection) ... B | Paro and Thimbu | Tibetan dialects |
| **Bismarck Archipelago** | 18,965 | 454,000 | 24 | Part of Papua New Guinea ... D | ........; Rabaul | Malay-Polynesian and Papuan languages |
| **Bolivia†** | 424,164 | 4,887,000 | 12 | Republic ... A | Sucre and La Paz; La Paz | Spanish, Quechua, Aymará |
| **Borneo, Indonesian (Kalimantan)** | 208,286 | 5,969,000 | 29 | Part of Indonesia ... D | ........; Banjarmasin | Indonesian |
| **Botswana (Bechuanaland)†** | 231,805 | 718,000 | 3.1 | Republic (Comm. of Nations) ... A | Gaborone; Francistown | Bechuana, other Bantu languages, English |
| **Brazil†** | 3,286,487 | 113,815,000 | 35 | Federal Republic ... A | Brasília; São Paulo | Portuguese |
| **Bremen** | 156 | 714,000 | 4,577 | State (Germany, Federal Republic of) ... E | Bremen | German |
| **British Antarctic Territory (excl. Antarctic mainland)** | 2,040 | Winter pop. 75 | | Colony (U.K.) ... C | Stanley, Falkland Islands | |
| **British Columbia** | 366,255 | 2,534,000 | 6.9 | Province (Canada) ... E | Victoria; Vancouver | English |
| **British Guiana, see Guyana** | | | | | | |
| **British Honduras, see Belize** | | | | | | |
| **British Indian Ocean Territory** | 18 | | | Colony (U.K.) ... C | Administered from London | English |
| **Brunei** | 2,226 | 190,000 | 85 | Sultanate (U.K. protection) ... B | Bandar Seri Begawan | Malay-Polynesian languages, English |
| **Bulgaria†** | 42,823 | 8,820,000 | 206 | People's Republic ... A | Sofija (Sofia) | Bulgarian |
| **Burma†** | 261,790 | 31,815,000 | 122 | Federal Republic ... A | Rangoon | Burmese, English |
| **Burundi (Urundi)†** | 10,747 | 4,003,000 | 372 | Republic ... A | Bujumbura | Bantu and Hamitic languages, French |
| **California** | 158,693 | 22,017,500 | 139 | State (U.S.) ... E | Sacramento; Los Angeles | |
| **Cambodia†** | 69,898 | 8,712,000 | 125 | People's Republic ... A | Phnum Pénh | Cambodian (Khmer), French |
| **Cameroon†** | 183,569 | 6,725,000 | 37 | Federal Republic ... A | Yaoundé; Douala | French, English, native languages |
| **Canada†** | 3,851,809 | 23,625,000 | 6.0 | Monarchy (Federal) (Comm. of Nations) ... A | Ottawa; Montréal | English, French |
| **Canal Zone** | 553 | 40,000 | 72 | Under U.S. Jurisdiction ... C | Balboa Heights; Balboa | English, Spanish |
| **Canary Is.** | 2,808 | 1,271,000 | 453 | Part of Spain (2 Provinces) ... D | ........; Las Palmas de Gran Canaria | Spanish |
| **Canton & Enderbury** | 27 | | | U.K.-U.S. Administration ... C | Canton Island | Malay-Polynesian languages, English |
| **Cape Verde†** | 1,557 | 314,000 | 202 | Republic ... A | Praia; Mindelo | Portuguese |
| **Caroline Is.** | 463 | 85,000 | 184 | Part of U.S. Pacific Is. Trust Ter. (4 Districts) ... D | | Malay-Polynesian languages, English |
| **Cayman Is.** | 100 | 12,000 | 120 | Colony (U.K.) ... C | Georgetown | English |
| **Celebes (Sulawesi)** | 72,987 | 9,891,000 | 136 | Part of Indonesia ... D | ........; Ujung Pandang | Malay-Polynesian languages, Indonesian |
| **Central African Empire** | 240,535 | 1,923,000 | 8 | Empire ... A | Bangui | French, native languages |
| **Central America** | 202,063 | 20,172,000 | 100 | | ........; Guatemala | Spanish, Indian languages |
| **Central Asia, Soviet** | 493,950 | 23,929,000 | 48 | Union of Soviet Socialist Republics | ........; Taškent | Uzbek, Russian, Kirghiz, Turkoman, Tadzhik |
| **Ceylon, see Sri Lanka** | | | | | | |
| **Chad†** | 495,800 | 4,255,000 | 8.6 | Republic ... A | Ndjamena | French, native languages |
| **Channel Is. (Guernsey, Jersey, etc.)** | 75 | 129,000 | 1,720 | | ........; St. Helier | English, French |
| **Chile†** | 292,258 | 10,740,000 | 37 | Republic ... A | Santiago | Spanish |
| **China (excl. Taiwan)†** | 3,691,500 | 855,546,000 | 232 | People's Republic ... A | Beijing (Peking); Shanghai | Chinese, Mongolian, Turkish, Tungus |
| **China (Nationalist), see Taiwan** | | | | | | |
| **Christmas I. (Indian Ocean)** | 52 | 3,600 | 69 | External Territory (Australia) ... C | | Chinese, Malay, English |
| **Cocos (Keeling) Is.** | 5 | 700 | 140 | External Territory (Australia) ... C | | Malay, English |

† Member of the United Nations (1978).

World Political Information Table (Continued)

| Region or Political Division | Area in sq. miles | Estimated Population 1/1/78 | Pop. per sq. mi. | Form of Government and Ruling Power | Capital; Largest City (unless same) | Predominant Languages |
|---|---|---|---|---|---|---|
| Colombia† | 439,737 | 25,460,000 | 58 | Republic...A | Bogotá | Spanish |
| Colorado | 104,247 | 2,644,400 | 25 | State (U.S.)...E | Denver | ................................ |
| Commonwealth of Nations | 10,713,229 | 999,352,000 | 93 | | London | |
| Comoros† | 694 | 314,000 | 452 | Republic...A | Moroni | Comoran, French |
| Congo† | 132,000 | 1,455,000 | 11 | Republic...A | Brazzaville | French, native languages |
| Congo, The, see Zaire | | | | | | |
| Connecticut | 5,009 | 3,142,500 | 627 | State (U.S.)...E | Hartford | |
| Cook Is. | 93 | 18,000 | 194 | Self-governing Territory, (New Zealand)...C | Avarua | Malay-Polynesian languages, English |
| Corsica | 3,352 | 292,000 | 87 | Part of France (2 Departments)...D | ........; Bastia | French, Italian |
| Costa Rica† | 19,600 | 2,079,000 | 106 | Republic...A | San José | Spanish |
| Cuba† | 44,218 | 9,678,000 | 219 | People's Republic...A | La Habana (Havana) | Spanish |
| Curaçao | 173 | 157,000 | 908 | Division of Netherlands Antilles (Neth.)...D | Willemstad | Dutch, Spanish, English, Papiamento |
| Cyprus† | 3,572 | 645,000 | 181 | Republic (Comm. of Nations)...A | Levkósia | Greek, Turkish, English |
| Czechoslovakia† | 49,373 | 15,095,000 | 306 | People's Republic...A | Praha (Prague) | Czech, Slovak |
| Dahomey, see Benin | | | | | | |
| Delaware | 2,057 | 587,600 | 286 | State (U.S.)...E | Dover;Wilmington | |
| Denmark† | 16,629 | 5,090,000 | 306 | Monarchy...A | København (Copenhagen) | Danish |
| Denmark and Possessions | 857,169 | 5,180,000 | 6.0 | | København (Copenhagen) | Danish, Faeroese, Greenlandic |
| District of Columbia | 67 | 689,000 | 10,283 | District (U.S.)...E | Washington | |
| Djibouti† | 8,900 | 152,000 | 17 | Republic...A | Djibouti | Arabic, French |
| Dominica | 290 | 77,000 | 266 | Associated State (U.K.)...B | Roseau | English, French |
| Dominican Republic† | 18,816 | 5,041,000 | 268 | Republic...A | Santo Domingo | Spanish |
| Ecuador† | 109,483 | 8,180,000 | 75 | Republic...A | Quito; Guayaquil | Spanish, Quechua |
| Egypt† | 386,661 | 39,320,000 | 102 | Republic‡‡...A | Al-Qāhirah (Cairo) | Arabic |
| Ellice Is., see Tuvalu | | | | | | |
| El Salvador† | 8,260 | 4,290,000 | 519 | Republic...A | San Salvador | Spanish |
| England (excl. Monmouthshire) | 50,332 | 46,386,000 | 922 | United Kingdom...E | ........; London | English |
| England & Wales | 58,348 | 49,151,000 | 842 | Administrative division of United Kingdom...E | London | English, Welsh |
| Equatorial Guinea† | 10,830 | 325,000 | 30 | Republic...A | Malabo | Spanish, native languages |
| Estonskaja (S.S.R.) | 17,400 | 1,456,000 | 84 | Soviet Socialist Republic (U.S.S.R.)...E | Tallinn | Estonian, Russian |
| Ethiopia† | 471,778 | 29,775,000 | 63 | Provisional Military Government...A | Addis Abeba | Amharic, Arabic, Hamitic dialects |
| Eurasia | 20,910,000 | 3,086,000,000 | 148 | | ........; Tōkyō | |
| Europe | 3,825,000 | 654,000,000 | 171 | | ........; London | |
| Faeroe Is. | 540 | 40,000 | 74 | Self-governing Territory (Denmark)...B | Tórshavn | Danish, Faeroese |
| Falkland Is. (excl. Deps) | 4,618 | 1,900 | 0.4 | Colony (U.K.)...C | Stanley | English |
| Fernando Poo, see Macías Nguema Biyogo | | | | | | |
| Fiji† | 7,055 | 595,000 | 84 | Monarchy (Federal) (Comm. of Nations)...A | Suva | English, Fijian, Hindustani |
| Finland† | 130,120 | 4,770,000 | 37 | Republic...A | Helsinki (Helsingfors) | Finnish, Swedish |
| Florida | 58,560 | 8,651,600 | 148 | State (U.S.)...E | Tallahassee; Miami | |
| France† | 211,207 | 53,208,000 | 252 | Republic...A | Paris | French |
| France and Possessions | 229,981 | 54,986,000 | 239 | | Paris | |
| Franklin | 549,253 | 7,000 | 0.01 | District of Northwest Territories, Canada...E | ........; Cambridge Bay | English, Eskimo, Indian |
| French Gulana | 35,100 | 66,000 | 1.9 | Overseas Department (France)...C | Cayenne | French |
| French Polynesia | 1,550 | 138,000 | 89 | Overseas Territory (France)...C | Papeete | Malay-Polynesian languages, French |
| French Somaliland, see Djibouti | | | | | | |
| French Southern & Antarctic Ter. (excl. Adélie Coast) | 2,918 | 90 | 0.03 | Overseas Territory (France)...C | ................ | French |
| French West Indies | 1,112 | 749,000 | 673 | | ........; Fort-de-France | French |
| Gabon† | 103,347 | 537,000 | 5.2 | Republic...A | Libreville | French, native languages |
| Galápagos Is. (Colon, Archipélago de) | 3,075 | 5,100 | 1.7 | Province (Ecuador)...D | Puerto Baquerizo Moreno | Spanish |
| Gambia† | 4,361 | 559,000 | 128 | Republic (Comm. of Nations)...A | Banjul | English, native languages |
| Georgia | 58,876 | 5,032,400 | 85 | State (U.S.)...E | Atlanta | |
| Germany (Entire) | 137,727 | 77,765,000 | 565 | | ........; Essen | German |
| German Democratic Republic† | 41,768 | 16,695,000 | 400 | People's Republic...A | Berlin (East) | German |
| Germany, Federal Republic of (incl. West Berlin)† | 95,968 | 61,070,000 | 636 | Federal Republic...A | Bonn; Essen | German |
| Ghana† | 92,100 | 10,905,000 | 118 | Republic (Comm. of Nations)...A | Accra | English, native languages |
| Gibraltar | 2 | 30,000 | 15,000 | Colony (U.K.)...C | Gibraltar | Spanish, English |
| Gilbert Islands | 331 | 58,000 | 175 | Colony (U.K.)...C | Bairiki | Malay-Polynesian languages, English |
| Great Britain & Northern Ireland, see United Kingdom | | | | | | |
| Greece† | 50,944 | 9,340,000 | 183 | Republic...A | Athínai (Athens) | Greek |
| Greenland | 840,000 | 50,000 | 0.06 | Overseas Territory (Denmark)...C | Godthåb | Greenlandic, Danish, Eskimo |
| Grenada† | 133 | 114,000 | 857 | Parliamentary State (Comm. of Nations)...A | Saint George's | English |
| Gruzinskaja (Georgia) S.S.R. | 26,900 | 5,046,000 | 188 | Soviet Socialist Republic (U.S.S.R.)...E | Tbilisi | Georgic, Armenian, Russian |
| Guadeloupe (incl. Dependencies) | 687 | 371,000 | 540 | Overseas Department (France)...C | Basse-Terre; Pointe-à-Pitre | French |
| Guam | 212 | 96,000 | 453 | Unincorporated Territory (U.S.)...C | Agana | English, Chamorro |
| Guatemala† | 42,042 | 6,525,000 | 155 | Republic...A | Guatemala | Spanish, Indian languages |
| Guernsey (incl. Dependencies) | 30 | 54,000 | 1,800 | Bailiwick (U.K.)...C | St. Peter Port | English, French |
| Guinea† | 94,964 | 4,695,000 | 49 | Republic...A | Conakry | French, native languages |
| Guinea-Bissau† | 13,948 | 539,000 | 39 | Republic...A | Bissau | Portuguese, native languages |
| Guyana† | 83,000 | 781,000 | 9.4 | Republic (Comm. of Nations)...A | Georgetown | English |
| Haiti† | 10,714 | 4,800,000 | 448 | Republic...A | Port-au-Prince | Creole, French |
| Hamburg | 288 | 1,710,000 | 5,938 | State (Germany, Federal Republic of)...E | Hamburg | German |
| Hawaii | 6,450 | 914,200 | 142 | State (U.S.)...E | Honolulu | English, Japanese, Hawaiian |
| Hessen (Hesse) | 8,150 | 5,496,000 | 674 | State (Germany, Federal Republic of)...E | Wiesbaden; Frankfurt am Main | German |
| Hispaniola | 29,530 | 9,841,000 | 333 | | ........; Santo Domingo | French, Spanish |
| Holland, see Netherlands | | | | | | |
| Honduras† | 43,277 | 2,946,000 | 68 | Republic...A | Tegucigalpa | Spanish |
| Hong Kong | 403 | 4,445,000 | 11,030 | Colony (U.K.)...C | Victoria (Xianggang) | Chinese, English |
| Hungary† | 35,920 | 10,690,000 | 298 | People's Republic...A | Budapest | Hungarian |
| Iceland† | 39,800 | 225,000 | 5.7 | Republic...A | Reykjavík | Icelandic |
| Idaho | 83,557 | 854,900 | 10 | State (U.S.)...E | Boise (Boise City) | |
| Illinois | 56,400 | 11,277,200 | 200 | State (U.S.)...E | Springfield; Chicago | |
| India (incl. part of Kashmir)† | 1,269,210 | 627,990,000 | 495 | Republic (Comm. of Nations)...A | New Delhi; Calcutta | Hindi and other Indo-Aryan languages, Dravidian languages, English |
| Indiana | 36,291 | 5,306,100 | 146 | State (U.S.)...E | Indianapolis | |
| Indonesia (incl. West Irian)† | 741,034 | 138,180,000 | 186 | Republic...A | Jakarta | Indonesian, Chinese, English |
| Iowa | 56,290 | 2,880,900 | 51 | State (U.S.)...E | Des Moines | |
| Iran (Persia)† | 636,300 | 34,160,000 | 54 | Monarchy...A | Tehrān | Farsi, Turkish dialects, Kurdish |
| Iraq† | 167,925 | 12,069,000 | 72 | Republic...A | Baghdād | Arabic, Kurdish |
| Ireland† | 27,137 | 3,210,000 | 118 | Republic...A | Dublin (Baile Átha Cliath) | English, Irish |
| Isle of Man | 227 | 64,000 | 282 | Possession (U.K.)...C | Douglas | English |
| Israel† | 8,019 | 3,610,000 | 450 | Republic‡‡...A | Yerushalayim; Tel Aviv-Yafo | Hebrew, Arabic, English |
| Italy† | 116,304 | 56,710,000 | 488 | Republic...A | Roma (Rome); Milano | Italian |
| Ivory Coast† | 124,504 | 7,095,000 | 57 | Republic...A | Abidjan | French, native languages |

† Member of the United Nations (1978).
‡‡ Areas for Egypt, Israel, Jordan and Syria do not reflect de facto changes which took place during 1967.

## World Political Information Table (Continued)

| Region or Political Division | Area in sq. miles | Estimated Population 1/1/78 | Pop. per sq. mi. | Form of Government and Ruling Power | Capital; Largest City (unless same) | Predominant Languages |
|---|---|---|---|---|---|---|
| Jamaica† | 4,232 | 2,080,000 | 491 | Parliamentary State (Comm. of Nations)........A | Kingston | English |
| Japan† | 143,751 | 114,650,000 | 798 | Monarchy........A | Tōkyō | Japanese |
| Java (Jawa) (incl. Madura) | 51,033 | 88,184,000 | 1,728 | Part of Indonesia........D | ........; Jakarta | Indonesian, Chinese, English |
| Jersey | 45 | 75,000 | 1,667 | Bailiwick (U.K.)........C | St. Helier | English, French |
| Jordan† | 37,738 | 2,900,000 | 77 | Monarchy‡‡ | 'Ammān | Arabic |
| Kansas | 82,264 | 2,337,200 | 28 | State (U.S.)........E | Topeka; Wichita | ........ |
| Kashmir, Jammu & | 86,024 | 5,275,000 | 61 | In dispute (India & Pakistan) | Srīnagar | Kashmiri, Punjabi |
| Kazachskaja (Kazakh) S.S.R. | 1,048,300 | 14,592,000 | 14 | Soviet Socialist Republic (U.S.S.R.)........E | Alma-Ata | Turkic languages, Russian |
| Keewatin | 228,160 | 4,000 | 0.02 | District of Northwest Territories, Canada......E | ........; Baker Lake | English, Eskimo, Indian |
| Kentucky | 40,395 | 3,482,400 | 86 | State (U.S.)........E | Frankfort; Louisville | ........ |
| Kenya† | 224,960 | 14,545,000 | 65 | Republic (Comm. of Nations)........A | Nairobi | English, Swahili, native languages |
| Kerguélen | 2,700 | 90 | 0.03 | Part of French Southern & Antarctic Ter. (Fr.)..D | ........ | French |
| Kirgizskaja (Kirghiz) S.S.R. | 76,650 | 3,433,000 | 45 | Soviet Socialist Republic (U.S.S.R.)........E | Frunze | Turkic languages, Persian, Russian |
| Korea (Entire)‡ | 85,052 | 53,590,000 | 630 | | ........; Sŏul (Seoul) | Korean |
| Korea, North | 46,540 | 16,855,000 | 362 | People's Republic........A | P'yŏngyang | Korean |
| Korea, South | 38,025 | 36,735,000 | 966 | Republic........A | Sŏul (Seoul) | Korean |
| Kuwait† | 6,880 | 1,091,000 | 159 | Sheikdom........A | Al-Kuwayt | Arabic |
| Labrador | 112,826 | 34,000 | 0.3 | Part of Newfoundland Province, Canada........D | ........; Labrador City | English, Eskimo |
| Laos† | 91,429 | 3,485,000 | 38 | People's Republic........A | Viangchan (Vientiane) | Lao, French |
| Latin America | 7,924,731 | 339,947,000 | 43 | | ........; Ciudad de México (Mexico City) | ........ |
| Latvijskaja (Latvia) S.S.R. | 24,600 | 2,601,000 | 106 | Soviet Socialist Republic (U.S.S.R.)........E | Rīga | Latvian, Russian |
| Lebanon† | 4,015 | 3,096,000 | 771 | Republic........A | Bayrūt (Beirut) | Arabic, French, English |
| Lesotho (Basutoland)† | 11,720 | 1,622,000 | 138 | Monarchy (Comm. of Nations)........A | Maseru | Sesotho, English |
| Liberia† | 43,000 | 1,810,000 | 42 | Republic........A | Monrovia | English, native languages |
| Libya† | 679,362 | 2,678,000 | 4.0 | Republic........A | Tarābulus (Tripoli) | Arabic |
| Liechtenstein | 62 | 25,000 | 403 | Principality........A | Vaduz | German |
| Litovskaja (Lithuania) S.S.R. | 25,150 | 3,381,000 | 134 | Soviet Socialist Republic (U.S.S.R.)........E | Vilnius | Lithuanian, Polish, Russian |
| Louisiana | 48,523 | 3,905,500 | 80 | State (U.S.)........E | Baton Rouge; New Orleans | ........ |
| Luxembourg† | 998 | 365,000 | 366 | Grand Duchy........A | Luxembourg | Luxembourgish, French, German |
| Macau | 6 | 284,000 | 47,333 | Overseas Province (Portugal)........C | Macau | Chinese, Portuguese |
| Macías Nguema Biyogo | 785 | 82,000 | 104 | Part of Equatorial Guinea........D | Malabo | Spanish, native languages |
| Mackenzie | 527,490 | 33,000 | 0.06 | District of Northwest Territories, Canada......E | ........; Yellowknife | English, Eskimo, Indian |
| Madagascar (Malagasy Republic)† | 226,658 | 8,399,000 | 37 | Republic........A | Antananarivo | French, Malagasy |
| Madeira Is. | 308 | 271,000 | 880 | Part of Portugal (Funchal District)........D | Funchal | Portuguese |
| Maine | 33,215 | 1,086,800 | 33 | State (U.S.)........E | Augusta; Portland | ........ |
| Malawi (Nyasaland)† | 45,747 | 5,385,000 | 118 | Republic (Comm. of Nations)........A | Lilongwe; Blantyre | Chichewa, English |
| Malaya | 50,700 | 10,805,000 | 213 | Part of Malaysia........D | ........; Kuala Lumpur | Malay, Chinese, English |
| Malaysia† | 128,430 | 12,845,000 | 100 | Constitutional Monarchy (Comm. of Nations)...A | Kuala Lumpur | Malay, Chinese, English |
| Maldives† | 115 | 141,000 | 1,226 | Republic........A | Male | Divehi, Arabic |
| Mali† | 478,655 | 6,050,000 | 13 | Republic........A | Bamako | French, Bambara |
| Malta† | 122 | 275,000 | 2,254 | Republic (Comm. of Nations)........A | Valletta | English, Maltese |
| Manitoba | 251,000 | 1,050,000 | 4.2 | Province (Canada)........E | Winnipeg | English |
| Mariana Is. (excl. Guam) | 184 | 16,000 | 87 | District of U.S. Pacific Is. Trust Ter........D | Saipan | Malay-Polynesian languages, English |
| Maritime Provinces (excl. Newfoundland) | 51,963 | 1,668,000 | 32 | Canada | ........; Halifax | English |
| Marshall Is. | 70 | 28,000 | 400 | District of U.S. Pacific Is. Trust Ter........D | Majuro | Malay-Polynesian languages, English |
| Martinique | 425 | 378,000 | 889 | Overseas Department (France)........C | Fort-de-France | French |
| Maryland | 10,577 | 4,190,200 | 396 | State (U.S.)........E | Annapolis; Baltimore | ........ |
| Massachusetts | 8,257 | 5,832,600 | 706 | State (U.S.)........E | Boston | ........ |
| Mauritania† | 397,950 | 1,484,000 | 3.7 | Republic........A | Nouakchott | Arabic, French |
| Mauritius (incl. Dependencies)† | 789 | 901,000 | 1,142 | Parliamentary State (Comm. of Nations)........A | Port Louis | English, French, Creole |
| Mayotte | 144 | 43,000 | 299 | Overseas Territory (France)........C | Dzaoudzi | French, Malagasy |
| Mexico† | 761,604 | 65,555,000 | 86 | Federal Republic........A | Ciudad de México (Mexico City) | Spanish |
| Michigan | 58,216 | 9,121,800 | 157 | State (U.S.)........E | Lansing; Detroit | ........ |
| Middle America | 1,054,731 | 113,947,000 | 108 | ........ | ........; Ciudad de México (Mexico City) | ........ |
| Midway Is. | 2 | 2,000 | 1,000 | Possession (U.S.)........C | ........ | English |
| Minnesota | 84,068 | 4,026,900 | 48 | State (U.S.)........E | St. Paul; Minneapolis | ........ |
| Mississippi | 47,716 | 2,379,200 | 50 | State (U.S.)........E | Jackson | ........ |
| Missouri | 69,686 | 4,800,800 | 69 | State (U.S.)........E | Jefferson City; St. Louis | ........ |
| Moldavskaja (Moldavia) S.S.R. | 13,000 | 3,902,000 | 300 | Soviet Socialist Republic (U.S.S.R.)........E | Kišin'ov (Kishinev) | Moldavian, Russian, Ukrainian |
| Monaco | 0.6 | 26,000 | 43,333 | Principality........A | Monaco | French, Italian |
| Mongolia† | 604,200 | 1,552,000 | 2.6 | People's Republic........A | Ulaanbaatar (Ulan Bator) | Mongolian |
| Montana | 147,138 | 763,800 | 5.2 | State (U.S.)........E | Helena; Billings | ........ |
| Montserrat | 39 | 14,000 | 359 | Colony (U.K.)........C | Plymouth | English |
| Morocco† | 172,415 | 18,575,000 | 108 | Monarchy........A | Rabat; Casablanca | Arabic, Berber, French |
| Mozambique† | 302,329 | 9,745,000 | 32 | People's Republic........A | Maputo (Lourenço Marques) | Portuguese, native languages |
| Namibia (excluding Walvis Bay) | 317,827 | 910,000 | 2.9 | Under South African Administration*........C | Windhoek | English, Afrikaans, Native languages, German |
| Nauru | 8 | 7,300 | 913 | Republic (Comm. of Nations)........A | ........ | Nauruan, English |
| Nebraska | 77,227 | 1,564,900 | 20 | State (U.S.)........E | Lincoln; Omaha | ........ |
| Nepal† | 54,362 | 13,280,000 | 244 | Monarchy........A | Kātmāndu | Nepali, Tibeto-Burman languages |
| Netherlands† | 15,770 | 13,945,000 | 884 | Monarchy........A | Amsterdam and s'-Gravenhage (The Hague); Amsterdam | Dutch |
| Netherlands and Possessions | 16,141 | 14,187,000 | 879 | ........ | Amsterdam and s'-Gravenhage; Amsterdam | ........ |
| Netherlands Antilles | 371 | 242,000 | 652 | Self-governing Territory (Netherlands)........C | Willemstad | Dutch, Spanish, English, Papiamento |
| Netherlands Guiana, see Surinam... | ........ | ........ | ........ | | | |
| Nevada | 110,540 | 637,000 | 5.8 | State (U.S.)........E | Carson City; Las Vegas | ........ |
| New Brunswick | 28,354 | 696,000 | 25 | Province (Canada)........E | Fredericton; Saint John | English, French |
| New Caledonia (incl. Deps.) | 7,358 | 141,000 | 19 | Overseas Territory (France)........C | Nouméa | Malay-Polynesian languages, French |
| New England | 66,608 | 12,306,000 | 185 | United States | ........; Boston | English |
| Newfoundland | 156,185 | 573,000 | 3.7 | Province (Canada)........E | St. John's | English |
| Newfoundland (excl. Labrador) | 43,359 | 539,000 | 12 | | ........; St. John's | English |
| New Hampshire | 9,304 | 838,000 | 90 | State (U.S.)........E | Concord; Manchester | ........ |
| New Hebrides | 5,700 | 100,000 | 18 | Condominium (France-U.K.)........C | Vila | Malay-Polynesian languages, French, English |
| New Jersey | 7,836 | 7,358,700 | 939 | State (U.S.)........E | Trenton; Newark | ........ |
| New Mexico | 121,666 | 1,201,600 | 9.9 | State (U.S.)........E | Santa Fe; Albuquerque | ........ |
| New South Wales | 309,433 | 4,886,000 | 16 | State (Australia)........E | Sydney | English |
| New York | 49,576 | 18,102,300 | 365 | State (U.S.)........E | Albany; New York | ........ |
| New Zealand† | 103,736 | 3,245,000 | 31 | Monarchy (Comm. of Nations)........A | Wellington; Auckland | English, Maori |
| Nicaragua† | 50,200 | 2,347,000 | 47 | Republic........A | Managua | Spanish |
| Niedersachsen (Lower Saxony) | 18,299 | 7,157,000 | 391 | State (Germany, Federal Republic of)........E | Hannover | German |
| Niger† | 489,200 | 4,925,000 | 10 | Republic........A | Niamey | Hausa, Arabic, French |
| Nigeria† | 356,669 | 66,190,000 | 186 | Republic (Comm. of Nations)........A | Lagos | Hausa, Ibo, Yoruba, English |
| Niue | 100 | 3,000 | 30 | Island Territory (New Zealand)........C | Alofi | Malay-Polynesian languages, English |
| Nordrhein-Westfalen (North Rhine Westphalia) | 13,145 | 16,977,000 | 1,292 | State (Germany, Federal Republic of)........E | Düsseldorf; Köln | German |
| Norfolk Island | 14 | 2,000 | 143 | External Territory (Australia)........C | Kingston | English |

† Member of the United Nations (1978).
‡ Includes 487 sq. miles of demilitarized zone, not included in North or South Korea figures.
‡‡ Areas for Egypt, Israel, Jordan and Syria do not reflect de facto changes which took place during 1967.

\* The United Nations declared an end to the mandate of South Africa over Namibia in October 1966. Administration of the territory by South Africa is not recognized by the United Nations.

## World Political Information Table (Continued)

| Region or Political Division | Area in sq. miles | Estimated Population 1/1/78 | Pop. per sq. mi. | Form of Government and Ruling Power | Capital; Largest City (unless same) | Predominant Languages |
|---|---|---|---|---|---|---|
| North America................. | 9,420,000 | 355,200,000 | 38 | ............................... | ........; New York | ............................... |
| North Borneo, see Sabah........... | | | | | | |
| North Carolina................. | 52,586 | 5,538,600 | 105 | State (U.S.).....................E | Raleigh; Charlotte | ............................... |
| North Dakota.................. | 70,665 | 650,500 | 9.2 | State (U.S.).....................E | Bismarck; Fargo | ............................... |
| Northern Ireland.............. | 5,463 | 1,537,000 | 281 | Administrative division of United Kingdom.....E | Belfast | English |
| Northern Rhodesia, see Zambia.... | | | | | | |
| Northern Territory............. | 520,280 | 100,000 | 0.2 | Territory (Australia)...................E | Darwin | English, Aboriginal languages |
| North Polar Regions.............. | | | | | | |
| Northwest Territories............. | 1,304,903 | 44,000 | 0.03 | Territory (Canada)...................E | Yellowknife | English, Eskimo, Indian |
| Norway†........................ | 125,181 | 4,060,000 | 32 | Monarchy........................A | Oslo | Norwegian (Riksmål and Landsmål) |
| Nova Scotia.................... | 21,425 | 851,000 | 40 | Province (Canada)...................E | Halifax | English |
| Nyasaland, see Malawi.......... | | | | | | |
| Oceania (incl. Australia)........... | 3,295,000 | 21,900,000 | 6.6 | ............................... | ........; Sydney | ............................... |
| Ohio.......................... | 41,222 | 10,669,100 | 259 | State (U.S.).....................E | Columbus; Cleveland | ............................... |
| Oklahoma..................... | 69,919 | 2,823,100 | 40 | State (U.S.).....................E | Oklahoma City | ............................... |
| Oman†........................ | 82,030 | 824,000 | 10 | Sultanate.......................A | Masqaṭ; Maṭraḥ | Arabic |
| Ontario....................... | 412,582 | 8,492,000 | 21 | Province (Canada)...................E | Toronto | English |
| Oregon....................... | 96,981 | 2,372,700 | 24 | State (U.S.).....................E | Salem; Portland | ............................... |
| Orkney Is..................... | 376 | 18,000 | 48 | Part of Scotland, U.K..............D | Kirkwall | English |
| Pacific Islands Trust Territory.... | 717 | 129,000 | 180 | Trust Territory (U.S.)..............C | Saipan | Malay-Polynesian languages, English |
| Pakistan (incl. part of Kashmir)†.. | 345,753 | 77,040,000 | 223 | Federal Republic..................A | Islāmābād; Karāchī | Urdu, English |
| Panama†...................... | 29,209 | 1,795,000 | 61 | Republic.........................A | Panamá | Spanish |
| Papua New Guinea†............ | 178,260 | 2,950,000 | 17 | Parliamentary State................A | Port Moresby | Papuan and Negrito languages, English |
| Paraguay†..................... | 157,048 | 2,839,000 | 18 | Republic.........................A | Asunción | Spanish, Guaraní |
| Pennsylvania.................. | 45,333 | 11,896,700 | 262 | State (U.S.).....................E | Harrisburg; Philadelphia | ............................... |
| Persia, see Iran................ | | | | | | |
| Peru†......................... | 496,224 | 16,795,000 | 34 | Republic.........................A | Lima | Spanish, Quechua |
| Philippines†................... | 116,000 | 44,505,000 | 384 | Republic.........................A | Manila | Pilipino, English |
| Pitcairn (excl. Dependencies)....... | 2 | 70 | 35 | Colony (U.K.)....................C | Adamstown | English |
| Poland†....................... | 120,725 | 34,865,000 | 289 | People's Republic..................A | Warszawa (Warsaw); Katowice | Polish |
| Portugal†..................... | 35,553 | 9,660,000 | 272 | Republic.........................A | Lisboa (Lisbon) | Portuguese |
| Portugal and Possessions.......... | 35,559 | 9,944,000 | 280 | | Lisboa (Lisbon) | |
| Portuguese Guinea, see Guinea-Bissau............. | | | | | | |
| Prairie Provinces.................. | 757,985 | 3,886,000 | 5.1 | Canada | ........; Winnipeg | English |
| Prince Edward Island............ | 2,184 | 121,000 | 55 | Province (Canada)...................E | Charlottetown | English |
| Puerto Rico................... | 3,435 | 3,435,000 | 974 | Commonwealth (U.S.)..............C | San Juan | Spanish, English |
| Qatar†........................ | 4,247 | 100,000 | 24 | Emirate.........................A | Ad-Dawḥah (Doha) | Arabic |
| Quebec....................... | 594,860 | 6,406,000 | 11 | Province (Canada)...................E | Québec; Montréal | French, English |
| Queensland................... | 667,000 | 2,084,000 | 3.1 | State (Australia)...................E | Brisbane | English |
| Reunion...................... | 969 | 525,000 | 542 | Overseas Department (France)..........C | St. Denis | French |
| Rheinland-Pfalz (Rhineland-Palatinate)................ | 7,657 | 3,628,000 | 474 | State (Germany, Federal Republic of)..........E | Mainz | German |
| Rhode Island.................. | 1,214 | 922,400 | 760 | State (U.S.).....................E | Providence | ............................... |
| Rhodesia..................... | 150,804 | 6,860,000 | 45 | Self-governing Colony (U.K.)*..........C | Salisbury | English, native languages |
| Rio Muni, see Equatorial Guinea.... | | | | | | |
| Rodrigues..................... | 42 | 27,000 | 643 | Dependency of Mauritius (U.K.)..........D | Port Mathurin | English, French |
| Romania†..................... | 91,699 | 21,760,000 | 237 | People's Republic..................A | București (Bucharest) | Romanian, Hungarian |
| Rossijskaja Sovetskaja Federativnaja Socialističeskaja Respublika............ | 6,592,850 | 137,053,000 | 21 | Soviet Federated Socialist Republic (U.S.S.R.)..E | Moskva (Moscow) | Russian, Finno-Ugric languages, various Turkic, Iranian, and Mongol languages |
| Rossijskaja S.F.S.R. in Europe...... | 1,527,350 | 100,559,000 | 66 | Union of Soviet Socialist Republics............... | ........; Moskva (Moscow) | Russian, Finno-Ugric languages |
| Rwanda†...................... | 10,169 | 4,421,000 | 435 | Republic.........................A | Kigali | Kinyarwanda, French |
| Saarland (Saar)............... | 992 | 1,081,000 | 1,090 | State (Germany, Federal Republic of)..........E | Saarbrücken | German |
| Sabah (North Borneo).......... | 29,388 | 849,000 | 29 | Administrative division of Malaysia..........E | Kota Kinabalu; Sandakan | Malay, Chinese, English |
| St. Helena (incl. Dependencies).... | 162 | 8,000 | 49 | Colony (U.K.)....................C | Jamestown | English |
| St. Kitts-Nevis................ | 103 | 48,000 | 466 | Associated State (U.K.)..............B | Basseterre | English |
| St. Lucia..................... | 238 | 117,000 | 492 | Associated State (U.K.)..............B | Castries | English |
| St. Pierre & Miquelon.......... | 93 | 6,000 | 65 | Overseas Territory (France)..........C | St. Pierre | French |
| St. Vincent................... | 150 | 117,000 | 780 | Associated State (U.K.)..............B | Kingstown | English |
| Samoa (Entire)................ | 1,173 | 203,000 | 173 | | ........; Apia | Samoan, English |
| San Marino................... | 24 | 21,000 | 875 | Republic.........................A | San Marino | Italian |
| Sao Tome & Principe†.......... | 372 | 83,000 | 223 | Republic.........................A | São Tomé | Portuguese, native languages |
| Sarawak...................... | 48,342 | 1,191,000 | 25 | Administrative division of Malaysia..........E | Kuching | Malay, Chinese, English |
| Sardinia...................... | 9,301 | 1,571,000 | 169 | Part of Italy.....................D | Cagliari | Italian |
| Saskatchewan................. | 251,700 | 947,000 | 3.8 | Province (Canada)...................E | Regina | English |
| Saudi Arabia†................. | 830,000 | 9,645,000 | 12 | Monarchy........................A | Ar-Riyāḍ (Riyadh) | Arabic |
| Scandinavia (incl. Finland and Iceland)..................... | 509,899 | 22,450,000 | 44 | | ........; København (Copenhagen) | Swedish, Danish, Norwegian, Finnish, Icelandic |
| Schleswig-Holstein............ | 6,046 | 2,541,000 | 420 | State (Germany, Federal Republic of)..........E | Kiel | German |
| Scotland...................... | 30,414 | 5,202,000 | 171 | Administrative division of United Kingdom.....E | Edinburgh; Glasgow | English, Gaelic |
| Senegal†...................... | 75,750 | 5,295,000 | 70 | Republic.........................A | Dakar | French, native languages |
| Seychelles†................... | 156 | 61,000 | 391 | Republic (Comm. of Nations)..........A | Victoria | English, Creole |
| Shetland Is................... | 550 | 19,000 | 35 | Part of Scotland, U.K..............D | Lerwick | English |
| Siam, see Thialand............. | | | | | | |
| Sicily........................ | 9,926 | 4,917,000 | 495 | Part of Italy (Sicilia Autonomous Region).......D | Palermo | Italian |
| Sierra Leone†................. | 27,699 | 3,252,000 | 117 | Republic (Comm. of Nations)..........A | Freetown | English, native languages |
| Singapore†.................... | 224 | 2,320,000 | 10,357 | Republic (Comm. of Nations)..........A | Singapore | Chinese, Malay, English, Tamil |
| Solomon Is. (Papua New Guinea)... | 4,100 | 128,000 | 31 | Part of Papua New Guinea..........D | Sohano; Kieta | Malay-Polynesian languages, English |
| Solomon Is.................... | 10,983 | 215,000 | 20 | Parliamentary state................A | Honiara | Malay-Polynesian languages, English |
| Somalia†...................... | 246,201 | 3,391,000 | 14 | Republic.........................A | Mogadisho | Somali |
| South Africa (incl. Walvis Bay)†.... | 471,879 | 27,061,000 | 57 | Federal Republic..................A | Pretoria, Cape Town, Bloem-fontein; Johannesburg | English, Afrikaans, native languages |
| South America................. | 6,870,000 | 226,000,000 | 33 | | ........; São Paulo | ............................... |
| South Australia................ | 380,070 | 1,273,000 | 3.3 | State (Australia)...................E | Adelaide | English |
| South Carolina................ | 31,055 | 2,900,500 | 93 | State (U.S.).....................E | Columbia | ............................... |
| South Dakota................. | 77,047 | 688,400 | 8.9 | State (U.S.).....................E | Pierre; Sioux Falls | ............................... |
| Southern Rhodesia, see Rhodesia... | | | | | | |
| Southern Yemen, see Yemen, People's Democratic Republic of.. | | | | | | |
| South Georgia................. | 1,450 | 20 | 0.01 | Dependency of Falkland Is. (U.K.)..........D | Grytviken | English, Norwegian |

† Member of the United Nations (1978).
* Rhodesia unilaterally declared its independence from the United Kingdom on November 11, 1965.
‡‡ Areas for Egypt, Israel, Jordan and Syria do not reflect de facto changes which took place during 1967.

## World Political Information Table (Continued)

| Region or Political Division | Area in sq. miles | Estimated Population 1/1/78 | Pop. per sq. mi. | Form of Government and Ruling Power | Capital; Largest City (unless same) | Predominant Languages |
|---|---|---|---|---|---|---|
| **South Polar Regions** | ... | ... | ... | ... | ... | ... |
| **South West Africa, see Namibia** | ... | ... | ... | ... | ... | ... |
| **Spain†** | 194,885 | 36,530,000 | 187 | Monarchy ... A | Madrid | Spanish, Catalan, Galician, Basque |
| **Spain and Possessions** | 194,897 | 36,646,000 | 188 | ... | Madrid | ... |
| **Spanish Possessions in North Africa** | 12 | 116,000 | 9,667 | Five Possessions (no central government) (Spain) ... C | ...; Ceuta | Spanish, Arabic, Berber |
| **Spitsbergen, see Svalbard** | ... | ... | ... | ... | ... | ... |
| **Sri Lanka (Ceylon)†** | 25,332 | 14,085,000 | 556 | Republic (Comm. of Nations) ... A | Colombo | Sinhala, Tamil, English |
| **Sudan†** | 967,499 | 16,726,000 | 17 | Republic ... A | Al-Kharṭūm (Khartoum) | Arabic, native languages, English |
| **Sumatra (Sumatera)** | 182,860 | 24,112,000 | 132 | Part of Indonesia ... D | ...; Medan | Indonesian, English, Chinese |
| **Surinam (Neth. Guiana)†** | 63,037 | 454,000 | 7.2 | Republic ... A | Paramaribo | Dutch, Creole |
| **Svalbard (Spitsbergen) and Jan Mayen** | 24,102 | Winter pop. ... | ... | Dependency (Norway) ... C | Longyearbyen | Norwegian, Russian |
| **Swaziland†** | 6,705 | 515,000 | 77 | Monarchy (Comm. of Nations) ... A | Mbabane | English, siSwati |
| **Sweden†** | 173,732 | 8,265,000 | 48 | Monarchy ... A | Stockholm | Swedish |
| **Switzerland** | 15,941 | 6,270,000 | 393 | Federal Republic ... A | Bern (Berne); Zürich | German, French, Italian |
| **Syria†** | 71,498 | 7,968,000 | 111 | Republic‡‡ ... A | Dimashq (Damascus) | Arabic, French |
| **Tadžikskaja (Tadzhik) S.S.R.** | 55,250 | 3,538,000 | 64 | Soviet Socialist Republic (U.S.S.R.) ... E | Dušhanbe | Tadzhik, Turkic languages, Russian |
| **Taiwan (Formosa) (Nationalist China)** | 13,885 | 16,770,000 | 1,208 | Republic ... A | T'aipei | Chinese |
| **Tanganyika, see Tanzania** | ... | ... | ... | ... | ... | ... |
| **Tanzania (Tanganyika & Zanzibar)†** | 364,900 | 16,154,000 | 44 | Republic (Comm. of Nations) ... A | Dar-es-Salaam | Swahili, English, Arabic |
| **Tasmania** | 26,383 | 412,000 | 16 | State (Australia) ... E | Hobart | English |
| **Tennessee** | 42,244 | 4,276,400 | 101 | State (U.S.) ... E | Nashville; Memphis | ... |
| **Texas** | 267,339 | 12,834,700 | 48 | State (U.S.) ... E | Austin; Houston | ... |
| **Thailand (Siam)†** | 198,500 | 44,600,000 | 235 | Monarchy ... A | Krung Thep (Bangkok) | Thai, Chinese |
| **Tibet (Xizang Zizhiqu)** | 471,700 | 1,710,000 | 3.6 | Autonomous Region (China) ... E | Lasa (Lhasa) | Tibetan, Chinese |
| **Togo†** | 21,600 | 2,366,000 | 110 | Republic ... A | Lomé | Native languages, French |
| **Tokelau (Union) Is.** | 4 | 1,600 | 400 | Island Territory (New Zealand) ... C | ...; Fakaofo | Malay-Polynesian languages, English |
| **Tonga** | 270 | 92,000 | 341 | Monarchy (Comm. of Nations) ... A | Nukualofa | Tongan, English |
| **Transcaucasia** | 71,850 | 13,733,000 | 191 | Union of Soviet Socialist Republics ... | ...; Baku | ... |
| **Trinidad & Tobago†** | 1,980 | 1,118,000 | 565 | Republic ... A | Port of Spain | English, Spanish |
| **Tristan da Cunha** | 40 | 300 | 7.5 | Dependency of St. Helena (U.K.) ... D | Edinburgh | English |
| **Trucial States, see United Arab Emirates** | ... | ... | ... | ... | ... | ... |
| **Tunisia†** | 63,170 | 5,875,000 | 93 | Republic ... A | Tunis | Arabic, French |
| **Turkey†** | 301,382 | 41,605,000 | 138 | Republic ... A | Ankara; İstanbul | Turkish, Kurdish, Arabic |
| **Turkey in Europe** | 9,121 | 3,591,000 | 394 | Turkey ... | ...; İstanbul | Turkish |
| **Turkmenskaja (Turkmen) S.S.R.** | 188,450 | 2,627,000 | 14 | Soviet Socialist Republic (U.S.S.R.) ... E | Ašchabad | Turkic languages, Russian |
| **Turks & Caicos Is.** | 166 | 5,000 | 30 | Colony (U.K.) ... C | Grand Turk | English |
| **Tuvalu (Ellice Is.)** | 9.5 | 7,000 | 737 | Parliamentary State ... A | Funafuti | Malay-Polynesian languages, English |
| **Uganda†** | 91,134 | 12,521,000 | 137 | Republic (Comm. of Nations) ... A | Kampala | English, Swahili |
| **Ukrainskaja (Ukraine) S.S.R.†** | 233,100 | 49,941,000 | 214 | Soviet Socialist Republic (U.S.S.R.) ... E | Kijev (Kiev) | Ukrainian, Russian |
| **Union of Soviet Socialist Republics (Soviet Union)†** | 8,649,500 | 260,110,000 | 30 | Federal Soviet Republics ... A | Moskva (Moscow) | Russian and other Slavic languages, various Finno-Ugric, Turkic and Mongol languages, Caucasian languages, Persian |
| **Union of Soviet Socialist Republics in Europe** | 1,920,750 | 171,360,000 | 89 | Union of Soviet Socialist Republics ... | ...; Moskva (Moscow) | Russian, Ruthenian, various Finno-Ugric and Caucasian languages |
| **United Arab Emirates (Trucial States)†** | 32,278 | 239,000 | 7.4 | Self-governing Union ... A | Abū Ẓaby; Dubayy | Arabic |
| **United Kingdom of Great Britain & Northern Ireland†** | 94,227 | 55,890,000 | 593 | Monarchy (Comm. of Nations) ... A | London | English, Welsh, Gaelic |
| **United Kingdom & Possessions** | 288,049 | 68,688,000 | 238 | ... | London | ... |
| **United States†** | *3,675,545 | 217,513,000 | 59 | Federal Republic ... A | Washington; New York | English |
| **United States and Possessions** | 3,680,713 | 221,262,000 | 60 | ... | Washington; New York | English, Spanish |
| **Upper Volta†** | 105,800 | 6,376,000 | 60 | Republic ... A | Ouagadougou | French, native languages |
| **Uruguay†** | 68,536 | 2,826,000 | 41 | Republic ... A | Montevideo | Spanish |
| **Utah** | 84,916 | 1,263,800 | 15 | State (U.S.) ... E | Salt Lake City | ... |
| **Uzbekskaja (Uzbek) S.S.R.** | 173,600 | 14,332,000 | 83 | Soviet Socialist Republic (U.S.S.R.) ... E | Taškent | Turkic languages, Sart, Russian |
| **Vatican City (Holy See)** | 0.2 | 1,000 | 5,000 | Ecclesiastical State ... A | Città del Vaticano (Vatican City) | Italian, Latin |
| **Venezuela†** | 352,144 | 13,047,000 | 37 | Federal Republic ... A | Caracas | Spanish |
| **Vermont** | 9,609 | 483,300 | 50 | State (U.S.) ... E | Montpelier; Burlington | ... |
| **Victoria** | 87,884 | 3,730,000 | 42 | State (Australia) ... E | Melbourne | English |
| **Vietnam†** | 128,402 | 48,475,000 | 378 | People's Republic ... A | Ha-noi; Thanh-pho Ho Chi Minh (Sai-gon) | Vietnamese |
| **Virginia** | 40,817 | 5,114,200 | 125 | State (U.S.) ... E | Richmond; Norfolk | ... |
| **Virgin Is., British** | 59 | 10,000 | 169 | Colony (U.K.) ... C | Road Town | English |
| **Virgin Is. of the U.S.** | 133 | 102,000 | 766 | Unincorporated Territory (U.S.) ... C | Charlotte Amalie | English |
| **Wake I.** | 3 | 1,000 | 333 | Possession (U.S.) ... C | ... | English |
| **Wales (incl. Monmouthshire)** | 8,016 | 2,765,000 | 345 | United Kingdom ... | Cardiff | English, Welsh |
| **Wallis & Futuna** | 77 | 9,500 | 123 | Overseas Territory (France) ... C | Mata-Utu | Malay-Polynesian languages, French |
| **Washington** | 68,192 | 3,697,200 | 54 | State (U.S.) ... E | Olympia; Seattle | ... |
| **Western Australia** | 975,920 | 1,171,000 | 1.2 | State (Australia) ... E | Perth | English |
| **Western Sahara** | 102,700 | 139,000 | 1.4 | Administered by Morocco and Mauritania ... C | El Aaiún | Arabic |
| **Western Samoa†** | 1,097 | 170,000 | 155 | Constitutional Monarchy (Comm. of Nations) ... A | Apia | Samoan, English |
| **West Indies** | 92,041 | 28,220,000 | 307 | ... | ...; La Habana (Havana) | ... |
| **West Virginia** | 24,181 | 1,846,100 | 76 | State (U.S.) ... E | Charleston | ... |
| **White Russia, see Belorusskaja** | ... | ... | ... | ... | ... | ... |
| **Wisconsin** | 56,154 | 4,616,500 | 82 | State (U.S.) ... E | Madison; Milwaukee | ... |
| **World** | 57,280,000 | 4,119,000,000 | 72 | ... | ...; Tōkyō | ... |
| **Wyoming** | 97,914 | 406,900 | 4.2 | State (U.S.) ... E | Cheyenne | ... |
| **Yemen†** | 75,300 | 5,690,000 | 76 | Republic ... A | Ṣan'ā' | Arabic |
| **Yemen, People's Democratic Republic of,†** | 111,075 | 1,825,000 | 16 | People's Republic ... A | Aden | Arabic, English |
| **Yugoslavia†** | 98,766 | 21,875,000 | 221 | Socialist Federal Republic ... A | Beograd (Belgrade) | Serbo-Croatian, Slovenian, Macedonian |
| **Yukon** | 207,076 | 22,000 | 0.1 | Territory (Canada) ... E | Whitehorse | English, Eskimo, Indian |
| **Zaire (Congo, The)†** | 905,567 | 26,705,000 | 29 | Republic ... A | Kinshasa | French, native languages |
| **Zambia (Northern Rhodesia)†** | 290,586 | 5,406,000 | 19 | Republic (Comm. of Nations) ... A | Lusaka | English, native languages |
| **Zanzibar** | 950 | 413,000 | 435 | Part of Tanzania ... D | Zanzibar | Arabic, English, Swahili |

† Member of the United Nations (1978).
‡‡ Areas for Egypt, Israel, Jordan and Syria do not reflect de facto changes which took place during 1967.
* Total area of the United States includes 3,536,855 square miles of land; 78,268 square miles of inland water; and 60,422 square miles of Great Lakes area, not included in any state.

# Largest Metropolitan Areas of the World, 1978

This table lists the major metropolitan areas of the world according to their estimated population on January 1, 1978. For convenience in reference, the areas are grouped by major region, and the number of areas in each region and size group is given.

There are 25 areas with more than 5,000,000 population each; these are listed in rank order of estimated population, with the world rank given in parentheses following the name. For example, New York's 1975 rank is second. Below the 5,000,000 level, the metropolitan areas are listed alphabetically within region, not in order of size.

For ease of comparison, each metropolitan area has been defined by Rand McNally & Company according to consistent rules. A metropolitan area includes a central city, neighboring communities linked to it by continuous built-up areas, and more distant communities if the bulk of their population is supported by commuters to the central city. Some metropolitan areas have more than one central city, for example Tōkyō-Yokohama or San Francisco-Oakland-San Jose.

| POPULATION CLASSIFICATION | UNITED STATES and CANADA | LATIN AMERICA | EUROPE (excl. U.S.S.R.) | U.S.S.R. | ASIA | AFRICA–OCEANIA |
|---|---|---|---|---|---|---|
| Over 15,000,000 (3) | New York (2) | | | | Tōkyō–Yokohama (1) Ōsaka–Kōbe–Kyōto (3) | |
| 10,000,000–15,000,000 (5) | | Ciudad de México (Mexico City) (4) São Paulo (7) | London (5) | Moskva (Moscow) (6) | Calcutta (8) | |
| 5,000,000–10,000,000 (17) | Los Angeles (12) Chicago (17) Philadelphia (23) | Buenos Aires (9) Rio de Janeiro (13) | Paris (10) Essen–Dortmund– Duisburg (The Ruhr) (21) | Leningrad (24) | Sŏul (Seoul) (11) Bombay (15) Shanghai (16) Jakarta (18) Manila (19) Delhi (20) Beijing (Peking) (22) Tehrān (25) | Al-Qāhirah (Cairo) (14) |
| 3,000,000–5,000,000 (27) | Boston Detroit– Windsor San Francisco– Oakland– San Jose Washington | Bogotá Caracas Lima Santiago | Athínai (Athens) Barcelona Berlin İstanbul Madrid Milano (Milan) Roma (Rome) | | Baghdād Chongqing (Chungking) Karāchi Krung Thep (Bangkok) Madras Nagoya Shenyang (Mukden) T'aipei (Taipei) Tianjin (Tientsin) Victoria Wuhan | Sydney |
| 2,000,000–3,000,000 (45) | Cleveland Dallas– Fort Worth Houston Miami–Fort Lauderdale Montréal Pittsburgh St. Louis San Diego–Tijuana Toronto | Belo Horizonte Guadalajara La Habana (Havana) Recife | Birmingham Bruxelles (Brussel) (Brussels) Bucureşti (Bucharest) Budapest Hamburg Katowice–Bytom– Gliwice Lisboa (Lisbon) Manchester Napoli (Naples) Warszawa (Warsaw) | Doneck (Donetsk)– Makejevka Kijev (Kiev) | Ahmādābād Bangalore Dacca Guangzhou (Canton) Haerbin (Harbin) Hyderābād Lahore Pusan Rangoon Singapore Surabaya Thanh–pho Ho Chi Minh (Saigon) X'ian (Sian) | Alexandria Alger (Algiers) Casablanca Johannesburg Kinshasa Lagos Melbourne |
| 1,500,000–2,000,000 (32) | Atlanta Baltimore Buffalo Minneapolis– St. Paul Seattle– Tacoma | Medellín Monterrey Pôrto Alegre San Juan | Amsterdam Frankfurt am Main Glasgow København (Copenhagen) Köln (Cologne) Leeds–Bradford Liverpool München (Munich) Stuttgart Torino (Turin) Wien (Vienna) | Baku Char'kov (Kharkov) Gor'kij (Gorki) Taškent (Tashkent) | Ankara Chengdu (Chengtu) Colombo Fukuoka Kānpur Kitakyūshū–Shimonoseki Nanjing (Nanking) Taiyuan | |
| 1,000,000–1,500,000 (81) | Cincinnati Denver El Paso–Ciudad Juárez Hartford Indianapolis Kansas City Milwaukee New Orleans Phoenix Portland Vancouver | Cali Córdoba Fortaleza Guatemala Guayaquil Montevideo Rosario Salvador | Antwerpen (Anvers) (Antwerp) Beograd (Belgrade) Düsseldorf Hannover Lille Łódź Lyon Mannheim Marseille Newcastle– Sunderland Nürnberg Porto Praha (Prague) Rotterdam Sofija (Sofia) Stockholm Valencia | Čel'abinsk (Chelyabinsk) Dnepropetrovsk Jerevan (Yerevan) Kazan' Kujbyšev (Kuybyshev) Minsk Novosibirsk Odessa Omsk Perm Rostov-na-Donu Saratov Sverdlovsk Tbilisi Volgograd | Anshan Bandung Bayrūt (Beirut) Changchun (Hsinking) Chittagong Dimashq (Damascus) Fushun Ha-noi Hiroshima–Kure İzmir Jinan (Tsinan) Kaohsiung Kunming Lanzhou (Lanchow) Lucknow Lüda (Dairen) Nāgpur Pune (Poona) P'yŏngyang Qingdao (Tsingtao) Sapporo Shijiazhuang (Shihchiachuang) Taegu Tel Aviv–Yafo Zhengzhou (Chengchow) | Addis Abeba (Addis Ababa) Brisbane Cape Town Durban Tunis |
| Total by Region (210) | 33 | 24 | 48 | 23 | 68 | 14 |

The index includes in a single alphabetical list some 16,000 names appearing on the maps. Each name is followed by a page reference and by the location of the feature on the map. The map location is designated by latitude and longitude coordinates. If a page contains several maps, a lowercase letter identifies the inset map. The page reference for two-page maps is always to the left hand page.

Most map features are indexed to the largest-scale map on which they appear. Countries, mountain ranges, and other extensive features are generally indexed to the map that shows them in their entirety.

The features indexed are of three types: *point*, *areal*, and *linear*. For *point* features (for example, cities, mountain peaks, dams), latitude and longitude coordinates give the location of the point on the map. For *areal* features (countries, mountain ranges, etc.), the coordinates generally indicate the approximate center of the feature. For *linear* features (rivers, canals, aqueducts), the coordinates locate a terminating point—for example, the mouth of a river, or the point at which a feature reaches the map margin.

**NAME FORMS** Names in the Index, as on the maps, are generally in the local language and insofar as possible are spelled according to official practice. Diacritical marks are included, except that those used to indicate tone, as in Vietnamese, are usually not shown. Most features that extend beyond the boundaries of one country have no single official name, and these are usually named in English. Many conventional English names and former names are cross referenced to the primary map name. All cross references are indicated by the symbol→. A name that appears in a shortened version on the map due to space limitations is given in full in the Index, with the portion that is omitted on the map enclosed in brackets, for example, Acapulco [de Juárez].

**TRANSLITERATION** For names in languages not written in the Roman alphabet, the locally official transliteration system has been used where one exists. Thus, names in the Soviet Union and Bulgaria have been transliterated according to the systems adopted by the academies of science of these countries. Similarly, the transliteration for mainland Chinese names follows the Pinyin system, which has been officially adopted in mainland China. For languages with no one locally accepted transliteration system, notably Arabic, transliteration in general follows closely a system adopted by the United States Board on Geographic Names.

**ALPHABETIZATION** Names are alphabetized in the order of the letters of the English alphabet. Spanish *ll* and *ch*, for example, are not treated as distinct letters. Furthermore, diacritical marks are disregarded in alphabetization—German or Scandinavian *ä* or *ö* are treated as *a* or *o*.

The names of physical features may appear inverted, since they are always alphabetized under the proper, not the generic, part of the name, thus: "Gibraltar, Strait of ". Otherwise every entry, whether consisting of one word or more, is alphabetized as a single continuous entity. "Lakeland," for example, appears after "La Crosse" and before "La Salle." Names beginning with articles (Le Havre, Den Helder, Al-Qāhirah, As-Suways) are not inverted. Names beginning "Mc" are alphabetized as though spelled "Mac," and names beginning "St." and "Sainte" as though spelled "Saint."

In the case of identical names, towns are listed first, then political divisions, then physical features. Entries that are completely identical (including symbols, discussed below) are distinguished by abbreviations of their official country names and are sequenced alphabetically by country name. The many duplicate names in Canada, the United Kingdom, and the United States are further distinguished by abbreviations of the names of their primary subdivisions. (See list of abbreviations on pages 110 and 111).

**ABBREVIATION AND CAPITALIZATION** Abbreviation and styling have been standardized for all languages. A period is used after every abbreviation even when this may not be the local practice. The abbreviation "St." is used only for "Saint." "Sankt" and other forms of the term are spelled out.

All names are written with an initial capital letter except for a few Dutch names, such as 's-Gravenhage. Capitalization of noninitial words in a name generally follows local practice.

**SYMBOL** The symbols that appear in the Index graphically represent the broad categories of the features named, for example, $\wedge$ for mountain (Everest, Mount $\wedge$). Superior numbers following some symbols in the Index indicate finer distinctions, for example, $\wedge^{1}$ for volcano (Fuji-san $\wedge^{1}$). A complete list of the symbols and those with superior numbers is given on page 111.

## LIST OF ABBREVIATIONS

| | LOCAL NAME | ENGLISH |
|---|---|---|
| **Afg.** | Afghānestān | Afghanistan |
| **Afr.** | — | Africa |
| **Ala., U.S.** | Alabama | Alabama |
| **Alaska, U.S.** | Alaska | Alaska |
| **Alg.** | Algérie | Algeria |
| **Alta., Can.** | Alberta | Alberta |
| **Am. Sam.** | American Samoa | American Samoa |
| **And.** | Andorra | Andorra |
| **Ang.** | Angola | Angola |
| **Anguilla** | Anguilla | Anguilla |
| **Ant.** | — | Antarctica |
| **Antig.** | Antigua | Antigua |
| **Arc. O.** | — | Arctic Ocean |
| **Arg.** | Argentina | Argentina |
| **Ariz., U.S.** | Arizona | Arizona |
| **Ark., U.S.** | Arkansas | Arkansas |
| **Ar. Sa.** | Al-'Arabīyah as-Sa'ūdīyah | Saudi Arabia |
| **As.** | — | Asia |
| **Atl. O.** | — | Atlantic Ocean |
| **Austl.** | Australia | Australia |
| **Ba.** | Bahamas | Bahamas |
| **Baḥr.** | Al-Baḥrayn | Bahrain |
| **Barb.** | Barbados | Barbados |
| **B.A.T.** | British Antarctic Territory | British Antarctic Territory |
| **B.C., Can.** | British Columbia | British Columbia |
| **Bdi.** | Burundi | Burundi |
| **Bel.** | Belgique België | Belgium |
| **Belize** | Belize | Belize |
| **Benin** | Benin | Benin |
| **Ber.** | Bermuda | Bermuda |
| **Ber. S.** | — | Bering Sea |
| **Bhārat** | Bhārat | India |
| **B.I.O.T.** | British Indian Ocean Territory | British Indian Ocean Territory |
| **Blg.** | Bâlgarija | Bulgaria |
| **Bngl.** | Bangladesh | Bangladesh |
| **Bol.** | Bolivia | Bolivia |
| **Bots.** | Botswana | Botswana |
| **Bra.** | Brasil | Brazil |
| **B.R.D.** | Bundesrepublik Deutschland | Federal Republic of Germany |
| **Bru.** | Brunei | Brunei |
| **Br. Vir. Is.** | British Virgin Islands | British Virgin Islands |
| **Calif., U.S.** | California | California |
| **Cam.** | Cameroun | Cameroon |
| **Can.** | Canada | Canada |
| **Can./End.** | Canton and Enderbury | Canton and Enderbury |
| **Carib. S.** | — | Caribbean Sea |
| **Cay. Is.** | Cayman Islands | Cayman Islands |
| **Centraf.** | Empire centrafricain | Central African Empire |
| **Česko.** | Československo | Czechoslovakia |
| **Chile** | Chile | Chile |
| **Christ. I.** | Christmas Island | Christmas Island |
| **C. Iv.** | Côte d'Ivoire | Ivory Coast |
| **C.M.I.K.** | Chosŏn Minjujuŭi In'min Konghwaguk | North Korea |
| **Cocos Is.** | Cocos (Keeling) Islands | Cocos (Keeling) Islands |
| **Col.** | Colombia | Colombia |
| **Colo., U.S.** | Colorado | Colorado |
| **Comores** | Comores | Comoros |
| **Congo** | Congo | Congo |
| **Conn., U.S.** | Connecticut | Connecticut |
| **Cook Is.** | Cook Islands | Cook Islands |
| **C.R.** | Costa Rica | Costa Rica |
| **Cuba** | Cuba | Cuba |
| **C.V.** | Cabo Verde | Cape Verde |
| **C.Z.** | Canal Zone | Canal Zone |
| **Dan.** | Danmark | Denmark |
| **D.C., U.S.** | District of Columbia | District of Columbia |
| **D.D.R.** | Deutsche Demokratische Republik | German Democratic Republic |
| **Del., U.S.** | Delaware | Delaware |
| **Den.** | Danmark | Denmark |
| **Djibouti** | Djibouti | Djibouti |
| **Dom.** | Dominica | Dominica |
| **D.Y.** | Druk-Yul | Bhutan |
| **Ec.** | Ecuador | Ecuador |
| **Eire** | Eire | Ireland |
| **Ellás** | Ellás | Greece |
| **El Sal.** | El Salvador | El Salvador |
| **Eng., U.K.** | England | England |
| **Esp.** | España | Spain |
| **Eur.** | — | Europe |
| **Falk. Is.** | Falkland Islands | Falkland Islands (Islas Malvinas) |
| **Fiji** | Fiji | Fiji |
| **Fla., U.S.** | Florida | Florida |
| **Før.** | Føroyar | Faeroe Islands |
| **Fr.** | France | France |
| **Ga., U.S.** | Georgia | Georgia |
| **Gabon** | Gabon | Gabon |
| **Gam.** | Gambia | Gambia |
| **Gaza** | — | Gaza Strip |
| **Ghana** | Ghana | Ghana |
| **Gib.** | Gibraltar | Gibraltar |
| **Gilb. Is.** | Gilbert Islands | Gilbert Islands |
| **Gren.** | Grenada | Grenada |
| **Grn.** | Grønland | Greenland |
| **Guad.** | Guadeloupe | Guadeloupe |
| **Guam.** | Guam | Guam |
| **Guat.** | Guatemala | Guatemala |
| **Guer.** | Guernsey | Guernsey |
| **Gui.-B.** | Guinea-Bissau | Guinea-Bissau |
| **Gui. Ecu.** | Guinea Ecuatorial | Equatorial Guinea |
| **Guinée** | Guinée | Guinea |
| **Guy.** | Guyana | Guyana |
| **Guy. fr.** | Guyane française | French Guiana |
| **Haï.** | Haïti | Haiti |
| **Haw., U.S.** | Hawaii | Hawaii |
| **H.K.** | Hong Kong | Hong Kong |
| **Hond.** | Honduras | Honduras |
| **H. Vol.** | Haute-Volta | Upper Volta |
| **Idaho, U.S.** | Idaho | Idaho |
| **I.I.A.** | Ittiḥād al-Imārāt al-'Arabīyah | United Arab Emirates |
| **Ill., U.S.** | Illinois | Illinois |
| **Ind., U.S.** | Indiana | Indiana |
| **Ind. O.** | — | Indian Ocean |
| **Indon.** | Indonesia | Indonesia |
| **I. of Man** | Isle of Man | Isle of Man |
| **Iowa, U.S.** | Iowa | Iowa |
| **Īrān** | Īrān | Iran |
| **'Irāq** | Al-'Irāq | Iraq |
| **Ísland** | Ísland | Iceland |
| **It.** | Italia | Italy |
| **Jam.** | Jamaica | Jamaica |
| **Jersey** | Jersey | Jersey |
| **Jugo.** | Jugoslavija | Yugoslavia |
| **Kam.** | Kampuchea | Cambodia |
| **Kans., U.S.** | Kansas | Kansas |
| **Kenya** | Kenya | Kenya |
| **Kípros** | Kípros Kıbrıs | Cyprus |
| **Kuwayt** | Al-Kuwayt | Kuwait |
| **Ky., U.S.** | Kentucky | Kentucky |
| **La., U.S.** | Louisiana | Louisiana |
| **Lao** | Lao | Laos |
| **Leso.** | Lesotho | Lesotho |
| **Liber.** | Liberia | Liberia |
| **Lībiyā** | Lībiyā | Libya |
| **Liech.** | Liechtenstein | Liechtenstein |
| **Lubnān** | Al-Lubnān | Lebanon |
| **Lux.** | Luxembourg | Luxembourg |
| **Macau** | Macau | Macau |
| **Madag.** | Madagasikara | Madagascar |
| **Magreb** | Al-Magreb | Morocco |
| **Magy.** | Magyarország | Hungary |
| **Maine, U.S.** | Maine | Maine |
| **Malawi** | Malawi | Malawi |
| **Malay.** | Malaysia | Malaysia |
| **Mald.** | Maldives | Maldives |
| **Mali** | Mali | Mali |
| **Malta** | Malta | Malta |
| **Man., Can.** | Manitoba | Manitoba |
| **Mart.** | Martinique | Martinique |
| **Mass., U.S.** | Massachusetts | Massachusetts |
| **Maur.** | Mauritanie | Mauritania |
| **Maus.** | Mauritius | Mauritius |
| **Md., U.S.** | Maryland | Maryland |
| **Medit. S.** | — | Mediterranean Sea |
| **Méx.** | México | Mexico |
| **Mich., U.S.** | Michigan | Michigan |
| **Mid. Is.** | Midway Islands | Midway Islands |
| **Minn., U.S.** | Minnesota | Minnesota |
| **Miṣr** | Miṣr | Egypt |
| **Miss., U.S.** | Mississippi | Mississippi |
| **Mo., U.S.** | Missouri | Missouri |
| **Moç.** | Moçambique | Mozambique |
| **Monaco** | Monaco | Monaco |
| **Mong.** | Mongol Ard Uls | Mongolia |
| **Mont., U.S.** | Montana | Montana |
| **Monts.** | Montserrat | Montserrat |
| **Mya.** | Myanma | Burma |
| **N.A.** | — | North America |
| **Namibia** | Namibia | Namibia |
| **Nauru** | Nauru | Nauru |
| **N.B., Can.** | New Brunswick | New Brunswick |
| **N.C., U.S.** | North Carolina | North Carolina |
| **N. Cal.** | Nouvelle-Calédonie | New Caledonia |
| **N. Dak., U.S.** | North Dakota | North Dakota |
| **Nebr., U.S.** | Nebraska | Nebraska |
| **Ned.** | Nederland | Netherlands |
| **Ned. Ant.** | Nederlandse Antillen | Netherlands Antilles |
| **Nepāl** | Nepāl | Nepal |
| **Nev., U.S.** | Nevada | Nevada |
| **Newf., Can.** | Newfoundland | Newfoundland |
| **N.H., U.S.** | New Hampshire | New Hampshire |
| **N. Heb.** | New Hebrides Nouvelles-Hébrides | New Hebrides |
| **Nic.** | Nicaragua | Nicaragua |
| **Nig.** | Nigeria | Nigeria |
| **Niger** | Niger | Niger |
| **Nihon** | Nihon | Japan |
| **N. Ire., U.K.** | Northern Ireland | Northern Ireland |
| **Niue** | Niue | Niue |
| **N.J., U.S.** | New Jersey | New Jersey |
| **N. Mex., U.S.** | New Mexico | New Mexico |
| **Nor.** | Norge | Norway |
| **Norf. I.** | Norfolk Island | Norfolk Island |
| **N.S., Can.** | Nova Scotia | Nova Scotia |
| **N.W. Ter., Can.** | Northwest Territories | Northwest Territories |
| **N.Y., U.S.** | New York | New York |
| **N.Z.** | New Zealand | New Zealand |
| **Oc.** | — | Oceania |
| **Ohio, U.S.** | Ohio | Ohio |
| **Okla., U.S.** | Oklahoma | Oklahoma |
| **Ont., Can.** | Ontario | Ontario |
| **Oreg., U.S.** | Oregon | Oregon |
| **Öst.** | Österreich | Austria |
| **Pa., U.S.** | Pennsylvania | Pennsylvania |
| **Pac. O.** | — | Pacific Ocean |
| **Pāk.** | Pākistān | Pakistan |
| **Pan.** | Panamá | Panama |
| **Pap. N. Gui.** | Papua New Guinea | Papua New Guinea |
| **Para.** | Paraguay | Paraguay |
| **P.E.I., Can.** | Prince Edward Island | Prince Edward Island |
| **Perú** | Perú | Peru |
| **Pil.** | Pilipinas | Philippines |
| **Pit.** | Pitcairn | Pitcairn |
| **P.I.T.T.** | Pacific Islands Trust Territory | Pacific Islands Trust Territory |
| **Pol.** | Polska | Poland |
| **Poly. fr.** | Polynésie française | French Polynesia |
| **Port.** | Portugal | Portugal |
| **P.R.** | Puerto Rico | Puerto Rico |
| **P.S.N.Á.** | Plazas de Soberanía en el Norte de África | Spanish North Africa |
| **Qaṭar** | Qaṭar | Qatar |
| **Que., Can.** | Québec | Quebec |
| **Rep. Dom.** | República Dominicana | Dominican Republic |
| **Réu.** | Réunion | Reunion |
| **Rh.** | Rhodesia | Rhodesia |
| **R.I., U.S.** | Rhode Island | Rhode Island |
| **Rom.** | România | Romania |
| **Rw.** | Rwanda | Rwanda |
| **S.A.** | — | South America |
| **S. Afr.** | South Africa Suid-Afrika | South Africa |
| **Sah. Occ.** | Sahara Occidentale | Western Sahara |
| **Sask., Can.** | Saskatchewan | Saskatchewan |
| **S.C., U.S.** | South Carolina | South Carolina |
| **S. Ch. S.** | — | South China Sea |
| **Schw.** | Schweiz; Suisse; Svizzera | Switzerland |
| **Scot., U.K.** | Scotland | Scotland |
| **S. Dak., U.S.** | South Dakota | South Dakota |
| **Sén.** | Sénégal | Senegal |
| **Sey.** | Seychelles | Seychelles |
| **Shq.** | Shqipëri | Albania |
| **Sing.** | Singapore | Singapore |
| **S.L.** | Sierra Leone | Sierra Leone |
| **S. Lan.** | Sri Lanka | Sri Lanka |
| **S. Mar.** | San Marino | San Marino |
| **Sol. Is.** | Solomon Islands | Solomon Islands |
| **Som.** | Somaliya | Somalia |
| **Sp.** | España | Spain |
| **S.S.R.** | Sovetskaja Socialističeskaja Respublika | Soviet Socialist Republic |
| **S.S.S.R.** | Sojuz Sovetskich Socialističeskich Respublik | Union of Soviet Socialist Republics |
| **St. Hel.** | St. Helena | St. Helena |
| **St. K.-N.** | St. Kitts-Nevis | St. Kitts-Nevis |
| **St. Luc.** | St. Lucia | St. Lucia |
| **S. Tom./P.** | São Tomé e Príncipe | Sao Tome and Principe |
| **St. P./M.** | St.-Pierre-et-Miquelon | St. Pierre and Miquelon |
| **St. Vin.** | St. Vincent | St. Vincent |
| **Sūd.** | As-Sūdān | Sudan |
| **Suomi** | Suomi | Finland |
| **Sur.** | Suriname | Surinam |
| **Sūriy.** | As-Sūrīyah | Syria |
| **Sval.** | Svalbard og Jan Mayen | Svalbard and Jan Mayen |
| **Sve.** | Sverige | Sweden |
| **Swaz.** | Swaziland | Swaziland |
| **T.a.a.f.** | Terres australes et antarctiques françaises | French Southern and Antarctic Territories |
| **Taehan** | Taehan-Min'guk | South Korea |
| **T'aiwan** | T'aiwan | Taiwan |
| **Tan.** | Tanzania | Tanzania |
| **Tchad** | Tchad | Chad |
| **T./C. Is.** | Turks and Caicos Islands | Turks and Caicos Islands |
| **Tenn., U.S.** | Tennessee | Tennessee |
| **Tex., U.S.** | Texas | Texas |
| **Thai.** | Prathet Thai | Thailand |
| **Togo** | Togo | Togo |
| **Tok. Is.** | Tokelau Islands | Tokelau Islands |
| **Tonga** | Tonga | Tonga |
| **Trin.** | Trinidad and Tobago | Trinidad and Tobago |
| **Tun.** | Tunisie | Tunisia |
| **Tür.** | Türkiye | Turkey |
| **Tuvalu** | Tuvalu | Tuvalu |
| **Ug.** | Uganda | Uganda |
| **U.K.** | United Kingdom | United Kingdom |
| **'Umān** | 'Umān | Oman |
| **Ur.** | Uruguay | Uruguay |
| **Urd.** | Al-Urdunn | Jordan |
| **U.S.** | United States | United States |
| **U.S.S.R.** | Sojuz Sovetskich Socialističeskich Respublik | Union of Soviet Socialist Republics |
| **Utah, U.S.** | Utah | Utah |
| **Va., U.S.** | Virginia | Virginia |
| **Vat.** | Città del Vaticano | Vatican City |
| **Ven.** | Venezuela | Venezuela |
| **Viet.** | Viet-nam | Vietnam |
| **Vir. Is., U.S.** | Virgin Islands | Virgin Islands (U.S.) |
| **Vt., U.S.** | Vermont | Vermont |
| **Wake I.** | Wake Island | Wake Island |
| **Wales, U.K.** | Wales | Wales |
| **Wal./F.** | Wallis et Futuna | Wallis and Futuna |
| **Wash., U.S.** | Washington | Washington |
| **Wis., U.S.** | Wisconsin | Wisconsin |
| **W. Sam.** | Western Samoa | Western Samoa |
| **W. Va., U.S.** | West Virginia | West Virginia |
| **Wyo., U.S.** | Wyoming | Wyoming |
| **Yai.** | Yaitopya | Ethiopia |
| **Yaman** | Al-Yaman | Yemen |
| **Yam. S.** | Al-Yaman ash-Sha'bīyah | People's Democratic Republic of Yemen |
| **Yis.** | Yisra'el | Israel |
| **Yukon, Can.** | Yukon | Yukon |
| **Zaïre** | Zaïre | Zaire |
| **Zam.** | Zambia | Zambia |
| **Zhg.** | Zhongguo | China |

## KEY TO SYMBOLS

| | | | |
|---|---|---|---|
| ▲ Mountain | ➤ Cape | •³ Isthmus | ∟ Waterfall, Rapids |
| ▲¹ Volcano | ➤¹ Peninsula | •⁴ Cliff | ⊔ Strait |
| ▲² Hill | ➤² Spit, Sand Bar | •⁵ Cave, Caves | C Bay, Gulf |
| ▲ Mountains | I Island | •⁶ Crater | C¹ Estuary |
| ▲¹ Plateau | I¹ Atoll | •⁷ Depression | C² Fjord |
| ▲² Hills | I² Rock | •⁸ Dunes | C³ Bight |
| )( Pass | II Islands | •⁹ Lava Flow | ⊘ Lake, Lakes |
| ∨ Valley, Canyon | II¹ Rocks | | ⊘¹ Reservoir |
| ≃ Plain | ≗ Other Topographic Features | | ≋ Swamp |
| ≃² Delta | •¹ Continent | | ⊠ Ice Features, Glacier |
| | •² Coast, Beach | | |

| | | |
|---|---|---|
| ▽ Other Hydrographic Features | □ Political Unit | ⩜ Cultural Institution |
| ▽¹ Ocean | □¹ Independent Nation | Religious Institution |
| ▽² Sea | □² Dependency | Educational Institution |
| ▽³ Anchorage | □³ State, Canton, Republic | Scientific, Industrial Facility |
| ▽⁴ Oasis, Well, Spring | □⁴ Province, Region, Oblast | ⊥ Historical Site |
| ⊹ Submarine Features | □⁵ Department, District, Prefecture | ▲ Recreational Site |
| •¹ Depression | □⁶ County | ⊠ Airport |
| •² Reef, Shoal | □⁷ City, Municipality | ■ Military Installation |
| •³ Mountain, Mountains | □⁸ Miscellaneous | |
| •⁴ Slope, Shelf | □⁹ Historical | |

| Miscellaneous |
|---|
| ⊹¹ Region |
| ⊹² Desert |
| ⊹³ Forest, Moor |
| ⊹⁴ Reserve, Reservation |
| ⊹⁵ Transportation |
| ⊹⁶ Dam |
| ⊹⁷ Mine, Quarry |
| ⊹⁸ Neighborhood |
| ⊹⁹ Shopping Center |

# Index to Political-Physical Maps

| Name | Page | Lat | Long |
|---|---|---|---|
| **A** | | | |
| Aachen | 66 | 50.47 N | 6.05 E |
| Aalen | 66 | 48.50 N | 10.05 E |
| Aalst (Alost) | 68 | 50.56 N | 4.02 E |
| Aarau | 68 | 47.23 N | 8.03 E |
| Aarschot | 68 | 50.59 N | 4.50 E |
| Aba | 86 | 5.06 N | 7.21 E |
| Abacaxis ≃ | 100 | 3.54 S | 58.47 W |
| Ābādān | 84 | 30.20 N | 48.16 E |
| Abakan | 78 | 53.43 N | 91.26 E |
| Abakan ≃ | 78 | 53.43 N | 91.30 E |
| Abaya, Lake ⊘ | 88 | 6.20 N | 37.55 E |
| Abbert ≃ | 54 | 53.26 N | 9.54 W |
| Abbeville | 68 | 50.06 N | 1.50 E |
| Abbeydorney | 60 | 52.19 N | 9.41 W |
| Abbeyfeale | 60 | 52.24 N | 9.18 W |
| Abbey Head ▲¹ | 56 | 54.46 N | 3.58 W |
| Abbeyleix | 60 | 52.55 N | 7.20 W |
| Abbey Town | 56 | 54.50 N | 3.17 W |
| Abbiategrasso | 72 | 45.24 N | 8.54 E |
| Abbotsbury | 54 | 50.40 N | 2.36 W |
| Abbots Langley | 54 | 51.43 N | 0.25 W |
| 'Abd al-Kūrī I | 84 | 12.12 N | 52.15 E |
| Abe, Lake ⊘ | 88 | 11.06 N | 41.50 E |
| Abéché | 84 | 13.49 N | 20.49 E |
| Abengourou | 86 | 6.44 N | 3.29 W |
| Abenrå | 64 | 55.02 N | 9.26 E |
| Abeokuta | 86 | 7.10 N | 3.26 E |
| Aberaman | 54 | 51.42 N | 3.25 W |
| Aberayron | 54 | 52.15 N | 4.15 W |
| Abercarn | 54 | 51.39 N | 3.08 W |
| Aberchirder | 58 | 57.33 N | 2.38 W |
| Aberdare | 54 | 51.43 N | 3.27 W |
| Aberdaron | 54 | 52.49 N | 4.43 W |
| Aberdeen, Scot., U.K. | 58 | 57.10 N | 2.04 W |
| Aberdeen, S. Dak., U.S. | 96 | 45.28 N | 98.29 W |
| Aberdeen, Wash., U.S. | 96 | 46.59 N | 123.50 W |
| Aberdeen Lake ⊘ | 94 | 64.27 N | 99.00 W |
| Aberdour | 58 | 56.03 N | 3.19 W |
| Aberdovey | 54 | 52.33 N | 4.02 W |
| Aberdulais | 54 | 51.41 N | 3.48 W |
| Aberfeldy | 58 | 56.37 N | 3.54 W |
| Aberfoyle | 58 | 56.11 N | 4.23 W |
| Abergavenny | 54 | 51.50 N | 3.00 W |
| Abergele | 56 | 53.17 N | 3.34 W |
| Abergwynfi | 54 | 51.40 N | 3.35 W |
| Abergwynolwyn | 54 | 52.40 N | 3.58 W |
| Aberlour | 58 | 57.28 N | 3.14 W |
| Abernethy | 58 | 56.20 N | 3.19 W |
| Aberporth | 54 | 52.09 N | 4.33 W |
| Abersoch | 54 | 52.50 N | 4.29 W |
| Abersychan | 54 | 51.44 N | 3.04 W |
| Abertillery | 54 | 51.45 N | 3.09 W |
| Aberuthven | 58 | 56.19 N | 3.39 W |
| Aberystwyth | 54 | 52.25 N | 4.05 W |
| Abhā | 84 | 18.13 N | 42.30 E |
| Abidjan | 86 | 5.19 N | 4.02 W |
| Abilene | 96 | 32.27 N | 99.44 W |
| Abingdon | 54 | 51.41 N | 1.17 W |
| Abington Reefs ⊹² | 92 | 18.00 S | 149.36 E |
| Āb-i-Panja (P'andž) ≃ | 76 | 37.06 N | 68.20 E |
| Abitau ≃ | 94 | 59.53 N | 109.03 W |
| Abitibi ≃ | 94 | 51.03 N | 80.55 W |
| Abitibi, Lake ⊘ | 94 | 48.42 N | 79.45 W |
| Abomey | 86 | 7.11 N | 1.59 E |
| Abony | 66 | 47.11 N | 20.01 E |
| Aborigen, Pik ▲ | 78 | 62.59 N | 149.19 E |
| Aboyne | 58 | 57.05 N | 2.50 W |
| Abriachan | 58 | 57.22 N | 4.24 W |
| Absaroka Range ▲ | 96 | 44.45 N | 109.50 W |
| Abū Alī I | 84 | 27.20 N | 49.33 E |
| Abū Madd, Ra's ➤ | 84 | 24.50 N | 37.07 E |
| Abū Mūsā, Jazīreh-ye I | 84 | 25.52 N | 55.03 E |
| Abunã ≃ | 100 | 9.41 S | 65.23 W |
| Abū Ẕaby | 84 | 24.28 N | 54.22 E |
| Acámbaro | 94 | 20.02 N | 100.44 W |
| Acapulco [de Juárez] | 94 | 16.51 N | 99.55 W |
| Acarai Mountains ▲ | 100 | 1.50 N | 57.40 W |
| Acarigua | 100 | 9.33 N | 69.12 W |
| Acay, Nevado de ▲ | 102 | 24.21 S | 66.12 W |
| Accra | 86 | 5.33 N | 0.13 W |
| Accrington | 56 | 53.46 N | 2.21 W |
| Acerra | 72 | 40.57 N | 14.22 E |
| Achalpur | 84 | 21.16 N | 77.31 E |
| Acharacle | 58 | 56.44 N | 5.47 W |
| Achavanich | 58 | 58.22 N | 3.24 W |
| Achill Head ▲¹ | 52 | 53.59 N | 10.13 W |
| Achill Island I | 52 | 54.00 N | 10.00 W |
| Achill Sound | 58 | 53.55 N | 9.58 W |
| Achnasaul | 58 | 56.58 N | 4.59 W |
| Achnasheen | 58 | 57.35 N | 5.05 W |
| Achosnich | 58 | 56.45 N | 6.06 W |
| Achtuba ≃ | 76 | 48.00 N | 46.00 E |
| Acinsk | 78 | 56.17 N | 90.30 E |
| Acireale | 72 | 37.37 N | 15.10 E |
| Acklins Island I | 98 | 22.26 N | 73.58 W |
| Acle | 54 | 52.38 N | 1.33 E |
| Aconcagua, Cerro ▲ | 102 | 32.39 S | 70.00 W |
| Açores (Azores) II | 8 | 38.30 N | 28.00 W |
| Acqui Terme | 72 | 44.41 N | 8.28 E |
| Acre | 100 | 8.45 S | 67.22 W |
| Acton Turville | 54 | 51.32 N | 2.17 W |
| Adair, Cape ➤ | 94 | 71.30 N | 71.24 W |
| Adam, Mount ▲ | 102 | 51.36 S | 59.55 W |
| Adamawa ▲ | 86 | 7.00 N | 12.00 E |
| Adams, Mount ▲ | 96 | 46.12 N | 121.28 W |
| Adams Bridge ⊹² | 84 | 9.04 N | 79.37 E |
| Adams Peak ▲ | 84 | 6.48 N | 80.30 E |
| Adana | 84 | 37.01 N | 35.18 E |
| Adare | 60 | 52.34 N | 8.48 W |
| Ad-Dahnā' ≃² | 84 | 24.30 N | 48.10 E |
| Ad-Dammām | 84 | 26.27 N | 50.06 E |
| Ad-Dawhah (Doha) | 84 | 25.17 N | 51.32 E |
| Addiewell | 58 | 55.51 N | 3.39 W |
| Addingham | 56 | 53.57 N | 1.53 W |
| Addis Abeba | 88 | 9.00 N | 38.50 E |
| Ad-Dīwānīyah | 84 | 31.59 N | 44.56 E |
| Adelaide | 92 | 34.55 S | 138.35 E |
| Adelaide Peninsula ➤¹ | 94 | 68.09 N | 97.43 W |
| Adèle Island I | 92 | 15.32 S | 123.09 E |
| Aden | 84 | 12.45 N | 45.12 E |
| Aden, Gulf of C | 88 | 12.30 N | 48.00 E |
| Adieu, Cape ➤ | 92 | 31.59 S | 132.09 E |
| Adirondack Mountains ▲ | 96 | 44.00 N | 74.00 W |
| Adlington | 56 | 53.37 N | 2.36 W |
| Admiralty Gulf C | 92 | 14.20 S | 125.50 E |
| Admiralty Inlet C | 94 | 73.00 N | 86.00 W |
| Admiralty Island I | 94 | 69.30 N | 101.00 W |
| Adonara, Pulau I | 82 | 8.20 S | 123.10 E |
| Ádoni | 84 | 15.38 N | 77.17 E |
| Adra | 70 | 36.44 N | 3.01 W |
| Adrano | 72 | 37.40 N | 14.50 E |
| Adrar ▲¹ | 86 | 20.30 N | 13.30 W |
| Adria | 72 | 45.03 N | 12.03 E |
| Adriatic Sea ▽² | 50 | 42.30 N | 16.00 E |
| Adrigole | 60 | 51.40 N | 9.42 W |
| Adur ≃ | 54 | 50.49 N | 0.16 W |
| Advie | 58 | 57.23 N | 3.27 W |
| Adwa | 88 | 14.10 N | 38.55 E |
| Adwick le Street | 56 | 53.34 N | 1.11 W |
| Adýca ≃ | 78 | 68.13 N | 134.41 E |
| Ae, Water of ≃ | 56 | 55.08 N | 3.27 W |
| Aegean Sea ▽² | 50 | 38.30 N | 25.00 E |
| A'erjinshanmai ▲ | 80 | 37.30 N | 86.30 E |
| Aeron ≃ | 54 | 52.14 N | 4.16 W |
| Affric ≃ | 58 | 57.19 N | 4.50 W |
| Affric, Glen ∨ | 58 | 57.17 N | 4.56 W |
| Afghanistan □¹ | 84 | 33.00 N | 65.00 E |
| Afikpo | 86 | 5.53 N | 7.56 E |
| Africa •¹ | 8 | 10.00 N | 22.00 E |
| Agadir | 86 | 30.26 N | 9.36 W |
| Agalega Islands II | 90 | 10.24 S | 56.37 E |
| Agana | 82 | 13.28 N | 144.45 E |
| Agartala | 84 | 23.50 N | 91.16 E |
| Agen | 70 | 44.12 N | 0.37 E |
| Aghā Jārī | 84 | 30.42 N | 49.50 E |
| Aghleam | 60 | 54.08 N | 10.07 W |
| Agira | 72 | 37.39 N | 14.32 E |
| Agnews Hill ▲² | 54 | 54.50 N | 6.54 W |
| Āgra | 84 | 27.11 N | 77.59 E |
| Agrigento | 72 | 37.19 N | 13.35 E |
| Agrinion | 74 | 38.37 N | 21.24 E |
| Agryz | 76 | 56.33 N | 53.00 E |
| Aguanus ≃ | 94 | 50.13 N | 62.05 W |
| Aguarico ≃ | 100 | 0.59 S | 75.11 W |
| Aguascalientes | 98 | 21.53 N | 102.18 W |
| Aguijan I | 82 | 14.51 N | 145.34 E |
| Aguilar | 70 | 37.31 N | 4.39 W |
| Aguilas | 70 | 37.24 N | 1.35 W |
| Agulhas, Cape ➤ | 90 | 34.52 S | 20.00 E |
| Agulhas Negras, Pico das ▲ | 100 | 22.23 S | 44.38 W |
| Agusan ≃ | 82 | 9.00 N | 125.31 E |
| Ahaggar ▲ | 86 | 23.00 N | 6.30 E |
| Ahascragh | 60 | 53.24 N | 8.20 W |
| Ahlen | 66 | 51.46 N | 7.53 E |
| Ahmadābād | 84 | 23.02 N | 72.35 E |
| Ahmadnagar | 84 | 19.05 N | 74.45 E |
| Ahmar Mountains ▲ | 88 | 9.15 N | 41.00 E |
| Ahrensburg | 66 | 53.40 N | 10.14 E |
| Ahvāz | 84 | 31.19 N | 48.42 E |
| Ahvenanmaa (Åland) II | 64 | 60.15 N | 20.00 E |
| Aibihu ⊘ | 80 | 44.55 N | 82.55 E |
| Aide ≃ | 54 | 52.10 N | 1.27 E |
| Aihun | 80 | 50.13 N | 127.33 E |
| Ailaoshan ▲ | 80 | 24.08 N | 101.25 E |
| Ailsa Craig I | 56 | 55.16 N | 5.07 W |
| Aimorés, Serra dos ▲ | 100 | 19.00 S | 41.00 W |
| Ainsdale | 56 | 53.37 N | 3.03 W |
| Airdrie | 58 | 55.52 N | 3.59 W |
| Aire ≃ | 56 | 53.44 N | 0.54 W |
| Air Force Island I | 94 | 67.55 N | 74.10 W |
| Airor | 58 | 57.04 N | 5.46 W |
| Aishihik Lake ⊘ | 94 | 61.25 N | 137.06 W |
| Aith | 58 | 60.16 N | 1.23 W |
| Aiud | 74 | 46.19 N | 23.44 E |
| Aix-en-Provence | 68 | 43.32 N | 5.26 E |
| Aix-les-Bains | 68 | 45.42 N | 5.55 E |
| Aiyion | 74 | 38.15 N | 22.05 E |
| Aizu-wakamatsu | 80 | 37.30 N | 139.56 E |
| Ajaccio | 72 | 41.55 N | 8.44 E |
| Ajaguz | 78 | 47.56 N | 80.23 E |
| Ajan | 78 | 70.10 N | 95.50 E |
| Ajdābiyah | 88 | 30.48 N | 20.14 E |
| Ajmer | 84 | 26.27 N | 74.40 E |
| Ajon, Ostrov I | 78 | 69.50 N | 168.40 E |
| Ajtos | 74 | 42.42 N | 27.15 E |
| Akademii, Zaliv C | 78 | 54.15 N | 138.05 E |
| Aken | 66 | 51.51 N | 12.02 E |
| Akharnai | 74 | 38.05 N | 23.43 E |
| Akhisar | 84 | 38.55 N | 27.51 E |
| Akimiski Island I | 94 | 53.00 N | 81.20 W |
| Akita | 80 | 39.43 N | 140.07 E |
| 'Akko | 84 | 32.55 N | 35.04 E |
| Akobo ≃ | 88 | 7.47 N | 33.01 E |
| Akola | 84 | 20.42 N | 77.00 E |
| Akpatok Island I | 94 | 60.25 N | 68.00 W |
| Akranes | 62a | 64.18 N | 22.02 W |
| Akreyri | 62a | 65.44 N | 18.08 W |
| Akron | 96 | 41.05 N | 81.31 W |
| Akt'ubinsk | 76 | 50.17 N | 57.10 E |
| Akt'ubinskij Chrebet ▲ | 76 | 39.45 N | 72.00 E |
| Alabama □³ | 96 | 32.50 N | 87.00 W |
| Alagoinhas | 100 | 12.07 S | 38.26 W |
| Alajskij Chrebet ▲ | 76 | 39.45 N | 72.00 E |
| Alakol', Ozero ⊘ | 78 | 46.10 N | 81.45 E |
| Alamagan I | 82 | 17.36 N | 145.50 E |
| Alaotra, Lac ⊘ | 90 | 17.30 S | 48.30 E |
| Alapajevsk | 76 | 57.52 N | 61.42 E |
| Al-'Arīsh | 88 | 31.08 N | 33.48 E |
| Alasdair, Sgurr ▲ | 58 | 57.12 N | 6.14 W |
| Alaska □³ | 96 | 64.00 N | 150.00 W |
| Alaska, Gulf of C | 96a | 58.00 N | 146.00 W |
| Alaska Range ▲ | 96a | 62.30 N | 150.00 W |
| Alassio | 72 | 44.00 N | 8.10 E |
| Alaw ≃ | 56 | 53.25 N | 4.30 W |
| Alaw, Llyn ⊘¹ | 56 | 53.18 N | 4.22 W |
| Alazeja ≃ | 78 | 70.51 N | 153.34 E |
| Alba | 72 | 44.42 N | 8.02 E |
| Alba-Iulia | 74 | 46.04 N | 23.35 E |
| Albacete | 70 | 38.59 N | 1.51 W |
| Albania □¹ | 50 | 41.00 N | 20.00 E |
| Albano Laziale | 72 | 41.44 N | 12.39 E |
| Albany, Ga., U.S. | 96 | 31.35 N | 84.10 W |
| Albany, N.Y., U.S. | 96 | 42.39 N | 73.45 W |
| Albany ≃ | 94 | 52.17 N | 81.31 W |
| Al-Basrah | 84 | 30.30 N | 47.47 E |
| Albatross Bay C | 92 | 12.45 S | 141.43 E |
| Albemarle Sound ⊔ | 96 | 36.03 N | 76.12 W |
| Albenga | 72 | 44.03 N | 8.13 E |
| Alberga Creek ≃ | 92 | 27.06 S | 135.33 E |
| Albert | 68 | 50.00 N | 2.39 E |
| Albert, Lake ⊘ | 90 | 1.40 N | 31.00 E |
| Alberta □⁴ | 94 | 54.00 N | 113.00 W |
| Albertirsa | 66 | 47.15 N | 19.38 E |
| Albertville | 68 | 45.41 N | 6.23 E |
| Albi | 68 | 43.56 N | 2.09 E |
| Albino | 72 | 45.46 N | 9.47 E |
| Alborán, Isla de I | 70 | 35.58 N | 3.02 W |
| Alborg | 64 | 57.03 N | 9.56 E |
| Alborz, Reshteh-ye Kūhhā-ye ▲ | 84 | 36.00 N | 53.00 E |
| Albrighton | 54 | 52.38 N | 2.16 W |
| Albuquerque | 96 | 35.05 N | 106.40 W |
| Albury | 92 | 36.05 S | 146.55 E |
| Alcalá de Guadaira | 70 | 37.20 N | 5.50 W |
| Alcalá de Henares | 70 | 40.29 N | 3.22 W |
| Álcamo | 72 | 37.59 N | 12.58 E |
| Alcañiz | 70 | 41.03 N | 0.08 W |
| Alcantarilla | 70 | 37.58 N | 1.13 W |
| Alcázar de San Juan | 70 | 39.24 N | 3.12 W |
| Alcester | 54 | 52.13 N | 1.52 W |
| Alcira | 70 | 39.09 N | 0.26 W |
| Alconbury Brook ≃ | 54 | 52.19 N | 0.12 W |
| Alcoy | 70 | 38.42 N | 0.28 W |
| Aldabra Islands I¹ | 90 | 9.25 S | 46.22 E |
| Aldan | 78 | 58.37 N | 125.24 E |
| Aldan ≃ | 78 | 63.28 N | 129.35 E |
| Aldbourne | 54 | 51.29 N | 1.37 W |
| Aldbrough | 56 | 53.50 N | 0.07 W |
| Aldbury | 54 | 51.48 N | 0.36 W |
| Alde ≃ | 52 | 52.03 N | 1.28 E |
| Aldeburgh | 54 | 52.09 N | 1.35 E |
| Alder, Ben ▲ | 58 | 56.48 N | 4.28 W |
| Alderley Edge | 56 | 53.18 N | 2.15 W |
| Aldermaston | 54 | 51.23 N | 1.09 W |
| Alderney I | 54 | 49.43 N | 2.12 W |
| Aldershot | 54 | 51.15 N | 0.47 W |
| Aldridge | 54 | 52.36 N | 1.55 W |
| Aled ≃ | 56 | 53.14 N | 3.34 W |
| Alejandro Selkirk, Isla (Isla Más Afuera) I | 102 | 33.45 S | 80.46 W |
| Alejsk | 78 | 52.58 N | 82.45 E |
| Aleksandrov | 62 | 56.24 N | 38.43 E |
| Aleksandrovsk-Sachalinskij | 78 | 50.54 N | 142.10 E |
| Aleksinac | 74 | 43.31 N | 37.05 E |
| Alençon | 70 | 48.26 N | 0.05 E |
| Alès | 68 | 44.08 N | 4.05 E |
| Alessandria | 72 | 44.54 N | 8.37 E |
| Ålesund | 64 | 62.28 N | 6.09 E |
| Aleutian Islands II | 96a | 52.00 N | 176.00 W |
| Alevina, Mys ➤ | 78 | 58.50 N | 151.20 E |
| Ale Water ≃ | 58 | 55.31 N | 2.35 W |
| Alexandra Falls L | 94 | 60.29 N | 116.18 W |
| Alexandria, Rom. | 74 | 43.58 N | 25.20 E |
| Alexandria, Scot., U.K. | 58 | 55.59 N | 4.36 W |
| Alexandria, Va., U.S. | 96 | 38.48 N | 77.03 W |
| Alexandrina, Lake ⊘ | 92 | 35.26 S | 139.10 E |
| Alexandroúpolis | 74 | 40.50 N | 25.52 E |
| Alfeld | 66 | 51.59 N | 9.50 E |
| Al-Fāshir | 88 | 13.38 N | 25.21 E |
| Al-Fayyūm | 88 | 29.19 N | 30.50 E |
| Alford, Eng., U.K. | 56 | 53.16 N | 0.10 E |
| Alford, Scot., U.K. | 58 | 57.13 N | 2.42 W |
| Alfreton | 54 | 53.06 N | 1.24 W |
| Algeciras | 70 | 36.08 N | 5.30 W |
| Algemesi | 70 | 39.11 N | 0.26 W |
| Alger (Algiers) | 86 | 36.47 N | 3.03 E |
| Al-Hillah | 84 | 32.29 N | 44.25 E |
| Alghero | 72 | 40.34 N | 8.19 E |
| Algorta | 70 | 43.22 N | 3.01 W |
| Al-Hamād ≃ | 84 | 32.00 N | 39.30 E |
| Al-Harūj al-Aswad ▲ | 88 | 27.00 N | 17.10 E |
| Alhaurín el Grande | 70 | 36.38 N | 4.41 W |
| Al-Hijāz ➤¹ | 84 | 24.30 N | 38.30 E |
| Al-Hillah | 84 | 32.29 N | 44.25 E |
| Al-Hudaydah | 84 | 14.48 N | 42.57 E |
| Al-Hufūf | 84 | 25.22 N | 49.34 E |
| Alicante | 70 | 38.21 N | 0.29 W |
| Alice Springs | 92 | 23.42 S | 133.53 E |
| Alicudi, Isola I | 72 | 38.32 N | 14.21 E |
| Alima ≃ | 86 | 1.36 S | 16.36 E |
| Alingsås | 64 | 57.56 N | 12.31 E |
| Al-Iskandarīyah (Alexandria) | 88 | 31.12 N | 29.54 E |
| Al-Ismāʿīlīyah | 88 | 30.35 N | 32.16 E |
| Al-Jabal al-Akhdar ▲ | 84 | 23.15 N | 57.20 E |
| Al-Jawf | 88 | 24.15 N | 23.15 E |
| Al-Jazīrah ≃ | 84 | 14.25 N | 33.00 E |
| Al-Jilf al-Kabīr, Hadabat ▲ | 88 | 23.27 N | 26.00 E |
| Al-Jīzah | 88 | 30.01 N | 31.13 E |
| Al-Khalīl | 84 | 31.32 N | 35.06 E |
| Al-Khamīs, Ash-Shallāl L | 88 | 18.23 N | 33.47 E |
| Al-Khandaq | 88 | 18.36 N | 30.34 E |
| Al-Khubar | 84 | 26.17 N | 50.12 E |
| Al-Khums | 88 | 32.39 N | 14.16 E |
| Al-Khurtūm (Khartoum) | 88 | 15.36 N | 32.32 E |
| Al-Lādhiqīyah | 84 | 35.31 N | 35.47 E |
| Allāḩābād | 84 | 25.27 N | 81.50 E |
| Allan Water ≃ | 58 | 56.09 N | 3.56 W |
| 'Allāq, Bi'r ▽⁴ | 88 | 31.45 N | 12.44 E |
| Allegheny Plateau ▲¹ | 96 | 41.30 N | 78.00 W |
| Allen, Lough ⊘ | 60 | 54.08 N | 8.08 W |
| Allendale Town | 56 | 54.54 N | 2.16 W |
| Allenheads | 56 | 54.48 N | 2.12 W |
| Alleppey | 84 | 9.29 N | 76.20 E |
| Allerston | 56 | 54.16 N | 0.40 W |
| Allgäu ▲ | 66 | 47.33 N | 10.05 E |
| Allier ≃ | 68 | 46.58 N | 3.04 E |
| Allihies | 60 | 51.38 N | 10.03 W |
| Alloa | 58 | 56.07 N | 3.49 W |
| Allonby | 56 | 54.46 N | 3.25 W |
| Alma-Ata | 76 | 43.15 N | 76.57 E |
| Almada | 70 | 38.41 N | 9.09 W |
| Almadén | 70 | 38.46 N | 4.50 W |
| Al-Madīnah (Medina) | 84 | 24.28 N | 39.36 E |
| Al-Mahallah al-Kubrā | 88 | 30.58 N | 31.10 E |
| Almalyk | 76 | 40.50 N | 69.35 E |
| Al-Manāmah | 84 | 26.13 N | 50.35 E |
| Almansa | 70 | 38.52 N | 1.05 W |
| Al-Manşūrah | 88 | 31.03 N | 31.23 E |
| Al-Marj | 88 | 32.30 N | 20.54 E |
| Almas, Pico das ▲ | 100 | 13.33 S | 41.56 W |
| Al-Maşīrah I | 84 | 20.25 N | 58.50 E |
| Al-Mawşil | 88 | 36.20 N | 43.08 E |
| Almelo | 66 | 52.21 N | 6.39 E |
| Almendralejo | 70 | 38.41 N | 6.24 W |
| Almería | 70 | 36.50 N | 2.27 W |
| Al'metjevsk | 62 | 54.53 N | 52.20 E |
| Al-Minyā | 88 | 28.06 N | 30.45 E |
| Almond ≃, Scot., U.K. | 58 | 56.25 N | 3.27 W |
| Almond ≃, Scot., U.K. | 58 | 55.58 N | 3.18 W |
| Almondsbury | 54 | 51.33 N | 2.34 W |
| Almonte | 70 | 37.15 N | 6.31 W |
| Al-Mubarraz | 84 | 25.25 N | 49.36 E |
| Al-Muharraq | 84 | 26.16 N | 50.37 E |
| Al-Mukallā | 84 | 14.32 N | 49.08 E |
| Al-Mukhā | 84 | 13.19 N | 43.15 E |
| Alne ≃ | 56 | 55.23 N | 1.37 W |
| Alne | 54 | 52.13 N | 1.52 W |
| Alness | 58 | 57.41 N | 4.15 W |
| Alnmouth | 56 | 55.23 N | 1.36 W |
| Alnwick | 56 | 55.25 N | 1.42 W |
| Alor, Pulau I | 82 | 8.15 S | 124.45 E |
| Alor Setar | 82 | 6.07 N | 100.22 E |
| Aloysius, Mount ▲ | 92 | 26.01 S | 128.34 E |
| Alphington | 54 | 50.42 N | 3.31 W |
| Alphonse Island I | 90 | 7.00 S | 52.45 E |
| Alps ▲ | 50 | 46.25 N | 10.00 E |
| Al-Qāhirah (Cairo) | 88 | 30.03 N | 31.15 E |
| Al-Qash (Gash) ≃ | 88 | 16.48 N | 35.51 E |
| Al-Qaţīf | 84 | 26.33 N | 50.00 E |
| Al-Qaţţārah, Munkhafaḍ ▽⁷ | 88 | 29.30 N | 27.30 E |
| Alsek ≃ | 94 | 59.10 N | 138.10 W |
| Alsh, Loch C | 58 | 57.15 N | 5.39 W |
| Alston | 56 | 54.49 N | 2.26 W |
| Altai ▲ | 78 | 48.00 N | 90.00 E |
| Altamaha ≃ | 96 | 31.19 N | 81.17 W |
| Altamura | 72 | 40.49 N | 16.33 E |
| Altarnun | 54 | 50.37 N | 4.30 W |
| Altdorf | 68 | 46.53 N | 8.39 E |
| Altenburg | 66 | 51.00 N | 12.26 E |
| Altiplano ▲¹ | 100 | 18.00 S | 68.00 W |
| Altnaharra | 58 | 58.16 N | 4.27 W |
| Alton, Eng., U.K. | 54 | 51.09 N | 0.59 W |
| Alton, Ill., U.S. | 96 | 38.54 N | 90.10 W |
| Altoona | 96 | 40.31 N | 78.24 W |
| Altrincham | 56 | 53.24 N | 2.21 W |
| Al-Ubayyid | 88 | 13.11 N | 30.13 E |
| Al-Uqşur (Luxor) | 88 | 25.41 N | 32.39 E |
| Alva | 58 | 56.09 N | 3.48 W |
| Alvechurch | 54 | 52.21 N | 1.57 W |
| Alveston | 54 | 51.36 N | 2.32 W |
| Alwar | 84 | 27.46 N | 76.37 E |
| Alwen ≃ | 56 | 53.05 N | 3.24 W |
| Alyth | 58 | 56.37 N | 3.14 W |
| Alytus | 66 | 54.24 N | 24.03 E |
| Amadeus, Lake ⊘ | 92 | 24.50 S | 130.45 E |
| Amadjuak Lake ⊘ | 94 | 65.00 N | 71.00 W |
| Amalfi | 72 | 40.38 N | 14.36 E |
| Amalias | 74 | 37.49 N | 21.23 E |
| Amambai, Serra de ▲ | 100 | 23.10 S | 55.30 W |
| Amami-Ō-shima I | 80 | 28.15 N | 129.20 E |
| Amarillo | 96 | 35.13 N | 101.49 W |
| Amazon (Solimões) (Amazonas) ≃ | 100 | 0.05 S | 50.00 W |
| Ambāla | 84 | 30.23 N | 76.46 E |
| Ambato | 100 | 1.15 S | 78.37 W |
| Ambelau, Pulau I | 82 | 3.51 S | 127.12 E |
| Amber ≃ | 54 | 53.01 N | 1.29 W |
| Amble | 56 | 55.20 N | 1.34 W |
| Amblecote | 54 | 52.27 N | 2.09 W |
| Ambleside | 56 | 54.26 N | 2.58 W |
| Amboise | 68 | 47.25 N | 0.59 E |
| Ambon | 82 | 3.43 S | 128.12 E |
| Ambon, Pulau I | 82 | 3.35 S | 128.10 E |
| Ambositra | 90 | 20.31 S | 47.15 E |
| Ambre, Cap d' ➤ | 90 | 11.57 S | 49.17 E |
| American Falls Reservoir ⊘¹ | 96 | 43.00 N | 113.00 W |
| Amersfoort | 66 | 52.09 N | 5.23 E |
| Amersham | 54 | 51.40 N | 0.38 W |
| Ames | 96 | 42.02 N | 93.37 W |
| Amesbury | 54 | 51.10 N | 1.45 W |
| Amfissa | 74 | 38.32 N | 22.22 E |
| Amga ≃ | 78 | 62.38 N | 134.32 E |
| Amiens | 68 | 49.54 N | 2.18 E |
| Amīndīvi Islands II | 84 | 11.23 N | 72.23 E |
| Amirante Islands II | 90 | 6.00 S | 53.10 E |
| Amlwch | 56 | 53.25 N | 4.20 W |
| Ammanford | 54 | 51.48 N | 3.59 W |
| Āmol | 84 | 36.28 N | 52.21 E |
| Amorgós I | 74 | 36.50 N | 25.59 E |
| Amos | 94 | 48.34 N | 78.07 W |
| Ampthill | 54 | 52.02 N | 0.30 W |
| Amrāvati | 84 | 20.56 N | 77.47 E |
| Amritsar | 84 | 31.35 N | 74.53 E |
| Amroha | 84 | 28.54 N | 78.38 E |
| Amsterdam | 66 | 52.22 N | 4.54 E |
| Amsterdam, Île I | 22 | 37.52 S | 77.32 E |
| Amstetten | 66 | 48.07 N | 14.53 E |
| Amu Darya (Amudarja) ≃ | 76 | 43.40 N | 59.01 E |
| Amundsen Gulf C | 94 | 71.00 N | 124.00 W |
| Amundsen Sea ▽² | 8 | 72.30 S | 112.00 W |
| Amuntai | 82 | 2.26 S | 115.15 E |
| Amur (Heilongjiang) ≃ | 78 | 52.56 N | 141.10 E |
| Anabar ≃ | 78 | 73.08 N | 113.36 E |
| Anadyr' | 78 | 64.55 N | 176.05 E |
| Anadyrskij Zaliv C | 78 | 64.00 N | 179.00 W |
| Anadyrskoje Ploskogorje ▲¹ | 78 | 67.00 N | 172.00 E |
| Anaheim | 96 | 33.51 N | 117.57 W |
| Anajás, Ilha I | 100 | 0.20 S | 50.30 W |
| Anambas, Kepulauan II | 82 | 3.00 N | 106.00 E |
| Ananjev | 66 | 47.40 N | 29.55 E |
| Anantapur | 84 | 14.41 N | 77.37 E |
| Anápolis | 100 | 16.20 S | 48.58 W |
| Anatahan I | 82 | 16.22 N | 145.40 E |
| Anauá ≃ | 100 | 0.58 N | 61.21 W |
| Anavilhanas, Arquipélago das II | 100 | 2.42 S | 60.45 W |
| Ancaster | 54 | 52.59 N | 0.32 W |
| Ancholme ≃ | 56 | 53.41 N | 0.32 W |
| Anchorage | 96a | 61.13 N | 149.53 W |
| Ancona | 72 | 43.38 N | 13.30 E |
| Ancrum | 58 | 55.31 N | 2.35 W |
| Ancud, Golfo de C | 102 | 42.05 S | 73.00 W |
| Andaman Islands II | 84 | 12.00 N | 92.45 E |
| Andaman Sea ▽² | 82 | 10.00 N | 95.00 E |
| Andernach | 66 | 50.26 N | 7.24 E |
| Anderson, Ind., U.S. | 96 | 40.10 N | 85.41 W |
| Anderson, S.C., U.S. | 96 | 34.31 N | 82.39 W |
| Anderson ≃ | 94 | 69.43 N | 128.58 W |
| Andes ▲ | 100 | 17.00 S | 70.00 W |
| Andikíthira I | 74 | 35.52 N | 23.18 E |
| Andizan | 76 | 40.45 N | 72.22 E |
| Andoas | 100 | 1.00 N | 76.25 W |
| Andong, Taehan | 80 | 36.35 N | 128.44 E |
| Andong, Zhg. | 80 | 40.08 N | 124.20 E |
| Andorra | 70 | 42.30 N | 1.31 E |
| Andorra □¹ | 70 | 42.30 N | 1.30 E |
| Andover | 54 | 51.13 N | 1.28 W |
| Andøya I | 50 | 69.08 N | 15.54 E |
| Andradina | 100 | 20.54 S | 51.23 W |
| Andria | 72 | 41.13 N | 16.18 E |
| Andros | 74 | 37.59 N | 24.56 E |
| Andros Island I | 98 | 24.26 N | 77.57 W |
| Andrychów | 66 | 49.52 N | 19.21 E |
| Andújar | 70 | 38.03 N | 4.04 W |
| Angamos, Punta ➤ | 102 | 23.01 S | 70.32 W |
| Angara ≃ | 78 | 58.06 N | 93.00 E |
| Angarsk | 78 | 52.34 N | 103.54 E |
| Angaur I | 82 | 6.54 N | 134.09 E |
| Angel, Salto (Angel Falls) L | 100 | 5.57 N | 62.30 W |
| Ángel de la Guarda, Isla I | 98 | 29.20 N | 113.25 W |
| Angeles | 82 | 15.09 N | 120.35 E |
| Ängelholm | 64 | 56.15 N | 12.51 E |
| Angermanälven ≃ | 64 | 62.48 N | 17.56 E |
| Angermünde | 66 | 53.01 N | 14.00 E |
| Angers | 68 | 47.28 N | 0.33 W |
| Angikuni Lake ⊘ | 94 | 62.12 N | 100.00 W |
| Anglesey I | 56 | 53.16 N | 4.22 W |
| Anglinghu ≃ | 80 | 31.40 N | 83.00 E |
| Angle | 54 | 51.41 N | 5.06 W |
| Angmering | 54 | 50.49 N | 0.29 W |
| Angoche, Ilha I | 90 | 16.20 S | 39.50 E |
| Angola □¹ | 90 | 12.30 S | 18.30 E |
| Angoulême | 68 | 45.39 N | 0.09 E |
| Angren | 76 | 41.01 N | 70.12 E |
| Anguilla □² | 98 | 18.14 N | 63.05 W |
| Anholt I | 64 | 56.42 N | 11.34 E |
| Animaqingshanmai ▲ | 80 | 34.24 N | 100.10 E |
| Anina | 74 | 45.05 N | 21.51 E |
| Aniva, Zaliv C | 78 | 46.16 N | 142.48 E |
| Anjiang | 80 | 27.21 N | 110.04 E |
| Anjou □⁹ | 68 | 47.20 N | 0.20 W |
| Anjouan I | 90 | 12.15 S | 44.25 E |
| Ankang | 80 | 32.41 N | 109.02 E |
| Ankara | 84 | 39.56 N | 32.52 E |
| Ankaratra ▲ | 90 | 19.25 S | 47.12 E |
| Anklam | 66 | 53.51 N | 13.41 E |
| Anlaby | 56 | 53.45 N | 0.27 W |
| Annaba (Bône) | 86 | 36.54 N | 7.46 E |
| Annaberg-Buchholz | 66 | 50.35 N | 13.00 E |
| An-Nafūd ≃² | 84 | 28.30 N | 41.00 E |
| Annagassan | 60 | 53.53 N | 6.20 W |
| An-Najaf | 84 | 31.59 N | 44.20 E |
| Annalee ≃ | 60 | 54.03 N | 7.24 W |
| Annan | 56 | 54.59 N | 3.16 W |
| Annandale ∨ | 56 | 55.12 N | 3.25 W |
| Annapolis | 96 | 38.59 N | 76.30 W |
| Annapurna ▲ | 84 | 28.34 N | 83.50 E |
| Ann Arbor | 96 | 42.18 N | 83.45 W |
| An-Nāşirīyah | 84 | 31.02 N | 46.16 E |
| Annecy | 68 | 45.54 N | 6.07 E |
| Annenkov Island I | 102 | 54.29 S | 37.05 W |
| Anner ≃ | 60 | 52.29 N | 7.44 W |
| Annestown | 60 | 52.07 N | 7.16 W |
| Anniston | 96 | 33.40 N | 85.50 W |
| Annonay | 68 | 45.14 N | 4.40 E |
| An-Nuhūd | 88 | 12.42 N | 28.26 E |
| Anqing | 80 | 30.31 N | 117.02 E |
| Anshan | 80 | 41.08 N | 122.59 E |
| Anshun | 80 | 26.11 N | 105.57 E |
| Anstey | 54 | 52.41 N | 1.11 W |
| Anstruther | 58 | 56.14 N | 2.42 W |
| Antakya | 84 | 36.14 N | 36.07 E |
| Antalya | 84 | 36.53 N | 30.42 E |
| Antalya Körfezi C | 84 | 36.30 N | 31.00 E |
| Antananarivo | 90 | 18.55 S | 47.31 E |
| Antarctica •¹ | 8 | 90.00 S | — |
| An Teallach ▲ | 58 | 57.48 N | 5.14 W |
| Antequera | 70 | 37.01 N | 4.33 W |
| Antibes | 68 | 43.35 N | 7.07 E |
| Anticosti, Île I | 94 | 49.30 N | 63.00 W |
| Antigua I | 98 | 17.03 N | 61.48 W |
| Antigua □² | 98 | 17.03 N | 61.48 W |
| Antofagasta | 102 | 23.39 S | 70.24 W |
| Antofalla, Salar de ≃ | 102 | 25.44 S | 67.45 W |
| Antongil, Baie d' C | 90 | 16.14 S | 49.54 E |
| António Enes | 90 | 16.14 S | 39.54 E |
| Antrim | 60 | 54.43 N | 6.13 W |
| Antrim, Mountains of ▲ | 60 | 55.00 N | 6.10 W |
| Antsirabe | 90 | 19.51 S | 47.02 E |
| Antsiranana | 90 | 12.16 S | 49.17 E |
| Antwerpen (Anvers) | 68 | 51.13 N | 4.25 E |
| An'ujskij Chrebet ▲ | 78 | 67.00 N | 165.00 E |
| Anyang | 80 | 36.06 N | 114.21 E |
| Anzero-Sudžensk | 78 | 56.07 N | 86.00 E |
| Anzin | 68 | 50.22 N | 3.30 E |
| Anzio | 72 | 41.27 N | 12.37 E |
| Anžu, Ostrova II | 78 | 75.30 N | 143.00 E |
| Aomori | 80 | 40.49 N | 140.45 E |
| Aóral, Phnum ▲ | 82 | 12.02 N | 104.10 E |
| Aosta | 72 | 45.44 N | 7.20 E |
| Aouk, Bahr ≃ | 88 | 8.51 N | 18.53 E |
| Aoukâr ≃¹ | 86 | 18.00 N | 9.30 W |
| Apa ≃ | 102 | 22.06 S | 58.00 W |
| Apalachee Bay C | 96 | 30.00 N | 84.13 W |
| Apalachicola ≃ | 96 | 29.44 N | 84.59 W |
| Apaporis ≃ | 100 | 1.23 S | 69.25 W |
| Apatin | 74 | 45.40 N | 18.59 E |
| Apatity | 62 | 67.34 N | 33.18 E |
| Ape Dale ∨ | 54 | 52.30 N | 2.45 W |
| Apeldoorn | 66 | 52.13 N | 5.58 E |
| Apiacás, Serra dos ▲ | 100 | 10.15 S | 57.15 W |
| Apo, Mount ▲ | 82 | 6.59 N | 125.16 E |
| Apolda | 66 | 51.01 N | 11.31 E |
| Aporé ≃ | 100 | 19.27 S | 50.57 W |
| Apostle Islands II | 96 | 46.50 N | 90.30 W |
| Appalachian Mountains ▲ | 96 | 41.00 N | 77.00 W |
| Appennino ▲ | 50 | 43.00 N | 13.00 E |
| Appleby | 56 | 54.36 N | 2.29 W |
| Applecross | 58 | 57.25 N | 5.49 W |
| Appledore | 54 | 51.03 N | 4.10 W |
| Appleton | 96 | 44.16 N | 88.25 W |
| Aprelevka | 62 | 55.33 N | 37.04 E |
| Apure ≃ | 100 | 7.37 N | 66.25 W |
| Apurímac ≃ | 100 | 11.48 S | 74.03 W |
| Aqaba, Gulf of C | 84 | 29.00 N | 34.40 E |
| Ara ≃ | 60 | 52.24 N | 7.56 W |
| Arabian Peninsula ➤¹ | 8 | 25.00 N | 45.00 E |
| Arabian Sea ▽² | 84 | 15.00 N | 65.00 E |
| Araç ≃ | 84 | 41.15 N | 33.00 E |
| Aracaju | 100 | 10.55 S | 37.04 W |
| Araçatuba | 100 | 21.12 S | 50.25 W |
| Arad | 74 | 46.11 N | 21.20 E |
| Araguaia ≃ | 100 | 5.21 S | 48.41 W |
| Araguari | 100 | 18.38 S | 48.11 W |
| Araguari ≃ | 100 | 1.15 N | 49.55 W |
| Arak | 84 | 34.05 N | 49.41 E |
| Arakan Yoma ▲ | 82 | 19.00 N | 94.40 E |
| Araks (Aras) ≃ | 84 | 40.01 N | 48.28 E |
| Aral'sk | 76 | 46.48 N | 61.40 E |
| Aral'skoje More ▽² | 76 | 45.00 N | 60.00 E |
| Aranda de Duero | 70 | 41.41 N | 3.41 W |
| Aran Fawddwy ▲ | 54 | 52.47 N | 3.41 W |
| Aran Island I | 60 | 54.58 N | 8.33 W |
| Aran Islands II | 60 | 53.07 N | 9.43 W |
| Aranjuez | 70 | 40.02 N | 3.36 W |
| Araraquara | 100 | 21.47 S | 48.10 W |
| Aras (Araks) ≃ | 84 | 40.01 N | 48.28 E |
| Arauca | 100 | 7.24 N | 66.35 W |
| Arauca ≃ | 100 | 7.24 N | 66.35 W |
| Araxá | 100 | 19.35 S | 46.55 W |
| Arboga | 64 | 59.24 N | 15.50 E |
| Arbroath | 58 | 56.34 N | 2.35 W |
| Arbuthnott | 58 | 56.54 N | 2.24 W |
| Arcachon | 68 | 44.40 N | 1.10 W |
| Archangel'sk | 62 | 64.34 N | 40.32 E |
| Archer Bay C | 92 | 13.25 S | 141.43 E |
| Arcos de la Frontera | 70 | 36.45 N | 5.48 W |
| Arctic Ocean ▽¹ | 8 | 85.00 N | 170.00 E |
| Arctic Red ≃ | 94 | 67.27 N | 133.46 W |
| Ard, Loch C | 58 | 56.11 N | 4.28 W |
| Ardabīl | 84 | 38.15 N | 48.18 E |
| Ardakān | 84 | 32.19 N | 54.01 E |
| Ardanaish, Rubh' ➤ | 58 | 56.17 N | 6.18 W |
| Ardara | 60 | 54.46 N | 8.25 W |
| Ardbeg | 58 | 55.38 N | 6.05 W |
| Ardcharnich | 58 | 57.51 N | 5.05 W |
| Ardee | 60 | 53.52 N | 6.33 W |
| Arden, Forest of ⊹³ | 54 | 52.23 N | 1.45 W |
| Ardennes ▲ | 68 | 50.10 N | 5.45 E |
| Ardentinny | 58 | 56.03 N | 4.55 W |
| Ardfern | 58 | 56.11 N | 5.32 W |
| Ardfert | 60 | 52.20 N | 9.47 W |
| Ardglass | 60 | 54.16 N | 5.37 W |
| Ardgroom | 60 | 51.43 N | 9.54 W |
| Ardingly | 54 | 51.03 N | 0.04 W |
| Ardivachar Point ➤ | 58 | 57.22 N | 7.25 W |
| Ardlui | 58 | 56.18 N | 4.43 W |
| Ardmolich | 58 | 56.49 N | 5.41 W |
| Ardmore | 60 | 51.57 N | 7.43 W |
| Ardmore Point ➤, Scot., U.K. | 58 | 56.39 N | 6.07 W |
| Ardmore Point ➤, Scot., U.K. | 58 | 55.42 N | 6.01 W |
| Ardnamurchan, Point of ➤ | 58 | 56.44 N | 6.14 W |
| Ardnave Point ➤ | 58 | 55.54 N | 6.20 W |
| Ardrahan | 60 | 53.09 N | 8.48 W |
| Ardrishaig | 58 | 56.01 N | 5.27 W |
| Ardrossan | 58 | 55.39 N | 4.49 W |
| Ardvasar | 58 | 57.03 N | 5.54 W |
| Arecibo | 98 | 18.28 N | 66.43 W |
| Arendal | 64 | 58.27 N | 8.48 E |
| Arenig Fawr ▲ | 54 | 52.55 N | 3.45 W |
| Arequipa | 100 | 16.24 S | 71.33 W |
| Arezzo | 72 | 43.25 N | 11.53 E |
| Arga-Sala ≃ | 78 | 68.30 N | 112.12 E |
| Argentan | 68 | 48.45 N | 0.01 W |
| Argentina □¹ | 102 | 34.00 S | 64.00 W |
| Argentino, Lago ⊘ | 102 | 50.13 S | 72.25 W |
| Argostólion | 74 | 38.10 N | 20.30 E |
| Argun ≃ | 78 | 53.20 N | 121.28 E |
| Argyle, Lake ⊘ | 92 | 16.15 S | 128.45 E |
| Århus | 64 | 56.09 N | 10.13 E |
| Ariano Irpino | 72 | 41.09 N | 15.05 E |
| Arica | 100 | 18.29 S | 70.20 W |
| Arid, Cape ➤ | 92 | 34.00 S | 123.09 E |
| Arinos ≃ | 100 | 10.25 S | 58.20 W |
| Arisaig | 58 | 56.55 N | 5.51 W |
| Arisaig, Sound of ⊔ | 58 | 56.50 N | 5.50 W |
| Arizona □³ | 96 | 34.00 N | 112.00 W |
| Arkaig, Loch ⊘ | 58 | 56.58 N | 5.08 W |
| Arkansas □³ | 96 | 34.50 N | 93.40 W |
| Arkansas ≃ | 96 | 33.48 N | 91.04 W |
| Arklow | 60 | 52.48 N | 6.09 W |

| Name | Page | Lat | Long |
|---|---|---|---|
| Arktičeskij, Mys ➤ | 78 | 81.15 N | 95.45 E |
| Arktičeskogo Instituta, Ostrova II | 78 | 75.20 N | 81.55 E |
| Arles | 96 | 43.40 N | 4.38 E |
| Arlington | 96 | 38.52 N | 77.05 W |
| Arlon | 66 | 49.41 N | 5.49 E |
| Armadale | 58 | 55.54 N | 3.42 W |
| Armagh | 60 | 54.21 N | 6.39 W |
| Arm'anskaja Sovetskaja Socialističeskaja Respublika □³ | 76 | 40.00 N | 45.00 E |
| Armavir | 76 | 45.00 N | 41.08 E |
| Armenia | 100 | 4.31 N | 75.41 W |
| Armentières | 68 | 50.41 N | 2.53 E |
| Armidale | 92 | 30.31 S | 151.39 E |
| Armstrong, Mount Λ | 94 | 63.12 N | 133.16 W |
| Armthorpe | 54 | 53.32 N | 1.03 W |
| Arnaud ≈ | 94 | 59.59 N | 69.46 W |
| Arney ≈ | 60 | 54.16 N | 7.37 W |
| Arnhem | 66 | 51.59 N | 5.55 E |
| Arnhem, Cape ➤ | 92 | 12.21 S | 136.21 E |
| Arnhem Land ◄¹ | 92 | 13.10 S | 134.30 E |
| Arnissa | 74 | 40.48 N | 21.50 E |
| Arnold | 54 | 53.00 N | 1.08 W |
| Arnsberg | 66 | 51.24 N | 8.03 E |
| Arnstadt | 66 | 50.50 N | 10.57 E |
| Arona | 66 | 45.46 N | 8.34 E |
| Ar-Rab' al-Khālī ◄² | 84 | 20.00 N | 51.00 E |
| Arrah | 84 | 25.33 N | 84.40 E |
| Arran, Island of I | 58 | 55.35 N | 5.15 W |
| Arras | 68 | 50.17 N | 2.47 E |
| Ar-Riyāḍ (Riyadh) | 84 | 24.38 N | 46.43 E |
| Arrochar | 58 | 56.12 N | 4.44 W |
| Arrow ≈, Eng., U.K. | 54 | 52.09 N | 1.53 W |
| Arrow ≈, Eng., U.K. | 54 | 52.12 N | 2.43 W |
| Arrow, Lough ⌷ | 60 | 54.04 N | 8.21 W |
| Arrowsmith Bay C | 94 | 68.00 N | 95.15 W |
| Arsenjev | 76 | 44.10 N | 133.15 E |
| Arta | 74 | 39.09 N | 20.59 E |
| Artigas | 102 | 30.24 S | 56.28 W |
| Artillery Lake ⌷ | 94 | 63.09 N | 107.52 W |
| Artney, Glen V | 58 | 56.20 N | 4.14 W |
| Art'om | 76 | 43.22 N | 132.13 E |
| Art'omovsk | 78 | 54.21 N | 93.26 E |
| Aru, Kepulauan II | 82 | 6.00 S | 134.30 E |
| Aru, Tanjung ➤ | 82 | 2.10 S | 116.34 E |
| Aruba I | 98 | 12.30 N | 69.58 W |
| Arun ≈ | 54 | 50.48 N | 0.33 W |
| Arundel | 54 | 50.51 N | 0.34 W |
| Arusha | 90 | 3.22 S | 36.41 E |
| Aruwimi ≈ | 90 | 1.13 N | 23.36 E |
| Arvagh | 60 | 53.55 N | 7.34 W |
| Arvika | 64 | 59.39 N | 12.36 E |
| Arzamas | 62 | 55.23 N | 43.50 E |
| Arzignano | 72 | 45.31 N | 11.20 E |
| Aš | 66 | 50.10 N | 12.10 E |
| Aša | 76 | 55.00 N | 57.16 E |
| Asahikawa | 80 | 43.46 N | 142.22 E |
| Asansol | 84 | 23.41 N | 86.58 E |
| Asbest | 76 | 57.00 N | 61.30 E |
| Ascension I | 8 | 7.57 S | 14.22 W |
| Aschabad | 76 | 37.57 N | 58.23 E |
| Aschaffenburg | 66 | 49.59 N | 9.09 E |
| Aschersleben | 66 | 51.45 N | 11.27 E |
| Ascoli Piceno | 72 | 42.51 N | 13.34 E |
| Ascot | 54 | 51.25 N | 0.41 W |
| Asenovgrad | 74 | 42.01 N | 24.52 E |
| Ash, Eng., U.K. | 54 | 51.15 N | 0.44 W |
| Ash, Eng., U.K. | 54 | 51.17 N | 1.16 E |
| Ash ≈ | 54 | 51.48 N | 0.24 W |
| Ashbourne, Eire | 60 | 53.31 N | 6.24 W |
| Ashbourne, Eng., U.K. | 56 | 53.02 N | 1.44 W |
| Ashburton | 54 | 50.31 N | 3.45 W |
| Ashburton ≈ | 92 | 21.40 S | 114.56 E |
| Ashby-de-la-Zouch | 54 | 52.46 N | 1.28 W |
| Ashdown Forest ◄³ | 54 | 51.04 N | 0.03 E |
| Asheville | 96 | 35.34 N | 82.33 W |
| Asheweig ≈ | 94 | 54.17 N | 87.12 W |
| Ashford | 54 | 51.08 N | 0.53 E |
| Ashikaga | 80 | 36.20 N | 139.27 E |
| Ashington | 56 | 55.11 N | 1.35 W |
| Ashland | 96 | 38.28 N | 82.38 W |
| Ashmore Islands II | 92 | 12.14 S | 123.05 E |
| Ashtabula | 96 | 41.52 N | 80.47 W |
| Ashtead | 54 | 51.19 N | 0.18 W |
| Ashton-in-Makerfield | 56 | 53.29 N | 2.39 W |
| Ashton-under-Lyne | 56 | 53.29 N | 2.06 W |
| Ashuanipi Lake ⌷ | 94 | 52.35 N | 66.10 W |
| Ashwater | 54 | 50.44 N | 4.16 W |
| Asia ◄¹ | 8 | 50.00 N | 100.00 E |
| Asia Minor ◄¹ | 38 | 39.00 N | 32.00 E |
| Asino | 78 | 57.00 N | 86.09 E |
| 'Asīr ◄¹ | 84 | 19.00 N | 42.00 E |
| Askeaton | 60 | 52.36 N | 8.58 W |
| Askern | 56 | 53.37 N | 1.09 W |
| Askival Λ | 58 | 56.59 N | 6.17 W |
| Askrigg | 54 | 54.19 N | 2.04 W |
| Asmera | 90 | 15.20 N | 38.53 E |
| Aspatria | 56 | 54.46 N | 3.20 W |
| Aspe | 70 | 38.21 N | 0.46 W |
| Assisi | 72 | 43.04 N | 12.37 E |
| As-Sulaymānīyah | 84 | 35.33 N | 45.26 E |
| Assumption Island I | | 9.45 S | 46.30 E |
| As-Suwaydā' | 84 | 32.42 N | 36.34 E |
| As-Suways (Suez) | 88 | 29.58 N | 32.33 E |
| Assynt, Loch ⌷ | 58 | 58.11 N | 5.06 W |
| Asti | 72 | 44.54 N | 8.12 E |
| Aston Clinton | 54 | 51.48 N | 0.44 W |
| Astorga | 70 | 42.27 N | 6.03 W |
| Astove Island I | 90 | 10.05 S | 47.45 E |
| Astrachan' | 76 | 46.21 N | 48.03 E |
| Asunción | 102 | 25.16 S | 57.40 W |
| Asunción Island I | 8 | 19.40 N | 145.24 E |
| Aswān | 88 | 24.05 N | 32.53 E |
| Asyūṭ | 88 | 27.11 N | 31.11 E |
| Atacama, Desierto de ⋌ | 102 | 24.30 S | 69.15 W |
| Atacama, Puna de ⋌¹ | 102 | 25.00 S | 68.00 W |
| Atacama, Salar de ⌷ | 102 | 23.30 S | 68.15 W |
| Atar | 86 | 20.31 N | 13.03 W |
| Ataúro, Ilha de I | 82 | 8.13 S | 125.35 E |
| 'Aṭbarah | 88 | 17.42 N | 33.59 E |
| 'Aṭbarah (Atbara) ≈ | 88 | 17.40 N | 33.56 E |
| Atbasar | 76 | 51.48 N | 68.20 E |
| Ath | 66 | 50.38 N | 3.47 E |
| Athabasca ≈ | 94 | 58.40 N | 110.50 W |
| Athabasca, Lake ⌷ | 94 | 59.07 N | 110.00 W |
| Athboy | 60 | 53.37 N | 6.55 W |
| Athea | 60 | 52.28 N | 9.17 W |
| Athenry | 60 | 53.18 N | 8.45 W |
| Atherstone | 54 | 52.35 N | 1.31 W |
| Atherton | 56 | 53.31 N | 2.30 W |
| Athínai (Athens) | 74 | 37.58 N | 23.43 E |
| Athleague | 60 | 53.34 N | 8.15 W |
| Athlone | 60 | 53.25 N | 7.56 W |
| Atholl, Forest of ◄³ | 58 | 56.50 N | 4.00 W |
| Athy | 60 | 53.00 N | 7.00 W |
| Atikonak Lake ⌷ | 94 | 52.40 N | 64.30 W |
| Atlanta | 96 | 33.45 N | 84.23 W |
| Atlantic City | 96 | 39.22 N | 74.26 W |
| Atlantic Ocean ▼¹ | 8 | 5.00 N | 25.00 W |
| Atlas Mountains ⋌ | 86 | 33.00 N | 2.00 W |
| Atlas Saharien ⋌ | 86 | 33.25 N | 1.20 E |
| Atrak (Atrek) ≈ | 84 | 37.28 N | 53.57 E |
| Atrato ≈ | 100 | 8.17 N | 76.58 W |
| Atrek (Atrak) ≈ | 84 | 37.28 N | 53.57 E |
| Aṭ-Ṭā'if | 84 | 21.16 N | 40.24 E |
| Attawapiskat Lake ⌷ | 94 | 52.18 N | 87.54 W |
| Attleborough | 54 | 52.31 N | 1.01 E |
| Attow, Ben Λ | 58 | 57.14 N | 5.17 W |
| Attymon | 60 | 53.19 N | 8.35 W |
| Atuel ≈ | 102 | 36.17 S | 66.50 W |
| Auasberge ⋌ | 90 | 22.45 S | 17.22 E |
| Aubagne | 68 | 43.17 N | 5.34 E |
| Aubry Lake ⌷ | 94 | 67.23 N | 126.30 W |
| Auburn | 96 | 42.56 N | 76.34 W |
| Aubusson | 68 | 45.57 N | 2.11 E |
| Auch | 68 | 43.39 N | 0.35 E |
| Auchenblae | 58 | 56.54 N | 2.26 W |
| Auchencairn | 56 | 54.51 N | 3.53 W |
| Auchinleck | 56 | 55.28 N | 4.17 W |
| Auchterarder | 58 | 56.18 N | 3.43 W |
| Auchterderran | 58 | 56.09 N | 3.16 W |
| Auchtermuchty | 58 | 56.17 N | 3.15 W |
| Auckland | 93A | 36.52 S | 174.46 E |
| Audincourt | 68 | 47.29 N | 6.50 E |
| Aue | 66 | 50.35 N | 12.42 E |
| Auerbach | 66 | 50.41 N | 12.54 E |
| Augher | 60 | 54.26 N | 7.09 W |
| Aughnacloy | 60 | 54.25 N | 6.58 W |
| Aughrim | 60 | 52.51 N | 6.17 W |
| Aughty, Slieve ⋌ | 60 | 53.05 N | 8.35 W |
| Augsburg | 66 | 48.23 N | 10.53 E |
| Augusta, Ga., U.S. | 96 | 33.29 N | 81.57 W |
| Augusta, It. | 72 | 37.13 N | 15.13 E |
| Augusta, Maine, U.S. | 96 | 44.19 N | 69.47 W |
| Augustów | 66 | 53.51 N | 22.59 E |
| Augustus, Mount Λ | 92 | 24.20 S | 116.50 E |
| Auld, Lake ⌷ | 92 | 22.32 S | 123.44 E |
| Auldearn | 58 | 57.34 N | 3.49 W |
| Aultbea | 58 | 57.50 N | 5.35 W |
| Aumale | 68 | 26.25 S | 20.35 E |
| Aurangābād | 84 | 19.53 N | 75.20 E |
| Aurich | 66 | 53.28 N | 7.29 E |
| Aurillac | 68 | 44.56 N | 2.26 E |
| Aurora, Colo., U.S. | 96 | 39.44 N | 104.52 W |
| Aurora, Ill., U.S. | 96 | 41.45 N | 88.19 W |
| Ausangate, Nevado Λ | 100 | 13.48 S | 71.14 W |
| Auskerry I | 58 | 59.02 N | 2.34 W |
| Austin, Minn., U.S. | 96 | 43.40 N | 92.59 W |
| Austin, Tex., U.S. | 96 | 30.16 N | 97.45 W |
| Austin, Lake ⌷ | 92 | 27.40 S | 118.00 E |
| Austin Channel ⋓ | 94 | 75.35 N | 103.25 W |
| Australes, Îles II | 8 | 23.00 S | 150.00 W |
| Australia □¹ | 92 | 25.00 S | 135.00 E |
| Austria □¹ | 66 | 47.20 N | 13.20 E |
| Autun | 68 | 46.57 N | 4.18 E |
| Auxerre | 68 | 47.48 N | 3.34 E |
| Auyán-Tepuí Λ | 100 | 5.55 N | 62.32 W |
| Avan ≈ | 78 | 51.35 N | 3.48 W |
| Avebury | 54 | 51.27 N | 1.51 W |
| Aveiro | 70 | 40.38 N | 8.39 W |
| Avellaneda | 102 | 34.39 S | 58.23 W |
| Avellino | 72 | 40.54 N | 14.47 E |
| Aves, Islas de II | 100 | 12.00 N | 67.30 W |
| Avesnes | 68 | 50.07 N | 3.56 E |
| Avesta | 64 | 60.09 N | 16.12 E |
| Avezzano | 72 | 42.02 N | 13.25 E |
| Avich, Loch ⌷ | 58 | 56.16 N | 5.20 W |
| Aviemore | 58 | 57.12 N | 3.50 W |
| Avignon | 68 | 43.57 N | 4.49 E |
| Ávila | 70 | 40.39 N | 4.42 W |
| Avilés | 70 | 43.33 N | 5.55 W |
| Avoca ≈ | 52 | 52.48 N | 6.09 W |
| Avola | 72 | 36.54 N | 15.09 E |
| Avon □⁶ | 54 | 51.30 N | 2.40 W |
| Avon ≈, Eng., U.K. | 54 | 52.25 N | 1.31 W |
| Avon ≈, Eng., U.K. | 54 | 50.43 N | 1.46 W |
| Avon ≈, Scot., U.K. | 58 | 56.00 N | 3.40 W |
| Avon ≈, Scot., U.K. | 58 | 57.25 N | 3.23 W |
| Avon, Ben Λ | 58 | 57.05 N | 3.27 W |
| Avonmore ≈ | 52 | 52.50 N | 6.13 W |
| Avonmouth | 54 | 51.31 N | 2.42 W |
| Avon Water ≈ | 58 | 55.47 N | 4.01 W |
| Avranches | 68 | 48.41 N | 1.22 W |
| Awash ≈ | 90 | 11.45 N | 41.05 E |
| Axbridge | 54 | 51.17 N | 2.49 W |
| Axe ≈ | 54 | 56.15 N | 5.15 W |
| Axios (Vardar) ≈ | 74 | 40.35 N | 22.50 E |
| Axminster | 54 | 50.47 N | 3.00 W |
| Axmouth | 54 | 50.42 N | 3.02 W |
| Ayacucho | 100 | 13.07 S | 74.13 W |
| Ayamonte | 70 | 37.51 N | 27.51 E |
| Ayers Rock Λ | 92 | 25.23 S | 131.05 E |
| Aydın | 74 | 35.11 N | 25.42 E |
| Aylesbury | 54 | 51.50 N | 0.50 E |
| Aylesford | 54 | 51.18 N | 0.29 E |
| Aylmer Lake ⌷ | 94 | 64.05 N | 108.30 W |
| Aylsham | 54 | 52.49 N | 1.15 E |
| Ayr | 58 | 55.28 N | 4.38 W |
| Ayr ≈ | 58 | 55.28 N | 4.38 W |
| Ayre, Point of ➤ | 56 | 54.26 N | 4.22 W |
| Aysgarth | 54 | 54.17 N | 2.00 W |
| Ayvalık | 74 | 39.18 N | 26.41 E |
| Azaouak, Vallée de l' | 86 | 15.30 N | 3.18 E |
| Azare | 86 | 11.40 N | 10.11 E |
| Azerbajdzanskaja Sovetskaja Socialističeskaja Respublika □³ | 76 | 40.30 N | 47.30 E |
| Azov | 76 | 47.07 N | 39.25 E |
| Azovskoje More ▼² | 76 | 46.00 N | 36.00 E |
| Azuaga | 70 | 38.16 N | 5.41 W |
| Azuero, Peninsula de ◄¹ | 98 | 7.40 N | 80.35 W |
| Azul | 102 | 36.47 S | 59.51 W |
| Az-Zahrān (Dhahran) | 84 | 26.18 N | 50.08 E |
| Az-Zaqāzīq | 84 | 30.35 N | 31.31 E |
| Az-Zarqā' | 84 | 32.05 N | 36.06 E |
| Ba, Loch ⌷ | 58 | 56.36 N | 4.44 W |
| Baarn | 66 | 52.13 N | 5.16 E |
| Babaeski | 74 | 41.26 N | 27.06 E |
| Babajevo | 62 | 59.23 N | 35.56 E |
| Babar, Pulau I | 82 | 7.50 S | 129.45 E |
| Babar, Kepulauan II | 82 | 7.55 S | 129.45 E |
| Babbacombe Bay C | 54 | 50.30 N | 3.25 W |
| Babelthuap I | 8 | 7.30 N | 134.36 E |
| Babine Lake ⌷ | 94 | 54.45 N | 126.00 W |
| Bābol | 84 | 36.34 N | 52.42 E |
| Babuyan Island I | 82 | 19.32 N | 121.57 E |
| Bacabal | 100 | 4.14 S | 44.47 W |
| Bacan, Pulau I | 82 | 0.35 S | 127.30 E |
| Bacău | 74 | 46.34 N | 26.55 E |
| Bačka Palanka | 74 | 45.15 N | 19.24 E |
| Bačka Topola | 74 | 45.49 N | 19.38 E |
| Backnang | 66 | 48.56 N | 9.25 E |
| Bac-Lieu (Vinh-loi) | 82 | 9.17 N | 105.44 E |
| Bacolod | 82 | 10.40 N | 122.57 E |
| Bacup | 56 | 53.42 N | 2.12 W |
| Badajoz | 70 | 38.53 N | 6.58 W |
| Badalona | 70 | 41.27 N | 2.15 E |
| Bad Doberan | 66 | 54.06 N | 11.53 E |
| Bad Dürkheim | 66 | 49.28 N | 8.11 E |
| Bad Ems | 66 | 50.20 N | 7.43 E |
| Baden, Öst. | 66 | 48.00 N | 16.14 E |
| Baden, Schw. | 66 | 47.28 N | 8.18 E |
| Baden-Baden | 66 | 48.46 N | 8.14 E |
| Badenoch ◄¹ | 58 | 57.01 N | 4.09 W |
| Bad Freienwalde | 66 | 52.47 N | 14.01 E |
| Bad Harzburg | 66 | 51.53 N | 10.33 E |
| Bad Hersfeld | 66 | 50.52 N | 9.42 E |
| Bad Homburg [vor der Höhe] | 66 | 50.14 N | 8.37 E |
| Bad Ischl | 66 | 47.43 N | 13.37 E |
| Bad Kissingen | 66 | 50.12 N | 10.04 E |
| Bad Kreuznach | 66 | 49.52 N | 7.51 E |
| Badlands ⋌ | 96 | 46.45 N | 103.30 W |
| Bad Langensalza | 66 | 51.06 N | 10.38 E |
| Bad Mergentheim | 66 | 49.30 N | 9.46 E |
| Bad Nauheim | 66 | 50.22 N | 8.44 E |
| Bad Oeynhausen | 66 | 52.12 N | 8.48 E |
| Bad Oldesloe | 66 | 53.48 N | 10.22 E |
| Bad Pyrmont | 66 | 51.59 N | 9.15 E |
| Bad Reichenhall | 66 | 47.43 N | 12.52 E |
| Bad Salzuflen | 66 | 52.05 N | 8.44 E |
| Bad Salzungen | 66 | 50.48 N | 10.13 E |
| Bad Schwartau | 66 | 53.55 N | 10.40 E |
| Bad Segeberg | 66 | 53.56 N | 10.17 E |
| Bad Tölz | 66 | 47.46 N | 11.34 E |
| Baena | 70 | 37.37 N | 4.19 W |
| Baffin Bay C | 94 | 73.00 N | 66.00 W |
| Baffin Island I | 94 | 68.00 N | 70.00 W |
| Bafing ≈ | 86 | 13.49 N | 10.50 W |
| Bagansiapi-api | 82 | 2.09 N | 100.49 E |
| Baggy Point ➤ | 54 | 51.09 N | 4.16 W |
| Baghdād | 84 | 33.21 N | 44.25 E |
| Bagheria | 72 | 38.05 N | 13.30 E |
| Bagnara Cálabra | 72 | 38.18 N | 15.49 E |
| Bagnères-de-Bigorre | 68 | 43.04 N | 0.09 E |
| Bagnols-sur-Cèze | 68 | 54.23 N | 20.39 E |
| Bagrationovsk | 66 | 54.23 N | 20.39 E |
| Bagshot | 54 | 51.22 N | 0.42 W |
| Baguio | 82 | 16.25 N | 120.36 E |
| Bagzane, Monts ⋌ | 86 | 17.43 N | 8.45 E |
| Bahamas □¹ | 98 | 24.15 N | 76.00 W |
| Bahawalpur | 84 | 29.24 N | 71.41 E |
| Bahia, Islas de la II | 98 | 16.20 N | 86.30 W |
| Bahía Blanca | 102 | 38.43 S | 62.17 W |
| Bahraich | 84 | 27.36 N | 81.36 E |
| Bahrain □¹ | 84 | 26.00 N | 50.30 E |
| Baia-Mare | 74 | 47.40 N | 23.35 E |
| Baicheng | 80 | 45.38 N | 122.46 E |
| Baidoa | 88 | 3.04 N | 43.48 E |
| Baildon | 56 | 53.52 N | 1.46 W |
| Bailén | 70 | 38.06 N | 3.46 W |
| Băileşti | 74 | 44.02 N | 23.21 E |
| Bailieborough | 60 | 53.54 N | 6.59 W |
| Bailique, Ilha I | 100 | 1.02 N | 49.58 W |
| Bailongjiang ≈ | 80 | 32.18 N | 105.42 E |
| Bain ≈ | 54 | 53.05 N | 0.12 W |
| Baird Peninsula ◄¹ | 94 | 69.00 N | 75.15 W |
| Baise ≈ | 68 | 44.17 N | 0.18 E |
| Bayinchang | 80 | 36.47 N | 104.07 E |
| Baja | 74 | 46.11 N | 18.57 E |
| Baja California ◄¹ | 98 | 28.00 N | 113.30 W |
| Bajdarackaja Guba C | 76 | 69.00 N | 67.30 E |
| Bajkal, Ozero (Lake Baykal) ⌷ | 78 | 69.00 N | 107.40 E |
| Bajram-Ali | 76 | 37.37 N | 62.10 E |
| Baker Lake | 94 | 64.10 N | 95.30 W |
| Baker, Mount Λ | 96 | 48.47 N | 121.49 W |
| Baker Lake ⌷ | 94 | 64.10 N | 95.30 W |
| Bakersfield | 96 | 35.23 N | 119.01 W |
| Bakewell | 56 | 53.13 N | 1.40 W |
| Bakırköy | 74 | 40.59 N | 28.52 E |
| Bakoye ≈ | 86 | 13.49 N | 10.50 W |
| Baku | 76 | 40.23 N | 49.51 E |
| Balabac Island I | 82 | 7.57 N | 117.01 E |
| Balabac Strait ⋓ | 82 | 7.35 N | 117.00 E |
| Balachna | 62 | 56.30 N | 43.36 E |
| Balakovo | 62 | 52.02 N | 47.47 E |
| Balallan | 58 | 58.05 N | 6.35 W |
| Balambangan, Pulau I | 82 | 7.15 N | 116.55 E |
| Balašov | 76 | 51.32 N | 43.08 E |
| Balaton ⌷ | 66 | 46.50 N | 17.45 E |
| Balboa Heights | 98 | 8.57 N | 79.33 W |
| Balbriggan | 60 | 53.37 N | 6.11 W |
| Balchaš | 76 | 46.49 N | 74.59 E |
| Balchaš, Ozero ⌷ | 76 | 46.00 N | 74.00 E |
| Balcombe | 54 | 51.04 N | 0.08 W |
| Balderton | 54 | 53.03 N | 0.47 W |
| Baldock | 54 | 51.59 N | 0.12 W |
| Baldock Lake ⌷ | 94 | 56.33 N | 97.57 W |
| Baldoyle | 60 | 53.24 N | 6.08 W |
| Baldy Peak Λ | 96 | 33.55 N | 109.35 W |
| Baleares, Islas (Balearic Islands) II | 70 | 39.30 N | 3.00 E |
| Baleine, Rivière à la ≈ | 94 | 58.15 N | 67.40 W |
| Balej | 76 | 51.36 N | 116.38 E |
| Balen | 66 | 51.10 N | 5.09 E |
| Balfour | 58 | 59.01 N | 2.55 W |
| Bali I | 82 | 8.20 S | 115.00 E |
| Bali, Selat ⋓ | 82 | 8.18 S | 114.25 E |
| Balıkesir | 74 | 39.39 N | 27.53 E |
| Balikpapan | 82 | 1.17 S | 116.50 E |
| Balintang Channel ⋓ | 82 | 19.49 N | 121.40 E |
| Balla | 60 | 53.48 N | 9.09 W |
| Ballachulish | 58 | 56.40 N | 5.10 W |
| Ballagh | 60 | 52.35 N | 7.59 W |
| Ballaghaderreen | 60 | 53.55 N | 8.35 W |
| Ballantrae | 58 | 55.06 N | 5.00 W |
| Ballarat | 92 | 37.34 S | 143.52 E |
| Ballard, Lake ⌷ | 92 | 29.27 S | 120.55 E |
| Ballater | 58 | 57.03 N | 3.03 W |
| Ballaugh | 56 | 54.20 N | 4.32 W |
| Ballina | 60 | 54.07 N | 9.09 W |
| Ballinakill | 60 | 52.54 N | 7.23 W |
| Ballinasloe | 60 | 53.20 N | 8.13 W |
| Ballinascarty | 60 | 51.40 N | 8.51 W |
| Ballindine | 60 | 53.39 N | 8.59 W |
| Ballindejoy | 60 | 51.44 N | 8.56 W |
| Ballingarry | 60 | 52.29 N | 8.21 W |
| Ballingeary | 60 | 51.49 N | 9.13 W |
| Ballinluig | 58 | 56.38 N | 3.42 W |
| Ballinrobe | 60 | 53.37 N | 9.13 W |
| Ballinskelligs Bay C | 60 | 51.50 N | 10.15 W |
| Ballintoy | 60 | 55.14 N | 6.21 W |
| Ballintra | 60 | 54.35 N | 8.07 W |
| Balloch | 58 | 57.29 N | 4.07 W |
| Balls Pyramid I | 92 | 31.45 S | 159.15 E |
| Ballybay | 60 | 54.08 N | 6.54 W |
| Ballybofey | 60 | 54.57 N | 7.47 W |
| Ballybogey | 60 | 55.05 N | 6.33 W |
| Ballybunion | 60 | 52.31 N | 9.40 W |
| Ballycanew | 60 | 52.37 N | 6.18 W |
| Ballycastle, Eire | 60 | 54.17 N | 9.23 W |
| Ballycastle, N. Ire., U.K. | 60 | 55.12 N | 6.15 W |
| Ballyclare | 60 | 54.46 N | 6.00 W |
| Ballyconneely | 60 | 53.27 N | 10.08 W |
| Ballyconnell | 60 | 54.07 N | 7.35 W |
| Ballycotton | 60 | 51.49 N | 8.01 W |
| Ballycroy | 60 | 54.02 N | 9.49 W |
| Ballyduff, Eire | 60 | 52.27 N | 9.40 W |
| Ballyduff, Eire | 60 | 52.09 N | 8.03 W |
| Ballyferriter | 60 | 52.10 N | 10.26 W |
| Ballyfinboy ≈ | 60 | 52.53 N | 8.05 W |
| Ballygar | 60 | 53.32 N | 8.20 W |
| Ballygawley | 60 | 54.28 N | 7.02 W |
| Ballyhaise | 60 | 54.03 N | 7.19 W |
| Ballyhaunis | 60 | 53.46 N | 8.46 W |
| Ballyheige | 60 | 52.23 N | 9.50 W |
| Ballyhoura Hills ⋌² | 60 | 52.18 N | 8.35 W |
| Ballyjamesduff | 60 | 53.52 N | 7.12 W |
| Ballymacoda | 60 | 51.53 N | 7.53 W |
| Ballymahon | 60 | 53.34 N | 7.45 W |
| Ballymena | 60 | 54.52 N | 6.17 W |
| Ballymoney | 60 | 55.04 N | 6.31 W |
| Ballymurphy | 60 | 52.35 N | 6.54 W |
| Ballynahinch | 60 | 54.24 N | 5.54 W |
| Ballynoe | 60 | 54.33 N | 5.54 W |
| Ballyquintin Point ➤ | 60 | 54.20 N | 5.30 W |
| Ballyragget | 60 | 52.47 N | 7.20 W |
| Ballysadare | 60 | 54.13 N | 8.31 W |
| Ballyshannon | 60 | 54.30 N | 8.11 W |
| Ballyvaughan | 60 | 53.07 N | 9.07 W |
| Ballyvoy | 60 | 55.12 N | 6.11 W |
| Ballywalter | 60 | 54.33 N | 5.30 W |
| Balmerino | 58 | 56.24 N | 3.02 W |
| Balmoral Castle | 58 | 57.20 N | 3.15 W |
| Balnacra | 58 | 57.28 N | 5.23 W |
| Bologoje | 62 | 57.54 N | 34.02 E |
| Balonne ≈ | 100 | 7.14 S | 44.33 W |
| Balsas ≈, Bra. | 100 | 7.14 S | 44.33 W |
| Balsas ≈, Méx. | 98 | 17.55 N | 102.10 W |
| Balsham | 54 | 52.08 N | 0.20 E |
| Baltasound | 58a | 60.45 N | 0.52 W |
| Baltic Sea ▼² | 64 | 57.00 N | 19.00 E |
| Baltijsk | 66 | 54.39 N | 19.55 E |
| Baltimore, Eire | 60 | 51.29 N | 9.22 W |
| Baltimore, Md., U.S. | 96 | 39.17 N | 76.37 W |
| Baltinglass | 60 | 52.55 N | 6.41 W |
| Baluchistan □⁹ | 84 | 28.00 N | 63.00 E |
| Balvicar | 58 | 56.14 N | 5.38 W |
| Bam | 84 | 29.06 N | 58.21 E |
| Bamako | 86 | 12.39 N | 8.00 W |
| Bambari | 88 | 5.45 N | 20.40 E |
| Bamberg | 66 | 49.53 N | 10.53 E |
| Bamburgh | 56 | 55.36 N | 1.42 W |
| Bamenda | 86 | 5.56 N | 10.10 E |
| Bamingui ≈ | 88 | 8.33 N | 19.05 E |
| Bampton, Eng., U.K. | 54 | 51.44 N | 1.33 W |
| Bampton, Eng., U.K. | 54 | 51.00 N | 3.29 W |
| Banagher | 60 | 53.11 N | 7.59 W |
| Banana | 90 | 6.01 S | 12.24 E |
| Bananal, Ilha do I | 100 | 11.30 S | 50.15 W |
| Banās, Ra's ➤ | 88 | 23.54 N | 35.48 E |
| Banbridge | 60 | 54.21 N | 6.16 W |
| Banbury | 54 | 52.04 N | 1.20 W |
| Banchory | 58 | 57.30 N | 2.30 W |
| Banda, Laut (Banda Sea) ▼² | 82 | 5.00 S | 128.00 E |
| Banda Aceh | 82 | 5.34 N | 95.20 E |
| Bandama ≈ | 86 | 5.10 N | 5.00 W |
| Bandar-e Pahlavī | 84 | 37.28 N | 49.27 E |
| Bandar Seri Begawan | 82 | 4.56 N | 114.55 E |
| Bandeira, Pico da Λ | 100 | 20.26 S | 41.47 W |
| Bandırma | 74 | 40.20 N | 27.58 E |
| Bandon | 60 | 51.44 N | 8.45 W |
| Bandon ≈ | 60 | 51.42 N | 8.30 W |
| Bandundu | 90 | 3.18 S | 17.20 E |
| Bandung | 82 | 6.54 S | 107.36 E |
| Banes | 98 | 20.58 N | 75.43 W |
| Banff | 58 | 57.40 N | 2.33 W |
| Bangalore | 84 | 12.58 N | 77.36 E |
| Banggai, Kepulauan II | 82 | 1.30 S | 123.15 E |
| Banggi, Pulau I | 82 | 7.17 N | 117.12 E |
| Banghāzī | 88 | 32.07 N | 20.04 E |
| Bangka, Selat ⋓ | 82 | 2.20 S | 105.45 E |
| Bangladesh □¹ | 84 | 24.00 N | 90.00 E |
| Bangor, N. Ire., U.K. | 60 | 54.40 N | 5.40 W |
| Bangor, Wales, U.K. | 56 | 53.13 N | 4.08 W |
| Bangor, Maine, U.S. | 96 | 44.49 N | 68.47 W |
| Bangor Erris | 60 | 54.09 N | 9.45 W |
| Bangweulu, Lake ⌷ | 90 | 11.05 S | 29.45 E |
| Bani ≈ | 86 | 14.30 N | 4.12 W |
| Banī Mazār | 88 | 28.30 N | 30.48 E |
| Banī Suwayf | 88 | 29.05 N | 31.05 E |
| Bania Luka | 74 | 44.46 N | 17.11 E |
| Banjarmasin | 82 | 3.20 S | 114.35 E |
| Banjul | 86 | 13.28 N | 16.39 W |
| Bankfoot | 58 | 56.30 N | 3.30 W |
| Banks Island I, Austl. | 92 | 10.12 S | 142.16 E |
| Banks Island I, B.C., Can. | 94 | 53.25 N | 130.10 W |
| Banks Island I, N.W. Ter., Can. | 94 | 73.15 N | 121.30 W |
| Banks Strait ⋓ | 92 | 40.40 S | 148.07 E |
| Bānkura | 84 | 23.14 N | 87.04 E |
| Bann ≈ | 60 | 55.10 N | 6.46 W |
| Bannockburn | 58 | 56.06 N | 3.55 W |
| Bannu | 84 | 32.59 N | 70.36 E |
| Bansha | 60 | 52.28 N | 8.04 W |
| Banská Bystrica | 66 | 48.44 N | 19.07 E |
| Banská Štiavnica | 66 | 48.28 N | 18.54 E |
| Banstead | 54 | 51.19 N | 0.12 W |
| Banteer | 60 | 52.07 N | 8.54 W |
| Bantry | 60 | 51.41 N | 9.27 W |
| Bantry Bay C | 60 | 51.38 N | 9.48 W |
| Banwell | 54 | 51.20 N | 2.52 W |
| Banwy ≈ | 54 | 52.42 N | 3.16 W |
| Banyak, Kepulauan II | 82 | 2.10 N | 97.15 E |
| Banyuwangi | 82 | 8.12 S | 114.21 E |
| Baoding | 80 | 38.52 N | 115.29 E |
| Baoji | 80 | 34.22 N | 107.14 E |
| Baoshan | 80 | 25.09 N | 99.09 E |
| Baotou | 80 | 40.40 N | 109.59 E |
| Barabinsk | 78 | 55.21 N | 78.21 E |
| Barabinskaja Step' ≃ | 78 | 55.00 N | 79.00 E |
| Baram ≈ | 82 | 4.36 N | 113.59 E |
| Baranoviči | 76 | 53.08 N | 26.02 E |
| Barat Daya, Kepulauan II | 82 | 7.25 S | 128.00 E |
| Baracena | 100 | 21.14 S | 43.46 W |
| Barbados □¹ | 98 | 13.10 N | 59.32 W |
| Barbas, Cabo ➤ | 86 | 22.18 N | 16.41 W |
| Barbastro | 70 | 42.02 N | 0.08 E |
| Barbate de Franco | 70 | 36.12 N | 5.55 W |
| Barbuda I | 98 | 17.38 N | 61.48 W |
| Barcellona Pozzo di Gotto | 72 | 38.09 N | 15.13 E |
| Barcelona, Esp. | 70 | 41.23 N | 2.11 E |
| Barcelona, Ven. | 100 | 10.08 N | 64.42 W |
| Barcoo ≈ | 92 | 25.30 S | 142.50 E |
| Bardejov | 66 | 49.18 N | 21.16 E |
| Bardney | 54 | 53.12 N | 0.21 W |
| Bardsey Island I | 56 | 52.45 N | 4.45 W |
| Bardsey Sound ⋓ | 56 | 52.47 N | 4.46 W |
| Bareilly | 84 | 28.21 N | 79.25 E |
| Barents Sea ▼² | 76 | 74.00 N | 36.00 E |
| Barguzin | 78 | 53.36 N | 109.02 E |
| Bari | 72 | 41.07 N | 16.52 E |
| Barīm I | 88 | 12.40 N | 43.25 E |
| Barinas | 100 | 8.38 N | 70.12 W |
| Baring, Cape ➤ | 94 | 70.01 N | 117.30 W |
| Barisāl | 84 | 22.42 N | 90.22 E |
| Barisan, Pegunungan ⋌ | 82 | 3.00 S | 102.15 E |
| Barito ≈ | 82 | 3.32 S | 114.29 E |
| Barka ≈ | 88 | 18.13 N | 37.35 E |
| Barking ◄⁸ | 54 | 51.33 N | 0.06 E |
| Barkley Sound ⋓ | 96 | 48.53 N | 125.20 W |
| Barkly Tableland ⋌¹ | 92 | 19.00 S | 136.00 E |
| Bar-le-Duc | 68 | 48.47 N | 5.10 E |
| Barlee, Lake ⌷ | 92 | 29.10 S | 119.30 E |
| Barletta | 72 | 41.19 N | 16.17 E |
| Barmouth | 56 | 52.43 N | 4.03 W |
| Barmouth Bay C | 56 | 52.42 N | 4.05 W |
| Barnard Castle | 56 | 54.33 N | 1.55 W |
| Barnaul | 78 | 53.22 N | 83.45 E |
| Barnby le Wold | 54 | 53.13 N | 0.26 W |
| Barnoldswick | 56 | 53.55 N | 2.11 W |
| Barnsley | 56 | 53.34 N | 1.28 W |
| Barnstaple | 54 | 51.05 N | 4.04 W |
| Barnstaple Bay C | 54 | 51.04 N | 4.20 W |
| Barnt Green | 54 | 52.21 N | 1.59 W |
| Baroda | 84 | 22.18 N | 73.12 E |
| Barotseland □⁹ | 90 | 16.00 S | 24.00 E |
| Barqah (Cyrenaica) ◄⁹ | 88 | 31.00 N | 22.30 E |
| Barquisimeto | 100 | 10.04 N | 69.19 W |
| Barra I | 58 | 56.58 N | 7.29 W |
| Barra, Ponta da ➤ | 90 | 23.47 S | 35.32 E |
| Barra, Sound of ⋓ | 58 | 57.04 N | 7.25 W |
| Barra Falsa, Ponta da ➤ | 90 | 22.55 S | 35.37 E |
| Barrafranca | 72 | 37.23 N | 14.13 E |
| Barra Head ➤ | 58 | 56.46 N | 7.38 W |
| Barra Mansa | 100 | 22.32 S | 44.11 W |
| Barranca | 100 | 10.45 S | 77.46 W |
| Barrancabermeja | 100 | 7.03 N | 73.52 W |
| Barranquilla | 100 | 10.59 N | 74.48 W |
| Barrhead | 58 | 55.48 N | 4.24 W |
| Barrhill | 56 | 55.07 N | 4.46 W |
| Barrier Range ⋌ | 92 | 31.25 S | 141.25 E |
| Barrow ≈ | 52 | 52.15 N | 7.00 W |
| Barrowford | 56 | 53.52 N | 2.13 W |
| Barrow-in-Furness | 56 | 54.07 N | 3.14 W |
| Barrow Island I | 92 | 20.48 S | 115.23 E |
| Barrow Strait ⋓ | 94 | 74.21 N | 94.10 W |
| Barry | 54 | 51.24 N | 3.18 W |
| Barth | 66 | 54.22 N | 12.43 E |
| Bartle Frere Λ | 92 | 17.23 S | 145.49 E |
| Barton Mills | 54 | 52.20 N | 0.31 E |
| Barton-under-Needwood | 54 | 52.45 N | 1.43 W |
| Barton-upon-Humber | 56 | 53.41 N | 0.27 W |
| Bartoszyce | 66 | 54.16 N | 20.49 E |
| Barun-Sibertuj, Gora Λ | 78 | 49.42 N | 109.59 E |
| Barvas | 58 | 58.22 N | 6.32 W |
| Barwell | 54 | 52.32 N | 1.21 W |
| Barwon ≈ | 92 | 30.00 S | 148.05 E |
| Barys | 66 | 53.39 N | 47.08 E |
| Basatongwulashan ⋌ | 80 | 33.05 N | 91.30 E |
| Bascuñán, Cabo ➤ | 102 | 28.51 S | 71.30 W |
| Basel (Bâle) | 66 | 47.33 N | 7.35 E |
| Basildon | 54 | 51.34 N | 0.29 E |
| Basilan | 82 | 6.34 N | 122.03 E |
| Basilan Island I | 82 | 6.34 N | 122.03 E |
| Basingstoke | 54 | 51.15 N | 1.05 W |
| Baskatong, Réservoir ⌷¹ | 94 | 46.48 N | 75.50 W |
| Baslow | 56 | 53.15 N | 1.38 W |
| Bassano del Grappa | 72 | 45.46 N | 11.44 E |
| Bassas da India ◄² | 90 | 21.25 S | 39.42 E |
| Bassein | 84 | 16.47 N | 94.44 E |
| Bassenthwaite | 56 | 54.41 N | 3.12 W |
| Bassenthwaite Lake ⌷ | 56 | 54.38 N | 3.13 W |
| Basse-Terre, Guad. | 98 | 16.00 N | 61.44 W |
| Basseterre, St. K.-N. | 98 | 17.18 N | 62.43 W |
| Bass Strait ⋓ | 92 | 39.20 S | 145.30 E |
| Basswood Lake ⌷ | 94 | 48.06 N | 91.40 W |
| Bastia | 68 | 42.42 N | 9.27 E |
| Bata | 90 | 1.51 N | 9.45 E |
| Batabanó, Golfo de C | 98 | 22.15 N | 82.30 W |
| Batajsk | 76 | 47.10 N | 39.44 E |
| Batala | 84 | 31.48 N | 75.13 E |
| Batanghari ≈ | 82 | 1.16 S | 104.05 E |
| Batan Island I | 82 | 20.26 N | 121.58 E |
| Batan Islands II | 82 | 20.30 N | 121.50 E |
| Batanta, Pulau I | 82 | 0.50 S | 130.40 E |
| Bātdâmbâng | 82 | 13.06 N | 103.12 E |
| Bath | 54 | 51.23 N | 2.22 W |
| Bathgate | 58 | 55.55 N | 3.39 W |
| Bathurst, Cape ➤ | 94 | 70.35 N | 128.00 W |
| Bathurst Inlet C | 94 | 66.50 N | 108.01 W |
| Bathurst Island I, Austl. | 92 | 11.37 S | 130.27 E |
| Bathurst Island I, N.W. Ter., Can. | 94 | 76.00 N | 100.30 W |
| Batley | 56 | 53.44 N | 1.37 W |
| Batna | 86 | 35.34 N | 6.11 E |
| Baton Rouge | 96 | 30.23 N | 91.11 W |
| Battambang | 82 | 13.06 N | 103.12 E |
| Batticaloa | 84 | 7.43 N | 81.42 E |
| Battle | 54 | 50.55 N | 0.30 E |
| Battle Creek | 96 | 42.19 N | 85.11 W |
| Batu Λ | 88 | 6.55 N | 39.46 E |
| Batu, Kepulauan II | 82 | 0.18 S | 98.28 E |
| Batumi | 76 | 41.38 N | 41.38 E |
| Batu Pahat | 82 | 1.51 N | 102.56 E |
| Bauchi | 86 | 10.19 N | 9.50 E |
| Bauld, Cape ➤ | 94 | 51.38 N | 55.25 W |
| Bautzen | 66 | 51.11 N | 14.26 E |
| Bawtry | 56 | 53.26 N | 1.01 W |
| Bay, Laguna de ⌷ | 82 | 14.23 N | 121.15 E |
| Bayamo | 98 | 20.23 N | 76.39 W |
| Bayamón | 98 | 18.24 N | 66.10 W |
| Bayble | 58 | 58.12 N | 6.13 W |
| Bay City | 96 | 43.36 N | 83.53 W |
| Bayeux | 68 | 49.16 N | 0.42 W |
| Bayhead | 58 | 57.33 N | 7.24 W |
| Bayonne | 68 | 43.29 N | 1.29 W |
| Bayreuth | 66 | 49.57 N | 11.35 E |
| Bayrūt | 84 | 33.53 N | 35.30 E |
| Bazaruto, Ilha do I | 90 | 21.30 S | 35.28 E |
| Beachy Head ➤ | 54 | 50.44 N | 0.16 E |
| Beacon Hill Λ | 54 | 51.10 N | 1.26 W |
| Beaconsfield | 54 | 51.37 N | 0.39 W |
| Beagh, Slieve ⋌² | 60 | 54.20 N | 7.12 W |
| Beagle Gulf C | 92 | 12.00 S | 130.20 E |
| Beagle Reef ⋌² | 92 | 15.20 S | 123.23 E |
| Beaminster | 54 | 50.49 N | 2.45 W |
| Bear Bay C | 94 | 75.47 N | 87.00 W |
| Bear Island I | 94 | 54.27 N | 83.53 W |
| Bear Lake ⌷ | 96 | 42.00 N | 111.20 W |
| Bearsden | 58 | 55.56 N | 4.20 W |
| Beas ≈ | 84 | 31.10 N | 74.59 E |
| Beata, Isla I | 98 | 17.35 N | 71.31 W |
| Beatrice, Cape ➤ | 92 | 14.15 S | 136.59 E |
| Beattock | 58 | 55.18 N | 3.28 W |
| Beaucaire | 68 | 43.48 N | 4.38 E |
| Beaufort Sea ▼² | 94 | 73.00 N | 140.00 W |
| Beaufort West | 90 | 32.18 S | 22.36 E |
| Beaulieu | 54 | 50.49 N | 1.27 W |
| Beauly | 58 | 57.29 N | 4.29 W |
| Beauly Firth C¹ | 58 | 57.30 N | 4.20 W |
| Beaumaris | 56 | 53.16 N | 4.05 W |
| Beaumont | 96 | 30.05 N | 94.06 W |
| Beaune | 68 | 47.02 N | 4.50 E |
| Beauvais | 68 | 49.26 N | 2.05 E |
| Beaver ≈, Can. | 94 | 59.43 N | 124.16 W |
| Beaver ≈, U.S. | 96 | 36.35 N | 100.01 W |
| Beawar | 84 | 26.06 N | 74.20 E |
| Bebington | 56 | 53.21 N | 3.01 W |
| Bečej | 74 | 45.37 N | 20.03 E |
| Béchar | 86 | 31.37 N | 2.13 W |
| Beckingham | 54 | 53.24 N | 0.49 W |
| Beckley | 96 | 37.46 N | 81.11 W |
| Beckum | 66 | 51.45 N | 8.02 E |
| Beddgelert | 56 | 53.01 N | 4.06 W |
| Bedford | 54 | 52.08 N | 0.29 W |
| Bedfordshire □⁶ | 54 | 52.05 N | 0.20 W |
| Bedlington | 56 | 55.08 N | 1.35 W |
| Bedwas | 54 | 51.36 N | 3.12 W |
| Bedworth | 54 | 52.29 N | 1.28 W |
| Beela ≈ | 56 | 54.11 N | 2.45 W |
| Beer | 54 | 50.42 N | 3.05 W |
| Beeston | 54 | 52.56 N | 1.12 W |
| Beeville | 96 | 28.24 N | 97.45 W |
| Behbehān | 84 | 30.36 N | 50.15 E |
| Beian | 80 | 48.15 N | 126.30 E |
| Beihai | 80 | 21.29 N | 109.05 E |
| Beijing (Peking) | 80 | 39.55 N | 116.23 E |
| Beipiao | 80 | 41.49 N | 120.46 E |
| Beira | 90 | 19.49 S | 34.52 E |
| Beja, Port. | 70 | 38.01 N | 7.52 W |
| Béja, Tun. | 72 | 36.44 N | 9.11 E |
| Bejaïa | 86 | 36.49 N | 5.04 E |
| Béjar | 70 | 40.23 N | 5.46 W |
| Békés | 66 | 46.46 N | 21.08 E |
| Békéscsaba | 66 | 46.41 N | 21.06 E |
| Bela Crkva | 74 | 44.54 N | 21.26 E |
| Belaja ≈ | 76 | 56.00 N | 54.32 E |
| Belaja Cerkov' | 76 | 49.49 N | 30.07 E |
| Belaja Cholunica | 62 | 58.50 N | 50.48 E |
| Belcher Islands II | 94 | 56.20 N | 79.30 W |
| Belgorod | 76 | 50.36 N | 36.35 E |
| Belitung I | 82 | 2.50 S | 107.55 E |
| Belize | 98 | 17.30 N | 88.12 W |
| Belize □² | 98 | 17.15 N | 88.45 W |
| Bell ⋌ | 78 | 75.32 N | 135.44 E |
| Bellac | 68 | 46.07 N | 1.04 E |
| Bellary | 84 | 15.09 N | 76.56 E |
| Belleek | 60 | 54.29 N | 8.06 W |
| Belle-Île I | 68 | 47.20 N | 3.10 W |
| Belle Isle I | 94 | 51.55 N | 55.20 W |
| Belle Isle, Strait of ⋓ | 94 | 51.35 N | 56.30 W |
| Bellingham, Eng., U.K. | 56 | 55.09 N | 2.16 W |
| Bellingham, Wash., U.S. | 96 | 48.49 N | 122.29 W |
| Bellinzona | 66 | 46.11 N | 9.02 E |
| Bello | 100 | 6.20 N | 75.33 W |
| Bellona Reefs ⋌² | 100 | 21.30 S | 159.00 E |
| Bell Peninsula ◄¹ | 94 | 63.50 N | 82.00 W |
| Belluno | 72 | 46.09 N | 12.13 E |
| Belmopan | 98 | 17.15 N | 88.46 W |
| Belmullet | 60 | 54.14 N | 10.00 W |
| Belo Horizonte | 100 | 19.55 S | 43.56 W |
| Beloit | 96 | 42.31 N | 89.02 W |
| Beloje, Ozero ⌷ | 62 | 60.11 N | 37.37 E |
| Beloje More (White Sea) ▼² | 76 | 65.30 N | 38.00 E |
| Belomorsk | 76 | 64.32 N | 34.48 E |
| Beloreck | 76 | 53.58 N | 58.24 E |
| Belot, Lac ⌷ | 94 | 66.55 N | 126.18 W |
| Belovo | 78 | 54.25 N | 86.18 E |
| Beloz'orsk | 62 | 60.02 N | 37.48 E |
| Belper | 56 | 53.02 N | 1.29 W |
| Beltra | 58 | 54.13 N | 8.37 W |
| Belturbet | 60 | 54.06 N | 7.28 W |
| Belucha, Gora Λ | 78 | 49.48 N | 86.40 E |
| Belvoir, Vale of V | 54 | 52.57 N | 0.53 W |
| Belyando ≈ | 92 | 21.38 S | 146.50 E |
| Belyj, Ostrov I | 76 | 73.10 N | 70.45 E |
| Bembridge | 54 | 50.41 N | 1.05 W |
| Benavente | 70 | 42.00 N | 5.41 W |
| Benbane Head ➤ | 60 | 55.15 N | 6.28 W |
| Benbecula I | 58 | 57.27 N | 7.20 W |
| Bendery | 76 | 46.48 N | 29.29 E |
| Bendigo | 92 | 36.46 S | 144.17 E |
| Bendorf | 66 | 50.25 N | 7.34 E |
| Beneraird Λ² | 58 | 55.04 N | 4.57 W |
| Benevento | 72 | 41.08 N | 14.45 E |
| Bengal, Bay of C | 84 | 15.00 N | 90.00 E |
| Bengbu | 80 | 32.58 N | 117.24 E |
| Benguela | 90 | 12.35 N | 13.25 E |
| Benguérua, Ilha I | 90 | 21.58 S | 35.28 E |
| Beni | 100 | 10.23 S | 65.24 W |
| Beni ≈ | 100 | 10.23 S | 65.24 W |
| Benicarló | 70 | 40.25 N | 0.26 E |
| Beni-Mellal | 86 | 32.22 N | 6.29 W |
| Benin □¹ | 86 | 9.30 N | 2.15 E |
| Benin, Bight of C³ | 86 | 5.30 N | 3.00 E |
| Benin City | 86 | 6.19 N | 5.41 E |
| Benllech | 56 | 53.19 N | 4.13 W |
| Benoni | 90 | 26.15 S | 28.27 E |
| Bénoué (Benue) ≈ | 86 | 7.48 N | 6.46 E |
| Bensheim | 66 | 49.41 N | 8.37 E |
| Benson | 54 | 51.38 N | 1.05 W |
| Bentinck Island I | 92 | 17.04 S | 139.30 E |
| Benton Harbor | 96 | 42.06 N | 86.27 W |
| Benue (Bénoué) ≈ | 86 | 7.48 N | 6.46 E |
| Benwee Head ➤ | 60 | 54.20 N | 9.50 W |
| Benxi | 80 | 41.18 N | 123.45 E |
| Beograd (Belgrade) | 74 | 44.50 N | 20.30 E |
| Beppu | 80 | 33.17 N | 131.30 E |
| Berat | 74 | 40.42 N | 19.57 E |
| Berau, Teluk C | 82 | 2.30 S | 132.30 E |
| Berbera | 88 | 10.25 N | 45.02 E |
| Berberati | 88 | 4.16 N | 15.47 E |
| Berbice ≈ | 100 | 6.17 N | 57.32 W |
| Berck | 68 | 50.24 N | 1.34 E |
| Berd'ansk | 76 | 46.45 N | 36.49 E |
| Berdičev | 76 | 49.54 N | 28.36 E |
| Berdsk | 78 | 54.47 N | 83.02 E |
| Bere Alston | 54 | 50.29 N | 4.12 W |
| Berens ≈ | 94 | 52.18 N | 97.02 W |
| Bere Regis | 54 | 50.46 N | 2.14 W |
| Berettyóujfalu | 66 | 47.14 N | 21.32 E |
| Berezniki | 76 | 59.24 N | 56.46 E |
| Bergama | 74 | 39.07 N | 27.10 E |
| Bergamo | 72 | 45.41 N | 9.43 E |
| Bergen [auf Rügen] | 66 | 54.25 N | 13.26 E |
| Bergen op Zoom | 66 | 51.30 N | 4.17 E |
| Bergerac | 68 | 44.51 N | 0.29 E |
| Bergisch Gladbach | 66 | 50.59 N | 7.07 E |
| Berhala, Selat ⋓ | 82 | 0.48 S | 104.25 E |
| Berhampore | 84 | 24.06 N | 88.15 E |
| Berhampur | 84 | 19.19 N | 84.48 E |
| Beringa, Ostrov I | 78 | 55.00 N | 166.00 E |
| Bering Sea ▼² | 78 | 60.00 N | 175.00 W |
| Berkeley, Eng., U.K. | 54 | 51.42 N | 2.27 W |
| Berkeley, Calif., U.S. | 96 | 37.57 N | 122.18 W |
| Berkeley, Vale of V | 54 | 51.43 N | 2.25 W |
| Berkhamsted | 54 | 51.46 N | 0.35 W |
| Berkshire □⁶ | 54 | 51.30 N | 1.20 W |
| Berkshire Downs ⋌² | 54 | 51.32 N | 1.30 W |
| Berlin (West), B.R.D. | 66 | 52.31 N | 13.24 E |
| Berlin, N.H., U.S. | 96 | 44.28 N | 71.10 W |
| Berlin (East), D.D.R. | 66 | 52.30 N | 13.25 E |
| Bermejo ≈, Arg. | 102 | 26.51 S | 58.23 W |
| Bermejo ≈, S.A. | 102 | 31.52 S | 67.22 W |
| Bermeo | 70 | 43.26 N | 2.43 W |
| Bermuda □² | 102 | 32.20 N | 64.45 W |
| Bern (Berne) | 66 | 46.57 N | 7.26 E |
| Bernalda | 72 | 40.24 N | 16.41 E |
| Bernau bei Berlin | 66 | 52.40 N | 13.35 E |
| Bernay | 68 | 49.06 N | 0.36 E |
| Bernburg | 66 | 51.48 N | 11.44 E |
| Berner Alpen ⋌ | 66 | 46.25 N | 7.30 E |
| Bernier Bay C | 94 | 71.08 N | 88.00 W |
| Bernier Island I | 92 | 24.52 S | 113.08 E |
| Bernisdale | 58 | 57.25 N | 6.24 W |
| Beroun | 66 | 49.58 N | 14.04 E |
| Ber'ozovo | 76 | 63.56 N | 65.01 E |
| Berriedale | 58 | 58.11 N | 3.30 W |
| Bertraghboy Bay C | 60 | 53.23 N | 9.53 W |
| Berwick-upon-Tweed | 56 | 55.46 N | 2.00 W |
| Berwyn ⋌² | 56 | 52.52 N | 3.24 W |
| Besançon | 68 | 47.15 N | 6.02 E |
| Bessbrook | 60 | 54.11 N | 6.24 W |
| Bethanien | 90 | 26.31 S | 17.09 E |
| Bethel | 94a | 60.48 N | 161.46 W |
| Bethesda | 56 | 53.11 N | 4.03 W |
| Bethlehem | 90 | 28.15 S | 28.15 E |
| Béthune | 68 | 50.32 N | 2.38 E |
| Betpak-Dala ≃² | 76 | 46.00 N | 70.00 E |
| Betsiamites ≈ | 94 | 49.25 N | 68.40 W |
| Betsiboka ≈ | 90 | 16.03 S | 46.36 E |
| Bette, Pic Λ | 88 | 22.00 N | 19.12 E |
| Bettyhill | 58 | 58.32 N | 4.14 W |
| Betws-y-Coed | 56 | 53.05 N | 3.48 W |
| Betzdorf | 66 | 50.47 N | 7.53 E |
| Beult ≈ | 54 | 51.13 N | 0.26 E |
| Beverley | 56 | 53.51 N | 0.26 W |
| Beverly Lake ⌷ | 94 | 64.36 N | 100.30 W |
| Beverwijk | 66 | 52.28 N | 4.40 E |
| Bewdley | 54 | 52.23 N | 2.19 W |
| Bexhill | 54 | 50.50 N | 0.29 E |
| Bexley ◄⁸ | 54 | 51.26 N | 0.09 E |
| Beykoz | 74 | 41.08 N | 29.06 E |
| Beypazarı | 74 | 40.10 N | 31.56 E |
| Beyşehir Gölü ⌷ | 74 | 37.47 N | 31.30 E |
| Bezeck | 62 | 57.47 N | 36.39 E |
| Béziers | 68 | 43.21 N | 3.15 E |
| Bhadravati | 84 | 13.52 N | 75.43 E |
| Bhāgalpur | 84 | 25.15 N | 87.00 E |
| Bhatinda | 84 | 30.12 N | 74.57 E |
| Bhātpāra | 84 | 22.52 N | 88.24 E |
| Bhaunagar | 84 | 21.46 N | 72.09 E |
| Bheigeir, Beinn Λ² | 58 | 55.44 N | 6.07 W |
| Bhilai | 84 | 21.13 N | 81.26 E |
| Bhilwāra | 84 | 25.21 N | 74.38 E |
| Bhima ≈ | 84 | 16.25 N | 77.17 E |
| Bhiwāni | 84 | 28.47 N | 76.08 E |
| Bhopāl | 84 | 23.15 N | 77.25 E |

| Name | Page | Lat ° ′ | Long ° ′ |
|---|---|---|---|
| Bhubaneswar | 84 | 20.15 N | 85.50 E |
| Bhuj | 84 | 23.17 N | 69.41 E |
| Bhusāwal | 84 | 21.03 N | 75.46 E |
| Bhutan □[1] | 84 | 27.30 N | 90.30 E |
| Bia, Phou ∧ | 82 | 18.59 N | 103.09 E |
| Biafra, Bight of C[3] | 86 | 4.00 N | 8.00 E |
| Biak I | 82 | 1.00 S | 136.00 E |
| Biała Podlaska | 66 | 52.02 N | 23.06 E |
| Białogard | 66 | 54.01 N | 16.00 E |
| Białystok | 66 | 53.09 N | 23.09 E |
| Bian, Bidean nam ∧ | 58 | 56.38 N | 5.02 W |
| Biarritz | 68 | 43.29 N | 1.34 W |
| Biberach an der Riss | 66 | 48.06 N | 9.47 E |
| Bicaz | 74 | 46.54 N | 26.05 E |
| Bicester | 54 | 51.54 N | 1.09 W |
| Bida | 86 | 9.05 N | 6.01 E |
| Biddeford | 96 | 43.30 N | 70.26 W |
| Biddenden | 54 | 51.07 N | 0.39 E |
| Biddulph | 56 | 53.08 N | 2.10 W |
| Bideford | 54 | 51.01 N | 4.13 W |
| Bidford-on-Avon | 54 | 52.10 N | 1.51 W |
| Bié | 90 | 12.22 S | 16.56 E |
| Bielawa | 66 | 50.41 N | 16.38 E |
| Biel [bienne] | 68 | 47.10 N | 7.12 E |
| Bielefeld | 66 | 52.01 N | 8.31 E |
| Bieler Lake ⊜ | 94 | 70.20 N | 73.00 W |
| Biella | 72 | 45.34 N | 8.03 E |
| Bielsko-Biała | 66 | 49.49 N | 19.02 E |
| Bielsk Podlaski | 66 | 52.47 N | 23.12 E |
| Bien-hoa | 82 | 10.57 N | 106.49 E |
| Bienville, Lac ⊜ | 94 | 55.05 N | 72.40 W |
| Bietigheim | 66 | 48.58 N | 9.07 E |
| Biga | 74 | 40.13 N | 27.14 E |
| Bigbury Bay C | 54 | 50.16 N | 3.48 W |
| Biggar | 58 | 55.38 N | 3.32 W |
| Biggin Hill ◆[8] | 54 | 51.18 N | 0.04 E |
| Biggleswade | 54 | 52.05 N | 0.17 W |
| Bighorn ≃ | 96 | 46.09 N | 107.28 W |
| Bighorn Mountains ∧∧ | 96 | 44.00 N | 107.30 W |
| Big Island I | 94 | 62.43 N | 70.43 W |
| Big Quill Lake ⊜ | 94 | 51.55 N | 104.22 W |
| Big Sand Lake ⊜ | 94 | 57.45 N | 99.42 W |
| Big Trout Lake ⊜ | 94 | 53.45 N | 90.00 W |
| Bihać | 72 | 44.49 N | 15.52 E |
| Bihār | 84 | 25.11 N | 85.31 E |
| Bija ≃ | 78 | 52.25 N | 85.05 E |
| Bijagós, Arquipélago dos II | 86 | 11.25 N | 16.20 W |
| Bijāpur | 84 | 16.50 N | 75.42 E |
| Bijeljina | 74 | 44.45 N | 19.13 E |
| Bijie | 80 | 27.18 N | 105.20 E |
| Bijsk | 78 | 52.34 N | 85.15 E |
| Bīkaner | 84 | 28.01 N | 73.18 E |
| Bikin ≃ | 78 | 46.51 N | 134.02 E |
| Bilāspur | 84 | 22.05 N | 82.08 E |
| Bilauktaung Range ∧∧ | 82 | 13.00 N | 99.00 E |
| Bilbao | 70 | 43.15 N | 2.58 W |
| Bilecik | 74 | 40.09 N | 29.59 E |
| Bílina | 66 | 50.35 N | 13.45 E |
| Biliran Island I | 82 | 11.35 N | 124.28 E |
| Billabong Creek ≃ | 92 | 35.06 S | 144.02 E |
| Billericay | 54 | 51.38 N | 0.25 E |
| Billesdon | 54 | 52.37 N | 0.55 W |
| Billingham | 56 | 54.36 N | 1.17 W |
| Billings | 96 | 45.47 N | 118.27 W |
| Billingshurst | 54 | 51.01 N | 0.28 W |
| Biloxi | 96 | 30.24 N | 88.53 W |
| Bilston | 54 | 52.34 N | 2.04 W |
| Binche | 66 | 50.24 N | 4.10 E |
| Binga, Monte ∧ | 90 | 19.45 S | 33.04 E |
| Bingen | 66 | 48.07 N | 9.16 E |
| Bingham | 54 | 52.57 N | 0.57 W |
| Binghamton | 96 | 42.08 N | 75.54 W |
| Bingley | 56 | 53.51 N | 1.50 W |
| Binjai | 82 | 3.36 N | 98.30 E |
| Binongko, Pulau I | 82 | 5.57 S | 124.02 E |
| Bintan, Pulau I | 82 | 1.05 N | 104.30 E |
| Binzert (Bizerte) | 86 | 37.17 N | 9.52 E |
| Bío-Bío ≃ | 102 | 36.49 S | 73.10 W |
| Birchington | 54 | 51.23 N | 1.19 E |
| Birch Mountains ∧∧[2] | 94 | 57.30 N | 112.30 W |
| Bird Island I | 102 | 54.00 S | 38.05 W |
| Bird Islet I | 92 | 22.10 S | 155.28 E |
| Bīrjand | 84 | 32.53 N | 59.13 E |
| Birkenhead | 56 | 53.24 N | 3.02 W |
| Birkerød | 64 | 55.50 N | 12.26 E |
| Bîrlad | 74 | 46.14 N | 27.40 E |
| Birmingham, Eng., U.K. | 54 | 52.30 N | 1.50 W |
| Birmingham, Ala., U.S. | 96 | 33.31 N | 86.49 W |
| Birobidžan | 78 | 48.48 N | 132.57 E |
| Birr | 60 | 53.05 N | 7.54 W |
| Birrie ≃ | 92 | 29.43 S | 146.37 E |
| Birstall | 54 | 52.41 N | 1.07 W |
| Birtley | 56 | 54.54 N | 1.34 W |
| Bir'usa ≃ | 78 | 57.34 N | 95.24 E |
| Bisa, Pulau I | 82 | 1.15 S | 127.28 E |
| Biscay, Bay of C | 50 | 44.00 N | 4.00 W |
| Bisceglie | 72 | 41.14 N | 16.31 E |
| Bischofswerda | 66 | 51.07 N | 14.10 E |
| Bishārah, Ma'ṭan ⊤[4] | 88 | 22.58 N | 22.39 E |
| Bishop Auckland | 56 | 54.40 N | 1.40 W |
| Bishop's Castle | 54 | 52.29 N | 3.00 W |
| Bishop's Cleeve | 54 | 51.57 N | 2.04 W |
| Bishops Frome | 54 | 52.08 N | 2.29 W |
| Bishops Lydeard | 54 | 51.04 N | 3.12 W |
| Bishop's Stortford | 54 | 51.53 N | 0.09 E |
| Bishopsteignton | 54 | 50.34 N | 3.31 W |
| Bishopstoke | 54 | 50.59 N | 1.19 W |
| Bishop's Waltham | 54 | 50.58 N | 1.12 W |
| Biskra | 86 | 34.51 N | 5.44 E |
| Bisley | 54 | 51.45 N | 2.08 W |
| Bismarck | 96 | 46.48 N | 100.47 W |
| Bissau | 86 | 11.51 N | 15.35 W |
| Bistrița | 74 | 47.08 N | 24.30 E |
| Bitola | 74 | 41.01 N | 21.20 E |
| Bitonto | 72 | 41.06 N | 16.42 E |
| Bitterfeld | 66 | 51.37 N | 12.20 E |
| Bitterroot Range ∧∧ | 96 | 47.06 N | 115.10 W |
| Biwa-ko ⊜ | 80 | 35.15 N | 136.05 E |
| Bjala Slatina | 74 | 43.28 N | 23.56 E |
| Bjelovar | 72 | 45.54 N | 16.51 E |
| Bjørnøya I | 8 | 74.25 N | 19.00 E |
| Black (Da) ≃ | 82 | 21.15 N | 105.20 E |
| Blackadder Water ≃ | 58 | 55.46 N | 2.15 W |
| Blackburn, Eng., U.K. | 56 | 53.45 N | 2.29 W |
| Blackburn, Scot., U.K. | 58 | 57.12 N | 2.18 W |
| Blackcraig Hill ∧ | 56 | 55.20 N | 4.08 W |
| Black Devon ≃ | 58 | 56.06 N | 3.47 W |
| Black Down Hills ∧∧[2] | 54 | 50.57 N | 3.09 W |
| Black Duck ≃ | 94 | 56.51 N | 89.02 W |
| Black Esk ≃ | 56 | 55.12 N | 5.10 W |
| Blackford | 58 | 56.15 N | 3.46 W |
| Blackhall Colliery | 56 | 54.44 N | 1.14 W |
| Black Head ≻, Eire | 60 | 53.08 N | 9.17 W |
| Black Head ≻, Eng., U.K. | 54 | 50.01 N | 5.06 W |
| Black Hills ∧∧ | 96 | 44.00 N | 104.00 W |
| Blackhope Star ∧ | 58 | 55.44 N | 3.05 W |
| Black Isle ≻[1] | 58 | 57.35 N | 4.15 W |
| Black Lake ⊜ | 94 | 59.10 N | 105.20 W |
| Blacklunans | 58 | 56.44 N | 3.22 W |
| Blackmoor ∧∧[1] | 54 | 50.24 N | 4.46 W |
| Blackmoor Vale ∨ | 54 | 50.56 N | 2.25 W |
| Black Mountain ∧ | 54 | 51.52 N | 3.46 W |
| Black Mountains ∧∧ | 54 | 51.57 N | 3.08 W |
| Blackpool | 56 | 53.50 N | 3.03 W |
| Blackrock ∧[2] | 60 | 52.18 N | 8.32 W |
| Black Rock I[2] | 60 | 54.05 N | 10.22 W |
| Black Rock II[1] | 102 | 53.39 S | 41.48 W |
| Black Rock Desert ◆[2] | 96 | 41.10 N | 119.00 W |
| Black Sea ⊤[2] | 50 | 43.00 N | 35.00 E |
| Blacksod Bay C | 52 | 54.08 N | 10.00 W |
| Black Volta (Volta Noire) ≃ | 86 | 8.41 N | 1.33 W |
| Blackwater | 60 | 52.26 N | 6.21 W |
| Blackwater ≃, Eire | 52 | 51.51 N | 7.50 W |
| Blackwater ≃, Eur. | 56 | 54.31 N | 6.34 W |
| Blackwater ≃, Eng., U.K. | 54 | 51.45 N | 1.00 E |
| Blackwaterfoot | 58 | 55.30 N | 5.19 W |
| Blackwater Lake ⊜ | 94 | 64.00 N | 123.05 W |
| Blackwater Reservoir ⊜[1] | 58 | 56.41 N | 4.46 W |
| Bladnoch ≃ | 56 | 54.51 N | 4.25 W |
| Blaenau Ffestiniog | 54 | 52.59 N | 3.56 W |
| Blaenavon | 54 | 51.48 N | 3.05 W |
| Blagdon | 54 | 51.20 N | 2.43 W |
| Blagoevgrad | 74 | 42.01 N | 23.06 E |
| Blagoveščensk | 78 | 50.17 N | 127.32 E |
| Blaina | 54 | 51.46 N | 3.10 W |
| Blair Atholl | 58 | 56.46 N | 3.51 W |
| Blairgowrie | 58 | 56.36 N | 3.21 W |
| Blakeney, Eng., U.K. | 54 | 52.58 N | 1.00 E |
| Blakeney, Eng., U.K. | 54 | 51.46 N | 2.29 W |
| Blanc, Cap ≻ | 86 | 20.46 N | 17.03 W |
| Blanc, Mont ∧ | 50 | 45.50 N | 6.52 E |
| Blanca, Bahía C | 102 | 38.55 S | 62.10 W |
| Blanca, Cordillera ∧∧ | 100 | 9.10 S | 77.35 W |
| Blanca Peak ∧ | 96 | 37.35 N | 105.29 W |
| Blanche, Lake ⊜ | 92 | 29.15 S | 139.39 E |
| Blanco, Cape ≻ | 96 | 42.50 N | 124.34 W |
| Blandford Forum | 54 | 50.52 N | 2.11 W |
| Blankenburg | 66 | 51.48 N | 10.58 E |
| Blansko | 66 | 49.22 N | 16.39 E |
| Blantyre | 90 | 15.47 S | 35.00 E |
| Blarney | 60 | 51.56 N | 8.34 W |
| Blaydon | 56 | 54.58 N | 1.42 W |
| Blaze, Point ≻ | 92 | 12.56 S | 130.12 E |
| Blean | 54 | 51.19 N | 1.02 E |
| Blessington | 60 | 53.10 N | 6.32 W |
| Bletchley | 54 | 52.00 N | 0.46 W |
| Bleus, Monts ∧∧, Afr. | 88 | 1.30 N | 30.30 E |
| Bleus, Monts ∧∧, Zaïre | 90 | 4.31 S | 21.02 E |
| Blida | 86 | 36.28 N | 2.50 E |
| Blitar | 82 | 8.06 S | 112.09 E |
| Blithe ≃ | 54 | 52.45 N | 1.50 W |
| Blithfield Reservoir ⊜[1] | 54 | 52.48 N | 1.53 W |
| Blockley | 54 | 52.01 N | 1.45 W |
| Bloemfontein | 90 | 29.12 S | 26.07 E |
| Blois | 68 | 47.35 N | 1.20 E |
| Bloodvein ≃ | 94 | 51.45 N | 96.44 W |
| Bloody Foreland ≻ | 52 | 55.09 N | 8.17 W |
| Bloom, Slieve ∧∧ | 60 | 53.05 N | 7.35 W |
| Bloomington, Ill., U.S. | 96 | 40.29 N | 89.00 W |
| Bloomington, Ind., U.S. | 96 | 39.10 N | 86.32 W |
| Blouberg ∧ | 90 | 23.01 S | 28.59 E |
| Bloxham | 54 | 52.02 N | 1.22 W |
| Bludenz | 66 | 47.09 N | 9.49 E |
| Blue Mountain Peak ∧ | 98 | 18.03 N | 76.35 W |
| Blue Mountains ∧∧ | 96 | 45.30 N | 118.15 W |
| Blue Nile (Al-Bahr al-Azraq) ≃ | 88 | 15.38 N | 32.31 E |
| Bluenose Lake ⊜ | 94 | 68.30 N | 119.35 W |
| Blue Ridge ∧∧ | 96 | 37.00 N | 82.00 W |
| Blue Stack Mountains ∧∧ | 60 | 54.45 N | 8.05 W |
| Bluff Knoll ∧ | 92 | 34.23 S | 118.20 E |
| Blyth | 56 | 55.07 N | 1.30 W |
| Blyth ≃ | 54 | 52.18 N | 1.40 E |
| Blyth Bridge | 58 | 55.42 N | 3.24 W |
| Bo | 86 | 7.56 N | 11.21 W |
| Boarhills | 58 | 56.19 N | 2.42 W |
| Boath | 58 | 57.44 N | 4.23 W |
| Boat of Garten | 58 | 57.20 N | 3.44 W |
| Boa Vista I | 86 | 16.05 N | 22.50 W |
| Böblingen | 66 | 48.41 N | 9.01 E |
| Bobo Dioulasso | 86 | 11.12 N | 4.18 W |
| Bobrujsk | 76 | 53.09 N | 29.14 E |
| Bochnia | 66 | 49.58 N | 20.26 E |
| Bocholt | 66 | 51.50 N | 6.36 E |
| Bochum | 66 | 51.28 N | 7.13 E |
| Bodajbo | 78 | 57.51 N | 114.10 E |
| Boddam, Scot., U.K. | 58 | 57.28 N | 1.47 W |
| Boddam, Scot., U.K. | 58 | 59.55 N | 1.17 W |
| Bodele ◆[1] | 88 | 16.30 N | 16.30 E |
| Boden | 64 | 65.50 N | 21.42 E |
| Bodensee ⊜ | 50 | 47.35 N | 9.25 E |
| Boderg, Lough ⊜ | 60 | 53.52 N | 7.58 W |
| Bodiam | 54 | 51.00 N | 0.33 E |
| Bodmin | 54 | 50.29 N | 4.43 W |
| Bodmin Moor ◆[3] | 52 | 50.33 N | 4.33 W |
| Bodø | 62 | 67.17 N | 14.23 E |
| Bogale | 82 | 16.17 N | 95.24 E |
| Bogan ≃ | 92 | 32.45 S | 148.08 E |
| Bogeduoshanmai ∧∧ | 80 | 43.30 N | 89.45 E |
| Boggeragh Mountains ∧∧ | 60 | 52.03 N | 8.55 W |
| Bognor Regis | 54 | 50.47 N | 0.41 W |
| Bogor | 82 | 6.35 S | 106.47 E |
| Bogorodsk | 62 | 56.06 N | 43.31 E |
| Bogotá | 100 | 4.36 N | 74.05 W |
| Bogotol | 78 | 56.12 N | 89.33 E |
| Bogrie Hill ∧[2] | 56 | 55.08 N | 3.55 W |
| Bohai C | 80 | 38.30 N | 120.00 E |
| Bohol I | 82 | 9.50 N | 124.10 E |
| Boigu Island I | 92 | 9.16 S | 142.12 E |
| Bois, Lac des ⊜ | 94 | 66.40 N | 125.15 W |
| Boisdale, Loch C | 58 | 57.08 N | 7.19 W |
| Boise | 96 | 43.37 N | 116.13 W |
| Boizenburg | 66 | 53.22 N | 10.43 E |
| Bojador, Cabo ≻ | 86 | 26.08 N | 14.30 W |
| Bojeador, Cape ≻ | 82 | 18.30 N | 120.34 E |
| Bojnūrd | 84 | 37.28 N | 57.19 E |
| Boksitogorsk | 62 | 59.28 N | 33.51 E |
| Bolbec | 68 | 49.34 N | 0.29 E |
| Boldon | 56 | 54.57 N | 1.27 W |
| Bolesławiec | 66 | 51.16 N | 15.34 E |
| Bolívar, Cerro ∧ | 100 | 7.28 N | 63.25 W |
| Bolívar, Pico ∧ | 100 | 8.30 N | 71.02 W |
| Bolivia □[1] | 100 | 17.00 S | 65.00 W |
| Bollin ≃ | 56 | 53.23 N | 2.28 W |
| Bollington | 56 | 53.18 N | 2.06 W |
| Bollnäs | 64 | 61.21 N | 16.25 E |
| Bollullos par del Condado | 70 | 37.20 N | 6.32 W |
| Bologna | 72 | 44.29 N | 11.20 E |
| Bol'šaja Balachn'a ≃ | 78 | 73.37 N | 107.05 E |
| Bol'šaja Čheta ≃ | 78 | 69.33 N | 84.15 E |
| Bol'šaja Čuja ≃ | 78 | 58.56 N | 112.13 E |
| Bol'ševik, Ostrov I | 78 | 78.40 N | 102.30 E |
| Bol'šezemel'skaja Tundra ◆[1] | 76 | 67.30 N | 56.00 E |
| Bol'šoj An'uj ≃ | 78 | 68.30 N | 160.49 E |
| Bol'šoj Begičev, Ostrov I | 78 | 74.20 N | 112.30 E |
| Bol'šoj Kavkaz (Caucasus) ∧∧ | 76 | 42.30 N | 45.00 E |
| Bol'šoj L'achovskij, Ostrov I | 78 | 73.35 N | 142.00 E |
| Bol'šoj Uzen' ≃ | 76 | 48.50 N | 49.40 E |
| Bolsover | 56 | 53.14 N | 1.18 W |
| Bolton | 56 | 53.35 N | 2.26 W |
| Bolton Abbey | 56 | 53.59 N | 1.53 W |
| Bolton Bridge | 56 | 53.58 N | 1.57 W |
| Bolton-le-Sands | 56 | 54.06 N | 2.47 W |
| Bolton upon Dearne | 56 | 53.31 N | 1.19 W |
| Bolus Head ≻ | 60 | 51.46 N | 10.21 W |
| Bolzano (Bozen) | 72 | 46.31 N | 11.22 E |
| Boma | 90 | 5.51 S | 13.03 E |
| Bombay | 84 | 18.58 N | 72.50 E |
| Bomberai, Jazirah ≻[1] | 82 | 3.00 S | 133.00 E |
| Bomu (Mbomou) ≃ | 88 | 4.08 N | 22.26 E |
| Bon, Cap ≻ | 86 | 37.05 N | 11.03 E |
| Bonaire I | 98 | 12.10 N | 68.15 W |
| Bonaparte Archipelago II | 92 | 14.17 S | 125.18 E |
| Bonarbridge | 58 | 53.33 N | 4.21 W |
| Bonavista Bay C | 94 | 48.45 N | 53.20 W |
| Bonawe | 58 | 56.26 N | 5.13 W |
| Bonchester Bridge | 56 | 55.24 N | 2.40 W |
| Bondeno | 72 | 44.53 N | 11.25 E |
| Bone, Teluk C | 82 | 4.00 S | 120.40 E |
| Bo'ness | 58 | 56.01 N | 3.37 W |
| Bonifacio, Strait of ⊔ | 50 | 41.20 N | 9.15 E |
| Bonn | 66 | 50.44 N | 7.05 E |
| Bonnet Plume ≃ | 94 | 65.55 N | 134.58 W |
| Bonny | 86 | 4.27 N | 7.10 E |
| Bonnyrigg | 58 | 55.52 N | 3.08 W |
| Boom | 66 | 51.05 N | 4.22 E |
| Boot | 56 | 54.24 N | 3.17 W |
| Boothia, Gulf of C | 94 | 71.00 N | 91.00 W |
| Boothia Peninsula ≻[1] | 94 | 70.30 N | 95.00 W |
| Bootle | 56 | 53.28 N | 3.00 W |
| Bor, Jugo. | 74 | 44.05 N | 22.07 E |
| Bor, S.S.S.R. | 62 | 56.22 N | 44.05 E |
| Borah Peak ∧ | 96 | 44.08 N | 113.48 W |
| Borås | 64 | 57.43 N | 12.55 E |
| Bordeaux | 68 | 44.50 N | 0.34 W |
| Borden Peninsula ≻[1] | 94 | 73.00 N | 83.00 W |
| Borders □[4] | 52 | 55.37 N | 3.15 W |
| Bordighera | 72 | 43.46 N | 7.39 E |
| Borehamwood | 54 | 51.40 N | 0.16 W |
| Boreray I | 58 | 57.42 N | 7.18 W |
| Borgå (Porvoo) | 64 | 60.24 N | 25.40 E |
| Borghorst | 66 | 52.07 N | 7.23 E |
| Borgomanero | 72 | 45.42 N | 8.28 E |
| Borgosesia | 72 | 45.43 N | 8.16 E |
| Borisoglebsk | 76 | 51.23 N | 42.06 E |
| Borisov | 76 | 54.15 N | 28.30 E |
| Borken | 66 | 51.51 N | 6.51 E |
| Borlänge | 64 | 60.29 N | 15.25 E |
| Borna | 66 | 51.19 N | 13.11 E |
| Borneo (Kalimantan) I | 82 | 0.30 N | 114.00 E |
| Bornholm I | 50 | 55.10 N | 15.00 E |
| Bornova | 74 | 38.27 N | 27.14 E |
| Boroughbridge | 56 | 54.06 N | 1.23 W |
| Borough Green | 54 | 51.17 N | 0.19 E |
| Boroviči | 62 | 58.24 N | 33.55 E |
| Borovoj | 62 | 59.55 N | 51.38 E |
| Borris | 60 | 52.35 N | 6.06 W |
| Borrisokane | 60 | 52.59 N | 8.07 W |
| Borrisoleigh | 60 | 52.45 N | 7.57 W |
| Borrowdale | 56 | 54.31 N | 3.10 W |
| Borșa | 74 | 47.39 N | 24.40 E |
| Borščovočnyj Chrebet ∧∧ | 78 | 52.00 N | 117.00 E |
| Borth | 54 | 52.29 N | 4.03 W |
| Borthwick Water ≃ | 56 | 55.24 N | 2.50 W |
| Borūjerd | 84 | 33.54 N | 48.46 E |
| Borve | 58 | 56.58 N | 7.32 W |
| Borz'a | 78 | 50.38 N | 115.38 E |
| Bosanski Novi | 72 | 45.03 N | 16.23 E |
| Boscastle | 54 | 50.41 N | 4.42 W |
| Boshan | 80 | 36.29 N | 117.50 E |
| Bositenghu ⊜ | 80 | 42.00 N | 87.00 E |
| Bosna ≃ | 50 | 45.04 N | 18.29 E |
| Bossangoa | 88 | 6.29 N | 17.27 E |
| Bosso, Dallol ∨ | 86 | 12.25 N | 2.50 E |
| Boston, Eng., U.K. | 54 | 52.59 N | 0.01 W |
| Boston, Mass., U.S. | 96 | 42.21 N | 71.04 W |
| Boston Mountains ∧∧ | 96 | 35.50 N | 93.20 W |
| Boteti ≃ | 90 | 20.08 S | 23.23 E |
| Bothnia, Gulf of C | 50 | 63.00 N | 20.30 E |
| Botley | 54 | 50.56 N | 1.18 W |
| Botoșani | 74 | 47.45 N | 26.40 E |
| Botswana □[1] | 90 | 22.00 S | 24.00 E |
| Bottesford | 54 | 52.56 N | 0.48 W |
| Bottrop | 66 | 51.31 N | 6.55 E |
| Botucatu | 100 | 22.52 S | 48.26 W |
| Bouaké | 86 | 7.41 N | 5.02 W |
| Bouar | 88 | 5.57 N | 15.36 E |
| Bougainville Reefs ✦[2] | 92 | 15.30 S | 147.06 E |
| Boughton Street | 54 | 51.18 N | 0.59 E |
| Boulder | 96 | 40.01 N | 105.17 W |
| Boulogne-Billancourt | 68 | 48.50 N | 2.15 E |
| Boulogne-sur-Mer | 68 | 50.43 N | 1.37 E |
| Boulsworth Hill ∧ | 56 | 53.48 N | 2.06 W |
| Boundary Peak ∧ | 96 | 37.51 N | 118.21 W |
| Bourg-en-Bresse | 68 | 46.12 N | 5.13 E |
| Bourges | 68 | 47.05 N | 2.24 E |
| Bourgoin | 68 | 45.35 N | 5.17 E |
| Bourne | 54 | 52.46 N | 0.23 W |
| Bourne ≃ | 54 | 51.02 N | 1.47 W |
| Bournemouth | 54 | 50.43 N | 1.54 W |
| Bourton-on-theWater | 54 | 51.53 N | 1.45 W |
| Bou Saâda | 86 | 35.12 N | 4.11 E |
| Bøvågen | 62 | 60.40 N | 4.58 E |
| Bøverdal | 62 | 61.43 N | 8.21 E |
| Bovey ≃ | 54 | 50.34 N | 3.37 W |
| Bovey Tracey | 54 | 50.36 N | 3.40 W |
| Bovingdon | 54 | 51.44 N | 0.32 W |
| Bow Brook ≃ | 54 | 52.04 N | 2.07 W |
| Bowgreave | 56 | 53.52 N | 2.45 W |
| Bowland, Forest of ◆[3] | 56 | 53.58 N | 2.32 W |
| Bowling Green | 96 | 37.00 N | 86.27 W |
| Bowman Bay C | 94 | 65.30 N | 73.40 W |
| Bowmont Water ≃ | 56 | 55.34 N | 2.09 W |
| Bowmore | 58 | 55.45 N | 6.17 W |
| Bowness-on-Windermere | 56 | 54.22 N | 2.55 W |
| Box | 54 | 51.26 N | 2.15 W |
| Boxian | 80 | 33.53 N | 115.45 E |
| Boyle | 60 | 53.58 N | 8.18 W |
| Boyne ≃ | 52 | 53.43 N | 6.15 W |
| Bozeman | 96 | 45.41 N | 111.02 W |
| Bozhen | 80 | 38.07 N | 116.32 E |
| Bra | 72 | 44.42 N | 7.51 E |
| Braan ≃ | 58 | 56.33 N | 3.35 W |
| Bracadale, Loch C | 58 | 57.19 N | 6.30 W |
| Bracebridge Heath | 56 | 53.13 N | 0.33 W |
| Brackley | 54 | 52.02 N | 1.09 W |
| Bracknell | 54 | 51.26 N | 0.45 W |
| Braco | 58 | 56.15 N | 3.53 W |
| Brad | 74 | 46.08 N | 22.47 E |
| Bradenton | 96 | 27.29 N | 82.34 W |
| Bradford | 56 | 53.48 N | 1.45 W |
| Bradford-on-Avon | 54 | 51.20 N | 2.15 W |
| Brading | 54 | 50.41 N | 1.09 W |
| Bradwell-on-Sea | 54 | 51.44 N | 0.54 E |
| Bradworthy | 54 | 50.54 N | 4.22 W |
| Brae | 58a | 60.23 N | 1.21 W |
| Braemar | 58 | 57.01 N | 3.23 W |
| Braga | 70 | 41.33 N | 8.26 W |
| Bragança | 70 | 41.49 N | 6.45 W |
| Bragar | 58 | 58.24 N | 6.40 W |
| Brahmaputra (Yaluzangbujiang) ≃ | 84 | 24.02 N | 90.55 E |
| Braich y Pwll ≻ | 52 | 52.48 N | 4.36 W |
| Brăila | 74 | 45.16 N | 27.58 E |
| Brain ≃ | 54 | 51.48 N | 0.39 E |
| Braine-l'Alleud | 66 | 50.41 N | 4.22 E |
| Braint ≃ | 56 | 53.08 N | 4.19 W |
| Braintree | 54 | 51.53 N | 0.32 E |
| Brake | 66 | 53.19 N | 8.28 E |
| Bramford | 54 | 52.04 N | 1.06 E |
| Brampton | 54 | 52.19 N | 0.14 W |
| Brancaster | 54 | 52.58 N | 0.39 E |
| Brancaster Roads ⊤[3] | 54 | 53.05 N | 0.45 W |
| Branco ≃ | 100 | 1.24 S | 61.51 W |
| Brandberg ∧ | 90 | 21.10 S | 14.33 E |
| Brandenburg | 66 | 52.24 N | 12.32 E |
| Brandon, Eng., U.K. | 54 | 52.27 N | 0.37 E |
| Brandon, Eng., U.K. | 56 | 54.46 N | 1.39 W |
| Brandon Bay C | 52 | 52.15 N | 10.05 W |
| Brandon Head ≻ | 60 | 52.16 N | 10.14 W |
| Brandon Mountain ∧ | 52 | 52.14 N | 10.15 W |
| Brandýs nad Labem | 66 | 50.10 N | 14.41 E |
| Braniewo | 66 | 54.24 N | 19.50 E |
| Br'ansk | 76 | 53.15 N | 34.22 E |
| Brantford | 94 | 43.08 N | 80.16 W |
| Bras d'Or Lake ⊜ | 94 | 45.52 N | 60.50 W |
| Brasília | 100 | 15.47 S | 47.55 W |
| Brașov | 74 | 45.39 N | 25.37 E |
| Bratislava | 66 | 48.09 N | 17.07 E |
| Bratsk | 78 | 56.05 N | 101.48 E |
| Bratskoje Vodochranilišče ⊜[1] | 78 | 56.10 N | 102.10 E |
| Braunau [am Inn] | 66 | 48.15 N | 13.02 E |
| Braunschweig | 66 | 52.16 N | 10.31 E |
| Braunton | 54 | 51.07 N | 4.10 W |
| Brava I | 86 | 14.52 N | 24.43 W |
| Bravo del Norte (Rio Grande) ≃ | 96 | 25.55 N | 97.09 W |
| Bray | 60 | 53.12 N | 6.06 W |
| Bray ≃ | 54 | 50.59 N | 3.53 W |
| Bray Head ≻ | 60 | 51.53 N | 10.26 W |
| Brazil □[1] | 100 | 10.00 S | 55.00 W |
| Brazos ≃ | 96 | 28.53 N | 95.23 W |
| Brazzaville | 90 | 4.16 S | 15.17 E |
| Brčko | 74 | 44.53 N | 18.48 E |
| Breamish ≃ | 56 | 55.31 N | 1.56 W |
| Bream's Eaves | 54 | 51.45 N | 2.34 W |
| Brechfa | 54 | 51.54 N | 4.36 W |
| Brechin | 58 | 56.44 N | 2.40 W |
| Breckland ◆[1] | 54 | 52.28 N | 0.37 E |
| Břeclav | 66 | 48.46 N | 16.53 E |
| Brecon | 54 | 51.57 N | 3.24 W |
| Brecon Beacons ∧ | 54 | 51.53 N | 3.31 W |
| Breda | 66 | 51.35 N | 4.46 E |
| Bredon Hill ∧[2] | 54 | 52.06 N | 2.03 W |
| Breedoge ≃ | 60 | 53.55 N | 8.27 W |
| Bregenz | 72 | 47.30 N | 9.46 E |
| Breiðafjördur C | 50 | 65.15 N | 23.15 W |
| Bremen | 66 | 53.04 N | 8.49 E |
| Bremerhaven | 66 | 53.33 N | 8.34 E |
| Bremerton | 96 | 47.34 N | 122.38 W |
| Brendon Hills ∧∧[2] | 54 | 51.07 N | 3.25 W |
| Brenish | 58 | 58.08 N | 7.08 W |
| Brenish, Aird ≻ | 58 | 58.08 N | 7.08 W |
| Brent ◆[8] | 54 | 51.34 N | 0.17 W |
| Brent ≃ | 54 | 51.28 N | 0.18 W |
| Brentwood | 54 | 51.38 N | 0.18 E |
| Brescia | 72 | 45.33 N | 13.15 E |
| Bressanone | 72 | 46.43 N | 11.39 E |
| Bressay I | 52 | 60.08 N | 1.05 W |
| Bressay Sound ⊔ | 58a | 60.07 N | 1.09 W |
| Brest, Fr. | 68 | 48.24 N | 4.29 W |
| Brest, S.S.S.R. | 66 | 52.06 N | 23.42 E |
| Brett ≃ | 54 | 51.58 N | 0.58 E |
| Brevoort Island I | 94 | 63.30 N | 64.20 W |
| Brewood | 54 | 52.41 N | 2.10 W |
| Brezno | 66 | 48.50 N | 19.39 E |
| Briançon | 68 | 44.54 N | 6.39 E |
| Bride | 56 | 54.22 N | 4.22 W |
| Bride ≃ | 60 | 52.04 N | 7.52 W |
| Bridgend, Scot., U.K. | 58 | 55.48 N | 6.16 W |
| Bridgend, Scot., U.K. | 58 | 56.48 N | 2.45 W |
| Bridgend, Wales, U.K. | 54 | 51.31 N | 3.35 W |
| Bridge of Allan | 58 | 56.09 N | 3.57 W |
| Bridge of Gaur | 58 | 56.41 N | 4.27 W |
| Bridge of Orchy | 58 | 56.30 N | 4.46 W |
| Bridge of Weir | 58 | 55.52 N | 4.35 W |
| Bridgeport | 96 | 41.11 N | 73.11 W |
| Bridgetown | 98 | 13.06 N | 59.37 W |
| Bridgnorth | 54 | 52.33 N | 2.25 W |
| Bridgwater | 54 | 51.08 N | 3.00 W |
| Bridgwater Bay C | 52 | 51.16 N | 3.12 W |
| Bridlington | 56 | 54.05 N | 0.12 W |
| Bridlington Bay C | 52 | 54.04 N | 0.08 W |
| Bridport | 54 | 50.44 N | 2.46 W |
| Brierfield | 56 | 53.50 N | 2.14 W |
| Brierley Hill | 54 | 52.29 N | 2.07 W |
| Brigg | 56 | 53.34 N | 0.30 W |
| Brighouse | 56 | 53.42 N | 1.47 W |
| Brighstone | 54 | 50.38 N | 1.24 W |
| Brightlingsea | 54 | 51.49 N | 1.02 E |
| Brighton | 54 | 50.50 N | 0.08 W |
| Brig o' Turk | 58 | 56.13 N | 4.22 W |
| Brill | 54 | 51.49 N | 1.03 W |
| Brilon | 66 | 51.24 N | 8.34 E |
| Brimfield | 54 | 52.18 N | 2.42 W |
| Brimington | 56 | 53.16 N | 1.23 W |
| Brindisi | 72 | 40.38 N | 17.56 E |
| Brinyan | 58 | 59.07 N | 2.59 W |
| Brisbane | 92 | 27.28 S | 153.02 E |
| Bristol, Eng., U.K. | 54 | 51.27 N | 2.35 W |
| Bristol, Tenn., U.S. | 96 | 36.36 N | 82.11 W |
| Bristol Channel ⊔ | 52 | 51.20 N | 4.00 W |
| British Columbia □[4] | 94 | 54.00 N | 125.00 W |
| British Indian Ocean Territory □[2] | 90 | 7.00 S | 72.00 E |
| British Isles II | 8 | 54.00 N | 4.00 W |
| British Mountains ∧∧ | 94 | 69.00 N | 140.20 W |
| Briton Ferry | 54 | 51.38 N | 3.49 W |
| Brittas | 60 | 53.14 N | 6.27 W |
| Brive-la-Gaillarde | 68 | 45.10 N | 1.32 E |
| Brixham | 54 | 50.24 N | 3.30 W |
| Brixworth | 54 | 52.20 N | 0.54 W |
| Brno | 66 | 49.12 N | 16.37 E |
| Broach | 84 | 21.42 N | 72.58 E |
| Broadback ≃ | 94 | 51.21 N | 78.52 W |
| Broad Bay C | 52 | 58.15 N | 6.15 W |
| Broad Chalke | 54 | 51.02 N | 1.57 W |
| Broad Clyst | 54 | 50.46 N | 3.26 W |
| Broadford | 58 | 57.14 N | 5.54 W |
| Broad Haven C | 52 | 54.18 N | 9.55 W |
| Broad Law ∧ | 52 | 55.30 N | 3.22 W |
| Broad Sound ⊔ | 92 | 22.10 S | 149.45 E |
| Broadstairs | 54 | 51.22 N | 1.27 E |
| Broadway | 54 | 52.02 N | 1.51 W |
| Broadwindsor | 54 | 50.49 N | 2.48 W |
| Brochel | 58 | 57.26 N | 6.01 W |
| Brock ≃ | 56 | 53.52 N | 2.47 W |
| Brockenhurst | 54 | 50.49 N | 1.34 W |
| Brockman, Mount ∧ | 92 | 22.28 S | 117.18 E |
| Brockworth | 54 | 51.51 N | 2.09 W |
| Brodeur Peninsula ≻[1] | 94 | 73.00 N | 88.00 W |
| Brodick | 58 | 55.35 N | 5.09 W |
| Brodnica | 66 | 53.16 N | 19.23 E |
| Broken Hill | 92 | 31.57 S | 141.27 E |
| Bromborough | 56 | 53.19 N | 2.59 W |
| Bromley ◆[8] | 54 | 51.24 N | 0.02 E |
| Brompton | 56 | 54.22 N | 1.25 W |
| Bromsgrove | 54 | 52.20 N | 2.03 W |
| Bromyard | 54 | 52.11 N | 2.30 W |
| Bronllys | 54 | 52.01 N | 3.16 W |
| Bronlund Peak ∧ | 94 | 57.26 N | 126.38 W |
| Bronte | 72 | 37.48 N | 14.50 E |
| Brookeborough | 60 | 54.19 N | 7.24 W |
| Brookland | 54 | 50.59 N | 0.50 E |
| Brooks Range ∧∧ | 96a | 68.00 N | 154.00 W |
| Broom, Little Loch C | 58 | 57.54 N | 5.22 W |
| Broom, Loch C | 58 | 57.52 N | 5.08 W |
| Brora | 58 | 58.01 N | 3.51 W |
| Brora ≃ | 52 | 58.01 N | 3.51 W |
| Broseley | 54 | 52.37 N | 2.29 W |
| Brosna ≃ | 60 | 53.13 N | 7.58 W |
| Brotton | 56 | 54.34 N | 0.56 W |
| Brough, Eng., U.K. | 56 | 54.32 N | 2.19 W |
| Brough, Eng., U.K. | 56 | 53.44 N | 0.35 W |
| Brough, Scot., U.K. | 58 | 58.39 N | 3.20 W |
| Brough Head ≻ | 58 | 59.08 N | 3.17 W |
| Broughshane | 60 | 54.54 N | 6.12 W |
| Broughton, Eng., U.K. | 54 | 52.23 N | 0.46 W |
| Broughton, Scot., U.K. | 58 | 55.37 N | 3.25 W |
| Broughton in Furness | 56 | 54.17 N | 3.12 W |
| Broughton Island I | 94 | 67.35 N | 63.50 W |
| Broughtown | 58 | 59.15 N | 2.36 W |
| Broughty Ferry | 58 | 56.28 N | 2.53 W |
| Brown Clee Hill ∧[2] | 54 | 52.28 N | 2.35 W |
| Brown Gelly ∧[2] | 54 | 50.32 N | 4.32 W |
| Brownhills | 54 | 52.39 N | 1.55 W |
| Brownsville | 96 | 25.54 N | 97.30 W |
| Brown Willy ∧[2] | 54 | 50.35 N | 4.36 W |
| Browse Island I | 92 | 14.07 S | 123.33 E |
| Bruay-en-Artois | 68 | 50.29 N | 2.33 E |
| Bruce, Mount ∧ | 92 | 22.36 S | 118.08 E |
| Bruchsal | 66 | 49.07 N | 8.35 E |
| Bruck an der Mur | 66 | 47.25 N | 15.16 E |
| Brue ≃ | 54 | 51.13 N | 3.00 W |
| Bruff | 60 | 52.29 N | 8.33 W |
| Brugge | 66 | 51.13 N | 3.14 E |
| Brûlé, Lac ⊜ | 94 | 52.17 N | 63.52 W |
| Brunei □[1] | 82 | 4.30 N | 114.40 E |
| Brunsbüttel | 66 | 53.54 N | 9.07 E |
| Brunswick | 96 | 31.10 N | 81.29 W |
| Brunswick, Península de ≻[1] | 102 | 53.30 S | 71.25 W |
| Bruntál | 66 | 49.59 N | 17.28 E |
| Bruree | 60 | 52.26 N | 8.36 W |
| Bruton | 54 | 51.07 N | 2.27 W |
| Bruxelles (Brussel) | 68 | 50.50 N | 4.20 E |
| Bryan | 96 | 30.40 N | 96.22 W |
| Bryher I | 54a | 49.57 N | 6.20 W |
| Brymbo | 54 | 53.06 N | 3.04 W |
| Brynamman | 54 | 51.49 N | 3.52 W |
| Bryn Brawd ∧[2] | 54 | 52.09 N | 3.54 W |
| Bryncethin | 54 | 51.33 N | 3.34 W |
| Brynmawr | 54 | 51.49 N | 3.11 W |
| Brzeg | 66 | 50.52 N | 17.27 E |
| Brzesko | 66 | 49.59 N | 20.36 E |
| Būbiyān I | 84 | 29.47 N | 48.10 E |
| Bucaramanga | 100 | 7.08 N | 73.09 W |
| Buccaneer Archipelago II | 92 | 16.17 S | 123.20 E |
| Buchanan | 86 | 5.57 N | 10.02 W |
| Buchan Gulf C | 94 | 71.47 N | 74.16 W |
| Buchan Ness ≻ | 52 | 57.32 N | 1.48 W |
| Buchara | 76 | 39.48 N | 64.25 E |
| Buckden, Eng., U.K. | 54 | 52.17 N | 0.16 W |
| Buckden, Eng., U.K. | 56 | 54.12 N | 2.05 W |
| Bückeburg | 66 | 52.16 N | 9.02 E |
| Buckfastleigh | 54 | 50.29 N | 3.46 W |
| Buckhaven | 58 | 56.11 N | 3.03 W |
| Buckie | 58 | 57.40 N | 2.58 W |
| Buckingham | 54 | 52.00 N | 1.00 W |
| Buckingham Bay C | 92 | 12.10 S | 135.46 E |
| Buckinghamshire □[6] | 52 | 51.45 N | 0.48 W |
| Buckland Brewer | 54 | 50.57 N | 4.14 W |
| Buckley | 56 | 53.09 N | 3.04 W |
| București | 74 | 44.26 N | 26.06 E |
| Budapest | 66 | 47.30 N | 19.05 E |
| Budaun | 84 | 28.03 N | 79.07 E |
| Bude | 54 | 50.50 N | 4.33 W |
| Bude Bay C | 52 | 50.50 N | 4.37 W |
| Budleigh Salterton | 54 | 50.38 N | 3.20 W |
| Buenaventura | 100 | 3.53 N | 77.04 W |
| Buenos Aires | 102 | 34.36 S | 58.27 W |
| Buenos Aires, Lago (Lago General Carrera) ⊜ | 102 | 46.35 S | 72.00 W |
| Buffalo | 96 | 42.54 N | 78.53 W |
| Buffalo ≃ | 94 | 60.55 N | 115.00 W |
| Buffalo Lake ⊜ | 94 | 60.10 N | 115.30 W |
| Bug ≃ | 50 | 52.31 N | 21.05 E |
| Buga | 100 | 3.54 N | 76.17 W |
| Bugle | 54 | 50.24 N | 4.47 W |
| Bugul'ma | 62 | 54.33 N | 52.48 E |
| Buguruslan | 76 | 53.39 N | 52.26 E |
| Buhuși | 74 | 46.43 N | 26.41 E |
| Buie, Loch C | 58 | 56.20 N | 5.52 W |
| Builth Wells | 54 | 52.09 N | 3.24 W |
| Buinsk | 62 | 54.57 N | 48.17 E |
| Buir Nuur ⊜ | 80 | 47.48 N | 117.42 E |
| Buj | 62 | 58.30 N | 41.30 E |
| Bujalance | 70 | 37.54 N | 4.22 W |
| Bujnaksk | 76 | 42.49 N | 47.07 E |
| Bujumbura | 90 | 3.23 S | 29.22 E |
| Bukavu | 90 | 2.30 S | 28.52 E |
| Bukittinggi | 82 | 0.19 S | 100.22 E |
| Bulawayo | 90 | 20.09 S | 28.36 E |
| Buldan | 74 | 38.03 N | 28.51 E |
| Bulgaria □[1] | 50 | 43.00 N | 25.00 E |
| Bulkington | 54 | 52.29 N | 1.25 W |
| Bulloo ≃ | 92 | 28.43 S | 142.30 E |
| Bull Shoals Lake ⊜[1] | 96 | 36.30 N | 92.50 W |
| Buluntuohai ⊜ | 80 | 47.15 N | 87.20 E |
| Bumpus, Mount ∧[2] | 94 | 69.33 N | 112.40 W |
| Bunbury | 92 | 33.19 S | 115.38 E |
| Bunclody | 60 | 52.38 N | 6.40 W |
| Buncrana | 60 | 55.08 N | 7.27 W |
| Bundaberg | 92 | 24.52 S | 152.21 E |
| Bundoran | 60 | 54.28 N | 8.17 W |
| Bunessan | 58 | 56.19 N | 6.14 W |
| Bungay | 54 | 52.28 N | 1.26 E |
| Bungo-suidō ⊔ | 80 | 33.00 N | 132.13 E |
| Bunguran Utara, Kepulauan II | 82 | 4.40 N | 108.00 E |
| Bunia | 90 | 1.34 N | 30.15 E |
| Bunker Group II | 92 | 23.48 S | 152.20 E |
| Bunnahowen | 60 | 54.11 N | 9.54 W |
| Buntingford | 54 | 51.57 N | 0.01 W |
| Buor-Chaja, Guba C | 78 | 71.30 N | 131.00 E |
| Buor-Chaja, Mys ≻ | 78 | 71.56 N | 132.40 E |
| Burao | 88 | 9.30 N | 45.30 E |
| Buraydah | 84 | 26.20 N | 43.59 E |
| Burbage | 54 | 52.31 N | 1.20 W |
| Burdekin ≃ | 92 | 19.39 S | 147.30 E |
| Burdwān | 84 | 23.14 N | 87.52 E |
| Bure ≃ | 54 | 52.37 N | 1.43 E |
| Bureinskij Chrebet ∧∧ | 78 | 50.35 N | 133.35 E |
| Bureja ≃ | 78 | 49.25 N | 129.35 E |
| Burford | 54 | 51.49 N | 1.38 W |
| Burgas | 74 | 42.30 N | 27.28 E |
| Burg [bei Magdeburg] | 66 | 52.16 N | 11.51 E |
| Burgdorf, B.R.D. | 66 | 52.27 N | 10.00 E |
| Burgdorf, Schw. | 68 | 47.04 N | 7.37 E |
| Burgess Hill | 54 | 50.57 N | 0.07 W |
| Burghausen | 66 | 48.09 N | 12.49 E |
| Burghead | 58 | 57.42 N | 3.30 W |
| Burgos | 70 | 42.21 N | 3.42 W |
| Burgstädt | 66 | 50.55 N | 12.49 E |
| Burgsteinfurt | 66 | 52.08 N | 7.20 E |
| Burhaniye | 74 | 39.30 N | 26.58 E |
| Burhānpur | 84 | 21.19 N | 76.14 E |
| Burjasot | 70 | 39.31 N | 0.25 W |
| Burke ≃ | 92 | 23.12 S | 139.33 E |
| Burlington, Iowa, U.S. | 96 | 40.49 N | 91.14 W |
| Burlington, Vt., U.S. | 96 | 44.29 N | 73.13 W |
| Burma □[1] | 82 | 22.00 N | 98.00 E |
| Burn ≃ | 56 | 54.12 N | 1.38 W |
| Burnham | 54 | 51.33 N | 0.39 W |
| Burnham Market | 54 | 52.57 N | 0.44 E |
| Burnham-on-Crouch | 54 | 51.38 N | 0.49 E |
| Burnham-on-Sea | 54 | 51.15 N | 3.00 W |
| Burnhaven | 58 | 57.29 N | 1.47 W |
| Burnie | 92 | 41.04 S | 145.54 E |
| Burnley | 56 | 53.48 N | 2.14 W |
| Burnmouth | 58 | 55.50 N | 2.04 W |
| Burnside ≃ | 94 | 66.51 N | 108.04 W |
| Burntisland | 58 | 56.03 N | 3.15 W |
| Burntwood ≃ | 94 | 56.08 N | 96.30 W |
| Burravoe | 58a | 60.32 N | 1.28 W |
| Burray I | 52 | 58.51 N | 2.48 W |
| Burriana | 70 | 39.53 N | 0.05 W |
| Burrow Head ≻ | 56 | 54.41 N | 4.24 W |
| Burry Holms I | 54 | 51.37 N | 4.18 W |
| Burry Port | 54 | 51.42 N | 4.15 W |
| Bursa | 74 | 40.11 N | 29.04 E |
| Būr Sa'īd (Port Said) | 88 | 31.16 N | 32.18 E |
| Burscough | 56 | 53.35 N | 2.51 W |
| Burslem | 54 | 53.02 N | 2.12 W |
| Būr Sūdān (Port Sudan) | 88 | 19.37 N | 37.14 E |
| Burton Fleming | 56 | 54.08 N | 0.20 W |
| Burton Latimer | 54 | 52.23 N | 0.41 W |
| Burton-upon-Trent | 54 | 52.49 N | 1.36 W |
| Buru I | 82 | 3.24 S | 126.40 E |
| Burundi □[1] | 90 | 3.15 S | 30.00 E |
| Burwell | 54 | 52.16 N | 0.19 E |
| Burwick | 58 | 58.44 N | 2.57 W |
| Bury, Eng., U.K. | 54 | 50.54 N | 0.34 W |
| Bury, Eng., U.K. | 56 | 53.36 N | 2.17 W |
| Bury Saint Edmunds | 54 | 52.15 N | 0.43 E |
| Būshehr | 84 | 28.59 N | 50.50 E |
| Bushey | 54 | 51.39 N | 0.22 W |
| Bushman Land □[9] | 90 | 29.15 S | 20.00 E |
| Bushmills | 60 | 55.12 N | 6.32 W |
| Busko Zdrój | 66 | 50.28 N | 20.44 E |
| Bussum | 66 | 52.16 N | 5.10 E |
| Busto Arsizio | 72 | 45.37 N | 8.51 E |
| Busuanga Island I | 82 | 12.05 N | 120.05 E |
| Bute, Island of I | 58 | 55.50 N | 5.06 W |
| Bute, Kyles of ⊔ | 58 | 55.53 N | 5.13 W |
| Bute, Sound of ⊔ | 58 | 55.44 N | 5.12 W |
| Butehaqi | 80 | 48.02 N | 122.43 E |
| Bute Inlet C | 94 | 50.37 N | 124.53 W |
| Butler | 96 | 40.52 N | 79.54 W |
| Butlers Bridge | 60 | 54.02 N | 7.22 W |
| Butte | 96 | 46.00 N | 112.32 W |
| Buttermere | 56 | 54.33 N | 3.17 W |
| Butterwick | 54 | 52.59 N | 0.05 E |
| Butterworth | 82 | 5.25 N | 100.24 E |
| Buttevant | 60 | 52.14 N | 8.40 W |
| Butuan | 82 | 8.57 N | 125.33 E |
| Butung, Pulau I | 82 | 5.00 S | 122.55 E |
| Bützow | 66 | 53.50 N | 11.59 E |
| Buxtehude | 66 | 53.28 N | 9.41 E |
| Buxton | 56 | 53.15 N | 1.55 W |
| Büyük Ağrı Dağı (Mount Ararat) ∧ | 50 | 39.42 N | 44.18 E |
| Buzău | 74 | 45.09 N | 26.49 E |
| Búzi ≃ | 90 | 19.50 S | 34.43 E |
| Buzuluk | 76 | 52.47 N | 52.15 E |
| Bwlch | 54 | 51.54 N | 3.15 W |
| Byam Channel ⊔ | 94 | 75.20 N | 105.20 W |
| Byam Martin Island I | 94 | 75.15 N | 104.00 W |
| Bydgoszcz | 66 | 53.08 N | 18.00 E |
| Byfield | 54 | 52.11 N | 1.14 W |
| Byfleet | 54 | 51.20 N | 0.29 W |
| Bylot Island I | 94 | 73.13 N | 78.34 W |
| Byron, Cape ≻ | 92 | 28.39 S | 153.38 E |
| Byron, Isla I | 102 | 47.47 S | 75.12 W |
| Byrranga, Gory ∧∧ | 78 | 75.00 N | 104.00 E |
| Bytantaj ≃ | 78 | 68.46 N | 134.20 E |
| Bytom (Beuthen) | 66 | 50.22 N | 18.54 E |
| Bytów | 66 | 54.11 N | 17.30 E |
| **C** | | | |
| Ca ≃ | 82 | 18.46 N | 105.47 E |
| Cabanatuan | 82 | 15.29 N | 120.58 E |
| Cabeza del Buey | 70 | 38.43 N | 5.13 W |
| Cabimas | 100 | 10.23 N | 71.28 W |
| Cabonga, Réservoir ⊜[1] | 94 | 47.20 N | 76.35 W |
| Cabot Strait ⊔ | 94 | 47.20 N | 59.30 W |
| Cabra | 70 | 37.28 N | 4.27 W |
| Cabrera I | 50 | 39.09 N | 2.56 E |
| Čačak | 74 | 43.53 N | 20.21 E |
| Cáceres | 70 | 39.29 N | 6.22 W |
| Cachimbo, Serra do ∧∧ | 100 | 8.30 S | 55.50 W |
| Cachoeiro de Itapemirim | 100 | 20.51 S | 41.06 W |
| Caçumba, Ilha I | 100 | 17.46 S | 39.17 W |
| Čadca | 66 | 49.26 N | 18.48 E |
| Cader Bronwyn ∧ | 54 | 52.54 N | 3.22 W |
| Cader Idris ∧ | 52 | 52.42 N | 3.54 W |
| Cádiz | 70 | 36.32 N | 6.18 W |
| Cadnam | 54 | 50.55 N | 1.35 W |
| Caen | 68 | 49.11 N | 0.21 W |
| Caergwrle | 56 | 53.07 N | 3.03 W |
| Caerleon | 54 | 51.37 N | 2.57 W |
| Caernarvon | 56 | 53.08 N | 4.16 W |
| Caernarvon Bay C | 52 | 53.05 N | 4.30 W |
| Caerphilly | 54 | 51.35 N | 3.14 W |
| Caersws | 54 | 52.31 N | 3.25 W |
| Cagayan de Oro | 82 | 8.29 N | 124.39 E |
| Cagayan Islands II | 82 | 9.40 N | 121.16 E |
| Cagayan Sulu Island I | 82 | 7.01 N | 118.30 E |
| Cagliari | 72 | 39.20 N | 9.00 E |
| Cagnes | 68 | 43.40 N | 7.09 E |
| Caguas | 98 | 18.14 N | 66.02 W |
| Caha Mountains ∧∧ | 52 | 51.45 N | 9.45 W |
| Caher | 60 | 52.21 N | 7.56 W |
| Caherdaniel | 60 | 51.45 N | 10.05 W |
| Cahirciveen | 60 | 51.57 N | 10.13 W |
| Cahore Point ≻ | 52 | 52.34 N | 6.11 W |
| Cahors | 68 | 44.27 N | 1.26 E |
| Caiabis, Serra dos ∧∧[1] | 100 | 11.30 S | 56.30 W |
| Caiapó, Serra ∧∧ | 100 | 17.00 S | 52.00 W |
| Caibarién | 98 | 22.31 N | 79.28 W |
| Caicos Islands II | 98 | 21.56 N | 71.58 W |
| Cain ≃ | 54 | 52.46 N | 3.08 W |
| Cairndow | 58 | 56.15 N | 4.56 W |
| Cairngorm Mountains ∧∧ | 52 | 57.06 N | 3.30 W |
| Cairnryan | 56 | 54.58 N | 5.02 W |
| Cairns | 92 | 16.55 S | 145.46 E |
| Cairnsmore of Carsphairn ∧ | 56 | 55.15 N | 4.12 W |
| Cairnsmore of Fleet ∧ | 56 | 54.59 N | 4.20 W |
| Cairn Table ∧ | 56 | 55.29 N | 4.02 W |
| Cairn Water ≃ | 56 | 55.07 N | 3.45 W |
| Cairo Montenotte | 72 | 44.24 N | 8.16 E |
| Caister-on-Sea | 54 | 52.39 N | 1.44 E |
| Caistor | 56 | 53.30 N | 0.20 W |
| Cajamarca | 100 | 7.10 S | 78.31 W |
| Cajàzeiras | 100 | 6.54 S | 38.34 W |
| Čajkovskij | 62 | 56.40 N | 54.10 E |
| Čakovec | 72 | 46.23 N | 16.26 E |
| Calabar | 86 | 4.57 N | 8.19 E |
| Calabozo | 100 | 8.56 N | 67.26 W |
| Calahorra | 70 | 42.18 N | 1.58 W |
| Calais | 68 | 50.57 N | 1.50 E |
| Calais, Pas de (Strait of Dover) ⊔ | 52 | 51.00 N | 1.30 E |
| Calama | 102 | 22.28 S | 68.56 W |
| Calamian Group II | 82 | 12.00 N | 120.00 E |
| Călărași | 74 | 44.11 N | 27.20 E |
| Calatayud | 70 | 41.21 N | 1.38 W |
| Calayan Island I | 82 | 19.20 N | 121.27 E |
| Calbe | 66 | 51.54 N | 11.46 E |
| Calcutta | 84 | 22.34 N | 88.20 E |
| Caldas da Rainha | 70 | 39.24 N | 9.08 W |
| Calder ≃ | 56 | 53.44 N | 1.21 W |
| Calder, Loch ⊜ | 58 | 58.31 N | 3.36 W |
| Calder Bridge | 56 | 54.27 N | 3.29 W |
| Caldew ≃ | 56 | 54.54 N | 2.56 W |
| Caldey Island I | 52 | 51.38 N | 4.41 W |
| Caldicot | 54 | 51.36 N | 2.45 W |
| Cale ≃ | 54 | 50.59 N | 2.20 W |
| Caledonian Canal ≊ | 52 | 57.20 N | 4.30 W |
| Calf of Man I | 52 | 54.03 N | 4.48 W |
| Calgary | 94 | 51.03 N | 114.05 W |
| Cali | 100 | 3.27 N | 76.31 W |
| Calicut | 84 | 11.15 N | 75.46 E |
| California □[3] | 96 | 37.30 N | 119.30 W |
| California, Golfo de C | 98 | 28.00 N | 112.00 W |
| Callabonna, Lake ⊜ | 92 | 29.45 S | 140.04 E |
| Callan | 60 | 52.33 N | 7.23 W |
| Callander | 58 | 56.15 N | 4.14 W |
| Callanish | 58 | 58.12 N | 6.43 W |
| Callao | 100 | 12.04 S | 77.09 W |
| Callington | 54 | 50.30 N | 4.18 W |
| Callosa de Segura | 70 | 38.08 N | 0.52 W |
| Calne | 54 | 51.27 N | 2.00 W |
| Calshot | 54 | 50.49 N | 1.19 W |
| Calstock | 54 | 50.30 N | 4.12 W |
| Caltagirone | 72 | 37.14 N | 14.31 E |
| Caltanissetta | 72 | 37.29 N | 14.04 E |
| Caltra | 60 | 53.26 N | 8.25 W |
| Calw | 66 | 48.43 N | 8.44 E |
| Cam ≃ | 52 | 52.21 N | 0.15 E |
| Camagüey | 98 | 21.23 N | 77.55 W |
| Camaiore | 72 | 43.56 N | 10.18 E |
| Camas | 70 | 37.24 N | 6.02 W |
| Ca-mau, Mui ≻ | 82 | 8.38 N | 104.44 E |
| Cambay | 84 | 22.19 N | 72.37 E |
| Camberley | 54 | 51.21 N | 0.45 W |
| Cambo | 56 | 55.10 N | 1.57 W |
| Cambodia □[1] | 82 | 13.00 N | 105.00 E |
| Cambois | 56 | 55.10 N | 1.31 W |
| Camborne | 54 | 50.12 N | 5.19 W |
| Cambrai | 68 | 50.10 N | 3.14 E |
| Cambrian Mountains ∧∧ | 52 | 52.35 N | 3.35 W |
| Cambridge, Ont., Can. | 94 | 43.22 N | 80.19 W |
| Cambridge, Eng., U.K. | 54 | 52.13 N | 0.08 E |
| Cambridge, Mass., U.S. | 96 | 42.22 N | 71.06 W |
| Cambridge Bay | 94 | 69.03 N | 105.05 W |
| Cambridge Fiord C[2] | 94 | 71.20 N | 74.44 W |
| Cambridgeshire □[6] | 52 | 52.20 N | 0.05 E |
| Camden | 96 | 39.57 N | 75.07 W |
| Camden ◆[8] | 54 | 51.33 N | 0.10 W |
| Camel ≃ | 54 | 50.33 N | 4.55 W |
| Camelford | 54 | 50.37 N | 4.41 W |
| Cameron Hills ∧∧[2] | 94 | 59.48 N | 118.00 W |
| Cameroon □[1] | 86 | 6.00 N | 12.00 E |
| Cameroun, Mont ∧ | 86 | 4.12 N | 9.11 E |
| Camiguin Island I | 82 | 18.56 N | 121.55 E |
| Camlad ≃ | 54 | 52.36 N | 3.10 W |
| Camowen ≃ | 60 | 54.36 N | 7.18 W |
| Campana, Isla I | 102 | 48.20 S | 75.15 W |
| Campbelltown | 58 | 57.34 N | 4.02 W |
| Campbeltown | 56 | 55.26 N | 5.36 W |
| Campeche | 98 | 19.51 N | 90.32 W |
| Campeche, Bahía de C | 98 | 20.00 N | 94.00 W |
| Cam-pha | 82 | 21.01 N | 107.19 E |
| Campina Grande | 100 | 7.13 S | 35.53 W |
| Campinas | 100 | 22.54 S | 47.05 W |
| Campobasso | 72 | 41.34 N | 14.39 E |
| Campo de Criptana | 70 | 39.24 N | 3.07 W |
| Campo Grande | 100 | 20.27 S | 54.37 W |
| Campos | 100 | 21.45 S | 41.18 W |
| Campsie Fells ∧∧[2] | 58 | 56.02 N | 4.12 W |
| Camrose | 54 | 51.51 N | 5.01 W |
| Camsell ≃ | 94 | 65.40 N | 118.07 W |
| Can ≃ | 54 | 51.48 N | 0.25 E |


Symbols in the index entries are identified on page 111.

| Name | Page | Lat | Long |
|---|---|---|---|
| Canada □¹ | 94 | 60.00 N | 95.00 W |
| Canadian ≃ | 96 | 35.27 N | 95.03 W |
| Çanakkale | 74 | 40.09 N | 26.24 E |
| Çanakkale Boğazı | 50 | 40.15 N | 26.25 E |
| Canal Zone □² | 98 | 9.10 N | 79.48 W |
| Canarias, Islas (Canary Islands) II | 86 | 28.00 N | 15.30 W |
| Canastra, Serra da ⋌² | 100 | 20.00 S | 46.20 W |
| Canaveral, Cape ➤ | 96 | 28.27 N | 80.32 W |
| Canberra | 92 | 35.17 S | 149.08 E |
| Cangzhou | 80 | 38.19 N | 116.51 E |
| Caniapiscau ≃ | 94 | 57.40 N | 69.30 W |
| Caniapiscau, Lac ⊜ | 94 | 54.10 N | 69.55 W |
| Canicattì | 72 | 37.21 N | 13.51 E |
| Canisp ⋀ | 58 | 58.07 N | 5.03 W |
| Canna I | 58 | 57.03 N | 6.33 W |
| Canna, Sound of ⋃ | 58 | 56.59 N | 6.40 W |
| Cannanore | 84 | 11.58 N | 75.21 E |
| Cannes | 68 | 43.33 N | 7.01 E |
| Cannich | 58 | 57.21 N | 4.46 W |
| Cannich ≃ | 58 | 57.21 N | 4.44 W |
| Cannington | 54 | 51.09 N | 3.04 W |
| Cannock | 54 | 52.42 N | 2.09 W |
| Canonbie | 56 | 55.05 N | 2.57 W |
| Canosa [di Puglia] | 72 | 41.13 N | 16.04 E |
| Cantábrica, Cordillera ⋌ | 50 | 43.00 N | 5.00 W |
| Canterbury | 54 | 51.17 N | 1.05 E |
| Can-tho | 82 | 10.02 N | 105.47 E |
| Cantù | 72 | 45.44 N | 9.08 E |
| Canvey | 54 | 51.30 N | 0.36 E |
| Canvey Island I | 54 | 51.33 N | 0.34 E |
| Çany, Ozero ⊜ | 78 | 54.50 N | 77.30 E |
| Çaolisport, Loch ⊂ | 58 | 55.54 N | 5.37 W |
| Capâjevsk | 62 | 52.58 N | 49.41 E |
| Capanaparo ≃ | 100 | 7.01 N | 67.07 W |
| Cape Barren Island I | 92 | 40.25 S | 148.12 E |
| Cape Breton Island I | 94 | 46.00 N | 60.30 W |
| Cape Coast | 86 | 5.05 N | 1.15 W |
| Capel Curig | 54 | 53.06 N | 3.54 W |
| Cape Town (Kaapstad) | 90 | 33.55 S | 18.22 E |
| Cape Verde □¹ | 86 | 16.00 N | 24.00 W |
| Cape York Peninsula ➤¹ | 92 | 14.00 S | 142.30 E |
| Cap-Haïtien | 98 | 19.45 N | 72.12 W |
| Capim ≃ | 100 | 1.40 S | 47.47 W |
| Cappamore | 60 | 52.37 N | 8.20 W |
| Cappoquin | 60 | 52.09 N | 7.50 W |
| Capri, Isola di I | 72 | 40.33 N | 14.13 E |
| Capricorn Group II | 92 | 23.28 S | 152.00 E |
| Capua | 72 | 41.06 N | 14.12 E |
| Caquetá (Japurá) ≃ | 100 | 3.08 S | 64.46 W |
| Çaç, Slieve ⋀ | 60 | 54.03 N | 9.40 W |
| Cara ≃ | 78 | 60.22 N | 70.02 E |
| Caracal | 74 | 44.07 N | 24.21 E |
| Caracas | 100 | 10.30 N | 66.56 W |
| Caragh, Lough ⊜ | 60 | 52.03 N | 9.52 W |
| Carajás, Serra dos ⋌ | 100 | 6.00 S | 51.20 W |
| Caransebeş | 74 | 45.25 N | 22.13 E |
| Caratasca, Laguna de ⊂ | 98 | 15.23 N | 83.55 W |
| Caratinga | 100 | 19.47 S | 42.08 W |
| Caravaca | 70 | 38.06 N | 1.51 W |
| Caravaggio | 72 | 45.30 N | 9.38 E |
| Carbonia | 72 | 39.11 N | 8.32 E |
| Carbost | 58 | 57.18 N | 6.22 W |
| Carcagente | 70 | 39.08 N | 0.27 W |
| Carcajou ≃ | 94 | 65.37 N | 128.43 W |
| Carcassonne | 68 | 43.13 N | 2.21 E |
| Cárdenas | 98 | 23.02 N | 81.12 W |
| Cardiel, Lago ⊜ | 102 | 48.55 S | 71.15 W |
| Cardiff | 54 | 51.29 N | 3.13 W |
| Cardigan | 54 | 52.06 N | 4.40 W |
| Cardigan Bay ⊂ | 54 | 52.30 N | 4.20 W |
| Cardigan Island I | 54 | 52.08 N | 4.41 W |
| Cardzou | 76 | 39.06 N | 63.34 E |
| Carei | 74 | 47.42 N | 22.28 E |
| Carey, Lake ⊜ | 92 | 29.05 S | 122.15 E |
| Cargill | 58 | 56.30 N | 3.22 W |
| Caribbean Sea ⊤² | 98 | 15.00 N | 73.00 W |
| Cariboo Mountains ⋌ | 94 | 53.00 N | 121.00 W |
| Caribou ≃ | 94 | 59.20 N | 94.44 W |
| Carini | 72 | 38.08 N | 13.11 E |
| Carinish | 58 | 57.31 N | 7.18 W |
| Carisbrooke | 54 | 50.41 N | 1.19 W |
| Carleton, Mount ⋀ | 94 | 47.23 N | 66.53 W |
| Carlingford Lough ⊂ | 60 | 54.04 N | 6.12 W |
| Carlisle | 56 | 54.54 N | 2.55 W |
| Carlow | 60 | 52.50 N | 6.55 W |
| Carlow □⁶ | 52 | 52.50 N | 7.00 W |
| Carloway | 58 | 58.17 N | 6.48 W |
| Carlton | 56 | 52.58 N | 1.05 W |
| Carluke | 56 | 55.45 N | 3.51 W |
| Carmagnola | 72 | 44.51 N | 7.43 E |
| Carmarthen | 54 | 51.52 N | 4.19 W |
| Carmarthen Bay ⊂ | 54 | 51.40 N | 4.30 W |
| Carmel Head ➤ | 54 | 53.24 N | 4.34 W |
| Carmen, Isla I | 98 | 25.57 N | 111.12 W |
| Carmona | 70 | 37.28 N | 5.38 W |
| Carnatic ⋌¹ | 84 | 12.30 N | 78.15 E |
| Carncastle | 60 | 54.54 N | 5.53 W |
| Carndonagh | 60 | 55.15 N | 7.15 W |
| Carnedd Llewelyn ⋀ | 54 | 53.10 N | 3.58 W |
| Carnedd Wen ⋀ | 54 | 52.41 N | 3.35 W |
| Carnegie, Lake ⊜ | 92 | 26.10 S | 122.30 E |
| Carnew | 60 | 52.43 N | 6.30 W |
| Carnforth | 56 | 54.08 N | 2.46 W |
| Carnlough | 60 | 54.59 N | 5.59 W |
| Carno | 54 | 52.33 N | 3.31 W |
| Carnoustie | 58 | 56.30 N | 2.44 W |
| Carnsore Point ➤ | 52 | 52.10 N | 6.22 W |
| Carnwath | 58 | 55.43 N | 3.38 W |
| Caroline Islands II | 8 | 8.00 N | 140.00 E |
| Caroni ≃ | 100 | 8.21 N | 62.43 W |
| Carpathian Mountains ⋌ | 50 | 48.00 N | 24.00 E |
| Carpaţii Meridionali ⋌ | 50 | 45.30 N | 24.15 E |
| Carpentaria, Gulf of ⊂ | 92 | 14.00 S | 139.00 E |
| Carpentras | 68 | 44.03 N | 5.03 E |
| Carpi | 72 | 44.47 N | 10.53 E |
| Carra, Lough ⊜ | 60 | 53.42 N | 9.16 W |
| Carradale | 58 | 55.35 N | 5.28 W |
| Carrantoohill ⋀ | 52 | 52.00 N | 9.45 W |
| Carrara | 72 | 44.05 N | 10.06 E |
| Carrauntoohill ⋀ | 52 | 52.00 N | 9.45 W |
| Carrbridge | 58 | 57.17 N | 3.49 W |
| Carreta, Punta ➤ | 100 | 14.13 S | 76.18 W |
| Carrick □⁹ | 58 | 55.12 N | 4.38 W |
| Carrickart | 60 | 55.10 N | 7.47 W |
| Carrickfergus | 60 | 54.43 N | 5.49 W |
| Carrickmacross | 60 | 53.57 N | 6.05 W |
| Carrick-on-Shannon | 60 | 53.57 N | 8.05 W |
| Carrick-on-Suir | 60 | 52.21 N | 7.25 W |
| Carrigahorig | 60 | 53.04 N | 8.09 W |
| Carrigaline | 60 | 51.48 N | 8.24 W |
| Carron ≃, Scot., U.K. | 58 | 57.53 N | 7.39 W |
| Carron ≃, Scot., U.K. | 58 | 57.53 N | 4.21 W |
| Carron, Loch ⊂ | 58 | 57.22 N | 5.31 W |
| Carronbridge | 56 | 55.16 N | 3.48 W |
| Carron Valley Reservoir ⊜¹ | 58 | 56.02 N | 4.05 W |
| Carrot ≃ | 94 | 53.50 N | 101.17 W |
| Carrowmore Lake ⊜ | 60 | 54.12 N | 9.47 W |
| Cartier Island I | 92 | 12.32 S | 123.32 E |
| Caruaru | 100 | 8.17 S | 35.58 W |
| Carúpano | 100 | 10.40 N | 63.14 W |
| Carvin | 68 | 50.29 N | 2.58 E |
| Cary ≃ | 54 | 51.09 N | 2.59 W |
| Casablanca (Dar-el-Beida) | 86 | 33.39 N | 7.35 W |
| Casale Monferrato | 72 | 45.08 N | 8.27 E |
| Casanare ≃ | 100 | 6.02 N | 69.51 W |
| Casarano | 72 | 40.00 N | 18.10 E |
| Cascade Range ⋌ | 96 | 49.00 N | 120.00 W |
| Cascais | 70 | 38.42 N | 9.25 W |
| Cascina | 72 | 43.41 N | 10.33 E |
| Caserta | 72 | 41.04 N | 14.20 E |
| Cashel, Eire | 60 | 53.25 N | 9.48 W |
| Cashel, Eire | 60 | 52.31 N | 7.53 W |
| Casiquiare, Brazo ≃ | 100 | 2.01 N | 67.07 W |
| Cáslav | 66 | 49.54 N | 15.23 E |
| Casper | 96 | 42.51 N | 106.19 W |
| Caspian Sea ⊤² | 76 | 42.00 N | 50.30 E |
| Cassai (Kasai) ≃ | 90 | 3.06 S | 16.57 E |
| Cassano allo Ionio | 72 | 39.47 N | 16.20 E |
| Cassia Mountains ⋌ | 96 | 59.00 N | 129.00 W |
| Cassino | 72 | 41.30 N | 13.49 E |
| Cassley ≃ | 58 | 57.58 N | 4.35 W |
| Castel | 55b | 49.28 N | 2.34 W |
| Castelfranco Veneto | 72 | 45.40 N | 11.55 E |
| Castellammare del Golfo ⊂ | 72 | 38.01 N | 12.53 E |
| Castellaneta | 72 | 40.42 N | 14.29 E |
| Castellón de la Plana | 70 | 39.59 N | 0.02 W |
| Castelo Branco | 70 | 39.49 N | 7.30 W |
| Castelsarrasin | 68 | 44.02 N | 1.06 E |
| Castelvetrano | 72 | 37.41 N | 12.47 E |
| Castilla | 100 | 5.12 S | 80.38 W |
| Castillo, Pampa del ⋌² | 102 | 45.58 S | 68.24 W |
| Castle Acre | 54 | 52.42 N | 0.41 E |
| Castlebar | 60 | 53.52 N | 9.17 W |
| Castlebay | 58 | 56.57 N | 7.29 W |
| Castlebellingham | 60 | 53.54 N | 6.23 W |
| Castleblayney | 60 | 54.07 N | 6.44 W |
| Castle Cary | 54 | 51.06 N | 2.31 W |
| Castlecomer | 60 | 52.48 N | 7.12 W |
| Castlederg | 60 | 54.42 N | 7.36 W |
| Castledermot | 60 | 52.55 N | 6.50 W |
| Castle Donington | 56 | 52.51 N | 1.19 W |
| Castle Douglas | 56 | 54.57 N | 3.56 W |
| Castlefin | 60 | 54.47 N | 7.35 W |
| Castleford | 56 | 53.44 N | 1.21 W |
| Castleisland | 60 | 52.14 N | 9.27 W |
| Castlemaine | 60 | 52.09 N | 9.43 W |
| Castlemartyr | 60 | 51.55 N | 8.03 W |
| Castlepollard | 60 | 53.40 N | 7.17 W |
| Castlerea | 60 | 53.46 N | 8.29 W |
| Castlereagh ≃ | 60 | 54.33 N | 5.48 W |
| Castlereagh ≃ | 92 | 30.12 S | 147.32 E |
| Castleside | 56 | 54.50 N | 1.52 W |
| Castleton, Eng., U.K. | 56 | 54.28 N | 0.56 W |
| Castleton, Eng., U.K. | 56 | 53.21 N | 1.46 W |
| Castletown, Eire | 60 | 53.26 N | 7.38 W |
| Castletown, I. of Man | 56 | 54.04 N | 4.40 W |
| Castletown, Scot., U.K. | 58 | 58.35 N | 3.23 W |
| Castletown Bere (Castletown Bearhaven) | 60 | 51.39 N | 9.55 W |
| Castletownroche | 60 | 52.10 N | 8.28 W |
| Castletownshend | 60 | 51.32 N | 9.11 W |
| Castlewellan | 60 | 54.16 N | 5.57 W |
| Castres | 68 | 43.36 N | 2.15 E |
| Castries | 98 | 14.01 N | 61.00 W |
| Castro del Rio | 70 | 37.41 N | 4.28 W |
| Catamarca | 102 | 28.28 S | 65.47 W |
| Catanduanes Island I | 82 | 13.45 N | 124.15 E |
| Catanduva | 100 | 21.08 S | 48.58 W |
| Catania | 72 | 37.30 N | 15.06 E |
| Catanzaro | 72 | 38.54 N | 16.36 E |
| Catastrophe, Cape ➤ | 92 | 34.59 S | 136.00 E |
| Catbalogan | 82 | 11.46 N | 124.53 E |
| Cat Island I | 98 | 24.27 N | 75.30 W |
| Catlodge | 58 | 57.00 N | 4.15 W |
| Catoche, Cabo ➤ | 98 | 21.35 N | 87.05 W |
| Cato Island I | 92 | 23.15 S | 155.32 E |
| Catrimani | 100 | 0.28 N | 61.44 W |
| Catrine | 58 | 55.30 N | 4.20 W |
| Catterick | 56 | 54.22 N | 1.38 W |
| Catterick Camp | 56 | 54.22 N | 1.43 W |
| Cattolica | 72 | 43.58 N | 12.44 E |
| Catton | 56 | 54.55 N | 2.15 W |
| Cauca ≃ | 100 | 8.54 N | 74.28 W |
| Cauldcleuch Head ⋀ | 56 | 55.18 N | 2.51 W |
| Caulkerbush | 56 | 54.54 N | 3.41 W |
| Caunskaja Guba ⊂ | 78 | 69.20 N | 170.00 E |
| Caura ≃ | 100 | 7.38 N | 64.53 W |
| Cava de' Tirreni | 72 | 40.42 N | 14.42 E |
| Cavaillon | 68 | 43.50 N | 5.02 E |
| Cavalla (Cavally) ≃ | 86 | 4.00 N | 7.21 W |
| Cavan | 60 | 54.00 N | 7.21 W |
| Cavan □⁶ | 52 | 53.55 N | 7.30 W |
| Caviana, Ilha I | 100 | 0.10 N | 50.10 W |
| Cavite | 82 | 14.29 N | 120.55 E |
| Cawdor | 58 | 57.31 N | 3.56 W |
| Cawood | 56 | 53.50 N | 1.07 W |
| Cawston | 56 | 52.46 N | 1.10 E |
| Caxias | 100 | 4.50 S | 43.21 W |
| Cayambe ⋀¹ | 100 | 0.02 N | 77.59 W |
| Cayenne | 100 | 4.56 N | 52.20 W |
| Cayman Brac I | 98 | 19.43 N | 79.49 W |
| Cayman Islands □² | 98 | 19.30 N | 80.40 W |
| Çeanannus Mór | 60 | 53.44 N | 6.53 W |
| Çeboksary | 62 | 56.09 N | 47.15 E |
| Cebu | 82 | 10.18 N | 123.54 E |
| Cebu I | 82 | 10.20 N | 123.30 E |
| Cechov | 62 | 55.09 N | 37.27 E |
| Cecina | 72 | 43.19 N | 10.31 E |
| Cedar Lake ⊜¹ | 94 | 53.10 N | 100.00 W |
| Cedar Rapids | 96 | 41.59 N | 91.40 W |
| Cedros, Isla I | 98 | 28.12 N | 115.15 W |
| Cefalù | 72 | 38.02 N | 14.01 E |
| Cefni ≃ | 56 | 53.14 N | 4.23 W |
| Ceglèd | 66 | 47.10 N | 19.48 E |
| Ceglie Messapico | 72 | 40.39 N | 17.31 E |
| Cehegín | 70 | 38.06 N | 1.48 W |
| Ceiriog ≃ | 56 | 52.57 N | 3.27 W |
| Cel´abinsk | 76 | 55.10 N | 61.24 E |
| Celaya | 98 | 20.31 N | 100.49 W |
| Celebes Sea ⊤² | 82 | 3.00 N | 122.00 E |
| Celinograd | 76 | 51.10 N | 71.30 E |
| Celje | 72 | 46.14 N | 15.16 E |
| Celkar | 76 | 47.50 N | 59.36 E |
| Cellar Head ➤ | 58 | 58.26 N | 6.10 W |
| Cel´uskin, Mys ➤ | 78 | 77.45 N | 104.20 E |
| Cemaes Head ➤ | 54 | 52.07 N | 4.44 W |
| Cemerno | 74 | 43.11 N | 18.37 E |
| Cemmaes | 54 | 52.37 N | 3.42 W |
| Cenderawasih, Teluk ⊂ | 82 | 2.30 S | 135.20 E |
| Cento | 72 | 44.43 N | 11.17 E |
| Central □⁴ | 52 | 56.15 N | 4.00 W |
| Central, Cordillera ⋌, Bol. | 100 | 18.30 S | 64.55 W |
| Central, Cordillera ⋌, Col. | 100 | 5.00 N | 75.00 W |
| Central, Cordillera ⋌, Perú | 100 | 8.00 S | 77.00 W |
| Central, Planalto ⋌¹ | 100 | 18.00 S | 47.00 W |
| Central, Sistema ⋌ | 50 | 40.30 N | 5.00 W |
| Central African Empire □¹ | 88 | 7.00 N | 20.00 E |
| Central Makrān Range ⋌ | 84 | 26.40 N | 64.30 E |
| Çerdyn | 62 | 60.23 N | 56.24 E |
| Çeremchovo | 78 | 53.09 N | 103.05 E |
| Çeremušskij | 62 | 61.16 N | 47.12 E |
| Çerepovec | 62 | 59.08 N | 37.54 E |
| Ceri | 54 | 52.03 N | 4.29 W |
| Çerignola | 72 | 41.16 N | 15.54 E |
| Çerkassy | 76 | 49.26 N | 32.04 E |
| Çerkessk | 76 | 44.14 N | 42.04 E |
| Çern'achovsk (Insterburg) | 66 | 54.38 N | 21.49 E |
| Çernavodă | 74 | 44.21 N | 28.01 E |
| Cerne Abbas | 54 | 50.49 N | 2.29 W |
| Çernigov | 76 | 51.30 N | 31.18 E |
| Çernogorsk | 78 | 53.49 N | 91.18 E |
| Çernovcy | 76 | 48.18 N | 25.56 E |
| Cerralvo, Isla I | 98 | 24.15 N | 109.55 W |
| Cerrigydrudion | 56 | 53.02 N | 3.33 W |
| Cerro de Pasco | 100 | 10.41 S | 76.16 W |
| Çerskogo, Chrebet ⋌ | 78 | 65.00 N | 145.00 E |
| Çerven Brjag | 74 | 43.16 N | 24.06 E |
| Cervia | 72 | 44.15 N | 12.22 E |
| Cesena | 72 | 44.08 N | 12.15 E |
| Çeská Lípa | 66 | 50.42 N | 14.32 E |
| Çeská Trebová | 66 | 49.54 N | 16.27 E |
| Çeské Budéjovice | 66 | 48.59 N | 14.28 E |
| Çeský Tešín | 66 | 49.45 N | 18.37 E |
| Çeskaja Guba ⊂ | 76 | 67.30 N | 46.30 E |
| Cessnock | 92 | 32.50 S | 151.21 E |
| Cestos ≃ | 86 | 5.40 N | 9.10 W |
| Çetinje | 74 | 42.23 N | 18.55 E |
| Cetlasskij Kamen', Gora ⋀² | 76 | 64.22 N | 50.45 E |
| Ceuta | 86 | 35.53 N | 5.19 W |
| Chabarovsk | 78 | 48.27 N | 135.06 E |
| Chacewater | 54 | 50.15 N | 5.10 W |
| Chachani, Nevado ⋀ | 100 | 16.12 S | 71.33 W |
| Chad □¹ | 88 | 15.00 N | 19.00 E |
| Chad, Lake (Lac Tchad) ⊜ | 88 | 13.20 N | 14.00 E |
| Chadderton | 56 | 53.33 N | 2.08 W |
| Chadileuvú ≃ | 102 | 37.46 S | 66.00 W |
| Chagos Archipelago II | 8 | 6.00 S | 72.00 E |
| Chaidamupendi ≃¹ | 80 | 37.00 N | 95.00 E |
| Chaîne Annamitique ⋌ | 82 | 17.00 N | 106.00 E |
| Chaîne des Mongos ⋌ | 88 | 8.40 N | 22.25 E |
| Chalfont Saint Peter | 54 | 51.37 N | 0.33 W |
| Chalford | 54 | 51.45 N | 2.09 W |
| Chal'mer-Ju | 62 | 67.58 N | 64.50 E |
| Châlons-sur-Marne | 68 | 48.57 N | 4.22 E |
| Chalon-sur-Saône | 68 | 46.47 N | 4.51 E |
| Chaltel, Cerro (Monte Fitzroy) ⋀ | 102 | 49.17 S | 73.05 W |
| Chalturin | 62 | 58.33 N | 48.50 E |
| Chambal ≃ | 84 | 26.30 N | 79.15 E |
| Chambéry | 68 | 45.34 N | 5.56 E |
| Chambo, Djebel ⋀ | 86 | 35.11 N | 8.42 E |
| Chamonix-Mont-Blanc | 68 | 45.55 N | 6.52 E |
| Champagne ≃¹ | 68 | 48.57 N | 4.30 E |
| Champaqui, Cerro ⋀ | 102 | 31.59 S | 64.56 W |
| Champlain, Lake ⊜ | 96 | 44.45 N | 73.15 W |
| Chandigarh | 84 | 30.44 N | 76.47 E |
| Chandler's Ford | 54 | 50.59 N | 1.23 W |
| Chandrapur | 84 | 19.57 N | 79.18 E |
| Changane ≃ | 90 | 24.43 S | 33.32 E |
| Changbaishan ⋀ | 82 | 42.05 N | 128.00 E |
| Changchun | 80 | 43.53 N | 125.19 E |
| Changde | 80 | 29.02 N | 111.40 E |
| Changdu | 80 | 31.11 N | 97.15 E |
| Changhua | 80 | 24.05 N | 120.32 E |
| Changjiang (Yangtze) ≃ | 80 | 31.48 N | 121.10 E |
| Changli | 80 | 39.43 N | 119.11 E |
| Changsha | 80 | 28.11 N | 113.01 E |
| Changshu | 80 | 31.39 N | 120.45 E |
| Changzhi | 80 | 36.11 N | 113.08 E |
| Changzhou | 80 | 31.47 N | 119.57 E |
| Channel Islands II, Eur. | 52 | 49.20 N | 2.20 W |
| Channel Islands II, Calif., U.S. | 96 | 34.00 N | 120.00 W |
| Chantilly | 68 | 49.12 N | 2.28 E |
| Chantrey Inlet ⊂ | 94 | 67.48 N | 96.20 W |
| Chanty-Mansijsk | 76 | 61.00 N | 69.06 E |
| Chaoan | 80 | 23.41 N | 116.38 E |
| Chao Phraya ≃ | 82 | 13.32 N | 100.36 E |
| Chapala, Lago de ⊜ | 98 | 20.15 N | 103.00 W |
| Chapel-en-le-Frith | 56 | 53.20 N | 1.54 W |
| Chapel Point ➤ | 54 | 52.45 N | 0.15 E |
| Chapman, Cape ➤ | 94 | 69.12 N | 88.59 W |
| Chapra | 84 | 23.31 N | 88.33 E |
| Char ≃ | 54 | 50.44 N | 2.54 W |
| Chard | 54 | 50.53 N | 2.58 W |
| Charing | 54 | 51.13 N | 0.48 E |
| Char'kov | 76 | 50.00 N | 36.15 E |
| Charlbury | 54 | 51.53 N | 1.29 W |
| Charleroi | 68 | 50.25 N | 4.26 E |
| Charleston, S.C., U.S. | 96 | 32.48 N | 79.57 W |
| Charleston, W. Va., U.S. | 96 | 38.21 N | 81.38 W |
| Charlestown | 60 | 53.57 N | 8.49 W |
| Charleville-Mézières | 68 | 49.46 N | 4.43 E |
| Charlotte | 96 | 35.14 N | 80.50 W |
| Charlotte Amalie | 98 | 18.21 N | 64.56 W |
| Charlottesville | 96 | 38.02 N | 78.29 W |
| Charlottetown | 94 | 46.14 N | 63.08 W |
| Charlton Kings | 54 | 51.53 N | 2.03 W |
| Charminster | 54 | 50.45 N | 2.35 W |
| Charmouth | 54 | 50.44 N | 2.54 W |
| Charwood Forest ≃³ | 54 | 52.43 N | 1.15 W |
| Charsk | 76 | 49.36 N | 81.30 E |
| Chartres | 68 | 48.27 N | 1.30 E |
| Char Us Nuur ⊜ | 80 | 48.00 N | 92.10 E |
| Chasavjurt | 76 | 43.15 N | 46.35 E |
| Chasetown | 54 | 52.40 N | 1.56 W |
| Chatanga | 78 | 72.55 N | 106.00 E |
| Chatangskij Zaliv ⊂ | 78 | 73.30 N | 109.00 E |
| Châteaubriant | 68 | 47.43 N | 1.23 W |
| Château-Thierry | 68 | 49.03 N | 3.24 E |
| Châtellerault | 68 | 46.49 N | 0.33 E |
| Chatham | 54 | 51.23 N | 0.32 E |
| Chattahoochee ≃ | 96 | 30.52 N | 84.57 W |
| Chattanooga | 96 | 35.02 N | 85.18 W |
| Chatteris | 54 | 52.27 N | 0.03 E |
| Chatton | 56 | 55.33 N | 1.55 W |
| Chauk | 84 | 20.54 N | 94.50 E |
| Chaumont | 68 | 48.07 N | 5.08 E |
| Chauny | 68 | 49.37 N | 3.13 E |
| Chaves | 70 | 41.44 N | 7.28 W |
| Cheadle, Eng., U.K. | 56 | 53.23 N | 2.13 W |
| Cheadle, Eng., U.K. | 56 | 53.24 N | 1.59 W |
| Cheadle Hulme | 56 | 53.22 N | 2.12 W |
| Chech, Erg ≃² | 86 | 25.00 N | 2.15 W |
| Cheddar | 54 | 51.17 N | 2.46 W |
| Cheduba Island I | 84 | 18.48 N | 93.38 E |
| Cheju | 80 | 33.31 N | 126.32 E |
| Cheju-do I | 80 | 33.20 N | 126.30 E |
| Chélia, Djebel ⋀ | 86 | 35.19 N | 6.42 E |
| Chellaston | 56 | 52.54 N | 1.27 W |
| Chelm | 66 | 51.10 N | 23.28 E |
| Chelmer ≃ | 54 | 51.48 N | 0.40 E |
| Chelmno | 66 | 53.22 N | 18.26 E |
| Chelmsford | 54 | 51.44 N | 0.28 E |
| Chelmza | 66 | 53.12 N | 18.37 E |
| Cheltenham | 54 | 51.54 N | 2.04 W |
| Chenāb ≃ | 84 | 29.23 N | 71.02 E |
| Chengde | 80 | 40.58 N | 117.53 E |
| Chengdu | 80 | 30.39 N | 104.04 E |
| Chengshanjiao ➤ | 80 | 37.23 N | 122.42 E |
| Chenxi | 80 | 28.01 N | 110.12 E |
| Chepstow | 54 | 51.39 N | 2.41 W |
| Cherbourg | 68 | 49.39 N | 1.39 W |
| Çeremchovo | 78 | 53.09 N | 103.05 E |
| Cherson | 76 | 46.38 N | 32.35 E |
| Chertsey | 54 | 51.24 N | 0.30 W |
| Cherwell ≃ | 54 | 51.44 N | 1.15 W |
| Chesapeake | 96 | 36.43 N | 76.15 W |
| Chesapeake Bay ⊂ | 96 | 38.40 N | 76.25 W |
| Chesham | 54 | 51.43 N | 0.38 W |
| Cheshire □⁶ | 52 | 53.23 N | 2.30 W |
| Cheshire Plain ≃ | 53 | 53.17 N | 2.40 W |
| Cheshunt | 54 | 51.43 N | 0.02 W |
| Chesil Beach ≃² | 54 | 50.38 N | 2.33 W |
| Chester | 56 | 53.12 N | 2.54 W |
| Chesterfield | 56 | 53.15 N | 1.25 W |
| Chesterfield, Île I | 90 | 16.20 S | 43.58 E |
| Chesterfield, Îles II | 92 | 19.30 S | 158.00 E |
| Chesterfield Inlet ⊂ | 94 | 63.25 N | 90.45 W |
| Chester-le-Street | 56 | 54.52 N | 1.34 W |
| Chet ≃ | 54 | 52.33 N | 1.32 E |
| Cheta ≃ | 78 | 71.54 N | 102.06 E |
| Chevington Drift | 56 | 55.17 N | 1.36 W |
| Cheviot Hills ⋌² | 56 | 55.22 N | 2.22 W |
| Chew Bahir (Lake Stefanie) ⊜ | 88 | 4.40 N | 36.50 E |
| Chew Magna | 54 | 51.22 N | 2.35 W |
| Cheyenne | 96 | 41.08 N | 104.49 W |
| Cheyenne ≃ | 96 | 44.40 N | 101.15 W |
| Chezhou | 80 | 25.48 N | 112.59 E |
| Chi ≃ | 82 | 15.11 N | 104.43 E |
| Chiai | 80 | 23.29 N | 120.27 E |
| Chiang Mai | 82 | 18.47 N | 98.59 E |
| Chiari | 72 | 45.32 N | 9.56 E |
| Chiavari | 72 | 44.19 N | 9.19 E |
| Chiba | 80 | 35.36 N | 140.07 E |
| Chicago | 96 | 41.53 N | 87.38 W |
| Chicapa ≃ | 90 | 6.25 S | 20.47 E |
| Chichester | 54 | 50.50 N | 0.48 W |
| Chickerell | 54 | 50.37 N | 2.30 W |
| Chiclana de la Frontera | 70 | 36.25 N | 6.08 W |
| Chiclayo | 100 | 6.46 S | 79.51 W |
| Chico | 96 | 39.44 N | 121.50 W |
| Chico ≃, Arg. | 102 | 49.56 S | 68.32 W |
| Chico ≃, Arg. | 102 | 43.48 S | 66.25 W |
| Chicoutimi | 94 | 48.26 N | 71.04 W |
| Chidley, Cape ➤ | 94 | 60.23 N | 64.26 W |
| Chieri | 72 | 45.01 N | 7.49 E |
| Chieti | 72 | 42.21 N | 14.10 E |
| Chieveley | 54 | 51.27 N | 1.19 W |
| Chigwell | 54 | 51.38 N | 0.05 E |
| Chihuahua | 98 | 28.38 N | 106.05 W |
| Chilcotin ≃ | 94 | 51.45 N | 122.24 W |
| Chilcott Island I | 92 | 16.58 S | 149.58 E |
| Chilham | 54 | 51.15 N | 0.57 E |
| Chililabombwe (Bancroft) | 90 | 12.18 S | 27.43 E |
| Chilka Lake ⊜ | 84 | 19.45 N | 85.25 E |
| Chillán | 102 | 36.36 S | 72.07 W |
| Chiloé, Isla de I | 102 | 42.30 S | 73.55 W |
| Chilok ≃ | 78 | 51.19 N | 106.59 E |
| Chilpancingo | 98 | 17.33 N | 99.30 W |
| Chiltern Hills ⋌² | 54 | 51.42 N | 0.48 W |
| Chilung | 80 | 25.08 N | 121.44 E |
| Chilwa, Lake ⊜ | 90 | 15.12 S | 35.50 E |
| Chimborazo ⋀¹ | 100 | 1.28 S | 78.48 W |
| Chimbote | 100 | 9.05 S | 78.36 W |
| China □¹ | 80 | 35.00 N | 105.00 E |
| Chinandega | 98 | 12.37 N | 87.09 W |
| Chincha, Islas de II | 100 | 13.38 S | 76.25 W |
| Chincha Alta | 100 | 13.27 S | 76.08 W |
| Chinchaga ≃ | 94 | 58.50 N | 118.20 W |
| Chinchorro, Banco ⋌⁴ | 98 | 18.35 N | 87.20 W |
| Chinde | 90 | 18.37 S | 36.24 E |
| Chindwin ≃ | 84 | 21.26 N | 95.15 E |
| Chingola | 90 | 12.32 S | 27.52 E |
| Chinhae | 80 | 35.09 N | 128.40 E |
| Chin Hills ⋌² | 84 | 22.30 N | 93.30 E |
| Chinju | 80 | 35.11 N | 128.05 E |
| Chinnor | 54 | 51.43 N | 0.56 W |
| Chioggia | 72 | 45.13 N | 12.17 E |
| Chippenham | 54 | 51.28 N | 2.07 W |
| Chippewa ≃ | 96 | 44.25 N | 92.10 W |
| Chipping Campden | 54 | 52.03 N | 1.46 W |
| Chipping Norton | 54 | 51.56 N | 1.32 W |
| Chipping Ongar | 54 | 51.43 N | 0.15 E |
| Chipping Sodbury | 54 | 51.33 N | 2.24 W |
| Chirgis Nuur ⊜ | 80 | 49.12 N | 93.24 E |
| Chiricahua Peak ⋀ | 96 | 31.52 N | 109.20 W |
| Chiriqui, Golfo de ⊂ | 98 | 8.00 N | 82.20 W |
| Chiriqui, Volcán de ⋀¹ | 98 | 8.48 N | 82.33 W |
| Chirk | 54 | 52.56 N | 3.03 W |
| Chirnside | 58 | 55.48 N | 2.12 W |
| Chirripó, Cerro ⋀ | 98 | 9.29 N | 83.30 W |
| Chiseldon | 54 | 51.31 N | 1.44 W |
| Chittagong | 84 | 22.20 N | 91.50 E |
| Chiume ≃ | 90 | 15.11 S | 21.12 E |
| Chiusi | 72 | 43.01 N | 11.57 E |
| Chiuta, Lake ⊜ | 90 | 14.55 S | 35.50 E |
| Chiva | 70 | 39.28 N | 0.43 W |
| Chivasso | 72 | 45.11 N | 7.53 E |
| Chmel'nickij | 76 | 49.25 N | 27.00 E |
| Chochis, Cerro ⋀ | 100 | 18.04 S | 60.03 W |
| Chodzież | 66 | 52.48 N | 59.25 E |
| Choiseul I | 92 | 7.05 S | 157.00 E |
| Chojnice | 66 | 53.42 N | 17.34 E |
| Chojnów | 66 | 51.17 N | 15.56 E |
| Cholet | 68 | 47.04 N | 0.53 W |
| Cholm | 62 | 57.09 N | 31.11 E |
| Cholmsk | 78 | 47.03 N | 142.03 E |
| Cholsey | 54 | 51.34 N | 1.10 W |
| Chomo Lhari ⋀ | 84 | 27.50 N | 89.15 E |
| Chomutov | 66 | 50.28 N | 13.26 E |
| Chon Buri | 82 | 13.22 N | 100.59 E |
| Ch'ŏngjin | 80 | 41.47 N | 129.50 E |
| Ch'ŏngju | 80 | 36.39 N | 127.31 E |
| Chongqing | 80 | 29.34 N | 106.27 E |
| Chŏnju | 80 | 35.49 N | 127.08 E |
| Chonos, Archipiélago de los II | 102 | 45.00 S | 74.00 W |
| Chop'or ≃ | 76 | 49.36 N | 42.19 E |
| Chor ≃ | 78 | 47.48 N | 134.43 E |
| Chorley | 56 | 53.39 N | 2.39 W |
| Choszczno | 66 | 53.10 N | 15.26 E |
| Chövsgöl Nuur ⊜ | 80 | 51.00 N | 100.30 E |
| Chovu | 78 | 51.37 N | 100.36 E |
| Chrisostomovo | 78 | 60.03 N | 88.57 E |
| Chroma ≃ | 78 | 71.36 N | 144.49 E |
| Chromtau | 76 | 50.09 N | 58.24 E |
| Chu ≃ | 76 | 45.00 N | 67.44 E |
| Chubut ≃ | 102 | 43.20 S | 65.03 W |
| Chudleigh | 54 | 50.36 N | 3.36 W |
| Chulmleigh | 54 | 50.54 N | 3.52 W |
| Chulucanas | 100 | 5.06 S | 80.10 W |
| Ch'unch'ŏn | 80 | 37.52 N | 127.44 E |
| Ch'ungju | 80 | 36.58 N | 127.56 E |
| Chuquicamata | 102 | 22.19 S | 68.56 W |
| Chur | 66 | 46.51 N | 9.32 E |
| Churchdown | 54 | 51.53 N | 2.09 W |
| Churchill ≃, Can. | 94 | 58.47 N | 94.12 W |
| Churchill ≃, Newf., Can. | 94 | 53.30 N | 60.10 W |
| Churchill, Cape ➤ | 94 | 58.46 N | 93.12 W |
| Churchill Falls ⊾ | 94 | 53.35 N | 64.27 W |
| Church Stretton | 54 | 52.32 N | 2.49 W |
| Churn ≃ | 54 | 51.38 N | 1.53 W |
| Churnet ≃ | 56 | 52.50 N | 1.48 W |
| Chuxiong | 80 | 25.02 N | 101.30 E |
| Chyrov | 78 | 52.09 N | 105.09 E |
| Cianjur | 82 | 6.49 S | 107.08 E |
| Ciche, Sgurr na ⋀ | 58 | 57.01 N | 5.27 W |
| Ciechanów | 66 | 52.53 N | 20.38 E |
| Ciego de Avila | 98 | 21.51 N | 78.46 W |
| Cienfuegos | 98 | 22.09 N | 80.27 W |
| Cieszyn | 66 | 49.45 N | 18.38 E |
| Cieza | 70 | 38.14 N | 1.25 W |
| Čikoj ≃ | 78 | 51.02 N | 106.39 E |
| Cilacap | 82 | 7.44 S | 109.00 E |
| Cimarron ≃ | 96 | 36.10 N | 96.17 W |
| Čimbaj | 76 | 42.57 N | 59.47 E |
| Čimkent | 76 | 42.18 N | 69.36 E |
| Ciml'anskoje Vodochranilišče ⊜¹ | 76 | 48.00 N | 43.00 E |
| Cîmpina | 74 | 45.08 N | 25.44 E |
| Cîmpulung | 74 | 45.16 N | 25.03 E |
| Cîmpulung Moldovenesc | 74 | 47.31 N | 25.34 E |
| Cina, Tanjung ➤ | 82 | 5.56 S | 104.45 E |
| Cincinnati | 96 | 39.06 N | 84.31 W |
| Cinderford | 54 | 51.50 N | 2.29 W |
| Çine | 74 | 37.36 N | 28.04 E |
| Cipolletti | 102 | 38.56 S | 67.59 W |
| Circik | 76 | 41.29 N | 69.35 E |
| Ciremay, Gunung ⋀¹ | 82 | 6.54 S | 108.24 E |
| Cirencester | 54 | 51.44 N | 1.59 W |
| Ciriè | 72 | 45.14 N | 7.36 E |
| Çirpan | 74 | 42.12 N | 25.20 E |
| Cistopol' | 62 | 55.21 N | 50.37 E |
| Čita | 78 | 52.03 N | 113.30 E |
| Citlaltépetl, Volcán ⋀¹ | 98 | 19.01 N | 97.16 W |
| Città di Castello | 72 | 43.27 N | 12.14 E |
| Cittanova | 72 | 38.21 N | 16.05 E |
| Ciudad Bolívar | 100 | 8.08 N | 63.33 W |
| Ciudad del Carmen | 98 | 18.38 N | 91.50 W |
| Ciudad de México (Mexico City) | 98 | 19.24 N | 99.09 W |
| Ciudad de Valles | 98 | 21.59 N | 99.01 W |
| Ciudadela | 70 | 40.02 N | 3.50 E |
| Ciudad Guayana | 100 | 8.22 N | 62.40 W |
| Ciudad Guzmán | 98 | 19.41 N | 103.29 W |
| Ciudad Juárez | 98 | 31.44 N | 106.29 W |
| Ciudad Mante | 98 | 22.44 N | 98.57 W |
| Ciudad Obregón | 98 | 27.29 N | 109.56 W |
| Ciudad Ojeda | 100 | 10.12 N | 71.19 W |
| Ciudad Real | 70 | 38.59 N | 3.56 W |
| Ciudad Rodrigo | 70 | 40.36 N | 6.32 W |
| Ciudad Victoria | 98 | 23.44 N | 99.08 W |
| Civil'sk | 62 | 55.53 N | 47.29 E |
| Civitanova Marche | 72 | 43.18 N | 13.44 E |
| Civitavecchia | 72 | 42.06 N | 11.48 E |
| Čkalovsk | 62 | 56.46 N | 43.16 E |
| Clachan | 58 | 55.45 N | 5.34 W |
| Clachnaharry | 58 | 57.30 N | 3.46 W |
| Clacton-on-Sea | 54 | 51.48 N | 1.09 E |
| Cladich | 58 | 56.21 N | 5.05 W |
| Claerwen ≃ | 54 | 52.14 N | 3.37 W |
| Claerwen Reservoir ⊜¹ | 54 | 52.17 N | 3.43 W |
| Claire, Lake ⊜ | 94 | 58.30 N | 112.00 W |
| Clane | 60 | 53.18 N | 6.41 W |
| Claonaig | 58 | 55.46 N | 5.22 W |
| Clara | 60 | 53.20 N | 7.37 W |
| Clarecastle | 60 | 52.49 N | 8.57 W |
| Clare ≃ | 60 | 53.20 N | 9.03 W |
| Clare □⁶ | 52 | 52.50 N | 9.00 W |
| Clare I | 60 | 53.47 N | 6.29 W |
| Clare Island I | 60 | 53.48 N | 10.00 W |
| Claremorris | 60 | 53.44 N | 9.00 W |
| Clarence Strait ⋃ | 92 | 12.00 S | 131.00 E |
| Clark Hill Lake ⊜¹ | 96 | 33.50 N | 82.20 W |
| Clarksburg | 96 | 39.17 N | 80.21 W |
| Claro ≃ | 100 | 19.08 S | 50.40 W |
| Clashmore | 58 | 57.50 N | 7.48 W |
| Claughton | 56 | 55.05 N | 4.17 W |
| Clausthal-Zellerfeld | 66 | 51.48 N | 10.20 E |
| Clay Cross | 56 | 53.11 N | 1.25 W |
| Claydon | 54 | 52.06 N | 1.07 E |
| Clayton | 56 | 53.47 N | 1.52 W |
| Clayton-le-Moors | 56 | 53.47 N | 2.23 W |
| Clear, Cape ➤ | 52 | 51.24 N | 9.30 W |
| Clear Island I | 52 | 51.26 N | 9.30 W |
| Clearwater | 96 | 27.58 N | 82.48 W |
| Clearwater ≃ | 94 | 56.44 N | 111.25 W |
| Cleator Moor | 56 | 54.31 N | 3.30 W |
| Clee Hills ⋌² | 54 | 52.25 N | 2.35 W |
| Cleethorpes | 56 | 53.34 N | 0.02 W |
| Cleeve Cloud ⋀² | 54 | 51.56 N | 2.00 W |
| Cleggan | 60 | 53.33 N | 10.09 W |
| Cleobury Mortimer | 54 | 52.23 N | 2.29 W |
| Clerke Rocks II¹ | | 55.01 S | 34.41 W |
| Clermont-Ferrand | 68 | 45.47 N | 3.05 E |
| Clevedon | 54 | 51.27 N | 2.51 W |
| Cleveland □⁶ | 52 | 54.33 N | 1.09 W |
| Cleveland | 96 | 41.30 N | 81.41 W |
| Cleveland, Cape ➤ | 92 | 19.11 S | 147.01 E |
| Cleveland Hills ⋌² | 56 | 54.23 N | 1.05 W |
| Cleveleys | 56 | 53.53 N | 3.03 W |
| Cley next the Sea | 54 | 52.57 N | 1.03 E |
| Clifden | 60 | 53.29 N | 10.01 W |
| Clifden Bay ⊂ | 60 | 53.28 N | 10.05 W |
| Cliffe | 54 | 51.28 N | 0.30 E |
| Clifton Gorge ∨ | 96 | 35.36 N | 83.37 W |
| Clingmans Dome ⋀ | 96 | 35.35 N | 83.30 W |
| Clinton | 96 | 41.51 N | 90.12 W |
| Clinton-Colden Lake ⊜ | 94 | 63.58 N | 107.27 W |
| Clipperton I¹ | 8 | 10.17 N | 109.13 W |
| Clisham ⋀ | 58 | 57.57 N | 6.49 W |
| Clitheroe | 56 | 53.53 N | 2.23 W |
| Cloates, Point ➤ | 92 | 22.43 S | 113.40 E |
| Cloghan, Eire | 60 | 53.13 N | 7.53 W |
| Cloghan, Eire | 60 | 54.51 N | 7.56 W |
| Clogheen | 60 | 52.16 N | 8.00 W |
| Clogher | 60 | 54.25 N | 7.10 W |
| Clogher Head ➤ | 60 | 53.48 N | 6.12 W |
| Cloghjordan | 60 | 52.57 N | 8.02 W |
| Clonakilty | 60 | 51.37 N | 8.54 W |
| Clonakilty Bay ⊂ | 60 | 51.35 N | 8.50 W |
| Clonbur | 60 | 53.32 N | 9.21 W |
| Clondalkin | 60 | 53.19 N | 6.24 W |
| Clones | 60 | 54.11 N | 7.15 W |
| Clonfert | 60 | 53.14 N | 8.05 W |
| Clonmel | 60 | 52.21 N | 7.42 W |
| Clonroche | 60 | 52.27 N | 6.43 W |
| Cloone | 60 | 53.57 N | 7.47 W |
| Cloppenburg | 66 | 52.50 N | 8.02 E |
| Clough | 60 | 54.19 N | 5.50 W |
| Clova, Glen ∨ | 58 | 56.50 N | 3.04 W |
| Clovelly | 54 | 50.58 N | 4.24 W |
| Clovenfords | 56 | 55.37 N | 2.58 W |
| Clowne | 56 | 53.17 N | 1.16 W |
| Cloyne | 60 | 51.52 N | 8.06 W |
| Cluanie, Loch ⊜ | 58 | 57.08 N | 5.05 W |
| Clun | 54 | 52.26 N | 3.02 W |
| Clun ≃ | 54 | 52.22 N | 2.53 W |
| Clun Forest ≃³ | 54 | 52.27 N | 3.07 W |
| Clunie Water ≃³ | 58 | 57.00 N | 3.23 W |
| Clwyd □⁶ | 52 | 53.05 N | 3.20 W |
| Clwyd ≃ | 56 | 53.19 N | 3.30 W |
| Clwyd, Vale of ∨ | 56 | 53.10 N | 3.25 W |
| Clydach | 54 | 51.42 N | 3.54 W |
| Clyde ≃ | 58 | 55.56 N | 4.29 W |
| Clyde, Firth of ⊂¹ | 58 | 55.42 N | 5.00 W |
| Clydebank | 58 | 55.54 N | 4.24 W |
| Clynnog-fawr | 56 | 53.01 N | 4.23 W |
| Cnoc Moy ⋀² | 58 | 55.18 N | 5.41 W |
| Coachford | 60 | 51.54 N | 8.48 W |
| Coahuila □³ | 98 | 27.00 N | 103.00 W |
| Coalburn | 56 | 55.36 N | 3.53 W |
| Coalisland | 60 | 54.32 N | 6.42 W |
| Coalville | 56 | 52.44 N | 1.20 W |
| Coari | 100 | 4.05 S | 63.08 W |
| Coast Mountains ⋌ | 94 | 55.00 N | 129.00 W |
| Coast Ranges ⋌ | 96 | 41.00 N | 123.30 W |
| Coatbridge | 58 | 55.52 N | 4.01 W |
| Coatzacoalcos | 98 | 18.09 N | 94.25 W |
| Cobalt | 96 | 47.24 N | 79.41 W |
| Cobán | 98 | 15.29 N | 90.19 W |
| Cobar | 92 | 31.27 S | 145.48 E |
| Cobh | 60 | 51.51 N | 8.17 W |
| Cobham | 54 | 51.20 N | 0.25 W |
| Cobham | 54 | 53.15 N | 93.58 W |
| Coburg Peninsula ➤¹ | 92 | 11.20 S | 132.15 E |
| Coburg | 66 | 50.15 N | 10.58 E |
| Cochabamba | 100 | 17.24 S | 66.09 W |
| Cochin | 84 | 9.58 N | 76.15 E |
| Cochrane, Lago (Lago Puyerredón) ⊜ | 102 | 47.20 S | 72.00 W |
| Cock Bridge | 58 | 57.09 N | 3.14 W |
| Cockburnspath | 58 | 55.56 N | 2.21 W |
| Cockenzie | 58 | 55.58 N | 2.58 W |
| Cockermouth | 56 | 54.40 N | 3.21 W |
| Coco ≃ | 98 | 15.00 N | 83.10 W |
| Coco, Isla del I | 98 | 5.32 N | 87.04 W |
| Cocoa | 96 | 28.21 N | 80.44 W |
| Coco Channel ⋃ | 82 | 13.45 N | 93.00 E |
| Cocos Islands II | 82 | 14.05 N | 93.18 E |
| Cod ≃ | 54 | 54.10 N | 1.22 W |
| Cod, Cape ➤ | 96 | 41.42 N | 70.15 W |
| Coddenham | 54 | 52.09 N | 1.08 E |
| Codó | 100 | 4.28 S | 43.53 W |
| Codogno | 72 | 45.09 N | 9.42 E |
| Codsall | 54 | 52.38 N | 2.12 W |
| Coetivy Island I | 7 | 7.08 S | 56.16 E |
| Coffin Bay ⊂ | 92 | 34.27 S | 135.19 E |
| Coggeshall | 54 | 51.52 N | 0.41 E |
| Cognac | 68 | 45.42 N | 0.20 W |
| Coiba, Isla de I | 98 | 7.27 N | 81.45 W |
| Coig (Coyle) ≃ | 102 | 50.58 S | 69.11 W |
| Coigeach, Rubha ➤ | 58 | 58.06 N | 5.26 W |
| Coimbatore | 84 | 11.00 N | 76.57 E |
| Coimbra | 70 | 40.12 N | 8.25 W |
| Coin | 70 | 36.40 N | 4.45 W |
| Coipasa, Salar de ≃ | 100 | 19.26 S | 68.09 W |
| Coire, Loch ⊜ | 58 | 58.13 N | 4.21 W |
| Cojbalsan | 80 | 48.04 N | 114.50 E |
| Colatina | 100 | 19.32 S | 40.37 W |
| Colchester | 54 | 51.54 N | 0.54 E |
| Coldbackie | 58 | 58.33 N | 4.23 W |
| Cold Fell ⋀ | 56 | 54.54 N | 2.36 W |
| Coldingham | 58 | 55.53 N | 2.10 W |
| Coldstream | 56 | 55.39 N | 2.15 W |
| Coleman ≃ | 92 | 15.06 S | 141.38 E |
| Coleraine | 60 | 55.08 N | 6.40 W |
| Coleshill | 54 | 52.30 N | 1.42 W |
| Colgrave Sound ⋃ | 58 | 60.37 N | 0.58 W |
| Colima | 98 | 19.14 N | 103.43 W |
| Coll I | 58 | 56.39 N | 6.34 W |
| Collier Bay ⊂ | 92 | 16.10 S | 124.15 E |
| Collier Law ⋀² | 56 | 54.46 N | 1.58 W |
| Collieston | 58 | 57.21 N | 1.56 W |
| Colligan ≃ | 60 | 52.06 N | 7.38 W |
| Collingbourne Kingston | 54 | 51.18 N | 1.13 W |
| Collon | 60 | 53.47 N | 6.29 W |
| Collooney | 60 | 54.11 N | 8.29 W |
| Colmar | 68 | 48.05 N | 7.22 E |
| Colmonell | 58 | 55.08 N | 4.55 W |
| Coln ≃ | 54 | 51.46 N | 1.45 W |
| Colne | 56 | 53.52 N | 2.09 W |
| Colne ≃ | 54 | 51.51 N | 1.02 E |
| Colnett, Cabo ➤ | 98 | 30.58 N | 116.19 W |
| Colombia □¹ | 100 | 4.00 N | 72.00 W |
| Colombo | 84 | 6.56 N | 79.51 E |
| Colonsay I | 58 | 56.05 N | 6.10 W |
| Coloradas, Lomas ⋌² | 102 | 43.24 S | 67.24 W |
| Colorado □³ | 96 | 39.30 N | 105.30 W |
| Colorado ≃, Arg. | 102 | 39.50 S | 62.08 W |
| Colorado ≃, N.A. | 98 | 31.54 N | 114.57 W |
| Colorado ≃, Tex., U.S. | 96 | 28.36 N | 95.58 W |
| Colorado Plateau ⋌¹ | 96 | 36.30 N | 108.00 W |
| Colorado Springs | 96 | 38.50 N | 104.49 W |
| Colsterworth | 54 | 52.48 N | 0.37 W |
| Coltishall | 54 | 52.44 N | 1.22 E |
| Columbia, Mo., U.S. | 96 | 38.57 N | 92.20 W |
| Columbia, S.C., U.S. | 96 | 34.00 N | 81.03 W |
| Columbia ≃ | 96 | 46.15 N | 124.05 W |
| Columbia, Mount ⋀ | 94 | 52.09 N | 117.25 W |
| Columbus, Ga., U.S. | 96 | 32.29 N | 84.59 W |
| Columbus, Ohio, U.S. | 96 | 39.57 N | 83.00 W |
| Colville ≃ | 94 | 70.25 N | 150.30 W |
| Colwell | 56 | 55.04 N | 2.04 W |
| Colwyn Bay | 56 | 53.18 N | 3.43 W |
| Colyton | 54 | 50.44 N | 3.04 W |
| Comacchio | 72 | 44.42 N | 12.11 E |
| Combe Martin | 54 | 51.13 N | 4.02 W |
| Comber | 60 | 54.33 N | 5.45 W |
| Comberton | 54 | 52.11 N | 0.02 E |
| Comfort, Cape ➤ | 94 | 64.13 N | 83.17 W |
| Comilla | 84 | 23.27 N | 91.12 E |
| Comiso | 72 | 36.56 N | 14.37 E |
| Comitán | 98 | 16.15 N | 92.08 W |
| Committee Bay ⊂ | 94 | 68.30 N | 86.30 W |
| Comodoro Rivadavia | 102 | 45.52 S | 67.30 W |
| Comorin, Cape ➤ | 84 | 8.04 N | 77.34 E |
| Comoros □¹ | 90 | 12.10 S | 44.15 E |
| Compiègne | 68 | 49.25 N | 2.50 E |
| Comprida, Ilha I | 100 | 24.50 S | 47.42 W |
| Cona ≃, S.S.S.R. | 78 | 52.54 N | 111.06 E |
| Cona ≃, Scot., U.K. | 58 | 56.51 N | 5.10 W |
| Conakry | 86 | 9.31 N | 13.43 W |
| Concarneau | 68 | 47.52 N | 3.55 W |
| Concepción, Chile | 102 | 36.50 S | 73.03 W |
| Concepción, Para. | 100 | 23.25 S | 57.17 W |
| Concepción, Laguna ⊜ | 100 | 17.29 S | 61.25 W |
| Concepción del Uruguay | 102 | 32.29 S | 58.14 W |
| Conception Bay ⊂, Newf., Can. | 94 | 47.45 N | 53.00 W |
| Conception Bay ⊂, Namibia | 90 | 23.53 S | 14.28 E |
| Conchos ≃ | 98 | 29.35 N | 104.25 W |
| Concord | 96 | 43.13 N | 71.32 W |
| Concordia | 102 | 31.24 S | 58.02 W |
| Conegliano | 72 | 45.53 N | 12.18 E |
| Confuso ≃ | 102 | 25.09 S | 57.34 W |
| Cong | 60 | 53.32 N | 9.19 W |
| Congleton | 56 | 53.10 N | 2.13 W |
| Congo (Zaire) (Zaïre) ≃ | 90 | 6.04 S | 12.24 E |
| Congresbury | 54 | 51.23 N | 2.48 W |
| Coningsby | 56 | 53.07 N | 0.10 W |
| Conisbrough | 56 | 53.29 N | 1.13 W |
| Coniston | 56 | 54.22 N | 3.05 W |
| Coniston Water ⊜ | 56 | 54.20 N | 3.04 W |
| Conjuror Bay ⊂ | 94 | 65.45 N | 118.07 W |
| Conn, Lough ⊜ | 60 | 54.04 N | 9.15 W |
| Connaught □⁹ | 60 | 53.45 N | 9.00 W |
| Connecticut □³ | 96 | 41.45 N | 72.45 W |
| Connecticut ≃ | 96 | 41.16 N | 72.21 W |
| Connel Park | 58 | 55.22 N | 4.12 W |
| Connemara ≃¹ | 60 | 53.30 N | 9.45 W |
| Connors Range ⋌ | 92 | 21.40 S | 149.10 E |
| Consett | 56 | 54.51 N | 1.49 W |
| Conselheiro Lafaiete | 100 | 20.40 S | 43.48 W |
| Con Son II | 82 | 8.43 N | 106.36 E |
| Constanţa | 74 | 44.11 N | 28.39 E |
| Constantine | 86 | 36.22 N | 6.37 E |
| Constantine Bay ⊂ | 54 | 50.32 N | 5.01 W |
| Consuegra | 70 | 39.28 N | 3.36 W |
| Contwoyto Lake ⊜ | 94 | 65.42 N | 110.50 W |
| Conway | 96 | 35.05 N | 92.26 W |
| Conway, Vale of ∨ | 56 | 53.17 N | 3.50 W |
| Cookham | 54 | 51.34 N | 0.43 W |
| Cook Islands II | 8 | 20.00 S | 158.00 W |
| Cookstown | 60 | 54.39 N | 6.45 W |
| Cook Strait ⋃ | 93 | 41.15 S | 174.30 E |
| Coolaney | 60 | 54.10 N | 8.37 W |
| Coolgreany | 60 | 52.46 N | 6.15 W |
| Coonoor | 84 | 11.21 N | 76.49 E |
| Cooper Creek ≃ | 92 | 28.29 S | 137.46 E |
| Cootehill | 60 | 54.04 N | 7.05 W |
| Cop | 78 | | |
| Copertino | 72 | 40.16 N | 18.03 E |
| Cope, Cape ➤ | 70 | 37.26 N | 1.30 W |

Symbols in the index entries are identified on page 111.

| Name | Page | Lat | Long |
|---|---|---|---|
| Copiapó I | 102 | 27.22 S | 70.20 W |
| Copinsay I | 58 | 58.54 N | 2.40 W |
| Copparo | 72 | 44.54 N | 11.49 E |
| Coppermine ≈ | 94 | 67.49 N | 115.04 W |
| Copplestone | 54 | 50.49 N | 3.45 W |
| Coquet ≈ | 56 | 55.22 N | 1.37 W |
| Coquet Dale V | 56 | 55.16 N | 1.50 W |
| Coquimbo | 102 | 29.58 S | 71.21 W |
| Corabia | 74 | 43.46 N | 24.30 E |
| Coral Sea ∓[2] | 92 | 15.00 S | 155.00 E |
| Corato | 72 | 41.09 N | 16.25 E |
| Corbeil-Essonnes | 68 | 48.36 N | 2.29 E |
| Corbiere Point ⅄ | 55b | 49.11 N | 2.15 W |
| Corby | 54 | 52.29 N | 0.40 W |
| Corcovado, Golfo ≈ | 102 | 43.30 S | 73.30 W |
| Corcovado, Volcán ▲[1] | 102 | 43.12 S | 72.48 W |
| Córdoba, Arg. | 102 | 31.24 S | 64.11 W |
| Córdoba, Esp. | 70 | 37.53 N | 4.46 W |
| Córdoba, Méx. | 98 | 18.53 N | 96.56 W |
| Corfe Castle | 54 | 50.38 N | 2.04 W |
| Coria del Río | 70 | 37.16 N | 6.03 W |
| Corigliano Calabro | 72 | 39.36 N | 16.31 E |
| Corixa Grande ≈ | 100 | 17.31 S | 57.52 W |
| Cork | 60 | 51.54 N | 8.28 W |
| Cork □[6] | 52 | 52.00 N | 8.30 W |
| Cork Harbour C | 52 | 51.45 N | 8.15 W |
| Corleone | 72 | 37.49 N | 13.18 E |
| Çorlu | 74 | 41.09 N | 27.48 E |
| Cornforth | 56 | 54.42 N | 1.31 W |
| Cornhill | 58 | 57.36 N | 2.42 W |
| Corn Islands II | 98 | 12.15 N | 83.00 W |
| Corno Grande ▲ | 54 | 42.27 N | 13.42 E |
| Cornwall | 94 | 45.02 N | 74.44 W |
| Cornwall □[6] | 52 | 50.30 N | 4.40 W |
| Cornwallis Island I | 94 | 75.15 N | 94.30 W |
| Coro | 100 | 11.25 N | 69.41 W |
| Corofin | 60 | 52.56 N | 9.03 W |
| Coromandel Coast ≈[2] | 84 | 13.30 N | 80.30 E |
| Coronation Gulf C | 94 | 68.25 N | 110.00 W |
| Coronel | 102 | 37.01 S | 73.08 W |
| Coropuna, Nevado ▲ | 100 | 15.31 S | 72.42 W |
| Corpus Christi | 96 | 27.48 N | 97.24 W |
| Corran | 58 | 56.43 N | 5.14 W |
| Corraum Peninsula ⅄[1] | 60 | 54.54 N | 9.53 W |
| Correggio | 72 | 44.46 N | 10.47 E |
| Corrente ≈ | 100 | 13.08 S | 43.28 W |
| Corrib, Lough ⊜ | 52 | 53.05 N | 9.10 W |
| Corrientes | 100 | 27.28 S | 58.50 W |
| Corrientes, Cabo ⅄, Col. | 100 | 5.30 N | 77.34 W |
| Corrientes, Cabo ⅄, Cuba | 98 | 21.45 N | 84.31 W |
| Corrientes, Cabo ⅄, Méx. | 98 | 20.25 N | 105.42 W |
| Corryvreckan, Gulf of ⊔ | 58 | 56.09 N | 5.44 W |
| Corse (Corsica) I | 72 | 42.00 N | 9.00 E |
| Corse, Cap ⅄ | 50 | 43.00 N | 9.25 E |
| Corserine ▲ | 56 | 55.09 N | 4.22 W |
| Corsham | 54 | 51.26 N | 2.11 W |
| Corsock | 56 | 55.04 N | 3.57 W |
| Cortachy | 58 | 56.43 N | 2.58 W |
| Cort Adelaer, Kap ⅄ | 94 | 62.00 N | 42.00 W |
| Cortina d'Ampezzo | 72 | 46.32 N | 12.08 E |
| Corton | 54 | 52.32 N | 1.44 E |
| Cortona | 72 | 43.16 N | 11.59 E |
| Corubal ≈ | 86 | 11.57 N | 15.06 W |
| Coruche | 70 | 41.36 N | 41.35 E |
| Çorum | 74 | 19.01 S | 57.39 W |
| Corumbá ≈ | 100 | 18.19 S | 48.55 W |
| Corvallis | 44 | 44.34 N | 123.16 W |
| Corve V | 54 | 52.22 N | 2.43 W |
| Corve Dale V | 54 | 52.29 N | 2.35 W |
| Corwen | 54 | 52.59 N | 3.22 W |
| Cosby | 54 | 52.33 N | 1.11 W |
| Coseley | 54 | 52.33 N | 2.09 W |
| Cosenza | 72 | 39.17 N | 16.15 E |
| Cosmoledo Group II | 90 | 9.43 S | 47.35 E |
| Cosne-sur-Loire | 68 | 47.24 N | 2.55 E |
| Costa Rica □[1] | 98 | 10.00 N | 84.00 W |
| Costelloe | 53 | 53.17 N | 9.32 W |
| Costessey | 54 | 52.40 N | 1.11 E |
| Coswig | 66 | 51.53 N | 12.26 E |
| Cotabato | 82 | 7.13 N | 124.15 E |
| Cothi ≈ | 54 | 51.52 N | 4.10 W |
| Cotonou | 86 | 6.21 N | 2.26 E |
| Cotopaxi ▲[1] | 100 | 0.40 S | 78.26 W |
| Cotswold Hills ≈[2] | 52 | 51.45 N | 2.10 W |
| Cottbus | 66 | 51.45 N | 14.19 E |
| Cottingham (Haltemprice) | 56 | 53.47 N | 0.24 W |
| Coulommiers | 68 | 48.49 N | 3.05 E |
| Council Bluffs | 96 | 41.16 N | 95.52 W |
| Cougar Angus | 58 | 56.33 N | 3.17 W |
| Couranyne (Corantijn) ≈ | 100 | 5.55 N | 57.05 W |
| Courcelles | 66 | 50.28 N | 4.22 E |
| Courtmacsherry | 60 | 51.38 N | 8.43 W |
| Courtmacsherry Bay C | 60 | 51.35 N | 8.40 W |
| Courtown Harbour C | 60 | 52.38 N | 6.13 W |
| Cove | 58 | 57.51 N | 5.42 W |
| Coventry | 54 | 52.25 N | 1.30 W |
| Cover ≈ | 56 | 54.17 N | 1.47 W |
| Covington | 96 | 39.05 N | 84.30 W |
| Cowal ▲[1] | 58 | 56.05 N | 5.08 W |
| Cowan, Lake ⊜ | 92 | 31.50 S | 121.50 E |
| Cowbridge | 54 | 51.28 N | 3.27 W |
| Cowdenbeath | 58 | 56.07 N | 3.21 W |
| Cowes | 54 | 50.45 N | 1.18 W |
| Cow Green Reservoir ⊜[1] | 56 | 54.40 N | 2.18 W |
| Cowie Water ≈ | 58 | 56.58 N | 2.12 W |
| Cowley | 54 | 51.43 N | 1.12 W |
| Cowplain | 54 | 50.54 N | 1.01 W |
| Coyle, Water of ≈ | 56 | 55.28 N | 4.32 W |
| Cozumel, Isla de I | 98 | 20.30 N | 86.55 W |
| Cradock | 90 | 32.08 S | 25.36 E |
| Craighouse | 58 | 55.51 N | 5.57 W |
| Craignish Point ⅄ | 58 | 56.09 N | 5.32 W |
| Craignure | 58 | 56.28 N | 5.42 W |
| Crail | 58 | 56.16 N | 2.38 W |
| Crailsheim | 66 | 49.08 N | 10.04 E |
| Craiova | 74 | 44.19 N | 23.48 E |
| Crake ≈ | 56 | 54.14 N | 3.03 W |
| Cramington | 56 | 55.05 N | 1.36 W |
| Cranborne Chase ≈[3] | 54 | 50.55 N | 2.05 W |
| Cranbrook, B.C., Can. | 94 | 49.31 N | 115.46 W |
| Cranbrook, Eng., U.K. | 54 | 51.06 N | 0.33 E |
| Cranfield | 54 | 52.04 N | 0.36 W |
| Cranleigh | 54 | 51.09 N | 0.30 W |
| Crateús | 100 | 5.10 S | 40.40 W |
| Crathie | 58 | 57.02 N | 3.12 W |
| Crato | 100 | 7.14 S | 39.23 W |
| Craufurd, Cape ⅄ | 94 | 73.43 N | 84.40 W |
| Craughwell | 60 | 53.13 N | 8.43 W |
| Craven Arms | 54 | 52.26 N | 2.51 W |
| Crawford | 56 | 55.28 N | 3.40 W |
| Crawley | 54 | 51.07 N | 0.12 W |
| Cray ≈ | 54 | 51.55 N | 0.18 E |
| Creagan | 58 | 56.33 N | 5.16 W |
| Creagorry | 58 | 57.26 N | 7.19 W |
| Crediton | 54 | 50.47 N | 3.39 W |
| Cree ≈, Sask., Can. | 94 | 59.00 N | 105.47 W |
| Cree ≈, Scot., U.K. | 56 | 54.52 N | 4.20 W |
| Cree Lake ⊜ | 94 | 57.30 N | 106.30 W |
| Creetown | 56 | 54.54 N | 4.23 W |
| Creeganbaun | 60 | 53.42 N | 9.51 W |
| Creil | 68 | 49.16 N | 2.29 E |
| Crema | 72 | 45.22 N | 9.41 E |
| Cremona | 72 | 45.07 N | 10.02 E |
| Crean, Loch ⊜ | 58 | 56.31 N | 5.00 W |
| Crescent Group II | 82 | 16.31 N | 111.38 E |
| Creswell | 56 | 53.16 N | 1.12 W |
| Creswell Bay C | 94 | 72.35 N | 93.25 W |
| Crevillente | 70 | 38.15 N | 0.48 W |
| Crewe | 54 | 53.06 N | 2.28 W |
| Crewkerne | 54 | 50.53 N | 2.48 W |
| Crianlarich | 58 | 56.23 N | 4.36 W |

| Name | Page | Lat | Long |
|---|---|---|---|
| Criccieth | 54 | 52.55 N | 4.14 W |
| Crick | 54 | 52.21 N | 1.07 W |
| Crickhowell | 54 | 51.53 N | 3.07 W |
| Cricklade | 54 | 51.39 N | 1.51 W |
| Crieff | 58 | 56.23 N | 3.52 W |
| Criffell ▲ | 56 | 54.57 N | 3.38 W |
| Crimmitschau | 66 | 50.49 N | 12.23 E |
| Crinan | 58 | 56.05 N | 5.35 W |
| Croachy | 58 | 57.59 N | 4.14 W |
| Crocketford | 56 | 55.02 N | 3.50 W |
| Croggan | 58 | 56.22 N | 5.42 W |
| Croglin | 56 | 54.49 N | 2.39 W |
| Croick | 58 | 57.53 N | 4.35 W |
| Croker Island I | 92 | 11.12 S | 132.32 E |
| Croker, Cape ⅄ | 92 | 10.58 S | 132.35 E |
| Cromarty | 58 | 57.40 N | 4.02 W |
| Cromarty Firth C[1] | 58 | 57.41 N | 4.07 W |
| Cromer | 54 | 52.56 N | 1.18 E |
| Cromore | 58 | 58.08 N | 6.29 W |
| Crook | 56 | 54.43 N | 1.44 W |
| Crooked Island I | 98 | 22.45 N | 74.13 W |
| Crook of Alves | 58 | 57.37 N | 3.27 W |
| Crookstown | 60 | 51.50 N | 8.50 W |
| Croom | 60 | 52.31 N | 8.42 W |
| Crosby | 54 | 53.30 N | 3.02 W |
| Crossbost | 58 | 58.08 N | 6.23 W |
| Cross Fell ▲ | 52 | 54.42 N | 2.29 W |
| Crossgar | 60 | 54.24 N | 5.45 W |
| Crosshaven | 60 | 51.48 N | 8.17 W |
| Crosshill | 56 | 55.19 N | 4.39 W |
| Cross Lake ⊜ | 94 | 54.45 N | 97.30 W |
| Crossmaglen | 60 | 54.05 N | 6.37 W |
| Crossmolina | 60 | 54.06 N | 9.20 W |
| Crouch ≈ | 54 | 51.37 N | 0.57 E |
| Crowborough | 54 | 51.03 N | 0.09 E |
| Crowland | 54 | 52.41 N | 0.11 W |
| Crowle | 56 | 53.37 N | 0.49 W |
| Crowlin Islands II | 58 | 57.20 N | 5.44 W |
| Crowthorne | 54 | 51.23 N | 0.49 W |
| Croxley Green | 54 | 51.39 N | 0.27 W |
| Croy | 58 | 57.31 N | 4.02 W |
| Croyde | 54 | 51.07 N | 4.13 W |
| Croydon ≈[8] | 92 | 18.12 S | 142.14 E |
| Cruach, Iles II | 8 | 46.00 S | 52.00 E |
| Cruachan, Ben ▲ | 58 | 56.25 N | 5.08 W |
| Cruden Bay | 58 | 57.25 N | 1.50 W |
| Crudgington | 54 | 52.46 N | 2.33 W |
| Crumlin | 60 | 54.37 N | 6.14 W |
| Crummock Water ⊜ | 56 | 54.34 N | 3.18 W |
| Crusheen | 60 | 52.58 N | 8.53 W |
| Cruz, Cabo ⅄ | 98 | 19.51 N | 77.44 W |
| Cruz del Eje | 102 | 30.44 S | 64.48 W |
| Crymmych | 54 | 51.59 N | 4.40 W |
| Csongrád | 74 | 46.43 N | 20.09 E |
| Ču ≈ | 76 | 43.36 N | 73.45 E |
| Ču ≈ | 76 | 45.00 N | 67.44 E |
| Cuando (Kwando) ≈ | 90 | 18.27 S | 23.32 E |
| Cuango (Kwango) ≈ | 90 | 3.14 S | 17.23 E |
| Cuanza ≈ | 90 | 9.19 S | 13.08 E |
| Cuarto ≈ | 102 | 33.25 S | 63.02 W |
| Cuba □[1] | 98 | 21.30 N | 80.00 W |
| Cubango (Okavango) ≈ | 90 | 18.50 S | 22.25 E |
| Čuchloma | 62 | 58.45 N | 42.41 E |
| Cuckfield | 54 | 51.00 N | 0.09 W |
| Cuckney | 56 | 53.15 N | 1.08 W |
| Cúcuta | 100 | 7.54 N | 72.31 W |
| Cuddalore | 84 | 11.45 N | 79.46 E |
| Cuddapah | 84 | 14.29 N | 78.50 E |
| Cudworth | 56 | 53.35 N | 1.25 W |
| Cuenca, Ec. | 100 | 2.53 S | 78.59 W |
| Cuenca, Esp. | 70 | 40.04 N | 2.08 W |
| Cuernavaca | 98 | 18.55 N | 99.15 W |
| Cuffley | 54 | 51.47 N | 0.07 W |
| Cugir | 74 | 45.50 N | 23.22 E |
| Cuiabá | 100 | 15.35 S | 56.05 W |
| Cuiabá ≈ | 100 | 17.05 S | 56.36 W |
| Cuilcagh ▲ | 60 | 54.10 N | 7.48 W |
| Cuillin, Lago de ⊜ | 90 | 3.22 S | 17.22 E |
| Cuito ≈ | 90 | 18.01 S | 20.48 E |
| Cuitzeo, Lago de ⊜ | 98 | 19.55 N | 101.05 W |
| Cukotskij, Mys ⅄ | 78 | 64.14 N | 173.10 W |
| Čukotskij Poluostrov ⅄[1] | 78 | 66.00 N | 175.00 W |
| Culdaff | 60 | 55.18 N | 7.11 W |
| Culdaff Bay C | 60 | 55.19 N | 7.10 W |
| Culiacán | 98 | 24.48 N | 107.24 W |
| Culion Island I | 82 | 11.50 N | 119.55 E |
| Cullen | 58 | 57.41 N | 2.49 W |
| Cullera | 70 | 39.10 N | 0.15 W |
| Cullicudden | 58 | 57.39 N | 4.13 W |
| Cullin, Lough ⊜ | 60 | 53.57 N | 9.12 W |
| Cullin Hills ▲[2] | 58 | 57.15 N | 6.15 W |
| Cullompton | 54 | 50.52 N | 3.24 W |
| Culm ≈ | 54 | 50.46 N | 3.31 W |
| Culrain | 58 | 57.55 N | 4.24 W |
| Cults | 58 | 57.07 N | 2.10 W |
| Culuene ≈ | 100 | 12.56 S | 52.51 W |
| Culvain ▲ | 58 | 56.56 N | 5.17 W |
| Culver, Point ⅄ | 92 | 32.54 S | 124.43 E |
| Cumaná | 100 | 10.28 N | 64.10 W |
| Cumbal, Volcán de ▲[1] | 100 | 0.57 N | 77.52 W |
| Cumberland ≈ | 96 | 39.39 N | 78.46 W |
| Cumberland Islands II | 92 | 20.40 S | 149.08 E |
| Cumberland Peninsula ⅄[1] | 94 | 66.50 N | 64.00 W |
| Cumberland Plateau ▲[1] | 96 | 36.00 N | 85.00 W |
| Cumberland Sound ⊔ | 94 | 65.10 N | 65.30 W |
| Cumbernauld | 58 | 55.58 N | 3.59 W |
| Cumbria □[6] | 54 | 54.30 N | 3.00 W |
| Cumbrian Mountains ▲ | 52 | 54.30 N | 3.05 W |
| Cuminapanema ≈ | 100 | 1.09 S | 54.54 W |
| Cuminestown | 58 | 57.32 N | 2.20 W |
| Cumnock | 56 | 55.27 N | 4.16 W |
| Cumnor | 54 | 51.44 N | 1.20 W |
| Cumwhinton | 56 | 54.52 N | 2.49 W |
| Cúnya ≈ | 78 | 53.31 N | 83.10 E |
| Cun'a ≈ | 78 | 61.36 N | 96.30 E |
| Cunene ≈ | 90 | 17.20 S | 11.50 E |
| Cuneo | 72 | 44.23 N | 7.32 E |
| Cunninghame ▲[9] | 52 | 55.40 N | 4.30 W |
| Cupar | 58 | 56.19 N | 3.00 W |
| Curaçao I | 100 | 12.11 N | 69.00 W |
| Curaray ≈ | 100 | 2.20 S | 74.05 W |
| Curepipe | 90 | 20.19 S | 57.31 E |
| Curicó | 102 | 34.55 S | 71.14 W |
| Currie | 58 | 55.53 N | 3.18 W |
| Curtea-de-Argeş | 74 | 45.08 N | 24.41 E |
| Curtis, Port ⅄[3] | 92 | 24.00 S | 151.30 E |
| Curtis Island I | 92 | 23.38 S | 151.09 E |
| Curuá, Ilha I | 100 | 0.50 N | 49.58 W |
| Curuá ≈ | 100 | 0.48 S | 55.00 W |
| Cushendall | 60 | 55.06 N | 6.04 W |
| Cushendun | 60 | 55.08 N | 6.02 W |
| Cushnie ≈ | 58 | 57.15 N | 7.05 W |
| Cutro | 72 | 39.02 N | 16.59 E |
| Cuttack | 84 | 20.26 N | 85.53 E |
| Cuvier, Cape ⅄ | 92 | 24.05 S | 113.22 E |
| Cuvo ≈ | 90 | 10.50 S | 13.47 E |
| Cuxhaven | 66 | 53.52 N | 8.42 E |
| Cuyo Islands II | 82 | 11.04 N | 120.57 E |
| Cuyuni ≈ | 100 | 6.23 N | 58.41 W |
| Cuzco | 100 | 13.31 S | 71.59 W |
| Cwmbran | 54 | 51.39 N | 3.00 W |
| Cynwyl Elfed | 54 | 51.55 N | 4.22 W |
| Cyprus □[1] | 50 | 35.00 N | 33.00 E |
| Cyrus Field Bay C | 94 | 62.50 N | 64.55 W |
| Czechoslovakia □[1] | 50 | 49.30 N | 17.00 E |
| Czechowice-Dziedzice | 66 | 49.54 N | 19.00 E |

| Name | Page | Lat | Long |
|---|---|---|---|
| Częstochowa | 66 | 50.49 N | 19.06 E |

**D**

| Name | Page | Lat | Long |
|---|---|---|---|
| Dabashan ≈ | 80 | 31.55 N | 109.05 E |
| Dacca | 84 | 23.43 N | 90.25 E |
| Dachau | 66 | 48.15 N | 11.27 E |
| Dagupan | 82 | 16.03 N | 120.20 E |
| Dahlak Archipelago II | 88 | 15.45 N | 40.30 E |
| Dahy, Nafūd ad- ≈[6] | 84 | 22.20 N | 45.35 E |
| Daimiel | 70 | 39.04 N | 3.37 W |
| Daingean | 60 | 53.18 N | 7.17 W |
| Dairsie | 58 | 56.20 N | 2.56 W |
| Dairy | 58 | 55.43 N | 4.43 W |
| Dajianshan ▲ | 80 | 26.42 N | 103.34 E |
| Dakar | 86 | 14.40 N | 17.26 W |
| Dakovica | 74 | 42.23 N | 20.25 E |
| Dalälven ≈ | 50 | 60.38 N | 17.27 E |
| Dalbeattie | 56 | 54.56 N | 3.49 W |
| Dalch ≈ | 54 | 50.52 N | 3.47 W |
| Dale | 54 | 51.43 N | 5.11 W |
| Dalhalvaig | 58 | 58.28 N | 3.53 W |
| Dalhousie, Cape ⅄ | 94 | 70.14 N | 129.42 W |
| Dalkeith | 58 | 55.54 N | 3.04 W |
| Dallas, Scot., U.K. | 58 | 57.33 N | 3.28 W |
| Dallas, Tex., U.S. | 96 | 32.47 N | 96.48 W |
| Dalmally | 58 | 56.24 N | 4.58 W |
| Dalmellington | 56 | 55.19 N | 4.24 W |
| Dalmaspidal | 58 | 56.50 N | 4.14 W |
| Daloa | 86 | 6.53 N | 6.27 W |
| Dalry, Scot., U.K. | 58 | 55.07 N | 4.10 W |
| Dalry, Scot., U.K. | 56 | 55.43 N | 4.44 W |
| Dalton-in-Furness | 56 | 54.09 N | 3.11 W |
| Dalwhinnie | 58 | 56.56 N | 4.14 W |
| Damanhūr | 88 | 31.02 N | 30.28 E |
| Damar, Pulau I | 82 | 7.09 S | 128.40 E |
| Damaraland ≈[3] | 90 | 21.00 S | 17.00 E |
| Damascus → Dimashq | 84 | 33.30 N | 36.18 E |
| Damāvand, Qolleh-ye ▲[1] | 84 | 35.56 N | 52.08 E |
| Damerham | 54 | 50.57 N | 1.52 W |
| Dampier, Selat ⊔ | 82 | 0.40 S | 130.40 E |
| Dampier Archipelago II | 92 | 20.35 S | 116.35 E |
| Danakil Plain ≈ | 88 | 12.25 N | 40.30 E |
| Da-nang | 82 | 16.04 N | 108.13 E |
| Danbury | 54 | 51.44 N | 0.33 E |
| Dane ≈ | 56 | 53.15 N | 2.31 W |
| Danube ≈ | 50 | 45.20 N | 29.40 E |
| Danville, Ill., U.S. | 96 | 40.08 N | 87.37 W |
| Danville, Va., U.S. | 96 | 36.35 N | 79.24 W |
| Danxian | 80 | 34.48 N | 116.03 E |
| Darabani | 74 | 48.11 N | 26.35 E |
| Darbhanga | 84 | 26.10 N | 85.56 E |
| Darchan | 80 | 49.28 N | 105.56 E |
| Dargle ≈ | 60 | 53.11 N | 6.04 W |
| Darjeeling | 84 | 27.02 N | 88.16 E |
| Darlaston | 54 | 52.34 N | 2.02 W |
| Darling ≈ | 92 | 34.07 S | 141.55 E |
| Darling Range ≈ | 92 | 32.00 S | 116.30 E |
| Darlington | 56 | 54.31 N | 1.34 W |
| Darłowo | 66 | 54.26 N | 16.23 E |
| Darmstadt | 66 | 49.53 N | 8.40 E |
| Darnah | 88 | 32.46 N | 22.39 E |
| Darnley, Cape ⅄ | 8 | 67.50 S | 69.30 E |
| Daroca | 70 | 41.07 N | 1.25 W |
| Dart ≈ | 54 | 50.24 N | 3.39 W |
| Dartford | 54 | 51.27 N | 0.14 E |
| Dartmoor ≈[3] | 52 | 50.35 N | 4.00 W |
| Dartmouth, N.S., Can. | 94 | 44.40 N | 63.34 W |
| Dartmouth, Eng., U.K. | 54 | 50.21 N | 3.35 W |
| Darton | 56 | 53.36 N | 1.32 W |
| Darvel | 58 | 55.37 N | 4.18 W |
| Darwen | 56 | 53.42 N | 2.28 W |
| Darwen ≈ | 56 | 53.45 N | 2.41 W |
| Darwin | 92 | 12.28 S | 130.50 E |
| Darwin, Monte ▲ | 102 | 54.45 S | 69.29 W |
| Dasht ≈ | 84 | 25.10 N | 61.40 E |
| Dasht-e Kavir ≈[7] | 84 | 34.40 N | 53.00 E |
| Datong ≈ | 80 | 40.08 N | 113.13 E |
| Datonghe ≈ | 80 | 36.20 N | 102.55 E |
| Datu, Tandjung ⅄ | 82 | 2.00 N | 109.39 E |
| Datu Piang | 82 | 7.01 N | 124.30 E |
| Daugai | 62 | 54.10 N | 24.20 E |
| Daule ≈ | 100 | 2.10 S | 79.52 W |
| Dauphin Lake ⊜ | 94 | 51.20 N | 99.48 W |
| Davangere | 84 | 14.28 N | 75.55 E |
| Davao | 82 | 7.04 N | 125.36 E |
| Davao Gulf C | 82 | 6.40 N | 125.55 E |
| Davenham | 56 | 53.14 N | 2.31 W |
| Davenport | 96 | 41.32 N | 90.41 W |
| Daventry | 54 | 52.16 N | 1.09 W |
| David | 98 | 8.25 N | 82.27 W |
| Davington | 58 | 55.18 N | 3.12 W |
| Daviot | 58 | 57.25 N | 4.08 W |
| Davis Mountains ▲ | 96 | 30.35 N | 104.00 W |
| Davis Strait ⊔ | 94 | 67.00 N | 57.00 W |
| Dawa (Daua) ≈ | 88 | 4.11 N | 42.06 E |
| Dawley | 54 | 52.40 N | 2.28 W |
| Dawlish | 54 | 50.35 N | 3.28 W |
| Dawna Range ≈ | 84 | 16.50 N | 98.15 E |
| Dawros Head ⅄ | 60 | 54.50 N | 8.34 W |
| Dawson, Isla I | 102 | 53.55 S | 70.45 W |
| Dawson Inlet C | 94 | 61.50 N | 93.25 W |
| Dawson Range ≈ | 94 | 62.40 N | 139.00 W |
| Dax | 68 | 43.43 N | 1.03 W |
| Daxian | 80 | 31.18 N | 107.30 E |
| Daxing'anlingshan ▲ | 80 | 49.40 N | 122.00 E |
| Daxueshan ▲ | 80 | 30.10 N | 101.50 E |
| Dayr az-Zawr | 84 | 35.20 N | 40.09 E |
| Dayrūt | 88 | 27.33 N | 30.49 E |
| Dayton | 96 | 39.45 N | 84.15 W |
| Daytona Beach | 96 | 29.12 N | 81.00 W |
| De Aar | 90 | 30.39 S | 24.00 E |
| Dead Sea ⊜ | 84 | 31.30 N | 35.30 E |
| Deal | 54 | 51.14 N | 1.24 E |
| Dean, Forest of ≈[3] | 54 | 51.48 N | 2.30 W |
| Dean Channel ⊔ | 94 | 52.33 N | 127.13 W |
| Deans Dundas Bay C | 94 | 72.15 N | 118.25 W |
| Dearg, Beinn ▲ | 58 | 56.54 N | 4.58 W |
| Dear Reservoir ⊜[1] | 58 | 55.30 N | 1.16 W |
| Dease ≈ | 94 | 59.54 N | 128.30 W |
| Dease Arm C | 94 | 66.52 N | 119.37 W |
| Dease Strait ⊔ | 94 | 68.40 N | 108.00 W |
| Death Valley V | 96 | 36.30 N | 117.00 W |
| Debica | 66 | 50.04 N | 21.24 E |
| Debenham | 54 | 52.13 N | 1.11 E |
| Deblin | 66 | 51.35 N | 21.50 E |
| Debrecen | 74 | 47.32 N | 21.38 E |
| Debre Markos | 88 | 10.20 N | 37.45 E |
| Decatur, Ala., U.S. | 96 | 34.36 N | 86.59 W |
| Decatur, Ill., U.S. | 96 | 39.51 N | 89.32 W |
| Decazeville | 68 | 44.34 N | 2.15 E |
| Děčín | 66 | 50.47 N | 14.12 E |
| Decize | 68 | 46.50 N | 3.27 E |
| Deddington | 54 | 51.59 N | 1.19 W |
| Dee ≈, Eire | 60 | 53.52 N | 6.21 W |
| Dee ≈, Eng., U.K. | 52 | 53.14 N | 3.08 W |
| Dee ≈, Scot., U.K. | 52 | 57.04 N | 2.07 W |
| Dee ≈, Wales, U.K. | 56 | 53.14 N | 3.18 W |
| Dee, Loch ⊜ | 56 | 55.05 N | 4.24 W |
| Deeping Fen ≈ | 54 | 52.44 N | 0.13 W |
| Deerpass Bay C | 94 | 65.58 N | 122.25 W |
| Deer Sound ⊔ | 58 | 58.58 N | 2.48 W |
| Deganwy | 54 | 53.18 N | 3.50 W |
| Degebe ≈ | 70 | 38.20 N | 7.16 W |
| Degendorf | 66 | 48.50 N | 12.57 E |
| De Grey ≈ | 92 | 20.12 S | 119.11 E |
| Dehiwala-Mount Lavinia | 84 | 6.51 N | 79.52 E |
| Dehra Dūn | 84 | 30.19 N | 78.02 E |
| Dej | 74 | 47.09 N | 23.52 E |
| Dej | 50 | 50.57 N | 4.42 W |
| Delabole | 54 | 50.37 N | 4.44 W |
| Delamere Forest ≈[3] | 56 | 53.14 N | 2.38 W |
| Delano ≈ | 96 | 39.10 N | 75.30 W |
| Delaware Bay C | 96 | 39.05 N | 75.15 W |
| Delémont | 68 | 47.22 N | 7.21 E |

| Name | Page | Lat | Long |
|---|---|---|---|
| Delft | 66 | 52.00 N | 4.21 E |
| Delfzijl | 66 | 53.19 N | 6.46 E |
| Delgado, Cabo ⅄ | 90 | 10.40 S | 40.35 E |
| Delhi | 84 | 28.37 N | 77.12 E |
| Delicias | 98 | 28.13 N | 105.28 W |
| Delitzsch | 66 | 51.31 N | 12.20 E |
| Dell | 58 | 58.30 N | 6.20 W |
| Delmenhorst | 66 | 53.03 N | 8.38 E |
| De-Longa, Ostrova II | 78 | 76.30 N | 153.00 E |
| Delorme, Lac ⊜ | 94 | 54.31 N | 69.52 W |
| Delta Peak ▲ | 94 | 56.39 N | 129.34 W |
| Delvin | 60 | 53.36 N | 7.05 W |
| Demidov | 62 | 55.16 N | 31.31 E |
| Demini ≈ | 100 | 0.46 S | 62.56 W |
| Demirci | 74 | 39.03 N | 28.40 E |
| Demjanka ≈ | 78 | 59.34 N | 69.17 E |
| Demmin | 66 | 53.54 N | 13.02 E |
| Dempo, Gunung ▲ | 82 | 4.02 S | 103.09 E |
| Denain | 66 | 50.20 N | 3.23 E |
| Denau | 76 | 38.16 N | 67.54 E |
| Denbigh | 54 | 53.11 N | 3.25 W |
| Denby Dale | 56 | 53.35 N | 1.38 W |
| Dendermonde | 66 | 51.02 N | 4.07 E |
| Denge Marsh ≈ | 54 | 50.57 N | 0.55 E |
| Denham, Mount ▲ | 98 | 18.13 N | 77.32 W |
| Denham Range ▲ | 92 | 21.55 S | 147.46 E |
| Den Helder | 66 | 52.54 N | 4.45 E |
| Denizli | 74 | 37.46 N | 29.06 E |
| Denmark □[1] | 50 | 56.00 N | 10.00 E |
| Dennis Head ⅄ | 58 | 59.23 N | 2.23 W |
| Denny | 58 | 56.02 N | 3.55 W |
| Denpasar | 82 | 8.39 S | 115.13 E |
| Denton | 56 | 53.27 N | 2.07 W |
| D Entrecasteaux, Point ⅄ | 92 | 34.50 S | 116.00 E |
| D'Entrecasteaux Islands II | 92 | 9.30 S | 150.40 E |
| Dera Ghāzi Khān | 84 | 30.03 N | 70.38 E |
| Dera Ismāîl Khān | 84 | 31.50 N | 70.54 E |
| Derbent | 76 | 42.03 N | 48.18 E |
| Derby | 54 | 52.55 N | 1.29 W |
| Derbyshire □[6] | 52 | 53.00 N | 1.33 W |
| Derev'anka ≈ | 62 | 61.34 N | 34.27 E |
| Derg ≈ | 60 | 54.44 N | 7.25 W |
| Derg, Lough ⊜ | 52 | 53.00 N | 8.20 W |
| Déroute, Passage de la ⊔ | 55b | 49.25 N | 2.00 W |
| Derravaragh, Lough ⊜ | 60 | 53.40 N | 7.24 W |
| Derrybrien | 60 | 53.04 N | 8.36 W |
| Derrykeevan | 60 | 55.08 N | 6.29 W |
| Derryveagh Mountains ▲ | 60 | 55.00 N | 8.05 W |
| Dersingham | 54 | 52.51 N | 0.30 E |
| Derventa | 72 | 44.58 N | 17.55 E |
| Derwent ≈, Eng., U.K. | 52 | 53.45 N | 0.57 W |
| Derwent ≈, Eng., U.K. | 52 | 52.50 N | 1.15 W |
| Derwent ≈, Eng., U.K. | 56 | 54.57 N | 1.41 W |
| Derwent ≈, Eng., U.K. | 56 | 54.38 N | 3.34 W |
| Derwent Reservoir ⊜[1] | 56 | 54.50 N | 2.00 W |
| Derwent Water ⊜ | 56 | 54.34 N | 3.08 W |
| Desaguadero ≈, Arg. | 102 | 34.13 S | 66.47 W |
| Desaguadero ≈, Bol. | 100 | 18.24 S | 67.05 W |
| Desborough | 54 | 52.27 N | 0.49 W |
| Deschutes ≈ | 96 | 45.38 N | 120.54 W |
| Dese | 88 | 11.05 N | 39.41 E |
| Deseado ≈ | 102 | 47.45 S | 65.54 W |
| Desengaño, Punta ⅄ | 102 | 49.15 S | 67.37 W |
| Desenzano del Garda | 72 | 45.28 N | 10.32 E |
| Desford | 54 | 52.39 N | 1.17 W |
| Des Moines | 96 | 41.35 N | 93.37 W |
| Des Moines ≈ | 96 | 40.22 N | 91.26 W |
| Desna ≈ | 62 | 50.33 N | 30.32 E |
| Desolación, Isla I | 102 | 53.00 S | 74.10 W |
| Dessau | 66 | 51.50 N | 12.14 E |
| Detmold | 66 | 51.56 N | 8.53 E |
| Deva | 74 | 45.53 N | 22.55 E |
| Dévánánya | 74 | 47.02 N | 20.58 E |
| Deventer | 66 | 52.15 N | 6.10 E |
| Deveron ≈ | 58 | 57.40 N | 2.31 W |
| Devil's Bridge | 54 | 52.23 N | 3.51 W |
| Devil's Water ≈ | 56 | 54.58 N | 2.07 W |
| Devizes | 54 | 51.22 N | 1.59 W |
| Devon □[6] | 52 | 50.45 N | 3.50 W |
| Devon ≈, Scot., U.K. | 58 | 56.06 N | 3.51 W |
| Devon Island I | 94 | 75.00 N | 87.00 W |
| Devonport, Austl. | 92 | 41.11 S | 146.21 E |
| Devonport, Eng., U.K. | 54 | 50.22 N | 4.11 W |
| Dewsbury | 56 | 53.42 N | 1.37 W |
| Dexterity Fiord C[2] | 94 | 71.11 N | 73.03 W |
| Dezhou | 80 | 37.27 N | 116.18 E |
| Dežneva, Mys ⅄ | 78 | 66.05 N | 169.45 W |
| Dhamār | 84 | 14.46 N | 44.23 E |
| Dhānbād | 84 | 23.48 N | 86.27 E |
| Dhaulāgiri ▲ | 84 | 28.42 N | 83.30 E |
| Dherue, Loch an ⊜ | 58 | 58.25 N | 4.27 W |
| Dhodhekánisos II | 74 | 36.10 N | 27.00 E |
| Dhomhnuill, Sgurr ▲ | 58 | 56.45 N | 5.27 W |
| Dhule | 84 | 20.54 N | 74.47 E |
| Diabaig | 58 | 57.34 N | 5.41 W |
| Diable, Ile du I | 100 | 5.17 N | 52.35 W |
| Diaka ≈[1] | 86 | 15.13 N | 4.14 W |
| Diamante ≈ | 102 | 34.30 S | 66.46 W |
| Diamantina | 100 | 18.15 S | 43.36 W |
| Diamantina ≈ | 92 | 26.45 S | 139.10 E |
| Diamond Islets II | 92 | 17.25 S | 150.58 E |
| Dibrugarh | 84 | 27.29 N | 94.54 E |
| Didcot | 54 | 51.37 N | 1.15 W |
| Diego de Almagro, Isla I | 102 | 51.25 S | 75.10 W |
| Diego Ramírez, Islas II | 102 | 56.30 S | 68.44 W |
| Diego-Suarez | 90 | 12.16 S | 49.17 E |
| Dieppe | 68 | 49.56 N | 1.05 E |
| Digby | 94 | 44.37 N | 65.46 W |
| Digne | 68 | 44.06 N | 6.14 E |
| Digoin | 68 | 46.29 N | 3.59 E |
| Digul ≈ | 82 | 7.07 S | 138.42 E |
| Dijon | 68 | 47.19 N | 5.01 E |
| Dikili | 74 | 39.04 N | 26.53 E |
| Dili | 82 | 8.33 S | 125.35 E |
| Dimashq (Damascus) | 84 | 33.30 N | 36.18 E |
| Dimitrovgrad, Blg. | 74 | 42.03 N | 25.36 E |
| Dimitrovgrad, S.S.S.R. | 62 | 54.14 N | 49.39 E |
| Dimlang ▲ | 86 | 8.24 N | 11.47 E |
| Dinan | 68 | 48.27 N | 2.02 W |
| Dinara ▲ | 72 | 44.00 N | 16.35 E |
| Dinard | 68 | 48.38 N | 2.04 W |
| Dinas ≈ | 54 | 52.02 N | 4.54 W |
| Dinas Head ⅄ | 54 | 52.02 N | 4.55 W |
| Dinas Powis | 54 | 51.25 N | 3.16 W |
| Dingalan Bay C | 82 | 15.18 N | 121.25 E |
| Dingle | 60 | 52.08 N | 10.15 W |
| Dingle Bay C | 52 | 52.05 N | 10.15 W |
| Dingle Peninsula ⅄[1] | 60 | 52.12 N | 10.05 W |
| Dingolfing | 66 | 48.38 N | 12.30 E |
| Dingwall | 58 | 57.35 N | 4.29 W |
| Dinkelsbühl | 66 | 49.04 N | 10.19 E |
| Dinnet | 58 | 57.03 N | 2.54 W |
| Dinnington | 56 | 53.22 N | 1.12 W |
| Diourbel | 86 | 14.40 N | 16.15 W |
| Dire Dawa | 88 | 9.37 N | 41.52 E |
| Dirk Hartog Island I | 92 | 25.48 S | 113.00 E |
| Disappointment, Cape ⅄, Falk. Is. | 102 | 54.53 S | 36.07 W |
| Disappointment, Cape ⅄, Wash., U.S. | 96 | 46.18 N | 124.03 W |
| Disappointment, Lake ⊜ | 92 | 23.30 S | 122.50 E |
| Disko I | 94 | 69.50 N | 53.30 W |
| Disko Bugt C | 94 | 69.15 N | 52.00 W |
| Dismal Lakes ⊜ | 94 | 67.26 N | 117.07 W |

| Name | Page | Lat | Long |
|---|---|---|---|
| Disna ≈ | 62 | 55.33 N | 28.10 E |
| Diss | 54 | 52.23 N | 1.07 E |
| Distington | 56 | 54.36 N | 3.32 W |
| Disûq | 88 | 31.08 N | 30.39 E |
| Ditton Priors | 54 | 52.30 N | 2.35 W |
| Divinópolis | 100 | 20.09 S | 44.54 W |
| Divisor, Serra do ▲[1] | 100 | 8.20 S | 73.30 W |
| Dixon Entrance ⊔ | 94 | 54.25 N | 132.30 W |
| Dizzard Point ⅄ | 54 | 50.45 N | 4.38 W |
| Dja ≈ | 90 | 2.02 N | 15.12 E |
| Djawa, Laut (Java Sea) ∓[2] | 82 | 5.00 S | 110.00 E |
| Djerba, Ile de I | 88 | 33.48 N | 10.54 E |
| Djerem ≈ | 86 | 5.20 N | 13.24 E |
| Djerid, Chott ≈≈ | 88 | 33.42 N | 8.26 E |
| Djibouti | 88 | 11.36 N | 43.09 E |
| Djibouti □[1] | 88 | 11.30 N | 43.00 E |
| Djursholm | 64 | 59.24 N | 18.05 E |
| Dmitrija Lapteva, Proliv ⊔ | 78 | 73.00 N | 142.00 E |
| Dmitrov | 62 | 56.21 N | 37.31 E |
| Dnepr ≈ | 76 | 46.30 N | 32.18 E |
| Dneprodzeržinsk | 76 | 48.30 N | 34.37 E |
| Dnepropetrovsk | 76 | 48.27 N | 34.59 E |
| Dnestr ≈ | 76 | 46.18 N | 30.17 E |
| Dno | 62 | 57.50 N | 29.59 E |
| Döbeln | 66 | 51.07 N | 13.07 E |
| Doberai, Jazirah ⅄[1] | 82 | 1.30 S | 132.30 E |
| Doboj | 72 | 44.44 N | 18.05 E |
| Dobromil' | 66 | 49.34 N | 22.47 E |
| Doce ≈ | 100 | 19.37 S | 39.49 W |
| Dochart ≈ | 58 | 56.28 N | 4.20 W |
| Docking | 54 | 52.55 N | 0.38 E |
| Dodman Point ⅄ | 54 | 50.13 N | 4.48 W |
| Dodoma | 90 | 6.11 S | 35.45 E |
| Dogai Coring ⊜ | 80 | 34.30 N | 89.00 E |
| Doetinchem | 66 | 51.58 N | 6.17 E |
| Dole | 68 | 47.06 N | 5.30 E |
| Dolgarrog | 54 | 53.11 N | 3.51 W |
| Dolgellau | 54 | 52.44 N | 3.53 W |
| Dolisie | 90 | 4.12 S | 12.41 E |
| Dollar | 58 | 56.09 N | 3.40 W |
| Dollar Law ▲ | 56 | 55.33 N | 3.17 W |
| Dolphin and Union Strait ⊔ | 94 | 69.05 N | 114.45 W |
| Dolton | 54 | 50.53 N | 4.02 W |
| Dolwyddelan | 54 | 53.03 N | 3.53 W |
| Dombóvár | 66 | 46.23 N | 18.08 E |
| Domeyko, Cordillera ≈ | 102 | 24.30 S | 69.00 W |
| Dominica □[1] | 98 | 15.30 N | 61.20 W |
| Dominican Republic □[1] | 98 | 19.00 N | 70.40 W |
| Dominion, Cape ⅄ | 94 | 66.13 N | 74.28 W |
| Domodossola | 72 | 46.40 N | 8.17 E |
| Domuyo, Volcán ▲[1] | 102 | 36.38 S | 70.26 W |
| Don ≈, S.S.S.R. | 76 | 47.04 N | 39.18 E |
| Don ≈, Eng., U.K. | 52 | 53.39 N | 0.59 W |
| Don ≈, Scot., U.K. | 58 | 57.10 N | 2.04 W |
| Donagadee | 60 | 54.39 N | 5.33 W |
| Donaghmore | 60 | 54.32 N | 6.49 W |
| Donard, Slieve ▲ | 60 | 54.11 N | 5.55 W |
| Donaueschingen | 66 | 47.57 N | 8.29 E |
| Don Benito | 70 | 38.57 N | 5.52 W |
| Doncaster | 56 | 53.32 N | 1.07 W |
| Dondra Head ⅄ | 84 | 5.55 N | 80.35 E |
| Doneck | 76 | 48.00 N | 37.48 E |
| Donegal | 60 | 54.50 N | 8.00 W |
| Donegal □[6] | 52 | 54.50 N | 8.00 W |
| Donegal Bay C | 52 | 54.30 N | 8.30 W |
| Doneraile | 60 | 52.13 N | 8.35 W |
| Donga ≈ | 86 | 8.19 N | 9.58 E |
| Dongchuan | 80 | 26.10 N | 103.01 E |
| Donggala | 82 | 0.40 S | 119.46 E |
| Dong-hai ∓[2] | 80 | 30.00 N | 126.00 E |
| Donghao | 80 | 34.34 N | 119.11 E |
| Dongjiang ≈ | 80 | 23.06 N | 114.00 E |
| Dong-nai ≈ | 82 | 10.45 N | 106.46 E |
| Dongshaqundao (Pratas Islands) II | 80 | 20.42 N | 116.43 E |
| Dongting ⊜ | 80 | 29.20 N | 112.54 E |
| Donjek ≈ | 94 | 62.55 N | 140.00 W |
| Donoughmore | 60 | 51.57 N | 8.45 W |
| Dooagh | 60 | 53.58 N | 10.07 W |
| Doon ≈ | 56 | 55.26 N | 4.41 W |
| Doon, Loch ⊜ | 56 | 55.15 N | 4.22 W |
| Doonbeg | 60 | 52.44 N | 9.32 W |
| Dora, Lake ⊜ | 92 | 22.05 S | 122.55 E |
| Dorain, Beinn ▲ | 58 | 56.30 N | 4.42 W |
| Dorback Burn ≈ | 58 | 57.31 N | 3.41 W |
| Dorchester, Eng., U.K. | 54 | 50.43 N | 2.26 W |
| Dorchester, Eng., U.K. | 54 | 51.39 N | 1.10 W |
| Dorchester, Cape ⅄ | 94 | 65.29 N | 77.30 W |
| Dordogne ≈ | 68 | 45.02 N | 0.35 W |
| Dordon | 54 | 52.36 N | 1.37 W |
| Dordrecht | 66 | 51.49 N | 4.40 E |
| Dore ≈ | 54 | 51.59 N | 2.54 W |
| Dore, Mont ▲ | 68 | 45.32 N | 2.49 E |
| Dorking | 54 | 51.14 N | 0.20 W |
| Dornbirn | 66 | 47.25 N | 9.44 E |
| Dornie | 58 | 57.16 N | 5.31 W |
| Dornoch | 58 | 57.52 N | 4.02 W |
| Dornoch Firth C[2] | 58 | 57.50 N | 4.04 W |
| Dorogobuž | 62 | 54.55 N | 33.18 E |
| Dorohoi | 74 | 47.57 N | 26.24 E |
| Dorre Island I | 92 | 25.09 S | 113.07 E |
| Dorridge | 54 | 52.22 N | 1.45 W |
| Dorset □[6] | 52 | 50.47 N | 2.28 W |
| Dortmund | 66 | 51.31 N | 7.28 E |
| Dos Bahías, Cabo ⅄ | 102 | 44.55 S | 65.32 W |
| Dos Hermanas | 70 | 37.17 N | 5.55 W |
| Dothan | 96 | 31.13 N | 85.24 W |
| Douai | 66 | 50.22 N | 3.04 E |
| Douala | 86 | 4.03 N | 9.42 E |
| Douarnenez | 68 | 48.06 N | 4.20 W |
| Douglas, I. of Man | 56 | 54.09 N | 4.28 W |
| Douglas, Scot., U.K. | 56 | 55.33 N | 3.51 W |
| Douglas ≈ | 56 | 53.43 N | 2.47 W |
| Douglas Channel ⊔ | 94 | 53.30 N | 129.12 W |
| Douglas Water ≈ | 56 | 55.38 N | 3.40 W |
| Doune | 58 | 56.12 N | 4.03 W |
| Dourada, Serra ▲[1] | 100 | 13.10 S | 48.45 W |
| Durango, Bol. | 72 | 43.10 S | 2.37 W |
| Durango, Méx. | 98 | 24.02 N | 104.40 W |
| Durazno | 102 | 33.22 S | 56.31 W |
| Durban | 90 | 29.55 S | 30.56 E |
| Düren | 66 | 50.48 N | 6.28 E |
| Durg | 84 | 21.11 N | 81.17 E |
| Durham, Eng., U.K. | 56 | 54.47 N | 1.34 W |
| Durham, N.C., U.S. | 96 | 36.00 N | 78.54 W |
| Durham Heights ▲ | 94 | 71.08 N | 122.56 W |
| Durham □[6] | 52 | 54.42 N | 1.45 W |
| Durmitor ▲ | 72 | 43.08 N | 19.01 E |
| Durness | 58 | 58.34 N | 4.45 W |
| Durness, Kyle of C | 58 | 58.34 N | 4.49 W |
| Durrës | 74 | 41.19 N | 19.26 E |
| Durrow | 60 | 52.50 N | 7.25 W |
| Dursey Head ⅄ | 60 | 51.34 N | 10.14 W |
| Dursley | 54 | 51.42 N | 2.21 W |
| Dury Voe ⊔[2] | 58 | 60.21 N | 1.08 W |
| Düsseldorf | 66 | 51.12 N | 6.47 E |
| Duyun | 80 | 26.12 N | 107.31 E |
| Dvuch Cirkjee, Gora ▲ | 78 | 67.35 N | 168.07 E |
| Dvůr Králové (nad Labem) | 66 | 50.26 N | 15.48 E |
| Dwyfor ≈ | 54 | 52.55 N | 4.27 W |
| Dyfi ≈ | 54 | 52.32 N | 4.03 W |
| Dyer, Cape ⅄ | 94 | 66.37 N | 61.18 W |
| Dyfed □[6] | 52 | 52.00 N | 4.30 W |
| Dyke | 58 | 57.37 N | 3.41 W |
| Dymchurch | 54 | 51.02 N | 1.00 E |
| Dymock | 54 | 51.59 N | 2.26 W |
| Dysart | 58 | 56.08 N | 3.07 W |
| Dzalal-Abad | 76 | 40.56 N | 73.00 E |
| Dżam-Abad | 76 | 35.48 N | 56.51 E |
| Džankoj | 76 | 45.42 N | 34.23 E |
| Dzaoudzi | 90 | 12.47 N | 45.17 E |
| Džetygara | 76 | 52.11 N | 61.12 E |
| Dzeržinsk | 62 | 56.15 N | 43.24 E |
| Dzeržinsk | 62 | 53.41 N | 27.08 E |
| Dzierżoniów (Reichenbach) | 66 | 50.44 N | 16.39 E |
| Dżizak | 76 | 40.06 N | 67.50 E |

| Name | Page | Lat ° ' | Long ° ' |
|---|---|---|---|
| Dzugdžur, Chrebet ⋏ | 78 | 58.00 N | 136.00 E |
| Džungarskij Alatau, Chrebet ⋏ | 76 | 45.00 N | 80.00 E |
| **E** | | | |
| Eagle ≈ | 94 | 53.35 N | 57.25 W |
| Eaglesfield | 56 | 55.03 N | 3.12 W |
| Eaglesham | 54 | 55.44 N | 4.18 W |
| Ealing ⌂8 | 54 | 51.31 N | 0.20 W |
| Eamont ≈ | 54 | 54.40 N | 2.39 W |
| Earby | 54 | 53.56 N | 2.08 W |
| Eardisley | 54 | 52.08 N | 2.59 W |
| Earlish | 58 | 57.34 N | 6.23 W |
| Earls Colne | 54 | 51.56 N | 0.42 E |
| Earl Shilton | 54 | 52.35 N | 1.20 W |
| Earl Soham | 54 | 52.14 N | 1.16 E |
| Earlston | 54 | 55.39 N | 2.40 W |
| Earn ≈ | 52 | 56.21 N | 3.19 W |
| Earn, Loch | 58 | 56.23 N | 4.14 W |
| Earsdon | 54 | 55.03 N | 1.29 W |
| Easington | 54 | 54.47 N | 1.19 W |
| Easingwold | 54 | 54.07 N | 1.11 W |
| Eask, Lough | 60 | 54.41 N | 8.03 W |
| Easky | 58 | 54.18 N | 8.58 W |
| East Aberthaw | 54 | 51.23 N | 3.22 W |
| East Allen ≈ | 54 | 54.55 N | 2.19 W |
| Eastbourne | 54 | 50.46 N | 0.17 E |
| East Calder | 54 | 55.54 N | 3.27 W |
| East China Sea ⫶2 | 50 | 30.00 N | 126.00 E |
| Eastchurch | 54 | 51.25 N | 0.52 E |
| East Cleddau ≈ | 54 | 51.46 N | 4.52 W |
| Eastleigh | 54 | 52.41 N | 0.56 E |
| Eastern Ghâts ⋏ | 84 | 16.00 N | 79.00 E |
| Eastern Isles II | 54a | 49.57 N | 6.15 W |
| East Falkland I | 102 | 51.55 S | 59.00 W |
| East Grinstead | 54 | 51.08 N | 0.01 W |
| East Harling | 54 | 52.26 N | 0.55 E |
| East Hoathly | 54 | 50.55 N | 0.10 E |
| East Horsley | 54 | 51.15 N | 0.26 W |
| East Ilsley | 54 | 51.32 N | 1.17 W |
| East Kilbride | 54 | 55.46 N | 4.10 W |
| Eastleigh | 54 | 50.58 N | 1.22 W |
| East Linton | 58 | 55.59 N | 2.39 W |
| East Loch Roag | 58 | 58.14 N | 6.48 W |
| East Loch Tarbert C | 58 | 57.52 N | 6.45 W |
| East London (Oos-Londen) | 90 | 33.00 S | 27.55 E |
| East Loof | 54 | 50.22 N | 4.27 W |
| Eastmain ≈ | 94 | 52.15 N | 78.35 W |
| East Markham | 54 | 53.15 N | 0.54 W |
| Easton | 54 | 50.32 N | 2.26 W |
| East Peckham | 54 | 51.15 N | 0.23 E |
| East Retford | 54 | 53.19 N | 0.56 W |
| Eastriggs | 54 | 54.59 N | 3.10 W |
| Eastry | 54 | 51.15 N | 1.18 E |
| East Saint Louis | 96 | 38.38 N | 90.09 W |
| East Stour ≈ | 54 | 51.08 N | 0.53 E |
| East Wittering | 54 | 50.41 N | 0.53 W |
| Eastwood | 54 | 53.01 N | 1.18 W |
| Eaton Socon | 54 | 52.13 N | 0.18 W |
| Eau ≈ | 54 | 53.31 N | 0.44 W |
| Eau Claire | 96 | 44.49 N | 91.31 W |
| Eau-Claire, Lac à l' | 94 | 56.10 N | 74.25 W |
| Eauripik I1 | 82 | 6.42 N | 143.03 E |
| Ebbw ≈ | 54 | 51.33 N | 2.59 W |
| Ebbw Vale | 54 | 51.47 N | 3.12 W |
| Eberbach | 66 | 49.28 N | 8.59 E |
| Eberswalde | 66 | 52.50 N | 13.49 E |
| Ebingen | 66 | 48.13 N | 9.01 E |
| Eboli | 72 | 40.37 N | 15.04 E |
| Ebro ≈ | 66 | 40.43 N | 0.54 E |
| Ecclefechan | 56 | 55.03 N | 3.17 W |
| Eccles | 54 | 53.29 N | 2.21 W |
| Ecclesfield | 54 | 53.27 N | 1.27 W |
| Eccleshall | 54 | 52.52 N | 2.15 W |
| Echt | 58 | 57.08 N | 2.26 W |
| Ecija | 70 | 37.32 N | 5.04 W |
| Eck, Loch | 58 | 56.05 N | 5.00 W |
| Eckernförde | 66 | 54.28 N | 9.50 E |
| Eckington | 54 | 53.19 N | 1.21 W |
| Eclipse Sound U | 94 | 72.38 N | 79.00 W |
| Ecuador □1 | 100 | 2.00 S | 77.30 W |
| Eday I | 52 | 59.11 N | 2.47 W |
| Edderton | 58 | 57.50 N | 4.10 W |
| Eddleston | 56 | 55.43 N | 3.13 W |
| Eddrachillis Bay C | 58 | 58.19 N | 5.15 W |
| Eddystone Rocks II | 54 | 50.12 N | 4.15 W |
| Ede, Ned. | 66 | 52.03 N | 5.40 E |
| Ede, Nig. | 86 | 7.44 N | 4.27 E |
| Eden ≈ | 54 | 54.43 N | 5.47 W |
| Eden ≈, Eng., U.K. | 52 | 54.57 N | 3.01 W |
| Eden ≈, Eng., U.K. | 54 | 51.10 N | 0.11 E |
| Eden ≈, Scot., U.K. | 56 | 56.22 N | 2.50 W |
| Eden ≈, Wales, U.K. | 54 | 52.53 N | 3.30 W |
| Edenbridge | 54 | 51.12 N | 0.04 E |
| Edenderry | 60 | 53.21 N | 7.35 W |
| Edenside V | 54 | 54.40 N | 2.35 W |
| Ederny | 60 | 54.32 N | 7.39 W |
| Edge Hill ▲2 | 54 | 52.08 N | 1.28 W |
| Edgeworthstown | 60 | 53.42 N | 7.36 W |
| Edhessa | 74 | 40.48 N | 22.03 E |
| Edinburgh | 56 | 55.57 N | 3.13 W |
| Edirne | 74 | 41.40 N | 26.34 E |
| Edmondbyers | 54 | 54.51 N | 1.58 W |
| Edmonton | 94 | 53.33 N | 113.28 W |
| Edremit | 74 | 39.35 N | 27.01 E |
| Edrengijn Nuruu ⋏ | 80 | 44.15 N | 97.45 E |
| Edward, Lake | 90 | 0.25 S | 29.30 E |
| Edwards Plateau ▲1 | 96 | 30.30 N | 101.00 W |
| Edwinstowe | 54 | 53.12 N | 1.04 W |
| Edzell | 58 | 56.48 N | 2.39 W |
| Eeklo | 66 | 51.11 N | 3.34 E |
| Eergu'nahe (Argun') ≈ | 78 | 53.20 N | 121.28 E |
| Egadi, Isole II | 72 | 37.56 N | 12.16 E |
| Egede og Rothes Fjord C2 | 94 | 66.00 N | 38.00 W |
| Eger | 74 | 47.54 N | 20.23 E |
| Egham | 54 | 51.26 N | 0.34 W |
| Eglsay | 58 | 59.09 N | 2.56 W |
| Eglinton | 60 | 55.01 N | 7.11 W |
| Egloskerry | 54 | 50.39 N | 4.27 W |
| Egremont | 54 | 54.29 N | 3.33 W |
| Eğridir Gölü | 74 | 38.02 N | 30.53 E |
| Egton | 54 | 54.26 N | 0.45 W |
| Egypt □1 | 86 | 27.00 N | 30.00 E |
| Ehen ≈ | 54 | 54.25 N | 3.30 W |
| Eibar | 70 | 43.11 N | 2.28 W |
| Eichstätt | 66 | 48.54 N | 11.12 E |
| Eigg I | 52 | 56.54 N | 6.10 W |
| Eigg, Sound of U | 58 | 56.51 N | 6.13 W |
| Eighe, Carn ▲ | 58 | 57.17 N | 5.07 W |
| Eighty Mile Beach ▲2 | 92 | 19.45 S | 121.00 E |
| Eilenburg | 66 | 51.27 N | 12.37 E |
| Eil Malk I | 82 | 7.09 N | 134.22 E |
| Einbeck | 66 | 51.49 N | 9.52 E |
| Eindhoven | 66 | 51.26 N | 5.28 E |
| Einsiedeln | 68 | 47.08 N | 8.45 E |
| Eisenach | 66 | 50.59 N | 10.19 E |
| Eisenberg | 66 | 50.58 N | 11.53 E |
| Eisenerz | 66 | 47.33 N | 14.53 E |
| Eisenhüttenstadt | 66 | 52.10 N | 14.38 E |
| Eisenstadt | 66 | 47.51 N | 16.32 E |
| Eishken | 58 | 58.02 N | 6.30 W |
| Eishort, Loch C | 58 | 57.10 N | 5.59 W |
| Eisleben | 66 | 51.31 N | 11.32 E |
| Eislingen | 66 | 48.42 N | 9.42 E |
| Eithon ≈ | 54 | 52.10 N | 3.28 W |
| Eitorf | 66 | 50.46 N | 7.26 E |
| Ejea de los Caballeros | 70 | 42.08 N | 1.08 W |
| Ekeren | 66 | 51.17 N | 4.25 E |
| Ekibastuz | 76 | 51.42 N | 75.22 E |
| El Aaiún | 86 | 27.09 N | 13.12 W |
| El Arahal | 70 | 37.16 N | 5.33 W |
| El Asnam | 86 | 36.10 N | 1.20 E |
| Elâziǧ | 84 | 38.41 N | 39.14 E |
| Elba, Isola d' I | 72 | 42.46 N | 10.17 E |
| El Banco | 100 | 9.00 N | 73.58 W |
| Elbasan | 74 | 41.06 N | 20.05 E |
| Elbe ≈ | 66 | 53.50 N | 9.00 E |
| Elbert, Mount ▲ | 96 | 39.07 N | 106.27 W |
| Elbeuf | 68 | 49.17 N | 1.00 E |
| Elblag (Elbing) | 66 | 54.10 N | 19.25 E |
| El'brus, Gora ▲ | 76 | 43.21 N | 42.26 E |
| El Cajon | 96 | 32.48 N | 116.58 W |
| El Capitan ▲ | 96 | 46.01 N | 114.23 W |
| Elche | 70 | 38.15 N | 0.42 W |
| Elda | 70 | 38.29 N | 0.47 W |
| El Djouf ⫶2 | 86 | 20.30 N | 8.00 W |
| Eldoret | 90 | 0.31 N | 35.17 E |
| Elektrostal' | 76 | 55.47 N | 38.28 E |
| Elephant Butte Reservoir ⌂1 | 96 | 33.19 N | 107.10 W |
| Eleuthera I | 98 | 25.10 N | 76.14 W |
| Elevsis | 74 | 38.02 N | 23.32 E |
| El Ferrol del Caudillo | 70 | 43.29 N | 8.14 W |
| Elgin, Scot., U.K. | 58 | 57.39 N | 3.20 W |
| Elgin, Ill., U.S. | 96 | 42.02 N | 88.17 W |
| Elgol | 58 | 57.09 N | 6.06 W |
| El Goléa | 86 | 30.30 N | 2.50 E |
| Elgon, Mount ▲ | 90 | 1.08 N | 34.33 E |
| Elham | 54 | 51.10 N | 1.07 E |
| El Hank ▲4 | 86 | 24.30 N | 7.00 W |
| Elhovo | 74 | 42.10 N | 26.34 E |
| Elinghu ≈ | 80 | 34.50 N | 97.35 E |
| Elista | 76 | 46.16 N | 44.14 E |
| Elizabeth | 92 | 34.43 S | 138.40 E |
| Elizabeth Reef I1 | 92 | 29.56 S | 159.04 E |
| El-Jadida | 86 | 33.16 N | 8.30 W |
| Elk | 66 | 53.50 N | 22.22 E |
| El Kairouan | 86 | 35.41 N | 10.07 E |
| Elkhart | 96 | 41.41 N | 85.58 W |
| Elland | 54 | 53.41 N | 1.50 W |
| Ellen ≈ | 54 | 54.43 N | 3.30 W |
| Ellesmere | 54 | 52.54 N | 2.54 W |
| Ellesmere Port | 54 | 53.17 N | 2.54 W |
| Ellice ≈ | 54 | 68.02 N | 103.26 W |
| Ellington | 58 | 55.13 N | 1.34 W |
| Ellon | 58 | 57.22 N | 2.05 W |
| Ellwangen | 66 | 48.57 N | 10.07 E |
| Elm | 54 | 52.38 N | 0.10 E |
| Elmira | 96 | 42.06 N | 76.49 W |
| Elmley ▲1 | 54 | 19.30 N | 7.00 W |
| Elmshorn | 66 | 53.45 N | 9.39 E |
| Elmswell | 54 | 52.15 N | 0.53 E |
| El Nevado, Cerro ▲ | 100 | 33.49 S | 74.04 W |
| Elobey, Islas II | 86 | 0.59 N | 9.30 E |
| El Oued | 86 | 33.20 N | 6.58 E |
| El Paso | 96 | 31.45 N | 106.29 W |
| Elphin | 58 | 53.51 N | 8.12 W |
| El Puerto de Santa Maria | 70 | 36.36 N | 6.13 W |
| El Salvador □1 | 98 | 13.50 N | 88.55 W |
| Elstead | 54 | 51.11 N | 0.43 W |
| Elsterwerda | 66 | 51.28 N | 13.31 E |
| Elstree | 54 | 51.39 N | 0.18 W |
| El Tigre | 100 | 8.55 N | 64.15 W |
| Elūru | 84 | 16.42 N | 81.07 E |
| Elvas | 70 | 38.53 N | 7.10 W |
| Elwy ≈ | 54 | 53.16 N | 3.26 W |
| Ely, Isle of ⌂1 | 54 | 52.24 N | 0.16 E |
| Emba ≈ | 76 | 46.38 N | 53.14 E |
| Embira ≈ | 100 | 7.19 S | 70.15 W |
| Embleton | 54 | 55.30 N | 1.37 W |
| Embo | 58 | 57.54 N | 3.59 W |
| Emden | 66 | 53.22 N | 7.00 E |
| Emmen | 66 | 52.47 N | 7.00 E |
| Emmendingen | 66 | 48.07 N | 7.50 E |
| Emmerich | 66 | 51.50 N | 6.15 E |
| Emneth | 54 | 52.38 N | 0.11 E |
| Empalme | 96 | 27.58 N | 110.51 W |
| Empoli | 72 | 43.43 N | 10.57 E |
| Emsdetten | 66 | 52.10 N | 7.31 E |
| Emsworth | 54 | 50.51 N | 0.56 W |
| Emyvale | 60 | 54.20 N | 6.59 W |
| Enard Bay C | 58 | 58.06 N | 5.24 W |
| Enborne ≈ | 54 | 51.24 N | 1.06 W |
| Encarnación | 102 | 27.20 S | 55.54 W |
| Encounter Bay C | 82 | 35.35 S | 138.44 E |
| Ende | 82 | 8.50 S | 121.39 E |
| Endeavour Strait U | 82 | 10.45 S | 142.15 E |
| Enderby | 54 | 52.36 N | 1.12 W |
| Ene ≈ | 100 | 11.09 S | 74.19 W |
| Enfield | 54 | 51.40 N | 0.05 W |
| Engel's | 76 | 51.30 N | 46.07 E |
| England □1 | 54 | 53.00 N | 2.00 W |
| Englefield, Cape ➤ | 94 | 69.51 N | 85.39 W |
| English Channel (La Manche) | 52 | 50.20 N | 1.00 W |
| Enid | 96 | 36.19 N | 97.48 W |
| Enkhuizen | 66 | 52.42 N | 5.17 E |
| Enköping | 64 | 59.38 N | 17.04 E |
| Enna | 72 | 37.34 N | 14.17 E |
| Ennadai Lake | 94 | 61.00 N | 101.15 W |
| Enmedi ▲1 | 88 | 17.15 N | 22.00 E |
| Ennell, Lough | 60 | 53.28 N | 7.24 W |
| Ennerdale Water | 54 | 54.31 N | 3.23 W |
| Ennis | 60 | 52.50 N | 8.59 W |
| Enniscorthy | 60 | 52.30 N | 6.34 W |
| Enniskillen | 60 | 54.21 N | 7.38 W |
| Ennistymon | 60 | 52.57 N | 9.15 W |
| Enns ≈ | 66 | 48.13 N | 14.29 E |
| Ensay I | 58 | 57.46 N | 7.05 W |
| Enschede | 66 | 52.12 N | 6.53 E |
| Ensenada | 96 | 31.52 N | 116.37 W |
| Entebbe | 90 | 0.04 N | 32.28 E |
| Enugu | 86 | 6.27 N | 7.27 E |
| Eólie, Isole II | 72 | 38.30 N | 15.00 E |
| Épernay | 68 | 49.02 N | 3.57 E |
| Épinal | 68 | 48.11 N | 6.27 E |
| Eport, Loch C | 58 | 57.33 N | 7.11 W |
| Epping | 54 | 51.43 N | 0.07 E |
| Epping Forest ⌂3 | 54 | 51.40 N | 0.03 E |
| Epsom | 54 | 51.20 N | 0.16 W |
| Epworth | 54 | 53.32 N | 0.49 W |
| Equatorial Guinea □1 | 86 | 2.00 N | 9.00 E |
| Erba | 72 | 45.49 N | 9.15 E |
| Erciyeş Daǧı ▲ | 84 | 38.32 N | 35.28 E |
| Erd | 66 | 47.23 N | 18.56 E |
| Erdek | 74 | 40.24 N | 27.48 E |
| Erding | 66 | 48.18 N | 11.54 E |
| Erfurt | 66 | 50.58 N | 11.01 E |
| Eriboll | 58 | 58.28 N | 4.41 W |
| Eriboll, Loch C | 58 | 58.32 N | 4.41 W |
| Erice | 72 | 38.02 N | 12.36 E |
| Erichsen Lake | 94 | 70.38 N | 80.31 W |
| Ericht, Loch | 58 | 56.50 N | 4.25 W |
| Erie | 96 | 42.08 N | 80.04 W |
| Erie, Lake | 96 | 42.15 N | 81.00 W |
| Erimo-misaki ➤ | 80 | 41.55 N | 143.15 E |
| Eriskay I | 58 | 57.04 N | 7.17 W |
| Erisort, Loch C | 58 | 58.07 N | 6.24 W |
| Erkelenz | 66 | 51.05 N | 6.19 E |
| Erkina ≈ | 60 | 52.51 N | 7.23 W |
| Erlangen | 66 | 49.36 N | 11.01 E |
| Ermelo | 90 | 26.31 S | 29.59 E |
| Ermoúpolis | 74 | 37.26 N | 24.56 E |
| Ernåkulam | 84 | 9.59 N | 76.17 E |
| Erne ≈ | 60 | 54.30 N | 8.16 W |
| Erne, Lower Lough | 52 | 54.10 N | 7.30 W |
| Erne, Upper Lough | 52 | 54.14 N | 7.32 W |
| Erode | 84 | 11.21 N | 77.43 E |
| Errigal ▲ | 60 | 55.02 N | 8.07 W |
| Erris Head ➤ | 60 | 54.19 N | 10.00 W |
| Errochty, Loch | 58 | 56.45 N | 4.12 W |
| Errogie | 58 | 57.16 N | 4.22 W |
| Erzincan | 84 | 39.44 N | 39.29 E |
| Erzurum | 84 | 39.55 N | 41.17 E |
| Esbjerg | 64 | 55.28 N | 8.27 E |
| Escarpada Point ➤ | 82 | 18.31 N | 122.13 E |
| Esch-sur-Alzette | 66 | 49.30 N | 5.59 E |
| Eschwege | 66 | 51.11 N | 10.04 E |
| Eschweiler | 66 | 50.49 N | 6.16 E |
| Escondido | 96 | 33.07 N | 117.05 W |
| Escrick | 54 | 53.53 N | 1.02 W |
| Escuintla | 98 | 14.18 N | 90.47 W |
| Esfahān | 84 | 32.40 N | 51.38 E |
| Esher | 54 | 51.23 N | 0.22 W |
| Esk ≈, Eng., U.K. | 54 | 54.21 N | 3.24 W |
| Esk ≈, Eng., U.K. | 54 | 54.29 N | 0.37 W |
| Esk ≈, Scot., U.K. | 56 | 55.57 N | 3.02 W |
| Eskdale ≈ | 56 | 55.12 N | 3.09 W |
| Eskilstuna | 64 | 59.22 N | 16.30 E |
| Eskimo Lakes | 94 | 69.15 N | 132.17 W |
| Eslöv | 64 | 55.50 N | 13.20 E |
| Esmeralda, Isla I | 102 | 48.57 S | 75.25 W |
| Esmeraldas | 100 | 0.59 N | 79.42 W |
| Esmeraldas ≈ | 100 | 0.58 N | 79.38 W |
| Esperance Bay C | 92 | 33.51 S | 121.53 E |
| Espinhaço, Serra do ▲ | 100 | 17.30 S | 43.30 W |
| Espinho | 70 | 41.00 N | 8.39 W |
| Espíritu Santo, Isla del I | 84 | 24.30 N | 110.22 W |
| Espoo (Esbo) | 64 | 60.13 N | 24.40 E |
| Esquel | 102 | 42.54 S | 71.19 W |
| Essaouira | 86 | 31.30 N | 9.47 E |
| Essen | 66 | 51.28 N | 7.01 E |
| Essendon, Mount ▲ | 92 | 24.59 S | 120.28 E |
| Essequibo ≈ | 100 | 6.59 N | 58.23 W |
| Essex ⌂6 | 54 | 51.48 N | 0.40 E |
| Esslingen | 66 | 48.45 N | 9.16 E |
| Est, Pointe de l' ➤ | 94 | 49.08 N | 61.41 W |
| Estacado, Llano ▲ | 96 | 33.30 N | 103.00 W |
| Estados, Isla de los | 102 | 54.47 S | 64.15 W |
| Este | 72 | 45.14 N | 11.39 E |
| Estepona | 70 | 36.26 N | 5.08 W |
| Eston | 54 | 54.34 N | 1.07 W |
| Estrondo, Serra do ▲1 | 100 | 9.00 S | 48.45 W |
| Esztergom | 74 | 47.48 N | 18.45 E |
| Étampes | 68 | 48.26 N | 2.09 E |
| Étaples | 68 | 50.31 N | 1.39 E |
| Etāwah | 84 | 26.33 N | 76.22 E |
| Ethiopia □1 | 88 | 8.00 N | 38.00 E |
| Etive, Loch C | 58 | 56.29 N | 5.09 W |
| Etna, Monte ▲1 | 72 | 37.46 N | 15.00 E |
| Eton | 54 | 51.31 N | 0.37 W |
| Etoshapan ▲ | 90 | 18.45 S | 16.15 E |
| Ettington | 54 | 52.09 N | 1.36 W |
| Ettlingen | 66 | 48.56 N | 8.24 E |
| Ettrick Forest ▲3 | 56 | 55.30 N | 3.00 W |
| Ettrick Pen ▲ | 56 | 55.21 N | 3.16 W |
| Ettrick Water ≈ | 56 | 55.31 N | 2.55 W |
| Eu | 68 | 50.03 N | 1.25 E |
| Eugene | 96 | 44.02 N | 123.05 W |
| Eugenia, Punta ➤ | 96 | 27.50 N | 115.05 W |
| Eupen | 66 | 50.38 N | 6.02 E |
| Euphrates (Al-Furāt) (Firāt) ≈ | 84 | 31.00 N | 47.25 E |
| Eureka | 96 | 40.47 N | 124.09 W |
| Europa, Île I | 90 | 22.20 S | 40.22 E |
| Europe ▲1 | 8 | 50.00 N | 28.00 E |
| Eutin | 66 | 54.08 N | 10.37 E |
| Eutsuk Lake | 94 | 53.20 N | 126.44 W |
| Evans, Lac | 94 | 50.55 N | 77.00 W |
| Evans Strait U | 94 | 63.15 N | 82.00 W |
| Evanston | 96 | 42.03 N | 87.42 W |
| Evansville | 96 | 37.58 N | 87.35 W |
| Evanton | 58 | 57.40 N | 4.20 W |
| Evenlode ≈ | 54 | 51.47 N | 1.21 W |
| Everard, Lake | 92 | 31.25 S | 135.05 E |
| Evercreech | 54 | 51.09 N | 2.30 W |
| Everest, Mount (Zhumulangmafeng) ▲ | 84 | 27.59 N | 86.56 E |
| Everett | 96 | 47.59 N | 122.31 W |
| Everett Mountains | 94 | 62.45 N | 67.12 W |
| Evergem | 66 | 51.07 N | 3.42 E |
| Evesham | 54 | 52.06 N | 1.50 W |
| Evesham, Vale of V | 54 | 52.06 N | 1.50 W |
| Évora | 70 | 38.34 N | 7.54 W |
| Évreux | 68 | 49.01 N | 1.09 E |
| Évvoia I | 74 | 38.34 N | 23.50 E |
| Ewe, Loch C | 58 | 57.48 N | 5.40 W |
| Ewes Water ≈ | 56 | 55.08 N | 3.00 W |
| Exe ≈ | 52 | 50.37 N | 3.25 W |
| Exeter | 54 | 50.43 N | 3.31 W |
| Exeter Sound U | 94 | 66.14 N | 62.00 W |
| Exford | 54 | 51.08 N | 3.38 W |
| Exminster | 54 | 50.41 N | 3.29 W |
| Exmoor ▲1 | 54 | 51.10 N | 3.45 W |
| Exmouth | 54 | 50.37 N | 3.25 W |
| Exmouth Gulf C | 92 | 22.00 S | 114.20 E |
| Exuma Sound U | 98 | 24.15 N | 76.00 W |
| Eyam | 54 | 53.17 N | 1.41 W |
| Eyasi, Lake | 90 | 3.40 S | 35.05 E |
| Eye, Eng., U.K. | 54 | 52.35 N | 0.10 W |
| Eye, Eng., U.K. | 54 | 52.19 N | 1.09 E |
| Eyemouth | 56 | 55.52 N | 2.06 W |
| Eye Peninsula ➤1 | 58 | 58.13 N | 6.05 W |
| Eye Water ≈ | 56 | 55.53 N | 2.06 W |
| Eynhallow Sound U | 58 | 59.08 N | 3.06 W |
| Eynort, Loch C | 58 | 57.13 N | 7.18 W |
| Eynsham | 54 | 51.48 N | 1.22 W |
| Eyrecourt | 60 | 53.11 N | 8.07 W |
| Eyre Creek ≈ | 82 | 26.40 S | 139.00 E |
| Eyre North, Lake | 82 | 28.40 S | 137.10 E |
| Eyre Peninsula ➤1 | 92 | 34.00 S | 135.45 E |
| Eyre South, Lake | 92 | 29.30 S | 137.20 E |
| Eythorne | 54 | 51.11 N | 1.17 E |
| Ezine | 74 | 39.47 N | 26.20 E |
| Ežva | 62 | 61.47 N | 50.40 E |
| **F** | | | |
| Fabriano | 72 | 43.20 N | 12.54 E |
| Fada, Lochan | 58 | 57.41 N | 5.18 W |
| Faddeja, Zaliv C | 78 | 76.40 N | 107.20 E |
| Faddejevskij, Ostrov | 78 | 75.30 N | 144.00 E |
| Faenza | 72 | 44.17 N | 11.53 E |
| Faeroe Islands ⌂2 | 50 | 62.00 N | 7.00 W |
| Făgăraş | 74 | 45.51 N | 24.58 E |
| Faguibine, Lac | 86 | 16.45 N | 4.00 W |
| Fahan | 60 | 55.05 N | 7.28 W |
| Failsworth | 54 | 53.31 N | 2.09 W |
| Fairbanks | 94 | 64.51 N | 147.43 W |
| Fairford | 54 | 51.44 N | 1.47 W |
| Fair Head ➤ | 52 | 55.13 N | 6.09 W |
| Fair Isle I | 52 | 59.30 N | 1.40 W |
| Fairlie | 56 | 55.46 N | 4.51 W |
| Fairlight | 54 | 50.53 N | 0.40 E |
| Fairweather, Mount ▲ | 94 | 58.54 N | 137.32 W |
| Fairy Water ≈ | 60 | 54.37 N | 7.20 W |
| Fais I | 82 | 9.46 N | 140.31 E |
| Faizābād, Afg. | 84 | 37.06 N | 70.34 E |
| Faizābād, Bhārat | 84 | 26.47 N | 82.08 E |
| Fakenham | 54 | 52.50 N | 0.51 E |
| Fal ≈ | 54 | 50.08 N | 5.02 W |
| Falconara Marittima | 72 | 43.37 N | 13.24 E |
| Falcon Reservoir ⌂1 | 96 | 26.37 N | 99.11 W |
| Faleme ≈ | 86 | 14.46 N | 12.14 W |
| Falkenberg | 64 | 56.54 N | 12.28 E |
| Falkensee | 66 | 52.33 N | 13.04 E |
| Falkenstein | 66 | 50.28 N | 12.22 E |
| Falkirk | 56 | 56.00 N | 3.48 W |
| Falkland | 56 | 56.15 N | 3.12 W |
| Falkland Islands ⌂2 | 102 | 51.45 S | 59.00 W |
| Falkland Sound U | 102 | 51.45 S | 59.25 W |
| Falköping | 64 | 58.10 N | 13.31 E |
| Fall River | 96 | 41.43 N | 71.08 W |
| Falmouth | 54 | 50.08 N | 5.04 W |
| Falmouth Bay C | 54 | 50.07 N | 5.03 W |
| Falster I | 64 | 54.48 N | 11.58 E |
| Fălticeni | 74 | 47.28 N | 26.18 E |
| Falun | 64 | 60.36 N | 15.38 E |
| Famatina, Nevado de ▲ | 102 | 29.00 S | 67.51 W |
| Fanad Head ➤ | 60 | 55.16 N | 7.38 W |
| Fane ≈, Éire | 60 | 53.56 N | 6.22 W |
| Fane ≈, Eur. | 60 | 53.57 N | 6.22 W |
| Fannich, Loch | 58 | 57.37 N | 5.00 W |
| Fan-si-pan ▲ | 80 | 22.15 N | 103.46 E |
| Faoileann, Bàgh nam C | 58 | 55.23 N | 7.14 W |
| Faraan, Jazā'ir II | 84 | 16.48 N | 41.54 E |
| Farafangana | 90 | 22.49 S | 47.50 E |
| Farah | 84 | 31.29 N | 61.24 E |
| Farallon de Medinilla I | 82 | 16.01 N | 146.04 E |
| Farallon de Pajaros I | 82 | 20.32 N | 144.54 E |
| Fareham | 54 | 50.51 N | 1.10 W |
| Fargo | 96 | 46.52 N | 96.48 W |
| Faribault, Lac | 94 | 59.00 N | 72.00 W |
| Faringdon | 54 | 51.40 N | 1.35 W |
| Farnborough | 54 | 51.17 N | 0.46 W |
| Farne Islands II | 56 | 55.38 N | 1.38 W |
| Farnham | 54 | 51.13 N | 0.49 W |
| Farnworth | 54 | 53.33 N | 2.24 W |
| Faro | 70 | 37.01 N | 7.56 W |
| Fårö I | 86 | 9.21 N | 12.55 E |
| Fårön I | 97 | 57.56 N | 19.08 E |
| Farquhar Group II | 90 | 10.10 S | 51.10 E |
| Farr | 58 | 57.34 N | 4.12 W |
| Farrar ≈ | 58 | 57.24 N | 4.50 W |
| Farrukhābād | 84 | 27.24 N | 79.35 E |
| Fartak, Ra's ➤ | 84 | 15.38 N | 52.15 E |
| Farvel, Kap ➤ | 94 | 59.45 N | 44.00 W |
| Fasano | 72 | 40.50 N | 17.22 E |
| Fastnet Rock I2 | 52 | 51.24 N | 9.35 W |
| Fauldhouse | 58 | 55.50 N | 3.37 W |
| Favara | 72 | 37.19 N | 13.40 E |
| Faversham | 54 | 51.20 N | 0.53 E |
| Fawley | 54 | 50.49 N | 1.20 W |
| Fawn ≈ | 94 | 55.22 N | 88.20 W |
| Faxaflói C | 50 | 64.30 N | 23.00 W |
| Fayetteville | 96 | 35.03 N | 78.54 W |
| Fazzān (Fezzan) ▲1 | 88 | 26.00 N | 14.00 E |
| Feale ≈ | 52 | 52.28 N | 9.40 W |
| Fear, Cape ➤ | 96 | 33.50 N | 77.58 W |
| Featherstone | 54 | 53.41 N | 1.21 W |
| Fécamp | 68 | 49.45 N | 0.22 E |
| Fedjedj, Chott el | 86 | 33.55 N | 9.10 E |
| Feeagh, Lough | 60 | 53.55 N | 9.36 W |
| Fehérgyarmat | 66 | 47.58 N | 22.32 E |
| Feia, Lagoa | 100 | 22.00 S | 41.20 W |
| Feira de Santana | 100 | 12.15 S | 38.57 W |
| Feldkirch | 66 | 47.14 N | 9.36 E |
| Felixstowe | 54 | 51.58 N | 1.20 E |
| Felling | 54 | 54.57 N | 1.33 W |
| Felpham | 54 | 50.47 N | 0.39 W |
| Feltre | 72 | 46.01 N | 11.54 E |
| Fen Ditton | 54 | 52.13 N | 0.10 E |
| Fengcheng | 80 | 40.28 N | 124.00 E |
| Fengzhen | 80 | 40.28 N | 113.09 E |
| Fenny Compton | 54 | 52.09 N | 1.20 W |
| Fenny Stratford | 54 | 52.00 N | 0.43 W |
| Fenyang | 80 | 37.18 N | 111.41 E |
| Feodosija | 76 | 45.02 N | 35.23 E |
| Ferdosija | — | — | — |
| Fermanagh ⌂9 | — | — | — |
| Fermo | 72 | 43.09 N | 13.43 E |
| Fernando de Noronha, Ilha I | 100 | 3.51 S | 32.25 W |
| Fernán-Núñez | 70 | 37.40 N | 4.43 W |
| Ferndown | 54 | 50.48 N | 1.55 W |
| Ferns | 60 | 52.35 N | 6.31 W |
| Ferrara | 72 | 44.33 N | 7.43 E |
| Ferryhill | 54 | 54.41 N | 1.33 W |
| Fès | 86 | 34.05 N | 4.57 W |
| Feshie ≈ | 58 | 57.08 N | 3.55 W |
| Fetcham | 54 | 51.17 N | 0.22 W |
| Feteşti | 74 | 44.24 N | 27.50 E |
| Fethaland, Point of ➤ | 58a | 60.38 N | 1.18 W |
| Fethard | 60 | 52.27 N | 7.41 W |
| Fethiye | 74 | 36.37 N | 29.07 E |
| Fetlar I | 52 | 60.37 N | 0.52 W |
| Fetteresso | 58 | 57.33 N | 2.01 W |
| Fettercairn | 58 | 56.51 N | 2.34 W |
| Feuilles, Baie aux C | 94 | 58.55 N | 69.20 W |
| Feuilles, Rivière aux ≈ | 94 | 58.47 N | 70.04 W |
| Feyzābād | 84 | 37.06 N | 70.34 E |
| Ffestiniog | 54 | 52.58 N | 3.55 W |
| Fforest Fawr ▲1 | 54 | 51.52 N | 3.36 W |
| Fianarantsoa | 90 | 21.26 S | 47.05 E |
| Fidenza | 72 | 44.52 N | 10.03 E |
| Fier | 74 | 40.43 N | 19.34 E |
| Fife ⌂4 | 52 | 56.13 N | 3.02 W |
| Fife Ness ➤ | 58 | 56.17 N | 2.36 W |
| Figueira da Foz | 70 | 40.09 N | 8.52 W |
| Figueras | 70 | 42.16 N | 2.58 E |
| Figuig | 86 | 32.06 N | 1.11 W |
| Fiji Islands II | 8 | 18.00 S | 178.00 E |
| Filby | 54 | 52.40 N | 1.40 E |
| Filey | 54 | 54.12 N | 0.17 W |
| Filey Bay C | 54 | 54.12 N | 0.16 W |
| Filton | 54 | 51.31 N | 2.35 W |
| Finale Ligure | 72 | 44.10 N | 8.20 E |
| Fincham | 54 | 52.37 N | 0.30 E |
| Findhorn | 58 | 57.38 N | 3.38 W |
| Findhorn ≈ | 58 | 57.38 N | 3.38 W |
| Findon | 54 | 50.54 N | 0.23 W |
| Finedon | 54 | 52.20 N | 0.39 W |
| Finisk ≈ | 60 | 52.08 N | 7.50 W |
| Finisterre, Cabo de ➤ | 70 | 42.53 N | 9.16 W |
| Finland □1 | 62 | 64.00 N | 26.00 E |
| Finland, Gulf of C | 62 | 60.00 N | 27.00 E |
| Finlas, Loch | 58 | 57.00 N | 4.25 W |
| Finlay ≈ | 94 | 57.00 N | 125.05 W |
| Finn ≈ | 60 | 54.43 N | 7.29 W |
| Finspång | 64 | 58.43 N | 15.47 E |
| Finsterwalde | 66 | 51.38 N | 13.42 E |
| Fintona | 60 | 54.30 N | 7.19 W |
| Finvoy | 60 | 55.00 N | 6.30 W |
| Fionn Loch | 58 | 57.46 N | 5.29 W |
| Firenze (Florence) | 72 | 43.46 N | 11.15 E |
| Firminy | 68 | 45.23 N | 4.18 E |
| Firozābād | 84 | 27.09 N | 78.24 E |
| Firozpur | 84 | 30.55 N | 74.38 E |
| Firth ≈ | 58 | 59.32 N | 139.20 W |
| Fish ≈ | 90 | 28.07 S | 17.45 E |
| Fishbourne | 54 | 50.44 N | 1.12 W |
| Fisher Strait U | 94 | 63.15 N | 83.30 W |
| Fishguard | 54 | 51.59 N | 4.59 W |
| Fitful Head ➤ | 58 | 59.54 N | 1.23 W |
| Fittleworth | 54 | 50.58 N | 0.35 W |
| Fitzroy ≈ | 92 | 17.31 S | 123.35 E |
| Fivemiletown | 60 | 54.23 N | 7.18 W |
| Five Penny Borve | 58 | 58.25 N | 6.25 W |
| Flagstaff | 96 | 35.12 N | 111.39 W |
| Flamborough Head ➤ | 56 | 54.07 N | 0.04 W |
| Flaming Gorge Reservoir ⌂1 | 96 | 41.15 N | 109.30 W |
| Flannan Islands II | 58 | 58.18 N | 7.36 W |
| Flat ≈ | 94 | 61.33 N | 125.18 W |
| Flathead Lake | 96 | 47.52 N | 114.08 W |
| Flat Holm I | 54 | 51.23 N | 3.07 W |
| Flattery, Cape ➤ | 96 | 48.23 N | 124.43 W |
| Fleet | 54 | 51.16 N | 0.50 W |
| Fleet ≈ | 58 | 57.57 N | 4.05 W |
| Fleetwood | 54 | 53.56 N | 3.01 W |
| Flimby | 54 | 54.41 N | 3.31 W |
| Flinders ≈ | 92 | 17.36 S | 140.36 E |
| Flinders Island I | 92 | 40.00 S | 148.00 E |
| Flinders Range ▲ | 92 | 31.00 S | 138.45 E |
| Flinders Reefs ▲2 | 92 | 17.37 S | 148.31 E |
| Flint, Wales, U.K. | 54 | 53.15 N | 3.10 W |
| Flint, Mich., U.S. | 96 | 43.01 N | 83.41 W |
| Flint ≈ | 96 | 30.52 N | 84.38 W |
| Flitwick | 54 | 52.00 N | 0.30 W |
| Flixton | 54 | 53.28 N | 2.22 W |
| Florence | 96 | 34.11 N | 79.46 W |
| Flores I | 82 | 8.30 S | 121.00 E |
| Flores, Laut (Flores Sea) ⫶2 | 82 | 8.00 S | 120.00 E |
| Floriano | 100 | 6.47 S | 43.01 W |
| Florianópolis | 102 | 27.35 S | 48.34 W |
| Florida □3 | 96 | 28.00 N | 82.00 W |
| Florida, Straits of U | 96 | 24.00 N | 79.45 W |
| Florida Keys II | 96 | 24.45 N | 81.00 W |
| Flórína | 74 | 40.48 N | 21.26 E |
| Flotta I | 58 | 58.50 N | 3.08 W |
| Foça | 74 | 38.39 N | 26.46 E |
| Focşani | 74 | 45.41 N | 27.11 E |
| Fochabers | 58 | 57.37 N | 3.05 W |
| Foday ⫶2 | 86 | 14.55 N | 24.25 W |
| Foggia | 72 | 41.27 N | 15.34 E |
| Fogo, Cabo ➤ | 86 | 14.55 N | 24.25 W |
| Fogo Island I | 94 | 49.40 N | 54.13 W |
| Foinaven ▲ | 58 | 58.25 N | 4.52 W |
| Foix | 68 | 42.57 N | 1.36 E |
| Foligno | 72 | 42.57 N | 12.42 E |
| Folkestone | 54 | 51.05 N | 1.11 E |
| Folkingham | 54 | 52.54 N | 0.24 W |
| Fond du Lac | 96 | 43.47 N | 88.27 W |
| Fond du Lac ≈ | 94 | 59.17 N | 106.00 W |
| Fondi | 72 | 41.21 N | 13.25 E |
| Fonseca, Golfo de C | 98 | 13.10 N | 87.40 W |
| Font ≈ | 56 | 55.10 N | 1.44 W |
| Fontainebleau | 68 | 48.24 N | 2.42 E |
| Fontas | 94 | 58.20 N | 121.50 W |
| Fontenay-le-Comte | 68 | 46.28 N | 0.49 W |
| Fontur ➤ | 50 | 66.23 N | 14.30 W |
| Forbach | 68 | 49.11 N | 6.54 E |
| Forchheim | 66 | 49.43 N | 11.04 E |
| Ford | 58 | 56.10 N | 5.26 W |
| Forden | 54 | 52.36 N | 3.08 W |
| Fordingbridge | 54 | 50.56 N | 1.47 W |
| Forel, Mont ▲ | 94 | 67.00 N | 37.00 W |
| Foreland Point ➤ | 54 | 51.16 N | 3.47 W |
| Forest Row | 54 | 51.06 N | 0.02 E |
| Forfar | 58 | 56.38 N | 2.54 W |
| Forli | 72 | 44.13 N | 12.03 E |
| Formby | 54 | 53.34 N | 3.05 W |
| Formby Point ➤ | 54 | 53.33 N | 3.06 W |
| Formentera I | 70 | 38.42 N | 1.28 E |
| Formia | 72 | 41.15 N | 13.37 E |
| Formosa | 102 | 26.11 S | 58.11 W |
| Formosa, Serra ▲1 | 100 | 12.00 S | 55.00 W |
| Formosa Strait U | 80 | 24.00 N | 119.00 E |
| Forres | 58 | 57.37 N | 3.38 W |
| Forst | 66 | 51.44 N | 14.39 E |
| Fortaleza | 100 | 3.43 S | 38.30 W |
| Fort Augustus | 58 | 57.09 N | 4.41 W |
| Fort Collins | 96 | 40.35 N | 105.05 W |
| Fort-Dauphin | 90 | 25.02 S | 47.00 E |
| Fort-de-France | 98 | 14.36 N | 61.05 W |
| Fort Dodge | 96 | 42.30 N | 94.10 W |
| Fortescue ≈ | 92 | 21.00 S | 116.06 E |
| Forth | 58 | 55.46 N | 3.41 W |
| Forth, Carse of V | 58 | 56.03 N | 3.44 W |
| Forth, Firth of C1 | 58 | 56.05 N | 2.55 W |
| Fort Lauderdale | 96 | 26.07 N | 80.08 W |
| Fort Myers | 96 | 26.37 N | 81.54 W |
| Fort Nelson | 94 | 59.30 N | 124.00 W |
| Fort Peck Lake | 96 | 47.45 N | 106.50 W |
| Fort Pierce | 96 | 27.27 N | 80.20 W |
| Fort Portal | 90 | 0.40 N | 30.17 E |
| Fortrose | 58 | 57.34 N | 4.09 W |
| Fort Smith | 96 | 35.23 N | 94.25 W |
| Fort Victoria | 90 | 20.05 S | 30.50 E |
| Fort Wayne | 96 | 41.04 N | 85.09 W |
| Fort William | 58 | 56.49 N | 5.07 W |
| Fort Worth | 96 | 32.45 N | 97.20 W |
| Forty Foot Drain ≈ | 54 | 52.30 N | 0.00 |
| Foshan | 80 | 23.03 N | 113.09 E |
| Foss ≈ | 54 | 53.58 N | 0.55 W |
| Fossano | 72 | 44.33 N | 7.43 E |
| Fotheringhay | 54 | 52.32 N | 0.27 W |
| Fougères | 68 | 48.21 N | 1.12 W |
| Foula I | 52 | 60.08 N | 2.05 W |
| Foulness ≈ | 54 | 53.47 N | 0.43 W |
| Foulness Island I | 54 | 51.36 N | 0.55 E |
| Foulness Point ➤ | 54 | 51.38 N | 0.57 E |
| Foulsham | 54 | 52.48 N | 1.01 E |
| Fouman | 84 | 37.13 N | 49.19 E |
| Fourmies | 68 | 50.00 N | 4.03 E |
| Fouta Djallon ▲1 | 86 | 11.30 N | 12.30 W |
| Foveaux Strait U | 93 | 46.40 S | 168.00 E |
| Fowey | 54 | 50.20 N | 4.38 W |
| Foxe Basin C | 94 | 68.25 N | 77.00 W |
| Foxe Channel U | 94 | 64.30 N | 80.00 W |
| Foxe Peninsula ➤1 | 94 | 65.00 N | 76.00 W |
| Foxford | 60 | 53.59 N | 9.08 W |
| Foxholes | 54 | 54.08 N | 0.28 W |
| Foyers | 58 | 57.15 N | 4.29 W |
| Foyle ≈ | 60 | 55.04 N | 7.15 W |
| Foyle, Lough C | 60 | 55.07 N | 7.08 W |
| Foynes | 60 | 52.35 N | 9.06 W |
| Framlingham | 54 | 52.13 N | 1.21 E |
| Frampton on Severn | 54 | 51.46 N | 2.22 W |
| Franca | 100 | 20.32 S | 47.24 W |
| Francavilla Fontana | 72 | 40.31 N | 17.35 E |
| France □1 | 50 | 46.00 N | 2.00 E |
| Francis Case, Lake | 96 | 43.15 N | 99.00 W |
| Francofonte | 72 | 37.13 N | 14.53 E |
| François Lake | 94 | 54.00 N | 125.40 W |
| Francs Peak ▲ | 96 | 43.58 N | 109.20 W |
| Frankenberg | 66 | 51.03 N | 13.01 E |
| Frankenthal | 66 | 49.32 N | 8.21 E |
| Frankfurt am Main | 66 | 50.07 N | 8.40 E |
| Frankfurt an der Oder | 66 | 52.20 N | 14.33 E |
| Franklin Bay C | 94 | 69.45 N | 125.35 W |
| Franklin Lake | 94 | 66.56 N | 96.03 W |
| Franklin Mountains | 94 | 65.00 N | 125.00 W |
| Franklin Strait U | 94 | 72.00 N | 96.00 W |
| Frascati | 72 | 41.48 N | 12.41 E |
| Fraser ≈, B.C., Can. | 94 | 49.09 N | 123.12 W |
| Fraser ≈, Newf., Can. | 94 | 56.35 N | 61.55 W |
| Fraserburgh | 58 | 57.42 N | 2.00 W |
| Fraser Island I | 92 | 25.15 S | 153.10 E |
| Fraser Plateau ▲1 | 94 | 51.30 N | 122.00 W |
| Frauenfeld | 68 | 47.34 N | 8.54 E |
| Fredericia | 64 | 55.35 N | 9.46 E |
| Frederick | 96 | 39.24 N | 77.25 W |
| Fredericton | 94 | 45.58 N | 66.39 W |
| Frederikshavn | 64 | 57.26 N | 10.32 E |
| Fredrikstad | 64 | 59.13 N | 10.57 E |
| Freels, Cape ➤ | 94 | 49.15 N | 53.28 W |
| Freemount | 60 | 52.16 N | 8.50 W |
| Freetown | 86 | 8.30 N | 13.15 W |
| Fregenal de la Sierra | 70 | 38.10 N | 6.39 W |
| Freiberg | 66 | 50.54 N | 13.20 E |
| Freiburg [im Breisgau] | 66 | 47.59 N | 7.51 E |
| Freising | 66 | 48.24 N | 11.44 E |
| Freital | 66 | 51.00 N | 13.39 E |
| Fréjus | 68 | 43.26 N | 6.44 E |
| Fremantle | 92 | 32.03 S | 115.45 E |
| Fremington | 54 | 51.04 N | 4.07 W |
| French Guiana ⌂2 | 100 | 4.00 N | 53.00 W |
| Frenchpark | 60 | 53.52 N | 8.24 W |
| French Polynesia ⌂2 | 8 | 15.00 S | 140.00 W |
| French Southern and Antarctic Territories ⌂2 | | | |
| Fresco ≈ | 86 | 5.03 N | 5.32 W |
| Freshford | 60 | 52.44 N | 7.24 W |
| Freshwater | 54 | 50.41 N | 1.30 W |
| Fresnillo | 96 | 23.10 N | 102.53 W |
| Fresno | 96 | 36.45 N | 119.45 W |
| Freudenstadt | 66 | 48.28 N | 8.25 E |
| Frewash ≈ | 54 | 52.52 N | 1.14 W |
| Freycinet Peninsula ➤1 | 92 | 42.13 S | 148.18 E |
| Fria, Cape ➤ | 90 | 18.26 S | 12.01 E |
| Fribourg (Freiburg) | 68 | 46.48 N | 7.09 E |
| Fridaythorpe | 54 | 54.01 N | 0.40 W |
| Friedrichshafen | 66 | 47.39 N | 9.28 E |
| Frinton-on-Sea | 54 | 51.50 N | 1.14 E |
| Frio, Cabo ➤ | 100 | 22.53 S | 42.00 W |
| Frisa, Loch | 58 | 56.33 N | 6.06 W |
| Frisian Islands II | 66 | 53.35 N | 6.40 E |
| Frizington | 54 | 54.33 N | 3.29 W |
| Frobisher Bay C | 94 | 62.30 N | 66.00 W |
| Frodsham | 54 | 53.18 N | 2.44 W |
| Frome | 54 | 51.14 N | 2.20 W |
| Frome ≈, Eng., U.K. | 54 | 50.41 N | 2.05 W |
| Frome ≈, Eng., U.K. | 54 | 50.44 N | 2.19 W |
| Frosinone | 72 | 41.38 N | 13.19 E |
| Frøya I | 64 | 63.45 N | 8.45 E |
| Frýdek-Místek | 66 | 49.41 N | 18.22 E |
| Fuday I | 58 | 57.03 N | 7.23 W |
| Fuengirola | 70 | 36.33 N | 4.37 W |
| Fuerteventura I | 86 | 28.20 N | 14.00 W |
| Fujian ⌂ | 80 | 26.00 N | 118.00 E |
| Fujin | 80 | 47.14 N | 132.02 E |
| Fuji-san ▲1 | 80 | 35.21 N | 138.44 E |
| Fukui | 80 | 36.04 N | 136.13 E |
| Fukuoka | 80 | 33.35 N | 130.24 E |
| Fukushima | 80 | 37.45 N | 140.28 E |
| Fülädï, Küh-e ▲ | 84 | 34.38 N | 67.32 E |
| Fulda | 66 | 50.33 N | 9.41 E |
| Fulda ≈ | 66 | 51.25 N | 9.39 E |
| Fuling | 80 | 29.42 N | 107.21 E |
| Fulwood | 54 | 53.46 N | 2.42 W |
| Funchal | 86 | 32.38 N | 16.54 W |
| Fundy, Bay of C | 94 | 45.00 N | 66.00 W |
| Funshinagh, Lough | 60 | 53.31 N | 8.07 W |
| Furmanov | 62 | 57.15 N | 41.07 E |
| Furnace | 58 | 56.09 N | 5.10 W |
| Furnas, Représa de ⌂1 | 100 | 20.45 S | 46.00 W |
| Furneaux Group II | 92 | 40.10 S | 148.05 E |
| Furness Fells ▲2 | 54 | 54.18 N | 3.07 W |
| Fürstenfeldbruck | 66 | 48.10 N | 11.15 E |
| Fürstenwalde | 66 | 52.21 N | 14.04 E |
| Fürth | 66 | 49.28 N | 10.59 E |
| Fushun | 80 | 41.52 N | 123.53 E |
| Füssen | 66 | 47.34 N | 10.42 E |
| Fuxian | 80 | 39.37 N | 122.01 E |
| Fuxinshi | 80 | 42.05 N | 121.46 E |
| Fuyang | 80 | 32.52 N | 115.42 E |
| Fuyu | 80 | 45.10 N | 124.50 E |
| Fuzhou, Zhg. | 80 | 28.01 N | 116.20 E |
| Fuzhou, Zhg. | 80 | 26.06 N | 119.17 E |
| Fyfield | 54 | 51.45 N | 0.16 E |
| Fylde ▲1 | 54 | 53.47 N | 2.56 W |
| Fyn I | 64 | 55.20 N | 10.30 E |
| Fyne, Loch C, Scot., U.K. | 58 | 56.00 N | 5.22 W |
| Fyne, Loch C, Scot., U.K. | 52 | 56.30 N | 5.20 W |
| Fyvie | 58 | 57.25 N | 2.23 W |
| **G** | | | |
| Gabès | 86 | 33.53 N | 10.07 E |
| Gabès, Golfe de C | 86 | 34.00 N | 10.25 E |
| Gabon □1 | 90 | 1.00 S | 11.45 E |
| Gaborone | 90 | 24.45 S | 25.55 E |
| Gabriel Strait U | 94 | 61.45 N | 65.30 W |
| Gabrovo | 74 | 42.52 N | 25.19 E |
| Gadag | 84 | 15.25 N | 75.38 E |
| Gadsden | 96 | 34.02 N | 86.00 W |
| Gaerwen | 56 | 53.13 N | 4.16 W |
| Gaeta | 72 | 41.12 N | 13.35 E |
| Gaferut I | 82 | 9.14 N | 145.23 E |
| Gafsa | 86 | 34.25 N | 8.48 E |
| Gagarin | 62 | 55.33 N | 35.00 E |
| Gaggenau | 66 | 48.48 N | 8.19 E |
| Gagnoa | 86 | 6.08 N | 5.56 W |
| Gainesville | 96 | 29.40 N | 82.20 W |
| Gainford | 54 | 54.32 N | 1.44 W |
| Gainsborough | 54 | 53.24 N | 0.46 W |
| Gairdner, Lake | 92 | 31.35 S | 136.00 E |
| Gairloch | 58 | 57.42 N | 5.40 W |
| Gairloch, Loch C | 58 | 57.44 N | 5.44 W |
| Gairsay I | 58 | 59.05 N | 2.59 W |
| Galán, Cerro ▲ | 102 | 25.55 S | 66.52 W |
| Galana ≈ | 90 | 3.09 S | 40.08 E |
| Galashiels | 56 | 55.37 N | 2.49 W |
| Galaţi | 74 | 45.26 N | 28.03 E |
| Galatina | 72 | 40.10 N | 18.10 E |
| Gala Water ≈ | 56 | 55.35 N | 2.47 W |
| Galera, Punta ➤ | 102 | 39.59 S | 73.43 W |
| Galesburg | 96 | 40.57 N | 90.22 W |
| Galič | 62 | 58.23 N | 42.21 E |
| Galka'yo | 88 | 6.49 N | 47.23 E |
| Gallan Head ➤ | 58 | 58.14 N | 7.03 W |
| Gallarate | 72 | 45.40 N | 8.47 E |
| Galle | 84 | 6.02 N | 80.13 E |
| Galley Head ➤ | 60 | 51.30 N | 8.57 W |
| Gallinas, Punta ➤ | 100 | 12.28 N | 71.40 W |
| Gallipoli | 72 | 40.03 N | 17.58 E |
| Gällivare | 62 | 67.07 N | 20.45 E |
| Galloway ⌂9 | 56 | 55.00 N | 4.25 W |
| Galloway, Mull of ➤ | 54 | 54.38 N | 4.50 W |
| Galston | 56 | 55.36 N | 4.22 W |
| Galtymore ▲ | 60 | 52.22 N | 8.10 W |
| Galty Mountains ▲ | 52 | 52.25 N | 8.10 W |
| Galveston | 96 | 29.18 N | 94.48 W |
| Galway | 60 | 53.16 N | 9.03 W |
| Galway ⌂6 | 60 | 53.20 N | 9.03 W |
| Gamba | 80 | 28.17 N | 88.31 E |
| Gambia (Gambie) □1 | 86 | 13.25 N | 16.00 W |
| Gambia (Gambie) ≈ | 86 | 13.28 N | 16.34 W |
| Gamph, Slieve ▲ | 60 | 54.05 N | 8.55 W |
| Gandak ≈ | 84 | 25.40 N | 85.13 E |
| Ganderkesee | 66 | 53.04 N | 8.33 E |
| Gandia | 70 | 38.58 N | 0.11 W |
| Ganges (Ganga) (Padma) ≈ | 84 | 23.22 N | 90.32 E |
| Gangtok | 84 | 27.20 N | 88.37 E |
| Gannett Peak ▲ | 96 | 43.11 N | 109.39 W |
| Ganu Mòr ▲ | 58 | 58.25 N | 4.53 W |
| Ganzhou | 80 | 25.51 N | 114.55 E |
| Gao | 86 | 16.16 N | 0.03 W |
| Gaoyouhu | 80 | 32.50 N | 119.20 E |
| Gap | 68 | 44.34 N | 6.05 E |
| Gara, Lough | 60 | 53.57 N | 8.25 W |
| Garanhuns | 100 | 8.54 S | 36.29 W |
| Garboldisham | 54 | 52.24 N | 0.56 E |
| Gardelegen | 66 | 52.31 N | 11.23 E |
| Gardone Val Trompia | 72 | 45.41 N | 10.11 E |
| Garelochhead | 58 | 56.05 N | 4.50 W |
| Garforth | 54 | 53.48 N | 1.24 W |
| Gargrave | 54 | 53.59 N | 2.06 W |
| Garies | 90 | 30.30 S | 17.59 E |
| Garlieston | 56 | 54.48 N | 4.22 W |
| Garmisch-Partenkirchen | 66 | 47.29 N | 11.05 E |
| Garmouth | 58 | 57.40 N | 3.07 W |
| Garnet Bay C | 94 | 65.17 N | 75.15 W |
| Garonne ≈ | 68 | 45.02 N | 0.36 W |
| Garoua | 86 | 9.18 N | 13.24 E |
| Garrison | 60 | 54.25 N | 8.05 W |
| Garron Point ➤ | 60 | 55.03 N | 5.55 W |
| Garros | 58 | 57.37 N | 6.42 W |
| Garry ≈ | 58 | 56.43 N | 3.47 W |
| Garry Bay C | 94 | 68.55 N | 85.05 W |
| Garry Lake | 94 | 66.00 N | 100.00 W |
| Garsdale Head | 54 | 54.19 N | 2.20 W |
| Garstang | 54 | 53.55 N | 2.47 W |
| Garvagh | 60 | 54.59 N | 6.42 W |
| Garvao | 70 | 37.42 N | 8.21 W |
| Garve | 58 | 57.37 N | 4.42 W |
| Garvellachs II | 58 | 56.14 N | 5.47 W |
| Gary | 96 | 41.36 N | 87.20 W |
| Gascoyne ≈ | 92 | 24.52 S | 113.37 E |
| Gash (Al-Qash) ≈ | 88 | 16.48 N | 35.51 E |
| Gastonia | 96 | 35.15 N | 81.11 W |
| Gata, Cabo de ➤ | 70 | 36.45 N | 2.11 W |
| Gatčina | 62 | 59.34 N | 30.08 E |
| Gateshead | 54 | 54.58 N | 1.37 W |
| Gatehouse of Fleet | 56 | 54.53 N | 4.11 W |
| Gatineau ≈ | 94 | 45.27 N | 75.40 W |
| Gauer Lake | 94 | 57.00 N | 97.50 W |
| Gauhati | 84 | 26.11 N | 91.45 E |
| Gaula ≈ | 64 | 63.21 N | 10.14 E |
| Gausta ▲ | 64 | 59.50 N | 8.35 E |
| Gävle | 64 | 60.40 N | 17.10 E |
| Gavrilov-Jam | 62 | 57.18 N | 39.51 E |
| Gawler Ranges ▲ | 92 | 32.30 S | 136.00 E |
| Gaya | 84 | 24.48 N | 85.03 E |
| Gaywood | 54 | 52.46 N | 0.26 E |
| Gaziantep | 84 | 37.05 N | 37.22 E |
| Gdańsk (Danzig) | 66 | 54.23 N | 18.40 E |
| Gdynia | 66 | 54.32 N | 18.33 E |
| Géba ≈ | 86 | 11.46 N | 15.36 W |
| Gebze | 74 | 40.48 N | 29.25 E |
| Gedaref | 88 | 14.02 N | 35.24 E |
| Gedling | 54 | 52.58 N | 1.06 W |
| Geel | 66 | 51.10 N | 4.59 E |
| Geelong | 92 | 38.08 S | 144.21 E |
| Geikie ≈ | 94 | 57.45 N | 103.52 W |
| Gejiu (Kokiu) | 80 | 23.22 N | 103.06 E |
| Gela | 72 | 37.03 N | 14.15 E |
| Gelasa, Selat U | 82 | 2.50 S | 107.15 E |
| Geleen | 66 | 50.58 N | 5.52 E |
| Gelibolu | 74 | 40.24 N | 26.40 E |
| Gelsenkirchen | 66 | 51.30 N | 7.05 E |
| Gelt ≈ | 54 | 54.56 N | 2.47 W |
| Gemlik | 74 | 40.26 N | 29.09 E |
| General Roca | 102 | 39.02 S | 67.35 W |

| Name | Page | Lat | Long |
|---|---|---|---|
| Geneva, Lake | 50 | 46.25 N | 6.30 E |
| Genève | 68 | 46.12 N | 6.09 E |
| Genk | 66 | 50.58 N | 5.30 E |
| Genova (Genoa) | 72 | 44.25 N | 8.57 E |
| Gent (Gand) | 66 | 51.03 N | 3.43 E |
| Genthin | 66 | 52.24 N | 12.09 E |
| Geographe Bay C | 92 | 33.35 S 115.15 E |
| Geographe Channel | 92 | 24.40 S 113.20 E |
| George | 90 | 58.49 N | 66.10 W |
| George, Lake | 90 | 0.00 N | 30.12 E |
| Georgetown, Cay. Is. | 98 | 19.18 N | 81.23 W |
| Georgetown, Guy. | 100 | 6.48 N | 58.10 W |
| Georgia | 94 | 32.50 N | 83.15 W |
| Georgia, Strait of | 94 | 49.00 N 123.20 W |
| Georgian Bay C | 94 | 45.15 N | 80.50 W |
| Gergina | 72 | 23.30 S 139.47 E |
| Georgiu-Dež | 76 | 50.59 N | 39.30 E |
| Gera | 66 | 50.52 N | 12.04 E |
| Geraardsbergen | 66 | 50.46 N | 3.52 E |
| Geral, Serra | 102 | 26.25 S | 51.25 W |
| Geral de Goiás, Serra | 100 | 13.00 S | 46.15 W |
| Geral do Paraná, Serra | 100 | 14.45 S | 47.30 W |
| Gerlachovský štít | 58 | 49.12 N | 20.08 E |
| German Democratic Republic (East Germany) | 66 | 52.00 N | 12.30 E |
| Germany, Federal Republic of (West Germany) | 66 | 51.00 N | 9.00 E |
| Germiston | 90 | 26.15 S | 28.05 E |
| Gerona | 70 | 41.59 N | 2.49 E |
| Getafe | 70 | 40.18 N | 3.43 W |
| Geyser, Banc du | 90 | 12.25 S | 46.25 E |
| Ghâghra | 84 | 25.47 N | 84.37 E |
| Ghana | 88 | 8.00 N | 2.00 W |
| Ghardaïa | 86 | 32.31 N | 3.37 E |
| Ghawdex | 50 | 0.00 |  |
| Ghazāl, Bahr al- | 88 | 9.31 N | 30.25 E |
| Ghazal, Bahr el | 88 | 13.01 N | 15.28 E |
| Ghāziābād | 84 | 28.40 N | 77.26 E |
| Ghaznî | 84 | 33.33 N | 68.26 E |
| Ghazzah | 84 | 31.30 N | 34.28 E |
| Gheorghe Gheorghiu-Dej | 74 | 46.14 N | 26.44 E |
| Gheorgheni | 74 | 46.43 N | 25.36 E |
| Ghio, Beinn a | 58 | 56.50 N | 3.43 W |
| Gia-dinh | 82 | 10.48 N 106.42 E |
| Gibraltar | 70 | 36.09 N | 5.21 W |
| Gibraltar | 50 | 36.11 N | 5.22 W |
| Gibraltar, Strait of | 70 | 35.57 N | 5.36 W |
| Gibraltar Point | 56 | 53.05 N | 0.19 E |
| Gibson Desert | 92 | 24.30 S 126.00 E |
| Gien | 68 | 47.42 N | 2.38 E |
| Giessen | 66 | 50.35 N | 8.40 E |
| Gifford | 58 | 55.54 N | 2.45 W |
| Gifford Fjord | 94 | 69.57 N | 81.55 W |
| Gifhorn | 66 | 52.29 N | 10.33 E |
| Gifu | 80 | 35.25 N 136.45 E |
| Giggleswick | 56 | 54.04 N | 2.17 W |
| Gigha, Sound of | 58 | 55.41 N | 5.44 W |
| Gigha Island | 58 | 55.41 N | 5.44 W |
| Gijón | 70 | 43.32 N | 5.40 W |
| Gila | 96 | 32.43 N 114.33 W |
| Gilbert | 92 | 16.35 S 141.15 E |
| Gilbert Islands | 8 | 0.30 S 174.00 E |
| Gilford | 60 | 54.23 N | 6.22 W |
| Gilgit | 84 | 35.44 N | 74.38 E |
| Gill, Lough | 60 | 54.16 N | 8.24 W |
| Gillen, Lake | 92 | 26.11 S 124.38 E |
| Gillian, Lake | 94 | 69.32 N | 75.23 W |
| Gillingham, Eng., U.K. | 54 | 51.24 N | 0.33 E |
| Gillingham, Eng., U.K. | 54 | 51.02 N | 2.17 W |
| Gilo | 88 | 8.10 N | 33.15 E |
| Gil'uj | 78 | 53.58 N 127.30 E |
| Gilwern | 54 | 51.51 N | 3.06 W |
| Ginosa | 72 | 40.34 N | 16.46 E |
| Gioia del Colle | 72 | 40.48 N | 16.56 E |
| Gioia Tauro | 72 | 38.26 N | 15.54 E |
| Gipping | 54 | 52.04 N | 1.10 E |
| Girardot | 100 | 4.18 N | 74.48 W |
| Girga | 88 | 26.19 N | 31.53 E |
| Girvan | 58 | 55.15 N | 4.51 W |
| Girvan, Water of | 58 | 55.15 N | 4.51 W |
| Girvas | 62 | 62.30 N | 33.40 E |
| Giugliano [in Campania] | 72 | 40.56 N | 14.12 E |
| Giulianova | 72 | 42.45 N | 13.57 E |
| Giurgiu | 74 | 43.53 N | 25.57 E |
| Givors | 68 | 45.35 N | 4.46 E |
| Giżycko | 58 | 54.03 N | 21.47 E |
| Gjirokastër | 74 | 40.05 N | 20.10 E |
| Gjøvik | 64 | 60.48 N | 10.42 E |
| Glace Bay | 94 | 46.12 N | 59.57 W |
| Gladbeck | 66 | 51.34 N | 6.59 E |
| Glâma | 58 | 59.12 N | 10.57 E |
| Glamis | 58 | 56.36 N | 3.00 W |
| Glanamman | 54 | 51.48 N | 3.54 W |
| Glascarnoch, Loch | 58 | 57.40 N | 4.50 W |
| Glasgow | 58 | 55.53 N | 4.15 W |
| Glaslyn | 54 | 52.56 N | 4.06 W |
| Glas Maol | 58 | 56.52 N | 3.22 W |
| Glasson | 56 | 54.00 N | 2.50 W |
| Glass, Loch | 58 | 57.43 N | 4.30 W |
| Glastonbury | 54 | 51.09 N | 2.43 W |
| Glauchau | 66 | 50.49 N | 12.32 E |
| Glaven | 54 | 52.58 N | 1.03 E |
| Glazov | 76 | 58.09 N | 52.40 E |
| Glemsford | 54 | 52.06 N | 0.40 E |
| Glen, Eng., U.K. | 54 | 52.51 N | 0.06 W |
| Glen, Eire | 60 | 54.38 N | 8.40 W |
| Glenamaddy | 60 | 53.37 N | 8.35 W |
| Glenamoy | 60 | 54.14 N | 9.42 W |
| Glenarm | 60 | 54.58 N | 5.57 W |
| Glenavy | 60 | 54.35 N | 6.13 W |
| Glenbeigh | 60 | 52.02 N | 9.58 W |
| Glencolumbkille | 60 | 54.43 N | 8.45 E |
| Glencoul, Loch C | 58 | 58.14 N | 4.58 W |
| Glendoe Forest | 57 | 57.06 N | 4.34 W |
| Glendowan | 60 | 54.58 N | 7.57 W |
| Glenelg | 58 | 57.13 N | 5.38 W |
| Glenelly | 60 | 54.45 N | 7.18 W |
| Glenfarg | 58 | 56.16 N | 3.24 W |
| Glenfinnan | 58 | 54.17 N | 7.59 W |
| Glenfield | 54 | 52.39 N | 1.12 W |
| Glenluce | 58 | 54.53 N | 4.49 W |
| Glenrothes | 58 | 56.12 N | 3.10 W |
| Glens Falls | 96 | 43.19 N | 73.39 W |
| Glenshee V | 58 | 56.45 N | 3.25 W |
| Glenties | 60 | 54.47 N | 8.17 W |
| Glenville | 54 | 52.03 N | 8.26 W |
| Glin | 60 | 52.34 N | 9.17 W |
| Glittertinden | 64 | 61.39 N | 8.33 E |
| Gliwice (Gleiwitz) | 58 | 50.17 N | 18.40 E |
| Głogów | 66 | 51.40 N | 16.05 E |
| Glorieuses, Îles | 90 | 11.30 S | 47.20 E |
| Glossop | 56 | 53.27 N | 1.57 W |
| Gloucester | 54 | 51.53 N | 2.14 W |
| Gloucester, Vale of | 54 | 51.55 N | 2.15 W |
| Gloucestershire | 54 | 51.47 N | 2.15 W |
| Głowno | 58 | 51.58 N | 19.44 E |
| Głuchołazy | 66 | 50.20 N | 17.22 E |
| Glyde | 60 | 53.52 N | 6.21 W |
| Glyder Fawr | 54 | 53.08 N | 4.02 W |
| Glyme | 54 | 51.49 N | 1.22 W |
| Glynneath | 54 | 51.46 N | 3.38 W |
| Gmünden | 66 | 47.55 N | 13.48 E |
| Gniezno | 66 | 52.31 N | 17.37 E |
| Gnjilane | 74 | 42.28 N | 21.29 E |
| Goat Fell | 58 | 55.39 N | 5.10 W |
| Goba | 88 | 54.23 N | 0.44 W |
| Goch | 66 | 51.40 N 105.00 E |
| Goce Delčev | 74 | 41.34 N | 23.44 E |
| Godalming | 54 | 51.11 N | 0.37 W |
| Godhra | 84 | 22.46 N | 73.36 E |
| Godmanchester | 54 | 52.19 N | 0.11 W |
| Gödöllő | 58 | 47.36 N | 19.22 E |
| Godoy Cruz | 102 | 32.55 S | 68.50 W |
| Gods | 94 | 56.22 N | 92.51 W |

| Name | Page | Lat | Long |
|---|---|---|---|
| Godshill | 54 | 50.38 N | 1.14 W |
| Gods Mercy, Bay of | 94 | 54.45 N | 94.00 W |
| Godstone | 54 | 51.15 N | 0.04 W |
| Godthåb | 94 | 64.11 N | 51.44 W |
| Godwin Austen (K2) | 84 | 35.53 N | 76.30 E |
| Goëland, Lac au | 94 | 49.47 N | 76.48 W |
| Goëlands, Lac aux | 94 |  |  |
| Goes | 66 | 55.27 N | 64.17 W |
| Goiana | 100 | 51.30 N | 3.54 E |
| Goiânia | 100 | 7.33 S | 34.59 W |
| Goiás | 100 | 16.40 S | 49.15 W |
| Goil, Loch C | 58 | 16.08 N | 49.52 W |
| Gôlcâk | 74 | 56.08 N | 4.52 W |
| Gölcük | 74 | 55.05 N | 8.22 W |
| Golden | 94 | 40.44 N | 29.48 E |
| Golden Hinde | 94 | 52.29 N | 7.58 W |
| Golden Valley V | 54 | 49.40 N 125.45 W |
| Golec-In'aptuk, Gora | 54 | 52.02 N | 2.56 W |
| Golec-Skalistyj, Gora | 78 | 56.22 N 110.11 E |
| Goleen | 60 | 56.24 N 119.12 E |
| Goleniów | 60 | 51.28 N | 9.43 W |
| Golspie | 66 | 53.36 N | 14.50 E |
| Gomel' | 58 | 57.58 N | 3.58 W |
| Gomera | 76 | 52.25 N | 31.00 E |
| Gometra I | 86 | 28.06 N | 17.08 W |
| Gómez Palacio | 58 | 56.29 N | 6.17 W |
| Gonam | 98 | 25.34 N 103.30 W |
| Gonâve, Île de la I | 78 | 57.17 N 131.14 E |
| Gonbad-e Qâbūs | 98 | 18.51 N | 73.03 W |
| Gonder | 84 | 37.15 N | 55.17 E |
| Gondomar | 88 | 12.40 N | 37.30 E |
| Gönen | 70 | 41.09 N | 8.32 W |
| Gonggashan | 74 | 40.06 N | 27.39 E |
| Gonggeershan | 80 | 29.35 N 101.51 E |
| Good Hope, Cape of | 80 | 38.37 N | 75.20 E |
| Good Hope Mountain | 90 | 34.24 S | 18.30 E |
| Goodwick | 54 | 51.09 N 124.10 W |
| Goole | 56 | 52.00 N | 5.00 W |
| Goose Lake | 96 | 53.42 N | 0.52 W |
| Göppingen | 66 | 41.57 N 120.25 W |
| Gorakhpur | 84 | 48.42 N | 9.40 E |
| Gorda, Punta | 98 | 26.45 N | 83.22 E |
| Gordon | 58 | 22.24 N | 82.10 W |
| Gorebridge | 58 | 55.41 N | 2.34 W |
| Gorey, Eire | 60 | 51.51 N | 6.18 W |
| Gorey, Jersey | 55b | 52.40 N | 6.18 W |
| Gorgân | 84 | 49.12 N | 2.02 W |
| Gorinchem | 66 | 36.50 N | 54.29 E |
| Goring | 54 | 51.50 N | 5.00 W |
| Goring-by-Sea | 54 | 52.32 N | 1.09 W |
| Goring Gap V | 54 | 50.49 N | 0.25 W |
| Gorizia | 72 | 51.32 N | 1.08 W |
| Gor'kij (Gorky) | 76 | 45.57 N | 13.38 E |
| Gor'kovskoje Vodochranilišče | 56 | 56.20 N | 44.00 E |
| Gorleston on Sea | 76 | 57.00 N | 43.10 E |
| Gorlice | 58 | 52.36 N | 1.43 E |
| Görlitz | 66 | 49.40 N | 21.10 E |
| Gorlovka | 76 | 51.10 N | 38.03 E |
| Gorm, Loch | 58 | 48.18 N | 6.25 W |
| Gorn'ackij | 76 | 55.48 N | 4.03 W |
| Gorna Orjahovica | 74 | 67.32 N | 64.03 E |
| Gorno-Altajsk | 78 | 43.07 N | 25.41 E |
| Gorodec | 62 | 51.58 N | 85.58 E |
| Gorodenka | 74 | 51.50 N | 3.52 W |
| Gorodišče | 58 | 48.41 N | 25.29 E |
| Gorodok | 58 | 53.17 N | 45.42 E |
| Gorontalo | 82 | 55.28 N | 29.59 E |
| Gorseinon | 54 | 0.33 N 123.03 E |
| Gort | 60 | 51.40 N | 4.02 W |
| Gortahork | 60 | 53.04 N | 8.50 W |
| Gorumna Island I | 60 | 55.08 N | 8.09 W |
| Gosforth, Eng., U.K. | 56 | 53.13 N | 9.40 W |
| Gosforth, Eng., U.K. | 56 | 55.01 N | 1.37 W |
| Goslar | 66 | 54.26 N | 3.27 W |
| Gosp[ort | 54 | 51.54 N | 10.25 E |
| Gossau | 54 | 50.48 N | 1.08 W |
| Gostivar | 74 | 50.37 N 134.51 E |
| Gostyń | 58 | 41.48 N | 20.54 E |
| Gostynin | 58 | 51.53 N | 17.00 E |
| Göteborg (Gothenburg) | 66 | 52.26 N | 19.29 E |
| Gotha | 66 | 57.43 N | 11.58 E |
| Gotland | 64 | 50.57 N | 10.41 E |
| Gotska Sandön | 58 | 58.23 N | 19.16 E |
| Göttingen | 66 | 51.32 N | 9.55 E |
| Gottwaldov | 66 | 49.13 N | 17.41 E |
| Gouda | 66 | 52.01 N | 4.43 E |
| Goudhurst | 54 | 51.07 N | 0.28 E |
| Gough Island I | 8 | 40.20 S | 10.00 W |
| Gouin, Réservoir | 94 | 48.38 N | 74.54 W |
| Goulburn | 92 | 34.45 S 149.43 E |
| Goulburn Islands II | 92 | 11.33 S 133.26 E |
| Goundam | 88 | 16.25 N | 3.40 W |
| Gourock | 58 | 55.58 N | 4.49 W |
| Governador Valadares | 100 | 18.51 S | 41.56 W |
| Gower I | 54 | 51.36 N | 4.10 W |
| Gowerton | 54 | 51.39 N | 4.01 W |
| Gowna, Lough | 60 | 53.51 N | 7.34 W |
| Gowy | 56 | 53.17 N | 2.51 W |
| Goya | 102 | 29.08 S | 59.16 W |
| Graaff-Reinet | 90 | 32.14 S | 24.32 E |
| Gračanica | 74 | 44.42 N | 18.19 E |
| Gracias a Dios, Cabo | 98 | 15.00 N | 83.10 W |
| Gradaús, Serra dos | 100 | 8.00 S | 50.45 W |
| Grado | 72 | 45.40 N | 13.23 E |
| Graemsay I | 58 | 58.56 N | 3.17 W |
| Grafham Water | 54 | 52.17 N | 0.20 W |
| Grafton | 92 | 29.41 S 152.56 E |
| Grafton, Cape | 92 | 16.52 S 145.55 E |
| Graham Island I | 94 | 53.40 N 132.30 W |
| Graham Moore Bay | 94 | 75.26 N 101.25 W |
| Grahamstown | 90 | 33.19 S | 26.31 E |
| Grain I | 54 | 51.28 N | 0.43 E |
| Grain, Isle of I | 54 | 51.27 N | 0.41 E |
| Grajaú | 100 | 5.49 S | 44.48 W |
| Grajewo | 58 | 53.39 N | 22.27 E |
| Grammichele | 72 | 37.13 N | 14.38 E |
| Grampian ⬜ | 58 | 57.15 N | 2.45 W |
| Grampian Mountains | 58 | 56.45 N | 4.00 W |
| Granada, Esp. | 70 | 37.13 N | 3.41 W |
| Granada, Nic. | 98 | 11.56 N | 85.57 W |
| Granard | 60 | 53.47 N | 7.30 W |
| Gran Canaria I | 86 | 28.00 N | 15.36 W |
| Gran Chaco | 102 | 23.00 S | 60.00 W |
| Grand Bahama I | 98 | 26.35 N | 78.00 W |
| Grand Canal C | 52 | 53.21 N | 6.14 W |
| Grand Canyon V | 96 | 36.10 N 112.45 W |
| Grand Cayman I | 98 | 19.20 N | 81.15 W |
| Grande, Bol. | 100 | 15.51 S | 64.39 W |
| Grande, Bra. | 100 | 11.05 S | 43.09 W |
| Grande, Bahía | 102 | 50.45 S | 68.45 W |
| Grande, Boca | 102 | 8.38 N | 60.30 W |
| Grande, Ilha I | 100 | 23.09 S | 44.14 W |
| Grande, Rio (Bravo del Norte) | 96 | 25.55 N | 97.09 W |
| Grande de Santiago | 98 | 21.35 N | 105.20 W |
| Grande de Tarija | 102 | 22.53 S | 64.21 W |
| Grande do Gurupá, Ilha I | 100 | 1.00 S | 51.30 W |
| Grand Erg de Bilma | 88 | 18.30 N | 14.00 E |
| Grand Erg Occidental | 86 | 30.30 N | 0.30 E |
| Grand Erg Oriental | 86 | 30.00 N | 7.00 E |
| Grandes, Salinas | 102 | 30.00 S | 65.00 W |
| Grand Forks | 96 | 47.55 N | 97.03 W |
| Grand, Lac | 94 | 63.59 N 119.00 W |
| Grandola | 70 | 38.10 N | 8.34 W |
| Grand Junction | 96 | 39.05 N 108.33 W |
| Grand Rapids | 96 | 42.58 N | 85.40 W |
| Grand Rivière de la Baleine | 94 | 55.16 N | 77.47 W |

| Name | Page | Lat | Long |
|---|---|---|---|
| Grand Teton | 96 | 43.44 N 110.48 W |
| Grandtully | 58 | 56.39 N | 3.49 W |
| Grand Turk | 98 | 21.28 N | 71.08 W |
| Graney, Lough | 60 | 52.59 N | 8.40 W |
| Grangemouth | 58 | 56.02 N | 3.44 W |
| Grange-over-Sands | 56 | 54.12 N | 2.55 W |
| Granite Peak | 96 | 45.10 N 109.48 W |
| Grannoch, Loch | 58 | 55.00 N | 4.17 W |
| Grannollers | 70 | 41.37 N | 2.18 E |
| Granta | 54 | 52.10 N | 0.06 E |
| Grantham | 54 | 52.55 N | 0.39 W |
| Granton | 58 | 55.59 N | 3.14 W |
| Grantown on Spey | 58 | 57.20 N | 3.58 W |
| Grant Range | 96 | 38.25 N 115.30 W |
| Grantshouse | 58 | 55.53 N | 2.19 W |
| Granville | 68 | 48.50 N | 1.36 W |
| Granville Lake | 94 | 56.18 N 100.30 W |
| Gras, Lac de | 94 | 64.30 N 110.30 W |
| Grasmere | 56 | 54.28 N | 3.02 W |
| Grasse | 68 | 43.40 N | 6.55 E |
| Grassington | 56 | 54.04 N | 1.59 W |
| Gravelly Point | 94 | 67.10 N | 76.43 W |
| Gravesend | 54 | 51.27 N | 0.24 E |
| Gravina in Puglia | 72 | 40.49 N | 16.25 E |
| Grayshott | 54 | 51.11 N | 0.45 W |
| Grays Peak | 96 | 39.37 N 105.45 W |
| Grays Thurrock | 54 | 51.29 N | 0.20 E |
| Graz | 66 | 47.05 N | 15.27 E |
| Gr'azovec | 58 | 58.53 N | 40.14 E |
| Great Abaco I | 98 | 26.28 N | 77.05 W |
| Great Artesian Basin | 92 | 25.00 S 143.00 E |
| Great Australian Bight | 92 | 35.00 S 130.00 E |
| Great Baddow | 54 | 51.43 N | 0.29 E |
| Great Barrier Reef | 92 | 18.00 S 145.50 E |
| Great Basin | 96 | 40.00 N 117.00 W |
| Great Bear Lake | 94 | 66.00 N 120.00 W |
| Great Bernera I | 58 | 58.13 N | 6.49 W |
| Great Blasket Island | 60 | 52.05 N | 10.32 W |
| Great Channel | 82 | 6.25 N | 94.20 E |
| Great Clifton | 56 | 54.38 N | 3.29 W |
| Great Cumbrae I | 58 | 55.46 N | 4.57 W |
| Great Cumbrae Island I | 58 | 55.46 N | 4.55 W |
| Great Dividing Range | 92 | 25.00 S 147.00 E |
| Great Dunmow | 54 | 51.53 N | 0.22 E |
| Great Eau | 56 | 53.16 N | 0.07 E |
| Greater Antilles II | 98 | 20.00 N | 74.00 W |
| Greater London ⬜² | 54 | 51.30 N | 0.10 W |
| Greater Manchester ⬜⁶ | 56 | 53.30 N | 2.20 W |
| Greater Sunda Islands II | 82 | 2.00 S 110.00 E |
| Great Exuma I | 98 | 23.32 N | 75.50 W |
| Great Falls | 96 | 47.30 N 111.17 W |
| Great Gable | 56 | 54.28 N | 3.12 W |
| Great Harwood | 56 | 53.48 N | 2.24 W |
| Great Inagua I | 98 | 21.05 N | 73.18 W |
| Great Indian Desert (Thar Desert) | 84 | 27.00 N | 71.00 E |
| Great Karroo | 90 | 32.25 S | 22.40 E |
| Great Malvern (Malvern) | 54 | 52.07 N | 2.19 W |
| Great Massingham | 54 | 52.46 N | 0.40 E |
| Great Missenden | 54 | 51.43 N | 0.43 W |
| Great Mis Tor | 54 | 50.34 N | 4.01 W |
| Great Ormes Head | 56 | 53.21 N | 3.52 W |
| Great Ouse | 54 | 52.47 N | 0.22 E |
| Great Plain of the Koukdjuak | 94 | 66.00 N | 73.00 W |
| Great Salt Lake | 96 | 41.10 N 112.30 W |
| Great Sandy Desert, Austl. | 92 | 21.30 S 125.00 E |
| Great Sandy Desert, Oreg., U.S. | 96 | 43.35 N 120.15 W |
| Great Shelford | 54 | 52.09 N | 0.09 E |
| Great Slave Lake | 94 | 61.30 N 114.00 W |
| Great Stour | 54 | 51.19 N | 1.15 E |
| Great Torrington | 54 | 50.57 N | 4.08 W |
| Great Victoria Desert | 92 | 28.30 S 127.45 E |
| Great Whernside | 56 | 54.09 N | 1.59 W |
| Great Yarmouth | 54 | 52.37 N | 1.44 E |
| Gréboun, Mont | 86 | 20.00 N | 8.35 E |
| Greece ⬜¹ | 50 | 39.00 N | 22.00 E |
| Greeley | 96 | 40.25 N 104.42 W |
| Green | 96 | 38.11 N 109.53 W |
| Green Bay | 96 | 45.00 N | 88.01 W |
| Green Bay C | 96 | 45.00 N | 87.30 W |
| Greencastle | 60 | 55.12 N | 6.59 W |
| Greenfield | 54 | 51.28 N | 3.13 W |
| Green Head | 92 | 30.05 S 114.58 E |
| Greenland | 50 | 70.00 N | 40.00 W |
| Greenland ⬜² | 94 | 70.00 N | 40.00 W |
| Greenlaw | 58 | 55.43 N | 2.28 W |
| Green Mountains | 96 | 43.45 N | 72.45 W |
| Greenock | 58 | 55.57 N | 4.45 W |
| Greenodd | 56 | 54.14 N | 3.04 W |
| Greenore Point | 60 | 52.15 N | 6.18 W |
| Greensboro | 96 | 36.04 N | 79.47 W |
| Greenstone Point | 57 | 57.55 N | 5.38 W |
| Greenville, Miss., U.S. | 96 | 33.25 N | 91.05 W |
| Greenville, S.C., U.S. | 96 | 34.51 N | 82.23 W |
| Greenwich ⬜ | 54 | 51.28 N | 0.02 E |
| Gregory Lake | 92 | 20.10 S 127.20 E |
| Gregory Range | 92 | 19.00 S 143.05 E |
| Greifswald | 66 | 54.05 N | 13.23 E |
| Greiz | 66 | 50.39 N | 12.12 E |
| Gremicha | 62 | 68.03 N | 39.27 E |
| Grenada ⬜¹ | 98 | 12.07 N | 61.40 W |
| Grenadine Islands II | 98 | 12.40 N | 61.15 W |
| Grenagh | 60 | 52.00 N | 8.37 W |
| Grenchen | 68 | 47.11 N | 7.24 E |
| Grenoble | 68 | 45.10 N | 5.43 E |
| Grenoside | 56 | 53.27 N | 1.30 W |
| Grenville, Cape | 92 | 11.58 S 143.14 E |
| Greta, Eng., U.K. | 56 | 54.36 N | 3.10 W |
| Greta, Eng., U.K. | 56 | 54.09 N | 2.36 W |
| Gretna | 56 | 54.59 N | 3.04 W |
| Gretna Green | 56 | 54.59 N | 3.04 W |
| Grevená | 74 | 40.05 N | 21.25 E |
| Grevenbroich | 66 | 51.05 N | 6.35 E |
| Grevesmühlen | 66 | 53.51 N | 11.10 E |
| Grey, Cape | 92 | 13.00 S 136.40 E |
| Grey Islands II | 94 | 50.50 N | 55.37 W |
| Grey Range | 92 | 27.00 S 143.35 E |
| Greystones | 60 | 53.09 N | 6.04 W |
| Gribbin Head | 54 | 50.19 N | 4.40 W |
| Griesheim | 66 | 49.50 N | 8.34 E |
| Griffith | 92 | 34.18 S 146.03 E |
| Grijalva | 98 | 18.36 N | 92.39 W |
| Grim, Cape | 92 | 40.41 S 144.41 E |
| Grimma | 66 | 51.14 N | 12.43 E |
| Grimmen | 66 | 54.07 N | 13.02 E |
| Grimsby | 56 | 53.35 N | 0.05 W |
| Grimsey | 64 | 66.34 N | 18.00 W |
| Grinnell Peninsula | 94 | 76.40 N | 95.00 W |
| Grizzly Bear Mountain | 94 | 65.22 N 121.00 W |
| Grodno | 58 | 53.41 N | 23.50 E |
| Grodzisk Mazowiecki | 58 | 52.07 N | 20.37 E |
| Gronau | 66 | 52.13 N | 7.01 E |
| Groningen | 66 | 53.13 N | 6.33 E |
| Groote Eylandt I | 92 | 14.00 S 136.40 E |
| Groot-Karasberge | 90 | 27.20 S | 18.40 E |
| Gros Morne | 90 | 49.36 N | 57.48 W |
| Grosne | 68 | 46.38 N | 4.44 E |
| Grossenhain | 66 | 51.17 N | 13.33 E |
| Grosseto | 72 | 42.46 N | 11.08 E |
| Grossglockner | 66 | 47.04 N | 12.42 E |
| Groswater Bay C | 94 | 54.20 N | 57.30 W |
| Grottaglie | 72 | 40.32 N | 17.26 E |
| Groundhog | 94 | 49.43 N | 81.58 W |
| Grovely Ridge V | 54 | 51.08 N | 2.04 W |

| Name | Page | Lat | Long |
|---|---|---|---|
| Groznyj | 76 | 43.20 N | 45.42 E |
| Grudziadz | 58 | 53.29 N | 18.45 E |
| Gruinard Bay C | 58 | 57.53 N | 5.31 W |
| Gruinart, Loch C | 58 | 55.52 N | 6.20 W |
| Grunavat, Loch C | 58 | 58.10 N | 6.55 W |
| Gruting | 58 | 60.14 N | 1.30 W |
| Gruzinskaja Sovetskaja Socialistićeskaja Respublika ⬜³ | 76 | 42.00 N | 44.00 E |
| Gryfice | 66 | 53.56 N | 15.12 E |
| Guacanayabo, Golfo de C | 98 | 20.28 N | 77.30 W |
| Guadalajara, Esp. | 70 | 40.38 N | 3.10 W |
| Guadalajara, Méx. | 98 | 20.40 N 103.20 W |
| Guadalcanal I | 8 | 9.32 S 160.12 E |
| Guadalquivir | 70 | 36.47 N | 6.22 W |
| Guadalupe Peak | 96 | 31.50 N 104.52 W |
| Guadeloupe ⬜² | 98 | 16.15 N | 61.35 W |
| Guadiana | 70 | 37.14 N | 7.22 W |
| Guadix | 70 | 37.18 N | 3.08 W |
| Guafo, Isla I | 102 | 43.36 S | 74.43 W |
| Guainia | 100 | 2.01 N | 67.07 W |
| Gualeguaychú | 102 | 33.01 S | 58.31 W |
| Gualicho, Salina | 102 | 40.24 S | 65.15 W |
| Guampí, Sierra de | 100 | 6.00 N | 65.35 W |
| Guanajuato | 98 | 21.01 N 101.15 W |
| Guang'an | 80 | 30.28 N 106.39 E |
| Guanghua | 80 | 32.25 N 111.36 E |
| Guangyuan | 80 | 32.23 N 105.58 E |
| Guangzhou (Canton) | 80 | 23.06 N 113.16 E |
| Guantánamo | 98 | 20.08 N | 75.12 W |
| Guanxian | 80 | 31.00 N 103.40 E |
| Guaporé (Iténez) | 100 | 11.54 S | 65.01 W |
| Guarda | 70 | 40.32 N | 7.16 W |
| Guatemala | 98 | 14.38 N | 90.31 W |
| Guatemala ⬜¹ | 98 | 15.30 N | 90.15 W |
| Guaviare | 100 | 4.03 N | 67.44 W |
| Guayaquil | 100 | 2.10 S | 79.50 W |
| Guaymallén | 102 | 32.54 S | 68.47 W |
| Guaymas | 98 | 27.56 N 110.54 W |
| Gubaha | 76 | 58.52 N | 57.36 E |
| Gubbio | 72 | 43.21 N | 12.35 E |
| Gubin | 66 | 51.56 N | 14.45 E |
| Gubkin | 76 | 51.18 N | 37.32 E |
| Guebwiller | 68 | 47.55 N | 7.12 E |
| Guelma | 86 | 36.28 N | 7.26 E |
| Guelph | 94 | 43.33 N | 80.15 W |
| Guéret | 68 | 46.10 N | 1.52 E |
| Guernsey ⬜² | 55b | 49.28 N | 2.35 W |
| Guge | 88 | 6.10 N | 37.26 E |
| Guguan I | 82 | 17.19 N 145.51 E |
| Guildford | 54 | 51.14 N | 0.35 W |
| Guildtown | 58 | 56.28 N | 3.24 W |
| Guilin | 80 | 25.11 N 110.09 E |
| Guillaume-Delisle, Lac C | 94 | 56.15 N | 76.17 W |
| Guisfield | 54 | 52.42 N | 3.09 W |
| Guinea ⬜¹ | 88 | 11.00 N | 10.00 W |
| Guinea, Gulf of C | 86 | 2.00 N | 2.30 E |
| Guinea-Bissau ⬜¹ | 88 | 12.00 N | 15.00 W |
| Guingamp | 68 | 48.33 N | 3.11 W |
| Güira de Melena | 98 | 22.48 N | 82.30 W |
| Guisborough | 56 | 54.32 N | 1.04 W |
| Guiseley | 56 | 53.53 N | 1.42 W |
| Guiyang | 80 | 26.35 N 106.43 E |
| Guizhou ⬜⁴ | 80 | 27.00 N 107.00 E |
| Gujan-Mestras | 68 | 44.38 N | 1.04 W |
| Gujarat ⬜³ | 84 | 22.00 N | 72.00 E |
| Gujranwala | 84 | 32.09 N | 74.11 E |
| Gujrat | 84 | 32.34 N | 74.05 E |
| Gulbarga | 84 | 17.20 N | 76.50 E |
| Gulfport | 96 | 30.22 N | 89.06 W |
| Gulian Rock II¹ | 58 | 50.34 N | 4.59 W |
| Gullane | 58 | 56.02 N | 2.50 W |
| Gullion, Slieve | 60 | 54.08 N | 6.26 W |
| Gummersbach | 66 | 51.02 N | 7.34 E |
| Gunnislake | 54 | 50.31 N | 4.12 W |
| Güntür | 84 | 16.18 N | 80.27 E |
| Günzburg | 66 | 48.27 N | 10.16 E |
| Gurjev | 76 | 47.07 N | 51.56 E |
| Gurjevsk | 76 | 54.17 N | 85.56 E |
| Gurupá | 100 | 1.13 S | 46.06 W |
| Gurupi, Serra do | 100 | 5.00 S | 47.30 W |
| Gurvan Sajchan Uul | 80 | 43.50 N 103.30 E |
| Gusau | 88 | 12.12 N | 6.40 E |
| Gus'-Chrustal'nyj | 76 | 55.37 N | 40.40 E |
| Gusev | 66 | 54.35 N | 22.12 E |
| Gustav Holm, Kap | 94 | 66.44 N | 34.00 W |
| Gutcher | 58 | 60.40 N | 1.00 W |
| Gütersloh | 66 | 51.54 N | 8.23 E |
| Guyana ⬜¹ | 100 | 5.00 N | 59.00 W |
| Gvardejsk | 66 | 54.39 N | 21.05 E |
| Gwalchmai | 56 | 53.15 N | 4.25 W |
| Gwalior | 84 | 26.13 N | 78.10 E |
| Gwash | 54 | 52.38 N | 0.27 W |
| Gwatar Bay C | 84 | 25.04 N | 61.36 E |
| Gweebarra | 60 | 54.50 N | 8.20 W |
| Gweebarra Bay C | 60 | 54.50 N | 8.30 W |
| Gweedore | 60 | 55.03 N | 8.14 W |
| Gweesalla | 60 | 54.07 N | 9.54 W |
| Gwelo | 90 | 19.27 S | 29.49 E |
| Gwendraeth Fâch | 54 | 51.44 N | 4.18 W |
| Gwent ⬜⁶ | 54 | 51.43 N | 3.00 W |
| Gwynedd ⬜⁶ | 54 | 53.00 N | 4.00 W |
| Gydanskaja Guba | 76 | 71.20 N | 76.30 E |
| Gydanskij Poluostrov | 78 | 70.50 N | 79.00 E |
| Gyldenløves Fjord | 94 | 64.30 N | 41.30 W |
| Gyöngyös | 66 | 47.47 N | 19.56 E |
| Györ | 66 | 47.42 N | 17.38 E |
| Gypsey Race | 56 | 54.06 N | 0.18 W |
| Gypsum Point | 94 | 61.53 N 114.35 W |
| Gyula | 74 | 46.39 N | 21.17 E |

| Name | Page | Lat | Long |
|---|---|---|---|
| **H** |  |  |  |
| Haapsalu | 62 | 58.56 N | 23.33 E |
| Haar | 66 | 48.06 N | 11.44 E |
| Haarlem | 66 | 52.23 N | 4.38 E |
| Hachinohe | 80 | 40.30 N 141.29 E |
| Hackettstown | 60 | 52.52 N | 6.33 W |
| Hackney | 54 | 51.33 N | 0.03 W |
| Hadd, Ra's al- | 84 | 22.32 N | 59.48 E |
| Haddenham, Eng., U.K. | 54 | 50.19 N | 4.40 W |
| Haddenham, Eng., U.K. | 54 | 51.46 N | 0.56 W |
| Haddington | 58 | 55.58 N | 2.47 W |
| Hadeng | 54 | 55.51 N | 4.30 W |
| Hadleigh | 54 | 52.03 N | 0.58 E |
| Hadley Bay C | 94 | 72.30 N 107.45 W |
| Hadlow | 54 | 51.14 N | 0.20 E |
| Hadramawt | 84 | 15.00 N | 50.00 E |
| Haerbin | 80 | 45.45 N 126.41 E |
| Hafnarfjördur | 64 | 64.03 N | 21.56 W |
| Hafun, Ras | 84 | 10.27 N | 51.26 E |
| Hagen | 66 | 51.22 N | 7.28 E |
| Hagerstown | 96 | 39.39 N | 77.43 W |
| Haggin, Mount | 96 | 46.10 N 113.15 W |
| Hagley | 54 | 52.26 N | 2.08 W |
| Hags Head | 60 | 52.57 N | 9.29 W |
| Hagueneau | 68 | 48.49 N | 7.47 E |
| Haicheng | 80 | 40.52 N 122.45 E |
| Haikou | 80 | 20.02 N 110.19 E |
| Haïl | 84 | 27.33 N | 41.42 E |
| Hailar | 80 | 49.12 N 119.42 E |
| Haile[...] | 60 | 54.00 N | 8.40 W |
| Hailsham | 54 | 50.52 N | 0.16 E |
| Hailun | 80 | 47.29 N 126.58 E |
| Haimen | 80 | 31.52 N 121.10 E |
| Hainandao | 80 | 19.00 N 109.30 E |
| Hai-phong | 82 | 20.52 N 106.41 E |
| Haiti ⬜¹ | 98 | 19.00 N | 72.25 W |

| Name | Page | Lat | Long |
|---|---|---|---|
| Hajdúböszörmény | 74 | 47.41 N | 21.30 E |
| Hajdúnánás | 66 | 47.51 N | 21.26 E |
| Hajdúszoboszló | 74 | 47.27 N | 21.24 E |
| Hajnówka | 58 | 52.45 N | 23.36 E |
| Hakodate | 80 | 41.45 N 140.43 E |
| Halab (Aleppo) | 84 | 36.12 N | 37.10 E |
| Halberton | 54 | 50.54 N | 3.25 W |
| Halberstadt | 66 | 51.54 N | 11.02 E |
| Halden | 64 | 59.09 N | 11.23 E |
| Haldensleben | 66 | 52.18 N | 11.24 E |
| Haleakala Crater | 96b | 20.43 N 156.13 W |
| Halesowen | 54 | 52.26 N | 2.05 W |
| Halesworth | 54 | 52.21 N | 1.30 E |
| Halfway | 54 | 56.10 N 121.35 W |
| Halifax, N.S., Can. | 94 | 44.39 N | 63.36 W |
| Halifax, Eng., U.K. | 56 | 53.44 N | 1.52 W |
| Halifax Bay C | 92 | 18.50 S 146.30 E |
| Halkirk | 58 | 58.33 N | 3.55 W |
| Halladale | 58 | 58.33 N 126.32 E |
| Halla-san | 80 | 50.44 N | 4.13 E |
| Halle, Bel. | 66 | 51.29 N | 11.58 E |
| Halle, D.D.R. | 66 | 47.41 N | 13.06 E |
| Hallein | 66 | 68.41 N | 81.52 W |
| Hall Lake | 94 | 63.30 N | 66.00 W |
| Hallstahammar | 64 | 59.37 N | 16.13 E |
| Halmahera I | 82 | 1.00 N 128.00 E |
| Halmahera, Laut (Halmahera Sea) | 82 | 1.00 S 129.00 E |
| Halmstad | 64 | 56.39 N | 12.50 E |
| Halstead | 54 | 51.57 N | 0.38 E |
| Haltern | 66 | 51.46 N | 7.10 E |
| Haltiatunturi | 62 | 69.18 N | 21.16 E |
| Haltwhistle | 56 | 54.58 N | 2.27 W |
| Halwell | 54 | 50.22 N | 3.43 W |
| Hamadãn | 84 | 34.48 N | 48.30 E |
| Hamâh | 84 | 35.08 N | 36.45 E |
| Hamamatsu | 80 | 34.42 N 137.44 E |
| Hamar | 64 | 60.48 N | 11.06 E |
| Hamble | 54 | 50.52 N | 1.19 W |
| Hambleton | 56 | 53.56 N | 1.04 W |
| Hambleton Hills | 56 | 54.16 N | 1.12 W |
| Hamburg | 66 | 53.33 N | 9.59 E |
| Hämeenlinna | 64 | 61.00 N | 24.27 E |
| Hameln | 66 | 52.06 N | 9.21 E |
| Hamersley Range | 92 | 21.53 S 116.46 E |
| Hamhŭng | 80 | 39.54 N 127.32 E |
| Hami | 80 | 42.47 N | 93.32 E |
| Hamilton, Ber. | 98 | 32.17 N | 64.46 W |
| Hamilton, Ont., Can. | 94 | 43.15 N | 79.51 W |
| Hamilton, N.Z. | 93a | 37.47 S 175.17 E |
| Hamilton, Scot., U.K. | 58 | 55.47 N | 4.03 W |
| Hamilton, Ohio, U.S. | 96 | 39.26 N | 84.30 W |
| Hamilton | 92 | 23.30 S 139.47 E |
| Hamilton Inlet C | 94 | 54.00 N | 57.30 W |
| Hamm | 66 | 51.41 N | 7.49 E |
| Hammâr, Hawr al- | 84 | 30.50 N | 47.10 E |
| Hammerfest | 62 | 70.40 N | 23.42 E |
| Hammersmith | 54 | 51.30 N | 0.14 W |
| Hammond | 96 | 41.35 N | 87.30 W |
| Hamra, Saguia el V | 86 | 27.24 N | 13.00 W |
| Hanau | 66 | 50.08 N | 8.55 E |
| Hanbury | 92 | 63.37 N 104.33 W |
| Handa | 58 | 58.22 N | 5.12 W |
| Handan | 80 | 36.37 N 114.29 E |
| Handlová | 66 | 48.44 N | 18.46 E |
| Hangingstone Hill | 54 | 50.39 N | 3.57 W |
| Hangzhou | 80 | 30.15 N 120.10 E |
| Hanish, Jazā'ir II | 84 | 13.45 N | 42.45 E |
| Hannah Bay C | 94 | 51.05 N | 79.45 W |
| Hannover | 66 | 52.22 N | 9.43 E |
| Ha-noi | 82 | 21.02 N 105.51 E |
| Hanshui | 80 | 30.35 N 114.17 E |
| Hantzsch | 94 | 67.33 N | 72.11 E |
| Hāpur | 84 | 28.44 N | 77.46 E |
| Harad | 84 | 25.20 N | 49.02 E |
| Harash, Bi'r al- | 84 | 28.00 N | 22.12 E |
| Hardangerfjorden | 64 | 60.10 N | 6.00 E |
| Hardenwijk | 66 | 52.21 N | 5.36 E |
| Hardisty Lake | 94 | 64.30 N 117.45 W |
| Hardwâr | 84 | 29.52 N | 78.10 E |
| Hare Indian | 94 | 66.16 N 128.38 W |
| Hareøen I | 94 | 70.25 N | 54.50 W |
| Harer | 88 | 9.20 N | 42.07 E |
| Hargeysa | 88 | 9.30 N | 44.03 E |
| Haringey ⬜⁸ | 54 | 51.35 N | 0.07 W |
| Hari Rūd (Tedžen) | 84 | 37.24 N | 60.38 E |
| Harlech | 54 | 52.52 N | 4.07 W |
| Harleston | 54 | 52.24 N | 1.18 E |
| Harlingen, Ned. | 66 | 53.10 N | 5.25 E |
| Harlingen, Tex., U.S. | 96 | 26.11 N | 97.42 W |
| Harlow | 54 | 51.47 N | 0.08 E |
| Harmanli | 74 | 41.56 N | 25.54 E |
| Harney Peak | 96 | 43.52 N 103.32 W |
| Härnösand | 64 | 62.38 N | 17.56 E |
| Haroldswick | 58 | 60.48 N | 0.50 W |
| Harpenden | 54 | 51.49 N | 0.22 W |
| Harper | 88 | 4.25 N | 7.43 W |
| Harper Town | 54 | 54.55 N | 2.01 W |
| Harray, Loch of C | 58 | 59.01 N | 3.13 W |
| Harriet[...] | 54 | 51.30 N | 2.39 W |
| Harrietsham | 54 | 51.15 N | 0.41 E |
| Harrington | 56 | 54.37 N | 3.34 W |
| Harris I | 58 | 57.53 N | 6.55 W |
| Harris, Lake | 92 | 31.08 S 135.14 E |
| Harris, Sound of | 58 | 57.45 N | 7.06 W |
| Harrisburg | 96 | 40.17 N | 76.52 W |
| Harrison, Cape | 94 | 54.55 N | 57.55 W |
| Harrison Islands II | 94 | 69.13 N | 90.30 W |
| Harrogate | 56 | 53.59 N | 1.32 W |
| Harrow ⬜⁸ | 54 | 51.36 N | 0.21 W |
| Harstad | 62 | 68.46 N | 16.30 E |
| Hart Fell | 58 | 55.25 N | 3.25 W |
| Hartford | 96 | 41.46 N | 72.41 W |
| Hartland | 54 | 50.59 N | 4.29 W |
| Hartland Point | 54 | 51.01 N | 4.32 W |
| Hartlepool | 56 | 54.42 N | 1.11 W |
| Hartshill | 54 | 52.32 N | 1.30 W |
| Hârūt | 84 | 31.35 N | 61.18 E |
| Harwich | 54 | 51.57 N | 1.17 E |
| Harz | 66 | 51.40 N | 10.40 E |
| Hascosay I | 58 | 60.37 N | 0.59 W |
| Hashâ, Jabal al- | 84 | 13.58 N | 44.31 E |
| Haskeir Islands II | 58 | 57.42 N | 7.40 W |
| Haslemere | 54 | 51.06 N | 0.43 W |
| Haslingden | 56 | 53.43 N | 2.18 W |
| Hasselt | 66 | 50.56 N | 5.20 E |
| Hässleholm | 64 | 56.09 N | 13.46 E |
| Hastings | 54 | 50.52 N | 0.36 E |
| Haswell | 56 | 54.42 N | 1.27 W |
| Hatfield | 54 | 51.46 N | 0.13 W |
| Hatfield Peverel | 54 | 51.47 N | 0.36 E |
| Hathersage | 56 | 53.20 N | 1.39 W |
| Hāthras | 84 | 27.36 N | 78.03 E |
| Hatteras, Cape | 96 | 35.13 N | 75.32 W |
| Hatton | 58 | 57.25 N | 1.54 W |
| Hatvan | 66 | 47.40 N | 19.41 E |
| Hat Yai | 82 | 7.01 N 100.28 E |
| Haugesund | 64 | 59.25 N | 5.18 E |
| Haugh of Urr | 58 | 54.59 N | 3.52 W |
| Haute Atlas | 86 | 31.30 N | 6.00 W |
| Hautmont | 68 | 50.15 N | 3.56 E |
| Havant | 54 | 50.51 N | 0.59 W |
| Haverfordwest | 54 | 51.49 N | 4.58 W |
| Haverhill | 54 | 52.05 N | 0.26 E |
| Havering ⬜⁸ | 54 | 51.34 N | 0.14 E |
| Haverø | 58 | 54.11 N | 2.17 E |
| Havířov | 66 | 49.47 N | 18.27 E |
| Havlíčkův Brod | 66 | 49.38 N | 15.35 E |
| Havre | 96 | 48.33 N 109.41 W |
| Havre St. Pierre | 94 | 50.14 N | 63.36 W |
| Hawaii ⬜³ | 96b | 20.00 N 157.45 W |
| Hawaii I | 96b | 19.30 N 155.30 W |
| Hawarden | 56 | 53.11 N | 3.02 W |
| Hawes | 56 | 54.18 N | 2.12 W |

| Name | Page | Lat | Long |
|---|---|---|---|
| Haweswater Reservoir | 56 | 54.32 N | 2.48 W |
| Hawick | 58 | 55.25 N | 2.47 W |
| Hawkhurst | 54 | 51.02 N | 0.30 E |
| Hay, Austl. | 92 | 25.14 S 138.00 E |
| Hay, Can. | 94 | 60.52 N 115.44 W |
| Hay, Cape | 94 | 74.25 N 113.00 W |
| Hayange | 68 | 49.20 N | 6.03 E |
| Haydock | 56 | 53.28 N | 2.39 W |
| Haydon Bridge | 56 | 54.58 N | 2.14 W |
| Hayes, Man., Can. | 94 | 57.03 N | 92.09 W |
| Hayes, N.W.Ter., Can. |  |  |  |
| Hay-on-Wye | 54 | 52.04 N | 3.07 W |
| Hayrabolu | 74 | 41.12 N | 27.06 E |
| Haywards Heath | 54 | 51.00 N | 0.06 W |
| Hazebrouck | 68 | 50.43 N | 2.32 E |
| Hazel Grove | 56 | 53.22 N | 2.07 W |
| Hazleton | 96 | 40.58 N | 75.59 W |
| Heacham | 54 | 52.55 N | 0.30 E |
| Headcorn | 54 | 51.11 N | 0.37 E |
| Headford | 60 | 53.28 N | 9.05 W |
| Headington | 54 | 51.45 N | 1.13 W |
| Headley | 54 | 51.07 N | 0.50 W |
| Heanor | 56 | 53.01 N | 1.22 W |
| Heath End | 54 | 51.22 N | 1.09 W |
| Heathfield | 54 | 50.59 N | 0.17 E |
| Hebburn | 56 | 54.59 N | 1.30 W |
| Hebden Bridge | 56 | 53.45 N | 2.00 W |
| Hebi | 80 | 35.59 N 114.11 E |
| Hebrides II | 52 | 57.00 N | 6.30 W |
| Hebrides, Sea of the | 52 | 57.00 N | 7.00 W |
| Hechuan | 80 | 30.00 N 106.16 E |
| Heckington | 54 | 52.59 N | 0.18 W |
| Hednesford | 54 | 52.43 N | 2.00 W |
| Hedon | 56 | 53.44 N | 0.12 W |
| Heerenveen | 66 | 52.57 N | 5.55 E |
| Heerlen | 66 | 50.54 N | 5.59 E |
| Hefa | 84 | 32.49 N | 35.00 E |
| Hefei | 80 | 31.51 N 117.17 E |
| Hegang | 80 | 47.24 N 130.17 E |
| Heide | 66 | 54.12 N | 9.06 E |
| Heidelberg | 66 | 49.25 N | 8.43 E |
| Heidenheim | 66 | 48.40 N | 10.44 E |
| Heilbronn | 66 | 49.09 N | 9.13 E |
| Heiligenstadt | 66 | 51.23 N | 10.09 E |
| Heilongjiang (Amur) | 78 | 52.56 N 141.10 E |
| Heisker Islands II | 58 | 57.32 N | 7.40 W |
| Hekla | 64 | 63.59 N | 19.39 W |
| Helagsfjället | 64 | 62.55 N | 12.27 E |
| Helena | 96 | 46.36 N 112.01 W |
| Helen Island I | 82 | 2.58 N 131.49 E |
| Helensburgh | 58 | 56.00 N | 4.44 W |
| Hellifield | 56 | 54.00 N | 2.12 W |
| Hellin | 70 | 38.31 N | 1.41 W |
| Helli Ness | 58 | 60.02 N | 1.10 W |
| Hell-Ville | 90 | 13.25 S | 48.16 E |
| Helmand | 84 | 31.12 N | 61.34 E |
| Helmond | 66 | 51.30 N | 5.40 E |
| Helmsdale | 58 | 58.07 N | 3.40 W |
| Helmsdale | 58 | 58.07 N | 3.40 W |
| Helmsley | 56 | 54.14 N | 1.04 W |
| Helsby | 56 | 53.16 N | 2.46 W |
| Helsingborg | 64 | 56.03 N | 12.42 E |
| Helsingør (Elsinore) | 64 | 56.02 N | 12.37 E |
| Helsinki (Helsingfors) | 64 | 60.10 N | 24.58 E |
| Helston | 54 | 50.05 N | 5.16 W |
| Helvellyn | 56 | 54.32 N | 3.01 W |
| Helvick Head | 60 | 52.03 N | 7.33 W |
| Hemel Hempstead | 54 | 51.46 N | 0.29 W |
| Hempnall | 54 | 52.30 N | 1.19 E |
| Hemsworth | 56 | 53.38 N | 1.21 W |
| Hendy | 54 | 51.43 N | 4.04 W |
| Henfield | 54 | 50.56 N | 0.17 W |
| Hengelo | 66 | 52.15 N | 6.45 E |
| Hengoed | 54 | 51.39 N | 3.10 W |
| Hengyang | 80 | 26.51 N 112.30 E |
| Henley-in-Arden | 54 | 52.17 N | 1.46 W |
| Henley-on-Thames | 54 | 51.32 N | 0.56 W |
| Henlow | 54 | 52.02 N | 0.18 W |
| Hennebont | 68 | 47.48 N | 3.17 W |
| Hennef | 66 | 50.46 N | 7.16 E |
| Hennigsdorf | 66 | 52.38 N | 13.12 E |
| Henrietta Maria, Cape | 94 | 55.09 N | 82.20 W |
| Henstridge | 54 | 50.59 N | 2.24 W |
| Henzada | 82 | 17.38 N | 95.28 E |
| Hepu | 80 | 21.39 N 109.11 E |
| Herât | 84 | 34.20 N | 62.07 E |
| Hereford | 54 | 52.04 N | 2.43 W |
| Hereford and Worcester ⬜⁶ | 54 | 52.10 N | 2.30 W |
| Herford | 66 | 52.06 N | 8.40 E |
| Herisau | 68 | 47.23 N | 9.17 E |
| Herma Ness | 58 | 60.50 N | 0.50 W |
| Hermosillo | 98 | 29.04 N 110.58 W |
| Herne | 66 | 51.32 N | 7.13 E |
| Herne Bay | 54 | 51.23 N | 1.08 E |
| Herning | 64 | 56.08 N | 8.59 E |
| Hersham | 54 | 51.22 N | 0.24 W |
| Herstal | 66 | 50.40 N | 5.38 E |
| Herstmonceux | 54 | 50.53 N | 0.20 E |
| Hertford | 54 | 51.48 N | 0.05 W |
| Hertfordshire ⬜⁶ | 54 | 51.51 N | 0.05 W |
| Hervey Bay C | 92 | 25.00 S 152.52 E |
| Hessle | 56 | 53.44 N | 0.26 W |
| Heswall | 56 | 53.20 N | 3.06 W |
| Hetianhe | 80 | 40.30 N | 80.45 E |
| Hetton-le-Hole | 56 | 54.49 N | 1.27 W |
| Hettstedt | 66 | 51.39 N | 11.30 E |
| Heves | 66 | 47.36 N | 20.17 E |
| Hexham | 56 | 54.58 N | 2.06 W |
| Heysham | 56 | 54.02 N | 2.54 W |
| Heywood | 56 | 53.36 N | 2.13 W |
| Hibaldstow | 56 | 53.31 N | 0.32 W |
| Hibernia Reef | 92 | 12.00 S 123.23 E |
| Hicks, Point | 92 | 37.48 S 149.17 E |
| Hidalgo del Parral | 98 | 26.56 N 105.40 W |
| Hierro I | 86 | 27.45 N | 18.00 W |
| Higham Ferrers | 54 | 52.18 N | 0.36 W |
| Higham Upshire | 54 | 51.25 N | 0.28 E |
| High Bentham | 56 | 54.07 N | 2.31 W |
| Highbridge | 54 | 51.13 N | 2.49 W |
| High Force L | 56 | 54.38 N | 2.13 W |
| Highland ⬜⁴ | 58 | 57.30 N | 5.00 W |
| High Peak ⬜¹ | 56 | 53.22 N | 1.48 W |
| High Plains | 58 | 38.30 N 100.00 W |
| High Seat | 56 | 54.23 N | 1.53 W |
| High Street | 56 | 54.30 N | 2.52 W |
| High Willhays | 54 | 50.41 N | 4.00 W |
| Highworth | 54 | 51.38 N | 1.43 W |
| High Wycombe | 54 | 51.38 N | 0.46 W |
| Hiiumaa I | 64 | 58.52 N | 22.40 E |
| Hijāz, Jabal al- | 84 | 19.45 N | 41.55 E |
| Hildburghausen | 66 | 50.25 N | 10.44 E |
| Hildesheim | 66 | 52.09 N | 9.57 E |
| Hilgay | 54 | 52.34 N | 0.24 E |
| Hillingdon ⬜⁸ | 54 | 51.32 N | 0.27 W |
| Hill Island Lake | 94 | 60.29 N 109.50 W |
| Hill of Fearn | 58 | 57.46 N | 3.58 W |
| Hillsborough | 60 | 54.28 N | 6.05 W |
| Hilltown | 60 | 54.12 N | 6.08 W |
| Hilo | 96b | 19.44 N 155.05 W |
| Hilpsford Point | 56 | 54.03 N | 3.12 W |
| Hilversum | 66 | 52.14 N | 5.10 E |
| Himalayas | 84 | 28.00 N | 84.00 E |
| Himeji | 80 | 34.49 N 134.42 E |
| Hinchinbrook Island | 92 | 18.23 S 146.17 E |
| Hinckley | 54 | 52.33 N | 1.21 W |
| Hindhead | 54 | 51.07 N | 0.44 W |
| Hindon | 54 | 51.05 N | 2.08 W |
| Hindu Kush | 84 | 36.00 N | 71.30 E |
| Hingol | 84 | 25.22 N | 65.28 E |
| Hinish Bay C | 58 | 56.28 N | 6.52 W |
| Hinnøya I | 62 | 68.30 N | 16.00 E |
| Hinojosa del Duque | 70 | 38.30 N | 5.09 W |
| Hirosaki | 80 | 40.35 N 140.28 E |
| Hiroshima | 80 | 34.24 N 132.27 E |

| Name | Page | Lat | Long |
|---|---|---|---|
| Hirson | 68 | 49.55 N | 4.05 E |
| Hirwaun | 54 | 51.45 N | 3.30 W |
| Hisār | 84 | 29.09 N | 75.44 E |
| Hispaniola I | 98 | 19.00 N | 71.00 W |
| Histon | 54 | 52.15 N | 0.06 E |
| Hitachi | 80 | 36.36 N | 140.39 E |
| Hitchin | 54 | 51.57 N | 0.17 W |
| Hitra I | 64 | 63.33 N | 8.45 E |
| Hjørring | 64 | 57.28 N | 9.59 E |
| Hlohovec | 68 | 48.25 N | 17.47 E |
| Hobart | 92 | 42.53 S | 147.19 E |
| Hoboken | 68 | 51.10 N | 4.21 E |
| Hockenheim | 66 | 49.19 N | 8.33 E |
| Hockley | 54 | 51.37 N | 0.40 E |
| Hodder ≈ | 54 | 53.50 N | 2.25 W |
| Hoddesdon | 54 | 51.46 N | 0.01 W |
| Hódmezóvásárhely | 74 | 46.25 N | 20.20 E |
| Hodna, Chott el ⊜ | 86 | 35.25 N | 4.45 E |
| Hodnet | 54 | 52.51 N | 2.35 W |
| Hodonin | 68 | 48.51 N | 17.08 E |
| Hof | 66 | 50.18 N | 11.55 E |
| Hofheim in Unterfranken | 66 | 50.08 N | 10.31 E |
| Hofors | 64 | 60.33 N | 16.17 E |
| Hofsjökull ⋈ | 64 | 64.48 N | 18.50 W |
| Hog, Tanjong ➤ | 82 | 5.18 N | 119.16 E |
| Hogs Back ⬩⁴ | 54 | 51.13 N | 0.40 W |
| Hohenlimburg | 66 | 51.21 N | 7.35 E |
| Hokkaidō I | 80 | 44.00 N | 143.00 E |
| Holbæk | 64 | 55.43 N | 11.43 E |
| Holbeach | 54 | 52.49 N | 0.01 E |
| Holbeach Marsh ⟐ | 54 | 52.52 N | 0.05 E |
| Holderness ➤¹ | 54 | 53.47 N | 0.10 W |
| Holguín | 98 | 20.53 N | 76.15 W |
| Hollam's Bird Island I | 90 | 24.45 S | 14.34 E |
| Holland | 68 | 42.47 N | 86.07 W |
| Holland Fen ⋍ | 54 | 53.00 N | 0.10 W |
| Holland-on-Sea | 54 | 51.48 N | 1.13 E |
| Hollandstoun | 58 | 59.21 N | 2.16 W |
| Hollywood, Eire | 58 | 53.06 N | 6.35 W |
| Hollywood, Fla., U.S. | 96 | 26.00 N | 80.09 W |
| Holme | 54 | 53.41 N | 1.43 W |
| Holmes Reefs ⋎² | 92 | 16.27 S | 148.00 E |
| Holmfirth | 54 | 53.35 N | 1.46 W |
| Holstebro | 64 | 56.21 N | 8.38 E |
| Holsworthy | 54 | 50.49 N | 4.21 W |
| Holt | 54 | 53.05 N | 2.53 W |
| Holycross | 60 | 52.38 N | 7.52 W |
| Holyhead | 54 | 53.19 N | 4.38 W |
| Holyhead Bay C | 54 | 53.23 N | 4.37 W |
| Holy Island I, Eng., U.K. | 56 | 55.41 N | 1.48 W |
| Holy Island I, Scot., U.K. | 58 | 55.32 N | 5.05 W |
| Holy Island I, Wales, U.K. | 52 | 53.18 N | 4.37 W |
| Holywell | 58 | 53.17 N | 3.13 W |
| Holywood | 66 | 51.50 N | 9.27 E |
| Holzminden | 86 | 15.16 N | 1.40 W |
| Hombori Tondo ⋀ | 102 | 25.23 S | 67.06 W |
| Hombre Muerto, Salar de | 66 | 49.19 N | 7.20 E |
| Homburg | 94 | 68.45 N | 67.10 W |
| Home Bay C | 54 | 51.54 N | 2.58 W |
| Hondu ⋍ | 98 | 15.00 N | 86.30 W |
| Honduras ⊡¹ | 98 | 16.10 N | 87.50 W |
| Honduras, Gulf of C | 64 | 60.10 N | 10.18 E |
| Hønefoss | 68 | 49.25 N | 0.14 E |
| Honfleur | 80 | 20.57 N | 107.05 E |
| Hon-gai | 80 | 29.48 N | 113.27 E |
| Honghu | 80 | 27.00 N | 109.51 E |
| Hongjiang | 80 | 22.15 N | 114.10 E |
| Hong Kong ⊡² | 94 | 49.15 N | 64.00 W |
| Honguedo, Détroit d' ⋃ | 80 | 33.16 N | 118.34 E |
| Hongzehu ⊜ | 96b | 9.26 S | 159.57 E |
| Honiara | 54 | 50.48 N | 3.13 W |
| Honiton | 96b | 21.19 N | 157.52 W |
| Honolulu | 80 | 36.00 N | 138.00 E |
| Honshū I | 96 | 45.23 N | 121.41 W |
| Hood, Mount ⋀ | 92 | 34.23 S | 119.34 E |
| Hood Point ➤ | 66 | 52.43 N | 6.29 E |
| Hoogeveen | 54 | 51.17 N | 0.58 W |
| Hook | 52 | 52.07 N | 6.56 W |
| Hook Head ➤ | 66 | 52.38 N | 5.04 E |
| Hoorn | 52 | 58.24 N | 4.36 W |
| Hope, Ben ⋀ | 58 | 58.27 N | 4.39 W |
| Hope, Loch ⊜ | 58 | 57.42 N | 3.25 W |
| Hopeman | 94 | 59.25 N | 69.40 W |
| Hopes Advance, Baie | 94 | 61.04 N | 69.34 W |
| Hopes Advance, Cap ➤ | 56 | 54.46 N | 1.18 W |
| Horden | 68 | 47.15 N | 8.36 E |
| Horgen | 54 | 51.11 N | 0.11 W |
| Horley | 84 | 26.34 N | 56.15 E |
| Hormuz, Strait of ⋃ | 66 | 66.28 N | 22.28 W |
| Horn ⋏ | 58 | 58.01 N | 4.02 W |
| Horn, Ben ⋀² | 94 | 69.22 N | 123.50 W |
| Hornaday ⋍ | 66 | 66.10 N | 17.30 E |
| Hornburg | 94 | 66.35 N | 117.50 W |
| Hornby Bay C | 54 | 53.13 N | 0.07 W |
| Horncastle | 54 | 50.55 N | 1.00 W |
| Horndean | 60 | 55.14 N | 7.59 W |
| Horn Head ➤ | 102 | 55.59 S | 67.16 W |
| Hornos, Cabo de (Cape Horn) ➤ | 94 | 62.15 N | 119.15 W |
| Horn Plateau ⋏¹ | 54 | 53.55 N | 0.10 W |
| Hornsea | 54 | 50.31 N | 4.05 W |
| Horrabridge | 54 | 55.52 N | 9.52 E |
| Horsens | 56 | 53.51 N | 1.39 W |
| Horsforth | 54 | 51.04 N | 0.21 W |
| Horsham | 54 | 52.41 N | 1.16 E |
| Horsham Saint Faith | 54 | 55.53 N | 12.30 E |
| Horsholm | 54 | 51.02 N | 0.01 W |
| Horsted Keynes | 64 | 59.25 N | 10.30 E |
| Horten | 54 | 54.09 N | 2.17 W |
| Horton in Ribblesdale | 94 | 67.30 N | 122.28 W |
| Horton Lake ⊜ | 56 | 53.37 N | 2.33 W |
| Horwich | 86 | 2.10 N | 13.15 E |
| Hosée Batandji ⋀ | 84 | 31.32 N | 75.54 E |
| Hoshiārpur | 84 | 15.16 N | 76.24 E |
| Hospet | 60 | 52.29 N | 8.25 W |
| Hospital | 70 | 41.22 N | 2.08 E |
| Hospitalet | 102 | 55.15 S | 69.00 W |
| Hoste, Isla I | 96 | 34.30 N | 93.03 W |
| Hot Springs National Park | 94 | 65.04 N | 118.29 W |
| Hottah Lake ⊜ | 56 | 54.51 N | 1.28 W |
| Houghton-le-Spring | 54 | 51.55 N | 0.31 W |
| Houghton Regis | 96 | 29.36 N | 90.43 W |
| Houma | 54 | 51.29 N | 0.22 W |
| Hounslow ⋏⁸ | 86 | 6.22 S | 39.18 W |
| Hourn, Loch ⋃ | 57 | 57.08 N | 5.36 W |
| Houston | 96 | 29.46 N | 95.22 W |
| Houtman Abrolhos II | 92 | 28.43 S | 113.48 E |
| Hove | 54 | 50.49 N | 0.10 W |
| Howardian Hills ⋏² | 54 | 54.07 N | 1.00 W |
| Howden | 56 | 53.45 N | 0.52 W |
| Howe, Cape ➤ | 92 | 37.31 S | 149.59 E |
| Howmore | 58 | 57.18 N | 7.23 W |
| Howrah | 84 | 22.35 N | 88.20 E |
| Höxter | 66 | 51.46 N | 9.23 E |
| Hoy I | 58 | 58.52 N | 3.18 W |
| Hoyerswerda | 66 | 51.26 N | 14.14 E |
| Hoylake | 56 | 53.23 N | 3.11 W |
| Hradec Králové | 66 | 50.12 N | 15.50 E |
| Hranice | 66 | 49.33 N | 17.44 E |
| Hronov | 66 | 50.29 N | 16.12 E |
| Hrubieszów | 68 | 50.49 N | 23.55 E |
| Hsinchu | 80 | 24.48 N | 120.58 E |
| Hsinkao Shan ⋀ | 80 | 23.28 N | 120.57 E |
| Huachi | 80 | 11.07 S | 77.37 W |
| Huadian | 80 | 42.56 N | 126.43 E |
| Huagaruancha, Cerro ⋀ | 100 | 10.32 S | 75.58 W |
| Huaian | 80 | 33.32 N | 119.10 E |
| Huaihe ⋍ | 80 | 32.58 N | 118.17 E |
| Huainan | 80 | 32.40 N | 117.00 E |
| Huajin | 80 | 33.35 N | 119.02 E |
| Hualien | 80 | 23.58 N | 121.36 E |
| Huallaga ⋍ | 100 | 5.07 S | 75.32 W |
| Huambo | 90 | 12.44 S | 15.47 E |
| Huancayo | 100 | 12.04 S | 75.14 W |
| Huanghuan | 80 | 32.09 N | 115.03 E |

| Name | Page | Lat | Long |
|---|---|---|---|
| Huanghe ⋍ | 80 | 37.32 N | 118.19 E |
| Huangshi | 80 | 30.13 N | 115.05 E |
| Huánuco | 100 | 9.55 S | 76.14 W |
| Huaraz | 100 | 9.32 S | 77.32 W |
| Huascarán, Nevado ⋀ | 100 | 9.07 S | 77.37 W |
| Hubli | 84 | 15.20 N | 75.08 E |
| Hucclecote | 54 | 51.51 N | 2.11 W |
| Hucknall | 54 | 53.02 N | 1.11 W |
| Huddersfield | 56 | 53.39 N | 1.47 W |
| Huddinge | 64 | 59.14 N | 17.59 E |
| Hudiksvall | 64 | 61.44 N | 17.07 E |
| Hudson ⋍ | 94 | 40.42 N | 74.02 W |
| Hudson Bay C | 94 | 60.00 N | 86.00 W |
| Hudson Strait ⋃ | 94 | 62.00 N | 72.00 W |
| Hue | 82 | 16.28 N | 107.36 E |
| Huelva | 70 | 37.16 N | 6.57 W |
| Huesca | 70 | 42.08 N | 0.25 W |
| Hugh Town | 54a | 49.55 N | 6.17 W |
| Huhehaote | 80 | 40.51 N | 111.40 E |
| Huila, Nevado del ⋀ | 100 | 3.00 N | 76.00 W |
| Huiyang | 80 | 23.05 N | 114.24 E |
| Hukayyim, Bi'r al- | 88 | 31.36 N | 23.29 E |
| Hulan | 80 | 46.00 N | 126.38 E |
| Hull | 94 | 45.26 N | 75.43 W |
| Hull ⋍ | 56 | 53.44 N | 0.19 W |
| Hullavington | 54 | 51.33 N | 2.09 W |
| Hullbridge | 54 | 51.37 N | 0.38 E |
| Hulunchi ⊜ | 80 | 49.01 N | 117.32 E |
| Humbe, Serra do ⋀ | 90 | 12.13 S | 15.25 E |
| Humber ⋍ | 52 | 53.40 N | 0.10 W |
| Humber, Mouth of ⋍ | 56 | 53.32 N | 0.08 E |
| Humberside ⊡⁶ | 52 | 53.50 N | 0.30 W |
| Humboldt ⋍ | 96 | 40.02 N | 118.31 W |
| Hume, Lake ⊜¹ | 92 | 36.06 S | 147.05 E |
| Humenné | 68 | 48.56 N | 21.55 E |
| Humphreys Peak ⋀ | 96 | 35.20 N | 111.40 W |
| Hunedoara | 74 | 45.45 N | 22.54 E |
| Hungary ⊡¹ | 50 | 47.00 N | 20.00 E |
| Hungerford | 54 | 51.26 N | 1.30 W |
| Húngnam | 80 | 39.50 N | 127.38 E |
| Hunish, Rubha ➤ | 58 | 57.41 N | 6.21 W |
| Hunsberge ⋏ | 90 | 27.45 S | 17.12 E |
| Hunstanton | 54 | 52.57 N | 0.30 E |
| Hunter Island I | 92 | 40.32 S | 144.45 E |
| Hunter's Quay | 58 | 55.58 N | 4.55 W |
| Huntingdon | 54 | 52.20 N | 0.12 W |
| Huntington, Eng., U.K. | 56 | 54.01 N | 1.04 W |
| Huntington, W. Va., U.S. | 96 | 38.25 N | 82.26 W |
| Huntly | 58 | 57.27 N | 2.47 W |
| Huntsville | 96 | 34.44 N | 86.35 W |
| Hunyani ⋍ | 90 | 15.37 S | 30.39 E |
| Hunyuan | 80 | 39.48 N | 113.41 E |
| Hurd, Cape ➤ | 94 | 45.13 N | 81.44 W |
| Hurlford | 58 | 55.36 N | 4.28 W |
| Hurliness | 58 | 58.47 N | 3.15 W |
| Huron, Lake ⊜ | 94 | 44.30 N | 82.15 W |
| Hursley | 54 | 51.02 N | 1.24 W |
| Hurstbourne Tarrant | 54 | 51.17 N | 1.23 W |
| Hurstpierpoint | 54 | 50.56 N | 0.11 W |
| Hürth | 66 | 50.52 N | 6.51 E |
| Husum | 54 | 46.40 N | 28.04 E |
| Huskvarna | 64 | 57.48 N | 14.16 E |
| Husum | 66 | 54.28 N | 9.03 E |
| Hutchinson | 96 | 38.05 N | 97.56 W |
| Huthwaite | 54 | 53.09 N | 1.17 W |
| Hüttental | 66 | 50.54 N | 8.02 E |
| Hutte Sauvage, Lac de la ⊜ | 94 | 56.15 N | 64.45 W |
| Huy | 66 | 50.31 N | 5.14 E |
| Huyton-with-Roby | 56 | 53.25 N | 2.52 W |
| Huzhou | 80 | 30.52 N | 120.06 E |
| Hvannadalshnúkur ⋀ | 50 | 64.01 N | 16.41 W |
| Hyde | 56 | 53.27 N | 2.04 W |
| Hyderābād, Bhārat | 84 | 17.23 N | 78.29 E |
| Hyderābād, Pāk. | 84 | 25.22 N | 68.22 E |
| Hyères | 68 | 43.07 N | 6.07 E |
| Hyland ⋍ | 94 | 59.50 N | 128.10 W |
| Hyndman Peak ⋀ | 96 | 43.50 N | 114.10 W |
| Hythe, Eng., U.K. | 54 | 50.51 N | 1.24 E |
| Hythe, Eng., U.K. | 54 | 51.05 N | 1.05 E |
| Hyvinkää | 64 | 60.38 N | 24.52 E |

| Name | Page | Lat | Long |
|---|---|---|---|
| Iaco (Yaco) ⋍ | 100 | 9.03 S | 68.34 W |
| Iaşi | 74 | 47.10 N | 27.35 E |
| Ibadan | 86 | 7.17 N | 3.30 E |
| Ibagué | 100 | 4.27 N | 75.14 W |
| Ibarra | 100 | 0.21 N | 78.07 W |
| Ibb | 84 | 14.01 N | 44.10 E |
| Ibenbüren | 66 | 52.16 N | 7.43 E |
| Ibérica, Península ⋏¹ | 50 | 40.00 N | 5.00 W |
| Iberville, Lac d' ⊜ | 94 | 55.55 N | 73.15 W |
| Iberville, Mont d' ⋀ | 94 | 58.53 N | 63.43 W |
| Ibiza | 70 | 38.54 N | 1.26 E |
| Ibiza I | 70 | 39.00 N | 1.25 E |
| Ibo | 90 | 12.20 S | 40.35 E |
| Iboundji, Mont ⋀ | 90 | 1.08 S | 11.48 E |
| Ibstock | 54 | 52.42 N | 1.23 W |
| Ica | 100 | 14.04 S | 75.42 W |
| Iça ⋍ | 100 | 14.54 S | 75.34 W |
| Iceland ⊡¹ | 50 | 65.00 N | 18.00 W |
| Ichalkaranji | 84 | 16.41 N | 74.28 E |
| Ich Bogd Uul ⋀ | 80 | 44.55 N | 100.20 E |
| Ichio ⋍ | 100 | 15.57 S | 64.42 W |
| Idaho ⊡³ | 96 | 45.00 N | 115.00 W |
| Idaho Falls | 96 | 43.30 N | 112.02 W |
| Idar-Oberstein | 66 | 49.42 N | 7.19 E |
| Idel | 54 | 64.08 N | 34.14 E |
| Iderijn ⋍ | 80 | 49.16 N | 100.41 E |
| Idfū | 88 | 24.58 N | 32.52 E |
| Idho Ōros ⋀ | 74 | 35.18 N | 24.43 E |
| Idrigill Point ➤ | 58 | 57.20 N | 6.35 W |
| Ieper | 68 | 50.51 N | 2.53 E |
| Ifalik I¹ | 82 | 7.15 N | 144.27 E |
| Ife | 86 | 7.30 N | 4.30 E |
| Iforas, Adrar des ⋏ | 86 | 20.00 N | 2.00 E |
| Igarka | 78 | 67.28 N | 86.35 E |
| Iglesias | 72 | 39.19 N | 8.32 E |
| Iguaçu, Saltos do (Iguassu Falls) ⋏ | 102 | 25.36 S | 54.36 W |
| Iguala | 102 | 25.41 S | 54.26 W |
| Igualada | 70 | 18.21 N | 99.32 W |
| Iguatu | 70 | 41.35 N | 1.38 E |
| Iguidi, Erg ⬩⁸ | 100 | 6.22 S | 39.18 W |
| Ihédy-Ode | 86 | 26.35 N | 5.40 W |
| IJmuiden | 86 | 6.56 N | 3.56 E |
| IJssel ⋍ | 86 | 22.38 N | 12.33 W |
| IJsselmeer ⋍² | 66 | 52.45 N | 5.25 E |
| Ikaria I | 74 | 37.41 N | 26.20 E |
| Ikerre | 86 | 7.31 N | 5.14 E |
| Ila | 86 | 8.01 N | 4.55 E |
| Ilan | 80 | 24.45 N | 121.44 E |
| Iława | 68 | 53.37 N | 19.33 E |
| Ile-à-la-Crosse, Lac ⊜ | 94 | 55.40 N | 107.45 W |
| Île Desroches I | 58 | 55.51 N | 53.41 E |
| Ilek ⋍ | 76 | 51.30 N | 53.22 E |
| Ilen ⋍ | 60 | 51.30 N | 9.19 W |
| Ilesha | 86 | 7.38 N | 4.45 E |
| Ileza | 76 | 60.43 N | 43.54 E |
| Ilfracombe | 54 | 51.13 N | 4.08 W |
| Ilhéus | 100 | 14.49 S | 39.02 W |
| Ili ⋍ | 78 | 45.24 N | 74.02 E |
| Iljinskij | 62 | 61.02 N | 32.41 E |
| Ilkeston | 54 | 52.59 N | 1.18 W |
| Ilkley | 56 | 53.55 N | 1.50 W |
| Illampu, Nevado ⋀ | 100 | 15.50 S | 68.34 W |
| Illimani, Nevado ⋀ | 100 | 16.39 S | 67.48 W |
| Illinois ⊡³ | 96 | 40.00 N | 89.00 W |
| Illinois ⋍ | 96 | 38.58 N | 90.27 W |
| Illminster | 54 | 50.56 N | 2.55 W |
| Il'men', Ozero ⊜ | 62 | 58.18 N | 31.20 E |
| Ilmenau ⋍ | 66 | 53.23 N | 9.17 E |
| Iloilo | 82 | 10.42 N | 122.34 E |
| Ilorin | 86 | 8.30 N | 4.32 E |
| Iman | 78 | 45.54 N | 133.43 E |
| Imandra, Ozero ⊜ | 78 | 67.30 N | 33.00 E |
| Imatra | 64 | 61.10 N | 28.46 E |

| Name | Page | Lat | Long |
|---|---|---|---|
| Ime, Beinn ⋀ | 58 | 56.14 N | 4.49 W |
| Immenstadt | 66 | 47.33 N | 10.13 E |
| Immingham Dock | 56 | 53.37 N | 0.12 W |
| Imola | 72 | 44.21 N | 11.42 E |
| Imperia | 72 | 43.53 N | 8.03 E |
| Imphāl | 84 | 24.49 N | 93.57 E |
| Inari ⊜ | 50 | 69.00 N | 28.00 E |
| Inca | 70 | 39.43 N | 2.54 E |
| Inch | 60 | 52.08 N | 9.59 W |
| Inchard, Loch C | 58 | 58.27 N | 5.04 W |
| Inchbare | 58 | 56.52 N | 2.39 W |
| Inchcape II¹ | 58 | 56.26 N | 2.47 W |
| Inchmarnock I | 58 | 55.46 N | 5.09 W |
| Inchnadamph | 58 | 58.09 N | 4.59 W |
| Inch'ŏn | 80 | 37.28 N | 126.38 E |
| Inchture | 58 | 56.26 N | 3.10 W |
| Indaal, Loch C | 58 | 55.45 N | 6.21 W |
| Indalsälven ⋍ | 64 | 62.31 N | 17.27 E |
| India ⊡¹ | 84 | 20.00 N | 77.00 E |
| Indiana ⊡³ | 96 | 40.00 N | 86.15 W |
| Indianapolis | 96 | 39.46 N | 86.09 W |
| Indian Ocean ⋍¹ | 8 | 10.00 S | 70.00 E |
| Indigirka ⋍ | 78 | 70.48 N | 148.54 E |
| Indispensable Reefs ⋎² | 92 | 12.40 S | 160.25 E |
| Indonesia ⊡¹ | 82 | 5.00 S | 120.00 E |
| Indore | 84 | 22.43 N | 75.50 E |
| Indus ⋍ | 84 | 24.20 N | 67.47 E |
| Inegöl | 74 | 40.05 N | 29.31 E |
| Infiernillo, Presa del ⊜¹ | 98 | 18.35 N | 101.45 W |
| Ingatestone | 54 | 51.41 N | 0.22 E |
| Ingelheim | 66 | 49.59 N | 8.05 E |
| Ingleborough ⋀ | 56 | 54.11 N | 2.23 W |
| Ingleton | 56 | 54.10 N | 2.27 W |
| Inglewood Forest ⋏³ | 56 | 54.45 N | 2.50 W |
| Ingolstadt | 66 | 48.46 N | 11.27 E |
| Inhaca, Ilha da I | 90 | 26.03 S | 32.57 E |
| Inhambane | 90 | 23.51 S | 35.29 E |
| Inharrime | 90 | 24.29 S | 35.01 E |
| Inírida ⋍ | 100 | 3.55 N | 67.52 W |
| Inishbofin I | 52 | 53.37 N | 10.15 W |
| Inisheer I | 52 | 53.02 N | 9.26 W |
| Inishmaan I | 52 | 53.05 N | 9.32 W |
| Inishmore I | 52 | 53.07 N | 9.45 W |
| Inishowen Peninsula ➤¹ | 60 | 55.12 N | 7.20 W |
| Inishowen Point ➤ | 60 | 55.14 N | 6.56 W |
| Inishshark I | 52 | 53.37 N | 10.18 W |
| Inishtrahull ⋍² | 52 | 55.26 N | 7.14 W |
| Inishturk I | 52 | 53.43 N | 10.08 W |
| Inistioge | 60 | 52.29 N | 7.04 W |
| Injasuti ⋀ | 90 | 29.09 S | 29.23 E |
| Inle Lake ⊜ | 82 | 20.30 N | 96.55 E |
| Inn ⋍ | 66 | 48.35 N | 13.28 E |
| Innellan | 58 | 55.54 N | 4.57 W |
| Inner Hebrides II | 52 | 57.00 N | 6.45 W |
| Innerleithen | 58 | 55.38 N | 3.05 W |
| Inner Sound ⋃ | 58 | 57.30 N | 5.55 W |
| Inniscrone | 60 | 54.12 N | 9.06 W |
| Innsbruck | 66 | 47.16 N | 11.24 E |
| Inny ⋍, Eire | 52 | 53.33 N | 7.48 W |
| Inny ⋍, Eng., U.K. | 54 | 50.35 N | 4.17 W |
| Inowrocław | 68 | 52.48 N | 18.15 E |
| In Salah | 86 | 27.12 N | 2.28 E |
| Inta | 78 | 66.02 N | 60.08 E |
| Interlaken | 68 | 46.41 N | 7.51 E |
| Inthanon, Doi ⋀ | 82 | 18.35 N | 98.29 E |
| Inukjuak | 94 | 58.28 N | 78.15 W |
| Inuvik | 94 | 68.25 N | 133.30 W |
| Inveraray | 58 | 56.13 N | 5.05 W |
| Inverbervie | 58 | 56.51 N | 2.17 W |
| Invercargill | 93a | 46.24 S | 168.21 E |
| Inverdruie | 58 | 57.10 N | 3.48 W |
| Invergarry | 58 | 57.02 N | 4.47 W |
| Invergordon | 58 | 57.42 N | 4.10 W |
| Inverkeilor | 58 | 56.38 N | 2.32 W |
| Inverkeithing | 58 | 56.02 N | 3.25 W |
| Inverkip | 58 | 55.54 N | 4.53 W |
| Invermoriston | 58 | 57.13 N | 4.38 W |
| Inverness | 58 | 57.27 N | 4.15 W |
| Inverurie | 58 | 57.17 N | 2.23 W |
| Investigator Group II | 92 | 33.45 S | 134.30 E |
| Investigator Strait ⋃ | 92 | 35.25 S | 137.10 E |
| Inyangani ⋀ | 90 | 18.20 S | 32.50 E |
| Inza | 62 | 53.51 N | 46.21 E |
| Ioánnina | 74 | 39.40 N | 20.50 E |
| Iona I | 58 | 56.19 N | 6.25 W |
| Iona, Sound of ⋃ | 58 | 56.19 N | 6.24 W |
| Ionian Sea ⋍² | 50 | 39.00 N | 19.00 E |
| Iónioi Nísoi II | 74 | 38.30 N | 20.30 E |
| Iony, Ostrov I | 78 | 56.26 N | 143.25 E |
| Iowa ⊡³ | 96 | 42.15 N | 93.30 W |
| Iowa City | 96 | 41.40 N | 91.32 W |
| Ipiales | 100 | 0.50 N | 77.37 W |
| Ipoh | 82 | 4.35 N | 101.05 E |
| Ipswich, Austl. | 92 | 27.36 S | 152.46 E |
| Ipswich, Eng., U.K. | 54 | 52.04 N | 1.10 E |
| Iquitos | 100 | 3.46 S | 73.15 W |
| Iráklion | 74 | 35.20 N | 25.09 E |
| Iran (Īrān) ⊡¹ | 84 | 32.00 N | 53.00 E |
| Iran, Pegunungan ⋏ | 82 | 2.05 N | 114.55 E |
| Irapuato | 98 | 20.41 N | 101.21 W |
| Iraq ⊡¹ | 84 | 33.00 N | 44.00 E |
| Irazú, Volcán ⋀¹ | 98 | 9.58 N | 83.53 W |
| Irbid | 84 | 32.33 N | 35.51 E |
| Irbīl | 84 | 36.11 N | 44.01 E |
| Irbit | 78 | 57.41 N | 63.03 E |
| Ireland ⊡¹ | 50 | 53.00 N | 8.00 W |
| Ireng ⋍ | 100 | 3.33 N | 59.51 W |
| Irfon ⋍ | 54 | 52.09 N | 3.24 W |
| Iri | 80 | 35.56 N | 126.57 E |
| Iringa | 90 | 7.46 S | 35.42 E |
| Iriri ⋍ | 100 | 3.52 S | 52.37 W |
| Irish Sea ⋍² | 52 | 53.30 N | 5.20 W |
| Irkutsk | 78 | 52.16 N | 104.20 E |
| Irlam | 56 | 53.28 N | 2.29 W |
| Iron Bridge | 54 | 52.38 N | 2.29 W |
| Irrawaddy ⋍ | 82 | 15.50 N | 95.06 E |
| Irt ⋍ | 56 | 54.22 N | 3.26 W |
| Irthing ⋍ | 56 | 54.55 N | 2.50 W |
| Irthlingborough | 54 | 52.20 N | 0.37 W |
| Irtyš ⋍ | 78 | 61.04 N | 68.52 E |
| Irvine | 58 | 55.37 N | 4.41 W |
| Irvinestown | 60 | 54.28 N | 7.38 W |
| Irwell ⋍ | 56 | 53.30 N | 2.17 W |
| Isabela, Cordillera ⋏ | 98 | 13.45 N | 85.15 W |
| Ísafjördur | 62a | 66.08 N | 23.13 W |
| Isana (Içana) ⋍ | 100 | 0.26 N | 67.19 W |
| Isbister | 58 | 60.36 N | 1.19 W |
| Ischia | 72 | 40.44 N | 13.57 E |
| Ischia, Isola d' I | 72 | 40.43 N | 13.54 E |
| Iserlohn | 66 | 51.22 N | 7.41 E |
| Isernia | 72 | 41.36 N | 14.14 E |
| Iset' ⋍ | 78 | 56.36 N | 66.24 E |
| Iseyin | 86 | 7.58 N | 3.36 E |
| Ishikari ⋍ | 80 | 43.15 N | 141.23 E |
| Ishinomaki | 80 | 38.25 N | 141.18 E |
| Ísim ⋍ | 78 | 56.09 N | 69.27 E |
| Íšim ⋍ | 78 | 57.45 N | 71.10 E |
| Íšimbaj | 76 | 53.28 N | 56.02 E |
| Ísimskaja Step' ≛ | 78 | 54.06 N | 69.00 E |
| Iskenderun | 84 | 36.37 N | 36.07 E |
| Iskenderun Körfezi C | 84 | 36.30 N | 35.40 E |
| Isla ⋍ | 58 | 56.19 N | 3.17 W |
| Islāmābād | 84 | 33.42 N | 73.10 E |
| Island Lake ⊜ | 94 | 53.47 N | 94.25 W |
| Islay I | 58 | 55.46 N | 6.10 W |
| Islay, Sound of ⋃ | 58 | 55.50 N | 6.06 W |
| Isleat, Sound of ⋃ | 58 | 57.05 N | 5.50 W |
| Isle of Man ⊡² | 52 | 54.15 N | 4.30 W |
| Isle of Wight ⊡⁶ | 54 | 50.40 N | 1.15 W |
| Islington ⋏⁸ | 54 | 51.33 N | 0.06 W |
| Islip | 54 | 51.50 N | 1.14 W |
| Isliv ⋍ | 58 | 58.05 N | 7.11 W |
| Ismaning | 66 | 48.14 N | 11.41 E |
| Israel ⊡¹ | 84 | 31.30 N | 35.00 E |

| Name | Page | Lat | Long |
|---|---|---|---|
| Issoire | 68 | 45.33 N | 3.15 E |
| Issoudun | 68 | 46.57 N | 2.00 E |
| Issyk-Kul', Ozero ⊜ | 76 | 42.25 N | 77.15 E |
| Istanbul | 74 | 41.01 N | 28.58 E |
| Istra | 62 | 55.55 N | 36.52 E |
| Itabuna | 100 | 14.48 S | 39.16 W |
| Itagüí | 100 | 6.10 N | 75.36 W |
| Itajubá | 100 | 22.26 S | 45.27 W |
| Italy ⊡¹ | 50 | 42.50 N | 12.50 E |
| Itapetininga | 100 | 23.36 S | 48.03 W |
| Itapicuru ⋍, Bra. | 100 | 2.52 S | 44.12 W |
| Itapicuru ⋍, Bra. | 100 | 11.47 S | 37.32 W |
| Itbayat Island I | 82 | 20.46 N | 121.50 E |
| Itchen Lake ⊜ | 94 | 65.33 N | 112.50 W |
| Ithaca | 96 | 42.27 N | 76.30 W |
| Itui ⋍ | 100 | 4.38 S | 70.19 W |
| Ituiutaba | 100 | 18.58 S | 49.28 W |
| Iturup, Ostrov (Etorofu-tō) I | 78 | 44.54 N | 147.30 E |
| Ituxi ⋍ | 100 | 7.18 S | 64.51 W |
| Itzehoe | 66 | 53.55 N | 9.31 E |
| Ivangorod | 62 | 59.24 N | 28.10 E |
| Ivangrad | 74 | 42.50 N | 19.52 E |
| Ivano-Frankovsk | 74 | 48.55 N | 24.43 E |
| Ivanovo | 76 | 57.00 N | 40.59 E |
| Ivdel' | 76 | 60.42 N | 60.24 E |
| Ivory Coast ⊡¹ | 86 | 8.00 N | 5.00 W |
| Ivrea | 72 | 45.28 N | 7.52 E |
| Ivybridge | 54 | 50.23 N | 3.56 W |
| Iwaki | 80 | 37.03 N | 140.55 E |
| Iwo | 86 | 7.38 N | 4.11 E |
| Ixworth | 54 | 52.18 N | 0.50 E |
| Izegem | 68 | 50.55 N | 3.12 E |
| Iževsk | 62 | 56.51 N | 53.14 E |
| Izmail | 76 | 45.19 N | 52.54 E |
| Izmir | 74 | 45.21 N | 28.50 E |
| Izmir (Kocaeli) | 74 | 38.25 N | 27.09 E |
| Iznik | 74 | 40.46 N | 29.55 E |
| Izozog, Bañados de ⊜ | 74 | 40.26 N | 29.43 E |
| Izu-shotō II | 100 | 18.48 S | 62.10 W |
| | 80 | 34.00 N | 140.00 E |

| Name | Page | Lat | Long |
|---|---|---|---|
| Jablonec nad Nisou | 66 | 50.44 N | 15.10 E |
| Jablonov | 74 | 48.24 N | 24.57 E |
| Jablonovyj Chrebet (Yablonovy Range) ⋏ | 78 | 53.30 N | 115.00 E |
| Jaboatão | 100 | 8.07 S | 35.01 W |
| Jacareí | 100 | 23.19 S | 45.58 W |
| Jackson, Mich., U.S. | 96 | 42.15 N | 84.24 W |
| Jackson, Miss., U.S. | 96 | 32.18 N | 90.12 W |
| Jacksonville, Fla., U.S. | 96 | 30.20 N | 81.40 W |
| Jacksonville, N.C., U.S. | 96 | 34.45 N | 77.26 W |
| Jacobābād | 84 | 28.17 N | 68.26 E |
| Jacques-Cartier, Détroit de ⋃ | 94 | 50.00 N | 63.30 W |
| Jacques-Cartier, Mont ⋀ | 94 | 48.59 N | 65.57 W |
| Jādū | 88 | 31.57 N | 12.01 E |
| Jaén | 70 | 37.46 N | 3.47 W |
| Jaffa, Cape ➤ | 92 | 36.58 S | 139.40 E |
| Jaffna | 84 | 9.40 N | 80.00 E |
| Jagādhri | 84 | 30.10 N | 77.18 E |
| Jaguaribe ⋍ | 100 | 4.25 S | 37.45 W |
| Jahrom | 84 | 28.31 N | 53.33 E |
| Jaipur | 84 | 26.55 N | 75.50 E |
| Jajce | 72 | 44.21 N | 17.16 E |
| Jakarta | 82 | 6.10 S | 106.48 E |
| Jakobstad (Pietarsaari) | 64 | 63.40 N | 22.42 E |
| Jalālābād | 84 | 34.26 N | 70.28 E |
| Jalapa Enríquez | 98 | 19.32 N | 96.55 W |
| Jālgaon | 84 | 21.01 N | 75.34 E |
| Jalón ⋍ | 70 | 41.47 N | 1.04 W |
| Jalpaiguri | 84 | 26.31 N | 88.44 E |
| Jalta | 76 | 44.30 N | 34.10 E |
| Jamaica ⊡¹ | 98 | 18.15 N | 77.30 W |
| Jamal, Poluostrov ➤¹ | 78 | 70.00 N | 70.00 E |
| Jambalpur ⋍ | 84 | 24.25 N | 86.40 E |
| Jamantau, Gora ⋀ | 76 | 54.15 N | 58.06 E |
| Jambes | 68 | 50.28 N | 4.52 E |
| Jambi | 82 | 1.36 S | 103.37 E |
| Jambol | 74 | 42.29 N | 26.30 E |
| Jambongan, Pulau I | 82 | 6.40 N | 117.27 E |
| James ⋍ | 96 | 42.52 N | 97.18 W |
| James Bay C | 94 | 53.30 N | 80.30 W |
| James Ross, Cape ➤ | 94 | 74.40 N | 114.25 W |
| James Ross Strait ⋃ | 94 | 69.40 N | 95.30 W |
| Jamestown, Eire | 58 | 53.55 N | 8.02 W |
| Jammerstown, N.Y., U.S. | 96 | 42.06 N | 79.14 W |
| Jammu | 84 | 32.44 N | 74.52 E |
| Jämmagar | 84 | 22.28 N | 70.04 E |
| Jamshedpur | 84 | 22.48 N | 86.11 E |
| Jana ⋍ | 78 | 71.31 N | 136.32 E |
| Janaúca, Ilha I | 100 | 3.00 N | 64.60 W |
| Janesville | 96 | 42.41 N | 89.01 W |
| Janjangl ⋏ | 84 | 34.02 N | 77.20 E |
| Jan Mayen I | 40 | 71.00 N | 8.20 W |
| Janskij Zaliv C | 78 | 71.50 N | 136.00 E |
| Jantarnyj (Palmnicken) | 68 | 54.52 N | 19.57 E |
| Japan ⊡¹ | 80 | 36.00 N | 138.00 E |
| Japan, Sea of ⋍² | 80 | 40.00 N | 135.00 E |
| Japurá (Caquetá) ⋍ | 100 | 3.08 S | 64.46 W |
| Jara ⋀ | 78 | 57.19 N | 47.54 E |
| Jarcevo | 62 | 55.55 N | 32.41 E |
| Jardines de la Reina II | 98 | 20.50 N | 78.55 W |
| Jaremča | 74 | 48.27 N | 24.34 E |
| Jari ⋍ | 100 | 1.09 S | 51.54 W |
| Jarocin | 68 | 51.59 N | 17.31 E |
| Jaroslavl' | 62 | 57.37 N | 39.52 E |
| Jarosław | 68 | 50.02 N | 22.42 E |
| Järvenpää | 64 | 60.28 N | 25.06 E |
| Jasło | 68 | 49.45 N | 21.29 E |
| Jasnogorsk | 62 | 54.29 N | 37.42 E |
| Jászapáti | 74 | 47.31 N | 20.09 E |
| Jászberény | 74 | 47.30 N | 19.56 E |
| Jat, Ras al- ➤ | 88 | 26.45 N | 15.03 E |
| Jatai | 100 | 17.53 S | 51.43 W |
| Jaú | 100 | 22.18 S | 48.33 W |
| Jaú ⋍ | 100 | 1.54 S | 61.26 W |
| Jauaperi ⋍ | 100 | 1.26 S | 61.35 W |
| Jaunpur | 84 | 25.44 N | 82.42 E |
| Javari (Yavari) ⋍ | 100 | 4.21 S | 70.02 W |
| Jawa (Java) I | 82 | 7.30 S | 110.00 E |
| Jaworzno | 68 | 50.13 N | 19.15 E |
| Jaya, Puncak ⋀ | 82 | 4.05 S | 137.11 E |
| Jayapura (Sukarnapura) | 82 | 2.32 S | 140.42 E |
| Jaywick | 54 | 51.47 N | 1.08 E |
| Jaz Mūriān, Hāmūn-e ⊜ | 84 | 27.20 N | 58.55 E |

| Name | Page | Lat | Long |
|---|---|---|---|
| Jedburgh | 58 | 55.29 N | 2.34 W |
| Jeddore Lake ⊜¹ | 94 | 48.03 N | 55.55 W |
| Jędrzejów | 68 | 50.39 N | 20.18 E |
| Jed Water ⋍ | 58 | 55.31 N | 2.33 W |
| Jefferson City | 96 | 38.34 N | 92.10 W |
| Jeffreys Bay | 90 | 34.02 S | 24.55 E |
| Jejsk | 76 | 46.42 N | 38.16 E |
| Jēkabpils | 62 | 56.30 N | 25.51 E |
| Jèkaterinyj, Proliv ⋃ | 78 | 50.53 N | 154.00 E |
| Jelabuga | 62 | 55.46 N | 52.04 E |
| Jelec | 62 | 52.37 N | 38.30 E |
| Jelenia Góra (Hirschberg) | 66 | 50.55 N | 15.46 E |
| Jelgava | 62 | 56.39 N | 23.43 E |
| Jelizavety, Mys ➤ | 78 | 54.24 N | 142.42 E |

| Name | Page | Lat | Long |
|---|---|---|---|
| Jeloguj ⋍ | 78 | 63.13 N | 87.45 E |
| Jember | 82 | 8.10 S | 113.42 E |
| Jemca | 62 | 63.04 N | 40.20 E |
| Jena | 66 | 50.56 N | 11.35 E |
| Jenisej ⋍ | 78 | 71.50 N | 82.40 E |
| Jenisejsk | 78 | 58.27 N | 92.10 E |
| Jenisejskij Kr'až ⋏ | 78 | 59.00 N | 93.00 E |
| Jenisejskij Zaliv C | 78 | 72.30 N | 80.00 E |
| Jequié | 100 | 13.51 S | 40.05 W |
| Jequitinhonha ⋍ | 100 | 15.51 S | 38.53 W |
| Jerez de la Frontera | 70 | 40.11 N | 44.30 E |
| Jerez de los Caballeros | 70 | 38.19 N | 6.46 W |
| Jergeni ⋏² | 76 | 47.00 N | 44.00 E |
| Jersey ⊡² | 54a | 49.15 N | 2.10 W |
| Jersey City | 96 | 40.44 N | 74.02 W |
| Jervis Bay C | 92 | 35.05 S | 150.44 E |
| Jesenice | 72 | 46.27 N | 14.04 E |
| Jessentuki | 76 | 44.03 N | 42.51 E |
| Jevpatorija | 76 | 45.12 N | 33.22 E |
| Jhang Maghiāna | 84 | 31.16 N | 72.19 E |
| Jhānsi | 84 | 25.27 N | 78.35 E |
| Jhelum | 84 | 32.56 N | 73.44 E |
| Jhelum ⋍ | 84 | 31.12 N | 72.08 E |
| Jialingjiang ⋍ | 80 | 30.02 N | 106.18 E |
| Jiamusi | 80 | 46.50 N | 130.21 E |
| Ji'an | 80 | 27.07 N | 114.58 E |
| Jiangmen | 80 | 22.35 N | 113.05 E |
| Jianou | 80 | 27.03 N | 118.19 E |
| Jianshui | 80 | 23.38 N | 102.49 E |
| Jiaohe | 80 | 43.42 N | 127.19 E |
| Jiaoxian | 80 | 36.18 N | 119.58 E |
| Jiaozuo | 80 | 35.14 N | 113.13 E |
| Jiaxing | 80 | 30.46 N | 120.45 E |
| Jičín | 66 | 50.26 N | 15.21 E |
| Jieyang | 80 | 23.33 N | 116.21 E |
| Jihlava | 66 | 49.24 N | 15.36 E |
| Jilin | 80 | 43.51 N | 126.33 E |
| Jima | 88 | 7.36 N | 36.50 E |
| Jimbolia | 74 | 45.47 N | 20.43 E |
| Jinan (Tsinan) | 80 | 36.40 N | 116.57 E |
| Jincheng | 80 | 35.30 N | 112.50 E |
| Jindřichův Hradec | 66 | 49.09 N | 15.00 E |
| Jingdezhen | 80 | 29.16 N | 117.11 E |
| Jinhua | 80 | 29.07 N | 119.39 E |
| Jining, Zhg. | 80 | 41.06 N | 112.58 E |
| Jining, Zhg. | 80 | 35.25 N | 116.36 E |
| Jinja | 90 | 0.26 N | 33.12 E |
| Jinshajiang ⋍ | 80 | 28.50 N | 104.36 E |
| Jinshi | 80 | 29.04 N | 111.40 E |
| Jinxian | 80 | 39.04 N | 121.40 E |
| Jinzhou | 80 | 41.07 N | 121.08 E |
| Jiparaná ⋍ | 100 | 8.03 S | 62.52 W |
| Jirjā | 88 | 26.20 N | 31.53 E |
| Jiujiang | 80 | 29.44 N | 115.59 E |
| Jiulingshan ⋀ | 80 | 28.40 N | 114.45 E |
| Jiuquan | 80 | 39.45 N | 98.34 E |
| Jixi | 80 | 45.17 N | 130.57 E |
| João Pessoa | 100 | 7.07 S | 34.52 W |
| Jódar | 70 | 37.50 N | 3.21 W |
| Jodhpur | 84 | 26.17 N | 73.01 E |
| Joensuu | 64 | 62.36 N | 29.46 E |
| Johannesburg | 90 | 26.15 S | 28.00 E |
| Johanngeorgenstadt | 66 | 50.26 N | 12.43 E |
| John O'groats | 58 | 58.38 N | 3.05 W |
| Johnshaven | 58 | 56.47 N | 2.20 W |
| Johnston | 54 | 51.46 N | 5.00 W |
| Johnston, Lake ⊜ | 92 | 32.25 S | 120.30 E |
| Johnstone | 58 | 55.50 N | 4.31 W |
| Johnston Island I | 8 | 16.45 N | 169.32 W |
| Johnstown | 96 | 40.19 N | 78.55 W |
| Johor Baharu | 82 | 1.28 N | 103.45 E |
| Joliet | 96 | 41.32 N | 88.05 W |
| Jolo | 82 | 6.03 N | 121.00 E |
| Jones Sound ⋃ | 94 | 76.00 N | 85.00 W |
| Jönköping | 64 | 57.47 N | 14.11 E |
| Jonquière | 94 | 48.25 N | 71.15 W |
| Joplin | 96 | 37.06 N | 94.31 W |
| Jordan ⊡¹ | 84 | 31.00 N | 36.00 E |
| Jos | 86 | 9.55 N | 8.53 E |
| Joseph Bonaparte Gulf C | 92 | 14.15 S | 128.30 E |
| Joškar-Ola | 62 | 56.38 N | 47.52 E |
| Jostedalsbreen ⋈ | 64 | 61.40 N | 7.00 E |
| Juan de Fuca, Strait of ⋃ | 96 | 48.18 N | 124.00 W |
| Juan de Nova, Île I | 90 | 17.03 S | 42.45 E |
| Juan Fernández, Islas II | 102 | 33.00 S | 80.00 W |
| Juàzeiro | 100 | 9.25 S | 40.30 W |
| Juàzeiro do Norte | 100 | 7.12 S | 39.20 W |
| Jūbā | 88 | 4.51 N | 31.37 E |
| Juby, Cap ➤ | 86 | 27.58 N | 12.55 W |
| Júcar ⋍ | 70 | 39.09 N | 0.14 W |
| Juchitán | 98 | 16.26 N | 95.01 W |
| Juchnov | 62 | 54.45 N | 35.14 E |
| Juddah (Jidda) | 84 | 21.30 N | 39.12 E |
| Judenburg | 66 | 47.10 N | 14.40 E |
| Judoma ⋍ | 78 | 59.08 N | 135.06 E |
| Juiz de Fora | 100 | 21.45 S | 43.20 W |
| Jujuy ⊡³ | 102 | 23.00 S | 66.00 W |
| Juliaca | 100 | 15.30 S | 70.08 W |
| Julianatop ⋀ | 100 | 3.41 N | 56.32 W |
| Jülich | 66 | 50.55 N | 6.21 E |
| Julundur | 84 | 31.19 N | 75.34 E |
| Jumentos Cays II | 98 | 23.05 N | 75.55 W |
| Jumet | 68 | 50.27 N | 4.26 E |
| Jumilla | 70 | 38.29 N | 1.17 W |
| Junagadh | 84 | 21.31 N | 70.28 E |
| Jundiai | 100 | 23.11 S | 46.52 W |
| Juneau | 94 | 58.20 N | 134.27 W |
| Junín | 102 | 34.35 S | 60.57 W |
| Junín, Lago de ⊜ | 100 | 11.02 S | 76.06 W |
| Jura I | 58 | 56.00 N | 5.50 W |
| Jura, Sound of ⋃ | 58 | 55.55 N | 5.45 W |
| Jurjevec | 62 | 57.19 N | 43.07 E |
| Jūrmala | 62 | 56.58 N | 23.42 E |
| Juruá ⋍ | 100 | 2.37 S | 65.44 W |
| Juruena ⋍ | 100 | 7.20 S | 58.03 W |
| Jutaí ⋍ | 100 | 2.43 S | 66.57 W |
| Jüterbog | 66 | 51.59 N | 13.04 E |
| Juža | 62 | 56.35 N | 42.02 E |
| Južno-Sachalinsk | 78 | 46.58 N | 142.42 E |
| Južnyj, Mys ➤ | 78 | 57.45 N | 156.45 E |
| Južnyj Bug ⋍ | 76 | 46.59 N | 31.58 E |
| Jyväskylä | 64 | 62.14 N | 25.44 E |

| Name | Page | Lat | Long |
|---|---|---|---|
| Kaap Plato ⋏¹ | 90 | 28.20 S | 23.57 E |
| Kabaena, Pulau I | 82 | 5.15 S | 121.55 E |
| Kabalo | 90 | 6.03 S | 26.55 E |
| Kabīr Kūh ⋏ | 84 | 33.25 N | 46.45 E |
| Kābul | 84 | 34.31 N | 69.11 E |
| Kabul ⋍ | 84 | 33.55 N | 72.14 E |
| Kaburuang, Pulau I | 82 | 3.48 N | 126.48 E |
| Kabwe (Broken Hill) | 90 | 14.27 S | 28.27 E |
| Kachovskoje Vodochranilišče ⊜¹ | 76 | 47.25 N | 34.10 E |
| Kadan Kyun I | 82 | 12.30 N | 98.22 E |
| Kadei ⋍ | 90 | 3.31 N | 16.05 E |
| Kadijevka | 76 | 48.34 N | 38.40 E |
| Kadiri | 84 | 14.07 N | 78.10 E |
| Kaédi | 86 | 16.09 N | 13.30 W |
| Kaesong | 80 | 37.59 N | 126.33 E |
| Kafue ⋍ | 90 | 15.56 S | 28.55 E |
| Kaga | 80 | 36.18 N | 136.18 E |
| Kagera ⋍ | 90 | 0.57 S | 31.47 E |
| Kagoshima | 80 | 31.36 N | 130.33 E |
| Kahayan ⋍ | 82 | 3.20 S | 114.04 E |
| Kahoolawe I | 96b | 20.33 N | 156.35 W |
| Kai, Kepulauan II | 82 | 5.35 S | 132.45 E |
| Kaieteur Fall ⋏ | 100 | 5.10 N | 59.28 W |
| Kaifeng | 80 | 34.51 N | 114.21 E |
| Kaikoura | 93a | 42.25 S | 173.41 E |
| Kaili | 80 | 26.34 N | 107.58 E |
| Kaimana | 82 | 3.39 S | 133.45 E |
| Kaipara Harbour C | 93a | 36.25 S | 174.13 E |
| Kairouan | 86 | 35.41 N | 10.07 E |
| Kaiserslautern | 66 | 49.26 N | 7.46 E |
| Kaixian | 80 | 31.11 N | 108.23 E |
| Kajaani | 64 | 64.14 N | 27.41 E |
| Kākināda | 84 | 16.57 N | 82.14 E |
| Kajrakkumskoje Vodochranilišče ⊜¹ | 84 | 40.15 N | 70.00 E |
| Kalahari Desert ⋍² | 90 | 24.00 S | 21.30 E |
| Kalámai | 74 | 37.04 N | 22.07 E |
| Kalamariá | 74 | 40.35 N | 22.58 E |
| Kalamazoo | 96 | 42.17 N | 85.37 W |
| Kalabáka | 74 | 52.15 N | 37.52 E |
| Kalb, Ra's al- ➤ | 84 | 14.02 N | 48.40 E |
| Kalemi (Albertville) | 90 | 5.56 S | 29.12 E |
| Kalevala | 62 | 65.13 N | 31.08 E |
| Kale Water ⋍ | 58 | 55.32 N | 2.28 W |
| Kalgoorlie | 92 | 30.45 S | 121.28 E |
| Kálimnos I | 74 | 36.57 N | 26.59 E |
| Kálimnos I | 74 | 36.57 N | 26.59 E |
| Kalinin | 62 | 56.52 N | 35.55 E |
| Kaliningrad (Königsberg) | 66 | 54.43 N | 20.30 E |
| Kalisz | 68 | 51.46 N | 18.06 E |
| Kalixälven ⋍ | 50 | 65.46 N | 22.22 E |
| Kalmar | 64 | 56.40 N | 16.22 E |
| Kalocsa | 66 | 46.32 N | 18.59 E |
| Kaluga | 62 | 54.31 N | 36.16 E |
| Kalvarija | 84 | 54.21 N | 23.14 E |
| Kalyān | 84 | 19.15 N | 73.08 E |
| Kama ⋍ | 76 | 55.45 N | 52.00 E |
| Kamaishi | 80 | 39.16 N | 141.53 E |
| Kamarān I | 84 | 15.21 N | 42.34 E |
| Kamčatka ⋍ | 78 | 56.15 N | 162.30 E |
| Kamčatka, Poluostrov ➤¹ | 78 | 56.00 N | 160.00 E |
| Kamčatskij Zaliv C | 78 | 55.35 N | 162.21 E |
| Kamen' ⋀ | 78 | 69.06 N | 94.48 E |
| Kamenec | 76 | 52.24 N | 23.49 E |
| Kamenec-Podol'skij | 76 | 48.41 N | 26.36 E |
| Kamen'-na-Obi | 78 | 53.47 N | 81.20 E |
| Kamennogorsk | 62 | 60.58 N | 29.07 E |
| Kamensk-Ural'skij | 76 | 56.28 N | 61.54 E |
| Kamenz | 66 | 51.16 N | 14.06 E |
| Kames | 58 | 55.54 N | 5.15 W |
| Kámet ⋀ | 84 | 30.54 N | 79.37 E |
| Kamienna Góra | 66 | 50.47 N | 16.07 E |
| Kamilukuak Lake ⊜ | 94 | 62.22 N | 101.40 W |
| Kamina | 90 | 8.44 S | 25.00 E |
| Kaminuriak Lake ⊜ | 94 | 63.00 N | 95.40 W |
| Kamloops | 94 | 50.40 N | 120.20 W |
| Kampala | 90 | 0.19 N | 32.25 E |
| Kampar ⋍ | 82 | 0.30 N | 103.08 E |
| Kampen | 66 | 52.33 N | 5.54 E |
| Kâmpóng Cham | 82 | 12.00 N | 105.27 E |
| Kâmpóng Saôm, Chhâk C | 82 | 10.50 N | 103.32 E |
| Kamrau, Teluk C | 82 | 3.32 S | 133.37 E |
| Kamskoje Vodochranilišče ⊜¹ | 76 | 58.52 N | 56.15 E |
| Kamyšin | 76 | 50.06 N | 45.24 E |
| Kanairiktok ⋍ | 94 | 55.05 N | 60.20 W |
| Kananga (Luluabourg) | 90 | 5.54 S | 22.25 E |
| Kanaš | 62 | 55.31 N | 47.32 E |
| Kanazawa | 80 | 36.34 N | 136.39 E |
| Kānchenjunga ⋀ | 84 | 27.42 N | 88.08 E |
| Kānchipuram | 84 | 12.50 N | 79.43 E |
| Kandalaksa | 62 | 67.09 N | 32.21 E |
| Kandangan | 82 | 2.47 S | 115.16 E |
| Kandy | 84 | 7.18 N | 80.38 E |
| Kaneohe | 96b | 21.25 N | 157.48 W |
| Kangaroo Island I | 92 | 35.50 S | 137.06 E |
| Kangding | 80 | 30.03 N | 102.02 E |
| Kangean, Kepulauan II | 82 | 6.55 S | 115.30 E |
| Kangnúng | 80 | 40.58 N | 126.34 E |
| Kangnúng | 80 | 37.45 N | 128.54 E |
| Kangto ⋀ | 84 | 27.52 N | 92.32 E |
| Kanin Nos, Mys ➤ | 76 | 68.00 N | 45.00 E |
| Kanin, Poluostrov ➤¹ | 76 | 68.00 N | 45.00 E |
| Kanjiža | 74 | 46.04 N | 20.04 E |
| Kankakee | 96 | 41.07 N | 87.52 W |
| Kankan | 86 | 10.23 N | 9.18 W |
| Kanmaw Kyun I | 82 | 11.40 N | 98.28 E |
| Kannapolis | 96 | 35.30 N | 80.37 W |
| Kano | 86 | 12.00 N | 8.30 E |
| Kānpur | 84 | 26.28 N | 80.21 E |
| Kansas ⊡³ | 96 | 38.45 N | 98.15 W |
| Kansas City, Kans., U.S. | 96 | 39.07 N | 94.39 W |
| Kansas City, Mo., U.S. | 96 | 39.05 N | 94.35 W |
| Kansk | 78 | 56.13 N | 95.41 E |
| Kanturk | 60 | 52.10 N | 8.55 W |
| Kanye | 90 | 24.59 S | 25.19 E |
| Kaohsiung | 80 | 22.38 N | 120.17 E |
| Kaokoveld ⋏¹ | 90 | 17.03 S | 14.20 E |
| Kaolack | 86 | 14.09 N | 16.04 W |
| Kapfenberg | 66 | 47.26 N | 15.18 E |
| Kapiskau ⋍ | 94 | 52.47 N | 81.55 W |
| Kapsvär | 74 | 46.22 N | 17.48 E |
| Kapuas ⋍ | 82 | 0.25 S | 109.40 E |
| Kapuas Hulu, Pegunungan ⋏ | 82 | 1.25 N | 113.15 E |
| Kapuskasing | 94 | 49.25 N | 82.26 W |
| Kara-Bogaz-Gol, Zaliv C | 76 | 41.00 N | 53.30 E |
| Karacabey | 74 | 40.13 N | 28.21 E |
| Karāchi | 84 | 24.52 N | 67.03 E |
| Karaganda | 78 | 49.50 N | 73.10 E |
| Karaginskij, Ostrov I | 78 | 58.50 N | 164.00 E |
| Karaginskij Zaliv C | 78 | 58.50 N | 164.00 E |
| Karagoš, Gora ⋀ | 78 | 51.44 N | 89.24 E |
| Karakoram Range ⋏ | 84 | 35.30 N | 77.00 E |
| Karakumskij Kanal ≛ | 84 | 37.35 N | 61.50 E |
| Karaman | 84 | 37.11 N | 33.13 E |
| Karamürsel | 74 | 40.42 N | 29.36 E |
| Karasuk | 78 | 53.44 N | 78.02 E |
| Karatau, Chrebet ⋏ | 84 | 43.00 N | 69.00 E |
| Karażal | 78 | 48.02 N | 70.49 E |
| Karbalā | 84 | 32.36 N | 44.02 E |
| Karcag | 74 | 47.19 N | 20.56 E |
| Kārdżali | 74 | 41.39 N | 25.22 E |
| Kargopol' | 62 | 61.30 N | 38.58 E |
| Karhula | 64 | 60.31 N | 26.57 E |
| Kariba, Lake ⊜¹ | 90 | 17.00 S | 28.00 E |
| Karimata, Kepulauan II | 82 | 1.25 S | 109.05 E |
| Karimata, Selat (Karimata Strait) ⋃ | 82 | 2.05 S | 108.40 E |
| Karl-Marx-Stadt (Chemnitz) | 66 | 50.50 N | 12.55 E |
| Karlovac | 72 | 45.29 N | 15.34 E |
| Karlovy Vary | 66 | 50.14 N | 12.52 E |
| Karlshamn | 64 | 56.10 N | 14.51 E |
| Karlskoga | 64 | 59.19 N | 14.31 E |
| Karlskrona | 64 | 56.10 N | 15.35 E |
| Karlstad | 64 | 59.22 N | 13.30 E |
| Karnāl | 84 | 29.41 N | 76.59 E |
| Karnataka ⊡³ | 84 | 13.00 N | 77.00 E |
| Karnobat | 74 | 42.39 N | 26.59 E |
| Karpasia ➤¹ | 84 | 35.40 N | 34.35 E |
| Karpinsk | 76 | 59.45 N | 60.01 E |
| Karrats Isfjord C² | 94 | 71.20 N | 54.00 W |
| Kars | 84 | 40.36 N | 43.05 E |
| Karši | 84 | 38.27 N | 27.07 E |
| Karskije Vorota, Proliv ⋃ | 76 | 70.30 N | 58.00 E |
| Karskoje More (Kara Sea) ⋍² | 78 | 76.00 N | 80.00 E |
| Kartaly | 76 | 53.03 N | 60.40 E |
| Kārūr | 84 | 10.57 N | 78.05 E |
| Kasai (Cassai) ⋍ | 90 | 3.06 S | 16.57 E |
| Kasba Lake ⊜ | 94 | 60.18 N | 102.07 W |
| Kashi (Kashgar) | 84 | 39.29 N | 75.59 E |
| Kasimov | 62 | 54.57 N | 41.24 E |
| Kaskattama ⋍ | 94 | 57.03 N | 90.07 W |
| Kásos I | 74 | 35.22 N | 26.55 E |
| Kasr, Ra's ➤ | 88 | 18.02 N | 38.35 E |

Symbols in the index entries are identified on page 111.

| Name | Page | Lat | Long |
|---|---|---|---|
| Kassalā | 88 | 15.28 N | 36.24 E |
| Kassel | 66 | 51.19 N | 9.29 E |
| Kastoria | 74 | 40.31 N | 21.15 E |
| Kasūr | 84 | 31.07 N | 74.27 E |

| Name | Page | Lat | Long |
|---|---|---|---|
| Lauritsala | 64 | 61.04 N | 28.16 E |
| Lausanne | 68 | 46.31 N | 6.38 E |
| Laut, Pulau I | 82 | 3.40 S | 116.10 E |
| Laut Kecil, Kepulauan II | 82 | 4.50 S | 115.45 E |
| Lavagh More ▲ | 54 | 54.45 N | 8.05 W |
| Laval, Qué., Can. | 94 | 45.33 N | 73.44 W |
| Laval, Fr. | 68 | 48.04 N | 0.46 W |
| Lavapié, Punta ➤ | 102 | 37.09 S | 73.35 W |
| La Vega | 98 | 19.13 N | 70.31 W |
| Lavello | 72 | 41.03 N | 15.48 E |
| Lavendon | 54 | 52.11 N | 0.40 W |
| Lavenham | 54 | 52.06 N | 0.47 E |
| Laver ≃ | 58 | 54.08 N | 1.30 W |
| Lawers, Ben ▲ | 52 | 56.33 N | 4.15 W |
| Lawrence, Kans., U.S. | 96 | 38.58 N | 95.14 W |
| Lawrence, Mass., U.S. | 96 | 42.42 N | 71.09 W |
| Lawton | 96 | 34.37 N | 98.25 W |
| Lawz, Jabal al- ▲ | 84 | 28.40 N | 35.18 E |
| Laxay | 58 | 58.09 N | 6.35 W |
| Laxey | 56 | 54.14 N | 4.23 W |
| Laxford, Loch C | 52 | 58.23 N | 5.06 W |
| Lazdijai | 66 | 54.14 N | 23.31 E |
| Lea ≃ | 54 | 51.30 N | 0.01 E |
| Leach ≃ | 54 | 51.41 N | 1.39 W |
| Leadburn | 58 | 55.47 N | 3.14 W |
| Leadenham | 54 | 53.05 N | 0.34 W |
| Leader Water ≃ | 58 | 55.36 N | 2.40 W |
| Leadgate | 58 | 54.52 N | 1.48 W |
| Leadhills | 54 | 55.25 N | 3.47 W |
| Leadon ≃ | 54 | 51.53 N | 2.16 W |
| League ≃ | 60 | 54.39 N | 8.44 W |
| Leam ≃ | 54 | 52.17 N | 1.14 W |
| Leane, Lough ⊜ | 52 | 52.05 N | 9.35 W |
| Leannan ≃ | 60 | 55.02 N | 7.38 W |
| Leatherhead | 54 | 51.18 N | 0.20 W |
| Leavenworth | 96 | 39.19 N | 94.55 W |
| Lebanon □¹ | 84 | 33.50 N | 35.50 E |
| Lebork | 66 | 54.33 N | 17.44 E |
| Lebrija | 70 | 36.55 N | 6.04 W |
| Le Cateau | 68 | 50.06 N | 3.33 E |
| Lecce | 72 | 40.23 N | 18.11 E |
| Lecco | 72 | 45.51 N | 9.23 E |
| Lechlade | 54 | 51.43 N | 1.41 W |
| Le Creusot | 68 | 46.48 N | 4.26 E |
| Łęczyca | 66 | 52.04 N | 19.13 E |
| Ledaig | 58 | 56.30 N | 5.23 W |
| Ledbury | 54 | 52.02 N | 2.25 W |
| Ledi, Ben ▲ | 58 | 56.15 N | 4.19 W |
| Lee ≃ | 60 | 51.54 N | 8.22 W |
| Leech Lake ⊜ | 96 | 47.09 N | 94.23 W |
| Leeds | 56 | 53.50 N | 1.35 W |
| Leedstown | 54 | 50.10 N | 5.22 W |
| Leek | 54 | 54.57 N | 1.11 W |
| Leenaun | 60 | 53.36 N | 9.45 W |
| Lee-on-the-Solent | 54 | 50.48 N | 1.12 W |
| Leer | 66 | 53.14 N | 7.26 E |
| Leeuwarden | 66 | 53.12 N | 5.46 E |
| Leeuwin, Cape ➤ | 88 | 34.22 S | 115.08 E |
| Leeward Islands II | 98 | 17.00 N | 63.00 W |
| Lefroy, Lake ⊜ | 92 | 31.15 S | 121.40 E |
| Legazpi | 82 | 13.08 N | 123.44 E |
| Legionowo | 66 | 52.25 N | 20.56 E |
| Legnago | 72 | 45.11 N | 11.18 E |
| Legnano | 72 | 45.36 N | 8.54 E |
| Legnica (Liegnitz) | 66 | 51.13 N | 16.09 E |
| Le Havre | 68 | 49.30 N | 0.08 E |
| Lehrte | 66 | 52.22 N | 9.59 E |
| Leicester | 54 | 52.38 N | 1.05 W |
| Leicestershire □⁶ | 54 | 52.40 N | 1.10 W |
| Leichhardt ≃ | 92 | 18.13 S | 139.48 E |
| Leiden | 66 | 52.09 N | 4.30 E |
| Leigh | 56 | 53.30 N | 2.33 W |
| Leighinbridge | 60 | 52.44 N | 6.59 W |
| Leigh-on-Sea | 54 | 51.33 N | 0.38 E |
| Leighton Buzzard | 54 | 51.55 N | 0.40 W |
| Leinster □⁹ | 52 | 53.05 N | 7.00 W |
| Leinster, Mount ▲ | 52 | 52.37 N | 6.44 W |
| Leintwardine | 54 | 52.22 N | 2.51 W |
| Leipzig | 66 | 51.19 N | 12.20 E |
| Leisler, Mount ▲ | 92 | 23.28 S | 129.17 E |
| Leith | 58 | 55.59 N | 3.10 W |
| Leith, Water of ≃ | 54 | 55.59 N | 3.11 W |
| Leith Hill ▲² | 54 | 51.11 N | 0.23 W |
| Leitrim □⁶ | 60 | 54.00 N | 8.04 W |
| Leixlip | 60 | 54.20 N | 8.20 W |
| Leizhoubandao ➤¹ | 80 | 21.15 N | 110.09 E |
| Lelant | 54 | 50.11 N | 5.26 W |
| Lelishan ▲ | 80 | 33.26 N | 81.42 E |
| Le Locle | 68 | 47.03 N | 6.45 E |
| Le Maire, Estrecho de ⋃ | 102 | 54.50 S | 65.00 W |
| Le Mans | 68 | 48.00 N | 0.12 E |
| Lemesos | 84 | 34.40 N | 33.02 E |
| Lemgo | 66 | 52.02 N | 8.54 E |
| Lemieux Islands II | 94 | 64.30 N | 64.40 W |
| Lena ≃ | 78 | 72.25 N | 126.40 E |
| Lenina, Pik ▲ | 76 | 39.20 N | 72.55 E |
| Leninabad | 76 | 40.17 N | 69.37 E |
| Leninakan | 76 | 40.48 N | 43.50 E |
| Leningrad | 62 | 59.55 N | 30.15 E |
| Leninogorsk, S.S.S.R. | 78 | 50.27 N | 83.32 E |
| Leninsk-Kuzneckij | 78 | 54.38 N | 86.10 E |
| Lenkoran' | 76 | 38.45 N | 48.50 E |
| Lennox □⁹ | 58 | 56.03 N | 4.15 W |
| Lennox, Isla I | 102 | 55.18 S | 66.50 W |
| Lennoxtown | 58 | 55.59 N | 4.12 W |
| Lens | 68 | 50.26 N | 2.50 E |
| Lensk | 78 | 61.00 N | 114.50 E |
| Lentini | 72 | 37.17 N | 15.00 E |
| Leoben | 66 | 47.23 N | 15.06 E |
| Leominster | 54 | 52.14 N | 2.45 W |
| León, Esp. | 70 | 42.36 N | 5.34 W |
| León, Méx. | 98 | 21.07 N | 101.40 W |
| León, Nic. | 98 | 12.26 N | 86.53 W |
| Leonberg | 66 | 48.48 N | 9.01 E |
| Leonforte | 72 | 37.39 N | 14.24 E |
| Lepe | 54 | 37.15 N | 7.12 W |
| Lepel' | 62 | 54.53 N | 28.42 E |
| Le Port | 90 | 20.55 S | 55.18 E |
| Le Puy | 68 | 45.02 N | 3.53 E |
| Leri ≃ | 54 | 52.32 N | 4.02 W |
| Lerici | 72 | 44.04 N | 9.55 E |
| Lérida | 70 | 41.37 N | 0.37 E |
| Lerwick | 50 | 60.09 N | 1.09 W |
| Lesbury | 56 | 55.24 N | 1.36 W |
| Leshan | 80 | 29.34 N | 103.45 E |
| Leskovac | 74 | 42.59 N | 21.57 E |
| Leslie | 58 | 56.12 N | 3.13 W |
| Lesmahagow | 58 | 55.39 N | 3.55 W |
| Lesotho □¹ | 90 | 29.30 S | 28.30 E |
| Lesozavodsk | 78 | 45.28 N | 133.27 E |
| Lesozavodskij | 62 | 66.44 N | 32.49 E |
| Les Sables-d'Olonne | 68 | 46.30 N | 1.47 W |
| Lesser Slave Lake ⊜ | 94 | 55.25 N | 115.30 W |
| Lésvos I | 50 | 39.10 N | 26.20 E |
| Leszno | 66 | 51.51 N | 16.35 E |
| Letchworth | 54 | 51.58 N | 0.14 W |
| Lethbridge | 94 | 49.42 N | 112.50 W |
| Leti, Kepulauan II | 82 | 8.13 S | 127.40 E |
| Letsök-aw Kyun I | 82 | 11.37 N | 98.15 E |
| Letterfrack | 53 | 53.33 N | 10.00 W |
| Letterkenny | 60 | 54.57 N | 7.44 W |
| Lettermullen | 60 | 53.13 N | 9.42 W |
| Letterston | 54 | 51.56 N | 5.00 W |
| Leuchars | 58 | 56.23 N | 2.53 W |
| Leuna | 66 | 51.19 N | 12.01 E |
| Leuven | 66 | 50.53 N | 4.42 E |
| Levádhia | 74 | 38.25 N | 22.54 E |
| Leven | 58 | 56.12 N | 3.00 W |
| Leven ≃ | 54 | 54.31 N | 1.21 W |
| Leven, Loch ⊜, Scot., U.K. | 58 | 56.12 N | 3.22 W |
| Leven, Loch C, Scot., U.K. | 58 | 56.41 N | 5.07 W |
| Leveque, Cape ➤ | 92 | 16.24 S | 122.56 E |
| Leverburgh | 57 | 57.45 N | 7.00 W |
| Leverkusen | 66 | 51.03 N | 6.59 E |
| Levice | 66 | 48.13 N | 18.37 E |
| Levkás I | 50 | 38.39 N | 20.41 E |
| Levkosía | 84 | 35.10 N | 33.22 E |
| Lewes | 54 | 50.52 N | 0.01 E |
| Lewis, Butt of ➤ | 50 | 58.31 N | 6.15 W |
| Lewis, Isle of I | 52 | 58.10 N | 6.40 W |
| Lewisham ✦⁸ | 52 | 51.27 N | 0.01 E |
| Lewis Range ▲ | 96 | 48.30 N | 113.15 W |
| Lewiston, Idaho, U.S. | 96 | 46.25 N | 117.01 W |
| Lewiston, Maine, U.S. | 96 | 44.06 N | 70.13 W |
| Lexington | 96 | 38.03 N | 84.30 W |
| Leyland | 56 | 53.42 N | 2.42 W |
| Leysdown-on-Sea | 54 | 51.24 N | 0.55 E |
| Leyte I | 82 | 10.50 N | 124.50 E |
| Leyte Gulf C | 82 | 10.50 N | 125.25 E |
| Lhanbryde | 58 | 57.37 N | 3.13 W |
| Lhokseumawe | 82 | 5.10 N | 97.08 E |
| Lhut ≃ | 84 | 29.20 N | 51.05 E |
| Lianxian | 80 | 24.41 N | 112.21 E |
| Liaocheng | 80 | 36.30 N | 115.59 E |
| Liaodongbandao ➤¹ | 80 | 40.00 N | 122.20 E |
| Liaodongwan C | 80 | 40.30 N | 121.30 E |
| Liaohe ≃ | 80 | 40.40 N | 122.09 E |
| Liaoyang | 80 | 41.17 N | 123.11 E |
| Liaoyuan | 80 | 42.54 N | 125.07 E |
| Liard ≃ | 94 | 61.52 N | 121.18 W |
| Liathach ▲ | 58 | 57.35 N | 5.29 W |
| Liberec | 66 | 50.46 N | 15.03 E |
| Liberia □¹ | 86 | 6.00 N | 10.00 W |
| Libourne | 68 | 44.55 N | 0.14 W |
| Libreville | 90 | 0.23 N | 9.27 E |
| Libya □¹ | 86 | 27.00 N | 17.00 E |
| Licata | 72 | 37.05 N | 13.56 E |
| Lichfield | 54 | 52.42 N | 1.48 W |
| Lichoslavl' | 62 | 57.07 N | 35.28 E |
| Lichtenburg | 90 | 26.08 S | 26.08 E |
| Lichtenfels | 66 | 50.09 N | 11.04 E |
| Lidzbark | 66 | 53.16 N | 19.49 E |
| Lidzbark Warmiński | 66 | 54.09 N | 20.35 E |
| Liechtenstein □¹ | 50 | 47.09 N | 9.35 E |
| Liège | 66 | 50.38 N | 5.34 E |
| Lienz | 66 | 46.50 N | 12.47 E |
| Liepāja | 62 | 56.31 N | 21.01 E |
| Lier | 66 | 51.08 N | 4.34 E |
| Liestal | 68 | 47.29 N | 7.44 E |
| Liévin | 68 | 50.25 N | 2.46 E |
| Lièvre, Rivière du ≃ | 94 | 45.31 N | 75.26 W |
| Lifford | 54 | 54.50 N | 7.29 W |
| Lifton | 54 | 50.39 N | 4.17 W |
| Ligonha ≃ | 90 | 16.54 S | 39.09 E |
| Ligurian Sea ⊽² | 50 | 43.30 N | 9.00 E |
| Lihou Reefs and Cays | 88 | 17.25 S | 151.40 E |
| Likasi (Jadotville) | 90 | 10.59 S | 26.44 E |
| Likoma Island I | 90 | 12.05 S | 34.45 E |
| Likouala ≃ | 90 | 0.50 S | 17.11 E |
| Lille | 68 | 50.38 N | 3.04 E |
| Lilleshall | 54 | 52.44 N | 2.23 W |
| Lillestrøm | 64 | 59.57 N | 11.05 E |
| Lilongwe | 90 | 13.59 S | 33.44 E |
| Lima, Perú | 100 | 12.03 S | 77.03 W |
| Lima, Ohio, U.S. | 96 | 40.46 N | 84.06 W |
| Limavady | 60 | 55.03 N | 6.57 W |
| Limay ≃ | 102 | 38.59 S | 68.00 W |
| Limburg an der Lahn | 66 | 50.23 N | 8.04 E |
| Limerick | 60 | 52.40 N | 8.38 W |
| Limerick □⁶ | 60 | 52.30 N | 9.00 W |
| Limfjorden C | 64 | 56.55 N | 9.10 E |
| Limmen Bight C³ | 92 | 14.45 S | 135.40 E |
| Limnos I | 50 | 39.54 N | 25.21 E |
| Limoges | 68 | 45.50 N | 1.16 E |
| Limoux | 68 | 43.04 N | 2.14 E |
| Limpopo ≃ | 90 | 25.15 S | 33.30 E |
| Limpsfield | 54 | 51.16 N | 0.01 E |
| Linares, Chile | 102 | 35.51 S | 71.36 W |
| Linares, Esp. | 70 | 38.05 N | 3.38 W |
| Lincoln, Eng., U.K. | 56 | 53.14 N | 0.33 W |
| Lincoln, Nebr., U.S. | 96 | 40.48 N | 96.42 W |
| Lincoln Heath ⋏² | 56 | 53.15 N | 0.32 W |
| Lincoln Marsh ⋏ | 56 | 53.17 N | 0.12 E |
| Lincolnshire □⁶ | 56 | 53.10 N | 0.10 W |
| Lincolnshire Wolds ⋏² | 56 | 53.20 N | 0.10 W |
| Lindau | 66 | 47.33 N | 9.41 E |
| Lindenows Fjord C² | 94 | 60.45 N | 43.30 W |
| Lindesnes ➤ | 64 | 58.00 N | 7.01 E |
| Lindfield | 54 | 51.01 N | 0.05 W |
| Lindi | 90 | 10.00 S | 39.43 E |
| Lindlar | 66 | 51.01 N | 7.23 E |
| Line Islands II | 8 | 0.05 N | 157.00 W |
| Linfen | 80 | 36.05 N | 111.31 E |
| Ling ≃ | 58 | 57.27 N | 5.27 W |
| Lingayen Gulf C | 82 | 16.15 N | 120.14 E |
| Lingen | 66 | 52.31 N | 7.19 E |
| Lingfield | 54 | 51.11 N | 0.01 W |
| Lingga, Kepulauan II | 82 | 0.05 S | 104.35 E |
| Lingga, Pulau I | 82 | 0.12 S | 104.35 E |
| Lingling | 80 | 26.11 N | 111.29 E |
| Linh, Ngoc ▲ | 82 | 15.04 N | 107.59 E |
| Linhai | 80 | 28.51 N | 121.07 E |
| Linjiang | 80 | 41.49 N | 126.54 E |
| Linköping | 64 | 58.25 N | 15.37 E |
| Linkou | 80 | 45.15 N | 130.16 E |
| Linlithgow | 58 | 55.59 N | 3.37 W |
| Linney Head ➤ | 54 | 51.38 N | 5.04 W |
| Linnhe, Loch C | 52 | 56.37 N | 5.25 W |
| Linru | 80 | 34.11 N | 112.49 E |
| Lins | 100 | 21.40 S | 49.45 W |
| Linslade | 54 | 51.55 N | 0.41 W |
| Lintao | 80 | 35.27 N | 103.46 E |
| Linton | 54 | 52.06 N | 0.17 E |
| Linxia | 80 | 35.34 N | 103.08 E |
| Linyi | 80 | 35.04 N | 118.22 E |
| Linz | 66 | 48.18 N | 14.18 E |
| Lion, Golfe du C | 68 | 43.00 N | 4.00 E |
| Lipa | 82 | 13.57 N | 121.10 E |
| Lipeck | 62 | 52.37 N | 39.35 E |
| Liphook | 54 | 51.05 N | 0.49 W |
| Lipno | 66 | 52.51 N | 19.10 E |
| Lipova | 74 | 46.05 N | 21.40 E |
| Lippstadt | 66 | 51.40 N | 8.20 E |
| Liptovský Mikuláš | 66 | 49.06 N | 19.37 E |
| Lisboa (Lisbon) | 70 | 38.43 N | 9.08 W |
| Lisburn | 60 | 54.30 N | 6.03 W |
| Liscannor Bay C | 52 | 52.55 N | 9.25 W |
| Lisdoonvarna | 60 | 53.01 N | 9.15 W |
| Lishui | 80 | 28.27 N | 119.54 E |
| Lishui ≃ | 80 | 29.24 N | 112.01 E |
| Lisičansk | 62 | 48.55 N | 38.26 E |
| Lisieux | 68 | 49.09 N | 0.14 E |
| Liskeard | 54 | 50.28 N | 4.28 W |
| Lismore, Austl. | 92 | 28.48 S | 153.17 E |
| Lismore, Eire | 60 | 52.08 N | 7.55 W |
| Lismore Island I | 52 | 56.30 N | 5.30 W |
| Lisnaskea | 60 | 54.15 N | 7.27 W |
| Liss | 54 | 51.03 N | 0.54 W |
| Listowel | 52 | 52.27 N | 9.29 W |
| Litang | 80 | 30.04 N | 100.30 E |
| Litcham | 54 | 52.44 N | 0.47 E |
| Litherland | 56 | 53.28 N | 2.59 W |
| Litomerice | 66 | 50.32 N | 14.09 E |
| Little Andaman I | 82 | 10.45 N | 92.30 E |
| Little Barford | 54 | 52.12 N | 0.18 W |
| Little Buffalo ≃ | 94 | 61.00 N | 113.46 W |
| Little Cayman I | 98 | 19.41 N | 80.03 W |
| Little Cumbrae Island I | 58 | 55.43 N | 4.57 W |
| Little Dart ≃ | 54 | 50.54 N | 3.51 W |
| Littlehampton | 54 | 50.48 N | 0.33 W |
| Little Inagua I | 98 | 21.30 N | 73.00 W |
| Little Karroo ≃¹ | 90 | 33.45 S | 21.30 E |
| Little Mecatina ≃ | 94 | 50.28 N | 59.35 W |
| Littlemill | 58 | 57.33 N | 3.49 W |
| Little Minch ⋃ | 52 | 57.35 N | 6.45 W |
| Little Missouri ≃ | 96 | 47.30 N | 102.25 W |
| Little Ouse ≃ | 54 | 52.28 N | 0.19 E |
| Little Rock | 96 | 34.44 N | 92.15 W |
| Little Scarcies ≃ | 86 | 8.51 N | 13.09 W |
| Little Walsingham | 54 | 52.54 N | 0.51 E |
| Litvinov | 66 | 50.37 N | 13.36 E |
| Liuan | 80 | 31.44 N | 116.31 E |
| Liuchonghe ≃ | 80 | 29.40 N | 107.25 E |
| Liuzhou | 80 | 24.22 N | 109.32 E |
| Liverpool | 56 | 53.25 N | 2.55 W |
| Liverpool, Cape ➤ | 94 | 73.38 N | 78.06 W |
| Liverpool Bay C | 56 | 53.30 N | 3.16 W |
| Livingston | 58 | 55.53 N | 3.32 W |
| Livingstone | 90 | 17.50 S | 25.53 E |
| Livingstone, Chutes de ⋏ | 90 | 4.50 S | 14.30 E |
| Livorno (Leghorn) | 72 | 43.33 N | 10.19 E |
| Lizard | 54 | 49.58 N | 5.12 W |
| Lizard Point ➤ | 52 | 49.56 N | 5.13 W |
| Ljubljana | 72 | 46.03 N | 14.31 E |
| Ljungby | 64 | 56.50 N | 13.56 E |
| Ljusnan ≃ | 50 | 61.12 N | 17.08 E |
| Llanaber | 54 | 52.45 N | 4.05 W |
| Llanaelhaiarn | 54 | 52.59 N | 4.24 W |
| Llanarth | 54 | 52.12 N | 4.18 W |
| Llanarthney | 54 | 51.52 N | 4.09 W |
| Llanbedrog | 54 | 52.52 N | 4.29 W |
| Llanberis, Pass of V | 54 | 53.06 N | 4.04 W |
| Llanbister | 54 | 52.21 N | 3.27 W |
| Llanboidy | 54 | 51.54 N | 4.36 W |
| Llanbrynmair | 54 | 52.37 N | 3.57 W |
| Llanbyther | 54 | 52.03 N | 4.10 W |
| Llancañelo, Salina ≃ | 102 | 35.40 S | 69.08 W |
| Llandaff | 54 | 51.30 N | 3.14 W |
| Llanddewi Brefi | 54 | 52.10 N | 3.57 W |
| Llandeilo | 54 | 51.53 N | 3.59 W |
| Llandinam | 54 | 52.29 N | 3.26 W |
| Llandissilio | 54 | 51.53 N | 4.44 W |
| Llandovery | 54 | 51.59 N | 3.48 W |
| Llandrindod Wells | 54 | 52.15 N | 3.23 W |
| Llandudno | 54 | 53.19 N | 3.49 W |
| Llandybie | 54 | 51.50 N | 4.00 W |
| Llandyssul | 54 | 52.02 N | 4.19 W |
| Llanelli | 54 | 51.42 N | 4.10 W |
| Llanenddwyn | 54 | 52.49 N | 4.06 W |
| Llanerchymedd | 54 | 53.20 N | 4.22 W |
| Llanfaethlu | 54 | 53.21 N | 4.32 W |
| Llanfair Caereinion | 54 | 52.39 N | 3.20 W |
| Llanfairfechan | 54 | 53.15 N | 3.58 W |
| Llanfairpwllgwyngyll | 54 | 53.13 N | 4.12 W |
| Llanfynydd | 54 | 51.56 N | 3.21 W |
| Llanfyllin | 54 | 52.46 N | 3.17 W |
| Llanfyrnach | 54 | 51.57 N | 4.35 W |
| Llangadog | 54 | 51.56 N | 3.53 W |
| Llangefni | 54 | 53.16 N | 4.18 W |
| Llangennech | 54 | 51.41 N | 4.04 W |
| Llangollen | 54 | 52.58 N | 3.10 W |
| Llangranog | 54 | 52.09 N | 4.29 W |
| Llangwyfon | 54 | 52.19 N | 4.03 W |
| Llangynog | 54 | 52.50 N | 3.25 W |
| Llanharan | 54 | 51.33 N | 3.25 W |
| Llanidloes | 54 | 52.27 N | 3.32 W |
| Llanilar | 54 | 52.21 N | 4.01 W |
| Llanllyfni | 54 | 53.03 N | 4.17 W |
| Llanon | 54 | 52.17 N | 4.10 W |
| Llanos ≃ | 100 | 5.00 N | 70.00 W |
| Llanpumsaint | 54 | 51.56 N | 4.18 W |
| Llanrhaeadr-ym-Mochnant | 54 | 52.51 N | 3.08 W |
| Llanrhidian | 54 | 51.37 N | 4.11 W |
| Llanrhystyd | 54 | 52.18 N | 4.09 W |
| Llanrwst | 54 | 53.08 N | 3.48 W |
| Llansantffraid-ym-Mechain | 54 | 52.47 N | 3.08 W |
| Llansawel | 54 | 52.01 N | 4.00 W |
| Llantrisant | 54 | 51.33 N | 3.23 W |
| Llantwit Major | 54 | 51.25 N | 3.30 W |
| Llanuwchllyn | 54 | 52.52 N | 3.41 W |
| Llanwenog | 54 | 52.06 N | 4.12 W |
| Llanwrda | 54 | 51.58 N | 3.53 W |
| Llanwrtyd Wells | 54 | 52.07 N | 3.38 W |
| Llay | 54 | 53.06 N | 2.59 W |
| Lleyn Peninsula ➤¹ | 54 | 52.54 N | 4.28 W |
| Lluchmayor | 70 | 39.29 N | 2.54 E |
| Llullaillaco, Volcán ▲¹ | 102 | 24.43 S | 68.33 W |
| Llyswen | 54 | 52.02 N | 3.17 W |
| Loa ≃ | 102 | 21.26 S | 70.04 W |
| Loange (Luange) ≃ | 90 | 4.17 S | 20.02 E |
| Loanhead | 58 | 55.53 N | 3.09 W |
| Loano | 72 | 44.07 N | 8.15 E |
| Lobatse | 90 | 25.13 S | 25.35 E |
| Lobau | 66 | 51.05 N | 14.40 E |
| Lobaye ≃ | 90 | 3.41 N | 18.35 E |
| Lobito | 90 | 12.20 S | 13.34 E |
| Lobos de Afuera, Islas II | 100 | 6.57 S | 80.42 W |
| Lobos de Tierra, Isla I | 100 | 6.27 S | 80.52 W |
| Lobstick Lake ⊜ | 94 | 54.00 N | 64.50 W |
| Locarno | 68 | 46.10 N | 8.48 E |
| Lochaber ⋏¹ | 58 | 56.57 N | 5.06 W |
| Lochailort | 58 | 56.53 N | 5.40 W |
| Lochaline | 58 | 56.32 N | 5.47 W |
| Lochboisdale | 58 | 57.09 N | 7.19 W |
| Lochcarron | 58 | 57.24 N | 5.30 W |
| Lochdonhead | 58 | 56.26 N | 5.41 W |
| Lochearnhead | 58 | 56.23 N | 4.17 W |
| Lochgair | 58 | 56.03 N | 5.20 W |
| Lochgelly | 58 | 56.08 N | 3.19 W |
| Lochgilphead | 58 | 56.03 N | 5.26 W |
| Lochgoilhead | 58 | 56.10 N | 4.54 W |
| Lochinch | 58 | 57.24 N | 6.13 W |
| Lochinver | 58 | 58.09 N | 5.15 W |
| Lochmaben | 58 | 55.08 N | 3.27 W |
| Lochmaddy | 58 | 57.36 N | 7.10 W |
| Lochnagar ▲ | 58 | 56.57 N | 3.16 W |
| Lochranza | 58 | 55.42 N | 5.18 W |
| Lochwinnoch | 58 | 55.48 N | 4.39 W |
| Lochy, Loch ⊜ | 58 | 56.57 N | 4.53 W |
| Lockerbie | 58 | 55.07 N | 3.22 W |
| Loddon | 54 | 52.32 N | 1.29 E |
| Loddon ≃ | 54 | 51.31 N | 0.53 W |
| Lodénoje Polje | 62 | 60.44 N | 33.32 E |
| Lodi | 72 | 45.19 N | 9.30 E |
| Łódź | 66 | 51.46 N | 19.30 E |
| Loffa ≃ | 86 | 6.36 N | 11.08 W |
| Lofoten II | 50 | 68.30 N | 15.00 E |
| Loftus | 56 | 54.33 N | 0.53 W |
| Logan | 96 | 41.44 N | 111.50 W |
| Logan, Mount ▲ | 94 | 60.34 N | 140.24 W |
| Logone ≃ | 88 | 12.06 N | 15.02 E |
| Logroño | 70 | 42.28 N | 2.27 W |
| Lohr | 66 | 50.00 N | 9.34 E |
| Loire ≃ | 68 | 47.16 N | 2.11 W |
| Loja, Ec. | 100 | 4.00 S | 79.13 W |
| Loja, Esp. | 70 | 37.10 N | 4.09 W |
| Lokeren | 66 | 51.06 N | 4.00 E |
| Loks Land I | 94 | 62.26 N | 64.38 W |
| Lolland I | 64 | 54.46 N | 11.30 E |
| Lom | 74 | 43.49 N | 23.14 E |
| Lom ≃ | 74 | 43.45 N | 23.14 E |
| Loma Mansa ▲ | 86 | 9.13 N | 11.07 W |
| Lomblen, Pulau I | 82 | 8.25 S | 123.30 E |
| Lombok I | 82 | 8.45 S | 116.30 E |
| Lomé | 86 | 6.08 N | 1.13 E |
| Lomond, Loch ⊜ | 58 | 56.08 N | 4.38 W |
| Lomonosov | 62 | 59.55 N | 29.46 E |
| Łomża | 66 | 53.11 N | 22.05 E |
| London, Ont., Can. | 94 | 42.59 N | 81.14 W |
| London, Eng., U.K. | 54 | 51.30 N | 0.10 W |
| Londonderry | 60 | 55.00 N | 7.19 W |
| Londonderry, Cape ➤ | 92 | 13.45 S | 126.55 E |
| Londonderry, Isla I | 102 | 55.03 S | 70.40 W |
| Longa, Loch C | 58 | 55.51 N | 5.52 W |
| Longá, Proliv ⋃ | 78 | 70.20 N | 178.00 E |
| Long Beach | 96 | 33.46 N | 118.11 W |
| Longbenton | 56 | 55.02 N | 1.34 W |
| Long Buckby | 54 | 52.19 N | 1.04 W |
| Long Crendon | 54 | 51.47 N | 1.00 W |
| Long Eaton | 54 | 52.54 N | 1.15 W |
| Longford | 60 | 53.44 N | 7.47 W |
| Longford □⁶ | 60 | 53.42 N | 7.45 W |
| Longframlington | 56 | 55.18 N | 1.47 W |
| Longhorsley | 56 | 55.15 N | 1.46 W |
| Longhoughton | 56 | 55.26 N | 1.37 W |
| Long Island I, Ba. | 98 | 23.15 N | 75.07 W |
| Long Island I, N.Y., U.S. | 96 | 40.50 N | 73.00 W |
| Long Island Sound ⋃ | 96 | 41.05 N | 72.58 W |
| Long Melford | 54 | 52.05 N | 0.43 E |
| Longli | 80 | 26.26 N | 106.58 E |
| Long Mountain ⋏² | 54 | 52.39 N | 3.09 W |
| Longmorn | 58 | 57.36 N | 3.17 W |
| Long Preston | 56 | 54.02 N | 2.15 W |
| Long Range Mountains ⋏ | 94 | 49.20 N | 57.30 W |
| Long Reef ⋆² | 92 | 13.58 S | 151.40 E |
| Longridge | 56 | 53.51 N | 2.36 W |
| Longs Peak ▲ | 96 | 40.15 N | 105.37 W |
| Long Sutton | 56 | 52.47 N | 0.08 E |
| Longton | 56 | 53.00 N | 2.09 W |
| Longtown | 54 | 55.01 N | 2.58 W |
| Longview, Tex., U.S. | 96 | 32.30 N | 94.44 W |
| Longview, Wash., U.S. | 96 | 46.08 N | 122.57 W |
| Longwy | 68 | 49.31 N | 5.46 E |
| Long-xuyen | 84 | 10.23 N | 105.25 E |
| Lons-le-Saunier | 68 | 46.40 N | 5.33 E |
| Lookout, Cape ➤ | 96 | 34.35 N | 76.32 W |
| Loop Head ➤ | 52 | 52.34 N | 9.56 W |
| Lopatina, Gora ▲ | 78 | 50.52 N | 143.10 E |
| Lopatka, Mys ➤ | 78 | 50.52 N | 156.40 E |
| Lopez, Cap ➤ | 90 | 0.38 S | 8.42 E |
| Lora, Hāmūn-i- ⊜ | 84 | 29.20 N | 64.50 E |
| Lora del Rio | 70 | 37.39 N | 5.32 W |
| Lorain | 96 | 41.28 N | 82.10 W |
| Lorca | 70 | 37.40 N | 1.42 W |
| Lord Howe Island I | 88 | 31.33 S | 159.05 E |
| Lorient | 68 | 47.45 N | 3.22 W |
| Lorn, Firth of C² | 52 | 56.20 N | 5.40 W |
| Lörrach | 66 | 47.37 N | 7.40 E |
| Los Angeles, Chile | 102 | 37.28 S | 72.21 W |
| Los Angeles, Calif., U.S. | 98 | 34.03 N | 118.15 W |
| Los Mochis | 98 | 25.45 N | 108.57 W |
| Los Palacios y Villafranca | 70 | 37.10 N | 5.56 W |
| Los Roques, Islas II | 70 | 11.50 N | 66.45 W |
| Lossie ≃ | 58 | 57.43 N | 3.16 W |
| Lossiemouth | 58 | 57.43 N | 3.18 W |
| Lostwithiel | 54 | 50.25 N | 4.40 W |
| Lota | 102 | 37.05 S | 73.10 W |
| Lothian □⁴ | 58 | 55.55 N | 3.00 W |
| Lotsane ≃ | 90 | 22.41 S | 28.11 E |
| Louangphrabang | 82 | 19.52 N | 102.08 E |
| Louga | 86 | 15.37 N | 16.13 W |
| Loughborough | 54 | 52.47 N | 1.11 W |
| Loughor | 54 | 51.40 N | 4.04 W |
| Loughor ≃ | 54 | 51.40 N | 4.04 W |
| Loughrea | 60 | 53.12 N | 8.34 W |
| Loughros More Bay C | 60 | 54.47 N | 8.35 W |
| Louisburgh | 60 | 53.46 N | 9.51 W |
| Louisiade Archipelago II | 88 | 11.00 S | 153.00 E |
| Louisiana □³ | 96 | 31.15 N | 92.15 W |
| Louis Trichardt | 90 | 23.01 S | 29.43 E |
| Louisville | 96 | 38.16 N | 85.45 W |
| Louis-XIV, Pointe ➤ | 94 | 54.37 N | 79.45 W |
| Louny | 66 | 50.21 N | 13.48 E |
| Lourdes | 68 | 43.06 N | 0.03 W |
| Louth, Eire | 60 | 53.57 N | 6.33 W |
| Louth, Eng., U.K. | 56 | 53.22 N | 0.01 W |
| Louth □⁶ | 60 | 53.55 N | 6.30 W |
| Lovviers | 68 | 49.13 N | 1.10 E |
| Lovat ≃ | 74 | 58.14 N | 31.28 E |
| Loveč | 74 | 43.08 N | 24.43 E |
| Low, Cape ➤ | 94 | 63.07 N | 85.18 W |
| Lowa ≃ | 90 | 1.24 S | 25.51 E |
| Lowell | 96 | 42.38 N | 71.18 W |
| Lower Lough Erne ⊜ | 60 | 54.26 N | 7.48 W |
| Lower Red Lake ⊜ | 96 | 48.00 N | 94.50 W |
| Lowestoft | 54 | 52.29 N | 1.45 E |
| Lowick, Eng., U.K. | 56 | 55.38 N | 2.00 W |
| Łowicz | 66 | 52.07 N | 19.56 E |
| Low Rocky Point ➤ | 92 | 43.00 S | 145.30 E |
| Lowther Hills ⋏² | 58 | 55.19 N | 3.38 W |
| Loyal, Loch ⊜ | 58 | 58.23 N | 4.22 W |
| Loyne, Loch ⊜ | 57 | 57.06 N | 5.00 W |
| Loznica | 74 | 44.32 N | 19.13 E |
| Lualaba ≃ | 90 | 0.26 N | 25.20 E |
| Luama ≃ | 90 | 4.46 S | 26.53 E |
| Luanda | 90 | 8.48 S | 13.14 E |
| Luangue (Loange) ≃ | 90 | 4.17 S | 20.02 E |
| Luangwa (Aruángua) ≃ | 90 | 15.11 S | 22.56 E |
| Luanhe ≃ | 80 | 39.25 N | 119.15 E |
| Luanshya | 90 | 13.08 S | 28.24 E |
| Luapula ≃ | 90 | 9.26 S | 28.33 E |
| Luban, Pol. | 66 | 51.08 N | 15.18 E |
| L'uban', S.S.S.R. | 62 | 59.21 N | 31.13 E |
| Lubango | 90 | 14.55 S | 13.30 E |
| Lübben | 66 | 51.56 N | 13.53 E |
| Lübbenau | 66 | 51.52 N | 13.57 E |
| Lubbock | 96 | 33.35 N | 101.51 W |
| Lübeck | 66 | 53.52 N | 10.40 E |
| L'ubercy | 62 | 55.41 N | 37.53 E |
| Lubin | 66 | 51.24 N | 16.13 E |
| Lublin | 66 | 51.15 N | 22.35 E |
| Lubliniec | 66 | 50.40 N | 18.41 E |
| Lubsko | 66 | 51.46 N | 14.59 E |
| Lubudi ≃ | 90 | 6.51 S | 21.18 E |
| Lubumbashi (Élisabethville) | 90 | 11.40 S | 27.28 E |
| Lucan | 60 | 53.22 N | 6.27 W |
| Lucania, Mount ▲ | 94 | 61.01 N | 140.28 W |
| Lucca | 72 | 43.50 N | 10.29 E |
| Luce, Water of ≃ | 54 | 54.52 N | 4.49 W |
| Luce Bay C | 52 | 54.47 N | 4.50 W |
| Lucena, Esp. | 70 | 37.24 N | 4.29 W |
| Lucena, Pil. | 82 | 13.56 N | 121.37 E |
| Lucera | 72 | 41.30 N | 15.20 E |
| Luchovicy | 62 | 54.59 N | 39.03 E |
| Luc'k | 62 | 50.44 N | 25.20 E |
| Luckenwalde | 66 | 52.05 N | 13.10 E |
| Lucknow | 84 | 26.50 N | 80.52 E |
| Lüda (Dairen) | 80 | 38.53 N | 121.35 E |
| Lüdenscheid | 66 | 51.13 N | 7.38 E |
| Ludgershall | 54 | 51.16 N | 1.37 W |
| Ludhiāna | 84 | 30.54 N | 75.51 E |
| Ludlow | 54 | 52.22 N | 2.43 W |
| Ludvika | 64 | 60.09 N | 15.11 E |
| Ludwigsburg | 66 | 48.53 N | 9.11 E |
| Ludwigsfelde | 66 | 52.18 N | 13.16 E |
| Ludwigslust | 66 | 53.19 N | 11.30 E |
| Ludwigshafen | 66 | 49.29 N | 8.26 E |
| Lufeng | 80 | 22.57 N | 115.38 E |
| Lufira ≃ | 90 | 8.16 S | 26.27 E |
| Luga | 62 | 58.44 N | 29.52 E |
| Lugano | 68 | 46.00 N | 8.58 E |
| Lugenda ≃ | 90 | 11.25 S | 38.33 E |
| Lugg ≃ | 54 | 52.02 N | 2.38 W |
| Lugnaquillia Mountain ▲ | 52 | 52.58 N | 6.28 W |
| Lugo, Esp. | 70 | 43.00 N | 7.34 W |
| Lugo, It. | 72 | 44.25 N | 11.54 E |
| Lugoj | 74 | 45.41 N | 21.54 E |
| Lui, Beinn ▲ | 58 | 56.24 N | 4.49 W |
| Luichart, Loch ⊜ | 58 | 57.37 N | 4.46 W |
| Luing I | 58 | 56.13 N | 5.39 W |
| Luino | 68 | 46.00 N | 8.44 E |
| Lukenie ≃ | 90 | 2.44 S | 18.09 E |
| Lukolela | 90 | 1.03 S | 17.12 E |
| Lukovit | 74 | 43.12 N | 24.10 E |
| Łuków | 66 | 51.56 N | 22.23 E |
| Lule ≃ | 50 | 65.35 N | 22.03 E |
| Luleå | 50 | 65.34 N | 22.10 E |
| Luleburgaz | 74 | 41.24 N | 27.21 E |
| Lulonga ≃ | 90 | 0.42 N | 18.26 E |
| Lulua ≃ | 90 | 5.02 S | 21.07 E |
| Lumberton | 96 | 34.37 N | 79.00 W |
| Lumphanan | 58 | 57.08 N | 2.52 W |
| Lumsden | 58 | 57.15 N | 2.52 W |
| Lumut, Tanjung ➤ | 82 | 3.50 S | 105.57 E |
| Lunan Bay C | 58 | 56.39 N | 2.28 W |
| Luncarty | 58 | 56.27 N | 3.28 W |
| Lund | 64 | 55.42 N | 13.11 E |
| Lundi ≃ | 90 | 21.43 S | 32.34 E |
| Lundy I | 52 | 51.10 N | 4.40 W |
| Lune ≃ | 54 | 54.02 N | 2.50 W |
| Lüneburg | 66 | 53.15 N | 10.23 E |
| Lünen | 66 | 51.36 N | 7.32 E |
| Lüneville | 68 | 48.36 N | 6.30 E |
| Lunga ≃ | 58 | 56.13 N | 5.42 W |
| Lungué-Bungo ≃ | 90 | 14.19 S | 23.14 E |
| Luobubo (Lop Nor) ⊜ | 80 | 40.20 N | 90.15 E |
| Luohe | 80 | 33.35 N | 114.01 E |
| Luohe ≃ | 80 | 34.42 N | 110.15 E |
| Luoyang | 80 | 34.41 N | 112.28 E |
| Lupeni | 74 | 45.22 N | 23.13 E |
| Lúrio | 90 | 13.35 S | 40.32 E |
| Lúrio ≃ | 90 | 13.32 S | 40.31 E |
| Lusaka | 90 | 15.25 S | 28.17 E |
| Lusambo | 90 | 4.58 S | 23.27 E |
| Lushan | 80 | 33.21 N | 115.58 E |
| Lushnje | 74 | 40.56 N | 19.42 E |
| Lushun (Port Arthur) | 80 | 38.47 N | 121.13 E |
| Lusk | 54 | 53.32 N | 6.10 W |
| Lüt, Dasht-e ⋈² | 84 | 33.00 N | 57.00 E |
| Luthrie | 58 | 56.21 N | 3.05 W |
| Luton | 54 | 51.53 N | 0.25 W |
| Lutterworth | 54 | 52.28 N | 1.10 W |
| Luxembourg | 66 | 49.36 N | 6.09 E |
| Luxembourg □¹ | 50 | 49.45 N | 6.05 E |
| Luza | 62 | 60.39 N | 47.10 E |
| Luzern | 68 | 47.03 N | 8.18 E |
| Luzhou | 80 | 28.54 N | 105.27 E |
| Luzon I | 82 | 16.00 N | 121.00 E |
| Luzon Strait ⋃ | 82 | 20.30 N | 121.00 E |
| L'vov | 76 | 49.50 N | 24.00 E |
| Lyallpur | 84 | 31.25 N | 73.05 E |
| Lybster | 58 | 58.18 N | 3.13 W |
| Lydd | 54 | 50.57 N | 0.55 E |
| Lydden V | 54 | 50.56 N | 2.22 W |
| Lydford | 54 | 50.39 N | 4.06 W |
| Lydham | 54 | 52.31 N | 2.58 W |
| Lydney | 54 | 51.44 N | 2.32 W |
| Lye | 54 | 52.28 N | 2.06 W |
| Lyme Bay C | 54 | 50.44 N | 2.57 W |
| Lyme Regis | 54 | 50.44 N | 2.57 W |
| Lyminge | 54 | 51.08 N | 1.05 E |
| Lymington | 54 | 50.46 N | 1.33 W |
| Lympne | 54 | 51.05 N | 1.02 E |
| Lynchburg | 96 | 37.24 N | 79.10 W |
| Lyndhurst | 54 | 50.53 N | 1.34 W |
| Lyne ≃ | 54 | 54.58 N | 3.01 W |
| Lyneham | 54 | 51.31 N | 1.58 W |
| Lynemouth | 56 | 55.12 N | 1.31 W |
| Lyne Water ≃ | 54 | 54.39 N | 3.16 W |
| Lynher ≃ | 54 | 50.27 N | 4.15 W |
| Lynmouth | 54 | 51.15 N | 3.50 W |
| Lynton | 54 | 51.15 N | 3.50 W |
| Lyon | 68 | 45.45 N | 4.51 E |
| Lyon, Glen V | 58 | 56.37 N | 4.01 W |
| Lyon, Loch ⊜ | 58 | 56.35 N | 4.20 W |
| Lyon Inlet C | 94 | 66.32 N | 83.53 W |
| Lyons ≃ | 92 | 25.02 S | 115.09 E |
| Lyracrumpane | 52 | 52.20 N | 9.30 W |
| Lyskovo | 62 | 56.04 N | 45.02 E |
| Lys'va | 76 | 58.07 N | 57.47 E |
| Lytham Saint Anne's | 56 | 53.45 N | 2.57 W |

## M

| Name | Page | Lat | Long |
|---|---|---|---|
| Ma ≃ | 82 | 19.47 N | 105.56 E |
| Maam Cross | 60 | 53.27 N | 9.31 W |
| Maanshan | 80 | 31.42 N | 118.30 E |
| Maas ≃ | 66 | 54.50 N | 8.22 W |
| Maastricht | 66 | 50.52 N | 5.43 E |
| Mababe Depression ≃⁷ | 90 | 18.50 S | 24.15 E |
| Maberry, Loch ⊜ | 58 | 55.02 N | 4.41 W |
| Mablethorpe | 56 | 53.21 N | 0.15 E |
| Macacos, Ilha dos I | 100 | 1.20 S | 50.35 W |
| McAllen | 96 | 26.12 N | 98.15 W |
| MacAlpine Lake ⊜ | 94 | 66.40 N | 103.15 W |
| Macapá | 100 | 0.02 N | 51.03 W |
| Macau (Aomen) | 80 | 22.14 N | 113.35 E |
| Macau □² | 80 | 22.10 N | 113.33 E |
| Macclesfield | 56 | 53.16 N | 2.07 W |
| Macdonald, Lake ⊜ | 92 | 23.30 S | 129.00 E |
| Macdonnell Ranges ⋏ | 92 | 23.45 S | 133.20 E |
| Macduff | 58 | 57.40 N | 2.29 W |
| Macdui, Ben ▲ | 58 | 57.04 N | 3.40 W |
| Maceió | 100 | 9.40 S | 35.43 W |
| Macerata | 72 | 43.18 N | 13.27 E |
| McFarlane ≃ | 94 | 59.12 N | 107.58 W |
| Macgillycuddy's Reeks ⋏ | 60 | 51.55 N | 9.45 W |
| Machačkala | 62 | 42.58 N | 47.30 E |
| Machala | 100 | 3.16 S | 79.58 W |
| Machilipatnam | 84 | 16.11 N | 81.08 E |
| Machynlleth | 54 | 52.35 N | 3.51 W |
| Macías Nguema Biyogo □² | 86 | 3.30 N | 8.40 E |
| Macina ≃ | 86 | 14.30 N | 5.00 W |
| Macintyre ≃ | 92 | 29.25 S | 148.45 E |
| Mackay | 92 | 21.09 S | 149.11 E |
| Mackay, Lake ⊜ | 92 | 22.30 S | 129.00 E |
| McKay Lake ⊜ | 94 | 63.55 N | 110.25 W |
| McKeand ≃ | 94 | 69.25 N | 68.10 W |
| Mackenzie ≃ | 94 | 69.15 N | 134.08 W |
| Mackenzie Bay C | 94 | 69.00 N | 136.30 W |
| Mackenzie Mountains ⋏ | 94 | 64.00 N | 130.00 W |
| Mackinac, Straits of ⋃ | 96 | 45.49 N | 84.42 W |
| McKinley Mount ▲ | 96a | 63.30 N | 151.00 W |
| Macleod, Lake ⊜ | 92 | 24.00 S | 113.35 E |
| McLeod Bay C | 94 | 62.53 N | 110.00 W |
| Macmillan ≃ | 94 | 62.52 N | 135.55 W |
| McMurdo Sound ⋃ | 67 | 77.30 S | 165.00 E |
| Macomer | 72 | 40.16 N | 8.46 E |
| Mâcon, Fr. | 68 | 46.18 N | 4.50 E |
| Macon, Ga., U.S. | 96 | 32.50 N | 83.38 W |
| Macroom | 60 | 51.54 N | 8.57 W |
| Madagascar □¹ | 90 | 19.00 S | 46.00 E |
| Madawaska ≃ | 94 | 45.30 N | 76.21 W |
| Maddaloni | 72 | 41.02 N | 14.23 E |
| Maddy, Loch C | 58 | 57.35 N | 7.08 W |
| Madeira ≃ | 100 | 3.22 S | 58.45 W |
| Madeira, Arquipélago da (Madeira Islands) II | 86 | 32.40 N | 16.45 W |
| Madeleine, Îles de la II | 94 | 47.30 N | 61.45 W |
| Madeley, Eng., U.K. | 54 | 52.38 N | 2.21 W |
| Madeley, Eng., U.K. | 54 | 52.59 N | 2.27 W |
| Madhya Pradesh □³ | 84 | 23.00 N | 79.00 E |
| Madïnat ash-Sha'b | 84 | 12.50 N | 44.56 E |
| Madison | 96 | 43.05 N | 89.22 W |
| Madras | 84 | 13.04 N | 80.16 E |
| Madre, Laguna C, Méx. | 98 | 25.00 N | 97.40 W |
| Madre, Laguna C, Tex., U.S. | 96 | 27.00 N | 97.35 W |
| Madre, Sierra ⋏ | 98 | 16.20 N | 92.00 W |
| Madre de Dios, Isla I | 102 | 50.15 S | 75.05 W |
| Madre del Sur, Sierra ⋏ | 98 | 17.10 N | 100.00 W |
| Madre Occidental, Sierra ⋏ | 98 | 25.00 N | 105.00 W |
| Madre Oriental, Sierra ⋏ | 98 | 22.00 N | 99.30 W |
| Madura I | 82 | 7.00 S | 113.20 E |
| Madurai | 84 | 9.56 N | 78.08 E |
| Mae Klong ≃ | 82 | 13.21 N | 100.00 E |
| Maenclochog | 54 | 51.54 N | 4.47 W |
| Maesteg | 54 | 51.37 N | 3.40 W |
| Mafeking | 90 | 25.53 S | 25.39 E |
| Magadan | 78 | 59.34 N | 150.48 E |
| Magallanes, Estrecho de (Strait of Magellan) ⋃ | 102 | 54.00 S | 71.00 W |
| Magangué | 100 | 9.14 N | 74.45 W |
| Magdalena | 100 | 11.06 N | 74.51 W |
| Magdalena, Isla I | 102 | 44.45 S | 73.10 W |
| Magdeburg | 66 | 52.07 N | 11.38 E |
| Magee, Island I ➤¹ | 60 | 54.49 N | 5.42 W |
| Magelang | 82 | 7.28 S | 110.13 E |
| Magenta | 72 | 45.28 N | 8.53 E |
| Maghera | 60 | 54.51 N | 6.40 W |
| Magherafelt | 60 | 54.45 N | 6.36 W |
| Maghull | 56 | 53.32 N | 2.57 W |
| Magnitogorsk | 76 | 53.27 N | 59.04 E |
| Magpie, Lac ⊜ | 94 | 51.00 N | 64.41 W |
| Maguarinho, Cabo ➤ | 100 | 0.15 S | 48.22 W |
| Maguse Lake ⊜ | 94 | 61.40 N | 95.10 W |
| Mahābhārat Range ⋏ | 84 | 27.40 N | 84.30 E |
| Mahajamba, Baie de la C | 90 | 15.24 S | 47.05 E |
| Mahakam ≃ | 82 | 0.35 S | 117.17 E |
| Mahébourg | 90 | 20.24 S | 57.42 E |
| Mahé Island I | 90 | 4.40 S | 55.28 E |
| Mahón | 70 | 39.53 N | 4.15 E |
| Maidenhead | 54 | 51.32 N | 0.44 W |
| Maiden Newton | 54 | 50.46 N | 2.35 W |
| Maidstone | 54 | 51.17 N | 0.32 E |
| Maiduguri | 86 | 11.51 N | 13.10 E |
| Maikala Range ⋏ | 84 | 22.30 N | 81.30 E |
| Maiko ≃ | 90 | 0.14 N | 25.33 E |
| Maikoor, Pulau I | 82 | 6.15 S | 134.15 E |
| Mai-Ndombe, Lac ⊜ | 90 | 2.00 S | 18.20 E |
| Maine □³ | 96 | 45.15 N | 69.15 W |
| Maine ≃ | 60 | 52.09 N | 9.45 W |
| Mainland I, Scot., U.K. | 52 | 59.00 N | 3.10 W |
| Mainland I, Scot., U.K. | 52 | 60.20 N | 1.22 W |
| Mainz | 66 | 50.01 N | 8.16 E |
| Maio I | 86 | 15.15 N | 23.10 W |
| Maipo, Volcán ▲¹ | 102 | 34.10 S | 69.50 W |
| Maipú | 102 | 36.52 S | 57.52 W |
| Maiquetia | 100 | 10.36 N | 66.57 W |
| Maitland | 92 | 32.44 S | 151.33 E |
| Majene | 82 | 3.33 S | 118.57 E |
| Majkop | 76 | 44.35 N | 40.07 E |
| Majunga | 90 | 15.43 S | 46.19 E |
| Makale | 82 | 3.06 S | 119.51 E |
| Makarjev | 62 | 57.52 N | 43.48 E |
| Makasar, Selat (Makassar Strait) ⋃ | 82 | 2.00 S | 117.30 E |
| Makejevka | 62 | 48.02 N | 37.58 E |
| Makeni | 86 | 8.53 N | 12.03 W |
| Makgadikgadi Pans ≃ | 90 | 20.45 S | 25.30 E |
| Makinsk | 76 | 52.37 N | 70.26 E |
| Makkah (Mecca) | 84 | 21.27 N | 39.49 E |
| Maklakovo | 78 | 58.16 N | 92.29 E |
| Makó | 66 | 46.13 N | 20.29 E |
| Makurdi | 86 | 7.45 N | 8.32 E |
| Malabar Coast ≃² | 84 | 11.00 N | 75.00 E |
| Malabo | 86 | 3.45 N | 8.47 E |
| Malacca, Strait of ⋃ | 82 | 2.30 N | 101.20 E |
| Malacky | 66 | 48.27 N | 17.01 E |
| Málaga | 70 | 36.43 N | 4.25 W |
| Malahide | 60 | 53.27 N | 6.09 W |
| Malaja Višera | 62 | 58.51 N | 32.14 E |
| Malakāl | 88 | 9.31 N | 31.39 E |
| Malange | 90 | 9.32 S | 16.20 E |
| Malaren ⊜ | 64 | 59.30 N | 17.12 E |
| Malatya | 84 | 38.21 N | 38.19 E |
| Malawi □¹ | 90 | 13.30 S | 34.00 E |
| Malay Peninsula ➤¹ | 82 | 6.00 N | 101.00 E |
| Malay Reef ⋆² | 92 | 17.59 S | 149.18 E |
| Malaysia □¹ | 82 | 2.30 N | 112.30 E |
| Malbork | 66 | 54.02 N | 19.01 E |
| Maldegem | 66 | 51.13 N | 3.27 E |
| Maldive Islands I | 84 | 5.00 N | 73.00 E |
| Maldon | 54 | 51.45 N | 0.40 E |
| Maléa, Ákra ➤ | 50 | 36.26 N | 23.12 E |
| Malegaon | 84 | 20.33 N | 74.32 E |
| Malen'ga | 62 | 63.50 N | 36.25 E |
| Mali □¹ | 86 | 17.00 N | 4.00 W |
| Mali Kyun I | 82 | 13.06 N | 98.16 E |
| Malin | 60 | 55.18 N | 7.15 W |
| Malin Beg | 60 | 54.40 N | 8.48 W |
| Malin Head ➤ | 60 | 55.23 N | 7.24 W |
| Malindi | 90 | 3.14 S | 40.07 E |
| Malin More | 60 | 54.42 N | 8.48 W |
| Mallaig | 58 | 57.00 N | 5.50 W |
| Mallawī | 88 | 27.44 N | 30.50 E |
| Mallorca I | 70 | 39.30 N | 3.00 E |
| Mallow | 60 | 52.08 N | 8.39 W |
| Malmberget | 62 | 67.10 N | 20.40 E |
| Malmesbury | 54 | 51.36 N | 2.06 W |
| Malmesbury, Vale of ⋁ | 54 | 51.32 N | 2.10 W |
| Malmö | 64 | 55.36 N | 13.00 E |
| Malmyž | 62 | 56.31 N | 50.40 E |
| Malpas | 54 | 53.01 N | 2.46 W |
| Malpaso, Presa de ⊜ | 98 | 17.10 N | 93.40 W |
| Malpelo, Isla de I | 100 | 3.59 N | 81.35 W |
| Maltby | 56 | 53.26 N | 1.11 W |
| Malton | 56 | 54.08 N | 0.48 W |
| Maluku, Laut (Molucca Sea) ⊽² | 82 | 2.00 N | 128.00 E |
| Maluku (Moluccas) II | 82 | 2.00 S | 125.00 E |
| Malvern Hills ⋏² | 54 | 52.05 N | 2.21 W |
| Malvern Link | 54 | 52.07 N | 2.18 W |
| Malyj Jenisej ≃ | 78 | 51.43 N | 94.26 E |
| Malyj Kavkaz ⋏ | 76 | 41.00 N | 44.35 E |
| Malyj Uzen' ≃ | 62 | 48.36 N | 49.14 E |
| Malyj Tajmyr, Ostrov I | 78 | 78.08 N | 107.12 E |
| Mamberamo ≃ | 82 | 1.26 S | 137.53 E |
| Mambéré ≃ | 90 | 3.31 N | 16.03 E |
| Mamoré ≃ | 100 | 10.23 S | 65.23 W |
| Mamou | 86 | 10.23 N | 12.05 W |
| Man | 86 | 7.24 N | 7.33 W |
| Mana ≃ | 100 | 5.45 N | 53.55 W |
| Managua | 98 | 12.09 N | 86.17 W |
| Managua, Lago de ⊜ | 98 | 12.20 N | 86.20 W |
| Manakara | 90 | 22.08 S | 48.01 E |
| Mananara | 90 | 16.10 S | 49.46 E |
| Mananjary | 90 | 21.13 S | 48.20 E |
| Manas ≃ | 84 | 26.12 N | 90.39 E |
| Manaus | 100 | 3.08 S | 60.01 W |
| Manchester, Eng., U.K. | 56 | 53.30 N | 2.15 W |
| Manchester, N.H., U.S. | 96 | 42.59 N | 71.28 W |
| Mandal | 64 | 58.02 N | 7.27 E |
| Mandalay | 84 | 22.00 N | 96.05 E |
| Mandan | 96 | 46.49 N | 100.53 W |
| Mandaon | 82 | 12.12 N | 123.18 E |
| Mandara Mountains ⋏ | 86 | 10.45 N | 13.40 E |
| Mandeb, Bāb el- ⋃ | 84 | 12.40 N | 43.20 E |
| Manduria | 72 | 40.24 N | 17.38 E |
| Manea | 54 | 52.30 N | 0.11 E |
| Manfalût | 88 | 27.19 N | 30.58 E |
| Manfredonia | 72 | 41.38 N | 15.55 E |
| Mangabeiras, Chapada das ⋏² | 100 | 10.00 S | 46.30 W |
| Mangalia | 74 | 43.48 N | 28.35 E |
| Mangalore | 84 | 12.52 N | 74.52 E |
| Mangerton Mountain ▲ | 52 | 51.57 N | 9.29 W |
| Mangkalihat, Tanjung ➤ | 82 | 1.02 N | 118.59 E |
| Mangoky ≃ | 90 | 23.27 S | 45.13 E |

Symbols in the index entries are identified on page 111.

| Name | Page | Lat | Long |
|---|---|---|---|
| Mangole, Pulau **I** | 82 | 1.53 S | 125.50 E |
| Mangotsfield | 54 | 51.28 N | 2.28 W |
| Manhattan | 94 | 39.11 N | 96.35 W |
| Manicouagan ≃ | 94 | 49.11 N | 68.13 W |
| Manicouagan, Réservoir ⊜¹ | 94 | 51.30 N | 68.19 W |
| Manifold ⊷ | 54 | 53.03 N | 1.47 W |
| Manihiki **I**¹ | 8 | 10.24 S | 161.01 W |
| Manila | 82 | 14.35 N | 121.00 E |
| Manila Bay **C** | 82 | 14.30 N | 120.45 E |
| Manipa, Selat **U** | 82 | 3.20 S | 127.23 E |
| Manisa | 74 | 38.36 N | 27.26 E |
| Manitoba □⁴ | 94 | 54.00 N | 97.00 W |
| Manitoba, Lake ⊜ | 94 | 51.00 N | 98.45 W |
| Manitoulin Island **I** | 94 | 45.45 N | 82.30 W |
| Manitowoc | 96 | 44.06 N | 87.40 W |
| Manizales | 100 | 5.05 N | 75.32 W |
| Mankato | 96 | 44.10 N | 94.01 W |
| Mannar, Gulf of **C** | 84 | 8.30 N | 79.00 E |
| Mannheim | 66 | 49.29 N | 8.29 E |
| Manningtree | 54 | 51.57 N | 1.04 E |
| Manono | 90 | 7.18 S | 27.25 E |
| Manorbier | 54 | 51.39 N | 4.48 W |
| Manorhamilton | 60 | 54.18 N | 8.10 W |
| Manouane, Lac ⊜ | 94 | 50.41 N | 70.45 W |
| Manresa | 70 | 41.44 N | 1.50 E |
| Mansel Island **I** | 94 | 62.00 N | 79.50 W |
| Mansfield, Eng., U.K. | 54 | 53.09 N | 1.11 W |
| Mansfield, Ohio, U.S. | 96 | 40.46 N | 82.31 W |
| Mansfield Woodhouse | 56 | 53.11 N | 1.12 W |
| Manta | 100 | 0.57 S | 80.44 W |
| Mantes-la-Jolie | 68 | 48.59 N | 1.43 E |
| Mantiqueira, Serra da ⊼¹ | 102 | 22.00 S | 44.45 W |
| Mantova | 72 | 45.09 N | 10.48 E |
| Manturovo | 62 | 58.20 N | 44.46 E |
| Manu ≃ | 100 | 12.16 S | 70.51 W |
| Manulla ⊷ | 60 | 53.57 N | 9.12 W |
| Manyč ⊷ | 76 | 47.15 N | 40.00 E |
| Manzanares | 70 | 39.00 N | 3.22 W |
| Manzanillo, Cuba | 98 | 20.21 N | 77.07 W |
| Manzanillo, Méx. | 98 | 19.03 N | 104.20 W |
| Manzhouli | 80 | 49.35 N | 117.22 E |
| Maoke, Pegunungan ⊼ | 82 | 4.00 S | 138.00 E |
| Maoming | 80 | 21.55 N | 110.52 E |
| Maouri, Dallol **V** | 86 | 12.05 N | 3.32 E |
| Mapuera ⊷ | 100 | 1.05 S | 57.02 W |
| Maputo (Lourenço Marques) | 90 | 25.58 S | 32.35 E |
| Mara ⊷ | 90 | 1.31 S | 33.56 E |
| Maracá, Ilha de **I** | 100 | 2.05 N | 50.25 W |
| Maracaibo | 100 | 10.40 N | 71.37 W |
| Maracaibo, Lago de ⊜ | 100 | 9.50 N | 71.30 W |
| Maracay | 100 | 10.15 N | 67.36 W |
| Maradi | 86 | 13.29 N | 7.06 E |
| Marāgheh | 84 | 37.23 N | 46.13 E |
| Marahuaca, Cerro ⊼ | 100 | 3.34 N | 65.27 W |
| Marajó, Baía de **C** | 100 | 1.00 S | 48.30 W |
| Marajó, Ilha de **I** | 100 | 1.00 S | 49.30 W |
| Maranoa ⊷ | 92 | 27.50 S | 148.37 E |
| Marano [di Napoli] | 72 | 40.54 N | 14.11 E |
| Marañón ⊷ | 84 | 4.30 S | 73.27 W |
| Maraş | 84 | 37.36 N | 36.55 E |
| Marburg an der Lahn | 66 | 50.49 N | 8.46 E |
| March | 54 | 52.33 N | 0.06 E |
| Marche ≃ | 78 | 63.28 N | 118.50 E |
| Marchena | 70 | 37.20 N | 5.24 W |
| Mar Chiquita, Laguna ⊜ | 102 | 30.42 S | 62.36 W |
| Mardān | 84 | 34.12 N | 72.02 E |
| Mar del Plata | 102 | 38.00 S | 57.33 W |
| Maree, Loch ⊜ | 52 | 57.40 N | 5.30 W |
| Marfleet | 56 | 53.45 N | 0.17 W |
| Mar Forest ⊷³ | 52 | 56.56 N | 3.45 W |
| Margam | 54 | 51.34 N | 3.44 W |
| Margarita, Isla de **I** | 100 | 11.00 N | 64.00 W |
| Margate | 54 | 51.24 N | 1.24 E |
| Margherita Peak ⊼ | 90 | 0.22 N | 29.51 E |
| Margilan | 78 | 40.29 N | 71.44 E |
| Mārgow, Dasht-e ⊷² | 84 | 30.45 N | 63.10 E |
| Mariana Islands **II** | 82 | 16.00 N | 145.30 E |
| Marianao | 98 | 23.05 N | 82.26 W |
| Marian Lake ⊜ | 94 | 63.00 N | 116.10 W |
| Mariánské Lázně | 66 | 49.59 N | 12.43 E |
| Mariato, Punta ⊁ | 98 | 7.13 N | 80.53 W |
| Maribor | 72 | 46.33 N | 15.39 E |
| Marie-Galante **I** | 98 | 15.56 N | 61.16 W |
| Mariestad | 64 | 58.43 N | 13.51 E |
| Marietta | 96 | 33.57 N | 84.33 W |
| Marignane | 68 | 43.25 N | 5.13 E |
| Mariinsk | 78 | 56.13 N | 87.45 E |
| Marília | 102 | 22.13 S | 49.56 W |
| Marinduque Island **I** | 82 | 13.24 N | 121.58 E |
| Marinette | 96 | 45.06 N | 87.38 W |
| Marino | 72 | 41.46 N | 12.39 E |
| Marinskij Posad | 62 | 56.07 N | 47.43 E |
| Marion, Ind., U.S. | 96 | 40.33 N | 85.40 W |
| Marion, Ohio, U.S. | 96 | 40.35 N | 83.08 W |
| Marion, Lake ⊜¹ | 96 | 33.30 N | 80.25 W |
| Marion Reef ⊷² | 92 | 19.10 S | 152.17 E |
| Maritime Alps ⊼ | 68 | 44.15 N | 7.10 E |
| Marka | 88 | 1.47 N | 44.52 E |
| Market Bosworth | 54 | 52.37 N | 1.24 W |
| Market Deeping | 54 | 52.41 N | 0.19 W |
| Market Drayton | 54 | 52.54 N | 2.29 W |
| Market Harborough | 54 | 52.29 N | 0.55 W |
| Market Lavington | 54 | 51.18 N | 1.59 W |
| Market Rasen | 56 | 53.24 N | 0.21 W |
| Market Weighton | 56 | 53.52 N | 0.40 W |
| Markham Bay **C** | 94 | 63.30 N | 71.48 W |
| Markinch | 58 | 56.12 N | 3.08 W |
| Markwitz | 66 | 50.00 N | 12.06 E |
| Marlborough | 54 | 51.26 N | 1.43 W |
| Marlborough Downs ⊼¹ | 54 | 51.30 N | 1.45 W |
| Marlow | 54 | 51.35 N | 0.48 W |
| Marmande | 68 | 44.30 N | 0.10 E |
| Marmelos, Rio dos ⊷ | 100 | 6.06 S | 61.46 W |
| Marnhull | 54 | 50.58 N | 2.18 W |
| Maromokotro ⊼ | 90 | 14.01 S | 48.59 E |
| Marovoay | 90 | 16.06 S | 46.39 E |
| Marowijne (Maroni) ⊷ | 100 | 5.45 N | 53.58 W |
| Marple | 56 | 53.24 N | 2.03 W |
| Marquette | 96 | 46.33 N | 87.24 W |
| Marquises, Îles **II** | 8 | 9.00 S | 139.30 W |
| Marrah, Jabal ⊼ | 88 | 13.04 N | 24.21 E |
| Marrakech | 86 | 31.38 N | 8.00 W |
| Marsala | 72 | 37.48 N | 12.26 E |
| Marseille | 68 | 43.18 N | 5.24 E |
| Marshfield | 54 | 51.28 N | 2.19 W |
| Marske-by-the-Sea | 56 | 54.36 N | 1.01 W |
| Märsta | 64 | 59.37 N | 17.51 E |
| Marston Moor ≃ | 56 | 53.57 N | 1.17 W |
| Martaban, Gulf of **C** | 82 | 16.30 N | 97.00 E |
| Marteg ⊷ | 54 | 52.20 N | 3.33 W |
| Martigny | 68 | 46.06 N | 7.04 E |
| Martigues | 68 | 43.24 N | 5.03 E |
| Martin, Isle **I** | 58 | 57.55 N | 5.14 W |
| Martina Franca | 72 | 40.42 N | 17.21 E |
| Martinique □² | 98 | 14.40 N | 61.00 W |
| Martinsville | 96 | 36.41 N | 79.52 W |
| Martock | 54 | 50.59 N | 2.46 W |
| Martos | 70 | 37.43 N | 3.58 W |
| Martre, Lac la **⊜** | 94 | 63.15 N | 116.55 W |
| Marungu ⊼ | 90 | 7.42 S | 30.00 E |
| Mary | 78 | 37.36 N | 61.50 E |
| Maryborough | 92 | 37.03 S | 143.45 E |
| Maryland □³ | 96 | 39.00 N | 76.45 W |
| Marypark | 58 | 57.26 N | 3.21 W |
| Maryport | 56 | 54.43 N | 3.30 W |
| Marysville | 96 | 39.09 N | 121.35 W |
| Marywell | 58 | 57.00 N | 2.42 W |
| Marzūq, Idehan ⊷² | 88 | 24.30 N | 13.00 E |
| Masai Steppe ⊼¹ | 90 | 4.45 S | 37.00 E |
| Masan | 80 | 35.11 N | 128.32 E |
| Masaya | 98 | 11.58 N | 86.06 W |
| Masbate Island **I** | 82 | 12.15 N | 123.30 E |
| Mascara | 86 | 35.24 N | 0.09 E |
| Mascarene Islands **II** | 16 | 21.00 S | 57.00 E |
| Maseru | 90 | 29.28 S | 27.30 E |

| Name | Page | Lat | Long |
|---|---|---|---|
| Mashābih **I** | 84 | 25.37 N | 36.29 E |
| Masham | 56 | 54.13 N | 1.40 W |
| Mashhad | 84 | 36.18 N | 59.36 E |
| Māshkel, Hāmūn-i- ⊜ | 84 | 28.15 N | 63.00 E |
| Maşīrah, Khalīj al- **C** | 84 | 20.10 N | 58.15 E |
| Masjed Soleymān | 84 | 31.58 N | 49.18 E |
| Masoala, Presqu'île ⊁¹ | 90 | 15.40 S | 50.12 E |
| Mason City | 96 | 43.09 N | 93.12 W |
| Masqat (Muscat) | 84 | 23.37 N | 58.35 E |
| Massa | 72 | 44.01 N | 10.09 E |
| Massachusetts □³ | 96 | 42.15 N | 71.50 W |
| Massafra | 72 | 40.35 N | 17.07 E |
| Massa Marittima | 72 | 43.03 N | 10.53 E |
| Massarosa | 72 | 43.52 N | 10.20 E |
| Massive, Mount ⊼ | 96 | 39.12 N | 106.28 W |
| Matabeleland ⊷¹ | 90 | 19.30 S | 26.00 E |
| Matadi | 90 | 5.49 S | 13.27 E |
| Matagalpa | 98 | 12.55 N | 85.55 W |
| Matamoros | 98 | 25.53 N | 97.30 W |
| Matandu ⊷ | 90 | 8.45 S | 39.19 E |
| Matanzas | 98 | 23.03 N | 81.35 W |
| Matara | 84 | 8.35 S | 116.07 E |
| Mataró | 70 | 41.32 N | 2.27 E |
| Matehuala | 98 | 23.39 N | 100.39 W |
| Matera | 72 | 40.40 N | 16.37 E |
| Mathry | 54 | 51.57 N | 5.05 W |
| Mathura | 84 | 27.30 N | 77.41 E |
| Matlock | 56 | 53.08 N | 1.32 W |
| Mato, Cerro ⊼ | 100 | 7.15 N | 65.14 W |
| Matočkin Šar, Proliv **U** | 76 | 73.20 N | 55.21 E |
| Mato Grosso, Planalto do ⊼¹ | 100 | 15.30 S | 56.00 W |
| Matopo Hills ⊼² | 90 | 20.36 S | 28.28 E |
| Matosinhos | 70 | 41.11 N | 8.42 W |
| Maţraḥ | 84 | 23.38 N | 58.34 E |
| Maţrūḥ | 88 | 31.21 N | 27.14 E |
| Matsue | 80 | 35.28 N | 133.04 E |
| Matsumoto | 80 | 36.14 N | 137.58 E |
| Matsu Shan **I** | 80 | 26.09 N | 119.56 E |
| Matsuyama | 80 | 33.50 N | 132.45 E |
| Mattagami ⊷ | 94 | 50.43 N | 81.29 W |
| Maturín | 100 | 9.45 N | 63.11 W |
| Maubeuge | 68 | 50.17 N | 3.58 E |
| Ma-ubin | 82 | 16.44 N | 95.39 E |
| Mauchline | 58 | 55.31 N | 4.24 W |
| Maud ⊷ | 58 | 57.31 N | 2.06 W |
| Maui **I** | 82 | 20.01 N | 145.13 E |
| Mauna Kea ⊼ | 96b | 20.45 N | 156.15 W |
| Maurice, Lake ⊜ | 92 | 29.28 S | 130.58 E |
| Mauritania □¹ | 86 | 20.00 N | 12.00 W |
| Mauritius □¹ | 90 | 20.17 S | 57.33 E |
| Maury Channel **U** | 94 | 75.44 N | 94.40 W |
| Mawgan ⊷ | 54 | 50.06 N | 5.06 W |
| Maxwell Bay **C** | 94 | 74.35 N | 89.00 W |
| Maxwelltown | 56 | 55.04 N | 3.38 W |
| May, Isle of **I** | 58 | 56.11 N | 2.34 W |
| Maybole | 58 | 55.21 N | 4.41 W |
| Mayen | 66 | 50.19 N | 7.13 E |
| Mayenne | 68 | 48.18 N | 0.37 W |
| Mayfield | 54 | 53.01 N | 1.45 W |
| Maykop | 76 | 44.35 N | 40.10 E |
| Maynooth | 60 | 53.23 N | 6.35 W |
| Mayo □⁶ | 60 | 53.50 N | 9.30 W |
| Mayon Volcano ⊼¹ | 82 | 13.15 N | 123.41 E |
| Mayotte ⊷² | 90 | 12.50 S | 45.10 E |
| Mazara del Vallo | 72 | 37.39 N | 12.36 E |
| Mazār-e Sharīf | 84 | 36.42 N | 67.06 E |
| Mazaruni ⊷ | 100 | 6.25 N | 58.38 W |
| Mazatlán | 98 | 23.13 N | 106.25 W |
| Mazoe ⊷ | 90 | 16.32 S | 33.25 E |
| Mbabane | 90 | 26.18 S | 31.06 E |
| Mbale | 90 | 1.05 N | 34.10 E |
| Mbandaka (Coquilhatville) | 90 | 0.04 N | 18.16 E |
| Mbari ⊷ | 88 | 4.34 N | 22.43 E |
| Mbeya ⊼ | 90 | 8.50 S | 33.22 E |
| Mbomou (Bomu) ⊷ | 88 | 4.08 N | 22.26 E |
| Mbuji-Mayi (Bakwanga) | 90 | 6.09 S | 23.38 E |
| M'Clintock Channel **U** | 94 | 71.00 N | 101.00 W |
| M'Clure, Cape ⊁ | 94 | 74.35 N | 121.08 W |
| M'Clure Strait **U** | 94 | 74.30 N | 116.00 W |
| Mead, Lake ⊜¹ | 96 | 36.05 N | 114.25 W |
| Meadie, Loch ⊜ | 58 | 58.05 N | 4.33 W |
| Mealasta Isle **I** | 58 | 58.05 N | 7.08 W |
| Measham | 54 | 52.43 N | 1.29 W |
| Meath □⁶ | 52 | 53.35 N | 6.40 W |
| Meath □⁹ | 52 | 53.40 N | 7.00 W |
| Meaux | 68 | 48.57 N | 2.52 E |
| Mechelen | 66 | 51.02 N | 4.28 E |
| Medanosa, Punta ⊁ | 102 | 48.06 S | 65.55 W |
| Medellín | 100 | 6.15 N | 75.35 W |
| Medford | 96 | 42.19 N | 122.52 W |
| Medgidia | 74 | 44.15 N | 28.16 E |
| Medias | 74 | 46.10 N | 24.21 E |
| Medicine Hat | 94 | 50.03 N | 110.40 W |
| Medina del Campo | 70 | 41.18 N | 4.55 W |
| Mediterranean Sea ⊷² | 8 | 35.00 N | 20.00 E |
| Mednogorsk | 76 | 51.24 N | 57.37 E |
| Mednyj, Ostrov **I** | 78 | 54.45 N | 167.35 E |
| Medstead | 54 | 51.08 N | 1.04 W |
| Medvedica ⊷ | 76 | 49.35 N | 42.41 E |
| Medveďjegorsk | 76 | 62.54 N | 34.23 E |
| Medvežʹi Ostrova **II** | 78 | 70.52 N | 161.26 E |
| Medway ⊷ | 54 | 51.27 N | 0.44 E |
| Medyn' | 62 | 54.58 N | 35.52 E |
| Meerane | 66 | 50.51 N | 12.28 E |
| Meerut | 84 | 28.59 N | 77.42 E |
| Mégara | 74 | 37.59 N | 23.20 E |
| Meghna ⊷ | 84 | 22.50 N | 90.50 E |
| Meig ⊷ | 58 | 57.34 N | 4.41 W |
| Meigle | 58 | 56.35 N | 3.09 W |
| Meikle Millyea ⊼ | 58 | 55.07 N | 4.19 W |
| Meikle Says Law ⊼ | 58 | 55.55 N | 2.40 W |
| Meiktila | 82 | 20.52 N | 95.52 E |
| Meiningen | 66 | 50.34 N | 10.25 E |
| Meissen | 66 | 51.10 N | 13.28 E |
| Meixian | 80 | 24.21 N | 116.08 E |
| Mekele | 88 | 13.33 N | 39.30 E |
| Meknès | 86 | 33.53 N | 5.37 W |
| Mekong ⊷ | 82 | 10.33 N | 105.24 E |
| Mékrou ⊷ | 86 | 12.24 N | 2.49 E |
| Melaka (Malacca) | 82 | 2.12 N | 102.15 E |
| Melanesia **II** | 8 | 13.00 S | 164.00 E |
| Melbost | 58 | 58.15 N | 6.22 W |
| Melbourn | 54 | 52.05 N | 0.01 E |
| Melbourne, Austl. | 92 | 37.49 S | 144.58 E |
| Melbourne, Eng., U.K. | 54 | 52.49 N | 1.25 W |
| Melbourne, Fla., U.S. | 96 | 28.05 N | 80.37 W |
| Melbourne Island **I** | 94 | 68.30 N | 104.45 W |
| Melcombe Regis | 54 | 50.36 N | 2.28 W |
| Melegnano | 72 | 45.21 N | 9.19 E |
| Melekess | 62 | 54.14 N | 49.39 E |
| Mélèzes, Rivière aux ⊷ | 94 | 57.40 N | 69.29 W |
| Melfi | 72 | 40.59 N | 15.40 E |
| Melfort, Loch **C**¹ | 58 | 56.15 N | 5.31 W |
| Melilla | 86 | 35.19 N | 2.58 W |
| Melitopol' | 76 | 46.50 N | 35.22 E |
| Melksham | 54 | 51.23 N | 2.09 W |
| Mellieha | 72 | 35.57 N | 14.21 E |
| Mellish Reef ⊷¹ | 92 | 17.25 S | 155.50 E |
| Mellon Udrigle | 58 | 57.55 N | 5.39 W |
| Melmerby | 56 | 54.44 N | 2.35 W |
| Melník | 66 | 50.21 N | 14.30 E |
| Melolo | 102 | 32.22 S | 54.11 W |
| Melrose | 58 | 55.36 N | 2.44 W |
| Melton Constable | 54 | 52.53 N | 1.01 E |
| Melton Mowbray | 54 | 52.46 N | 0.53 W |
| Melun | 68 | 48.32 N | 2.40 E |
| Melvaig | 58 | 57.48 N | 5.49 W |
| Melvich | 58 | 58.33 N | 3.55 W |
| Melville, Lake ⊜ | 94 | 53.45 N | 59.30 W |
| Melville Hills ⊼² | 94 | 69.20 N | 122.00 W |

| Name | Page | Lat | Long |
|---|---|---|---|
| Melville Island **I**, Austl. | 92 | 11.40 S | 131.00 E |
| Melville Island **I**, N.W. Ter., Can. | 94 | 75.15 N | 110.00 W |
| Melville Peninsula ⊁¹ | 94 | 68.00 N | 84.00 W |
| Melville Sound **U** | 94 | 68.05 N | 107.30 W |
| Melvin, Lough **⊜**, Eur. | 60 | 54.26 N | 8.10 W |
| Melvin, Lough **⊜**, N. Ire., U.K. | 52 | 54.26 N | 8.10 W |
| Melzo | 72 | 43.09 N | 9.25 E |
| Memmingen | 66 | 47.59 N | 10.11 E |
| Memphis | 96 | 35.08 N | 90.03 W |
| Memsie | 58 | 57.39 N | 2.02 W |
| Menai Bridge | 56 | 53.14 N | 4.10 W |
| Menai Strait **U** | 56 | 53.12 N | 4.12 W |
| Mendawai ⊷ | 82 | 3.17 S | 113.21 E |
| Mende | 68 | 44.30 N | 3.30 E |
| Menden | 66 | 51.26 N | 7.47 E |
| Mendip Hills ⊼² | 54 | 51.15 N | 2.40 W |
| Mendlesham | 54 | 52.16 N | 1.05 E |
| Mendocino, Cape ⊁ | 96 | 40.25 N | 124.25 W |
| Mendoza | 102 | 32.53 S | 68.49 W |
| Menemen | 74 | 38.36 N | 27.04 E |
| Menèn | 68 | 50.48 N | 3.07 E |
| Menfi | 72 | 37.36 N | 12.58 E |
| Menggala | 82 | 4.28 S | 105.17 E |
| Mengzi | 80 | 23.22 N | 103.20 E |
| Menihek Lakes ⊜ | 94 | 54.00 N | 66.35 W |
| Menorca **I** | 70 | 40.00 N | 4.00 E |
| Mentawai, Kepulauan **II** | 82 | 2.00 S | 99.30 E |
| Mentawai, Selat **U** | 82 | 1.56 S | 100.12 E |
| Menton | 68 | 43.47 N | 7.30 E |
| Menzel Bourguiba | 86 | 37.10 N | 9.48 E |
| Menzelinsk | 62 | 55.43 N | 53.08 E |
| Meon ⊷ | 54 | 50.48 N | 1.15 W |
| Mepal | 54 | 52.24 N | 0.07 E |
| Meppel | 66 | 52.42 N | 6.11 E |
| Merano (Meran) | 72 | 46.40 N | 11.09 E |
| Merced | 96 | 37.18 N | 120.29 W |
| Mercedes, Arg. | 102 | 33.40 S | 65.28 W |
| Mercedes, Ur. | 102 | 33.16 S | 58.01 W |
| Merchants Bay **C** | 94 | 67.10 N | 62.50 W |
| Mere | 54 | 51.06 N | 2.16 W |
| Mergui | 82 | 12.26 N | 98.36 E |
| Mergui Archipelago **II** | 82 | 12.00 N | 98.00 E |
| Mérida, Esp. | 70 | 38.55 N | 6.20 W |
| Mérida, Méx. | 98 | 20.58 N | 89.37 W |
| Mérida, Ven. | 100 | 8.36 N | 71.08 W |
| Mérida, Cordillera de ⊼ | 100 | 8.40 N | 71.00 W |
| Meriden | 54 | 52.26 N | 1.37 W |
| Meridian | 96 | 32.22 N | 88.42 W |
| Mérignac | 68 | 44.50 N | 0.42 W |
| Merir **I** | 82 | 4.19 N | 132.19 E |
| Merrick ⊼ | 58 | 55.08 N | 4.29 W |
| Merriott | 54 | 50.54 N | 2.48 W |
| Mersea Island **I** | 54 | 51.47 N | 0.55 E |
| Merseburg | 66 | 51.21 N | 11.59 E |
| Mersey ⊷ | 56 | 53.25 N | 3.00 W |
| Merseyside □⁶ | 56 | 53.25 N | 2.50 W |
| Mersin | 84 | 36.48 N | 34.38 E |
| Merthyr Tydfil | 54 | 51.46 N | 3.23 W |
| Merton ⊷⁸ | 54 | 51.25 N | 0.12 W |
| Meru ⊼ | 90 | 3.14 S | 36.45 E |
| Merzig | 66 | 49.27 N | 6.36 E |
| Mesa | 96 | 33.25 N | 111.50 W |
| Mesagne | 72 | 40.33 N | 17.49 E |
| Meschede | 66 | 51.20 N | 8.17 E |
| Mesewa (Massaua) | 88 | 15.38 N | 39.28 E |
| Mesolóngion | 74 | 38.21 N | 21.17 E |
| Mesopotamia ⊷¹ | 84 | 34.00 N | 44.00 E |
| Messalo ⊷ | 90 | 11.40 S | 40.46 E |
| Messina, Italy | 72 | 38.11 N | 15.33 E |
| Messina, S. Afr. | 90 | 22.23 S | 30.00 E |
| Messina, Stretto di **U** | 72 | 38.15 N | 15.35 E |
| Messíni | 74 | 37.04 N | 22.00 E |
| Mes/ojacha ⊷ | 78 | 67.52 N | 77.27 E |
| Mestre | 72 | 45.29 N | 12.15 E |
| Meta ⊷ | 100 | 6.12 N | 67.28 W |
| Methil | 58 | 56.10 N | 3.01 W |
| Methlick | 58 | 57.25 N | 2.14 W |
| Methwold | 54 | 52.31 N | 0.32 E |
| Mettingham | 54 | 52.26 N | 1.28 E |
| Mettmann | 66 | 51.15 N | 6.58 E |
| Metz | 68 | 49.08 N | 6.10 E |
| Meuse ⊷ | 50 | 51.49 N | 5.01 E |
| Mevagissey | 54 | 50.16 N | 4.48 W |
| Mexborough | 56 | 53.30 N | 1.17 W |
| Mexiana, Ilha **I** | 100 | 0.02 S | 49.35 W |
| Mexicali | 98 | 32.40 N | 115.29 W |
| Mexico □¹ | 98 | 23.00 N | 102.00 W |
| Mexico, Gulf of **C** | 98 | 25.00 N | 90.00 W |
| Mezdurečensk | 78 | 53.42 N | 88.03 E |
| Mezen' ⊷ | 76 | 66.11 N | 43.59 E |
| Mezöberény | 66 | 46.50 N | 21.02 E |
| Mezökövesd | 66 | 47.50 N | 20.34 E |
| Mezötúr | 66 | 47.00 N | 20.37 E |
| Mgun, Irhil ⊼ | 86 | 31.31 N | 6.25 W |
| Mhlanga, Punta de ⊁ | 90 | 26.45 S | 4.18 W |
| Mhòir, Beinn ⊼ | 58 | 57.17 N | 7.19 W |
| Mhòr, Loch **⊜** | 58 | 57.14 N | 4.26 W |
| Miami | 96 | 25.46 N | 80.12 W |
| Miami Beach | 96 | 25.47 N | 80.08 W |
| Mianyang | 80 | 30.23 N | 113.25 E |
| Miass | 76 | 54.59 N | 60.06 E |
| Michajlov | 62 | 54.14 N | 39.02 E |
| Michajlovka | 76 | 50.04 N | 43.15 E |
| Michalovce | 66 | 48.45 N | 21.55 E |
| Micheldever | 54 | 51.09 N | 1.15 W |
| Michigan □³ | 96 | 44.00 N | 85.00 W |
| Michigan, Lake ⊜ | 96 | 44.00 N | 87.00 W |
| Michigan City | 96 | 41.43 N | 86.54 W |
| Michikamau Lake ⊜ | 94 | 54.00 N | 64.00 W |
| Michipicoten Island **I** | 94 | 47.45 N | 85.45 W |
| Mickle Fell ⊼ | 56 | 54.37 N | 2.18 W |
| Mickleover | 54 | 52.55 N | 1.30 W |
| Micurinsk | 76 | 52.54 N | 40.30 E |
| Middelburg | 66 | 51.30 N | 3.37 E |
| Middle Andaman **I** | 84 | 12.30 N | 92.50 E |
| Middle Level Main Drain ⊷ | 54 | 52.43 N | 0.22 E |
| Middlesbrough | 56 | 54.35 N | 1.14 W |
| Middleton, Eng., U.K. | 56 | 52.43 N | 0.28 E |
| Middleton, Eng., U.K. | 56 | 53.45 N | 1.32 W |
| Middleton, Eng., U.K. | 56 | 53.33 N | 2.13 W |
| Middleton in Teesdale | 56 | 54.38 N | 2.04 W |
| Middleton-on-the-Wolds | 56 | 53.56 N | 0.33 W |
| Middleton Reef ⊷¹ | 92 | 29.28 S | 159.06 E |
| Middletown, N. Ire., U.K. | 60 | 54.18 N | 6.50 W |
| Middletown, Ohio, U.S. | 96 | 39.29 N | 84.25 W |
| Midhurst | 54 | 50.59 N | 0.44 W |
| Mid Glamorgan □⁶ | 54 | 51.40 N | 3.30 W |
| Midland, Mich., U.S. | 96 | 43.37 N | 84.14 W |
| Midland, Tex., U.S. | 96 | 32.00 N | 102.05 W |
| Midleton | 60 | 51.55 N | 8.10 W |
| Midnapore | 84 | 22.25 N | 87.20 E |
| Midsomer Norton | 54 | 51.18 N | 2.28 W |
| Miedzyrzec Podlaski | 66 | 52.00 N | 22.47 E |
| Miedzyrzecz | 66 | 52.28 N | 15.35 E |
| Mielec | 66 | 50.18 N | 21.25 E |
| Mieres | 70 | 43.15 N | 5.46 W |
| Miguel Alemán, Presa ⊜¹ | 98 | 18.13 N | 96.32 W |

| Name | Page | Lat | Long |
|---|---|---|---|
| Mildenhall | 54 | 52.21 N | 0.30 E |
| Milford | 54 | 51.11 N | 1.38 W |
| Milford Haven | 54 | 51.40 N | 5.02 W |
| Milford Haven **C** | 54 | 51.42 N | 5.03 W |
| Milford-on-Sea | 54 | 50.44 N | 1.36 W |
| Milk ⊷ | 96 | 48.05 N | 106.15 W |
| Milk Hill ⊼² | 54 | 51.22 N | 1.51 W |
| Millau | 68 | 44.06 N | 3.05 E |
| Millbrook | 54 | 50.20 N | 4.13 W |
| Mille Lacs, Lac des ⊜ | 94 | 48.50 N | 90.30 W |
| Mille Lacs Lake ⊜ | 96 | 46.15 N | 93.40 W |
| Milleur Point ⊁ | 52 | 55.01 N | 5.06 W |
| Milford | 54 | 55.07 N | 7.43 W |
| Millom | 56 | 54.13 N | 3.18 W |
| Millport | 58 | 55.46 N | 4.55 W |
| Mills Lake ⊜ | 94 | 61.30 N | 118.10 W |
| Milne Bay **C** | 92 | 10.22 S | 150.30 E |
| Milngavie | 58 | 55.57 N | 4.20 W |
| Milnrow | 56 | 53.37 N | 2.06 W |
| Milnthorpe | 56 | 54.14 N | 2.46 W |
| Milos **I** | 74 | 36.41 N | 24.15 E |
| Milton Abbot | 54 | 50.35 N | 4.15 W |
| Miltown Malbay | 60 | 52.50 N | 9.23 W |
| Milverton | 54 | 51.02 N | 3.16 W |
| Milwaukee | 96 | 43.02 N | 87.55 W |
| Minahasa ⊁¹ | 82 | 1.00 N | 124.35 E |
| Minami-Daitō-jima **I** | 80 | 25.50 N | 131.15 E |
| Minard | 58 | 56.07 N | 5.15 W |
| Minas | 102 | 34.23 S | 55.14 W |
| Minatitlán | 98 | 17.59 N | 94.31 W |
| Minchinhampton | 54 | 51.42 N | 2.10 W |
| Mindanao **I** | 82 | 8.00 N | 125.00 E |
| Mindanao ≃ | 82 | 7.20 N | 124.24 E |
| Mindanao Sea ⊷² | 82 | 9.10 N | 124.25 E |
| Mindelo | 86 | 16.53 N | 25.00 W |
| Minden | 66 | 52.17 N | 8.55 E |
| Mindoro **I** | 82 | 12.50 N | 121.05 E |
| Mindoro Strait **U** | 82 | 12.20 N | 120.40 E |
| Minehead | 54 | 51.13 N | 3.29 W |
| Minervino Murge | 72 | 41.05 N | 16.05 E |
| Mingäçaur | 76 | 40.45 N | 47.03 E |
| Mingo Lake ⊜ | 94 | 64.35 N | 72.10 W |
| Mingulay **I** | 58 | 56.50 N | 7.40 W |
| Minicoy Island **I** | 84 | 8.17 N | 73.04 E |
| Miniwgal, Lake ⊜ | 92 | 29.35 S | 123.12 E |
| Minjiang ⊷ | 80 | 26.05 N | 119.32 E |
| Minna | 86 | 9.37 N | 6.33 E |
| Minneapolis | 96 | 44.59 N | 93.13 W |
| Minnesota □³ | 96 | 46.00 N | 94.15 W |
| Minnesota ⊷ | 96 | 44.54 N | 93.10 W |
| Minnigaff | 58 | 54.58 N | 4.30 W |
| Minnoch, Water of ⊷ | 58 | 55.02 N | 4.33 W |
| Minot | 96 | 48.14 N | 101.18 W |
| Minshan ⊼ | 80 | 33.15 N | 103.15 E |
| Minsk | 76 | 53.54 N | 27.34 E |
| Mińsk Mazowiecki | 66 | 52.11 N | 21.34 E |
| Minster, Eng., U.K. | 54 | 51.26 N | 0.49 E |
| Minster, Eng., U.K. | 54 | 51.20 N | 1.19 E |
| Minsterley | 54 | 52.39 N | 2.55 W |
| Mintlaw | 58 | 57.31 N | 2.00 W |
| Minto, Lac ⊜ | 94 | 57.13 N | 74.00 W |
| Minto Inlet **C** | 94 | 71.20 N | 117.00 W |
| Minturno | 72 | 41.15 N | 13.45 E |
| Minusinsk | 78 | 53.43 N | 91.42 E |
| Minxian | 80 | 34.22 N | 104.08 E |
| Mira ⊷ | 92 | 45.26 N | 12.08 E |
| Miraj | 84 | 16.50 N | 74.38 E |
| Miramichi Bay **C** | 94 | 47.08 N | 65.08 W |
| Miranda | 96 | 19.25 S | 57.20 W |
| Miranda de Ebro | 70 | 42.41 N | 2.57 W |
| Mirandola | 72 | 44.53 N | 11.04 E |
| Mirfield | 56 | 53.41 N | 1.41 W |
| Mirim, Lagoa (Laguna Merín) **C** | 102 | 32.45 S | 52.50 W |
| Mirnyj | 78 | 62.33 N | 69.00 E |
| Mīrpur Khās | 84 | 25.09 N | 82.35 E |
| Mirzāpur | 84 | 25.09 N | 82.35 E |
| Mīshān, Bi'r ⊷⁴ | 88 | 22.12 N | 27.57 E |
| Mishmi Hills ⊼² | 84 | 29.00 N | 96.00 E |
| Misilmeri | 72 | 38.03 N | 13.27 E |
| Misima Island **I** | 92 | 10.40 S | 152.45 E |
| Miskitos, Cayos **II** | 98 | 14.23 N | 82.46 W |
| Miskolc | 66 | 48.06 N | 20.47 E |
| Misool, Pulau **I** | 82 | 1.52 S | 130.10 E |
| Mişrātah | 88 | 32.23 N | 15.06 E |
| Missinaibi ⊷ | 94 | 50.44 N | 81.29 W |
| Missinaibi Lake ⊜ | 94 | 48.23 N | 83.40 W |
| Mississippi □³ | 96 | 32.50 N | 89.30 W |
| Mississippi ⊷ | 96 | 29.00 N | 89.15 W |
| Mississippi Delta ⊷² | 96 | 29.10 N | 89.15 W |
| Missoula | 96 | 46.52 N | 114.01 W |
| Missouri □³ | 96 | 38.30 N | 93.30 W |
| Missouri ⊷ | 96 | 38.50 N | 90.08 W |
| Mistassibi ⊷ | 94 | 48.53 N | 72.13 W |
| Mistassini, Lac ⊜ | 94 | 51.00 N | 73.37 W |
| Misterbianco | 72 | 37.31 N | 15.01 E |
| Misterton, Eng., U.K. | 54 | 50.52 N | 2.47 W |
| Misterton, Eng., U.K. | 56 | 53.27 N | 0.51 W |
| Misti, Volcán ⊼¹ | 100 | 16.18 S | 71.24 W |
| Mistretta | 72 | 37.56 N | 14.22 E |
| Mita, Punta de ⊁ | 98 | 20.47 N | 105.33 W |
| Mitchelstown | 60 | 51.53 N | 2.30 W |
| Mitchell ⊷ | 92 | 15.12 S | 141.35 E |
| Mitchell, Mount ⊼ | 96 | 35.46 N | 82.16 W |
| Mitchelstown | 60 | 52.16 N | 8.16 W |
| Mitilíni | 74 | 39.06 N | 26.32 E |
| Mito | 80 | 36.22 N | 140.28 E |
| Mittweida | 66 | 50.59 N | 12.59 E |
| Mitumba, Monts ⊼ | 90 | 6.00 S | 29.00 E |
| Miyako-jima **I** | 80 | 24.47 N | 125.20 E |
| Miyakonojō | 80 | 31.44 N | 131.04 E |
| Miyazaki | 80 | 31.54 N | 131.26 E |
| Mizen Head ⊁ | 60 | 51.27 N | 9.49 W |
| Mjölby | 64 | 58.19 N | 15.08 E |
| Mjøsa ⊜ | 64 | 60.40 N | 11.00 E |
| Mława | 66 | 53.06 N | 20.23 E |
| Mladá Boleslav | 66 | 50.26 N | 14.59 E |
| Mljet **I** | 72 | 42.44 N | 17.30 E |
| Mo i Rana | 64 | 66.19 N | 14.08 E |
| Moa, Pulau **I** | 82 | 8.10 S | 127.56 E |
| Moa Island **I** | 92 | 10.12 S | 142.16 E |
| Moate | 60 | 53.24 N | 7.43 W |
| Mobile | 96 | 30.41 N | 88.02 W |
| Moçambique | 90 | 15.03 S | 40.42 E |
| Moçâmedes | 90 | 15.12 S | 12.08 E |
| Mocha, Isla ⊷¹ | 102 | 38.22 S | 73.56 W |
| Mochudi | 90 | 24.28 S | 26.05 E |
| Môco, Serra ⊼ | 90 | 12.28 S | 15.10 E |
| Modbury | 54 | 50.21 N | 3.53 W |
| Modena | 72 | 44.40 N | 10.55 E |
| Modesto | 96 | 37.39 N | 121.00 W |
| Modica | 72 | 36.51 N | 14.46 E |
| Mödling | 66 | 48.05 N | 16.17 E |
| Moe | 92 | 38.10 S | 146.15 E |
| Moel Fferna ⊼ | 54 | 52.57 N | 3.19 W |
| Moers | 66 | 51.27 N | 6.37 E |
| Moffat | 58 | 55.20 N | 3.27 W |
| Moffat Water ⊷ | 58 | 55.23 N | 3.21 W |
| Mogadiscio | 88 | 2.01 N | 45.20 E |
| Mogi das Cruzes | 102 | 23.31 S | 46.11 W |
| Mogi'ov | 76 | 53.54 N | 30.21 E |
| Mogi-Guaçu ⊷ | 102 | 20.53 S | 48.10 W |
| Mogil'ov | 76 | 53.11 N | 23.07 E |
| Mogocha | 78 | 53.44 N | 119.44 E |
| Mogoton, Cerro ⊼ | 98 | 13.45 N | 86.23 W |
| Mohács | 66 | 45.59 N | 18.42 E |
| Mohammedia | 86 | 33.44 N | 7.24 W |
| Moheli **I** | 90 | 12.15 S | 43.45 E |
| Moineşti | 74 | 46.28 N | 26.29 E |
| Moira | 60 | 54.30 N | 6.17 W |
| Mojave Desert ⊷² | 96 | 35.00 N | 117.00 W |
| Mojjero ⊷ | 78 | 68.44 N | 103.42 E |
| Moksa ⊷ | 62 | 54.44 N | 41.53 E |
| Mol | 66 | 51.11 N | 5.06 E |
| Mola di Bari | 72 | 41.04 N | 17.05 E |
| Mold | 56 | 53.10 N | 3.08 W |
| Moldoveanu ⊼ | 74 | 45.36 N | 24.44 E |
| Molepolole | 90 | 24.25 S | 25.30 E |
| Molfetta | 72 | 41.12 N | 16.36 E |
| Molina de Segura | 70 | 38.03 N | 1.12 W |
| Moline | 96 | 41.30 N | 90.31 W |

| Name | Page | Lat | Long |
|---|---|---|---|
| Molina de Rey | 70 | 41.25 N | 2.01 E |
| Mollendo | 100 | 17.02 S | 72.01 W |
| Mölln | 66 | 53.37 N | 10.41 E |
| Mölndal | 64 | 57.39 N | 12.01 E |
| Molodečno | 76 | 54.19 N | 26.49 E |
| Molokai **I** | 96b | 21.07 N | 157.00 W |
| Moma ⊷ | 78 | 28.30 N | 20.13 E |
| Mombasa | 90 | 4.03 S | 39.40 E |
| Møn **I** | 54 | 55.00 N | 12.20 E |
| Mona, Canal de la **U** | 98 | 18.30 N | 67.45 W |
| Mona, Isla **I** | 98 | 18.05 N | 67.54 W |
| Monach, Sound of **U** | 58 | 57.30 N | 7.43 W |
| Monaco □¹ | 50 | 43.45 N | 7.25 E |
| Monadhliath Mountains ⊼ | 58 | 57.15 N | 4.10 W |
| Monaghan ≃ | 52 | 54.15 N | 6.58 W |
| Monaghan □⁶ | 52 | 54.10 N | 7.00 W |
| Monamolin | 60 | 52.33 N | 6.20 W |
| Monar, Loch ⊜ | 58 | 57.25 N | 5.06 W |
| Monashee Mountains ⊼ | 94 | 50.30 N | 118.30 W |
| Monasterevin | 60 | 53.07 N | 7.02 W |
| Moncalieri | 72 | 45.00 N | 7.41 E |
| Monçegorsk | 62 | 67.54 N | 32.58 E |
| Mönchengladbach | 66 | 51.12 N | 6.28 E |
| Monclova | 98 | 26.54 N | 101.25 W |
| Moncton | 94 | 46.06 N | 64.47 W |
| Mondovì | 72 | 44.23 N | 7.49 E |
| Mondragone | 72 | 41.07 N | 13.53 E |
| Moneygall | 60 | 52.53 N | 7.57 W |
| Moneymore | 60 | 54.42 N | 6.41 W |
| Monfalcone | 72 | 45.49 N | 13.32 E |
| Monforte de Lemos | 70 | 42.31 N | 7.30 W |
| Monger, Lake ⊜ | 92 | 29.15 S | 117.05 E |
| Monghyr | 84 | 25.23 N | 86.29 E |
| Mongol Altaj Nuruu ⊼ | | | |
| Mongolia □¹ | 80 | 47.00 N | 92.00 E |
| Moniaive | 58 | 55.12 N | 3.55 W |
| Monifieth | 58 | 56.29 N | 2.49 W |
| Monimail | 58 | 56.19 N | 3.06 W |
| Monivea | 60 | 53.23 N | 8.43 W |
| Monmouth | 54 | 51.50 N | 2.43 W |
| Mono ⊷ | 86 | 6.17 N | 1.51 E |
| Mono Lake ⊜ | 96 | 38.00 N | 119.00 W |
| Monopoli | 72 | 40.57 N | 17.19 E |
| Monor | 66 | 47.21 N | 19.27 E |
| Monreale | 72 | 38.05 N | 13.17 E |
| Monroe | 96 | 32.33 N | 92.07 W |
| Monrovia | 86 | 6.18 N | 10.47 W |
| Mons | 66 | 50.27 N | 3.56 E |
| Montana □³ | 96 | 47.00 N | 110.00 W |
| Montargis | 68 | 48.00 N | 2.45 E |
| Montauban | 68 | 44.01 N | 1.21 E |
| Montbéliard | 68 | 47.31 N | 6.48 E |
| Montbrison | 68 | 45.36 N | 4.03 E |
| Montceau-[-les-Mines] | 68 | 46.40 N | 4.22 E |
| Mont-de-Marsan | 68 | 43.53 N | 0.30 W |
| Montebello Islands **II** | 92 | 20.25 S | 115.32 E |
| Montecatini Terme | 72 | 43.53 N | 10.46 E |
| Monte Cristo, Cerro ⊼ | 98 | 14.25 N | 89.21 W |
| Montego Bay | 98 | 18.28 N | 77.55 W |
| Montelimar | 68 | 44.34 N | 4.45 E |
| Monte Lindo ⊷ | 102 | 23.56 S | 57.12 W |
| Montereau-faut-Yonne | 68 | 48.23 N | 2.57 E |
| Monterey | 96 | 36.37 N | 121.55 W |
| Monterey Bay **C** | 96 | 36.45 N | 121.55 W |
| Montería | 100 | 8.46 N | 75.53 W |
| Monterotondo | 72 | 42.03 N | 12.37 E |
| Monterrey | 98 | 25.40 N | 100.19 W |
| Montes Claros | 100 | 16.43 S | 43.52 W |
| Montevarchi | 72 | 43.31 N | 11.34 E |
| Montevideo | 102 | 34.53 S | 56.11 W |
| Montgomery, Wales, U.K. | 54 | 52.33 N | 3.03 W |
| Montgomery, Ala., U.S. | 96 | 32.23 N | 86.18 W |
| Montichiari | 72 | 45.25 N | 10.23 E |
| Montijo, Esp. | 70 | 38.55 N | 6.37 W |
| Montijo, Port. | 70 | 38.42 N | 8.58 W |
| Montilla | 70 | 37.35 N | 4.38 W |
| Montluçon | 68 | 46.21 N | 2.36 E |
| Montmagny | 94 | 46.59 N | 70.33 W |
| Montpelier | 96 | 44.16 N | 72.34 W |
| Montpellier | 68 | 43.36 N | 3.53 E |
| Montréal | 94 | 45.31 N | 73.34 W |
| Montrose | 96 | 46.26 N | 6.55 E |
| Montrose | 58 | 56.43 N | 2.29 W |
| Montserrat □² | 98 | 16.45 N | 62.12 W |
| Monymusk | 58 | 57.13 N | 2.31 W |
| Monywa | 82 | 22.05 N | 95.08 E |
| Monza | 72 | 45.35 N | 9.16 E |
| Moore, Lake ⊜ | 92 | 29.50 S | 117.35 E |
| Moorfoot Hills ⊼² | 58 | 55.45 N | 3.02 W |
| Moorhead | 96 | 46.51 N | 96.46 W |
| Moosburg | 66 | 48.28 N | 11.57 E |
| Moosehead Lake ⊜ | 96 | 45.40 N | 69.40 W |
| Moose Jaw | 94 | 50.23 N | 105.32 W |
| Mopti | 86 | 14.30 N | 4.12 W |
| Mór | 66 | 47.23 N | 18.12 E |
| Mor, Glen **V** | 58 | 57.10 N | 4.40 W |
| Mor, Sgùrr ⊼ | 58 | 57.42 N | 5.03 W |
| Mora | 64 | 61.00 N | 14.33 E |
| Morádābád | 84 | 28.50 N | 78.47 E |
| Morahalom | 66 | 46.13 N | 19.54 E |
| Moraleda, Canal **U** | 102 | 44.30 S | 73.30 W |
| Morant Cays **II** | 98 | 17.24 N | 75.59 W |
| Morar, Loch ⊜ | 58 | 56.55 N | 5.43 W |
| Moratalla | 70 | 38.12 N | 1.53 W |
| Moratuwa | 84 | 6.46 N | 79.53 E |
| Moray Firth **C**¹ | 58 | 57.50 N | 3.30 W |
| More, Ben ⊼, Scot., U.K. | 58 | 56.23 N | 4.31 W |
| More, Ben ⊼, Scot., U.K. | 58 | 56.25 N | 6.01 W |
| More, Loch ⊜ | 58 | 58.17 N | 4.51 W |
| More Assynt, Ben ⊼ | 58 | 58.07 N | 4.51 W |
| Morecambe | 56 | 54.04 N | 2.53 W |
| Morecambe Bay **C** | 56 | 54.07 N | 3.00 W |
| Moree | 92 | 29.28 S | 149.51 E |
| Morella | 70 | 40.37 N | 0.06 W |
| Morelia | 98 | 19.42 N | 101.07 W |
| Morena, Sierra ⊼ | 70 | 38.00 N | 5.00 W |
| Moresby Island **I** | 94 | 52.45 N | 131.55 W |
| Moretonhampstead | 54 | 50.40 N | 3.45 W |
| Moreton-in-Marsh | 54 | 51.59 N | 1.42 W |
| Moreton Island **I** | 92 | 27.10 S | 153.25 E |
| Morfa Nefyn | 54 | 52.56 N | 4.33 W |
| More, Loch ⊜ | 58 | 58.30 N | 4.00 W |
| Morioka | 80 | 39.42 N | 141.09 E |
| Moriston ⊷ | 58 | 57.12 N | 4.36 W |
| Morjärv | 64 | 66.10 N | 22.45 E |
| Morkoka ⊷ | 78 | 65.10 N | 115.53 E |
| Morlaix | 68 | 48.35 N | 3.50 W |
| Morley | 56 | 53.46 N | 1.36 W |
| Morningstar ⊷ | 60 | 52.30 N | 8.40 W |
| Mornington, Isla ⊷¹ | 102 | 49.45 S | 75.23 W |
| Mornington Island **I** | 92 | 16.33 S | 139.24 E |
| Morocco □¹ | 86 | 32.00 N | 5.50 W |
| Morogoro | 90 | 6.49 S | 37.40 E |
| Moro Gulf **C** | 82 | 6.51 N | 123.00 E |
| Morón, Cuba | 98 | 22.06 N | 78.38 W |
| Morón de la Frontera | 70 | 37.08 N | 5.27 W |
| Morona ⊷ | 100 | 4.45 S | 77.04 W |
| Moron | 80 | 49.36 N | 100.10 E |
| Moronvilliers | 54 | 50.57 N | 3.02 W |
| Moro, Punta ⊁ | 102 | 33.53 S | 71.37 W |
| Morpeth | 56 | 55.10 N | 1.41 W |
| Morro, Punta ⊁ | 102 | 27.07 S | 70.57 W |
| Mørsvik | 64 | 67.54 N | 15.50 E |
| Mortes, Rio das ⊷ | 100 | 11.45 S | 50.44 W |
| Morvan ⊼ | 68 | 47.05 N | 4.00 E |
| Morven ⊼, Scot., U.K. | 58 | 58.13 N | 3.42 W |
| Morven ⊼, Scot., U.K. | 58 | 57.07 N | 3.02 W |
| Morvern ⊷¹ | 58 | 56.37 N | 5.45 W |
| Morwell | 92 | 38.14 S | 146.24 E |
| Mosal'sk | 62 | 54.29 N | 34.59 E |
| Mosbach | 66 | 49.21 N | 9.08 E |
| Moshi | 90 | 3.21 S | 37.20 E |

| Name | Page | Lat | Long |
|---|---|---|---|
| Moskva (Moscow) | 62 | 55.45 N | 37.35 E |
| Mosonmagyaróvár | 66 | 47.51 N | 17.17 E |
| Mosquitos, Golfo de los **C** | 98 | 9.00 N | 81.15 W |
| Moss | 64 | 59.26 N | 10.42 E |
| Mossbank | 58 | 60.02 N | 1.12 W |
| Mosselbaai | 90 | 34.11 S | 22.08 E |
| Mossley | 56 | 53.32 N | 2.02 W |
| Mossoró | 100 | 5.11 S | 37.20 W |
| Mostaganem | 86 | 35.51 N | 0.07 E |
| Mostar | 72 | 43.20 N | 17.49 E |
| Møsting, Kap ⊁ | 94 | 64.00 N | 41.00 W |
| Mostiska | 66 | 49.48 N | 23.09 E |
| Mostyn | 56 | 53.19 N | 3.16 W |
| Motagua ⊷ | 98 | 15.44 N | 88.14 W |
| Motala | 64 | 58.33 N | 15.03 E |
| Motherwell | 58 | 55.48 N | 4.00 W |
| Motril | 70 | 36.45 N | 3.31 W |
| Motru | 74 | 44.50 N | 23.00 E |
| Mottisfont | 54 | 51.02 N | 1.32 W |
| Moulins | 68 | 46.34 N | 3.20 E |
| Moulmein | 82 | 16.30 N | 97.38 E |
| Moulouya, Oued ≃ | 86 | 35.05 N | 2.25 W |
| Moundou | 88 | 8.34 N | 16.05 E |
| Mountain ⊷ | 56 | 65.41 N | 128.50 W |
| Mountain Ash | 54 | 51.42 N | 3.24 W |
| Mountain Nile (Baḥr al-Jabal) ⊷ | 88 | 9.30 N | 30.30 E |
| Mount Bellew Bridge | 60 | 53.28 N | 8.29 W |
| Mount Gambier | 92 | 37.50 S | 140.46 E |
| Mount Isa | 92 | 20.44 S | 139.30 E |
| Mountmellick | 60 | 53.07 N | 7.20 W |
| Mountnorth | 60 | 53.00 N | 7.27 W |
| Mount's Bay **C** | 54 | 50.03 N | 5.25 W |
| Mountsorrel | 54 | 52.44 N | 1.07 W |
| Mourdi, Dépression du ⊷⁷ | 88 | 18.10 N | 23.00 E |
| Mourne ⊷ | 60 | 54.49 N | 7.28 W |
| Mourne Beg ≃ | 60 | 54.41 N | 7.39 W |
| Mourne Mountains ⊼ | 52 | 54.10 N | 6.04 W |
| Mousa **I** | 58 | 60.00 N | 1.11 W |
| Mouscron | 68 | 50.44 N | 3.13 E |
| Moville | 60 | 55.11 N | 7.03 W |
| Moxos, Llanos de ⊷ | 100 | 15.00 S | 65.00 W |
| Moy ⊷ | 56 | 54.27 N | 6.42 W |
| Moy ≃ | 52 | 54.12 N | 9.08 W |
| Moycullen | 60 | 53.21 N | 9.09 W |
| Moyen Atlas ⊼ | 86 | 33.30 N | 5.00 W |
| Moyeuvre-Grande | 68 | 49.15 N | 6.02 E |
| Moyle ≃ | 52 | 55.10 N | 6.15 W |
| Moyo, Pulau **I** | 82 | 8.15 S | 117.34 E |
| Možajsk | 62 | 55.30 N | 36.01 E |
| Mozambique □¹ | 90 | 18.15 S | 35.00 E |
| Mozambique Channel **U** | 90 | 19.00 S | 41.00 E |
| Možga | 62 | 56.23 N | 52.17 E |
| Mozyr' | 76 | 52.03 N | 29.14 E |
| Mrągowo | 66 | 53.52 N | 21.19 E |
| Mtwara | 90 | 10.16 S | 40.11 E |
| Muar | 82 | 2.02 N | 102.34 E |
| Muasdale | 58 | 55.36 N | 5.41 W |
| Much Dewchurch | 54 | 51.59 N | 2.46 W |
| Muchinga Mountains ⊼ | 90 | 12.00 S | 31.45 E |
| Much Wenlock | 54 | 52.36 N | 2.34 W |
| Muck **I** | 58 | 56.50 N | 6.14 W |
| Muckle Roe **I** | 58a | 60.22 N | 1.27 W |
| Mucuri ⊷ | 100 | 18.05 S | 39.34 W |
| Mudanjiang | 80 | 44.35 N | 129.36 E |
| Mufulira | 90 | 12.33 S | 28.14 E |
| Mugla | 74 | 37.12 N | 28.22 E |
| Mugodžary ⊷¹ | 76 | 49.00 N | 58.40 E |
| Muhammad, Ra's ⊁ | 88 | 27.44 N | 34.15 E |
| Mühlacker | 66 | 48.57 N | 8.50 E |
| Mühldorf | 66 | 48.15 N | 12.32 E |
| Mühlhausen | 66 | 51.12 N | 10.27 E |
| Muick, Loch ⊜ | 58 | 56.55 N | 3.09 W |
| Muine Bheag | 60 | 52.41 N | 6.58 W |
| Muirdrum | 58 | 56.31 N | 2.42 W |
| Muirkirk | 58 | 55.31 N | 4.04 W |
| Muir of Ord | 58 | 57.31 N | 4.27 W |
| Muiron Islands **II** | 92 | 21.35 S | 114.20 E |
| Mukačevo | 66 | 48.27 N | 22.45 E |
| Mulben | 58 | 57.31 N | 3.06 W |
| Mulhacén ⊼ | 70 | 37.03 N | 3.19 W |
| Mülhouse | 68 | 47.45 N | 7.20 E |
| Mulkear ⊷ | 60 | 52.40 N | 8.20 W |
| Mull, Island of **I** | 58 | 56.27 N | 6.00 W |
| Mull, Sound of **U** | 58 | 56.30 N | 5.50 W |
| Mullaghareirk Mountains ⊼ | 60 | 52.20 N | 9.10 W |
| Mullaghcleevaun ⊼ | 60 | 53.06 N | 6.23 W |
| Mullaghmore ⊷ | 60 | 54.52 N | 6.50 W |
| Muller, Pegunungan ⊼ | 82 | 0.40 N | 113.50 E |
| Mullet Peninsula ⊁¹ | 60 | 54.12 N | 10.00 W |
| Mull Head ⊁, Scot., U.K. | 58 | 58.58 N | 2.43 W |
| Mull Head ⊁, Scot., U.K. | 58 | 59.23 N | 2.54 W |
| Mullinahone | 60 | 52.30 N | 7.30 W |
| Mullinavat | 60 | 52.22 N | 7.10 W |
| Mullingar | 60 | 53.32 N | 7.20 W |
| Mull of Galloway ⊁ | 56 | 54.38 N | 4.52 W |
| Multán | 84 | 30.11 N | 71.29 E |
| Mulen | 66 | 50.36 N | 8.01 W |
| Mumbles Head ⊁ | 54 | 51.35 N | 3.59 W |
| Mun ⊷ | 82 | 15.19 N | 105.30 E |
| Muna, Pulau **I** | 82 | 5.00 S | 122.30 E |
| München (Munich) | 66 | 48.08 N | 11.34 E |
| Münchberg | 66 | 50.11 N | 11.47 E |
| Müncheberg | 66 | 52.31 N | 14.08 E |
| Mundesley | 54 | 52.53 N | 1.26 E |
| Munku-Sardyk, Gora ⊼ | 78 | 51.45 N | 100.32 E |
| Munlochy | 58 | 57.32 N | 4.15 W |
| Münster, B.R.D. | 66 | 52.00 N | 10.05 E |
| Münster, B.R.D. | 66 | 51.57 N | 7.37 E |
| Munster □⁹ | 52 | 52.30 N | 8.20 W |
| Muonio | 64 | 67.57 N | 23.42 E |
| Muradiye | 74 | 39.00 N | 43.42 E |
| Muradnagar | 84 | 28.47 N | 77.22 E |
| Murakami | 80 | 38.14 N | 139.30 E |
| Murallón ⊼ | 102 | 49.48 S | 73.25 W |
| Murat | 68 | 45.07 N | 2.52 E |
| Murchison ⊷ | 92 | 27.42 S | 114.09 E |
| Murcia | 70 | 37.59 N | 1.07 W |
| Mürgab (Morghāb) ⊷ | 84 | 38.18 N | 61.12 E |
| Mürgab ⊷ | 78 | 38.10 N | 73.59 E |
| Murmansk | 62 | 68.58 N | 33.05 E |
| Murom | 62 | 55.34 N | 42.02 E |
| Muroran | 80 | 42.18 N | 140.59 E |
| Murray ⊷ | 92 | 35.22 S | 139.22 E |
| Murrumbidgee ⊷ | 92 | 34.43 S | 143.12 E |
| Murud, Gunong ⊼ | 82 | 3.52 N | 115.30 E |
| Murwara | 84 | 23.50 N | 80.24 E |
| Mürzzuschlag | 66 | 47.36 N | 15.41 E |
| Mus-Chaja, Gora ⊼ | 78 | 62.35 N | 140.50 E |
| Mushin | 86 | 6.31 N | 3.21 E |
| Musisahan ⊼ | 80 | 43.05 N | 104.56 E |
| Muskegon | 96 | 43.13 N | 86.16 W |
| Muskogee | 96 | 35.44 N | 95.21 W |
| Musselburgh | 58 | 55.57 N | 3.04 W |
| Mustafakemalpaşa | 74 | 40.03 N | 28.25 E |
| Muthill | 58 | 56.20 N | 3.50 W |
| Muzaffarnagar | 84 | 29.28 N | 77.42 E |
| Mweelrea ⊼ | 52 | 53.38 N | 9.50 W |
| Mweru, Lake ⊜ | 90 | 9.00 S | 28.45 E |
| Myanaung | 82 | 18.17 N | 95.19 E |
| Myaungmya | 82 | 16.36 N | 94.56 E |
| Mycielin | 66 | 52.30 N | 18.15 E |
| Myingyan | 82 | 21.28 N | 95.23 E |
| Myitkyina | 82 | 25.23 N | 97.24 E |
| Myjava | 66 | 48.45 N | 17.34 E |
| Mymensingh | 84 | 24.45 N | 90.24 E |
| Mynydd Bach ⊷² | 54 | 52.15 N | 4.05 W |
| Mynydd Eppynt ⊷ | 54 | 52.05 N | 3.30 W |

| Name | Page | Lat | Long |
|---|---|---|---|
| Mynydd Hiraethog ▲ | 54 | 53.05 N | 3.33 W |
| Mynydd Pencarreg ▲² | 54 | 52.04 N | 4.04 W |
| Mynydd Prescelly ▲ | 54 | 51.58 N | 4.42 W |
| Myski | 78 | 53.42 N | 87.48 E |
| Myślenice | 66 | 49.51 N | 19.56 E |
| Mysłowice | 66 | 50.15 N | 19.07 E |
| Mysore | 84 | 12.18 N | 76.39 E |
| Myszków | 66 | 50.36 N | 19.20 E |
| My-tho | 82 | 10.21 N | 106.21 E |
| Mytišci | 62 | 55.55 N | 37.46 E |
| Mzuzu | 90 | 11.27 S | 33.55 E |
| **N** | | | |
| Naas | 60 | 53.13 N | 6.39 W |
| Nabadwīp | 84 | 23.25 N | 88.22 E |
| Naberežnyje Čelny | 62 | 55.42 N | 52.19 E |
| Nabi Shu'ayb, Jabal an- ▲ | 84 | 15.18 N | 43.59 E |
| Nābulus | 84 | 32.13 N | 35.15 E |
| Nāchod | 66 | 50.25 N | 16.10 E |
| Nachodka | 78 | 42.48 N | 132.52 E |
| Nachvak Fiord C² | 94 | 59.03 N | 63.45 W |
| Nacka | 64 | 59.18 N | 18.10 E |
| Nadder ≈ | 54 | 51.03 N | 1.48 W |
| Nadiād | 84 | 22.42 N | 72.52 E |
| Nădlac | 74 | 46.10 N | 20.45 E |
| Nadym ≈ | 78 | 66.12 N | 72.00 E |
| Næstved | 64 | 55.14 N | 11.46 E |
| Naga | 82 | 13.37 N | 123.11 E |
| Nagano | 80 | 36.39 N | 138.11 E |
| Nagaoka | 80 | 37.27 N | 138.51 E |
| Nāgappattinam | 84 | 10.46 N | 79.50 E |
| Nagasaki | 80 | 32.48 N | 129.55 E |
| Nāgercoil | 84 | 8.11 N | 77.26 E |
| Nagles Mountains ▲ | 60 | 52.05 N | 8.30 W |
| Nagorsk | 62 | 59.18 N | 50.48 E |
| Nagoya | 80 | 35.10 N | 136.55 E |
| Nāgpur | 84 | 21.08 N | 79.04 E |
| Nagykanizsa | 74 | 46.27 N | 17.00 E |
| Nagykáta | 74 | 47.25 N | 19.45 E |
| Nagykörös | 74 | 47.02 N | 19.43 E |
| Naha | 80 | 26.13 N | 127.40 E |
| Nahuel Huapi, Lago ⬩ | 102 | 40.58 S | 71.30 W |
| Nailsea | 54 | 51.26 N | 2.43 W |
| Nailsworth | 54 | 51.42 N | 2.14 W |
| Nairn | 58 | 57.35 N | 3.53 W |
| Nairn ≈ | 58 | 57.35 N | 3.52 W |
| Nairobi | 90 | 1.17 S | 36.49 E |
| Najafābād | 84 | 32.37 N | 51.21 E |
| Najin | 80 | 42.15 N | 130.18 E |
| Najramdal Uul ▲ | 80 | 49.10 N | 87.52 W |
| Nakhon Pathom | 82 | 13.49 N | 100.03 E |
| Nakhon Ratchasima | 82 | 14.58 N | 102.07 E |
| Nakhon Sawan | 82 | 15.41 N | 100.07 E |
| Nakhon Si Thammarat | 82 | 8.26 N | 99.58 E |
| Nakło nad Notecia | 66 | 53.08 N | 17.35 E |
| Nakskov | 64 | 54.50 N | 11.09 E |
| Nakuru | 90 | 0.17 S | 36.04 E |
| Nal'čik | 76 | 43.29 N | 43.37 E |
| Namak, Daryācheh-ye ⬩ | 84 | 34.45 N | 51.36 E |
| Namangan | 76 | 41.00 N | 71.40 E |
| Namib Desert ≈² | 90 | 23.00 S | 15.00 E |
| Namibia □² | 90 | 22.00 S | 17.00 E |
| Namoi ≈ | 92 | 30.00 S | 148.07 E |
| Namp'o | 80 | 38.45 N | 125.23 E |
| Nampula | 90 | 15.07 S | 39.15 E |
| Namsos | 62 | 64.29 N | 11.30 E |
| Namuchabawashan ▲ | 80 | 29.38 N | 95.04 E |
| Namuhu | 80 | 30.42 N | 90.30 E |
| Namur | 66 | 50.28 N | 4.52 E |
| Namysłów | 66 | 51.05 N | 17.42 E |
| Nan ≈ | 82 | 15.42 N | 100.09 E |
| Nanaimo | 94 | 49.10 N | 123.56 W |
| Nanchang | 80 | 28.41 N | 115.53 E |
| Nanchong | 80 | 30.48 N | 106.04 E |
| Nancy | 68 | 48.41 N | 6.12 E |
| Nanda Devi ▲ | 84 | 30.23 N | 79.59 E |
| Nānded | 84 | 19.09 N | 77.20 E |
| N'andoma | 62 | 61.40 N | 40.12 E |
| Nanduhe ≈ | 80 | 20.04 N | 110.22 E |
| Nanga Parbat ▲ | 84 | 35.14 N | 74.36 E |
| Nanjing | 80 | 32.03 N | 118.47 E |
| Nanling | 80 | 25.00 N | 112.00 E |
| Nanning | 80 | 22.48 N | 108.20 E |
| Nanping | 80 | 26.38 N | 118.10 E |
| Nansei-shotō (Ryukyu Islands) II | 80 | 26.30 N | 128.00 E |
| Nantais, Lac ⬩ | 94 | 60.59 N | 74.00 W |
| Nant Bran ≈ | 54 | 51.57 N | 3.28 W |
| Nantes | 68 | 47.13 N | 1.33 W |
| Nantong | 80 | 32.02 N | 120.53 E |
| Nantucket Island I | 96 | 41.16 N | 70.03 W |
| Nantwich | 56 | 53.04 N | 2.32 W |
| Nant-y-moch Reservoir ⬩¹ | 54 | 52.27 N | 3.50 W |
| Nanuque | 100 | 17.50 S | 40.21 W |
| Nanxiong | 80 | 25.10 N | 114.20 E |
| Nanyang | 80 | 33.00 N | 112.32 E |
| Nao, Cabo de la ➤ | 70 | 38.44 N | 0.14 E |
| Náousa | 74 | 40.37 N | 22.05 E |
| Napier | 93a | 39.29 S | 176.55 E |
| Napo ≈ | 100 | 3.20 S | 72.40 W |
| Napoli (Naples) | 72 | 40.51 N | 14.17 E |
| Napton on the Hill | 54 | 52.15 N | 1.24 W |
| Nar ≈ | 54 | 52.45 N | 0.24 E |
| Nara | 80 | 34.41 N | 135.50 E |
| Nārāyanganj | 84 | 23.37 N | 90.30 E |
| Narberth | 54 | 51.48 N | 4.45 W |
| Narbonne | 68 | 43.11 N | 3.00 E |
| Nardò | 72 | 40.11 N | 18.02 E |
| Narew ≈ | 66 | 52.26 N | 20.42 E |
| Narjan-Mar | 62 | 67.39 N | 53.00 E |
| Narmada ≈ | 84 | 21.38 N | 72.36 E |
| Narni | 72 | 42.31 N | 12.31 E |
| Naro | 72 | 37.17 N | 13.48 E |
| Narodnaja, Gora ▲ | 62 | 65.04 N | 60.09 E |
| Naro-Fominsk | 62 | 55.23 N | 36.43 E |
| Narva | 62 | 59.23 N | 28.12 E |
| Narvik | 62 | 68.26 N | 17.25 E |
| Naryn | 76 | 41.26 N | 75.59 E |
| Naryn ≈ | 76 | 40.54 N | 71.45 E |
| Naseby | 54 | 52.25 N | 0.58 W |
| Nashua | 96 | 42.45 N | 71.27 W |
| Nashville | 96 | 36.09 N | 86.48 W |
| Nāsik | 84 | 19.59 N | 73.47 E |
| Naskaupi ≈ | 94 | 53.45 N | 60.50 W |
| Nass ≈ | 94 | 55.00 N | 129.50 W |
| Nassau | 98 | 25.05 N | 77.21 W |
| Nasser, Lake ⬩¹ | 88 | 22.40 N | 32.00 E |
| Nässjö | 64 | 57.39 N | 14.41 E |
| Nastapoca ≈ | 94 | 56.55 N | 76.33 W |
| Nastapoka Islands II | 94 | 57.00 N | 76.50 W |
| Natal | 100 | 5.47 S | 35.13 W |
| Natashquan ≈ | 94 | 50.06 N | 61.49 W |
| Natron, Lake ⬩ | 90 | 2.25 S | 36.00 E |
| Natuna Besar I | 82 | 4.00 N | 108.15 E |
| Naturaliste, Cape ➤ | 92 | 33.32 S | 115.01 E |
| Naturaliste Channel ⋃ | 92 | 25.25 S | 113.00 E |
| Nauen | 66 | 52.36 N | 12.52 E |
| Naumburg | 66 | 51.09 N | 11.48 E |
| Naust | 58 | 57.45 N | 5.37 W |
| Navarin, Mys ➤ | 78 | 62.16 N | 179.10 E |
| Navarino, Isla I | 102 | 55.05 S | 67.40 W |
| Naver ≈ | 58 | 58.32 N | 4.15 W |
| Naver, Loch ⬩ | 58 | 58.17 N | 4.22 W |
| Navoi | 76 | 40.15 N | 65.15 E |
| Navojoa | 98 | 27.06 N | 109.26 W |
| Návpaktos | 74 | 38.24 N | 21.50 E |
| Návplion | 74 | 37.34 N | 22.48 E |
| Navsāri | 84 | 20.57 N | 72.56 E |
| Nawābshāh | 84 | 26.15 N | 68.25 E |
| Naxos I | 74 | 37.02 N | 25.35 E |
| Nayland | 54 | 51.58 N | 0.52 E |
| Nazareth ➤ | 84 | 32.42 N | 35.18 E |
| Naze | 80 | 28.23 N | 129.30 E |
| Nazilli | 74 | 37.55 N | 28.21 E |
| Ndjamena (Fort-Lamy) | 88 | 12.07 N | 15.03 E |
| Ndola | 90 | 12.58 S | 28.38 E |
| Neagh, Lough ⬩ | 60 | 54.38 N | 6.24 W |
| Neale, Lake ⬩ | 92 | 24.22 S | 130.00 E |
| Neath | 54 | 51.40 N | 3.48 W |
| Neath ≈ | 54 | 51.37 N | 3.50 W |
| Nebine Creek ≈ | 92 | 29.07 S | 146.56 E |
| Nebit-Dag | 76 | 39.30 N | 54.22 E |
| Nebraska □³ | 96 | 41.30 N | 100.00 W |
| Nechako ≈ | 94 | 53.56 N | 122.42 W |
| Neckar ≈ | 66 | 49.12 N | 9.13 E |
| Neckarsulm | 66 | 49.11 N | 9.14 E |
| Needham Market | 54 | 52.09 N | 1.03 E |
| Nefern ≈ | 54 | 52.02 N | 4.50 W |
| Nefyn | 54 | 52.57 N | 4.31 W |
| Negombo | 84 | 7.13 N | 79.50 E |
| Negra, Cordillera ▲ | 100 | 9.25 S | 77.40 W |
| Negra, Punta ➤ | 100 | 6.06 S | 81.09 W |
| Negro ≈, Arg. | 102 | 41.02 S | 62.47 W |
| Negro ≈, Bol. | 100 | 14.11 S | 63.07 W |
| Negro ≈, S.A. | 100 | 3.08 S | 59.55 W |
| Negros I | 82 | 10.00 N | 123.00 E |
| Neheim-Hüsten | 66 | 51.27 N | 7.57 E |
| Neiges, Piton des ▲ | 90 | 21.05 S | 55.29 E |
| Neijiang | 80 | 29.35 N | 105.03 E |
| Neilston | 58 | 55.47 N | 4.27 W |
| Neiva | 100 | 2.56 N | 75.18 W |
| Neja | 62 | 58.18 N | 43.54 E |
| Nelidovo | 62 | 56.13 N | 32.46 E |
| Nellore | 84 | 14.26 N | 79.59 E |
| Nelson, N.Z. | 93a | 41.17 S | 173.17 E |
| Nelson, Eng., U.K. | 56 | 53.51 N | 2.13 W |
| Nelson ≈ | 94 | 57.04 N | 92.30 W |
| Nelson, Cape ➤ | 92 | 38.26 S | 141.33 E |
| Nelspruit | 90 | 25.30 S | 30.58 E |
| Neman | 62 | 55.02 N | 22.02 E |
| Neman (Nemunas) ≈ | 76 | 55.18 N | 21.23 E |
| Nemunas (Neman) ≈ | 76 | 55.18 N | 21.23 E |
| Nemuro | 80 | 43.20 N | 145.35 E |
| Nenagh | 60 | 52.52 N | 8.12 W |
| Nenagh ≈ | 60 | 52.56 N | 8.17 W |
| Nene ≈ | 54 | 52.48 N | 0.13 E |
| Nepa ≈ | 78 | 59.16 N | 108.16 E |
| Nepal (Nepāl) □¹ | 84 | 28.00 N | 84.00 E |
| Nephin ▲ | 60 | 54.01 N | 9.22 W |
| Nephin Beg Range ▲ | 60 | 54.00 N | 9.35 W |
| Nerastro, Sarīr ≈² | 88 | 24.20 N | 20.37 E |
| Nerča ≈ | 78 | 51.56 N | 116.40 E |
| Nerechta | 62 | 57.28 N | 40.34 E |
| Nerva | 70 | 37.42 N | 6.32 W |
| Ness, Loch ⬩ | 58 | 57.15 N | 4.30 W |
| Nesselrode, Mount ▲ | 94 | 58.58 N | 134.18 W |
| Nesterov | 66 | 54.38 N | 22.34 E |
| Neston | 56 | 53.18 N | 3.04 W |
| Netanya | 84 | 32.20 N | 34.51 E |
| Nethan ≈ | 58 | 55.42 N | 3.52 W |
| Netherlands □¹ | 52 | 52.15 N | 5.30 E |
| Netherlands Antilles □² | 98 | 12.15 N | 69.00 W |
| Nethy Bridge | 58 | 57.16 N | 3.38 W |
| Nethy Marsh | 58 | 50.53 N | 1.27 W |
| Nettilling Fiord C² | 94 | 66.02 N | 68.12 W |
| Nettilling Lake ⬩ | 94 | 66.30 N | 70.40 W |
| Nettlebed | 54 | 51.35 N | 1.00 W |
| Netturno | 72 | 41.27 N | 12.39 E |
| Neubrandenburg | 66 | 53.33 N | 13.15 E |
| Neuburg an der Donau | 66 | 48.44 N | 11.11 E |
| Neuchâtel | 68 | 46.59 N | 6.56 E |
| Neu-Isenburg | 66 | 50.03 N | 8.41 E |
| Neumarkt in der Oberpfalz | 66 | 49.16 N | 11.28 E |
| Neumünster | 66 | 54.04 N | 9.59 E |
| Neunkirchen | 66 | 47.43 N | 16.05 E |
| Neunkirchen / saar | 66 | 49.20 N | 7.10 E |
| Neuquén | 102 | 38.57 S | 68.00 W |
| Neuruppin | 66 | 52.55 N | 12.48 E |
| Neuss | 66 | 51.12 N | 6.41 E |
| Neustadt [an aisch] | 66 | 49.34 N | 10.37 E |
| Neustadt an der Weinstrasse | 66 | 49.21 N | 8.08 E |
| Neustadt in Holstein | 66 | 54.06 N | 10.48 E |
| Neustrelitz | 66 | 53.21 N | 13.04 E |
| Neu-Ulm | 66 | 48.23 N | 10.01 E |
| Neuwied | 66 | 50.25 N | 7.27 E |
| Nevada □³ | 96 | 39.00 N | 117.00 W |
| Nevada, Sierra ▲ | 96 | 38.00 N | 119.15 W |
| Nevado, Cerro ▲ | 102 | 35.35 S | 68.30 W |
| Nevel' | 62 | 56.02 N | 29.55 E |
| Nevinnomyssk | 76 | 44.38 N | 41.56 E |
| Nevis I | 98 | 17.10 N | 62.34 W |
| Nevis, Ben ▲ | 58 | 56.50 N | 5.00 W |
| Nevis, Loch ⬩ | 58 | 57.01 N | 5.43 W |
| New Abbey | 58 | 54.59 N | 3.38 W |
| New Alresford | 54 | 51.06 N | 1.10 W |
| New Amsterdam | 100 | 6.15 N | 57.31 W |
| Newark, N.J., U.S. | 96 | 40.44 N | 74.10 W |
| Newark, Ohio, U.S. | 96 | 40.04 N | 82.24 W |
| Newark-upon-Trent | 56 | 53.05 N | 0.49 W |
| New Bedford | 96 | 41.38 N | 70.56 W |
| New Bern | 96 | 35.07 N | 77.03 W |
| Newbiggin-by-the-Sea | 56 | 55.11 N | 1.30 W |
| Newborough | 54 | 53.09 N | 4.22 W |
| Newbridge on Wye | 54 | 52.13 N | 3.27 W |
| New Brunswick □⁴ | 94 | 46.30 N | 66.15 W |
| Newburgh, Scot., U.K. | 58 | 57.18 N | 2.00 W |
| Newburgh, Scot., U.K. | 58 | 56.20 N | 3.15 W |
| Newburn | 56 | 54.59 N | 1.43 W |
| Newbury | 54 | 51.25 N | 1.20 W |
| Newby | 54 | 54.20 N | 0.28 W |
| Newby Bridge | 56 | 54.16 N | 2.58 W |
| Newcastle, Austl. | 92 | 32.56 S | 151.46 E |
| Newcastle, Eire | 60 | 52.16 N | 7.48 W |
| Newcastle, S. Afr. | 90 | 27.49 S | 29.55 E |
| Newcastle, Eng., U.K. | 54 | 52.26 N | 3.06 W |
| Newcastle, N. Ire., U.K. | 60 | 54.12 N | 5.54 W |
| Newcastle Emlyn | 54 | 52.02 N | 4.28 W |
| Newcastle, Ariz., U.S. | 96 | 41.10 N | 104.11 W |
| Newcastle, Pa., U.S. | 96 | 55.11 N | 2.49 W |
| Newcastleton | 58 | 55.11 N | 2.49 W |
| Newcastle-under-Lyme | 56 | 53.00 N | 2.14 W |
| Newcastle upon Tyne | 56 | 54.59 N | 1.35 W |
| Newcastle West | 60 | 52.27 N | 9.03 W |
| Newcestown | 60 | 51.47 N | 8.51 W |
| Newchurch | 54 | 52.09 N | 3.08 W |
| New Cumnock | 58 | 55.24 N | 4.12 W |
| New Deer | 58 | 57.30 N | 2.12 W |
| New Delhi | 84 | 28.36 N | 77.15 E |
| Newent | 54 | 51.56 N | 2.24 W |
| New Forest ≈ | 54 | 50.53 N | 1.35 W |
| Newfoundland □⁴ | 94 | 52.00 N | 56.00 W |
| Newfoundland I | 94 | 48.30 N | 56.00 W |
| New Galloway | 58 | 55.05 N | 4.10 W |
| New Georgia I | 94 | 8.15 S | 157.30 E |
| New Glasgow | 94 | 45.35 N | 62.39 W |
| Newhall | 54 | 52.48 N | 1.34 W |
| New Hampshire □³ | 96 | 43.35 N | 71.40 W |
| New Haven, Conn., U.S. | 96 | 41.18 N | 72.56 W |
| New Hebrides II | 8 | 16.00 S | 167.00 E |
| New Holland | 56 | 53.42 N | 0.22 W |
| New Inn | 54 | 51.50 N | 1.08 E |
| New London | 96 | 41.21 N | 72.07 W |
| Newlyn | 54 | 50.06 N | 5.33 W |
| Newlyn East | 54 | 50.22 N | 5.03 W |
| Newmachar | 58 | 57.16 N | 2.11 W |
| Newmains | 58 | 55.47 N | 3.53 W |
| Newmarket, Eire | 60 | 52.13 N | 9.00 W |
| Newmarket, Eng., U.K. | 54 | 52.15 N | 0.25 E |
| Newmarket-on-Fergus | 60 | 52.45 N | 8.53 W |
| New Mexico □³ | 96 | 34.30 N | 106.00 W |
| New Mills | 56 | 53.23 N | 2.00 W |
| Newmilns | 58 | 55.37 N | 4.20 W |
| New Milton | 54 | 50.44 N | 1.40 W |
| Newnham | 54 | 51.49 N | 2.27 W |
| New Orleans | 96 | 29.58 N | 90.07 W |
| Newport, Eire | 60 | 53.53 N | 9.34 W |
| Newport, Eire | 60 | 52.42 N | 8.24 W |
| Newport, Eng., U.K. | 54 | 52.47 N | 2.22 W |
| Newport, Eng., U.K. | 54 | 50.42 N | 1.18 W |
| Newport, Wales, U.K. | 54 | 51.35 N | 3.00 W |
| Newport, Wales, U.K. | 54 | 52.01 N | 4.51 W |
| Newport, R.I., U.S. | 96 | 41.13 N | 71.18 W |
| Newport News | 96 | 37.04 N | 76.28 W |
| Newport-on-Tay | 58 | 56.26 N | 2.55 W |
| Newport Pagnell | 54 | 52.05 N | 0.44 W |
| New Providence I | 98 | 25.02 N | 77.24 W |
| Newquay, Eng., U.K. | 54 | 50.25 N | 5.05 W |
| New Quay, Wales, U.K. | 54 | 52.13 N | 4.22 W |
| New Romney | 54 | 50.59 N | 0.57 E |
| New Ross | 60 | 52.24 N | 6.56 W |
| New Rossington | 56 | 53.29 N | 1.04 W |
| Newton | 56 | 54.11 N | 6.20 W |
| Newton Abbot | 54 | 50.32 N | 3.36 W |
| Newton Arlosh | 56 | 54.53 N | 3.15 W |
| Newton Aycliffe | 54 | 54.36 N | 1.32 W |
| Newton Ferrers | 54 | 50.18 N | 4.02 W |
| Newton Flotman | 54 | 52.32 N | 1.16 E |
| Newtongrange | 58 | 55.52 N | 3.04 W |
| Newton-le-Willows | 56 | 53.28 N | 2.37 W |
| Newtonmore | 58 | 57.04 N | 4.08 W |
| Newton Stewart | 58 | 54.58 N | 4.29 W |
| Newtown | 54 | 52.32 N | 3.19 W |
| Newtownabbey | 60 | 54.36 N | 5.54 W |
| Newtownards | 60 | 54.36 N | 5.41 W |
| Newtownbutler | 60 | 54.12 N | 7.23 W |
| Newtown Crommelin | 60 | 54.59 N | 6.13 W |
| Newtown Forbes | 60 | 53.46 N | 7.50 W |
| Newtownhamilton | 60 | 54.11 N | 6.35 W |
| Newtown Saint Boswells | 58 | 55.34 N | 2.40 W |
| Newtownsteward | 60 | 54.43 N | 7.24 W |
| New Tredegar | 54 | 51.43 N | 3.14 W |
| New Westminster | 94 | 49.12 N | 122.55 W |
| New York | 96 | 40.43 N | 74.01 W |
| New York □³ | 96 | 43.00 N | 75.00 W |
| New Zealand □¹ | 93a | 41.00 S | 174.00 E |
| Neyland | 54 | 51.43 N | 4.57 W |
| Nežin | 76 | 51.03 N | 31.54 E |
| Ngami, Lake ⬩ | 90 | 20.37 S | 22.40 E |
| Ngoko ≈ | 90 | 1.40 N | 16.03 E |
| Ngulu I¹ | 82 | 8.27 N | 137.29 E |
| Nguru | 88 | 12.52 N | 10.27 E |
| Nhamundá ≈ | 100 | 2.12 S | 56.41 W |
| Nha-trang | 82 | 12.15 N | 109.11 E |
| Niagara Falls, Ont., Can. | 96 | 58.58 N | 134.18 W |
| Niagara Falls, N.Y., U.S. | 96 | 43.06 N | 79.04 W |
| Niamey | 88 | 13.31 N | 2.07 E |
| Nias, Pulau I | 82 | 1.05 N | 97.35 E |
| Nica ≈ | 82 | 53.29 N | 64.33 E |
| Nicaragua □¹ | 98 | 13.00 N | 85.00 W |
| Nicaragua, Lago de ⬩ | 98 | 11.30 N | 85.30 W |
| Nicastro (Lamezia Terme) | 72 | 38.59 N | 16.20 E |
| Nice | 68 | 43.42 N | 7.15 E |
| Nicholson ≈ | 92 | 17.31 S | 139.36 E |
| Nicobar Islands II | 82 | 8.00 N | 93.30 E |
| Nicosia | 72 | 37.45 N | 14.24 E |
| Nicoya, Península de ➤¹ | 98 | 10.00 N | 85.25 W |
| Nidd ≈ | 56 | 54.01 N | 1.12 W |
| Nidzica | 66 | 53.22 N | 20.26 E |
| Nienburg | 66 | 52.38 N | 9.13 E |
| Nieŕ ≈ | 66 | 52.17 N | 7.48 W |
| Nièvre □⁵ | 68 | 16.00 N | 8.00 E |
| Nigde | 76 | 5.33 N | 6.33 E |
| Niger □¹ | 88 | 16.00 N | 8.00 E |
| Niger ≈ | 88 | 5.33 N | 6.33 E |
| Nigeria □¹ | 88 | 10.00 N | 8.00 E |
| Nigrita | 74 | 40.55 N | 23.30 E |
| Niigata | 80 | 37.55 N | 139.03 E |
| Niihau I | 96 | 21.55 N | 160.10 W |
| Nijmegen | 66 | 51.50 N | 5.50 E |
| Nikel' | 62 | 69.24 N | 30.12 E |
| Nikolajev | 76 | 46.58 N | 32.00 E |
| Nikolajevsk-na-Amure | 78 | 53.08 N | 140.44 E |
| Nikol'sk | 62 | 59.32 N | 45.05 E |
| Nikopol' | 76 | 47.35 N | 34.25 E |
| Nile (Nahr an-Nīl) ≈ | 88 | 30.10 N | 31.06 E |
| Nimba, Mont ▲ | 88 | 7.37 N | 8.25 W |
| Nimba Mountains ▲ | 88 | 7.30 N | 8.30 W |
| Nîmes | 68 | 43.50 N | 4.21 E |
| Nina Bang Lake ⬩ | 94 | 70.51 N | 79.07 W |
| Nine Degree Channel ⋃ | 84 | 9.00 N | 73.00 E |
| Ninety Mile Beach ⋅ | 92 | 38.13 S | 147.23 E |
| Ninfield | 54 | 50.53 N | 0.25 E |
| Ningbo | 80 | 29.52 N | 121.31 E |
| Ninove | 66 | 50.50 N | 4.01 E |
| Niobrara ≈ | 96 | 42.45 N | 98.00 W |
| Niort | 68 | 46.19 N | 0.27 W |
| Nipigon, Lake ⬩ | 94 | 49.50 N | 88.30 W |
| Nipissing, Lake ⬩ | 94 | 46.17 N | 80.00 W |
| Niš | 74 | 43.19 N | 21.54 E |
| Niscemi | 72 | 37.08 N | 14.24 E |
| Nisling ≈ | 94 | 62.27 N | 139.30 W |
| Niterói | 100 | 22.53 S | 43.07 W |
| Nith ≈ | 58 | 55.00 N | 3.35 W |
| Nithsdale ∨ | 58 | 55.14 N | 3.46 W |
| Niton | 54 | 50.35 N | 1.16 W |
| Nitra | 66 | 48.20 N | 18.05 E |
| Nivelles (Nijvel) | 66 | 50.36 N | 4.20 E |
| Nizāmābād | 84 | 18.40 N | 78.06 E |
| Nizānkovici | 66 | 49.40 N | 22.47 E |
| Nižn'aja Omra | 62 | 62.46 N | 55.46 E |
| Nižn'aja Pojma | 78 | 56.11 N | 97.13 E |
| Nižn'aja Tunguska ≈ | 78 | 65.48 N | 88.04 E |
| Niznekamsk | 62 | 55.38 N | 51.58 E |
| Nizneudinsk | 78 | 54.54 N | 99.03 E |
| Nižnij Tagil | 76 | 57.55 N | 59.57 E |
| Nobeoka | 80 | 32.35 N | 131.40 E |
| Nocera [Inferiore] | 72 | 40.44 N | 14.38 E |
| Nogales, Méx. | 98 | 31.20 N | 110.56 W |
| Nogales, Ariz., U.S. | 96 | 31.20 N | 110.56 W |
| Nogent-le-Rotrou | 68 | 48.19 N | 0.50 E |
| Noginsk | 62 | 55.51 N | 38.27 E |
| Nogoa ≈ | 92 | 23.33 S | 148.32 E |
| Noirmoutier, Île de I | 68 | 47.00 N | 2.15 W |
| Nokia | 64 | 61.28 N | 23.30 E |
| Nola | 72 | 57.33 N | 14.33 E |
| Nolinsk | 62 | 57.33 N | 49.57 E |
| Noname Lake ⬩ | 94 | 75.00 N | 142.00 E |
| Nong'an | 80 | 44.25 N | 125.10 E |
| Nong Khai | 82 | 17.52 N | 102.44 E |
| Nootka Island I | 94 | 49.32 N | 126.42 W |
| Norden | 66 | 53.36 N | 7.12 E |
| Nordenham | 66 | 53.29 N | 8.29 E |
| Norderney I | 66 | 53.42 N | 7.15 E |
| Nordhausen | 66 | 51.30 N | 10.47 E |
| Nordhorn | 66 | 52.27 N | 7.05 E |
| Nordkapp ➤ | 62 | 71.11 N | 25.48 E |
| Nordre Strømfjord C² | 94 | 67.45 N | 52.30 W |
| Nore ≈ | 60 | 52.25 N | 6.58 W |
| Norfolk | 96 | 36.50 N | 76.14 W |
| Norfolk □⁶ | 54 | 52.40 N | 1.00 E |
| Norfolk Broads ⬩¹ | 54 | 52.42 N | 1.30 E |
| Norfolk Island I | 8 | 29.02 S | 167.57 E |
| Norham | 56 | 55.43 N | 2.10 W |
| Noril'sk | 78 | 69.20 N | 88.06 E |
| Norman ≈ | 92 | 17.28 S | 140.49 E |
| Noranda | 94 | 48.15 N | 79.01 W |
| Norrbottens □⁵ | 62 | 67.00 N | 19.00 E |
| Norresundby | 64 | 57.04 N | 9.56 E |
| Norrköping | 64 | 58.36 N | 16.11 E |
| Norrtälje | 64 | 59.46 N | 18.42 E |
| Norte, Canal do ⋃ | 100 | 0.10 N | 50.30 W |
| Norte, Serra do ▲ | 100 | 11.00 S | 59.00 W |
| North ≈ | 94 | 57.20 N | 109.55 W |
| North, Cape ➤² | 94 | 47.02 N | 60.25 W |
| Northallerton | 56 | 54.20 N | 1.26 W |
| Northam | 54 | 51.02 N | 4.12 W |
| North America ⬩¹ | 8 | 45.00 N | 100.00 W |
| Northampton | 54 | 52.14 N | 0.54 W |
| Northamptonshire □⁶ | 52 | 52.20 N | 0.50 W |
| North Andaman I | 84 | 13.15 N | 92.55 E |
| North Aulatsivik Island I | 94 | 59.50 N | 64.00 W |
| North Bay | 94 | 46.19 N | 79.28 W |
| North Berwick | 58 | 56.04 N | 2.44 W |
| North Caribou Lake ⬩ | | | |
| North Carolina □³ | 96 | 35.30 N | 80.00 W |
| North Channel ⋃, Ont., Can. | 94 | 46.02 N | 82.50 W |
| North Channel ⋃, U.K. | 52 | 55.10 N | 5.40 W |
| North Dakota □³ | 96 | 47.30 N | 100.15 W |
| North Dorset Downs ⬩² | 54 | 50.47 N | 2.30 W |
| North Down Cbangor | 60 | 54.40 N | 5.40 W |
| North Downs ≈² | 54 | 51.20 N | 0.10 E |
| Northeim | 66 | 51.42 N | 10.00 E |
| Northern Indian Lake ⬩ | | | |
| Northern Ireland □⁸ | 52 | 54.40 N | 6.45 W |
| North Esk ≈, Scot., U.K. | | | |
| North Esk ≈, Scot., U.K. | 58 | 55.54 N | 3.04 W |
| Northfleet | 54 | 51.27 N | 0.21 E |
| North Foreland ➤ | 54 | 51.23 N | 1.27 E |
| North Frisian Islands II | | | |
| North Henik Lake ⬩ | 94 | 61.45 N | 97.40 W |
| North Hill | 54 | 50.34 N | 4.25 W |
| North Hinksey | 54 | 51.45 N | 1.16 W |
| North Island I | 93a | 39.00 S | 176.00 E |
| Northleach | 54 | 51.51 N | 1.50 W |
| North Petherton | 54 | 51.06 N | 3.01 W |
| North Platte | 96 | 41.15 N | 100.45 W |
| North Queensferry | 58 | 56.01 N | 3.25 W |
| North Ronaldsay I | 52 | 59.23 N | 2.30 W |
| North Ronaldsay Firth ⋃ | 58 | 59.20 N | 2.25 W |
| North Saskatchewan ≈ | | | |
| North Sea ≈² | 52 | 55.20 N | 3.00 E |
| North Seaton Colliery | 56 | 55.11 N | 1.32 W |
| North Somercotes | 56 | 53.28 N | 0.08 E |
| North Sound ⋃, Eire | 60 | 53.11 N | 9.43 W |
| North Sound ⋃, Scot., U.K. | 58 | 59.18 N | 2.45 W |
| North Spicer Island I | | | |
| North Stradbroke Island I | 92 | 27.35 S | 153.28 E |
| North Sunderland | 56 | 55.35 N | 1.39 W |
| North Tawton | 54 | 50.48 N | 3.53 W |
| North Thompson ≈ | 94 | 50.41 N | 120.21 W |
| North Tidworth | 54 | 51.16 N | 1.40 W |
| North Tolsta | 58 | 58.20 N | 6.13 W |
| North Tyne ≈ | 56 | 54.59 N | 2.08 W |
| North Uist I | 52 | 57.37 N | 7.22 W |
| Northumberland □⁶ | 52 | 55.15 N | 2.05 W |
| Northumberland Isles II | | | |
| Northumberland Strait ⋃ | 92 | 21.40 S | 150.00 E |
| Northwall | 58 | 59.16 N | 2.17 W |
| North Walsham | 58 | 52.50 N | 1.24 E |
| North Weald Bassett | 54 | 51.43 N | 0.10 E |
| North West Cape ➤ | 92 | 21.45 S | 114.10 E |
| Northwest Territories □⁴ | 94 | 70.00 N | 100.00 W |
| Northwich | 56 | 53.16 N | 2.32 W |
| Northwold | 54 | 52.33 N | 0.35 E |
| North York Moors ⬩⁸ | | | |
| North Yorkshire □⁶ | 56 | 54.15 N | 1.30 W |
| Norton | 56 | 54.09 N | 0.47 W |
| Norton Canes | 54 | 52.41 N | 1.59 W |
| Norton Fitzwarren | 54 | 51.02 N | 3.09 W |
| Norway □¹ | 62 | 62.00 N | 10.00 E |
| Norway Bay C | 94 | 71.08 N | 104.35 W |
| Norwegian Sea ≈² | 50 | 70.00 N | 2.00 E |
| Norwich | 54 | 52.38 N | 1.18 E |
| Noss, Isle of I | 58a | 60.09 N | 1.01 W |
| Noss Head ➤ | 58 | 58.28 N | 3.04 W |
| Nossi-Bé I | 90 | 13.20 S | 48.15 E |
| Nossob (Nossop) ≈ | 90 | 26.55 S | 20.37 E |
| Noto | 72 | 36.53 N | 15.05 E |
| Noto-hantō ➤¹ | 80 | 37.20 N | 137.00 E |
| Notre Dame, Monts ▲ | 94 | 48.10 N | 68.00 W |
| Notre Dame Bay C | 94 | 49.45 N | 55.15 W |
| Nottaway ≈ | 94 | 51.22 N | 79.55 W |
| Nottingham | 56 | 52.58 N | 1.10 W |
| Nottingham Island I | 94 | 63.20 N | 77.55 W |
| Nottinghamshire □⁶ | 52 | 53.00 N | 1.00 W |
| Nouadhibou | 88 | 20.54 N | 17.04 W |
| Nouakchott | 88 | 18.06 N | 15.57 W |
| Nouveau-Québec, Cratère du ≈⁶ | 94 | 61.17 N | 73.40 W |
| Nouvelle-France, Cap de ➤ | 94 | 62.27 N | 73.42 W |
| Nova Friburgo | 100 | 22.16 S | 42.32 W |
| Novaja Ladoga | 62 | 60.05 N | 32.16 E |
| Novaja Sibir', Ostrov I | | | |
| Novaja Zeml'a II | 78 | 75.00 N | 149.00 E |
| Nova Lisboa | 78 | 74.00 N | 57.00 E |
| Nova Scotia □⁴ | 94 | 45.00 N | 63.00 W |
| Nova Zagora | 74 | 42.29 N | 26.01 E |
| Novelda | 70 | 38.23 N | 0.46 W |
| Nové Mesto nad Váhom | 66 | 48.46 N | 17.49 E |
| Nové Zámky | 66 | 47.59 N | 18.11 E |
| Novgorod | 62 | 58.31 N | 31.17 E |
| Novi Bečej | 74 | 45.36 N | 20.08 E |
| Novi Ligure | 72 | 44.46 N | 8.47 E |
| Novi Pazar, Blg. | 74 | 43.21 N | 27.12 E |
| Novi Pazar, Jugo. | 74 | 43.08 N | 20.31 E |
| Novi Sad | 74 | 45.15 N | 19.50 E |
| Novoaleksandrovsk | 76 | 45.30 N | 41.14 E |
| Novočeboksarsk | 62 | 56.08 N | 47.29 E |
| Novočerkassk | 76 | 47.25 N | 40.06 E |
| Novokazalinsk | 76 | 45.50 N | 62.10 E |
| Novokujbyševsk | 62 | 53.07 N | 49.58 E |
| Novokuzneck | 78 | 53.45 N | 87.06 E |
| Novomoskovsk | 62 | 54.05 N | 38.13 E |
| Novorossijsk | 76 | 44.45 N | 37.45 E |
| Novošachtinsk | 76 | 47.47 N | 39.56 E |
| Novosibirsk | 78 | 55.02 N | 82.55 E |
| Novosibirskije Ostrova II | 78 | 75.00 N | 142.00 E |
| Novosibirskoje Vodochranilišče ⬩¹ | 78 | 54.30 N | 82.30 E |
| Novosokol'niki | 62 | 56.21 N | 30.10 E |
| Novotroick | 76 | 51.12 N | 58.20 E |
| Novov'atsk | 62 | 58.29 N | 49.44 E |
| Novy Bohumín | 66 | 49.56 N | 18.20 E |
| Nový Jičín | 66 | 49.36 N | 18.00 E |
| Nova Ruda | 66 | 50.34 N | 16.30 E |
| Nowa Sól (Neusalz) | 66 | 51.48 N | 15.44 E |
| Nowgong | 84 | 26.21 N | 92.42 E |
| Nowshak ▲ | 84 | 36.26 N | 71.50 E |
| Nowy Dwór Mazowiecki | 66 | 52.26 N | 20.43 E |
| Nowy Sacz | 66 | 49.38 N | 20.42 E |
| Nowy Targ | 66 | 49.29 N | 20.02 E |
| Noyon | 68 | 49.35 N | 3.00 E |
| Ntem ≈ | 88 | 2.15 N | 9.45 E |
| Nūbah, Jibāl an- ▲ | 88 | 12.00 N | 30.45 E |
| Nubian Desert ≈² | 88 | 20.30 N | 33.00 E |
| Nueltin Lake ⬩ | 94 | 60.30 N | 99.30 W |
| Nueva, Isla I | 102 | 55.13 S | 66.30 W |
| Nueva Rosita | 98 | 27.57 N | 101.13 W |
| Nuevitas | 98 | 21.33 N | 77.16 W |
| Nuevo, Golfo C | 102 | 42.42 S | 64.36 W |
| Nuevo Laredo | 98 | 27.30 N | 99.31 W |
| Nuevo Mundo, Cerro ▲ | 100 | 21.55 S | 66.53 W |
| Nûgssuaq ➤¹ | 94 | 71.45 N | 53.00 W |
| N'uja ≈ | 78 | 60.32 N | 116.20 E |
| Nukus | 76 | 42.50 N | 59.29 E |
| Nullarbor Plain ≅ | 92 | 31.00 S | 129.00 E |
| Numazu | 80 | 35.06 N | 138.52 E |
| Numfoor, Pulau I | 82 | 1.03 S | 134.54 E |
| Nuneaton | 54 | 52.32 N | 1.28 W |
| Nuomiņhe ≈ | 80 | 48.06 N | 124.26 E |
| Nuoro | 72 | 40.19 N | 9.20 E |
| Nura ≈ | 76 | 50.30 N | 69.59 E |
| Nurlat | 62 | 54.26 N | 50.48 E |
| Nürnberg | 66 | 49.27 N | 11.04 E |
| Nürtingen | 66 | 48.38 N | 9.20 E |
| Nusa Tenggara (Lesser Sunda Islands) II | 82 | 9.00 S | 120.00 E |
| Nushan ▲ | 88 | 26.50 N | 99.03 E |
| Nyala | 88 | 12.03 N | 24.53 E |
| Nyasa, Lake ⬩ | 90 | 12.00 S | 34.30 E |
| Nyborg | 64 | 55.19 N | 10.48 E |
| Nybro | 64 | 56.45 N | 15.54 E |
| Nyfer ≈ | 54 | 52.02 N | 4.50 W |
| Nyíregyháza | 74 | 47.59 N | 21.43 E |
| Nykøbing | 64 | 54.46 N | 11.53 E |
| Nyköping | 64 | 58.45 N | 17.00 E |
| Nymburk | 66 | 50.11 N | 15.03 E |
| Nynäshamn | 64 | 58.54 N | 17.57 E |
| Nyong ≈ | 88 | 3.17 N | 9.54 E |
| Nyon | 68 | 46.23 N | 6.14 E |
| Nysa | 66 | 50.29 N | 17.20 E |
| Nytva | 62 | 57.56 N | 55.20 E |
| Nzi ≈ | 88 | 5.57 N | 4.50 W |
| **O** | | | |
| Oa, Mull of ➤ | 58 | 55.35 N | 6.19 W |
| Oadby | 54 | 52.36 N | 1.04 W |
| Oahe, Lake ⬩¹ | 96 | 45.30 N | 100.25 W |
| Oahu I | 96b | 21.30 N | 158.00 W |
| Oakengates | 54 | 52.42 N | 2.28 W |
| Oakham | 54 | 52.40 N | 0.43 W |
| Oaxaca | 98 | 37.47 N | 122.13 W |
| Ob' ≈ | 78 | 66.45 N | 69.30 E |
| Oban | 58 | 56.25 N | 5.29 W |
| Oberhausen | 66 | 51.28 N | 6.50 E |
| Oberursel | 66 | 50.11 N | 8.35 E |
| Obi, Kepulauan II | 82 | 1.30 S | 127.45 E |
| Obi, Pulau I | 82 | 1.30 S | 127.45 E |
| Obihiro | 80 | 42.55 N | 143.12 E |
| Obilatu, Pulau I | 82 | 1.25 S | 127.20 E |
| Obninsk | 62 | 55.05 N | 36.37 E |
| Obščij Syrt ▲² | 76 | 52.00 N | 51.30 E |
| Observatoire, Caye de l' ⬩² | 92 | 21.25 S | 158.50 E |
| Obskaja Guba C | 78 | 69.00 N | 73.00 E |
| Obuasi | 88 | 6.14 N | 1.39 W |
| Occidental, Cordillera ▲, Col. | 100 | 5.00 N | 76.00 W |
| Occidental, Cordillera ▲, Perú | 100 | 14.00 S | 74.00 W |
| Oceanside | 96 | 33.12 N | 117.23 W |
| Oċer | 62 | 57.53 N | 54.42 E |
| Ocha | 78 | 53.34 N | 142.56 E |
| Ochil Hills ▲² | 58 | 56.14 N | 3.40 W |
| Ochiltree | 58 | 55.28 N | 4.23 W |
| Ochota ≈ | 78 | 59.20 N | 143.04 E |
| Ochotsk | 78 | 59.23 N | 143.18 E |
| Ochtrup | 66 | 52.13 N | 7.11 E |
| Ock ≈ | 54 | 51.39 N | 1.17 W |
| Ocoña ≈ | 100 | 16.28 S | 73.07 W |
| Ocotlán | 98 | 20.21 N | 102.46 W |
| Ōdemiş | 74 | 38.13 N | 27.59 E |
| Odendaalsrus | 90 | 27.48 S | 26.45 E |
| Odense | 64 | 55.24 N | 10.23 E |
| Oder (Odra) ≈ | 52 | 53.32 N | 14.38 E |
| Odessa, S.S.S.R. | 76 | 46.28 N | 30.44 E |
| Odessa, Tex., U.S. | 96 | 31.51 N | 102.22 W |
| Odiham | 54 | 51.15 N | 0.57 W |
| Odorheiu Secuiesc | 74 | 46.18 N | 25.18 E |
| Oelde | 66 | 51.49 N | 8.08 E |
| Oelsnitz | 66 | 50.24 N | 12.10 E |
| Ofally □⁶ | 60 | 53.15 N | 7.30 W |
| Offenbach | 66 | 50.06 N | 8.47 E |
| Offenburg | 66 | 48.28 N | 7.57 E |
| O'Flynn, Lough ⬩ | 60 | 53.48 N | 8.40 W |
| Ogasawara-guntō (Bonin Islands) II | 8 | 27.00 N | 142.10 E |
| Ogbomosho | 88 | 8.08 N | 4.15 E |
| Ogilvie Mountains ▲ | 94 | 65.00 N | 139.30 W |
| Ogmore ≈ | 54 | 51.28 N | 3.38 W |
| Ogmore Vale | 54 | 51.38 N | 3.31 W |
| Ogooué ≈ | 90 | 0.49 S | 9.00 E |
| Ohio □³ | 96 | 40.15 N | 82.45 W |
| Ohio ≈ | 96 | 36.59 N | 89.08 W |
| Ohře ≈ | 66 | 50.32 N | 14.08 E |
| Ohrid | 74 | 41.07 N | 20.47 E |
| Ōita | 80 | 33.14 N | 131.36 E |
| Ojos del Salado, Cerro ▲ | 102 | 27.06 S | 68.32 W |
| Oka ≈, S.S.S.R. | 62 | 56.20 N | 43.59 E |
| Oka ≈, S.S.S.R. | 78 | 55.15 N | 102.10 E |
| Okanagan Lake ⬩ | 94 | 50.00 N | 119.28 W |
| Okara | 84 | 30.49 N | 73.27 E |
| Okavango (Cubango) ≈ | 90 | 18.50 S | 22.25 E |
| Okavango Swamp ≅ | 90 | 19.30 S | 23.00 E |
| Okayama | 80 | 34.39 N | 133.55 E |
| Okeechobee, Lake ⬩ | 96 | 26.55 N | 80.45 W |
| Okehampton | 54 | 50.44 N | 4.00 W |
| Okene | 88 | 7.33 N | 6.15 E |
| Okha | 84 | 22.28 N | 69.05 E |
| Okhotsk, Sea of (Ochotskoje More) ≈² | 78 | 53.00 N | 150.00 E |
| Okinawa-jima I | 80 | 26.30 N | 128.00 E |
| Okino-Tori-Shima I | 8 | 20.25 N | 136.00 E |
| Oklahoma □³ | 96 | 35.30 N | 98.00 W |
| Oklahoma City | 96 | 35.28 N | 97.32 W |
| Okt'abr'sk | 76 | 49.28 N | 57.25 E |
| Okt'abr'skoj Revol'ucii, Ostrov I | 78 | 79.30 N | 97.00 E |
| Okulovka | 62 | 58.26 N | 33.18 E |
| Öland I | 64 | 56.45 N | 16.38 E |
| Olavarría | 102 | 36.54 S | 60.17 W |
| Oława | 66 | 50.57 N | 17.17 E |
| Olbia | 72 | 40.55 N | 9.29 E |
| Ol'chon, Ostrov I | 78 | 53.09 N | 107.24 E |
| Old Bedford ≈ | 54 | 52.34 N | 0.20 E |
| Oldcastle | 60 | 53.46 N | 7.10 W |
| Old Colwyn | 56 | 53.18 N | 3.40 W |
| Old Crow | 94 | 67.35 N | 139.50 W |
| Oldenburg [in Oldenburg] | 66 | 53.08 N | 8.13 E |
| Oldenburg [in Holstein] | 66 | 54.17 N | 10.52 E |
| Old Fletton | 54 | 52.33 N | 0.15 W |
| Old Howe ≈ | 56 | 53.51 N | 0.19 W |
| Oldham | 56 | 53.33 N | 2.07 W |
| Oldmeldrum | 58 | 57.20 N | 2.19 W |
| Old Nene ≈ | 54 | 52.34 N | 0.13 E |
| Olds | 94 | 51.47 N | 114.06 W |
| Olekma ≈ | 78 | 60.22 N | 120.42 E |
| Olenij, Ostrov I | 78 | 72.25 N | 77.45 E |
| Olen'okskij Zaliv C | 78 | 73.00 N | 121.00 E |
| Olga, Mount ▲ | 92 | 25.19 S | 130.46 E |
| Olhão | 70 | 37.02 N | 7.50 W |
| Olimarao I¹ | 82 | 7.41 N | 145.52 E |
| Ólimbos ▲: Éllás | 74 | 40.05 N | 22.21 E |
| Ólimbos ▲: Kípros | 74 | 34.56 N | 32.52 E |
| Olinda | 100 | 8.01 S | 34.51 W |
| Oliva | 70 | 38.55 N | 0.07 W |
| Oliva de la Frontera | 70 | 38.16 N | 6.55 W |
| Ollatrim ≈ | 60 | 52.52 N | 8.13 W |
| Ollerton | 56 | 53.12 N | 1.00 W |
| Olney | 54 | 52.09 N | 0.42 W |
| Oloj ≈ | 78 | 66.29 N | 159.29 E |
| Ol'okma ≈ | 60 | 60.22 N | 120.42 E |
| Olomouc | 66 | 49.36 N | 17.16 E |
| Olonec | 62 | 61.00 N | 32.57 E |
| Olongapo | 82 | 14.50 N | 120.16 E |
| Oloron-Sainte-Marie | 68 | 43.12 N | 0.36 W |
| Olot | 70 | 42.11 N | 2.29 E |
| Olpe | 66 | 51.02 N | 7.52 E |
| Olsztyn (Allenstein), Pol. | 66 | 53.48 N | 20.29 E |
| Olsztyn, Pol. | 66 | 53.48 N | 20.29 E |
| Olt ≈ | 74 | 43.43 N | 24.51 E |
| Olten | 68 | 47.21 N | 7.54 E |
| Oltenița | 74 | 44.05 N | 26.38 E |
| Oluan Pi ➤ | 80 | 21.54 N | 120.51 E |
| Olympia | 96 | 47.03 N | 122.53 W |
| Olympus, Mount ▲ | 96 | 47.48 N | 123.43 W |
| Oma ≈ | 62 | 54.59 N | 73.22 E |
| Omagh | 60 | 54.36 N | 7.18 W |
| Omaha | 96 | 41.16 N | 95.57 W |
| Oman □¹ | 84 | 22.00 N | 58.00 E |
| Oman, Gulf of C | 84 | 24.30 N | 58.30 E |
| Ombersley | 54 | 52.17 N | 2.13 W |
| Omegna | 72 | 45.53 N | 8.24 E |
| Ometepe, Isla de I | 98 | 11.30 N | 85.35 W |
| Omineca ≈ | 94 | 56.05 N | 124.30 W |
| Omineca Mountains ▲ | | | |
| Ommanney Bay C | 94 | 73.07 N | 100.11 W |
| Omo ≈ | 88 | 4.32 N | 36.04 E |
| Omoloj ≈ | 78 | 71.10 N | 132.08 E |
| Omolon ≈ | 78 | 68.42 N | 158.36 E |
| Omsk | 78 | 55.00 N | 73.24 E |
| Ōmuta | 80 | 33.02 N | 130.27 E |
| Omutninsk | 62 | 58.40 N | 52.12 E |
| Onda | 70 | 39.58 N | 0.15 W |
| Ondo | 88 | 7.04 N | 4.47 E |
| Onega | 62 | 63.55 N | 38.05 E |
| Onega ≈ | 62 | 63.58 N | 37.55 E |
| Onekotan, Ostrov I | 78 | 49.25 N | 154.45 E |
| Onežskoje Ozero ⬩ | 62 | 61.30 N | 35.45 E |
| Onich | 58 | 56.42 N | 5.13 W |
| Onitsha | 88 | 6.09 N | 6.47 E |
| Onny ≈ | 54 | 52.23 N | 2.45 W |
| Onon ≈ | 78 | 51.42 N | 115.50 E |
| Ontario □⁴ | 94 | 51.00 N | 88.00 W |
| Ontario, Lake ⬩ | 96 | 43.45 N | 78.00 W |
| Onteniente | 70 | 38.49 N | 0.37 W |
| Oostende (Ostende) | 66 | 51.13 N | 2.55 E |
| Oosterhout | 66 | 51.38 N | 4.51 E |
| Ootacamund | 84 | 11.25 N | 76.43 E |
| Oparino | 62 | 59.52 N | 48.17 E |
| Opava | 66 | 49.56 N | 17.54 E |
| Opinaca ≈ | 94 | 52.15 N | 78.02 W |
| Opinan | 58 | 57.43 N | 5.47 W |
| Opladen | 66 | 51.04 N | 7.00 E |
| Opočka | 62 | 56.43 N | 28.38 E |
| Opoczno | 66 | 51.23 N | 20.17 E |
| Opole (Oppeln) | 66 | 50.41 N | 17.55 E |
| Oradea | 74 | 47.03 N | 21.57 E |
| Öræfajökull ⚠ | 62 | 64.00 N | 16.39 W |
| Oran | 88 | 35.43 N | 0.43 W |
| Orange, Austl. | 92 | 33.17 S | 149.06 E |
| Orange, Fr. | 68 | 44.08 N | 4.48 E |
| Orange (Oranje) ≈ | 90 | 28.41 S | 16.28 E |
| Orange, Cabo ➤ | 100 | 4.24 N | 51.33 W |
| Oranje Gebergte ▲ | 100 | 3.00 N | 55.05 W |
| Oranjestad | 98 | 12.33 N | 70.06 W |
| Oranmore | 60 | 53.16 N | 8.54 W |
| Orăştie | 74 | 45.50 N | 23.12 E |
| Orbetello | 72 | 42.27 N | 11.13 E |
| Orchon ≈ | 80 | 50.21 N | 106.05 E |
| Ord ≈ | 92 | 15.30 S | 128.21 E |
| Ord, Mount ▲ | 92 | 17.20 S | 125.34 E |
| Ordžonikidze | 76 | 43.03 N | 44.40 E |
| Öre ≈ | 62 | 63.30 N | 19.40 E |
| Örebro | 64 | 59.17 N | 15.13 E |
| Orechovo-Zujevo | 62 | 55.49 N | 38.59 E |
| Oregon □³ | 96 | 44.00 N | 121.00 W |
| Orenburg | 76 | 51.54 N | 55.06 E |
| Orense | 70 | 42.20 N | 7.51 W |
| Orestias | 74 | 41.30 N | 26.31 E |
| Orford | 54 | 52.05 N | 1.32 E |
| Orford Ness ➤ | 52 | 52.05 N | 1.34 E |
| Oriental, Cordillera ▲, Col. | 100 | 6.00 N | 73.00 W |
| Oriental, Cordillera ▲, Perú | 100 | 13.00 S | 72.00 W |
| Orihuela | 70 | 38.05 N | 0.57 W |
| Orinoco ≈ | 100 | 8.37 N | 62.15 W |
| Oristano | 72 | 39.54 N | 8.36 E |
| Orizaba | 98 | 18.51 N | 97.06 W |
| Ork, Ness of ➤ | 58 | 59.05 N | 2.48 W |
| Orkney Islands II⁴ | 52 | 59.00 N | 3.00 W |
| Orlando | 96 | 28.32 N | 81.23 W |
| Orléans | 68 | 47.55 N | 1.54 E |
| Orlová | 66 | 49.52 N | 18.24 E |
| Ormesby Saint Margaret | 54 | 52.40 N | 1.42 E |
| Ormoc | 82 | 11.00 N | 124.37 E |
| Ormskirk | 56 | 53.35 N | 2.54 W |
| Örnsköldsvik | 62 | 63.18 N | 18.43 E |
| Or'ol | 62 | 52.59 N | 36.05 E |
| Oronsay I | 58 | 56.01 N | 6.14 W |
| Orosháza | 74 | 46.34 N | 20.40 E |
| Orrin ≈ | 58 | 57.30 N | 4.29 W |
| Orrin, Loch ⬩ | 58 | 57.30 N | 4.45 W |
| Orşa | 62 | 54.31 N | 30.24 E |
| Orsk | 76 | 51.12 N | 58.34 E |
| Orta Nova | 72 | 41.19 N | 15.42 E |
| Ortegal, Cabo ➤ | 70 | 43.46 N | 7.53 W |
| Ortona | 72 | 42.21 N | 14.24 E |
| Oruro | 100 | 17.59 S | 67.09 W |
| Orvieto | 72 | 42.43 N | 12.07 E |
| Orwell ≈ | 54 | 51.57 N | 1.17 E |
| Osa, Península de ➤¹ | 98 | 8.34 N | 83.31 W |
| Ōsaka | 80 | 34.40 N | 135.30 E |
| Oschersleben | 66 | 52.02 N | 11.13 E |
| Oshawa | 94 | 43.54 N | 78.51 W |
| Oshkosh | 96 | 44.00 N | 88.33 W |
| Oshogbo | 88 | 7.47 N | 4.34 E |
| Osijek | 74 | 45.33 N | 18.41 E |
| Osinniki | 78 | 53.37 N | 87.21 E |
| Oskarshamn | 64 | 57.16 N | 16.26 E |
| Oslo | 64 | 59.55 N | 10.45 E |
| Osmington | 54 | 50.38 N | 2.22 W |
| Osnabrück | 66 | 52.16 N | 8.02 E |
| Osorno | 102 | 40.34 S | 73.09 W |
| Osprey Reef ≈² | 92 | 13.55 S | 146.38 E |
| Oss | 66 | 51.46 N | 5.31 E |
| Ossa, Mount ▲ | 92 | 41.54 S | 146.01 E |
| Ossett | 56 | 53.41 N | 1.35 W |
| Ossian, Loch ⬩ | 58 | 56.46 N | 4.38 W |
| Ostaškov | 62 | 57.09 N | 33.06 E |
| Osterholz-Scharmbeck | 66 | 53.14 N | 8.47 E |
| Osterode | 66 | 51.44 N | 10.11 E |
| Östersund | 62 | 63.11 N | 14.39 E |
| Ostrava | 66 | 49.50 N | 18.17 E |
| Ostróda | 66 | 53.43 N | 19.59 E |
| Ostrołeka | 66 | 53.06 N | 21.34 E |
| Ostrov | 62 | 57.20 N | 28.22 E |
| Ostrov, S.S.S.R. | 78 | 46.21 N | 143.10 E |
| Ostrów Świętokrzyski | 66 | 50.57 N | 21.23 E |
| Ostrów Mazowiecka | 66 | 52.49 N | 21.54 E |
| Ostrów Wielkopolski | 66 | 51.39 N | 17.49 E |
| Ostuni | 72 | 40.44 N | 17.35 E |
| Ōsumi-shotō II | 80 | 30.30 N | 130.00 E |
| Oświęcim | 66 | 50.03 N | 19.12 E |
| Oswaldtwistle | 56 | 53.44 N | 2.24 W |
| Oswestry | 54 | 52.52 N | 3.04 W |

| Name | Page | Lat | Long |
|---|---|---|---|
| Oświęcim | 66 | 50.03 N | 19.12 E |
| Otaru | 80 | 43.13 N | 141.00 E |
| Otford | 54 | 51.19 N | 0.12 E |
| Othery | 54 | 51.05 N | 2.53 W |
| Oti ≃ | 84 | 8.40 N | 0.13 E |
| Otish, Monts ↗ | 94 | 52.22 N | 70.30 W |
| Otjiwarongo | 90 | 20.29 S | 16.36 E |
| Otley | 56 | 53.54 N | 1.41 W |
| Otoskwin ≃ | 94 | 52.13 N | 88.06 W |
| Otra ≃ | 58 | 58.09 N | 8.00 E |
| Otradnyj | 62 | 53.22 N | 51.21 E |
| Otrokovice | 66 | 49.13 N | 17.31 E |
| Ōtsu | 80 | 35.00 N | 135.52 E |
| Ottawa | 94 | 45.25 N | 75.42 W |
| Ottawa ≃ | 94 | 45.20 N | 73.58 W |
| Ottawa Islands II | 94 | 59.30 N | 80.10 W |
| Otter ≃ | 54 | 50.46 N | 3.17 W |
| Otterburn | 56 | 55.14 N | 2.10 W |
| Ottery ≃ | 54 | 50.39 N | 4.20 W |
| Ottery Saint Mary | 54 | 50.45 N | 3.17 W |
| Ottumwa | 96 | 41.01 N | 92.25 W |
| Otway, Cape ❯ | 92 | 38.52 S | 143.31 E |
| Otwock | 66 | 52.07 N | 21.16 E |
| Ou ≃, Afr. | 84 | | |
| Ou ≃, Lao | 82 | 20.04 N | 102.13 E |
| Ouachita Mountains ↗ | 96 | 34.40 N | 94.25 W |
| Ouagadougou | 84 | 12.22 N | 1.31 W |
| Ouahigouya | 84 | 13.35 N | 2.25 W |
| Ouaka ≃ | 88 | 4.59 N | 19.56 E |
| Ouarane ≃¹ | 84 | 21.00 N | 10.30 W |
| Ouargla | 84 | 31.59 N | 5.25 E |
| Oudenaarde | 68 | 50.51 N | 3.36 E |
| Oudtshoorn | 90 | 33.35 S | 22.14 E |
| Ouémé ≃ | 84 | 6.29 N | 2.32 E |
| Ouezzane | 84 | 34.52 N | 5.35 W |
| Oughter, Lough ⊕ | 60 | 54.00 N | 7.30 W |
| Oughterard | 60 | 53.25 N | 9.17 W |
| Ouidah | 84 | 6.22 N | 2.05 E |
| Oujda | 84 | 34.41 N | 1.45 W |
| Oulton Broad | 54 | 52.31 N | 1.42 E |
| Oulu | 50 | 65.01 N | 25.28 E |
| Oulujärvi ⊕ | 50 | 64.20 N | 27.15 E |
| Oum er Rbia, Oued ≃ | 84 | 33.19 N | 8.21 W |
| Oundle | 54 | 52.29 N | 0.29 W |
| Ouro Prêto | 100 | 20.23 S | 43.30 W |
| Ouse, Rivière aux ≃ | 52 | 52.20 N | 0.41 W |
| Outardes, Rivière aux ≃ | 94 | 49.04 N | 68.28 W |
| Outer Hebrides II | 52 | 57.50 N | 7.32 W |
| Out Skerries II | 58a | 60.25 N | 0.42 W |
| Outwell | 54 | 52.37 N | 0.14 E |
| Outwood | 56 | 53.42 N | 1.30 W |
| Ovalle | 102 | 30.36 S | 71.12 W |
| Overseal | 54 | 52.44 N | 1.34 W |
| Overstrand | 54 | 52.56 N | 1.20 E |
| Overton | 54 | 51.09 N | 1.15 W |
| Over Wallop | 54 | 51.09 N | 1.35 W |
| Oviedo | 70 | 43.22 N | 5.50 W |
| Owel, Lough ⊕ | 60 | 53.34 N | 7.25 W |
| Owenboy ≃ | 60 | 51.48 N | 8.18 W |
| Owenea ≃ | 60 | 54.47 N | 8.26 W |
| Owenkillew ≃ | 60 | 54.44 N | 7.18 W |
| Owenmore ≃ | 60 | 54.07 N | 9.50 W |
| Owensboro | 96 | 37.46 N | 87.07 W |
| Owen Sound | 94 | 44.34 N | 80.56 W |
| Owen Stanley Range ↗ | 92 | 9.20 S | 147.55 E |
| Owl ≃ | 94 | 57.51 N | 92.44 W |
| Owo | 86 | 7.15 N | 5.37 E |
| Oxelösund | 58 | 58.40 N | 17.06 E |
| Oxford | 54 | 51.46 N | 1.15 W |
| Oxford Lake ⊕ | 94 | 54.51 N | 95.37 W |
| Oxfordshire □⁶ | 52 | 51.50 N | 1.15 W |
| Oxnard | 96 | 34.12 N | 119.11 W |
| Oxted | 54 | 51.16 N | 0.01 W |
| Oyapock (Oiapoque) ≃ | 100 | 4.08 N | 51.40 W |
| Oykel ≃ | 58 | 57.56 N | 4.25 W |
| Oykel Bridge | 58 | 57.58 N | 4.44 W |
| Oyo | 86 | 7.15 N | 3.56 E |
| Oyonnax | 68 | 46.15 N | 5.40 E |
| Ozamiz | 82 | 8.08 N | 123.50 E |
| Ozark Plateau ↗¹ | 96 | 38.10 N | 92.30 W |
| Ozarks, Lake of the ⊕¹ | 96 | 38.10 N | 92.50 W |
| Ózd | 66 | 48.13 N | 20.18 E |
| Ozieri | 74 | 40.34 N | 9.00 E |
| Ozogino, Ozero ⊕ | 78 | 69.16 N | 146.36 E |
| Ozorków | 66 | 51.58 N | 19.19 E |
| Oz'orsk | 66 | 54.25 N | 22.01 E |
| **P** | | | |
| Paarl | 90 | 33.45 S | 18.56 E |
| Pabbay I., Scot., U.K. | 52 | 57.47 N | 7.20 W |
| Pabbay I., Scot., U.K. | 58 | 56.51 N | 7.35 W |
| Pabianice | 66 | 51.40 N | 19.22 E |
| Pacaás Novos, Serra dos ↗ | 100 | 10.45 S | 64.15 W |
| Pachino | 72 | 36.42 N | 15.06 E |
| Pachitea ≃ | 100 | 8.46 S | 74.32 W |
| Pachuca | 98 | 20.07 N | 98.44 W |
| Pacific Islands Trust Territory □² | 82 | 10.00 N | 143.00 E |
| Pacific Ocean ≃¹ | 8 | 10.00 S | 150.00 W |
| Padang | 82 | 0.57 S | 100.21 E |
| Padangpanjang | 82 | 0.27 S | 100.25 E |
| Padangsidempuan | 82 | 1.22 N | 99.16 E |
| Paddock Wood | 54 | 51.11 N | 0.23 E |
| Paderborn | 66 | 51.43 N | 8.45 E |
| Padiham | 56 | 53.49 N | 2.19 W |
| Padloping Island I | 94 | 67.07 N | 62.35 W |
| Padova | 72 | 45.25 N | 11.53 E |
| Padstow | 54 | 50.33 N | 4.56 W |
| Paducah | 96 | 37.05 N | 88.36 W |
| Paektu-san ∧ | 80 | 42.00 N | 128.03 E |
| Pagai Selatan, Pulau I | 82 | 3.00 S | 100.20 E |
| Pagai Utara, Pulau I | 82 | 2.42 S | 100.07 E |
| Pagalu I | 90 | 1.25 S | 5.36 E |
| Pagan I | 82 | 18.07 N | 145.46 E |
| Paget, Mount ∧ | 102 | 54.26 S | 36.33 W |
| Pahang ≃ | 82 | 3.32 N | 103.28 E |
| Paignton | 54 | 50.26 N | 3.34 W |
| Painscastle | 54 | 52.07 N | 3.12 W |
| Painswick | 54 | 51.48 N | 2.11 W |
| Painted Desert ≃² | 96 | 36.00 N | 111.00 W |
| Paisley | 58 | 55.50 N | 4.26 W |
| Paj-Choj ↗² | 76 | 69.00 N | 63.00 E |
| Pajjer, Gora ∧² | 76 | 66.42 N | 64.25 E |
| Pakanbaru | 82 | 0.32 N | 101.27 E |
| Pakaraima Mountains ↗ | 100 | 5.30 N | 60.40 W |
| Pakistan (Pākistān) □¹ | 84 | 30.00 N | 70.00 E |
| Pakokku | 82 | 21.20 N | 95.05 E |
| Paks | 66 | 46.39 N | 18.53 E |
| P'akupur ≃, S.S.S.R. | 76 | 32.15 N | 97.43 W |
| P'akupur ≃, S.S.S.R. | 76 | 64.30 N | 77.28 E |
| Palagiano | 72 | 37.19 N | 14.45 E |
| Palaguža, Otoci I | 72 | 42.24 N | 16.15 E |
| Palau Islands II | 82 | 7.30 N | 134.30 E |
| Palawan I | 82 | 9.30 N | 118.30 E |
| Pālayankottai | 84 | 8.43 N | 77.44 E |
| Palembang | 82 | 2.55 S | 104.45 E |
| Palencia | 70 | 42.01 N | 4.32 W |
| Palermo | 74 | 38.07 N | 13.21 E |
| Pālghāt | 84 | 10.46 N | 76.40 E |
| Palk Strait ≃ | 84 | 10.00 N | 79.45 E |
| Pallas Grean | 60 | 52.33 N | 8.22 W |
| Pallaskenry | 60 | 52.39 N | 8.52 W |
| Palma del Río | 70 | 37.42 N | 5.17 W |
| Palma [de Mallorca] | 70 | 39.34 N | 2.39 E |
| Palma di Montechiaro | 72 | 37.11 N | 13.46 E |
| Palmas, Cape ❯ | 84 | 4.22 N | 7.44 W |
| Palma Soriano | 98 | 20.13 N | 76.00 W |
| Palmerston, Cape ❯ | 92 | 21.32 S | 149.29 E |
| Palmerston North | 93a | 40.21 S | 175.37 E |
| Palmi | 72 | 38.21 N | 15.51 E |
| Palopo | 82 | 3.00 S | 120.12 E |
| Pamekasan | 82 | 7.10 S | 113.28 E |

| Name | Page | Lat | Long |
|---|---|---|---|
| Pamiers | 68 | 43.07 N | 1.36 E |
| Pamir ↗, As. | 76 | 38.00 N | 73.00 E |
| Pamir ↗, S.S.S.R. | 76 | 38.00 N | 73.00 E |
| Pamlico Sound ⋃ | 96 | 35.20 N | 75.55 W |
| Pampas ≃ | 100 | 13.23 S | 73.15 W |
| Pampas ≃¹ | 102 | 35.00 S | 63.00 W |
| Pamplona, Col. | 100 | 7.23 N | 72.39 W |
| Pamplona, Esp. | 70 | 42.49 N | 1.38 W |
| Panaji (Panjim) | 84 | 15.29 N | 73.50 E |
| Panamá | 98 | 8.58 N | 79.32 W |
| Panamá □¹ | 98 | 9.00 N | 80.00 W |
| Panama, Gulf of C | 98 | 8.00 N | 79.30 W |
| Panama, Isthmus of ≃ | 98 | 9.00 N | 80.00 W |
| Panama City | 96 | 30.10 N | 85.41 W |
| Panay I | 82 | 11.15 N | 122.30 E |
| Panay Gulf C | 82 | 10.15 N | 122.15 E |
| Pančevo | 74 | 44.52 N | 20.39 E |
| Panevėžys | 62 | 55.44 N | 24.21 E |
| Panfilov | 76 | 44.10 N | 80.01 E |
| Pangani | 90 | 5.26 S | 38.58 E |
| Pangbourne | 54 | 51.29 N | 1.05 W |
| Pangkalpinang | 82 | 2.08 S | 106.08 E |
| Pangnirtung Fiord C² | 94 | 66.06 N | 65.58 W |
| Pangutaran Group II | 82 | 6.15 N | 120.30 E |
| Pānīpat | 84 | 29.25 N | 76.59 E |
| Pantar, Pulau I | 82 | 8.25 S | 124.07 E |
| Pantelleria, Isola di I | 50 | 36.47 N | 12.00 E |
| Paola | 72 | 39.22 N | 16.03 E |
| Pāpa | 66 | 47.19 N | 17.28 E |
| Papa, Sound of ⋃ | 58a | 60.18 N | 1.41 W |
| Papantla | 98 | 20.27 N | 97.19 W |
| Papa Stour I | 58a | 60.20 N | 1.42 W |
| Papa Westray I | 52 | 59.22 N | 2.54 W |
| Papenburg | 66 | 53.05 N | 7.23 E |
| Paps, of Jura ∧ | 58 | 55.55 N | 6.00 W |
| Papua, Gulf of C | 92 | 9.00 S | 145.00 E |
| Papua New Guinea □¹ | 82 | 6.00 S | 143.00 E |
| Par | 54 | 50.21 N | 4.43 W |
| Pará ≃ | 100 | 1.30 S | 48.55 W |
| Paracatu ≃ | 100 | 16.35 S | 45.06 W |
| Paracel Islands II | 82 | 16.30 N | 112.15 E |
| Paraćin | 74 | 43.52 N | 21.24 E |
| Paraguá ≃, Bol. | 100 | 13.34 S | 61.53 W |
| Paraguá ≃, Ven. | 100 | 6.55 N | 62.55 W |
| Paraguaçu ≃ | 100 | 12.45 S | 38.54 W |
| Paraguaná, Peninsula de ❯¹ | 100 | 11.55 N | 70.00 W |
| Paraguay □¹ | 102 | 23.00 S | 58.00 W |
| Paraguay ≃ | 102 | 27.18 S | 58.38 W |
| Paraíba do Sul ≃ | 100 | 21.37 S | 41.03 W |
| Paramaribo | 100 | 5.50 N | 55.10 W |
| Paramillo ∧ | 100 | 7.04 N | 75.55 W |
| Paramušir, Ostrov I | 78 | 50.25 N | 155.50 E |
| Paraná | 102 | 31.44 S | 60.32 W |
| Paraná ≃, Bra. | 100 | 12.30 S | 48.14 W |
| Paraná ≃, S.A. | 102 | 33.43 S | 59.15 W |
| Paranaíba | 100 | 19.40 S | 51.11 W |
| Parangaba | 100 | 3.45 S | 38.33 W |
| Paray-le-Monial | 68 | 46.27 N | 4.07 E |
| Parchim | 66 | 53.25 N | 11.51 E |
| Pardo ≃, Bra. | 100 | 21.46 S | 52.09 W |
| Pardo ≃, Bra. | 100 | 15.39 S | 38.57 W |
| Pardubice | 66 | 50.02 N | 15.47 E |
| Parecis, Serra dos ↗ | 100 | 13.00 S | 60.00 W |
| Paren' ≃ | 78 | 62.25 N | 163.10 E |
| Parepare | 82 | 4.01 S | 119.38 E |
| Parícutin ∧¹ | 98 | 19.28 N | 102.15 W |
| Parima, Sierra ↗ | 100 | 2.30 N | 64.00 W |
| Pariñas, Punta ❯ | 100 | 4.49 N | 75.43 W |
| Paris | 68 | 48.52 N | 2.20 E |
| Parker, Cape ❯ | 94 | 75.04 N | 79.40 W |
| Parkersburg | 96 | 39.17 N | 81.32 W |
| Parma | 72 | 44.48 N | 10.20 E |
| Parnaíba | 100 | 2.54 S | 41.47 W |
| Parnaíba ≃ | 100 | 3.00 S | 41.50 W |
| Parnassós ∧ | 50 | 38.32 N | 22.35 E |
| Pärnu | 62 | 58.24 N | 24.32 E |
| Paro | 84 | 27.26 N | 89.25 E |
| Paroo ≃ | 92 | 31.28 S | 143.32 E |
| Páros I | 50 | 37.08 N | 25.12 E |
| Parramatta | 92 | 33.49 S | 151.00 E |
| Parrett ≃ | 54 | 51.13 N | 3.01 W |
| Parry, Cape ❯ | 94 | 70.08 N | 124.24 W |
| Parry Bay C | 94 | 68.07 N | 82.00 W |
| Parsnip ≃ | 94 | 55.10 N | 123.00 W |
| Parthenay | 68 | 46.39 N | 0.15 W |
| Partille | 64 | 57.44 N | 12.07 E |
| Partinico | 72 | 38.03 N | 13.07 E |
| Parton | 56 | 54.33 N | 3.35 W |
| Partree | 58 | 53.41 N | 9.19 W |
| Pas, The | 94 | 53.50 N | 101.15 W |
| Pasadena | 96 | 34.09 N | 118.09 W |
| Pascagoula | 96 | 30.23 N | 88.31 W |
| Pașcani | 66 | 47.15 N | 26.44 E |
| Pasco | 96 | 46.14 N | 119.06 W |
| Pasewalk | 66 | 53.30 N | 14.00 E |
| P'asinskij Zaliv C | 78 | 73.50 N | 87.10 E |
| Pasirian | 82 | 74.00 N | 86.00 E |
| Pasley Bay C | 94 | 70.40 N | 96.27 W |
| Passage East | 60 | 52.13 N | 6.59 W |
| Passage West | 60 | 51.52 N | 8.20 W |
| Passau | 66 | 48.35 N | 13.28 E |
| Passero, Capo ❯ | 50 | 36.40 N | 15.09 E |
| Passos | 100 | 20.43 S | 46.37 W |
| Pasto | 100 | 1.13 N | 77.17 W |
| Pasuruan | 82 | 7.38 S | 112.54 E |
| Patagonia ≃¹ | 102 | 44.00 S | 68.00 W |
| Pātan | 84 | 23.51 N | 72.06 E |
| Pateley Bridge | 56 | 54.05 N | 1.45 W |
| Paterson | 70 | 39.30 N | 0.26 E |
| Paternò | 72 | 37.34 N | 14.54 E |
| Paterson | 96 | 40.55 N | 74.10 W |
| Pathānkot | 84 | 32.17 N | 75.40 E |
| Path of Condie | 58 | 56.15 N | 3.30 W |
| Patiāla | 84 | 30.19 N | 76.23 E |
| Patna | 84 | 25.36 N | 85.07 E |
| Patos | 100 | 7.01 S | 37.16 W |
| Patos de Minas | 100 | 18.35 S | 46.32 W |
| Pátrai | 50 | 38.15 N | 21.44 E |
| Patricio Lynch, Isla I | 102 | 48.37 S | 75.26 W |
| Patrington | 56 | 53.41 N | 0.02 W |
| Patterdale | 56 | 54.32 N | 2.56 W |
| Patu | 100 | 15.50 N | 84.17 W |
| Patuca ≃ | 98 | 43.18 N | 0.22 W |
| Pau | 68 | 43.18 N | 0.22 W |
| Paulo Afonso | 100 | 9.21 S | 38.14 W |
| Pavlograd | 62 | 48.32 N | 35.52 E |
| Pausania | 72 | 40.55 N | 9.06 E |
| Pavia | 72 | 45.10 N | 9.10 E |
| Pavlodar | 76 | 52.18 N | 76.57 E |
| Pavlovo | 62 | 55.58 N | 43.04 E |
| Payakumbuh | 82 | 0.14 S | 100.38 E |
| Payne, Baie C | 94 | 60.00 N | 70.00 W |
| Payne, Lac ⊕ | 94 | 59.25 N | 74.00 W |
| Paysandú | 102 | 32.19 S | 58.05 W |
| Pazardžik | 74 | 42.12 N | 24.20 E |
| P'azijeva Sel'ga | 62 | 59.00 N | 111.25 W |
| Peace ≃ | 94 | 59.00 N | 111.25 W |
| Peacehaven | 54 | 50.47 N | 0.00 |
| Peacock Hills ∧² | 94 | 66.05 N | 110.45 W |
| Peak, The ∧ | 56 | 53.24 N | 1.53 W |
| Peat Inn | 58 | 56.17 N | 2.53 W |
| Pec | 74 | 42.39 N | 20.19 E |
| Pečenga | 62 | 69.33 N | 31.07 E |
| Pečora ≃ | 62 | 68.13 N | 54.15 E |
| Pečora | 76 | 65.10 N | 57.11 E |
| Pečorskaja Guba C | 62 | 68.40 N | 54.45 E |
| Pečorskoje More ≃² | 62 | 70.00 N | 54.00 E |
| Pecos | 96 | 29.42 N | 101.22 W |
| Pécs | 66 | 46.05 N | 18.13 E |
| Peebles | 58 | 55.39 N | 3.12 W |
| Pee Dee ≃ | 96 | 33.21 N | 79.16 W |

| Name | Page | Lat | Long |
|---|---|---|---|
| Peel | 56 | 54.13 N | 4.40 W |
| Peel ≃ | 94 | 67.37 N | 134.40 W |
| Peel Fell ∧ | 56 | 55.17 N | 2.35 W |
| Peel Fell ∧ | 58 | 55.17 N | 2.35 W |
| Peel Point ❯ | 94 | 73.22 N | 114.35 W |
| Peel Sound ⋃ | 94 | 73.15 N | 96.30 W |
| Pegswood | 56 | 55.11 N | 1.38 W |
| Pegu | 82 | 17.20 N | 96.29 E |
| Pegu Yoma ↗ | 82 | 19.00 N | 95.50 E |
| Pegwell Bay C | 54 | 51.18 N | 1.26 E |
| Peixe, Rio do ≃ | 100 | 52.19 N | 10.13 E |
| Pekalongan | 82 | 21.31 S | 51.58 W |
| Pelagie, Isole II | 50 | 35.40 N | 12.40 E |
| Peleliu I | 82 | 7.01 N | 134.15 E |
| Peleng, Pulau I | 82 | 1.20 S | 123.10 E |
| Pelhřimov | 66 | 49.26 N | 15.13 E |
| Pelly ≃ | 94 | 62.47 N | 137.19 W |
| Pelly Bay C | 94 | 68.53 N | 89.51 W |
| Pelly Lake ⊕ | 94 | 65.59 N | 101.12 W |
| Pelly Mountains ↗ | 94 | 62.00 N | 133.00 W |
| Pelopónnisos ≃¹ | 50 | 37.30 N | 22.00 E |
| Pematangsiantar | 82 | 2.57 N | 99.03 E |
| Pemba Island I | 90 | 7.31 S | 39.25 E |
| Pembrey | 54 | 51.42 N | 4.16 W |
| Pembroke | 54 | 51.41 N | 4.55 W |
| Pembroke, Cape ❯ | 94 | 62.56 N | 81.55 W |
| Pembroke Dock | 54 | 51.42 N | 4.56 W |
| Pembuang ≃ | 82 | 3.24 S | 112.33 E |
| Pembury | 54 | 51.09 N | 0.20 E |
| Peñarroya-Pueblonuevo | 70 | 38.18 N | 5.16 W |
| Penarth | 54 | 51.27 N | 3.11 W |
| Peñas, Golfo de C | 102 | 47.22 S | 74.50 W |
| Pencader | 54 | 52.01 N | 4.14 W |
| Pencoed | 54 | 51.32 N | 3.30 W |
| Pendjari ≃ | 86 | 10.54 N | 0.51 E |
| Pendle Hill ∧² | 56 | 53.52 N | 2.17 W |
| Pend Oreille, Lake ⊕ | 96 | 48.10 N | 116.11 W |
| P'enghu Liehtao II | 80 | 23.30 N | 119.30 E |
| Penicuik | 58 | 55.50 N | 3.14 W |
| Penistone | 56 | 53.32 N | 1.37 W |
| Penmaenmawr | 56 | 53.16 N | 3.54 W |
| Pennines ↗ | 52 | 54.10 N | 2.05 W |
| Pennsylvania □³ | 96 | 40.45 N | 77.30 W |
| Penobscot ≃ | 96 | 44.30 N | 68.50 W |
| Penrhyn Bay | 54 | 53.19 N | 3.45 W |
| Penrhyndeudraeth | 54 | 52.56 N | 4.04 W |
| Penrith | 56 | 54.40 N | 2.44 W |
| Penryn | 54 | 50.09 N | 5.06 W |
| Pensacola | 96 | 30.25 N | 87.13 W |
| Penshaw | 56 | 54.53 N | 1.29 W |
| Pentire Point ❯ | 54 | 50.36 N | 4.55 W |
| Pentland Firth ⋃ | 58 | 58.44 N | 3.07 W |
| Pentland Hills ∧² | 58 | 55.46 N | 3.25 W |
| Pentraeth | 56 | 53.17 N | 4.12 W |
| Pen-y-Ghent ∧ | 56 | 54.10 N | 2.14 W |
| Penygroes, Wales, U.K. | 54 | 51.49 N | 4.02 W |
| Penygroes, Wales, U.K. | 56 | 53.04 N | 4.17 W |
| Penza | 76 | 53.13 N | 45.00 E |
| Penzance | 54 | 50.07 N | 5.33 W |
| Penzina ≃ | 78 | 62.28 N | 165.18 E |
| Penžinskaja Guba C | 78 | 61.00 N | 162.00 E |
| Penžinskij Chrebet ↗ | 78 | 62.30 N | 167.00 E |
| Peoria | 96 | 40.42 N | 89.36 W |
| Perabumulih | 82 | 3.27 S | 104.15 E |
| Perak ≃ | 82 | 3.58 N | 100.53 E |
| Perece | 100 | 4.49 N | 75.43 W |
| Pereira | 100 | 4.49 N | 75.43 W |
| Pereslavl'-Zalesskij | 62 | 56.44 N | 38.51 E |
| Pergamino | 102 | 33.53 S | 60.35 W |
| Pergine Valsugana | 72 | 46.04 N | 11.14 E |
| Péribonca ≃ | 94 | 48.45 N | 72.05 W |
| Périgueux | 68 | 45.11 N | 0.43 E |
| Perija, Sierra de ↗ | 100 | 10.00 N | 73.00 W |
| Perkam, Tanjung ❯ | 82 | 1.28 S | 137.54 E |
| Perleberg | 66 | 53.04 N | 11.51 E |
| Perm' | 76 | 58.00 N | 56.15 E |
| Pernik | 74 | 42.36 N | 23.02 E |
| Perpignan | 68 | 42.41 N | 2.53 E |
| Perranporth | 54 | 50.20 N | 5.09 W |
| Pershore | 54 | 52.07 N | 2.05 W |
| Persian Gulf C | 84 | 27.00 N | 51.00 E |
| Perth, Austl. | 92 | 31.56 S | 115.50 E |
| Perth, Scot., U.K. | 58 | 56.24 N | 3.28 W |
| Peru □¹ | 100 | 10.00 S | 76.00 W |
| Perugia | 72 | 43.08 N | 12.22 E |
| Pervomajsk | 62 | 54.53 N | 43.49 E |
| Pervoural'sk | 76 | 56.54 N | 59.58 E |
| Pervoural'sk | 76 | 56.54 N | 59.58 E |
| Pescara | 72 | 42.28 N | 14.13 E |
| Pescia | 72 | 43.54 N | 10.41 E |
| Peshāwar | 84 | 34.01 N | 71.33 E |
| Pesqueira | 100 | 8.22 S | 36.42 W |
| Pessac | 68 | 44.48 N | 0.38 W |
| Pestera | 74 | 42.02 N | 24.18 E |
| Pestovo | 62 | 58.36 N | 35.48 E |
| Petah Tiqwa | 84 | 32.05 N | 34.53 E |
| Peterborough, Ont., Can. | 94 | 44.18 N | 78.19 W |
| Peterborough, Eng., U.K. | 54 | 52.35 N | 0.15 W |
| Peterculter | 58 | 57.05 N | 2.16 W |
| Peterhead | 58 | 57.30 N | 1.49 W |
| Peter Hill ∧ | 58 | 56.58 N | 2.42 W |
| Peter Lake ⊕ | 94 | 63.08 N | 92.48 W |
| Peterlee | 56 | 54.46 N | 1.19 W |
| Peter Pond Lake ⊕ | 94 | 55.55 N | 108.44 W |
| Petersburg | 96 | 37.13 N | 77.24 W |
| Petersfield | 54 | 51.00 N | 0.56 W |
| Petilia Policastro | 72 | 39.07 N | 16.47 E |
| Petite Rivière de La Baleine ≃ | 94 | 56.00 N | 76.45 W |
| Petit-Mecatina, Rivière du ≃ | 94 | 50.40 N | 59.30 W |
| Petitot ≃ | 94 | 60.14 N | 123.29 W |
| Petitsikapau Lake ⊕ | 94 | 54.45 N | 66.25 W |
| Petra Velikogo, Zaliv C | 78 | 43.00 N | 132.00 E |
| Petrič | 74 | 41.24 N | 23.13 E |
| Petrila | 74 | 45.27 N | 23.25 E |
| Petrinja | 72 | 45.26 N | 16.17 E |
| Petrodvorec | 62 | 59.53 N | 29.54 E |
| Petrokrepost' | 62 | 59.57 N | 31.02 E |
| Petrolina | 100 | 9.24 S | 40.30 W |
| Petropavlovsk | 76 | 54.54 N | 69.06 E |
| Petropavlovsk-Kamčatskij | 78 | 53.01 N | 158.39 E |
| Petrópolis | 100 | 22.31 S | 43.10 W |
| Petroșani | 74 | 45.25 N | 23.22 E |
| Petrovsk-Zabajkal'skij | 78 | 51.17 N | 108.50 E |
| Petrozavodsk | 62 | 61.47 N | 34.20 E |
| Petteril ≃ | 56 | 54.53 N | 2.49 W |
| Pettigo | 60 | 54.33 N | 7.50 W |
| Petworth | 54 | 50.59 N | 0.38 W |
| Pevensey | 54 | 50.49 N | 0.20 E |
| Pevensey Levels ≃ | 54 | 50.51 N | 0.23 E |
| Pewsey | 54 | 51.21 N | 1.46 W |
| Pewsey, Vale of ≃ | 54 | 51.20 N | 1.48 W |
| Pezinok | 66 | 48.18 N | 17.17 E |
| Pforzheim | 66 | 48.54 N | 8.42 E |
| Pfungstadt | 66 | 49.48 N | 8.36 E |
| Phangan, Ko I | 82 | 9.45 N | 100.04 E |
| Phan-rang | 82 | 11.34 N | 108.59 E |
| Phan-thiet | 82 | 10.56 N | 108.06 E |
| Phetchabun, Thiu Khao ↗ | 82 | 16.20 N | 100.55 E |
| Philadelphia | 96 | 39.57 N | 75.07 W |
| Philippines □¹ | 82 | 13.00 N | 122.00 E |
| Philippine Sea ≃² | 82 | 20.00 N | 135.00 E |
| Phillip Island I | 82 | 38.29 S | 145.14 E |
| Phitsanulok | 82 | 16.50 N | 100.15 E |
| Phnum Pénh | 82 | 11.33 N | 104.55 E |
| Phoenix | 96 | 33.27 N | 112.05 W |
| Phoenix Islands II | 82 | 4.00 S | 172.00 W |
| Phrae | 82 | 18.09 N | 100.08 E |

| Name | Page | Lat | Long |
|---|---|---|---|
| Phra Nakhon Si Ayutthaya | 82 | 14.21 N | 100.33 E |
| Phuket | 82 | 7.53 N | 98.24 E |
| Phuket, Ko I | 82 | 8.00 N | 98.22 E |
| Phu-quoc, Dao I | 82 | 10.12 N | 104.00 E |
| Piacenza | 72 | 45.01 N | 9.40 E |
| Piatra-Neamţ | 66 | 46.56 N | 26.22 E |
| Piazza Armerina | 72 | 37.23 N | 14.22 E |
| Pibor ≃ | 88 | 8.26 N | 33.13 E |
| Pickering | 56 | 54.14 N | 0.46 W |
| Pickering, Vale of ≃ | 56 | 54.12 N | 0.45 W |
| Picton, Isla I | 102 | 55.02 S | 66.57 W |
| Piddle ≃ | 54 | 50.42 N | 2.04 W |
| Piddletrenthide | 54 | 50.48 N | 2.25 W |
| Pidurutalagala ∧ | 84 | 7.00 N | 80.46 E |
| Piedras Negras | 98 | 28.42 N | 100.31 W |
| Piekšämäki | 50 | 62.18 N | 27.08 E |
| Pierowall | 58 | 59.20 N | 2.59 W |
| Pierre | 96 | 44.22 N | 100.21 W |
| Pieśt'any | 66 | 48.36 N | 17.50 E |
| Pietermaritzburg | 90 | 29.37 S | 30.16 E |
| Pietersburg | 90 | 23.54 S | 29.25 E |
| Pietrasanta | 72 | 43.57 N | 10.14 E |
| Pikal'ovo | 62 | 59.31 N | 34.06 E |
| Pikes Peak ∧ | 96 | 38.51 N | 105.03 W |
| Piła (Schneidemühl) | 66 | 53.10 N | 16.44 E |
| Pilcomayo ≃ | 102 | 25.21 S | 57.42 W |
| Pilibhīt | 84 | 28.38 N | 79.48 E |
| Pinang (George Town) | 82 | 5.25 N | 100.20 E |
| Pinang, Pulau I | 82 | 5.24 N | 100.19 E |
| Pinar del Rio | 98 | 22.25 N | 83.42 W |
| Pindaré ≃ | 100 | 3.17 S | 44.47 W |
| Pindhos Óros ↗ | 50 | 39.49 N | 21.14 E |
| Pine ≃ | 94 | 56.08 N | 120.41 W |
| Pine Bluff | 96 | 34.13 N | 92.01 W |
| Pinega ≃ | 62 | 64.08 N | 41.54 E |
| Pinehouse Lake ⊕ | 94 | 55.32 N | 106.35 W |
| Pinerolo | 72 | 44.53 N | 7.21 E |
| Ping ≃ | 82 | 15.42 N | 100.09 E |
| Pingdingshan | 80 | 33.44 N | 113.18 E |
| Pingliang | 80 | 35.27 N | 107.10 E |
| Pingtung | 80 | 22.40 N | 120.29 E |
| Pingxiang | 80 | 22.09 N | 106.43 E |
| Pingyao | 80 | 37.16 N | 112.09 E |
| Pinhoe | 54 | 50.44 N | 3.27 W |
| Pinneberg | 66 | 53.40 N | 9.47 E |
| Pinos, Isla de I | 98 | 21.40 N | 82.50 W |
| Pinsk | 62 | 52.07 N | 26.04 E |
| Pinwherry | 56 | 55.09 N | 4.50 W |
| Pinxton | 54 | 53.05 N | 1.19 W |
| Piombino | 72 | 42.55 N | 10.32 E |
| Pioner, Ostrov I | 78 | 79.50 N | 92.30 E |
| Pionki | 66 | 51.30 N | 21.27 E |
| Piorini ≃ | 100 | 3.23 S | 63.30 W |
| Piotrków Trybunalski | 66 | 51.25 N | 19.42 E |
| Pipestone ≃ | 94 | 52.53 N | 89.23 W |
| Pipmuacan, Réservoir ⊕¹ | 94 | 49.35 N | 70.30 W |
| Piracicaba | 100 | 22.43 S | 47.38 W |
| Piraiévs (Piraeus) | 50 | 37.57 N | 23.38 E |
| Pirapora | 100 | 17.21 S | 44.56 W |
| Pirgos | 50 | 37.41 N | 21.28 E |
| Pirmasens | 66 | 49.12 N | 7.36 E |
| Pirot | 74 | 43.09 N | 22.35 E |
| Pisa | 72 | 43.43 N | 10.23 E |
| Pisco | 100 | 13.42 S | 76.13 W |
| Pisek | 66 | 49.19 N | 14.10 E |
| Pisticci | 72 | 40.23 N | 16.34 E |
| Pistoia | 72 | 43.55 N | 10.54 E |
| Piteå | 64 | 65.20 N | 21.30 E |
| Piteälven ≃ | 50 | 65.14 N | 21.32 E |
| Pitești | 74 | 44.52 N | 24.52 E |
| Pit'käranta | 62 | 61.34 N | 31.27 E |
| Pitlochry | 58 | 56.43 N | 3.45 W |
| Pittenweem | 58 | 56.12 N | 2.44 W |
| Pitt Island I | 93b | 44.18 S | 176.05 E |
| Pittsburgh | 96 | 40.26 N | 80.00 W |
| Piu, Cerro ∧ | 98 | 13.38 N | 84.52 W |
| Piura | 100 | 5.12 S | 80.38 W |
| Placentia Bay C | 94 | 47.15 N | 54.30 W |
| Placetas | 98 | 22.19 N | 79.40 W |
| Plata, Rio de la C¹ | 102 | 35.00 S | 57.00 W |
| Platte ≃ | 96 | 41.04 N | 95.53 W |
| Platte Island I | 90 | 5.52 S | 55.23 E |
| Plauen | 66 | 50.30 N | 12.08 E |
| Playgreen Lake ⊕ | 94 | 54.00 N | 98.11 W |
| Pleven | 74 | 43.25 N | 24.37 E |
| Pljevlja | 74 | 43.21 N | 19.21 E |
| Płock | 66 | 52.33 N | 19.43 E |
| Ploiești | 74 | 44.56 N | 26.02 E |
| Płońsk | 66 | 52.38 N | 20.23 E |
| Plovdiv | 74 | 42.09 N | 24.45 E |
| Plumbridge | 60 | 54.46 N | 7.15 W |
| Plym ≃ | 54 | 50.22 N | 4.05 W |
| Plymouth, Monts. | 98 | 16.42 N | 62.13 W |
| Plymouth, Eng., U.K. | 54 | 50.23 N | 4.10 W |
| Plympton | 54 | 50.23 N | 4.04 W |
| Plymstock | 54 | 50.22 N | 4.04 W |
| Plynlimon ∧ | 54 | 52.28 N | 3.47 W |
| Plzeň | 66 | 49.45 N | 13.23 E |
| Pobeda, Gora ∧ | 78 | 65.12 N | 146.12 E |
| Pobedy, Pik ∧ | 76 | 42.02 N | 80.05 E |
| Pocatello | 96 | 42.52 N | 112.27 W |
| Pochinki | 62 | 54.41 N | 44.50 E |
| Pochinok | 62 | 54.23 N | 32.28 E |
| Pocklington | 56 | 53.56 N | 0.46 W |
| Poços de Caldas | 100 | 21.48 S | 46.34 W |
| Poděbrady | 66 | 50.08 N | 15.07 E |
| Podkamennaja Tunguska ≃ | 78 | 61.36 N | 90.18 E |
| Podol'sk | 62 | 55.26 N | 37.33 E |
| Podporožje | 62 | 60.55 N | 34.10 E |
| Poggibonsi | 72 | 43.28 N | 11.09 E |
| P'ohang | 80 | 36.03 N | 129.22 E |
| Pointe-à-Pitre | 98 | 16.14 N | 61.32 W |
| Pointe-Noire | 90 | 4.48 S | 11.51 E |
| Poissy | 68 | 48.56 N | 2.03 E |
| Poitiers | 68 | 46.35 N | 0.20 E |
| Poland □¹ | 66 | 52.00 N | 19.00 E |
| Pol'arnyj | 62 | 69.13 N | 33.23 E |
| Polden Hills ↗² | 54 | 51.08 N | 2.50 W |
| Polegate | 54 | 50.49 N | 0.15 E |
| Polesje ≃¹ | 62 | 52.00 N | 27.00 E |
| Polessk | 66 | 54.52 N | 21.05 E |
| Polesworth | 54 | 52.37 N | 1.37 W |
| Polgár | 66 | 47.52 N | 21.08 E |
| Police | 66 | 53.35 N | 14.35 E |
| Polillo Islands II | 82 | 14.50 N | 122.05 E |
| Polistena | 72 | 38.24 N | 16.05 E |
| Pollaphuca Reservoir ⊕¹ | 60 | 53.08 N | 6.31 W |
| Polock | 62 | 55.29 N | 28.48 E |
| Polperro | 54 | 50.19 N | 4.31 W |
| Polruan | 54 | 50.19 N | 4.38 W |
| Poltava | 62 | 49.35 N | 34.34 E |
| Polunočnoje | 76 | 60.53 N | 60.25 E |
| Polynesia ≃¹ | 8 | 4.00 S | 156.00 W |
| Pomeroy | 60 | 54.36 N | 6.56 W |
| Pompei | 72 | 40.45 N | 14.30 E |
| Ponce | 98 | 18.01 N | 66.37 W |
| Pondcherry | 84 | 11.56 N | 79.50 E |
| Pond Inlet ⋃ | 94 | 72.40 N | 77.00 W |
| Ponferrada | 70 | 42.33 N | 6.35 W |
| Pongola ≃ | 90 | 26.54 S | 32.02 E |
| Ponoj ≃ | 62 | 66.59 N | 41.17 E |
| Ponta Grossa | 100 | 25.05 S | 50.09 W |
| Pont-à-Mousson | 68 | 48.54 N | 6.03 E |
| Pontardawe | 54 | 51.44 N | 3.51 W |
| Pontardulais | 54 | 51.43 N | 4.03 W |
| Pontarlier | 68 | 46.54 N | 6.22 E |
| Pontassieve | 72 | 43.46 N | 11.26 E |
| Pontchartrain, Lake ⊕ | 96 | 30.10 N | 90.10 W |
| Pontedera | 72 | 43.40 N | 10.38 E |
| Ponteeland | 56 | 55.03 N | 1.44 W |
| Pontefract | 56 | 53.42 N | 1.18 W |
| Ponteland | 56 | 55.03 N | 1.45 W |
| Ponte Nova | 100 | 20.24 S | 42.54 W |
| Ponterwyd | 54 | 52.25 N | 3.51 W |

| Name | Page | Lat | Long |
|---|---|---|---|
| Pontesbury | 54 | 52.39 N | 2.54 W |
| Pontevedra | 70 | 42.26 N | 8.38 W |
| Pontiac | 96 | 42.37 N | 83.18 W |
| Pontianak | 82 | 0.02 S | 109.20 E |
| Pontivy | 68 | 48.04 N | 2.59 E |
| Pontoise | 68 | 49.03 N | 2.06 E |
| Pontremoli | 72 | 44.22 N | 9.53 E |
| Pontrhydfendigaid | 54 | 52.17 N | 3.51 W |
| Pontyberem | 54 | 51.17 N | 4.09 W |
| Pontycymmer | 54 | 51.37 N | 3.34 W |
| Pontypool | 54 | 51.43 N | 3.02 W |
| Pontypridd | 54 | 51.37 N | 3.22 W |
| Ponziane, Isole II | 50 | 40.55 N | 12.57 E |
| Poole | 54 | 50.43 N | 1.59 W |
| Poole Bay C | 54 | 50.42 N | 1.52 W |
| Poolewe | 58 | 57.45 N | 5.37 W |
| Poopó, Lago de ⊕ | 100 | 18.45 S | 67.07 W |
| Popayán | 100 | 2.27 N | 76.36 W |
| Poperinge | 68 | 50.51 N | 2.43 E |
| Popham Bay C | 94 | 64.10 N | 65.10 W |
| Popigaj ≃ | 78 | 72.54 N | 106.36 E |
| Poplar ≃ | 94 | 53.00 N | 97.19 W |
| Popocatépetl, Volcán ∧¹ | 98 | 19.02 N | 98.38 W |
| Popomanaseu, Mount ∧ | 92 | 9.42 S | 160.04 E |
| Popovo | 74 | 43.21 N | 26.13 E |
| Poprad | 66 | 49.03 N | 20.18 E |
| Porbandar | 84 | 21.38 N | 69.36 E |
| Porcher Island I | 94 | 53.57 N | 130.30 W |
| Porchov | 62 | 57.46 N | 29.34 E |
| Porcuna | 70 | 37.52 N | 4.11 W |
| Porcupine ≃ | 94 | 66.34 N | 145.14 W |
| Poronajsk | 78 | 49.14 N | 143.04 E |
| Porsgrunn | 64 | 59.09 N | 9.40 E |
| Portacloy | 60 | 54.19 N | 9.48 W |
| Portadown | 60 | 54.26 N | 6.27 W |
| Portaferry | 60 | 54.23 N | 5.33 W |
| Portalegre | 70 | 39.17 N | 7.26 W |
| Portarlington | 60 | 53.10 N | 7.11 W |
| Port Arthur | 96 | 29.55 N | 93.55 W |
| Port Askaig | 58 | 55.51 N | 6.07 W |
| Port-au-Prince | 98 | 18.32 N | 72.20 W |
| Port Bannatyne | 58 | 55.52 N | 5.05 W |
| Port Blair | 84 | 11.40 N | 92.45 E |
| Port Elizabeth | 90 | 33.58 S | 25.40 E |
| Port Ellen | 58 | 55.39 N | 6.12 W |
| Port Erin | 56 | 54.06 N | 4.44 W |
| Porteynon | 54 | 51.33 N | 4.13 W |
| Porteynon Point ❯ | 54 | 51.32 N | 4.12 W |
| Port-Gentil | 90 | 0.43 S | 8.47 E |
| Port Glasgow | 58 | 55.57 N | 4.41 W |
| Portglenone | 60 | 54.53 N | 6.27 W |
| Porth | 54 | 51.36 N | 3.25 W |
| Port Harcourt | 86 | 4.43 N | 7.05 E |
| Porthcawl | 54 | 51.29 N | 3.42 W |
| Port Huron | 96 | 42.58 N | 82.27 W |
| Portimão | 70 | 37.08 N | 8.32 W |
| Port Isaac | 54 | 50.35 N | 4.50 W |
| Portishead | 54 | 51.30 N | 2.46 W |
| Portknockie | 58 | 57.41 N | 2.51 W |
| Portland, Maine, U.S. | 96 | 43.39 N | 70.17 W |
| Portland, Oreg., U.S. | 96 | 45.31 N | 122.36 W |
| Portland, Bill of ❯ | 52 | 50.31 N | 2.27 W |
| Portland, Isle of I | 54 | 50.32 N | 2.27 W |
| Portlaoighise | 60 | 53.02 N | 7.17 W |
| Portlaw | 60 | 52.17 N | 7.19 W |
| Port Logan | 56 | 54.43 N | 4.56 W |
| Port Louis | 90 | 20.10 S | 57.32 E |
| Port Moresby | 92 | 9.30 S | 147.10 E |
| Portnaguiran | 58 | 58.17 N | 6.13 W |
| Portnahaven | 58 | 55.41 N | 6.31 W |
| Pôrto | 70 | 41.11 N | 8.36 W |
| Pôrto Alegre | 102 | 30.04 S | 51.11 W |
| Porto Amélia | 90 | 12.58 S | 40.30 E |
| Port Talbot | 54 | 51.35 N | 3.47 W |
| Porto Empedocle | 72 | 37.17 N | 13.32 E |
| Port of Ness | 58 | 58.29 N | 6.13 W |
| Port of Spain | 98 | 10.39 N | 61.31 W |
| Portogruaro | 72 | 45.47 N | 12.50 E |
| Porto Sant Giorgio | 72 | 43.11 N | 13.48 E |
| Porto Sant'Elpidio | 72 | 43.15 N | 13.45 E |
| Porto Torres | 72 | 40.50 N | 8.23 E |
| Porto-Vecchio | 50 | 41.35 N | 9.17 E |
| Porto Velho | 100 | 8.46 S | 63.54 W |
| Portovoje | 62 | 1.03 S | 80.27 W |
| Portpatrick | 56 | 54.51 N | 5.07 W |
| Port Phillip Bay C | 92 | 38.07 S | 144.48 E |
| Portree | 58 | 57.24 N | 6.12 W |
| Portrush | 60 | 55.12 N | 6.40 W |
| Portsalon | 60 | 55.12 N | 7.37 W |
| Port Seton | 58 | 55.58 N | 2.57 W |
| Portslade | 54 | 50.50 N | 0.11 W |
| Portsmouth, Eng., U.K. | 54 | 50.48 N | 1.05 W |
| Portsmouth, N.H., U.S. | 96 | 43.04 N | 70.46 W |
| Portsmouth, Ohio, U.S. | 96 | 38.44 N | 82.59 W |
| Portsmouth, Va., U.S. | 96 | 36.50 N | 76.18 W |
| Portsoy | 58 | 57.41 N | 2.41 W |
| Portstewart | 60 | 55.11 N | 6.43 W |
| Port Talbot | 54 | 51.35 N | 3.47 W |
| Portugal □¹ | 70 | 39.30 N | 8.00 W |
| Portugalete | 70 | 43.19 N | 3.01 W |
| Port-Vladimir | 62 | 69.25 N | 33.06 E |
| Port William | 56 | 54.46 N | 4.35 W |
| Porz | 66 | 50.53 N | 7.03 E |
| Posadas | 102 | 27.23 S | 55.53 W |
| Posechonje-Volodarsk | 62 | 58.30 N | 39.07 E |
| Pössneck | 66 | 50.42 N | 11.37 E |
| Postavy | 62 | 55.07 N | 26.50 E |
| Potchefstroom | 90 | 26.41 S | 27.01 E |
| Potenza | 72 | 40.38 N | 15.48 E |
| Poti | 62 | 42.09 N | 41.40 E |
| Potomac ≃ | 96 | 38.00 N | 76.18 W |
| Potosi | 100 | 19.35 S | 65.45 W |
| Potsdam | 66 | 52.24 N | 13.04 E |
| Potter Heigham | 54 | 52.44 N | 1.33 E |
| Potters Bar | 54 | 51.42 N | 0.11 W |
| Potter Street | 54 | 51.46 N | 0.08 E |
| Potton | 54 | 52.08 N | 0.14 W |
| Poughkeepsie | 96 | 41.42 N | 73.56 W |
| Poulaphouca Reservoir ⊕¹ | 60 | 53.08 N | 6.31 W |
| Poulton-le-Fylde | 56 | 53.51 N | 2.59 W |
| Poundstock | 54 | 50.46 N | 4.34 W |
| Poûthisăt | 82 | 12.32 N | 103.55 E |
| Považská Bystrica | 66 | 49.08 N | 18.27 E |
| Póvoa de Varzim | 70 | 41.23 N | 8.46 W |
| Povungnituk, Rivière ≃ | 94 | 60.03 N | 77.15 W |
| Powder ≃ | 96 | 46.44 N | 105.26 W |
| Powell, Lake ⊕¹ | 96 | 37.25 N | 110.45 W |
| Powys, Vale of ∨ | 54 | 52.19 N | 3.08 W |
| Poyang Hu ⊕ | 80 | 29.00 N | 116.25 E |
| Poynton | 56 | 53.21 N | 2.07 W |
| Poyntzpass | 60 | 54.17 N | 6.23 W |
| Poza Rica de Hidalgo | 98 | 20.33 N | 97.27 W |
| Poznań | 66 | 52.25 N | 16.55 E |
| Pozoblanco | 70 | 38.22 N | 4.51 W |
| Pozza | 72 | 40.49 N | 14.02 E |
| Pozzuoli | 72 | 40.49 N | 14.07 E |
| Praha (Prague) | 66 | 50.05 N | 14.26 E |
| Praia | 86 | 14.55 N | 23.31 W |
| Prat de Llobregat | 70 | 41.20 N | 2.06 E |
| Prawle Point ❯ | 54 | 50.13 N | 3.43 W |
| Pra'iza | 72 | 61.42 N | 33.15 E |
| Preetz | 66 | 54.14 N | 10.16 E |
| Premnitz | 66 | 52.32 N | 12.20 E |
| Preparis Island I | 82 | 14.52 N | 93.41 E |
| Preparis North Channel ⋃ | 82 | 15.27 N | 94.05 E |
| Preparis South Channel ⋃ | 82 | 14.40 N | 94.00 E |

| Name | Page | Lat | Long |
|---|---|---|---|
| Přerov | 66 | 49.27 N | 17.27 E |
| Prescot | 56 | 53.26 N | 2.48 W |
| Prescott Island I | 94 | 73.01 N | 96.50 W |
| Presidente Prudente | 100 | 22.07 S | 51.22 W |
| Prešov | 66 | 49.00 N | 21.15 E |
| Prestatyn | 56 | 53.20 N | 3.24 W |
| Presteigne | 54 | 52.17 N | 3.00 W |
| Preston, Eng., U.K. | 56 | 53.46 N | 0.12 W |
| Preston, Eng., U.K. | 56 | 53.46 N | 2.42 W |
| Prestonpans | 58 | 55.57 N | 3.00 W |
| Prestwich | 56 | 53.32 N | 2.17 W |
| Prestwick | 58 | 55.30 N | 4.37 W |
| Pretoria | 90 | 25.45 S | 28.10 E |
| Préveza | 74 | 38.57 N | 20.44 E |
| Přibram | 66 | 49.42 N | 14.01 E |
| Priego de Córdoba | 70 | 37.26 N | 4.11 W |
| Priest Island I | 58 | 57.58 N | 5.30 W |
| Prievidza | 66 | 48.47 N | 18.37 E |
| Prijedor | 72 | 44.59 N | 16.43 E |
| Prikaspijskaja Nizmennost' ≃ | 76 | 48.00 N | 52.00 E |
| Prilep | 74 | 41.20 N | 21.33 E |
| Primorje | 76 | 50.36 N | 32.24 E |
| Primorsk, S.S.S.R. | 66 | 54.57 N | 20.00 E |
| Primorsk, S.S.S.R. | 64 | 60.22 N | 28.36 E |
| Primrose Lake ⊕ | 94 | 54.55 N | 109.45 W |
| Prince Albert | 94 | 53.12 N | 105.46 W |
| Prince Albert Sound ⋃ | 94 | 70.25 N | 115.00 W |
| Prince Charles Island I | 94 | 67.50 N | 76.00 W |
| Prince-de-Galles, Cap du ❯ | 94 | 61.36 N | 71.30 W |
| Prince Edward Island □ | 94 | 46.20 N | 63.20 W |
| Prince of Wales Island I, Austl. | 92 | 10.40 S | 142.10 E |
| Prince of Wales Island I, N.W. Ter., Can. | 94 | 72.40 N | 99.00 W |
| Prince of Wales Strait ⋃ | 94 | 73.00 N | 117.00 W |
| Prince Regent Inlet ⋃ | 94 | 73.00 N | 90.30 W |
| Princes Risborough | 54 | 51.44 N | 0.51 W |
| Princess Royal Island I | 94 | 52.57 S | 128.49 W |
| Princetown | 54 | 50.33 N | 4.00 W |
| Principe I | 90 | 1.37 N | 7.25 E |
| Prioz'orsk | 62 | 61.03 N | 30.04 E |
| Pripjat' ≃ | 62 | 51.21 N | 30.09 E |
| Priština | 74 | 42.39 N | 21.10 E |
| Pritzwalk | 66 | 53.09 N | 12.10 E |
| Privodino | 62 | 61.05 N | 46.28 E |
| Privolžskaja Vozvyšennost' ≃¹ | 52 | 52.00 N | 46.00 E |
| Probolinggo | 82 | 7.45 S | 113.13 E |
| Probus | 54 | 50.17 N | 4.57 W |
| Proddatūr | 84 | 14.44 N | 78.33 E |
| Professor Dr. Ir. W.J. Van Blommesten Meer ⊕¹ | 100 | 4.45 N | 55.00 W |
| Progreso | 98 | 21.17 N | 89.40 W |
| Prokopjevsk | 76 | 53.53 N | 86.45 E |
| Prokuplje | 74 | 43.14 N | 21.36 E |
| Prome (Pyè) | 82 | 18.49 N | 95.13 E |
| Prophet ≃ | 94 | 58.48 N | 122.45 W |
| Prostéjov | 66 | 49.29 N | 17.07 E |
| Providencia | 74 | 43.11 N | 22.05 E |
| Providence | 96 | 41.50 N | 71.25 W |
| Providence Island I | 90 | 9.14 S | 51.02 E |
| Provins | 68 | 48.33 N | 3.18 E |
| Provo | 96 | 40.14 N | 111.39 W |
| Prudhoe | 56 | 54.58 N | 1.51 W |
| Prudnik | 66 | 50.19 N | 17.34 E |
| Pruszków | 66 | 52.11 N | 20.48 E |
| Prutul (Prut) ≃ | 66 | 45.28 N | 28.12 E |
| Prysor ≃ | 54 | 52.56 N | 4.00 W |
| Przasnysz | 66 | 53.01 N | 20.55 E |
| Przemyśl | 66 | 49.47 N | 22.47 E |
| Przeval'sk | 76 | 42.29 N | 78.24 E |
| Pskov | 62 | 57.50 N | 28.20 E |
| Pszczyna | 66 | 50.00 N | 18.57 E |
| Ptolemais | 74 | 40.31 N | 21.41 E |
| Ptuj | 72 | 46.25 N | 15.52 E |
| Pucallpa | 100 | 8.23 S | 74.32 W |
| Pučež | 62 | 56.59 N | 43.11 E |
| Puddletown | 54 | 50.45 N | 2.21 W |
| Pudsey | 56 | 53.48 N | 1.39 W |
| Pudukkottai | 84 | 10.23 N | 78.49 E |
| Puebla | 98 | 19.03 N | 98.12 W |
| Pueblo | 96 | 38.16 N | 104.37 W |
| Puente-Genil | 70 | 37.23 N | 4.47 W |
| Puerto Berrio | 100 | 6.29 N | 74.24 W |
| Puerto Cabello | 100 | 10.28 N | 68.01 W |
| Puerto Cortés | 98 | 15.48 N | 87.56 W |
| Puerto la Cruz | 100 | 10.13 N | 64.38 W |
| Puerto Montt | 102 | 41.28 S | 72.57 W |
| Puerto Natales | 102 | 51.44 S | 72.31 W |
| Puerto Plata | 98 | 19.48 N | 70.41 W |
| Puerto Real | 70 | 36.32 N | 6.11 W |
| Puerto Rico □² | 98 | 18.15 N | 66.30 W |
| Puksoozero | 62 | 62.38 N | 40.36 E |
| Pula | 72 | 44.52 N | 13.50 E |
| Pulaj ≃ | 62 | 61.04 N | 48.07 E |
| Pulborough | 54 | 50.58 N | 0.31 W |
| Pulham Market | 54 | 52.25 N | 1.14 E |
| Pula Anna I | 82 | 4.40 N | 131.58 E |
| Pulog, Mount ∧ | 82 | 16.36 N | 120.54 E |
| Pultusk | 66 | 52.43 N | 21.05 E |
| Pumpsaint | 54 | 52.03 N | 3.58 W |
| Puná, Isla I | 100 | 2.50 S | 80.08 W |
| Pune (Poona) | 84 | 18.32 N | 73.52 E |
| Punta Alta | 102 | 38.53 S | 62.05 W |
| Punta Arenas | 102 | 53.09 S | 70.55 W |
| Punta Negra, Salar de ⊕ | 102 | 24.35 S | 69.00 W |
| Puntarenas | 98 | 9.58 N | 84.50 W |
| Punto Fijo | 100 | 11.42 N | 70.13 W |
| Pur ≃ | 76 | 67.31 N | 77.55 E |
| Purfleet | 54 | 51.29 N | 0.15 E |
| Puri | 84 | 19.48 N | 85.51 E |
| Purton | 54 | 51.35 N | 1.52 W |
| Purus (Purús) ≃ | 100 | 3.42 S | 61.28 W |
| Purwakarta | 82 | 6.34 S | 107.26 E |
| Purwokerto | 82 | 7.25 S | 109.14 E |
| Pusan | 80 | 35.06 N | 129.03 E |
| Puškin | 62 | 59.43 N | 30.25 E |
| Puškino | 62 | 56.01 N | 37.51 E |
| Püspökladány | 66 | 47.19 N | 21.07 E |
| Pustoška | 62 | 56.20 N | 29.22 E |
| Puting, Tanjung ❯ | 82 | 3.31 S | 111.46 E |
| Putoran, Plato ∧¹ | 78 | 69.00 N | 95.00 E |
| Putumayo (Içá) ≃ | 100 | 3.07 S | 67.58 W |
| Pwllheli | 54 | 52.53 N | 4.25 W |
| Pyhäjärvi ⊕ | 50 | 61.00 N | 22.20 E |
| Pyinmana | 82 | 19.44 N | 96.13 E |
| Pyle | 54 | 51.32 N | 3.42 W |
| Pyŏngyang | 80 | 39.01 N | 125.45 E |
| Pyramid Lake ⊕ | 96 | 40.00 N | 119.35 W |
| Pyrénées ↗ | 70 | 42.40 N | 1.00 E |
| Pyskowice | 66 | 50.24 N | 18.38 E |
| **Q** | | | |
| Qal'at Bīshah | 84 | 20.01 N | 42.36 E |
| Qamar, Ghubbat al- C | 84 | 16.00 N | 52.30 E |
| Qandahār | 84 | 31.32 N | 65.30 E |
| Qārūn, Birkat ⊕ | 88 | 29.28 N | 30.40 E |
| Qatar (Qaṭar) □¹ | 84 | 25.00 N | 51.10 E |
| Qeqertaq | 72 | 36.16 N | 27.06 E |
| Qeshm I | 84 | 26.45 N | 55.45 E |
| Qeys, Jazīreh-ye I | 84 | 26.32 N | 53.56 E |
| Qijiang | 80 | 29.00 N | 106.39 E |
| Qilianshan ∧ | 80 | 38.57 N | 99.07 E |

Symbols in the index entries are identified on page 111.

| Name | Page | Lat ° ' | Long ° ' |
|---|---|---|---|
| Qilianshanmai (Nanshan) ⋀ | 80 | 39.06 N | 98.40 E |
| Qilinhu @ | 80 | 31.50 N | 89.00 E |
| Qinā | 88 | 26.10 N | 32.43 E |
| Qingdao (Tsingtao) | 80 | 36.06 N | 120.19 E |
| Qinghai @ | 80 | 36.50 N | 100.20 E |
| Qinhuangdao | 80 | 39.56 N | 119.36 E |
| Qinlingshanmai ⋀ | 80 | 34.00 N | 108.00 E |
| Qionglai | 80 | 30.25 N | 103.27 E |
| Qiongzhouhaixia ⋃ | 80 | 20.10 N | 110.15 E |
| Qiqihaer (Tsitsihar) | 80 | 47.19 N | 123.55 E |
| Qom | 84 | 34.39 N | 50.54 E |
| Qondūz ≃ | 84 | 37.00 N | 68.16 E |
| Quantock Hills ⋀[2] | 54 | 51.07 N | 3.10 W |
| Quanzhou | 80 | 24.54 N | 118.35 E |
| Qu'Appelle ≃ | 94 | 50.25 N | 101.20 W |
| Quartu Sant'Elena | 72 | 39.14 N | 9.11 E |
| Quartz Lake @ | 94 | 70.55 N | 80.33 W |
| Qūchān | 84 | 37.06 N | 58.30 E |
| Queanbeyan | 92 | 35.21 S | 149.14 E |
| Québec | 94 | 46.49 N | 71.14 W |
| Quebec (Québec) □[4] | 94 | 52.00 N | 72.00 W |
| Quedlinburg | 66 | 51.48 N | 11.09 E |
| Queenborough | 54 | 51.26 N | 0.45 E |
| Queen Charlotte Islands II | 94 | 53.00 N | 132.00 W |
| Queen Charlotte Sound ⋃ | 94 | 51.30 N | 129.30 W |
| Queen Charlotte Strait ⋃ | 94 | 50.50 N | 127.25 W |
| Queen Maud Gulf C | 94 | 68.25 N | 102.30 W |
| Queensbury | 56 | 53.46 N | 1.50 W |
| Queens Channel II | 94 | 76.11 N | 96.00 W |
| Queens Channel ⋃ | 92 | 14.46 S | 129.24 E |
| Queensferry, Scot., U.K. | 58 | 55.59 N | 3.25 W |
| Queensferry, Wales, U.K. | 56 | 53.12 N | 3.01 W |
| Queenstown | 90 | 31.52 S | 26.52 E |
| Quelimane | 90 | 17.53 S | 36.51 E |
| Que Que | 90 | 18.55 S | 29.49 E |
| Querétaro | 98 | 20.36 N | 100.23 W |
| Quesnel Lake @ | 94 | 52.32 N | 121.05 W |
| Quetta | 84 | 30.12 N | 67.00 E |
| Quevedo | 100 | 1.02 S | 79.29 W |
| Quezaltenango | 98 | 14.50 N | 91.31 W |
| Quezon City | 82 | 14.38 N | 121.00 E |
| Quibdó | 100 | 5.42 N | 76.40 W |
| Quillota | 102 | 32.53 S | 71.16 W |
| Quilon | 84 | 8.53 N | 76.36 E |
| Quilty | 60 | 52.47 N | 9.26 W |
| Quimper | 68 | 48.00 N | 4.06 W |
| Quimperlé | 68 | 47.52 N | 3.33 W |
| Quincy | 96 | 39.56 N | 91.23 W |
| Qui-nhon | 82 | 13.46 N | 109.14 E |
| Quito | 100 | 0.13 S | 78.30 W |
| Quoich ≃ | 94 | 64.00 N | 93.30 W |
| Quoich, Loch @ | 58 | 57.04 N | 5.17 W |
| Quorndon | 54 | 52.45 N | 1.09 W |
| Quoyness | 58 | 58.54 N | 3.18 W |
| Quxian | 80 | 28.58 N | 118.52 E |
| **R** | | | |
| Raasay I | 52 | 57.25 N | 6.04 W |
| Raasay, Sound of ⋃ | 58 | 57.27 N | 6.06 W |
| Raba | 82 | 8.27 S | 118.46 E |
| Rabat, Magreb | 86 | 34.02 N | 6.51 W |
| Rabat (Victoria), Malta | 72 | 36.02 N | 14.14 E |
| Rabka | 66 | 49.36 N | 19.56 E |
| Raboćeostrovsk | 62 | 64.02 N | 34.46 E |
| Race, Cape > | 94 | 46.40 N | 53.10 W |
| Rach-gia | 82 | 10.01 N | 105.05 E |
| Racibórz (Ratibor) | 66 | 50.06 N | 18.13 E |
| Racine | 96 | 42.43 N | 87.48 W |
| Rackwick | 58 | 58.52 N | 3.23 W |
| Rădăuţi | 74 | 47.51 N | 25.55 E |
| Radcliffe | 56 | 53.34 N | 2.20 W |
| Radcliffe-on-Trent | 54 | 52.57 N | 1.03 W |
| Radeberg | 66 | 51.07 N | 13.55 E |
| Radebeul | 66 | 51.06 N | 13.40 E |
| Radevormwald | 66 | 51.12 N | 7.21 E |
| Radlett | 54 | 51.42 N | 0.20 W |
| Radnor Forest ∧ | 54 | 52.18 N | 3.10 W |
| Radolfzell | 66 | 47.44 N | 8.58 E |
| Radom | 66 | 51.25 N | 21.10 E |
| Radomsko | 66 | 51.05 N | 19.25 E |
| Radstock | 54 | 51.18 N | 2.28 W |
| Radstock, Cape > | 92 | 33.12 S | 134.20 E |
| Raḍwā, Jabal ∧ | 84 | 24.34 N | 38.18 E |
| Rae ≃ | 94 | 67.55 N | 115.30 W |
| Raeside, Lake @ | 92 | 29.30 S | 122.00 E |
| Rafaela | 102 | 31.16 S | 61.29 W |
| Rafsanjān | 84 | 30.24 N | 56.01 E |
| Raglan | 54 | 51.47 N | 2.51 W |
| Ragusa | 72 | 36.55 N | 14.44 E |
| Rahad, Nahr ar- ≃ | 88 | 14.28 N | 33.31 E |
| Rāichūr | 84 | 16.12 N | 77.21 E |
| Rainford | 56 | 53.30 N | 2.48 W |
| Rainham | 54 | 51.23 N | 0.36 E |
| Rainham ◆[8] | 54 | 51.31 N | 0.11 E |
| Rainhill | 56 | 53.26 N | 2.46 W |
| Rainier, Mount ∧ | 96 | 46.52 N | 121.46 W |
| Rainworth | 56 | 53.07 N | 1.08 W |
| Rainy Lake @ | 94 | 48.42 N | 93.10 W |
| Raipur | 84 | 21.14 N | 81.38 E |
| Rājahmundry | 84 | 17.01 N | 81.48 E |
| Rajang ≃ | 82 | 2.04 N | 111.12 E |
| Rājapālaiyam | 84 | 9.27 N | 77.33 E |
| Rajčichinsk | 78 | 49.46 N | 129.25 E |
| Rājkot | 84 | 22.18 N | 70.47 E |
| Rājshāhi | 84 | 24.22 N | 88.36 E |
| Rakaposhi ∧ | 84 | 36.09 N | 74.28 E |
| Rakovník | 66 | 50.05 N | 13.43 E |
| Rakvere | 62 | 59.22 N | 26.20 E |
| Raleigh | 96 | 35.47 N | 78.39 W |
| Ramasaig | 58 | 57.24 N | 6.44 W |
| Rambouillet | 68 | 48.39 N | 1.50 E |
| Rame Head > | 54 | 50.19 N | 4.13 W |
| Ramm, Jabal ∧ | 84 | 29.35 N | 35.24 E |
| Ramor, Lough @ | 60 | 53.49 N | 7.05 W |
| Ramparts ≃ | 94 | 66.11 N | 129.03 W |
| Rampside | 56 | 54.05 N | 3.10 W |
| Rāmpur | 84 | 28.48 N | 79.03 E |
| Ramree Island I | 82 | 19.06 N | 93.48 E |
| Ramsbottom | 56 | 53.40 N | 2.19 W |
| Ramsey, I. of Man | 56 | 54.20 N | 4.21 W |
| Ramsey, Eng., U.K. | 54 | 51.56 N | 1.14 E |
| Ramsey, Eng., U.K. | 54 | 52.27 N | 0.07 W |
| Ramsey Island I | 54 | 51.52 N | 5.10 W |
| Ramsgate | 54 | 51.20 N | 1.25 E |
| Rancagua | 102 | 34.10 S | 70.45 W |
| Rānchī | 84 | 23.22 N | 85.19 E |
| Randalstown | 60 | 54.45 N | 6.18 W |
| Randers | 64 | 56.28 N | 10.03 E |
| Ranfurly | 58 | 55.52 N | 4.33 W |
| Rangoon | 82 | 16.47 N | 96.10 E |
| Rannoch, Loch @ | 52 | 56.41 N | 4.20 W |
| Rannoch Moor ◆[3] | 58 | 56.38 N | 4.40 W |
| Rann of Kutch ⊻ | 84 | 24.00 N | 70.00 E |
| Ranongga I | 92 | 8.05 S | 156.34 E |
| Rantauprapat | 82 | 2.06 N | 99.50 E |
| Rantekombola, Bulu ∧ | 82 | 3.21 S | 120.01 E |
| Rapallo | 72 | 44.21 N | 9.14 E |
| Raphoe | 60 | 54.52 N | 7.36 W |
| Rapid City | 96 | 44.05 N | 103.14 W |
| Rapness | 58 | 59.14 N | 2.51 W |
| Rápulo ≃ | 100 | 13.43 S | 65.32 W |
| Ras Dashen ∧ | 88 | 13.10 N | 38.26 E |
| Rashīd | 88 | 31.24 N | 30.25 E |
| Rasht | 84 | 37.16 N | 49.36 E |
| Rastatt | 66 | 48.51 N | 8.12 E |
| Rastede | 66 | 53.15 N | 8.11 E |
| Rathangan | 60 | 53.12 N | 6.59 W |
| Rathcormack | 60 | 52.54 N | 8.17 W |
| Rathdowney | 60 | 52.50 N | 7.34 W |
| Rathdrum | 60 | 52.56 N | 6.13 W |
| Rathen | 58 | 57.38 N | 2.02 W |
| Rathenow | 66 | 52.36 N | 12.20 E |
| Rathfriland | 60 | 54.14 N | 6.10 W |
| Rathkeale | 60 | 52.32 N | 8.56 W |
| Rathlin Island I | 52 | 55.18 N | 6.13 W |
| Rathlin Sound ⋃ | 60 | 55.16 N | 6.17 W |
| Ráth Luirc | 60 | 52.21 N | 8.41 W |
| Rathmelton | 60 | 55.02 N | 7.38 W |
| Rathmore | 60 | 52.03 N | 9.13 W |
| Rathmullen | 60 | 55.06 N | 7.33 W |
| Rathnew | 60 | 53.00 N | 6.05 W |
| Rathowen | 60 | 53.40 N | 7.31 W |
| Ratingen | 66 | 51.18 N | 6.51 E |
| Ratlām | 84 | 23.28 N | 75.00 E |
| Rattray Head > | 58 | 57.37 N | 1.49 W |
| Ratz, Mount ∧ | 94 | 57.23 N | 132.19 W |
| Ratzeburg | 66 | 53.42 N | 10.46 E |
| Rauma | 64 | 61.08 N | 21.30 E |
| Rauma ≃ | 50 | 62.33 N | 7.43 E |
| Raunds | 54 | 52.21 N | 0.33 W |
| Raurkela | 84 | 22.14 N | 84.54 E |
| Ravanusa | 72 | 37.16 N | 13.58 E |
| Ravenglass | 56 | 54.21 N | 3.24 W |
| Ravenna | 72 | 44.25 N | 12.12 E |
| Ravensburg | 66 | 47.47 N | 9.37 E |
| Ravensthorpe | 56 | 53.42 N | 1.35 W |
| Rāwalpindi | 84 | 33.36 N | 73.04 E |
| Rawicz | 66 | 51.37 N | 16.52 E |
| Rawmarsh | 56 | 53.27 N | 1.21 W |
| Rawtenstall | 56 | 53.42 N | 2.18 W |
| Ray ≃, Eng., U.K. | 54 | 51.38 N | 1.49 W |
| Ray ≃, Eng., U.K. | 54 | 51.48 N | 1.15 W |
| Raya, Bukit ∧ | 82 | 0.40 S | 112.41 E |
| Rayleigh | 54 | 51.36 N | 0.36 E |
| R'azan' | 62 | 54.38 N | 39.44 E |
| Razdel'naja | 74 | 46.51 N | 30.05 E |
| Razgrad | 74 | 43.32 N | 26.31 E |
| Ré, Île de I | 50 | 46.12 N | 1.25 W |
| Rea ≃, Eng., U.K. | 54 | 52.30 N | 1.51 W |
| Rea ≃, Eng., U.K. | 54 | 52.18 N | 2.32 W |
| Reading, Eng., U.K. | 54 | 51.28 N | 0.59 W |
| Reading, Pa., U.S. | 96 | 40.20 N | 75.56 W |
| Real, Cordillera ⋀ | 100 | 17.00 S | 67.10 W |
| Reay | 58 | 58.33 N | 3.47 W |
| Reay Forest ◆[3] | 58 | 58.19 N | 4.47 W |
| Recherche, Archipelago of the II | 92 | 34.05 S | 122.45 E |
| Rečica | 76 | 52.22 N | 30.25 E |
| Recife | 100 | 8.03 S | 34.54 W |
| Recklinghausen | 66 | 51.36 N | 7.13 E |
| Red (Hong) (Yuanjiang) ≃, As. | 80 | 20.17 N | 106.34 E |
| Red ≃, N.A. | 96 | 50.24 N | 96.48 W |
| Red ≃, U.S. | 96 | 31.00 N | 91.40 W |
| Redang, Pulau I | 82 | 5.47 N | 103.00 E |
| Redbourn | 54 | 51.48 N | 0.24 W |
| Redbridge ◆[8] | 54 | 51.34 N | 0.05 E |
| Redcar | 56 | 54.37 N | 1.04 W |
| Redcliffe, Mount ∧ | 92 | 28.25 S | 121.32 E |
| Red Deer | 94 | 52.16 N | 113.48 W |
| Red Deer ≃, Can. | 94 | 52.53 N | 101.01 W |
| Red Deer ≃, Can. | 94 | 50.56 N | 109.54 W |
| Red Dial | 56 | 54.48 N | 3.10 W |
| Redding | 96 | 40.35 N | 122.24 W |
| Redditch | 54 | 52.19 N | 1.56 W |
| Rede ≃ | 56 | 55.08 N | 2.13 W |
| Redesdale V | 56 | 55.17 N | 2.16 W |
| Redhill | 54 | 51.14 N | 0.11 W |
| Redland | 58 | 59.05 N | 3.05 W |
| Redon | 68 | 47.39 N | 2.05 W |
| Redruth | 54 | 50.13 N | 5.14 W |
| Red Sea ⊤[2] | 88 | 20.00 N | 38.00 E |
| Redstone ≃ | 94 | 64.17 N | 124.33 W |
| Red Wharf Bay C | 56 | 53.18 N | 4.10 W |
| Ree, Lough @ | 52 | 53.35 N | 8.00 W |
| Reepham | 54 | 52.46 N | 1.07 E |
| Regensburg | 66 | 49.01 N | 12.06 E |
| Reggio di Calabria | 72 | 38.07 N | 15.39 E |
| Reggio nell'Emilia | 72 | 44.43 N | 10.36 E |
| Reghin | 74 | 46.47 N | 24.42 E |
| Regina | 94 | 50.25 N | 104.39 W |
| Rehovot | 84 | 31.53 N | 34.48 E |
| Reichenbach | 66 | 50.37 N | 12.18 E |
| Reigate | 54 | 51.14 N | 0.13 W |
| Reims | 68 | 49.15 N | 4.02 E |
| Reina Adelaida, Archipiélago II | 102 | 52.10 S | 74.25 W |
| Reindeer Lake @ | 94 | 57.15 N | 102.40 W |
| Reinosa | 70 | 43.00 N | 4.08 W |
| Reiss | 58 | 58.28 N | 3.10 W |
| Remiremont | 68 | 48.01 N | 6.35 E |
| Remscheid | 66 | 51.11 N | 7.11 E |
| Rendova I | 92 | 8.32 S | 157.20 E |
| Rendsburg | 66 | 54.18 N | 9.40 E |
| Renfrew | 58 | 55.53 N | 4.24 W |
| Renish Point > | 58 | 57.44 N | 6.59 W |
| Rennell I | 92 | 11.40 S | 160.10 E |
| Rennes | 68 | 48.05 N | 1.41 W |
| Reno | 96 | 39.31 N | 119.48 W |
| Rentería | 70 | 43.19 N | 1.54 W |
| Republican ≃ | 96 | 39.03 N | 96.48 W |
| Resipol, Beinn ∧ | 58 | 56.43 N | 5.39 W |
| Resistencia | 102 | 27.27 S | 58.59 W |
| Reşiţa | 74 | 45.17 N | 21.53 E |
| Resolution Island I | 94 | 61.30 N | 65.00 W |
| Resolven | 54 | 51.42 N | 3.42 W |
| Resort, Loch C | 58 | 58.03 N | 7.06 W |
| Reston | 58 | 55.51 N | 2.11 W |
| Rethel | 68 | 49.31 N | 4.22 E |
| Réthimnon | 74 | 35.22 N | 24.29 E |
| Reunion (Réunion) □[2] | 90 | 21.06 S | 55.36 E |
| Reus | 70 | 41.09 N | 1.07 E |
| Reutlingen | 66 | 48.29 N | 9.11 E |
| Revda | 76 | 56.48 N | 59.57 E |
| Revillagigedo, Islas de II | 98 | 19.00 N | 111.30 W |
| Rewa | 84 | 24.32 N | 81.17 E |
| Rey | 84 | 35.35 N | 51.25 E |
| Rey, Isla del I | 98 | 8.22 N | 78.55 W |
| Reykjavík | 62a | 64.09 N | 21.51 W |
| Reynosa | 98 | 26.07 N | 98.18 W |
| Reẕā'īyeh | 84 | 37.33 N | 45.04 E |
| Reẕā'īyeh, Daryācheh-ye @ | 84 | 37.40 N | 45.30 E |
| Rezé | 68 | 47.12 N | 1.34 W |
| Rēzekne | 62 | 56.30 N | 27.19 E |
| Rhayader | 54 | 52.18 N | 3.30 W |
| Rhdsneigr | 56 | 53.14 N | 4.31 W |
| Rheda-Wiedenbrück | 66 | 51.50 N | 8.18 E |
| Rheidol ≃ | 54 | 52.25 N | 4.05 W |
| Rheine | 66 | 52.17 N | 7.26 E |
| Rheinfelden | 66 | 47.33 N | 7.47 E |
| Rheinhausen | 66 | 51.24 N | 6.44 E |
| Rheydt | 66 | 51.10 N | 6.25 E |
| Rhine ≃ | 50 | 51.52 N | 6.02 E |
| Rhinns of Kells ⋀ | 56 | 55.07 N | 4.22 W |
| Rhir, Cap > | 86 | 30.38 N | 9.55 W |
| Rhiw ≃ | 54 | 52.36 N | 3.11 W |
| Rho | 72 | 45.32 N | 9.02 E |
| Rhode Island □[3] | 96 | 41.40 N | 71.30 W |
| Rhodesia □[1] | 90 | 20.00 S | 30.00 E |
| Rhodope Mountains ⋀ | 50 | 41.30 N | 24.30 E |
| Rhondda | 54 | 51.40 N | 3.27 W |
| Rhône ≃ | 50 | 43.20 N | 4.50 E |
| Rhosllanerchrugog | 54 | 53.00 N | 3.03 W |
| Rhos-on-Sea | 56 | 53.19 N | 3.45 W |
| Rhossilli | 54 | 51.34 N | 4.17 W |
| Rhuddlan | 56 | 53.18 N | 3.27 W |
| Rhum I | 52 | 57.00 N | 6.20 W |
| Rhum, Sound of ⋃ | 58 | 56.56 N | 6.14 W |
| Rhyl | 56 | 53.19 N | 3.29 W |
| Rhymney | 54 | 51.46 N | 3.18 W |
| Rhymney ≃ | 54 | 51.28 N | 3.10 W |
| Rhynie | 58 | 57.19 N | 2.50 W |
| Riau, Kepulauan II | 82 | 1.00 N | 104.30 E |
| Rib ≃ | 54 | 51.48 N | 0.04 W |
| Ribble ≃ | 52 | 53.44 N | 2.50 W |
| Ribeirão Prêto | 100 | 21.10 S | 47.48 W |
| Ribera | 72 | 37.30 N | 13.16 E |
| Ribnitz-Damgarten | 66 | 54.15 N | 12.28 E |
| Riccall | 56 | 53.50 N | 1.04 W |
| Riccione | 72 | 43.59 N | 12.39 E |
| Richard Collinson Inlet C | 94 | 72.45 N | 113.45 W |
| Richard's Bay C | 90 | 28.50 S | 32.02 E |
| Richards Island I | 94 | 69.20 N | 134.30 W |
| Richardson ≃ | 94 | 58.30 N | 111.30 W |
| Richardson Mountains ⋀ | 94 | 67.15 N | 136.30 W |
| Richland | 96 | 46.17 N | 119.18 W |
| Richmond, Eng., U.K. | 56 | 54.24 N | 1.44 W |
| Richmond, Ind., U.S. | 96 | 39.50 N | 84.54 W |
| Richmond, Va., U.S. | 96 | 37.30 N | 77.28 W |
| Richmond ◆[8] | 54 | 51.28 N | 0.18 W |
| Rickmansworth | 54 | 51.39 N | 0.29 W |
| Riddon, Loch C | 58 | 55.58 N | 5.12 W |
| Riecawr, Loch @ | 56 | 55.13 N | 4.27 W |
| Riesa | 66 | 51.18 N | 13.17 E |
| Riesco, Isla I | 102 | 53.00 S | 72.30 W |
| Riesi | 72 | 37.17 N | 14.05 E |
| Rieti | 72 | 42.24 N | 12.51 E |
| Rif ⋀ | 86 | 35.00 N | 4.00 W |
| Rift Valley V | 90 | 3.00 S | 29.00 E |
| Rīga | 62 | 56.57 N | 24.06 E |
| Rīgestān ◆[1] | 84 | 31.00 N | 65.00 E |
| Riihimäki | 64 | 60.45 N | 24.46 E |
| Rijeka | 72 | 45.20 N | 14.27 E |
| Rijssen | 66 | 52.18 N | 6.30 E |
| Rikeze | 80 | 29.17 N | 88.53 E |
| Rillington | 56 | 54.09 N | 0.42 W |
| Rima ≃ | 86 | 13.04 N | 5.10 E |
| Rimavská Sobota | 66 | 48.23 N | 20.02 E |
| Rimini | 72 | 44.04 N | 12.34 E |
| Rîmnicu-Sărat | 74 | 45.23 N | 27.03 E |
| Rîmnicu-Vîlcea | 74 | 45.06 N | 24.22 E |
| Rinca, Pulau I | 82 | 8.41 S | 119.42 E |
| Ringford | 56 | 54.54 N | 4.03 W |
| Ringmer | 54 | 50.53 N | 0.04 E |
| Ringvassøya I | 50 | 69.55 N | 19.15 E |
| Ringville | 60 | 52.02 N | 7.34 W |
| Ringwood | 54 | 50.51 N | 1.47 W |
| Rinjani, Gunung ∧ | 82 | 8.24 S | 116.28 E |
| Rinnes, Ben ∧ | 58 | 57.23 N | 3.15 W |
| Rinns of Islay ⋀ | 58 | 55.45 N | 6.25 W |
| Rinns Point > | 52 | 55.40 N | 6.30 W |
| Riobamba | 100 | 1.40 S | 78.38 W |
| Rio Branco | 100 | 9.58 S | 67.48 W |
| Rio Claro | 100 | 22.24 S | 47.33 W |
| Río Cuarto | 102 | 33.08 S | 64.21 W |
| Rio de Janeiro | 100 | 22.54 S | 43.14 W |
| Río Gallegos | 102 | 51.38 S | 69.13 W |
| Riom | 68 | 45.54 N | 3.07 E |
| Rio Negro, Embalse del @[1] | 102 | 32.45 S | 56.00 W |
| Rio Negro, Pantanal do ☷ | 100 | 19.00 S | 56.00 W |
| Rionero in Vulture | 72 | 40.56 N | 15.41 E |
| Ripley | 54 | 53.03 N | 1.24 W |
| Ripon | 56 | 54.08 N | 1.31 W |
| Ripponden | 56 | 53.41 N | 1.57 W |
| Risca | 54 | 51.37 N | 3.07 W |
| Riva | 72 | 45.53 N | 10.50 E |
| Rive-de-Gier | 68 | 45.32 N | 4.37 E |
| Rivera | 102 | 30.54 S | 55.31 W |
| Riverina ◆[1] | 92 | 35.30 S | 145.30 E |
| Riverside | 96 | 33.59 N | 117.22 W |
| Rivoli | 72 | 45.04 N | 7.31 E |
| Rižskij Zaliv C | 50 | 57.30 N | 23.35 E |
| Roadhead | 56 | 55.04 N | 2.46 W |
| Roan Fell ∧ | 56 | 55.13 N | 2.52 W |
| Roanne | 68 | 46.02 N | 4.04 E |
| Roanoke | 96 | 37.16 N | 79.57 W |
| Roanoke ≃ | 96 | 35.56 N | 76.43 W |
| Roaringwater Bay C | 60 | 51.25 N | 9.35 W |
| Roatán, Isla de I | 98 | 16.23 N | 86.30 W |
| Robe ≃ | 52 | 53.37 N | 9.16 W |
| Robertsbridge | 54 | 50.59 N | 0.29 E |
| Roberts Peak ∧ | 94 | 52.57 N | 120.32 W |
| Robertstown | 60 | 53.15 N | 6.59 W |
| Robin Hood's Bay | 56 | 54.25 N | 0.33 W |
| Róbinson Crusoe, Isla (Isla Más A Tierra) I | 102 | 33.38 S | 78.52 W |
| Robinson Ranges ⋀ | 92 | 25.45 S | 119.00 E |
| Robson, Mount ∧ | 94 | 53.07 N | 119.09 W |
| Roca Partida, Isla I | 98 | 19.01 N | 112.02 W |
| Rocas, Atol das I[1] | 100 | 3.52 S | 33.59 W |
| Roch ≃ | 56 | 53.34 N | 2.18 W |
| Rochdale | 56 | 53.38 N | 2.09 W |
| Roche | 54 | 50.24 N | 4.48 W |
| Rochefort | 68 | 45.57 N | 0.58 W |
| Rochester, Eng., U.K. | 56 | 55.16 N | 2.16 W |
| Rochester, Minn., U.S. | 96 | 44.02 N | 92.29 W |
| Rochester, N.Y., U.S. | 96 | 43.10 N | 77.36 W |
| Rochford | 54 | 51.36 N | 0.43 E |
| Rochfort Bridge | 60 | 53.23 N | 7.17 W |
| Rockcorry | 60 | 54.07 N | 7.01 W |
| Rockford | 96 | 42.17 N | 89.06 W |
| Rockhampton | 92 | 23.23 S | 150.31 E |
| Rockingham Forest ◆[3] | 54 | 52.30 N | 0.37 W |
| Rock Island | 96 | 41.30 N | 90.34 W |
| Rocky Mount | 96 | 35.56 N | 77.48 W |
| Rocky Mountains ⋀ | 96 | 48.00 N | 116.00 W |
| Rodel | 58 | 57.41 N | 7.05 W |
| Roden ≃ | 54 | 52.43 N | 2.36 W |
| Rodez | 68 | 44.21 N | 2.35 E |
| Ródhos (Rhodes) | 74 | 36.26 N | 28.13 E |
| Ródhos (Rhodes) I | 50 | 36.10 N | 28.00 E |
| Roding ≃ | 54 | 51.31 N | 0.06 E |
| Rodniki | 62 | 57.06 N | 41.44 E |
| Roermond | 66 | 51.12 N | 6.00 E |
| Roeselare | 68 | 50.57 N | 3.08 E |
| Roes Welcome Sound ⋃ | 94 | 64.00 N | 88.00 W |
| Rogagua, Lago @ | 100 | 13.43 S | 66.54 W |
| Rogan's Seat ∧ | 56 | 54.25 N | 2.07 W |
| Rogart | 58 | 58.00 N | 4.08 W |
| Rogers, Mount ∧ | 96 | 36.39 N | 81.33 W |
| Rogoaguado, Lago @ | 100 | 12.52 S | 65.43 W |
| Rohtak | 84 | 28.54 N | 76.35 E |
| Rokan ≃ | 82 | 2.00 N | 100.52 E |
| Rokycany | 66 | 49.45 N | 13.36 E |
| Roma (Rome) | 72 | 41.54 N | 12.29 E |
| Romaine ≃ | 94 | 50.18 N | 63.47 W |
| Roman | 74 | 46.55 N | 26.56 E |
| Roman ≃ | 54 | 51.51 N | 0.57 E |
| Romang, Pulau I | 82 | 7.35 S | 127.26 E |
| Romania (România) □[1] | 50 | 46.00 N | 25.30 E |
| Roman-Koš, Gora ∧ | 76 | 44.37 N | 34.15 E |
| Romano, Cayo I | 98 | 22.04 N | 77.50 W |
| Romans[-sur-Isère] | 68 | 45.03 N | 5.03 E |
| Rome, Ga., U.S. | 96 | 34.16 N | 85.11 W |
| Rome, N.Y., U.S. | 96 | 43.13 N | 75.27 W |
| Romilly-sur-Seine | 68 | 48.31 N | 3.43 E |
| Romney Marsh ☷ | 54 | 51.03 N | 0.55 E |
| Romorantin-Lanthenay | 68 | 47.22 N | 1.45 E |
| Romsey | 54 | 50.59 N | 1.30 W |
| Rona I, Scot., U.K. | 52 | 59.07 N | 5.49 W |
| Rona I, Scot., U.K. | 58 | 57.34 N | 5.59 W |
| Ronas Hill ∧[2] | 52 | 60.31 N | 1.28 W |
| Ronas Voe C | 58 | 60.32 N | 1.29 W |
| Ronay I | 52 | 57.28 N | 7.07 W |
| Roncador, Serra do ⋀[1] | 100 | 12.00 S | 52.00 W |
| Ronda | 70 | 36.44 N | 5.10 W |
| Ronge, Lac la @ | 94 | 55.10 N | 105.00 W |
| Ron-ma, Mui > | 82 | 18.07 N | 106.22 E |
| Rønne | 64 | 55.06 N | 14.42 E |
| Ronneburg | 66 | 50.51 N | 12.10 E |
| Ronneby | 64 | 56.12 N | 15.18 E |
| Ronse | 68 | 50.45 N | 3.36 E |
| Ronuro ≃ | 100 | 11.56 S | 53.33 W |
| Roosevelt ≃ | 100 | 7.35 S | 60.20 W |
| Roper ≃ | 92 | 14.43 S | 135.27 E |
| Rora Head > | 58 | 58.52 N | 3.25 W |
| Roraima, Mount ∧ | 100 | 5.12 N | 60.44 W |
| Rorschach | 68 | 47.29 N | 9.30 E |
| Rosario | 102 | 32.57 S | 60.40 W |
| Rosarno | 72 | 38.29 N | 15.59 E |
| Roscommon | 60 | 53.38 N | 8.11 W |
| Roscommon □[6] | 52 | 53.40 N | 8.30 W |
| Roscrea | 60 | 52.57 N | 7.47 W |
| Roseau | 98 | 15.18 N | 61.24 W |
| Rosehearty | 58 | 57.42 N | 2.07 W |
| Rosenheim | 66 | 47.51 N | 12.07 E |
| Rosignano Marittimo | 72 | 43.24 N | 10.28 E |
| Roşiori-de-Vede | 74 | 44.07 N | 25.00 E |
| Roskilde | 64 | 55.39 N | 12.05 E |
| Roslags-Näsby | 64 | 59.26 N | 18.04 E |
| Roslavl' | 76 | 53.57 N | 32.52 E |
| Rossano | 72 | 39.35 N | 16.39 E |
| Rossan Point > | 52 | 54.42 N | 8.48 W |
| Rosscarbery | 60 | 51.35 N | 9.01 W |
| Rossel Island I | 92 | 11.21 S | 154.09 E |
| Rossendale V | 56 | 53.45 N | 2.47 W |
| Rosses Bay C | 60 | 55.10 N | 8.27 W |
| Rosses Point | 60 | 54.18 N | 8.33 W |
| Rosslare | 60 | 52.17 N | 6.23 W |
| Rosslare Harbour | 60 | 52.15 N | 6.22 W |
| Rosslau | 66 | 51.53 N | 12.14 E |
| Rosslea | 60 | 54.14 N | 7.11 W |
| Ross-on-Wye | 54 | 51.55 N | 2.35 W |
| Røst II | 50 | 67.28 N | 11.59 E |
| Rostock | 66 | 54.05 N | 12.07 E |
| Rostov | 62 | 57.11 N | 39.25 E |
| Rostov-na-Donu | 76 | 47.14 N | 39.42 E |
| Rostrevor | 60 | 54.06 N | 6.12 W |
| Roswell | 96 | 33.24 N | 104.32 W |
| Rosyth | 58 | 56.03 N | 3.26 W |
| Rota | 70 | 36.37 N | 6.21 W |
| Rota I | 82 | 14.10 N | 145.12 E |
| Rotenburg | 66 | 53.06 N | 9.24 E |
| Rothbury | 56 | 55.19 N | 1.55 W |
| Rothbury Forest ◆[3] | 56 | 55.18 N | 1.54 W |
| Rothenburg ob der Tauber | 66 | 49.23 N | 10.10 E |
| Rother ≃ | 54 | 50.57 N | 0.32 W |
| Rotherham | 56 | 53.26 N | 1.20 W |
| Rothes | 58 | 57.31 N | 3.13 W |
| Rothesay | 58 | 55.51 N | 5.03 W |
| Rothwell, Eng., U.K. | 54 | 52.25 N | 0.48 W |
| Rothwell, Eng., U.K. | 56 | 53.46 N | 1.29 W |
| Roti, Pulau I | 82 | 10.45 S | 123.10 E |
| Rotorua | 93a | 38.09 S | 176.15 E |
| Rotterdam | 66 | 51.55 N | 4.28 E |
| Rottingdean | 54 | 50.48 N | 0.04 W |
| Rottweil | 66 | 48.10 N | 8.37 E |
| Roubaix | 68 | 50.42 N | 3.10 E |
| Roudnice | 66 | 50.22 N | 14.16 E |
| Rouen | 68 | 49.26 N | 1.05 E |
| Round Mountain ∧ | 92 | 30.27 S | 152.14 E |
| Roundstone | 60 | 53.23 N | 9.53 W |
| Roundwood | 60 | 53.04 N | 6.13 W |
| Rousay I | 52 | 59.01 N | 3.02 W |
| Rovato | 72 | 45.34 N | 10.00 E |
| Rovereto | 72 | 45.53 N | 11.02 E |
| Rovigo | 72 | 45.04 N | 11.47 E |
| Rovno | 76 | 50.37 N | 26.15 E |
| Rowlands Gill | 56 | 54.54 N | 1.45 W |
| Rowley ≃ | 94 | 70.16 N | 77.45 W |
| Rowley Island I | 94 | 69.08 N | 78.50 W |
| Rowley Regis | 54 | 52.29 N | 2.03 W |
| Rowley Shoals ⊹[2] | 92 | 17.30 S | 119.00 E |
| Roxas (Capiz) | 82 | 11.35 N | 122.45 E |
| Roxburgh | 58 | 55.34 N | 2.30 W |
| Royal Canal ☰ | 52 | 53.21 N | 6.15 W |
| Royale, Isle I | 96 | 48.00 N | 89.00 W |
| Royal Leamington Spa | 54 | 52.18 N | 1.31 W |
| Royan | 68 | 45.37 N | 1.01 W |
| Roydon | 54 | 51.46 N | 0.03 E |
| Royston, Eng., U.K. | 54 | 52.03 N | 0.01 W |
| Royston, Eng., U.K. | 56 | 53.37 N | 1.27 W |
| Royton | 56 | 53.34 N | 2.08 W |
| Rozel | 55b | 49.14 N | 2.03 W |
| Rožňava | 66 | 48.40 N | 20.32 E |
| Ruabon | 54 | 52.59 N | 3.02 W |
| Ruathair, Lochan @ | 58 | 58.18 N | 3.56 W |
| Rubcovsk | 78 | 51.33 N | 81.10 E |
| Rubery | 54 | 52.24 N | 2.00 W |
| Ruby Mountains ⋀ | 96 | 40.25 N | 115.35 W |
| Ruda Śląska | 66 | 50.18 N | 18.51 E |
| Rudn'a | 62 | 54.57 N | 31.06 E |
| Rudnyj | 76 | 52.57 N | 63.07 E |
| Rudolf, Lake @ | 88 | 3.30 N | 36.00 E |
| Rudolstadt | 66 | 50.43 N | 11.20 E |
| Rufisque | 86 | 14.43 N | 17.17 W |
| Rugby | 54 | 52.23 N | 1.15 W |
| Rugeley | 54 | 52.46 N | 1.55 W |
| Rügen I | 50 | 54.25 N | 13.24 E |
| Ruian | 80 | 27.49 N | 120.38 E |
| Rukwa, Lake @ | 90 | 8.00 S | 32.25 E |
| Ruma | 74 | 45.00 N | 19.49 E |
| Rumbling Bridge | 58 | 56.10 N | 3.35 W |
| Rum Cay I | 98 | 23.40 N | 74.53 W |
| Rumia | 66 | 54.35 N | 18.25 E |
| Rumney | 54 | 51.31 N | 3.07 W |
| Runan | 80 | 33.01 N | 114.22 E |
| Runcorn | 56 | 53.20 N | 2.44 W |
| Rupert, Rivière de ≃ | 94 | 51.29 N | 78.45 W |
| Ruse | 74 | 43.50 N | 25.57 E |
| Rush | 60 | 53.32 N | 6.06 W |
| Rushden | 54 | 52.17 N | 0.36 W |
| Russell, Cape > | 94 | 75.15 N | 117.35 W |
| Russell Island I | 94 | 73.55 N | 98.25 W |
| Russell Islands II | 92 | 9.04 S | 159.12 E |
| Russell Point > | 94 | 73.30 N | 115.00 W |
| Rüsselsheim | 66 | 50.00 N | 8.25 E |
| Russkij, Ostrov I | 78 | 77.00 N | 96.00 E |
| Rustavi | 76 | 41.33 N | 45.02 E |
| Rustenburg | 90 | 25.37 S | 27.08 E |
| Rustington | 54 | 50.48 N | 0.31 W |
| Ruteng | 82 | 8.36 S | 120.27 E |
| Rutherglen | 58 | 55.50 N | 4.12 W |
| Ruthin | 56 | 53.07 N | 3.18 W |
| Ruvuma (Rovuma) ≃ | 90 | 10.29 S | 40.28 E |
| Ruyton-Eleven-Towns | 54 | 52.48 N | 2.54 W |
| Ruzajevka | 62 | 54.04 N | 44.57 E |
| Ružomberok | 66 | 49.06 N | 19.18 E |
| Rwanda □[1] | 90 | 2.30 S | 30.00 E |
| Ryan, Loch C | 56 | 54.58 N | 5.02 W |
| Rybačij (Rossitten) | 66 | 55.09 N | 20.51 E |
| Rybačij, Poluostrov >[1] | 76 | 69.42 N | 32.36 E |
| Rybačje | 78 | 46.27 N | 81.32 E |
| Rybinsk | 62 | 58.03 N | 38.52 E |
| Rybinskoje Vodochranilišče @[1] | 76 | 58.30 N | 38.25 E |
| Rybnik | 66 | 50.06 N | 18.32 E |
| Rybnoje | 62 | 54.44 N | 39.30 E |
| Ryde | 54 | 50.44 N | 1.10 W |
| Ryder's Hill ∧[2] | 54 | 50.31 N | 3.53 W |
| Rye | 54 | 50.57 N | 0.44 E |
| Rye ≃ | 56 | 54.10 N | 0.45 W |
| Ryhope | 56 | 54.52 N | 1.21 W |
| Ryton | 56 | 54.59 N | 1.46 W |
| Ryton ≃ | 56 | 53.25 N | 1.00 W |
| Ryton-on-Dunsmore | 54 | 52.22 N | 1.26 W |
| Rzeszów | 66 | 50.03 N | 22.00 E |
| Ržev | 62 | 56.16 N | 34.20 E |
| **S** | | | |
| Saalfeld | 66 | 50.39 N | 11.22 E |
| Saarbrücken | 66 | 49.14 N | 6.59 E |
| Saaremaa I | 76 | 58.25 N | 22.30 E |
| Saarlouis | 66 | 49.21 N | 6.45 E |
| Şab, Tônlé @ | 82 | 13.00 N | 104.00 E |
| Šabac | 74 | 44.45 N | 19.42 E |
| Sabadell | 70 | 41.33 N | 2.06 E |
| Sābarmati ≃ | 84 | 22.25 N | 73.20 E |
| Şāberī, Hāmūn-e @ | 84 | 31.30 N | 61.20 E |
| Şabhah | 88 | 27.03 N | 14.26 E |
| Sabi (Save) ≃ | 90 | 21.00 S | 35.02 E |
| Sabine ≃ | 96 | 30.00 N | 93.45 W |
| Sabine Bay C | 94 | 75.35 N | 109.30 W |
| Sabine Peninsula >[1] | 94 | 76.20 N | 109.30 W |
| Sable, Cape >, N.S., Can. | 94 | 43.25 N | 65.35 W |
| Sable, Cape >, Fla., U.S. | 96 | 25.12 N | 81.05 W |
| Sable, Île de I | 92 | 19.15 S | 159.56 E |
| Sable Island I | 94 | 43.55 N | 59.50 W |
| Sabzevār | 84 | 36.13 N | 57.42 E |
| Săcele | 74 | 45.37 N | 25.42 E |
| Sachalin, Ostrov (Sakhalin) I | 78 | 51.00 N | 143.00 E |
| Şachalinskij Zaliv C | 78 | 53.45 N | 141.30 E |
| Şachrisabz | 76 | 39.03 N | 66.50 E |
| Şachty | 76 | 47.42 N | 40.13 E |
| Şachunja | 62 | 57.40 N | 46.37 E |
| Şack | 62 | 54.01 N | 41.43 E |
| Säckingen | 66 | 47.33 N | 7.56 E |
| Sacramento | 96 | 38.35 N | 121.30 W |
| Sacramento ≃ | 96 | 38.03 N | 121.56 W |
| Sacramento Mountains ⋀ | 96 | 33.10 N | 105.50 W |
| Şa'dah | 84 | 16.52 N | 43.37 E |
| Saddleback ∧ | 56 | 54.38 N | 3.03 W |
| Saddleworth | 56 | 53.33 N | 1.59 W |
| Şado I | 80 | 38.00 N | 138.25 E |
| Šadrinsk | 76 | 56.05 N | 63.38 E |
| Säffle | 64 | 59.08 N | 12.56 E |
| Saffron Walden | 54 | 52.01 N | 0.15 E |
| Safi | 86 | 32.20 N | 9.17 W |
| Safīd Kūh, Selseleh-ye ⋀ | 84 | 34.30 N | 63.30 E |
| Safonovo | 62 | 55.06 N | 33.15 E |
| Saga | 80 | 33.15 N | 130.18 E |
| Saganaga Lake @ | 96 | 48.14 N | 90.52 W |
| Saganthit Kyun I | 82 | 11.56 N | 98.29 E |
| Sāgar | 84 | 23.50 N | 78.45 E |
| Saginaw | 96 | 43.25 N | 83.58 W |
| Saginaw Bay C | 96 | 43.50 N | 83.40 W |
| Saglek Bay C | 94 | 58.35 N | 63.00 W |
| Sagua la Grande | 98 | 22.49 N | 80.05 W |
| Saguenay ≃ | 94 | 48.08 N | 69.44 W |
| Sagunto | 70 | 39.41 N | 0.16 W |
| Sahara ◆[2] | 88 | 26.00 N | 13.00 E |
| Sahāranpur | 84 | 29.57 N | 77.48 E |
| Sāhīwāl | 84 | 30.40 N | 73.06 E |
| Saibai I | 92 | 9.24 S | 142.40 E |
| Saïda | 86 | 34.50 N | 0.09 E |
| Saidpur | 84 | 25.47 N | 88.54 E |
| Saimaa @ | 50 | 61.15 N | 28.15 E |
| Saint Abb's Head > | 52 | 55.54 N | 2.09 W |
| Saint Agnes | 54 | 50.18 N | 5.13 W |
| Saint Agnes I | 54a | 49.54 N | 6.20 W |
| Saint Albans | 54 | 51.46 N | 0.21 W |
| Saint Aldhelm's Head > | 52 | 50.34 N | 2.04 W |
| Saint-Amand-les-Eaux | 68 | 50.26 N | 3.26 E |
| Saint-Amand-Mont-Rond | 68 | 46.44 N | 2.30 E |
| Saint-André, Cap > | 90 | 16.11 S | 44.27 E |
| Saint Andrews | 58 | 56.20 N | 2.48 W |
| Saint Andrews Bay C | 58 | 56.22 N | 2.50 W |
| Saint Anne | 55b | 49.42 N | 2.12 W |
| Saint Anne's | 56 | 53.45 N | 3.02 W |
| Saint Ann's Head > | 54 | 51.41 N | 5.10 W |
| Saint Arvans | 54 | 51.40 N | 2.41 W |
| Saint Asaph | 56 | 53.16 N | 3.26 W |
| Saint Athan | 54 | 51.24 N | 3.25 W |
| Saint Aubin | 55b | 49.11 N | 2.10 W |
| Saint-Augustin ≃ | 94 | 51.14 N | 58.41 W |
| Saint Austell | 54 | 50.20 N | 4.48 W |
| Saint-Avold | 68 | 49.06 N | 6.42 E |
| Saint-Barthélemy I | 98 | 17.54 N | 62.50 W |
| Saint Bees Head > | 56 | 54.32 N | 3.38 W |
| Saint Blazey | 54 | 50.22 N | 4.43 W |
| Saint Brides Bay C | 54 | 51.48 N | 5.15 W |
| Saint Bride's Major | 54 | 51.28 N | 3.38 W |
| Saint-Brieuc | 68 | 48.31 N | 2.47 W |
| Saint Catherine's Point > | 52 | 50.34 N | 1.15 W |
| Saint-Chamond | 68 | 45.28 N | 4.30 E |
| Saint Christopher I | 98 | 17.20 N | 62.45 W |
| Saint-Claude | 68 | 46.23 N | 5.52 E |
| Saint Clears | 54 | 51.50 N | 4.30 W |
| Saint Cloud | 96 | 45.33 N | 94.10 W |
| Saint Columb Major | 54 | 50.26 N | 5.03 W |
| Saint Combs | 58 | 57.39 N | 1.54 W |
| Saint Croix I | 98 | 17.45 N | 64.45 W |
| Saint David's | 54 | 51.54 N | 5.16 W |
| Saint David's Head > | 52 | 51.55 N | 5.19 W |
| Saint-Denis, Fr. | 68 | 48.56 N | 2.22 E |
| Saint-Denis, Réu. | 90 | 20.52 S | 55.28 E |
| Saint Dennis | 54 | 50.23 N | 4.53 W |
| Saint-Dié | 68 | 48.17 N | 6.57 E |
| Saint-Dizier | 68 | 48.38 N | 4.57 E |
| Saint Dogmaels | 54 | 52.05 N | 4.40 W |
| Saint Elias, Mount ∧ | 94 | 60.18 N | 140.55 W |
| Saintfield | 60 | 54.28 N | 5.47 W |
| Saint Fillans | 58 | 56.23 N | 4.07 W |
| Saint George's | 98 | 12.03 N | 61.45 W |
| Saint George's Bay C | 94 | 48.20 N | 59.00 W |
| Saint George's Channel ⋃ | 52 | 52.00 N | 6.00 W |
| Saint-Germain | 68 | 48.54 N | 2.05 E |
| Saint Germans | 54 | 50.24 N | 4.18 W |
| Saint Govan's Head > | 54 | 51.36 N | 4.55 W |
| Saint Helena I | 8 | 15.57 S | 0.54 W |
| Saint Helena Bay C | 90 | 32.43 S | 18.05 E |
| Saint Helens, Eng., U.K. | 54 | 50.42 N | 1.06 W |
| Saint Helens, Eng., U.K. | 56 | 53.28 N | 2.44 W |
| Saint Helier | 55b | 49.12 N | 2.37 W |
| Saint Ignace Island I | 94 | 48.48 N | 87.55 W |
| Saint Ives, Eng., U.K. | 54 | 50.12 N | 5.29 W |
| Saint Ives, Eng., U.K. | 54 | 52.20 N | 0.05 W |
| Saint Ives Bay C | 54 | 50.14 N | 5.28 W |
| Saint James, Cape > | 94 | 51.56 N | 131.01 W |
| Saint-Jean | 94 | 45.19 N | 73.16 W |
| Saint-Jean, Lac @ | 94 | 48.35 N | 72.05 W |
| Saint-Jean-d'Angély | 68 | 45.57 N | 0.31 W |
| Saint-Jean-de-Luz | 68 | 43.23 N | 1.40 W |
| Saint John, N.B., Can. | 94 | 45.16 N | 66.03 W |
| Saint John, Jersey | 55b | 49.15 N | 2.08 W |
| Saint John ≃ | 94 | 45.15 N | 66.04 W |
| Saint John, Cape > | 94 | 50.00 N | 55.32 W |
| Saint Johns, Antig. | 98 | 17.06 N | 61.51 W |
| Saint John's, Newf., Can. | 94 | 47.34 N | 52.43 W |
| Saint Joseph | 96 | 39.46 N | 94.51 W |
| Saint Joseph, Lake @ | 94 | 51.05 N | 90.35 W |
| Saint-Junien | 68 | 45.53 N | 0.54 E |
| Saint Just | 54 | 50.07 N | 5.42 W |
| Saint Keverne | 54 | 50.03 N | 5.06 W |
| Saint Kilda I | 52 | 57.49 N | 8.36 W |
| Saint Kitts-Nevis □[2] | 98 | 17.20 N | 62.45 W |
| Saint Lawrence ≃ | 94 | 49.30 N | 67.00 W |
| Saint Lawrence, Gulf of C | 94 | 48.00 N | 62.00 W |
| Saint Leonards | 54 | 50.51 N | 0.34 E |
| Saint-Lô | 68 | 49.07 N | 1.05 W |
| Saint-Louis, Sén. | 86 | 16.02 N | 16.30 W |
| Saint Louis, Mo., U.S. | 96 | 38.38 N | 90.11 W |
| Saint Lucia □[2] | 98 | 13.53 N | 60.58 W |
| Saint Lucia, Lake @ | 90 | 28.05 S | 32.26 E |
| Saint Magnus Bay C | 52 | 60.25 N | 1.35 W |
| Saint-Malo | 68 | 48.39 N | 2.01 W |
| Saint Margaret's at Cliffe | 54 | 51.09 N | 1.24 E |
| Saint Margaret's Hope | 58 | 58.49 N | 2.57 W |
| Sainte-Marguerite ≃ | 94 | 50.09 N | 66.36 W |
| Sainte-Marie, Cap > | 90 | 25.36 S | 45.08 E |
| Sainte-Marie, Île I | 90 | 16.50 S | 49.55 E |
| Saint-Martin I | 98 | 18.04 N | 63.04 W |
| Saint Martin, Lake @ | 94 | 51.37 N | 98.29 W |
| Saint Martin's I | 54a | 49.58 N | 6.20 W |
| Saint Mary Bourne | 54 | 51.16 N | 1.24 W |
| Saint Mary Peak ∧ | 92 | 31.30 S | 138.33 E |
| Saint Mary's I | 54a | 49.55 N | 6.18 W |
| Saint Mary's, Cape > | 94 | 46.49 N | 54.12 W |
| Saint Mary's Bay | 54 | 51.00 N | 0.58 E |
| Saint Mary's Bay C | 94 | 46.50 N | 53.47 W |
| Saint-Maur[-des-Fossés] | 68 | 48.48 N | 2.30 E |
| Saint-Maurice ≃ | 94 | 46.21 N | 72.31 W |
| Saint Mawes | 54 | 50.09 N | 5.01 W |
| Saint Mawgan | 54 | 50.28 N | 4.58 W |
| Saint Merryn | 54 | 50.31 N | 4.58 W |
| Saint Monance | 58 | 56.12 N | 2.46 W |
| Saint-Nazaire | 68 | 47.17 N | 2.12 W |
| Saint Neots | 54 | 52.14 N | 0.17 W |
| Saint-Omer | 68 | 50.45 N | 2.15 E |
| Saint Paul | 96 | 44.58 N | 93.07 W |
| Saint-Paul ≃, Can. | 94 | 51.26 N | 57.40 W |
| Saint Paul ≃, Liber. | 86 | 7.10 N | 10.00 W |
| Saint-Paul, Île I | 8 | 38.43 S | 77.29 E |
| Saint Peter Island I | 92 | 32.17 S | 133.35 E |
| Saint Peter Port | 55b | 49.27 N | 2.32 W |
| Saint Petersburg | 96 | 27.46 N | 82.38 W |
| Saint Pierre and Miquelon □[2] | 94 | 46.55 N | 56.10 W |
| Saint Pierre Island I | 90 | 9.19 S | 50:43 E |
| Saint-Quentin | 68 | 49.51 N | 3.17 E |
| Saint-Raphaël | 68 | 43.25 N | 6.46 E |
| Saintes | 68 | 45.45 N | 0.52 W |
| Saint Sampson | 55b | 49.29 N | 2.31 W |
| Saint Saviour | 55b | 49.11 N | 2.06 W |
| Saint-Sébastien, Cap > | 90 | 12.26 S | 48.44 E |
| Saint Thomas I | 98 | 18.21 N | 64.55 W |
| Saint Tudy | 54 | 50.33 N | 4.43 W |
| Saint Vincent □[2] | 98 | 13.15 N | 61.12 W |
| Saint Vincent, Gulf C | 92 | 35.00 S | 138.05 E |
| Saipan I | 82 | 15.12 N | 145.45 E |
| Sairecábur, Cerro ∧ | 102 | 22.43 S | 67.54 W |
| Sajama, Nevado ∧ | 100 | 18.06 S | 68.54 W |
| Sajószentpéter | 66 | 48.13 N | 20.44 E |
| Sakakawea, Lake @[1] | 96 | 47.50 N | 102.20 W |
| Sakami ≃ | 94 | 53.40 N | 76.40 W |
| Sakami, Lac @ | 94 | 53.15 N | 76.45 W |
| Sakania | 90 | 12.45 S | 28.34 E |
| Sakarya ≃ | 50 | 41.07 N | 30.39 E |
| Sakata | 80 | 38.55 N | 139.50 E |
| Sakishima-guntō II | 80 | 24.46 N | 124.00 E |
| Sal I | 86 | 16.45 N | 22.55 W |
| Sal ≃ | 76 | 47.31 N | 40.45 E |
| Salado ≃, Arg. | 102 | 31.42 S | 60.44 W |
| Salado ≃, Arg. | 102 | 38.49 S | 64.57 W |
| Salado ≃, Méx. | 98 | 26.52 N | 99.19 W |
| Salaguolehe ≃ | 80 | 40.28 N | 94.30 E |
| Salamanca, Esp. | 70 | 40.58 N | 5.39 W |
| Salamanca, Méx. | 98 | 20.34 N | 101.12 W |
| Salamís | 74 | 37.59 N | 23.28 E |
| Salatiga | 82 | 7.19 S | 110.30 E |
| Salavat | 76 | 53.21 N | 55.55 E |
| Salawati I | 82 | 1.07 S | 130.52 E |
| Salcombe | 54 | 50.13 N | 3.47 W |
| Salé, Magreb | 86 | 34.04 N | 6.50 W |
| Sale, Eng., U.K. | 56 | 53.26 N | 2.19 W |
| Salebabu, Pulau I | 82 | 3.55 N | 126.40 E |
| Salechard | 78 | 66.33 N | 66.40 E |
| Salem, Bhārat | 84 | 11.39 N | 78.10 E |
| Salem, Oreg., U.S. | 96 | 44.57 N | 123.01 W |
| Salen, Scot., U.K. | 58 | 56.43 N | 5.47 W |
| Salen, Scot., U.K. | 58 | 56.31 N | 5.57 W |
| Salerno | 72 | 40.41 N | 14.47 E |
| Salford | 56 | 53.28 N | 2.18 W |
| Salgótarján | 74 | 48.07 N | 19.48 E |
| Salihli | 74 | 38.29 N | 28.09 E |
| Salina | 96 | 38.50 N | 97.37 W |
| Salina Cruz | 98 | 16.10 N | 95.12 W |
| Salinas | 96 | 36.40 N | 121.38 W |
| Salisbury, Rh. | 90 | 17.50 S | 31.03 E |
| Salisbury, Eng., U.K. | 54 | 51.05 N | 1.48 W |
| Salisbury Island I | 94 | 63.30 N | 77.00 W |
| Salisbury Plain ⊻ | 52 | 51.12 N | 1.55 W |
| Salmon ≃ | 96 | 45.51 N | 116.46 W |
| Salmon River Mountains ⋀ | 96 | 44.45 N | 115.00 W |
| Salo | 64 | 60.23 N | 23.08 E |
| Salon-de-Provence | 68 | 43.38 N | 5.06 E |
| Salonta | 74 | 46.48 N | 21.40 E |
| Salop □[6] | 52 | 52.40 N | 2.40 W |
| Saloum ≃ | 86 | 13.50 N | 16.45 W |
| Sal'sk | 76 | 46.28 N | 41.33 E |
| Salt ≃ | 96 | 33.23 N | 112.18 W |
| Salta | 102 | 24.47 S | 65.25 W |
| Saltash | 54 | 50.24 N | 4.12 W |
| Saltburn-by-the-Sea | 56 | 54.35 N | 0.58 W |
| Saltcoats | 58 | 55.38 N | 4.47 W |
| Saltee Islands II | 52 | 52.07 N | 6.36 W |
| Saltillo | 98 | 25.25 N | 101.00 W |
| Salt Lake City | 96 | 40.46 N | 111.53 W |
| Salto | 102 | 31.23 S | 57.58 W |
| Salton Sea @ | 96 | 33.19 N | 115.50 W |
| Saluzzo | 72 | 44.39 N | 7.29 E |
| Salvador | 100 | 12.59 S | 38.31 W |
| Salween ≃ | 82 | 16.31 N | 97.37 E |
| Salzburg | 66 | 47.48 N | 13.02 E |
| Salzgitter | 66 | 52.10 N | 10.25 E |
| Salzwedel | 66 | 52.51 N | 11.09 E |
| Samālūt | 88 | 28.18 N | 30.42 E |
| Samar I | 82 | 12.00 N | 125.00 E |
| Samara ≃ | 76 | 53.10 N | 50.04 E |
| Samarinda | 82 | 0.30 S | 117.09 E |
| Samarkand | 76 | 39.40 N | 66.48 E |
| Sambhal | 84 | 28.35 N | 78.34 E |
| Sambor | 66 | 49.32 N | 23.11 E |
| Samoa Islands II | 8 | 14.00 S | 171.00 W |
| Samoded | 62 | 63.38 N | 40.29 E |
| Samokov | 74 | 42.20 N | 23.33 E |
| Sámos I | 50 | 37.48 N | 26.44 E |
| Samosir, Pulau I | 82 | 2.35 N | 98.50 E |
| Sampford Peverell | 54 | 50.56 N | 3.22 W |
| Sampit | 82 | 2.32 S | 112.57 E |
| Sam Rayburn Reservoir @[1] | 96 | 31.27 N | 94.37 W |
| Samson I | 54a | 49.56 N | 6.22 W |
| Samui, Ko I | 82 | 9.30 N | 100.00 E |
| San | 86 | 13.18 N | 4.54 W |
| Şan'ā' | 84 | 15.23 N | 44.12 E |
| Sanaga ≃ | 86 | 3.35 N | 9.38 E |
| San Agustin, Cape > | 82 | 6.16 N | 126.11 E |
| San Ambrosio, Isla I | 102 | 26.21 S | 79.52 W |
| Sanana, Pulau I | 82 | 2.12 S | 125.55 E |
| Sanandaj | 84 | 35.19 N | 47.00 E |
| San Andrés, Isla de I | 100 | 12.32 N | 81.42 W |
| San Andrés Tuxtla | 98 | 18.27 N | 95.13 W |
| San Angelo | 96 | 31.28 N | 100.26 W |
| San Antonio, Chile | 102 | 33.35 S | 71.38 W |
| San Antonio, Tex., U.S. | 96 | 29.28 N | 98.31 W |
| San Antonio, Cabo >, Arg. | 102 | 36.40 S | 56.42 W |
| San Antonio, Cabo >, Cuba | 98 | 21.52 N | 84.57 W |
| San Baudilio de Llobregat | 70 | 41.21 N | 2.03 E |
| San Benedetto del Tronto | 72 | 42.57 N | 13.53 E |
| San Benedicto, Isla I | 98 | 19.18 N | 110.49 W |
| San Bernardino | 96 | 34.06 N | 117.17 W |
| San Bernardo | 102 | 33.36 S | 70.43 W |
| San Blas, Cape > | 96 | 29.40 N | 85.22 W |
| San Carlos | 82 | 15.55 N | 120.20 E |
| San Carlos de Bariloche | 102 | 41.09 S | 71.18 W |
| San Cataldo | 72 | 37.29 N | 14.04 E |
| San Clemente Island I | 96 | 32.54 N | 118.29 W |
| San Cristóbal | 100 | 7.46 N | 72.14 W |
| San Cristóbal las Casas | 98 | 16.45 N | 92.38 W |
| Sancti-Spíritus | 98 | 21.56 N | 79.27 W |
| Sancy, Puy de ∧ | 50 | 45.30 N | 2.45 E |
| Sanda Island I | 52 | 55.18 N | 5.34 W |
| Sandakan | 82 | 5.50 N | 118.07 E |
| Sanday I | 52 | 59.15 N | 2.30 W |
| Sanday Sound C | 58 | 59.11 N | 2.31 W |
| Sandbach | 56 | 53.09 N | 2.22 W |
| Sandbank | 58 | 55.59 N | 4.58 W |
| Sandefjord | 64 | 59.08 N | 10.14 E |
| Sandgate | 54 | 51.05 N | 1.08 E |
| Sandhead | 56 | 54.48 N | 4.58 W |
| Sandhurst | 54 | 51.19 N | 0.48 W |
| San Diego | 96 | 32.43 N | 117.09 W |
| San Diego, Cabo > | 102 | 54.38 S | 65.07 W |
| Sandnes | 64 | 58.51 N | 5.44 E |
| Sandness | 58a | 60.17 N | 1.38 W |
| Sandomierz | 66 | 50.41 N | 21.45 E |
| San Donà di Piave | 72 | 45.38 N | 12.34 E |
| Sandown | 54 | 50.39 N | 1.09 W |
| Sandray I | 52 | 56.54 N | 7.25 W |
| Sandringham | 54 | 52.50 N | 0.30 E |
| Sandusky | 96 | 41.27 N | 82.42 W |
| Sandviken | 64 | 60.37 N | 16.46 E |
| Sandwich | 54 | 51.17 N | 1.20 E |
| Sandwich Bay C | 94 | 53.35 N | 57.15 W |
| Sandwick | 58a | 60.00 N | 1.15 W |
| Sand Wick C | 58 | 60.42 N | 0.52 W |
| Sandy | 54 | 52.08 N | 0.18 W |
| Sandy Cape >, Austl. | 92 | 24.42 S | 153.17 E |


Symbols in the index entries are identified on page 111.

| Name | Page | Lat | Long |
|---|---|---|---|
| Sandy Cape ➤, Austl. | 92 | 41.25 S | 144.45 E |
| Sandy Lake ⊜ | 94 | 53.00 N | 93.07 W |
| San Felipe | 100 | 10.20 N | 68.44 W |
| San Feliu de Guixols | 70 | 41.47 N | 3.02 E |
| San Félix, Isla I | 102 | 26.17 S | 80.05 W |
| San Fernando, Chile | 102 | 34.35 S | 71.00 W |
| San Fernando, Esp. | 70 | 36.28 N | 6.12 W |
| San Fernando, Pil. | 82 | 15.01 N | 120.41 E |
| San Fernando, Pil. | 82 | 16.37 N | 120.19 E |
| San Fernando, Trin. | 98 | 10.17 N | 61.28 W |
| San Fernando de Apure | 100 | 7.54 N | 67.28 W |
| San Francisco, Arg. | 102 | 31.26 S | 62.05 W |
| San Francisco, Calif., U.S. | 96 | 37.48 N | 122.24 W |
| San Francisco, Cabo de ➤ | 100 | 0.40 N | 80.05 W |
| San Francisco de Macoris | 98 | 19.18 N | 70.15 W |
| San Francisco Mountains ⋏ | 96 | 33.45 N | 109.00 W |
| Sangay, Volcán ⋏¹ | 100 | 2.00 S | 78.20 W |
| Sangayán, Isla de I | 100 | 13.51 S | 76.28 W |
| Sangerhausen | 66 | 51.28 N | 11.17 E |
| Sangganhe ≃ | 80 | 40.21 N | 115.21 E |
| Sangha ≃ | 80 | 1.13 S | 16.49 E |
| Sangihe, Kepulauan II | 82 | 3.00 N | 125.30 E |
| Sangihe, Pulau I | 82 | 3.35 N | 125.32 E |
| San Giovanni in Fiore | 74 | 39.16 N | 16.42 E |
| San Giovanni in Persiceto | 72 | 44.38 N | 11.11 E |
| San Giovanni Rotondo | 72 | 41.42 N | 15.44 E |
| San Giovanni Valdarno | 72 | 43.34 N | 11.32 E |
| Sangli | 84 | 16.52 N | 74.34 E |
| San Gorgonio Mountain ⋏ | 96 | 34.06 N | 116.50 W |
| Sangue, Rio do ≃ | 100 | 11.01 S | 58.39 W |
| San Isidro | 102 | 34.27 S | 58.30 W |
| San Joaquin Valley V | 96 | 36.50 N | 120.10 W |
| San Jorge, Golfo C | 102 | 46.00 S | 67.00 W |
| San José, B.R. | 98 | 9.56 N | 84.05 W |
| San Jose, Calif., U.S. | 96 | 37.20 N | 121.53 W |
| San Jose, Isla I | 98 | 25.00 N | 110.38 W |
| San José de Mayo | 102 | 34.20 S | 56.42 W |
| San Juan, Arg. | 102 | 31.32 S | 68.31 W |
| San Juan, P.R. | 98 | 18.28 N | 66.07 W |
| San Juan ≃, Arg. | 102 | 32.17 S | 67.22 W |
| San Juan ≃, N.A. | 96 | 37.16 N | 110.26 W |
| San Juan ≃, U.S. | 96 | 37.11 N | 110.54 W |
| San Juan de los Morros | 100 | 9.55 N | 67.21 W |
| San Juan Mountains ⋏ | 96 | 37.35 N | 107.10 W |
| Sankt Gallen | 68 | 47.25 N | 9.23 E |
| Sankt Ingbert | 66 | 49.17 N | 7.06 E |
| Sankt Pölten | 66 | 48.12 N | 15.37 E |
| Sankt Veit an der Glan | 66 | 46.46 N | 14.21 E |
| San Lázaro, Cabo ➤ | 98 | 24.48 N | 112.19 W |
| San Lorenzo, Isla I | 102 | 12.05 S | 77.15 W |
| Sanlúcar de Barrameda | 70 | 36.47 N | 6.21 W |
| San Lucas, Cabo ➤ | 98 | 22.52 N | 109.53 W |
| San Luis | 100 | 8.56 N | 61.40 W |
| San Luis, Lago de ⊜ | 100 | 13.45 S | 64.00 W |
| San Luis Potosi | 98 | 22.09 N | 100.59 W |
| San Luis Rio Colorado | 98 | 32.29 N | 114.48 W |
| San Marino | 72 | 43.56 N | 12.28 E |
| San Marino □¹ | 50 | 43.56 N | 12.25 E |
| San Martin ≃ | 102 | 33.08 S | 63.43 W |
| San Matias, Golfo C | 102 | 41.30 S | 64.15 W |
| Sanmenxia | 80 | 34.45 N | 111.05 E |
| San Miguel | 98 | 13.29 N | 88.11 W |
| San Miguel ≃ | 100 | 13.52 S | 63.56 W |
| San Miguel de Tucumán | 102 | 26.49 S | 65.13 W |
| San Miniato | 72 | 43.41 N | 10.51 E |
| Sannicandro Garganico | 72 | 41.50 N | 15.34 E |
| San Nicolás de los Arroyos | 102 | 33.20 S | 60.13 W |
| San Nicolas Island I | 96 | 33.15 N | 119.31 W |
| Sanok | 66 | 49.34 N | 22.13 E |
| San Pablo | 82 | 14.04 N | 121.19 E |
| San Pablo, Punta ➤ | 98 | 27.14 N | 114.29 W |
| San Pedro, Punta ➤ | 102 | 25.30 S | 70.38 W |
| San Pedro, Volcán ⋏¹ | 102 | 21.53 S | 68.25 W |
| San Pedro de las Colonias | 98 | 25.45 N | 102.59 W |
| San Pedro de Macoris | 98 | 18.27 N | 69.18 W |
| San Pedro Mártir, Sierra ⋏ | 98 | 30.45 N | 115.13 W |
| San Pedro Sula | 98 | 15.27 N | 88.02 W |
| Sanquhar | 56 | 55.22 N | 3.56 W |
| San Quintín, Cabo ➤ | 98 | 30.21 N | 116.00 W |
| San Rafael | 102 | 34.36 S | 68.20 W |
| San Remo | 72 | 43.49 N | 7.46 E |
| San Salvador | 98 | 13.42 N | 89.12 W |
| San Salvador (Watling Island) I | 98 | 24.02 N | 74.28 W |
| San Salvador de Jujuy | 102 | 24.11 S | 65.18 W |
| San Sebastián | 102 | 43.19 N | 1.59 W |
| Sansepolcro | 72 | 43.34 N | 12.08 E |
| San Severo | 72 | 41.41 N | 15.23 E |
| Sanshawan C | 80 | 26.35 N | 119.50 E |
| Santa ≃ | 100 | 8.58 S | 78.39 W |
| Santa Ana, El Sal. | 98 | 13.59 N | 89.34 W |
| Santa Ana, Calif., U.S. | 96 | 33.43 N | 117.54 W |
| Santa Ana, Cuchilla de ⋏² | 102 | 31.15 S | 55.15 W |
| Santa Bárbara, Méx. | 98 | 26.48 N | 105.49 W |
| Santa Bárbara, Calif., U.S. | 96 | 34.25 N | 119.42 W |
| Santa Catalina Island I | 96 | 33.23 N | 118.26 W |
| Santa Clara, Cuba | 98 | 22.24 N | 79.58 W |
| Santa Clara, Calif. | 96 | 33.42 S | 79.00 W |
| Santa Cruz, Bol. | 100 | 17.48 S | 63.10 W |
| Santa Cruz, Calif., U.S. | 96 | 36.58 N | 122.01 W |
| Santa Cruz ≃ | 102 | 50.08 S | 68.20 W |
| Santa Cruz de Tenerife | 86 | 28.27 N | 16.14 W |
| Santa Cruz Island I | 96 | 34.01 N | 119.45 W |
| Santa Fe, Arg. | 102 | 31.38 S | 60.42 W |
| Santa Fe, N. Mex., U.S. | 96 | 35.42 N | 106.57 W |
| Santai | 80 | 31.10 N | 105.02 E |
| Santa Inés, Isla I | 102 | 53.45 S | 72.45 W |
| Santa Isabel I | 92 | 8.00 S | 159.00 E |
| Santa Luzia I | 86 | 16.46 N | 24.45 W |
| Santa Magdalena, Isla I | 98 | 24.55 N | 112.15 W |
| Santa Margherita Ligure | 72 | 44.20 N | 9.12 E |
| Santa María | 72 | 34.57 N | 120.26 W |
| Santa Maria, Cabo de ➤ | 90 | 13.25 S | 12.32 E |
| Santa Maria Capua Vetere | 72 | 41.05 N | 14.15 E |
| Santa Marta | 100 | 11.15 N | 74.13 W |
| Santander | 70 | 43.28 N | 3.48 W |
| Santarém, Bra. | 100 | 2.26 S | 54.42 W |
| Santarém, Port. | 70 | 39.14 N | 8.41 W |
| Santa Rosa, Arg. | 102 | 32.20 S | 65.12 W |
| Santa Rosa, Calif., U.S. | 96 | 38.26 N | 122.43 W |
| Santa Rosa Island I | 96 | 33.58 N | 120.06 W |

| Name | Page | Lat | Long |
|---|---|---|---|
| Santiago, Chile | 102 | 33.27 S | 70.40 W |
| Santiago, Rep. Dom. | 98 | 19.27 N | 70.42 W |
| Santiago de Compostela | 70 | 42.53 N | 8.33 W |
| Santiago de Cuba | 98 | 20.01 N | 75.49 W |
| Santiago del Estero | 102 | 27.47 S | 64.16 W |
| Santo Antão I | 86 | 17.05 N | 25.10 W |
| Santo Domingo | 98 | 18.28 N | 69.54 W |
| Santos | 100 | 23.57 S | 46.20 W |
| San Valentin, Monte ⋏ | 102 | 46.36 S | 73.20 W |
| San Vicente de Baracaldo | 70 | 43.18 N | 2.59 W |
| San Vito dei Normanni | 72 | 40.39 N | 17.42 E |
| São Carlos | 100 | 22.01 S | 47.54 W |
| São Francisco ≃ | 100 | 10.30 S | 36.24 W |
| São João da Boa Vista | 100 | 21.58 S | 46.47 W |
| São João da Madeira | 70 | 40.54 N | 8.30 W |
| São João del Rei | 100 | 21.09 S | 44.16 W |
| São José do Rio Prêto | 100 | 20.48 S | 49.23 W |
| São José dos Campos | 100 | 23.11 S | 45.53 W |
| São Lourenço ≃ | 100 | 17.53 S | 57.27 W |
| São Lourenço, Pantanal de ⧢ | 100 | 17.30 S | 56.30 W |
| São Luis | 100 | 2.31 S | 44.16 W |
| São Nicolau I | 86 | 16.35 N | 24.15 W |
| São Paulo | 100 | 23.32 S | 46.37 W |
| São Roque, Cabo de ➤ | 100 | 5.29 S | 35.16 W |
| Saorre, Mount ⋏ | 94 | 64.27 N | 84.30 W |
| São Sebastião, Ilha de I | 100 | 23.50 S | 45.18 W |
| São Sebastião, Ponta ➤ | 90 | 22.07 S | 35.30 E |
| São Tiago I | 86 | 15.05 N | 23.40 W |
| São Tomé I | 90 | 0.12 N | 6.39 E |
| São Tomé, Cabo de ➤ | 100 | 21.59 S | 40.59 W |
| São Tomé, Pico de ⋏ | 90 | 0.16 N | 6.33 E |
| Sao Tome and Principe □¹ | 50 | 1.00 N | 7.00 E |
| São Vicente I | 100 | 23.58 S | 46.23 W |
| São Vicente, Cabo de ➤ | 50 | 37.01 N | 9.00 W |
| Sapele | 86 | 5.54 N | 5.41 E |
| Sapitwa ⋏ | 90 | 15.57 S | 35.36 E |
| Sapporo | 80 | 43.03 N | 141.21 E |
| Sapt Kosi ≃ | 84 | 26.31 N | 86.58 E |
| Sarajevo | 74 | 43.52 N | 18.25 E |
| Saran' | 78 | 49.46 N | 72.52 E |
| Saransk | 62 | 54.11 N | 45.11 E |
| Sarapul | 62 | 56.28 N | 53.48 E |
| Sarasota | 96 | 27.20 N | 82.34 W |
| Saratov | 76 | 51.34 N | 46.02 E |
| Sarayköy | 74 | 37.55 N | 28.58 E |
| Sarclet | 58 | 58.23 N | 3.07 W |
| Sardegna (Sardinia) I | 50 | 40.00 N | 9.00 E |
| Sargodha | 84 | 32.05 N | 72.40 E |
| Sarh | 88 | 9.09 N | 18.23 E |
| Sārī | 84 | 36.34 N | 53.04 E |
| Sarigan I | 82 | 16.42 N | 145.47 E |
| Sarīwŏn | 80 | 38.31 N | 125.45 E |
| Sarja ≃ | 62 | 58.24 N | 45.30 E |
| Sark I | 52 | 49.26 N | 2.21 W |
| Sarmiento, Monte ⋏ | 102 | 54.27 S | 70.50 W |
| Sarnia | 94 | 42.58 N | 82.23 W |
| Sarno | 72 | 40.49 N | 14.37 E |
| Saronno | 72 | 45.38 N | 9.02 E |
| Sarpsborg | 64 | 59.17 N | 11.07 E |
| Sarrebourg | 66 | 48.44 N | 7.03 E |
| Sarreguemines | 66 | 49.06 N | 7.03 E |
| Sartang ≃ | 78 | 67.44 N | 133.12 E |
| Sárvár | 66 | 47.15 N | 16.57 E |
| Sarysu ≃ | 76 | 45.12 N | 66.36 E |
| Sarzana | 72 | 44.07 N | 9.58 E |
| Sasebo | 80 | 33.10 N | 129.43 E |
| Saskatchewan □⁴ | 94 | 54.00 N | 105.00 W |
| Saskatchewan ≃ | 94 | 53.12 N | 99.16 W |
| Saskatoon | 94 | 52.07 N | 106.38 W |
| Sasovo | 62 | 54.21 N | 41.54 E |
| Sassandra ≃ | 86 | 4.58 N | 6.05 W |
| Sassari | 72 | 40.44 N | 8.33 E |
| Sassnitz | 66 | 54.31 N | 13.38 E |
| Sassuolo | 72 | 44.33 N | 10.47 E |
| Sātāra | 84 | 17.41 N | 73.59 E |
| Satka | 76 | 55.03 N | 59.01 E |
| Sátoraljaújhely | 74 | 48.24 N | 21.39 E |
| Sātpura Range ⋏ | 84 | 22.00 N | 78.00 E |
| Satsunan-shotō II | 80 | 29.00 N | 130.00 E |
| Satu Mare | 74 | 47.48 N | 22.53 E |
| Satura | 62 | 55.34 N | 39.32 E |
| Saudi Arabia □¹ | 84 | 25.00 N | 45.00 E |
| Sault Sainte Marie | 94 | 46.31 N | 84.20 W |
| Sault Ste. Marie | 94 | 46.28 N | 84.20 W |
| Saumarez Reef ⋏² | 92 | 21.50 S | 153.40 E |
| Saumur | 68 | 47.16 N | 0.05 W |
| Saundersfoot | 54 | 51.43 N | 4.43 W |
| Sava, It. | 72 | 40.24 N | 17.34 E |
| Sava, S.S.S.R. ≃ | 72 | 44.50 N | 20.26 E |
| Sava ≃ | 58 | 58.01 N | 6.23 E |
| Savannah | 96 | 32.04 N | 81.05 W |
| Savannah ≃ | 96 | 32.02 N | 80.53 W |
| Savannakhét | 82 | 16.33 N | 104.45 E |
| Save (Sabi) ≃ | 90 | 21.00 S | 35.02 E |
| Savé ≃ | 86 | 8.02 N | 2.29 E |
| Savernake Forest ✦³ | 54 | 51.24 N | 1.38 W |
| Saverne | 72 | 48.44 N | 7.22 E |
| Savigliano | 72 | 44.38 N | 7.40 E |
| Savona | 72 | 44.17 N | 8.30 E |
| Savory Creek ≃ | 92 | 23.22 S | 122.37 E |
| Sawbridgeworth | 54 | 51.50 N | 0.09 E |
| Sawdā', Jabal as- ⋏² | 88 | 29.00 N | 15.30 E |
| Sawel Mountain ⋏ | 84 | 34.18 N | 36.07 E |
| Sawhāj | 88 | 26.33 N | 31.42 E |
| Sawqarah, Dawhat C | 84 | 18.35 N | 57.15 E |
| Sawston | 54 | 52.07 N | 0.10 E |
| Sawtry | 54 | 52.27 N | 0.17 W |
| Sawu, Laut (Savu Sea) ⋯² | 82 | 9.40 S | 122.00 E |
| Sawu, Pulau I | 82 | 10.30 S | 121.54 E |
| Saxilby | 56 | 53.17 N | 0.40 W |
| Saxmundham | 54 | 52.13 N | 1.29 E |
| Sayan Mountains (Sajany) ⋏ | 76 | 52.45 N | 96.00 E |
| Say'ūn | 84 | 15.56 N | 48.47 E |
| Scafell Pikes ⋏ | 56 | 54.27 N | 3.12 W |
| Scalasaig | 58 | 56.04 N | 6.11 W |
| Scalby | 56 | 54.18 N | 0.27 W |
| Scalloway | 58a | 60.08 N | 1.18 W |
| Scalpay I, Scot., U.K. | 58 | 57.18 N | 6.00 W |
| Scalpay I, Scot., U.K. | 58 | 57.52 N | 6.40 W |
| Scandinavian Peninsula ⋏¹ | 50 | 65.00 N | 16.00 E |
| Scapa Flow ⋯³ | 58a | 58.54 N | 3.05 W |
| Scapegoat Mountain ⋏ | 96 | 47.19 N | 112.50 W |
| Scarba I | 58 | 56.11 N | 5.42 W |
| Scarborough | 56 | 54.17 N | 0.24 W |
| Scarinish | 58 | 56.31 N | 6.48 W |
| Scarp I | 58 | 58.02 N | 7.05 W |
| Scarriff | 60 | 52.55 N | 8.31 W |
| Scavaig, Loch C | 58 | 57.09 N | 6.10 W |
| Ščeljajur | 62 | 65.21 N | 53.21 E |
| Schaffhausen | 68 | 47.42 N | 8.38 E |
| Schenectady | 96 | 42.47 N | 73.53 W |
| Scheveningen | 66 | 52.06 N | 4.06 W |
| Schiedam | 66 | 51.55 N | 4.24 E |
| Schiltigheim | 68 | 48.36 N | 7.45 E |
| Schmölln | 66 | 50.53 N | 12.20 E |
| Schneeberg | 66 | 50.36 N | 12.38 E |
| Schönebeck | 66 | 52.01 N | 11.44 E |
| Schongau | 66 | 47.48 N | 10.54 E |
| Schramberg | 66 | 48.13 N | 8.23 E |
| Schull | 60 | 51.32 N | 9.33 W |

| Name | Page | Lat | Long |
|---|---|---|---|
| Schultz Lake ⊜ | 94 | 64.45 N | 97.30 W |
| Schwabach | 66 | 49.20 N | 11.01 E |
| Schwäbisch Gmünd | 66 | 48.48 N | 9.47 E |
| Schwäbisch Hall | 66 | 49.07 N | 9.44 E |
| Schwandorf in Bayern | 66 | 49.20 N | 12.08 E |
| Schwaner, Peguungan ⋏ | 82 | 0.40 S | 112.40 E |
| Schwechat | 66 | 48.08 N | 16.29 E |
| Schwedt | 66 | 53.03 N | 14.17 E |
| Schweinfurt | 66 | 50.03 N | 10.14 E |
| Schwerin | 66 | 53.38 N | 11.25 E |
| Schwetzingen | 66 | 49.23 N | 8.34 E |
| Schwyz | 68 | 47.02 N | 8.40 E |
| Sciacca | 72 | 37.30 N | 13.06 E |
| Scicli | 72 | 36.47 N | 14.43 E |
| Scilly, Isles of II | 52 | 49.55 N | 6.20 W |
| Scokino | 76 | 54.01 N | 37.31 E |
| Scole | 54 | 52.22 N | 1.10 E |
| Scott Head ➤ | 54 | 52.58 N | 0.42 E |
| Scoria | 82 | 37.18 N | 14.51 E |
| Scotland □⁸ | 52 | 57.00 N | 4.00 W |
| Scott Reef ⋏² | 92 | 14.00 S | 121.50 E |
| Scottsdale | 96 | 33.30 N | 111.56 W |
| Scour ⋏ | 58 | 55.13 N | 3.46 W |
| Scourie | 58 | 58.20 N | 5.08 W |
| Scranton | 96 | 41.24 N | 75.40 W |
| Scremerston | 56 | 55.44 N | 1.59 W |
| Scridain, Loch C | 58 | 56.21 N | 6.07 W |
| Scrooby | 56 | 53.25 N | 1.01 W |
| Scunthorpe | 56 | 53.36 N | 0.38 W |
| Scurrival Point ➤ | 58 | 57.04 N | 7.31 W |
| Seaford | 54 | 50.46 N | 0.06 E |
| Seaforth, Loch C | 58 | 57.54 N | 6.40 W |
| Seaham | 56 | 54.52 N | 1.20 W |
| Seahorse Point ➤ | 94 | 63.47 N | 80.09 W |
| Seahouses | 56 | 55.35 N | 1.38 W |
| Sea Islands II | 96 | 31.20 N | 81.20 W |
| Seal ≃ | 94 | 59.04 N | 94.48 W |
| Seal Lake ⊜ | 94 | 54.18 N | 61.40 W |
| Seascale | 56 | 54.24 N | 3.29 W |
| Seaton, Eng., U.K. | 54 | 50.43 N | 3.05 W |
| Seaton, Eng., U.K. | 54 | 54.41 N | 3.33 W |
| Seaton, Eng., U.K. | 56 | 53.54 N | 0.14 W |
| Seattle | 96 | 47.36 N | 122.20 W |
| Seaton Delaval | 56 | 55.04 N | 1.31 W |
| Sebastián Vizcaino, Bahia C | 98 | 28.00 N | 114.30 W |
| Sebes | 74 | 45.58 N | 23.34 E |
| Sebnitz | 66 | 50.58 N | 14.16 E |
| Sedan | 68 | 49.42 N | 4.57 E |
| Sedbergh | 56 | 54.20 N | 2.31 W |
| Sedgefield | 56 | 54.39 N | 1.26 W |
| Sedgley | 54 | 52.33 N | 2.08 W |
| Sedova, Pik ⋏ | 78 | 73.29 N | 54.58 E |
| Segama ≃ | 82 | 5.27 N | 118.48 E |
| Ségou | 86 | 13.27 N | 6.16 W |
| Segovia | 70 | 40.57 N | 4.07 W |
| Seil I | 58 | 56.18 N | 5.39 W |
| Seinäjoki | 64 | 62.47 N | 22.50 E |
| Seine ≃, Ont., Can. | 94 | 48.48 N | 92.49 W |
| Seine ≃, Fr. | 50 | 49.26 N | 0.26 E |
| Sejm ≃ | 76 | 51.27 N | 32.34 E |
| Sekondi-Takoradi | 86 | 4.59 N | 1.43 W |
| Selangor □³ | 82 | 4.10 S | 114.38 E |
| Selayar, Pulau I | 82 | 6.05 S | 120.30 E |
| Selborne | 54 | 51.06 N | 0.56 W |
| Selby | 56 | 53.48 N | 1.04 W |
| Selçuk | 74 | 37.56 N | 27.22 E |
| Selenga (Selenge Mörön) ≃ | 78 | 52.16 N | 106.16 E |
| Sélestat | 68 | 48.16 N | 7.27 E |
| Seletyteniz, Ozero ⊜ | 76 | 53.15 N | 73.15 E |
| Selkirk | 58 | 55.33 N | 2.50 W |
| Selkirk Mountains ⋏ | 94 | 51.00 N | 117.40 W |
| Selly Oak ✦⁸ | 54 | 52.25 N | 1.52 W |
| Selsey | 54 | 50.44 N | 0.48 W |
| Selsey Bill ➤ | 54 | 50.43 N | 0.48 W |
| Selston | 56 | 53.04 N | 1.20 W |
| Selvagens, Ilhas II | 86 | 30.05 N | 15.55 W |
| Selvas ⋯ | 100 | 5.00 S | 68.00 W |
| Selwyn Lake ⊜ | 94 | 59.55 N | 104.35 W |
| Selwyn Mountains ⋏ | 94 | 63.10 N | 130.20 W |
| Selwyn Range ⋏ | 92 | 21.35 S | 140.35 E |
| Semarang | 82 | 6.58 S | 110.25 E |
| Semau, Pulau I | 82 | 10.13 S | 123.22 E |
| Semeru, Gunung ⋏ | 82 | 8.06 S | 112.55 E |
| Seminole, Lake ⊜¹ | 96 | 30.45 N | 84.50 W |
| Sempalatinsk | 78 | 50.28 N | 80.13 E |
| Semliki ≃ | 90 | 1.14 S | 30.28 E |
| Sem'onov | 62 | 56.48 N | 44.30 E |
| Sendai | 80 | 38.15 N | 140.53 E |
| Senegal □¹ | 86 | 14.00 N | 14.00 W |
| Sénégal ≃ | 86 | 15.48 N | 16.32 W |
| Senftenberg | 66 | 51.31 N | 14.00 E |
| Senghenydd | 54 | 51.36 N | 3.16 W |
| Senica | 66 | 48.41 N | 17.22 E |
| Senigallia | 72 | 43.43 N | 13.13 E |
| Senja I | 62 | 69.20 N | 17.30 E |
| Senkursk | 62 | 62.08 N | 42.53 E |
| Sennar | 88 | 13.33 N | 33.38 E |
| Sennen | 52 | 50.04 N | 5.42 W |
| Sennestadt | 66 | 51.59 N | 8.37 E |
| Senno | 76 | 54.49 N | 29.43 E |
| Sennybridge | 54 | 51.57 N | 3.34 W |
| Sens | 74 | 48.12 N | 3.17 E |
| Seraing | 66 | 50.36 N | 5.29 E |
| Seram (Ceram) I | 82 | 3.00 S | 129.00 E |
| Seram, Laut (Ceram Sea) ⋯² | 82 | 2.30 S | 128.00 E |
| Serang | 82 | 6.07 S | 106.09 E |
| Seremban | 82 | 2.43 N | 101.56 E |
| Serengeti Plain ⋯ | 90 | 2.50 S | 35.00 E |
| Sergač | 62 | 55.32 N | 45.28 E |
| Sergeja Kirova, Ostrova II | 78 | 77.12 N | 89.30 E |
| Seria | 82 | 4.39 N | 114.23 E |
| Sérifos I | 74 | 37.11 N | 24.31 E |
| Sérigny ≃ | 94 | 56.47 N | 66.00 W |
| Serov | 76 | 59.29 N | 60.31 E |
| Serowe | 90 | 22.25 S | 26.44 E |
| Serpuchov | 76 | 54.55 N | 37.25 E |
| Serrai | 74 | 41.05 N | 23.32 E |
| Serpa, Pulau I | 82 | 6.18 S | 130.01 E |
| Serui | 82 | 1.53 S | 136.14 E |
| Sesayap ≃ | 82 | 3.36 N | 117.15 E |
| Sessa Aurunca | 72 | 41.14 N | 13.56 E |
| Sestao | 70 | 43.18 N | 3.00 W |
| Sestri Levante | 72 | 44.16 N | 9.24 E |
| Sestroreck | 62 | 60.06 N | 29.58 E |
| Sète | 68 | 43.24 N | 3.41 E |
| Sete Lagoas | 100 | 19.27 S | 44.14 W |
| Sete Quedas, Salto das ⌖ | 100 | 24.02 S | 54.16 W |
| Sétif | 86 | 36.09 N | 5.26 E |
| Seto-naikai ⋯² | 80 | 34.20 N | 133.30 E |
| Sette-Daban, Chrebet ⋏ | 78 | 62.00 N | 138.00 E |

| Name | Page | Lat | Long |
|---|---|---|---|
| Severnaja Sos'va ≃ | 78 | 64.10 N | 65.28 E |
| Severnaja Zeml'a II | 78 | 79.30 N | 98.00 E |
| Severnyj | 62 | 67.38 N | 64.06 E |
| Severnyj Uvaly ⋏² | 76 | 59.30 N | 49.00 E |
| Severodvinsk | 62 | 64.34 N | 39.50 E |
| Severomorsk | 62 | 69.05 N | 33.24 E |
| Severo-Sibirskaja Nizmennost' ⋯ | 78 | 73.00 N | 100.00 E |
| Severskij Donec ≃ | 76 | 48.20 N | 40.15 E |
| Sevier ≃ | 96 | 39.04 N | 113.06 W |
| Sevier Lake ⊜ | 96 | 38.55 N | 113.09 W |
| Sevilla, Col. | 100 | 4.16 N | 75.57 W |
| Sevilla, Esp. | 70 | 37.23 N | 5.59 W |
| Sevlievo | 74 | 43.01 N | 25.06 E |
| Seward | 96a | 60.06 N | 149.26 W |
| Seychelles □¹ | 4 | 4.53 S | 55.40 E |
| Sfax | 86 | 34.44 N | 10.46 E |
| Sfintu-Gheorghe | 74 | 45.52 N | 25.47 E |
| 's-Gravenhage ('s-Hague) | 66 | 52.06 N | 4.18 E |
| Sgrithéall, Beinn ⋏ | 58 | 57.08 N | 5.35 W |
| Shabani | 90 | 20.20 S | 30.02 E |
| Shaftesbury | 54 | 51.01 N | 2.12 W |
| Shag Rocks II¹ | 50 | 53.33 S | 42.02 W |
| Shahdad, Namakzār- ⋯ | 84 | 30.30 N | 58.30 E |
| Shāhjahānpur | 84 | 27.53 N | 79.55 E |
| Shahreza | 84 | 32.01 N | 51.52 E |
| Shāhrūd | 84 | 36.25 N | 55.01 E |
| Shaki | 86 | 8.39 N | 3.25 E |
| Shaler Mountains ⋏ | 94 | 72.35 N | 110.45 W |
| Shām, Bādiyat ash- ⋯ | 84 | 32.00 N | 40.00 E |
| Shām, Jabal ash- ⋏ | 84 | 23.13 N | 57.16 E |
| Shandongbandao ⋏¹ | 80 | 36.42 N | 33.26 E |
| Shangani ≃ | 58 | 18.41 S | 27.10 E |
| Shanghai | 80 | 31.14 N | 121.28 E |
| Shangqiu | 80 | 34.27 N | 115.42 E |
| Shangrao | 80 | 28.26 N | 117.58 E |
| Shangshui | 80 | 33.39 N | 114.39 E |
| Shanklin | 54 | 50.38 N | 1.10 W |
| Shannon ≃ | 52 | 52.36 N | 9.41 W |
| Shannon, Mouth of the ≃¹ | 52 | 52.30 N | 9.50 W |
| Shantou (Swatow) | 80 | 23.23 N | 116.41 E |
| Shaoguan | 80 | 24.50 N | 113.37 E |
| Shaoxing | 80 | 30.00 N | 120.35 E |
| Shaoyang | 80 | 27.06 N | 111.25 E |
| Shap | 56 | 54.32 N | 2.41 W |
| Shapinsay I | 58a | 59.03 N | 2.51 W |
| Shark Bay C | 92 | 25.30 S | 113.30 E |
| Sharktooth Mountain ⋏ | 94 | 58.35 N | 127.57 W |
| Sharon ≃ | 84 | 41.14 N | 80.31 W |
| Shashi | 80 | 22.14 S | 29.20 E |
| Shasta, Mount ⋏¹ | 96 | 41.20 N | 122.20 W |
| Shasta Lake ⊜¹ | 96 | 40.50 N | 122.25 W |
| Shaunavon | 94 | 49.40 N | 108.25 W |
| Shawinigan | 94 | 46.33 N | 72.45 W |
| Shaybārā I | 84 | 25.27 N | 36.48 E |
| Shaykh, Jabal ash- ⋏ | 84 | 33.26 N | 35.51 E |
| Shaykh 'Uthmān | 84 | 12.52 N | 44.59 E |
| Sheaf ≃ | 56 | 53.23 N | 1.26 W |
| Shebele (Shebelle) ≃ | 88 | 0.50 N | 43.10 E |
| Sheboygan | 96 | 43.46 N | 87.36 W |
| Shedfield | 54 | 50.54 N | 1.16 W |
| Sheelin, Lough ⊜ | 60 | 53.48 N | 7.22 W |
| Sheep Haven C | 60 | 55.10 N | 7.52 W |
| Sheerness | 54 | 51.27 N | 0.45 E |
| Sheffield | 56 | 53.23 N | 1.30 W |
| Shefford | 54 | 52.02 N | 0.20 W |
| Shehy Mountains ⋏ | 60 | 51.47 N | 9.15 W |
| Shelagyote Peak ⋏ | 94 | 55.58 N | 127.12 W |
| Shell, Loch C | 58 | 58.00 N | 6.30 W |
| Shenyang (Mukden) | 80 | 41.48 N | 123.27 E |
| Shepherd Bay C | 94 | 68.56 N | 93.40 W |
| Sheppey, Isle of I | 54 | 51.24 N | 0.50 E |
| Shepton Mallet | 54 | 51.12 N | 2.33 W |
| Sherborne | 54 | 50.57 N | 2.31 W |
| Sherborne Saint John | 54 | 51.18 N | 1.07 W |
| Sherbro Island I | 86 | 7.45 N | 12.55 W |
| Sherbrooke | 94 | 45.24 N | 71.54 W |
| Shercock | 60 | 54.00 N | 6.54 W |
| Sheringham | 54 | 52.57 N | 1.12 E |
| Sherman | 96 | 33.38 N | 96.36 W |
| Sherwood Forest ✦³ | 56 | 53.10 N | 1.08 W |
| Shetland Islands □⁴ | 58a | 60.30 N | 1.30 W |
| Shetland Islands II | 52 | 60.30 N | 1.30 W |
| Sheyenne ≃ | 96 | 47.02 N | 96.50 W |
| Sheykh Sho'eyb, Jazīreh-ye I | 84 | 26.48 N | 53.15 E |
| Shiant, Sound of ⋃ | 58 | 57.55 N | 6.25 W |
| Shiant Islands II | 58 | 57.54 N | 6.30 W |
| Shibām | 84 | 16.54 N | 48.38 E |
| Shibetsu | 80 | 44.11 N | 142.23 E |
| Shibīn al-Kawm | 88 | 30.33 N | 31.01 E |
| Shiel, Loch ⊜ | 58 | 56.48 N | 5.33 W |
| Shiel Bridge | 58 | 57.12 N | 5.25 W |
| Shieldaig | 58 | 57.31 N | 5.39 W |
| Shifnal | 54 | 52.40 N | 2.22 W |
| Shijiazhuang | 80 | 38.03 N | 114.28 E |
| Shikārpur | 84 | 27.57 N | 68.38 E |
| Shikoku I | 80 | 33.45 N | 133.30 E |
| Shildon | 56 | 54.38 N | 1.39 W |
| Shillelagh | 60 | 52.45 N | 6.32 W |
| Shillingstone | 54 | 50.54 N | 2.15 W |
| Shillong | 84 | 25.35 N | 91.53 E |
| Shimoga | 84 | 13.56 N | 75.35 E |
| Shimonoseki | 80 | 33.57 N | 130.57 E |
| Shin, Loch ⊜ | 58 | 58.07 N | 4.32 W |
| Shinkolobwe | 90 | 11.02 S | 26.35 E |
| Shinnel Water ≃ | 58 | 55.13 N | 3.49 W |
| Shinness | 58 | 58.05 N | 4.26 W |
| Shipdham | 54 | 52.37 N | 0.53 E |
| Shipley | 56 | 53.50 N | 1.47 W |
| Shipston-on-Stour | 54 | 52.04 N | 1.37 W |
| Shīrāz | 84 | 29.36 N | 52.32 E |
| Shire ≃ | 88 | 17.42 S | 35.19 E |
| Shirebrook | 56 | 53.12 N | 1.13 W |
| Shiretoko-misaki ➤ | 80 | 44.14 N | 145.17 E |
| Shirrell Heath | 54 | 50.54 N | 1.13 W |
| Shizuoka | 80 | 34.58 N | 138.23 E |
| Shkodër | 74 | 42.05 N | 19.30 E |
| Shoeburyness | 54 | 51.32 N | 0.48 E |
| Sholāpur | 84 | 17.40 N | 75.55 E |
| Shona, Eilean I | 58 | 56.48 N | 5.51 W |
| Shoreham-by-Sea | 54 | 50.49 N | 0.16 W |
| Shoshone Mountains ⋏ | 96 | 39.25 N | 117.15 W |
| Shotley Gate | 54 | 51.57 N | 1.17 E |
| Shotton Colliery | 56 | 54.44 N | 1.23 W |
| Shotts | 58 | 55.49 N | 3.48 W |
| Shournagh ≃ | 60 | 51.53 N | 8.35 W |
| Shreveport | 96 | 32.30 N | 93.45 W |
| Shrewsbury | 54 | 52.43 N | 2.45 W |
| Shrewton | 54 | 51.12 N | 1.55 W |
| Shrivenham | 54 | 51.36 N | 1.39 W |
| Shrule | 60 | 53.31 N | 9.06 W |
| Shuangcheng | 80 | 45.26 N | 126.18 E |
| Shuangliao | 80 | 43.31 N | 123.30 E |
| Shuangyashan | 80 | 46.40 N | 131.22 E |
| Shulehe ≃ | 80 | 40.50 N | 94.10 E |
| Shushtar | 84 | 32.03 N | 48.51 E |
| Shuswap Lake ⊜ | 94 | 50.57 N | 119.15 W |
| Shwebo | 82 | 22.34 N | 95.42 E |
| Siālkot | 84 | 32.30 N | 74.31 E |

| Name | Page | Lat | Long |
|---|---|---|---|
| Sichote-Alin' ⋏ | 78 | 48.00 N | 138.00 E |
| Sicilia (Sicily) I | 50 | 37.30 N | 14.00 E |
| Sidi bel Abbès | 86 | 35.13 N | 0.10 W |
| Sidi Ifni | 86 | 29.24 N | 10.12 W |
| Sidlaw Hills ⋏² | 58 | 56.32 N | 3.10 W |
| Sidmouth | 54 | 50.41 N | 3.15 W |
| Sidney Lanier, Lake ⊜¹ | 96 | 34.15 N | 83.57 W |
| Siedlce | 66 | 52.11 N | 22.16 E |
| Siegburg | 66 | 50.47 N | 7.12 E |
| Siegen | 66 | 50.52 N | 8.02 E |
| Siemianowice Śląskie | 66 | 50.19 N | 19.01 E |
| Siena | 72 | 43.19 N | 11.21 E |
| Sieradz | 66 | 51.36 N | 18.45 E |
| Sierpc | 66 | 52.52 N | 19.41 E |
| Sierra Leone □¹ | 68 | 8.30 N | 11.30 W |
| Sierre | 68 | 46.18 N | 7.32 E |
| Sifnos I | 50 | 36.59 N | 24.40 E |
| Sighetul Marmaţiei | 74 | 47.56 N | 23.54 E |
| Sighişoara | 74 | 46.13 N | 24.48 E |
| Sighty Crag ⋏ | 56 | 55.07 N | 2.37 W |
| Siglufjörður | 62a | 66.10 N | 18.56 W |
| Sigmaringen | 66 | 48.05 N | 9.13 E |
| Sikanni Chief ≃ | 94 | 58.20 N | 121.50 W |
| Sīkar | 84 | 27.36 N | 75.08 E |
| Sikaram ⋏ | 84 | 34.50 N | 69.55 E |
| Sikasso | 86 | 11.19 N | 5.40 W |
| Sikhote ⋏ | 74 | 36.46 N | 22.56 E |
| Silchar | 84 | 24.49 N | 92.48 E |
| Silhouette I | 90 | 4.29 S | 55.14 E |
| Siliguri | 84 | 26.43 N | 88.27 E |
| Silistra | 74 | 44.07 N | 27.16 E |
| Siljan ⊜ | 50 | 60.50 N | 14.45 E |
| Šilka | 78 | 51.51 N | 116.02 E |
| Šilka ≃, S.S.S.R. | 78 | 53.20 N | 119.15 E |
| Šilka ≃, S.S.S.R. | 64 | 56.10 N | 9.34 E |
| Silem Island I | 94 | 70.55 N | 71.30 W |
| Silloth | 56 | 54.52 N | 3.23 W |
| Silsden | 56 | 53.55 N | 1.55 W |
| Silsilah ⋏ | 84 | 22.05 N | 55.23 E |
| Silvermine Mountains ⋏ | 60 | 52.45 N | 8.15 W |
| Silvermines | 60 | 52.47 N | 8.13 W |
| Silverstone | 54 | 52.05 N | 1.02 W |
| Silverton | 96 | 37.48 N | 107.39 W |
| Šimanovsk | 78 | 52.00 N | 127.42 E |
| Simeria | 74 | 45.51 N | 23.01 E |
| Simeulue, Pulau I | 82 | 2.35 N | 96.00 E |
| Simferopol' | 76 | 44.57 N | 34.06 E |
| Simi | 74 | 36.35 N | 27.52 E |
| Simla | 84 | 31.06 N | 77.10 E |
| Simnas | 66 | 54.24 N | 23.39 E |
| Simonsbath | 54 | 51.09 N | 3.45 W |
| Simpson Desert ⋯² | 92 | 25.00 S | 137.00 E |
| Simpson Peninsula ⋏¹ | 94 | 68.34 N | 88.45 W |
| Simpson Strait ⋃ | 94 | 68.27 N | 97.45 W |
| Simusir, Ostrov I | 78 | 46.58 N | 152.02 E |
| Sinai (Sina Peninsula), Shib Jazīrat ⋏¹ | 88 | ... | ... |
| Sinaia | 74 | 45.21 N | 25.33 E |
| Sincelejo | 100 | 9.18 N | 75.24 W |
| Sinclair's Bay C | 58 | 58.31 N | 3.03 W |
| Sindelfingen | 66 | 48.42 N | 9.00 E |
| Sinë ≃ | 82 | 10.16 N | 16.28 W |
| Singapore | 82 | 1.17 N | 103.51 E |
| Singapore □¹ | 82 | 1.22 N | 103.48 E |
| Singapore, Pulau I | 82 | 8.07 S | 115.06 E |
| Singkang | 82 | 4.08 S | 120.01 E |
| Singkawang | 82 | 0.54 N | 109.00 E |
| Singkep, Pulau I | 82 | 0.30 S | 104.25 E |
| Singleton | 54 | 50.55 N | 0.46 W |
| Sinijärvi | 60 | 51.23 N | 8.52 W |
| Sinking ≃ | 84 | 54.05 N | 20.38 E |
| Sinnicolau Mare | 74 | 46.05 N | 20.38 E |
| Sinnūris | 88 | 29.25 N | 30.52 E |
| Sint-Niklaas | 66 | 51.10 N | 4.08 E |
| Sint-Truiden | 66 | 50.48 N | 5.12 E |
| Sion | 68 | 46.14 N | 7.21 E |
| Sioux City | 96 | 42.30 N | 96.23 W |
| Sioux Falls | 96 | 43.32 N | 96.43 W |
| Siping | 80 | 43.12 N | 124.20 E |
| Sipura, Pulau I | 82 | 2.12 S | 99.40 E |
| Siquijor Island I | 82 | 9.11 N | 123.34 E |
| Siracusa | 72 | 37.04 N | 15.17 E |
| Sir Edward Pellew Group II | 92 | 15.40 S | 136.48 E |
| Siret ≃ | 74 | 45.24 N | 28.01 E |
| Sirhān, Wādī as- ⋏² | 84 | 31.00 N | 37.30 E |
| Sir James MacBrien, Mount ⋏ | 94 | 62.07 N | 127.41 W |
| Síros I | 74 | 37.26 N | 24.54 E |
| Sirrī, Jazīreh-ye I | 84 | 25.55 N | 54.32 E |
| Sisak | 72 | 45.29 N | 16.23 E |
| Sīstān, Daryācheh-ye ⊜ | 84 | 31.00 N | 61.15 E |
| Sītāpur | 84 | 27.34 N | 80.41 E |
| Sitidgi Lake ⊜ | 94 | 68.32 N | 132.42 W |
| Sittang ≃ | 82 | 17.10 N | 96.58 E |
| Sittard | 66 | 51.00 N | 5.53 E |
| Sittingbourne | 54 | 51.21 N | 0.44 E |
| Sittwe (Akyab) | 82 | 20.09 N | 92.54 E |
| Sivas | 84 | 39.45 N | 37.02 E |
| Sixmilecross | 60 | 54.34 N | 7.08 W |
| Sjælland I | 64 | 55.30 N | 11.45 E |
| Skagen | 64 | 57.44 N | 10.36 E |
| Skagerrak ⋃ | 50 | 57.45 N | 9.00 E |
| Skarżysko-Kamienna | 66 | 51.08 N | 20.53 E |
| Skawina | 66 | 49.59 N | 19.49 E |
| Skeena ≃ | 94 | 54.09 N | 130.02 W |
| Skeena Mountains ⋏ | 94 | 57.00 N | 128.30 W |
| Skegness | 56 | 53.10 N | 0.21 E |
| Skellefteälven ≃ | 62 | 64.46 N | 20.57 E |
| Skellig Rocks II¹ | 60 | 51.48 N | 10.31 W |
| Skelmersdale | 56 | 53.33 N | 2.48 W |
| Skelmorlie | 58 | 55.51 N | 4.53 W |
| Skelton, Eng., U.K. | 54 | 54.33 N | 0.59 W |
| Skelton, Eng., U.K. | 56 | 54.43 N | 2.51 W |
| Skerne ≃ | 56 | 54.40 N | 1.34 W |
| Skerryvore ⋏⁵ | 58 | 56.19 N | 7.07 W |
| Skewen | 54 | 51.40 N | 3.51 W |
| Skibbereen | 60 | 51.33 N | 9.15 W |
| Skiddaw ⋏ | 56 | 54.38 N | 3.08 W |
| Skien | 64 | 59.12 N | 9.36 E |
| Skierniewice | 66 | 51.58 N | 20.08 E |
| Skipness | 58 | 55.46 N | 5.20 W |
| Skipton | 56 | 53.58 N | 2.01 W |
| Skirfare ≃ | 56 | 54.10 N | 2.03 W |
| Skive | 64 | 56.34 N | 9.02 E |
| Skokholm Island I | 54 | 51.42 N | 5.16 W |
| Skomer Island I | 54 | 51.44 N | 5.19 W |
| Skopje | 74 | 41.59 N | 21.26 E |
| Skovorodino | 78 | 53.59 N | 123.56 E |
| Skreen | 60 | 54.15 N | 8.45 W |
| Skull ⋏ | 58 | 57.18 N | 6.05 W |
| Skye, Island of I | 58 | 57.15 N | 6.10 W |
| Skyring, Seno ⋃ | 102 | 52.35 S | 72.00 W |
| Slagelse | 64 | 55.24 N | 11.22 E |
| Slamet, Gunung ⋏ | 82 | 7.14 S | 109.12 E |
| Slaney ≃ | 60 | 52.21 N | 6.30 W |
| Slatina | 74 | 44.26 N | 24.22 E |
| Slav'ansk | 76 | 48.52 N | 37.37 E |
| Slav'ansk-na-Kubani | 76 | 45.15 N | 38.08 E |
| Slave ≃ | 94 | 61.18 N | 113.39 W |
| Slavgorod | 78 | 52.59 N | 78.38 E |
| Slavonska Požega | 72 | 45.20 N | 17.41 E |
| Slavonski Brod | 74 | 45.10 N | 18.01 E |
| Sleaford | 56 | 53.00 N | 0.24 W |
| Slea Head ➤ | 60 | 52.06 N | 10.27 W |
| Sleat, Point of ➤ | 58 | 57.01 N | 6.02 W |

| Name | Page | Lat | Long |
|---|---|---|---|
| Sleat, Sound of ⋃ | 58 | 57.06 N | 5.49 W |
| Sledmere | 56 | 54.04 N | 0.35 W |
| Sliabh Gaoil ⋏ | 58 | 55.55 N | 5.28 W |
| Sliedrecht | 66 | 51.49 N | 4.45 E |
| Slievenaman ⋏ | 60 | 52.25 N | 7.34 W |
| Sligo | 60 | 54.17 N | 8.28 W |
| Sligo □⁶ | 60 | 54.10 N | 8.40 W |
| Sligo Bay C | 60 | 54.20 N | 8.40 W |
| Slioch ⋏ | 58 | 57.41 N | 5.22 W |
| Sliven | 74 | 42.40 N | 26.19 E |
| Slobodskoj | 62 | 58.42 N | 50.12 E |
| Slobozia | 74 | 44.34 N | 27.23 E |
| Slough | 54 | 51.31 N | 0.36 W |
| Slud'anka | 78 | 51.38 N | 103.42 E |
| Słupsk (Stolp) | 66 | 54.28 N | 17.01 E |
| Slyne Head ➤ | 52 | 53.24 N | 10.13 W |
| Smederevo | 74 | 44.40 N | 20.56 E |
| Smela | 76 | 49.14 N | 31.53 E |
| Smerwick Harbour C | 60 | 52.12 N | 10.24 W |
| Smethwick (Warley) | 54 | 52.30 N | 1.58 W |
| Šmidta, Ostrov I | 78 | 81.08 N | 90.48 E |
| Smite ≃ | 54 | 52.57 N | 0.53 W |
| Smith Arm C | 94 | 66.15 N | 124.00 W |
| Smithfield | 54 | 54.59 N | 2.52 W |
| Smoky ≃ | 94 | 56.10 N | 117.21 W |
| Smoky Cape ➤ | 92 | 30.56 S | 153.05 E |
| Smolensk | 62 | 54.47 N | 32.03 E |
| Smoljan | 74 | 41.35 N | 24.41 E |
| Smythe, Mount ⋏ | 94 | 57.54 N | 124.53 W |
| Snaefell ⋏ | 56 | 54.16 N | 4.27 W |
| Snake ≃, Yukon, Can. | 94 | 65.58 N | 134.10 W |
| Snake ≃, U.S. | 96 | 46.12 N | 119.02 W |
| Sneek | 66 | 53.02 N | 5.40 E |
| Snettisham | 54 | 52.53 N | 0.30 E |
| Snina | 66 | 48.59 N | 22.07 E |
| Snizort, Loch C | 58 | 57.34 N | 6.28 W |
| Snodland | 54 | 51.20 N | 0.27 E |
| Snæfellsnes ⋏¹ | 50 | 66.38 N | 14.02 W |
| Snowbird Lake ⊜ | 94 | 60.41 N | 103.00 W |
| Snowdon ⋏ | 52 | 53.04 N | 4.05 W |
| Snowy ≃ | 92 | 37.48 S | 148.32 E |
| Snowy Mountains ⋏ | 92 | 36.30 S | 148.20 E |
| Soay I | 58 | 57.08 N | 6.14 W |
| Sobat ≃ | 88 | 9.22 N | 31.33 E |
| Sobral | 100 | 3.42 S | 40.21 W |
| Sochaczew | 66 | 52.14 N | 20.14 E |
| Soči | 76 | 43.35 N | 39.45 E |
| Société, Îles de la II | 8 | 17.00 S | 150.00 W |
| Socorro, Isla I | 98 | 18.45 N | 110.58 W |
| Scoullamos | 70 | 39.17 N | 2.48 W |
| Sodankylä | 62 | 67.29 N | 26.32 E |
| Söderhamn | 64 | 61.18 N | 17.03 E |
| Södertälje | 64 | 59.12 N | 17.37 E |
| Soe | 82 | 9.52 S | 124.17 E |
| Soest, B.R.D. | 66 | 51.34 N | 8.07 E |
| Soest, Ned. | 66 | 52.09 N | 5.18 E |
| Sofija (Sofia) | 74 | 42.41 N | 23.19 E |
| Sogamoso | 100 | 5.43 N | 72.56 W |
| Sognafjorden C² | 50 | 61.06 N | 5.10 E |
| Soham | 54 | 52.20 N | 0.20 E |
| Soissons | 68 | 49.22 N | 3.20 E |
| Sôjôsôn-man C | 80 | 39.20 N | 124.50 E |
| Sŏkch'o | 80 | 37.45 N | 128.36 E |
| Söke | 74 | 37.45 N | 27.24 E |
| Sokodé | 86 | 8.59 N | 1.08 E |
| Sokol | 62 | 59.28 N | 40.10 E |
| Sokol'ka | 66 | 53.25 N | 23.31 E |
| Sokolov | 66 | 50.09 N | 12.40 E |
| Sokółka | 66 | 53.24 N | 23.07 E |
| Sokoto | 86 | 13.04 N | 5.16 E |
| Solbad Hall in Tirol | 66 | 47.17 N | 11.31 E |
| Soledad | 100 | 10.55 N | 74.46 W |
| Solihull | 54 | 52.25 N | 1.45 W |
| Solikamsk | 62 | 59.39 N | 56.47 E |
| Solingen | 66 | 51.10 N | 7.05 E |
| Sollentuna | 64 | 59.26 N | 17.57 E |
| Solna | 64 | 59.22 N | 18.01 E |
| Solnečnogorsk | 76 | 56.11 N | 36.59 E |
| Solomon Islands □¹ | 92 | 8.00 S | 159.00 E |
| Solomon Sea ⋯² | 92 | 8.00 S | 155.00 E |
| Solothurn | 68 | 47.13 N | 7.32 E |
| Sol'vyčegodsk | 62 | 61.19 N | 46.56 E |
| Solway Firth C² | 52 | 54.50 N | 3.35 W |
| Soma | 74 | 39.11 N | 27.36 E |
| Somalia □¹ | 88 | 10.00 N | 49.00 E |
| Sombor | 74 | 45.46 N | 19.07 E |
| Somerset □⁶ | 52 | 51.08 N | 3.00 W |
| Somerset Island I | 94 | 73.15 N | 93.30 W |
| Somersham | 54 | 52.23 N | 0.00 |
| Somerton | 54 | 51.04 N | 2.44 W |
| Somonauk | 90 | 14.26 S | 29.38 E |
| Sønderborg | 64 | 54.55 N | 9.47 E |
| Sondershausen | 66 | 51.22 N | 10.52 E |
| Sondre Strømfjord | 94 | 67.00 N | 50.40 W |
| Songhua ≃ | 72 | 46.10 N | 9.52 E |
| Songhuahu ⊜¹ | 80 | 43.32 N | 127.00 E |
| Songhuajiang ≃ | 80 | 47.44 N | 132.32 E |
| Songkhla | 82 | 7.12 N | 100.36 E |
| Songnim | 80 | 38.45 N | 125.38 E |
| Sonmiāni Bay C | 84 | 25.15 N | 66.30 E |
| Sonora □³ | 98 | 50.22 N | 110.20 W |
| Sonora ≃ | 98 | 51.29 N | 0.09 W |
| Sonsbeck | 54 | 51.29 N | 0.44 W |
| Sonsonate | 98 | 28.48 N | 111.33 W |
| Sonsorol Islands II | 82 | 5.20 N | 132.13 E |
| Sopot | 66 | 54.28 N | 18.34 E |
| Sopron | 66 | 47.41 N | 16.36 E |
| Sora | 72 | 41.43 N | 13.37 E |
| Sorbie | 56 | 54.46 N | 4.27 W |
| Sorel, Cape ➤ | 92 | 42.12 S | 145.10 E |
| Sorel Point ➤ | 55b | 49.16 N | 2.10 W |
| Soria | 70 | 41.46 N | 2.28 W |
| Sorocaba | 100 | 23.29 S | 47.27 W |
| Sorol I¹ | 82 | 8.08 N | 140.23 E |
| Soroti | 90 | 1.43 N | 33.37 E |
| Sørøya I | 62 | 70.36 N | 22.46 E |
| Sorrento | 72 | 40.37 N | 14.22 E |
| Sŏsan | 80 | 36.47 N | 126.27 E |
| Sosnogorsk | 62 | 63.37 N | 53.51 E |
| Sosnovka | 62 | 56.17 N | 51.17 E |
| Sosnowiec | 66 | 50.18 N | 19.08 E |
| Sotteville | 68 | 49.25 N | 1.06 E |
| Sŏul (Seoul) | 80 | 37.33 N | 126.58 E |
| Souris ≃ | 96 | 49.39 N | 99.34 W |
| Sousse | 86 | 35.49 N | 10.38 E |
| South Africa □¹ | 90 | 30.00 S | 26.00 E |
| South America ⋏¹ | 4 | 15.00 S | 60.00 W |
| Southampton | 54 | 50.55 N | 1.25 W |
| Southampton, Cape ➤ | 94 | 62.09 N | 83.40 W |
| Southampton Island I | 94 | 64.20 N | 84.40 W |
| South Andaman I | 82 | 11.45 N | 92.45 E |
| South Aulatsivik Island I | 94 | 56.45 N | 61.30 W |
| South Barrule ⋏² | 56 | 54.16 N | 4.40 W |
| South Bend | 96 | 41.41 N | 86.15 W |
| South Benfleet | 54 | 51.33 N | 0.34 E |
| South Brent | 54 | 50.25 N | 3.50 W |
| South Bruny I | 92 | 43.25 S | 147.17 E |
| South Carolina □³ | 96 | 34.00 N | 81.00 W |
| South China Sea ⋯² | 58 | 10.00 N | 113.00 E |
| South Dakota □³ | 96 | 44.15 N | 100.00 W |
| South Dorset Downs ⋏² | 54 | 50.40 N | 2.25 W |
| South Downs ⋏² | 54 | 50.55 N | 0.25 W |
| South East Cape ➤ | 92 | 43.39 S | 146.50 E |
| Southend | 58 | 55.20 N | 5.38 W |
| Southend-on-Sea | 54 | 51.33 N | 0.43 E |
| Southern Alps ⋏ | 93a | 43.30 S | 170.30 E |

| Name | Page | Lat°′ | Long°′ |
|---|---|---|---|

Southern Indian Lake ⊜ 94 57.10 N 98.40 W
Southery 54 52.32 N 0.23 E
South Esk ≏, Scot., U.K. 58 56.42 N 2.32 W
South Esk ≏, Scot., U.K. 55.53 N 3.04 W
South Foreland ➤ 54 51.09 N 1.23 E
South Forty Foot Drain ≏ 22.56 N 0.15 W
South Georgia I 102 54.15 S 36.45 W
South Glamorgan □⁶ 54 51.30 N 3.25 W
South Hams ≙ 54 50.22 N 3.50 W
South Hayling 54 50.47 N 0.59 W
South Henik Lake ⊜ 94 61.30 N 97.30 W
South Island I 93a 43.00 S 171.00 E
South Kirkby 54 53.34 N 1.20 W
Southminster 54 51.40 N 0.50 E
South Molton 54 51.01 N 3.50 W
South Nahanni ≏ 94 61.03 N 123.20 W
South Ockendon 54 51.32 N 0.18 E
South Orkney Islands I 8 60.35 S 45.30 W
South Petherton 54 50.58 N 2.49 W
South Platte ≏ 96 41.00 N 100.42 W
South Point ➤ 92 39.00 S 146.20 E
Southport, Austl. 92 27.58 S 153.25 E
Southport, Eng., U.K. 54 53.39 N 3.01 W
South Ronaldsay I 58 58.46 N 2.50 W
South Saskatchewan ≏ 94 53.15 N 105.05 W
South Shetland Islands I 8 62.00 S 58.00 W
South Shields 56 55.00 N 1.25 W
South Sound ≡ 60 53.02 N 9.28 W
South Spicer Island I 94 68.06 N 79.13 W
South Tyne ≏ 54 54.59 N 2.08 W
South Uist I 58 57.15 N 7.24 W
Southwark ≙⁸ 54 51.30 N 0.06 W
South West Cape ➤ 92 43.34 S 146.02 E
Southwick 54 50.50 N 0.13 W
Southwold 54 52.20 N 1.40 E
South Woodham Ferrers 54 51.39 N 0.37 E
South Yorkshire □⁶ 56 53.30 N 1.15 W
South Zeal 54 50.44 N 3.54 W
Sovetsk, S.S.S.R. 62 57.37 N 48.58 E
Sovetsk (Tilsit), S.S.S.R. 66 54.52 N 21.53 E
Sovetskaja Gavan' 78 48.58 N 140.18 E
Sow ≏ 54 52.48 N 2.00 W
Sowerby 54 54.13 N 1.21 W
Sowerby Bridge 56 53.43 N 1.54 W
Spa 66 50.30 N 5.52 E
Spalding 54 52.47 N 0.10 W
Spanish North Africa □² 86 35.53 N 5.19 W
Sparkford 54 51.02 N 2.34 W
Spartanburg 96 34.57 N 81.55 W
Sparti (Sparta) 74 37.05 N 22.27 E
Spartivento, Capo ➤ 50 38.53 N 8.50 E
Spas-Demensk 62 54.25 N 34.01 E
Spask-Klepiki 62 55.08 N 40.13 E
Spassk-Dal'nij 78 44.37 N 132.48 E
Spassk-R'azanskij 62 54.24 N 40.23 E
Spean, Glen V 58 56.53 N 4.45 W
Spean Bridge 58 56.53 N 4.54 W
Spelve, Loch C 58 56.22 N 5.46 W
Spencer, Cape ➤ 92 35.18 S 136.53 E
Spencer Gulf C 92 34.00 S 137.00 E
Spennymoor 54 54.42 N 1.35 W
Sperrin Mountains ⋀ 60 54.50 N 7.05 W
Spey ≏ 52 57.40 N 3.06 W
Spey Bay C 58 57.41 N 3.00 W
Speyer 66 49.19 N 8.26 E
Spišská Nová Ves 66 48.57 N 20.34 E
Spithead ≡ 54 50.45 N 1.05 W
Spitsbergen I 8 78.45 N 16.00 E
Spittal an der Drau 66 46.48 N 13.30 E
Spittal of Glenshee 58 56.48 N 3.28 W
Split 72 43.31 N 16.27 E
Split Lake ⊜ 94 56.08 N 96.15 W
Spokane 96 47.40 N 117.23 W
Spoleto 72 42.44 N 12.44 E
Spondon 54 52.54 N 1.25 W
Spratly Island I 82 8.38 N 111.55 E
Spremberg 66 51.34 N 14.22 E
Springfield, Ill., U.S. 96 39.47 N 89.40 W
Springfield, Mass., U.S. 96 42.07 N 72.36 W
Springfield, Mo., U.S. 96 37.14 N 93.17 W
Springfield, Ohio, U.S. 96 39.56 N 83.49 W
Spring Mountains ⋀ 96 36.10 N 115.40 W
Springs 90 26.13 S 28.25 E
Sprint ≏ 54 54.22 N 2.45 W
Spruce Knob ⋀ 96 38.42 N 79.32 W
Spurn Head ➤ 54 53.34 N 0.07 W
Squinzano 72 40.26 N 18.03 E
Srbobran 74 45.33 N 19.48 E
Sredinnyj Chrebet ⋀ 78 56.00 N 158.00 E
Srednerusskaja Vozvyšennost' ⋀¹ 62 52.00 N 38.00 E
Srednesibirskoje Ploskogorje ⋀¹ 78 65.00 N 105.00 E
Šrem 66 52.08 N 17.01 E
Sremska Mitrovica 74 44.58 N 19.37 E
Sri Gangānagar 84 29.55 N 73.53 E
Sri Lanka □¹ 84 7.00 N 81.00 E
Šrīnagar 84 34.05 N 74.49 E
Środa Wielkopolski 66 52.14 N 17.17 E
Staaten ≏ 92 16.24 S 141.17 E
Stack, Loch ⊜ 58 58.20 N 4.55 W
Stackpole Head ➤ 54 51.37 N 4.54 W
Stack Skerry I² 58 59.01 N 4.31 W
Stade 66 53.36 N 9.28 E
Stadskanaal 66 53.00 N 6.55 E
Stadthagen 66 52.19 N 9.13 E
Staffa I 58 56.26 N 6.21 W
Staffin 58 57.37 N 6.12 W
Stafford 54 52.48 N 2.07 W
Staffordshire □⁶ 52 52.50 N 2.00 W
Staines 54 51.26 N 0.31 W
Stainforth 56 53.36 N 1.01 W
Stainmore Forest ←³ 54 54.30 N 2.10 W
Stalbridge 54 50.58 N 2.23 W
Stalham 54 52.47 N 1.31 E
Stalin (Kuçovë) 74 40.48 N 19.54 E
Stamford 54 52.39 N 0.29 W
Stamford Bridge 56 53.59 N 0.55 W
Standerton 90 26.58 S 29.07 E
Standish 56 53.36 N 2.41 W
Standon 54 51.53 N 0.02 E
Stanford le Hope 54 51.31 N 0.26 E
Stanhope 54 54.45 N 2.01 W
Stanke Dimitrov 74 42.16 N 23.07 E
Stanley, Falk. Is. 102 51.42 S 57.51 W
Stanley, Eng., U.K. 54 54.52 N 1.42 W
Stanley, Scot., U.K. 58 56.33 N 3.27 W
Stanley Falls L 90 0.15 N 25.30 E
Stanlow 54 53.17 N 2.52 W
Stannington 56 55.07 N 1.41 W
Stanovoj Chrebet ⋀ 78 56.20 N 126.00 E
Stanovoje Nagorje (Stanovoy Mountains) ⋀ 78 56.00 N 114.00 E
Stansted Abbots 54 51.47 N 0.01 E
Stansted Mountfitchet 54 51.54 N 0.12 E
Stanton 54 52.19 N 0.53 E
Stanwix 56 54.54 N 2.55 W
Stapleford 54 52.56 N 1.16 W
Staplehurst 54 51.10 N 0.33 E
Starachowice 66 51.03 N 21.04 E
Staraja Russa 62 58.00 N 31.23 E
Stara Planina ⋀ 58 43.15 N 25.00 E
Stara Zagora 74 42.25 N 25.38 E
Starcross 54 50.38 N 3.27 W
Stargard Szczeciński (Stargard in Pommern) 66 53.20 N 15.02 E

---

Starica 62 56.30 N 34.56 E
Starnberg 66 48.00 N 11.20 E
Starogard Gdański 66 53.59 N 18.33 E
Start Bay C 54 50.17 N 3.36 W
Start Point ➤ 52 50.13 N 3.38 W
Staryj Sambor 66 49.27 N 22.59 E
Stassfurt 66 51.51 N 11.34 E
Stavanger 58 58.58 N 5.45 E
Staveley 56 53.16 N 1.20 W
Stavropol' 76 45.02 N 41.59 E
Staxigoe 58 58.28 N 3.04 W
Steep Holm I 54 51.21 N 3.07 W
Steeping ≏ 56 53.06 N 0.18 E
Steep Point ➤ 92 26.08 S 113.08 E
Stefansson Island I 94 73.17 N 106.45 W
Steinkjer 62 64.01 N 11.30 E
Stellenbosch 90 33.58 S 18.50 E
Stendal 66 52.36 N 11.51 E
Stenhousemuir 58 56.02 N 3.48 W
Stenness, Loch of ⊜ 59.00 N 3.15 W
Stepancevo 62 56.08 N 41.42 E
Sterling 96 41.48 N 89.42 W
Sterlitamak 62 53.37 N 55.58 E
Šternberk 66 49.44 N 17.18 E
Steubenville 96 40.22 N 80.37 W
Stevenage 54 51.55 N 0.14 W
Stevenston 58 55.39 N 4.45 W
Stewart ≏ 94 63.18 N 139.25 W
Stewart I 93a 47.00 S 167.58 E
Stewarton 58 55.41 N 4.31 W
Stewartstown 60 54.35 N 6.41 W
Steyning 54 50.53 N 0.20 W
Steyr 66 48.03 N 14.25 E
Stikine ≏ 94 56.40 N 132.30 W
Stikine Ranges ⋀ 94 58.45 N 130.00 W
Stinchar ≏ 58 55.06 N 5.00 W
Štip 74 41.44 N 22.12 E
Stiperstones ⋀ 54 52.35 N 2.56 W
Stirling, Austl. 92 31.54 S 115.57 E
Stirling, Scot., U.K. 58 56.07 N 3.57 W
Stockbridge 54 51.07 N 1.29 W
Stockerau 66 48.23 N 16.13 E
Stockholm 66 59.20 N 18.03 E
Stockport 56 53.25 N 2.10 W
Stocksbridge 56 53.27 N 1.34 W
Stockton 96 37.57 N 121.17 W
Stockton-on-Tees 54 54.34 N 1.19 W
Stockton Plateau ⋀¹ 96 30.30 N 102.30 W
Stoer 58 58.12 N 5.20 W
Stoer, Point of ➤ 58 58.15 N 5.23 W
Stoke Golding 54 52.34 N 1.24 W
Stokenchurch 54 51.40 N 0.55 W
Stoke-on-Trent 54 53.00 N 2.10 W
Stokesley 54 54.28 N 1.11 W
Stolberg 66 50.46 N 6.13 E
Stone 54 52.54 N 2.10 W
Stonehaven 58 56.58 N 2.13 W
Stonehouse, Eng., U.K. 54 51.45 N 2.17 W
Stonehouse, Scot., U.K. 58 55.43 N 4.00 W
Stoneleigh 54 52.21 N 1.31 W
Stony Stratford 54 52.04 N 0.51 W
Storkerson Bay C 94 73.00 N 124.50 W
Storkerson Peninsula ✗¹ 94 72.30 N 106.30 W
Stornoway 58 58.12 N 6.23 W
Storrington 54 50.55 N 0.28 W
Storsjön ⊜ 62 63.12 N 14.18 E
Stotfold 54 52.01 N 0.14 W
Stour ≏, Eng., U.K. 54 51.18 N 1.22 E
Stour ≏, Eng., U.K. 54 51.52 N 1.16 E
Stour ≏, Eng., U.K. 54 52.20 N 2.15 W
Stour ≏, Eng., U.K. 54 51.18 N 1.22 E
Stourbridge 54 52.27 N 2.09 W
Stourport-on-Severn 54 52.21 N 2.16 W
Stowmarket 54 52.11 N 1.00 E
Stow-on-the-Wold 54 51.56 N 1.44 W
Strabane 60 54.49 N 7.27 W
Strachan 58 57.01 N 2.32 W
Strachur 58 56.10 N 5.04 W
Stradbally 54 52.19 N 1.16 E
Stradbroke 72 52.19 N 1.16 E
Stradella 72 45.05 N 9.18 E
Stradone 60 53.58 N 7.14 W
Strakonice 66 49.16 N 13.55 E
Stralsund 66 54.19 N 13.05 E
Stranda 54 53.11 N 8.36 W
Strangford 60 54.22 N 5.34 W
Strangford Lough C 52 54.26 N 5.36 W
Stranorlar 54 54.48 N 7.46 W
Stranraer 54 54.55 N 5.02 W
Strasbourg 66 48.35 N 7.45 E
Stratford 54 52.12 N 1.41 W
Stratford-upon-Avon 54 52.11 N 1.42 W
Strathaven 58 55.40 N 4.04 W
Strathbogie V 58 57.25 N 2.45 W
Strathdon 58 57.11 N 3.02 W
Strathearn V 58 56.18 N 3.45 W
Strathkanaird 58 57.59 N 5.11 W
Strathmore V 58 56.35 N 3.00 W
Strathpeffer 58 57.35 N 4.33 W
Strathy ≙ 58 58.34 N 4.00 W
Strathy Point ➤ 58 58.35 N 4.01 W
Stratton 54 50.50 N 4.31 W
Stratton Saint Margaret 54 51.35 N 1.45 W
Straubing 66 48.53 N 12.34 E
Strausberg 66 52.35 N 13.54 E
Streaky Bay C 92 32.48 S 134.13 E
Street 54 51.07 N 2.42 W
Stretford 72 53.27 N 2.19 W
Stretton 54 53.21 N 2.35 W
Stretton, Eng., U.K. 54 57.34 N 0.20 W
Strichen 58 57.34 N 2.05 W
Striven, Loch C 58 55.58 N 5.09 W
Stroeketown 54 53.47 N 8.08 W
Stroma I 58 58.42 N 3.04 W
Stromeferry 58 57.21 N 5.34 W
Stromness 58 58.57 N 3.18 W
Stronsay I 58 59.08 N 2.38 W
Stronsay Firth ≡ 58 59.05 N 2.45 W
Strontian 58 56.41 N 5.34 W
Strood 54 51.24 N 0.28 E
Stroud 54 51.45 N 2.12 W
Strule ≏ 54 54.43 N 7.25 W
Strumble Head ➤ 54 52.02 N 5.04 W
Strumica 74 41.26 N 22.38 E
Stry ≏ 66 57.24 N 4.30 W
Strzegom 66 50.58 N 16.21 E
Strzelce Opolskie 66 50.31 N 18.19 E
Strzelecki Creek ≏ 92 29.37 S 139.59 E
Stuart Lake ⊜ 94 54.32 N 124.35 W
Studholme 54 54.53 N 3.27 W
Studland 54 50.39 N 1.58 W
Studley 54 52.16 N 1.52 W
Stupino 62 54.53 N 38.05 E
Sturminster Newton 54 50.55 N 2.18 W
Sturt Desert ←² 28.30 S 141.00 E
Stuttgart 66 48.46 N 9.11 E
Subotica 74 46.06 N 19.40 E
Sučan 78 43.08 N 133.09 E
Suceava 74 47.39 N 26.19 E
Suchona ≏ 76 60.46 N 46.24 E
Suchumi 76 43.01 N 41.02 E
Suck ≏ 60 53.16 N 8.03 W
Sudan □¹ 88 15.00 N 30.00 E
Sudbury, Ont., Can. 94 46.30 N 81.00 W
Sudbury, Eng., U.K. 54 52.02 N 0.44 E
Sudd ≏ 88 7.41 N 28.03 E
Sueca 70 39.12 N 0.19 W
Suez, Canal do U 88 30.40 N 32.20 E
Suffolk □⁶ 52 52.10 N 1.00 E
Sugarloaf Point ➤ 92 32.26 S 152.33 E
Sugoj ≏ 78 64.15 N 154.29 E
Suhl 66 50.37 N 10.41 E
Suihua 80 46.37 N 127.00 E
Suining 80 30.31 N 105.34 E
Suir ≏ 60 52.15 N 7.00 W
Suizhong 80 40.20 N 120.19 E

---

Šuja 76 56.50 N 41.23 E
Sukabumi 82 6.55 S 106.56 E
Sukkozero 62 63.11 N 32.18 E
Sukkur 84 27.42 N 68.52 E
Sul, Canal do U 100 0.10 S 49.30 W
Sula, Kepulauan II 82 1.52 S 125.22 E
Sulaimān Range ⋀ 84 30.30 N 70.10 E
Sulawesi (Celebes) I 82 2.00 S 121.00 E
Sulechów 66 52.06 N 15.37 E
Sule Skerry I² 58 59.05 N 4.26 W
Sulitelma ⋀ 62 67.08 N 16.24 E
Sullana 100 4.53 S 80.41 W
Sullane ≏ 60 51.53 N 8.56 W
Sulmona 72 42.03 N 13.55 E
Sulu Archipelago II 82 6.00 N 121.00 E
Sulu Sea ⩪² 82 8.00 N 120.00 E
Sulzbach 66 49.18 N 7.07 E
Sulzbach-Rosenberg 66 49.30 N 11.45 E
Sumatera (Sumatra) I 82 0.05 S 102.00 E
Sumba I 82 10.00 S 120.00 E
Sumbawa I 82 8.40 S 118.00 E
Sumbawa Besar 82 8.30 S 117.26 E
Sumburgh Head ➤ 58 59.51 N 1.16 W
Sumburgh Roost U 58 59.49 N 1.19 W
Sumen 74 43.16 N 26.55 E
Sumerl'a 62 55.30 N 46.26 E
Sumgait 76 40.36 N 49.38 E
Summer Bridge 56 54.03 N 1.41 W
Summerhill 60 53.29 N 6.44 W
Summer Isles II 58 58.02 N 5.28 W
Šumperk 66 49.58 N 16.58 E
Sumter 96 33.55 N 80.20 W
Sumy 76 50.55 N 34.45 E
Sunart, Loch C 58 56.41 N 5.43 W
Sunda, Selat U 82 6.00 S 105.45 E
Sundarbans ≙ 84 22.00 N 89.00 E
Sundbyberg 62 59.22 N 17.58 E
Sunderland 54 54.55 N 1.23 W
Sundsvall 62 62.23 N 17.18 E
Sungaipenuh 82 2.05 S 101.23 E
Suninghill 54 51.25 N 0.40 W
Suntar-Chajata, Chrebet ⋀ 78 62.00 N 143.00 E
Suoche (Yarkand) 80 38.25 N 77.16 E
Suoguohu ⊜ 80 42.18 N 101.08 E
Suojarvi 62 62.05 N 32.21 E
Superior 96 46.44 N 92.05 W
Superior, Lake ⊜ 96 48.00 N 88.00 W
Superior Upland ⋀¹ 96 46.00 N 90.30 W
Suquṭrā I 84 12.30 N 54.00 E
Sura ≏ 76 56.06 N 46.00 E
Surabaya 82 7.15 S 112.45 E
Surakarta 82 7.35 S 110.50 E
Surat 84 21.12 N 72.50 E
Surat Thani 84 9.08 N 99.19 E
Surendranagar 84 22.43 N 71.38 E
Surgut 78 61.14 N 73.20 E
Surigao 82 9.45 N 125.30 E
Surinam □¹ 100 4.00 N 56.00 W
Surrey □⁶ 52 51.10 N 0.20 W
Surt, Khalīj C 88 31.30 N 18.00 E
Surtsey I 50 63.16 N 20.32 W
Surud Ad ⋀ 88 10.41 N 47.18 E
Sussex, East □⁶ 52 50.55 N 0.15 E
Sussex, Vale of V 54 50.57 N 0.17 W
Susurluk 74 39.54 N 28.10 E
Sutlej (Satluj) (Langchuhe) ≏ 84 29.23 N 71.02 E
Sutton 54 29.23 N 0.07 E
Sutton, Eng., U.K. 54 51.21 N 0.12 W
Sutton Bridge 54 52.46 N 0.12 E
Sutton Coldfield 54 52.34 N 1.48 W
Sutton Courtenay 54 51.39 N 1.17 W
Sutton-in-Ashfield 56 53.08 N 1.15 W
Sutton-on-Sea 56 53.19 N 0.17 E
Sutton on Trent 56 53.10 N 0.49 W
Sutton Scotney 54 51.10 N 1.21 W
Sutton Valence 54 51.12 N 0.36 E
Sutton Veny 54 51.11 N 2.08 W
Suwałki 66 54.07 N 22.56 E
Suways, Khalīj as- C 88 29.00 N 32.50 E
Suways, Qanāt as- ≡ 88 29.55 N 32.33 E
Suwŏn 80 37.17 N 127.01 E
Suzdal' 62 56.25 N 40.26 E
Suzhou 80 31.18 N 120.37 E
Svalbard II 8 78.00 N 20.00 E
Svartenhuk ➤¹ 94 71.55 N 55.00 W
Sv'atoj Nos, Mys ➤, S.S.S.R. 76 68.10 N 39.45 E
Sv'atoj Nos, Mys ➤, S.S.S.R. 78 72.52 N 140.42 E
Svendborg 64 55.03 N 10.37 E
Sverdlovsk, S.S.S.R. 76 48.05 N 39.40 E
Sverdlovsk, S.S.S.R. 76 56.51 N 60.36 E
Svetogorsk [Rauschen] 66 54.57 N 20.10 E
Svetly] [Peyse] 66 54.51 N 20.08 E
Svetogorsk 62 61.07 N 28.51 E
Svilengrad 74 41.46 N 26.12 E
Svir' ≏ 62 60.30 N 32.48 E
Svištov 74 43.37 N 25.20 E
Svitavy 74 49.45 N 16.27 E
Svobodnyj 78 51.24 N 128.08 E
Swadlincote 54 52.46 N 1.33 W
Swaffham 54 52.39 N 0.41 E
Swain Reefs ⩪² 92 21.40 S 152.15 E
Swakopmund 90 22.41 S 14.34 E
Swale ≏ 54 54.06 N 1.20 W
Swaledale V 54 54.23 N 2.00 W
Swan Island II 92 17.25 N 83.55 W
Swanley 54 51.24 N 0.12 E
Swanlinbar 60 54.10 N 7.42 W
Swansea 54 51.38 N 3.57 W
Swansea Bay C 54 51.35 N 3.52 W
Sway 54 50.47 N 1.38 W
Swaziland □¹ 90 26.30 S 31.30 E
Sweden □¹ 62 62.00 N 15.00 E
Świdnica (Schweidnitz) 66 50.51 N 16.29 E
Świdnik 66 51.14 N 22.41 E
Świdwin 66 53.47 N 15.47 E
Świebodzice 66 50.52 N 16.19 E
Świebodzin 66 52.15 N 15.32 E
Świecie 66 53.25 N 18.26 E
Swift ≏ 54 54.57 N 7.42 W
Swilly, Lough C 54 55.10 N 7.38 W
Swilly, Lough C 60 55.10 N 7.38 W
Swinburne, Cape ➤ 94 71.14 N 98.34 W
Swindon 54 51.34 N 1.47 W
Świnoujście (Swinemünde) 66 53.53 N 14.16 E
Swinton, Eng., U.K. 56 53.28 N 1.20 W
Swinton, Scot., U.K. 58 55.43 N 2.15 W
Switzerland □¹ 66 47.00 N 8.00 E
Swords 60 53.28 N 6.13 W
Syčovka 62 55.50 N 34.17 E
Sydney 92 33.52 S 151.13 E
Syktyvkar 76 61.40 N 50.46 E
Sylhet 84 24.54 N 91.52 E
Syracuse 96 43.03 N 76.09 W
Syr-dar'ja (Syr-Darya) ≏ 76 46.03 N 61.00 E
Syre 58 58.23 N 4.14 W
Syria □¹ 76 35.00 N 38.00 E
Syston 54 52.42 N 1.04 W
Syzran' 62 53.09 N 48.27 E
Szamotuły 66 52.37 N 16.35 E
Szarvas 66 46.52 N 20.34 E
Szczecin (Stettin) 66 53.24 N 14.32 E
Szczecinek (Neustettin) 66 53.43 N 16.42 E
Szczytno 66 53.34 N 21.00 E
Szeged 66 46.15 N 20.09 E
Székesfehérvár 66 47.12 N 18.25 E
Szekszárd 66 46.21 N 18.42 E
Szentendre 66 47.40 N 19.05 E
Szentes 66 46.39 N 20.16 E
Szolnok 66 47.10 N 20.12 E
Szombathely 66 47.14 N 16.38 E
Szprotawa 66 51.34 N 15.33 E

---

**T**
Tabatinga, Serra da ⋀¹ 100 10.25 S 44.00 W
Tabernes de Valldigna 70 39.04 N 0.16 W
Tablas Island I 82 12.24 N 122.02 E
Tábor 66 49.25 N 14.41 E
Tabora 90 5.01 S 32.48 E
Tabrīz 86 38.05 N 46.18 E
Tacloban 82 11.15 N 125.00 E
Tacna 100 18.01 S 70.15 W
Tacoma 96 47.15 N 122.27 W
Tacuarembó 102 31.44 S 55.59 W
Tacutu (Takutu) ≏ 100 3.01 N 60.29 W
Tadcaster 54 53.53 N 1.16 W
Tademaït, Plateau du ⋀¹ 86 28.30 N 2.00 E
Tadley 54 51.21 N 1.08 W
Tadoule Lake ⊜ 94 58.36 N 98.20 W
Tadworth 54 51.17 N 0.14 W
Taegu 80 35.52 N 128.35 E
Taejŏn 80 36.20 N 127.26 E
Taff ≏ 86 21.20 N 10.10 E
Taganrog 76 47.12 N 38.56 E
Taghmon 60 52.18 N 6.39 W
Tagish Lake ⊜ 94 59.45 N 134.15 W
Tagula Island I 92 11.30 S 153.30 E
Tagus ≏ 70 38.40 N 9.24 W
Tahan, Gunong ⋀ 84 4.38 N 102.14 E
Tahoe, Lake ⊜ 96 38.58 N 120.00 W
Taiarapu ≡ 86 14.54 N 5.16 E
Taian 80 36.12 N 117.07 E
Taibaishan ⋀ 80 33.54 N 107.46 E
T'aichung 82 24.09 N 120.41 E
Taihu ⊜ 80 31.15 N 120.10 E
Tain 58 57.48 N 4.04 W
T'ainan 80 23.00 N 120.11 E
Tainaron, Ákra ➤ 80 25.03 N 121.30 E
T'aipei 82 25.03 N 121.30 E
Taiping 82 4.51 N 100.44 E
Taisetsu-zan ⋀ 80a 43.30 N 142.57 E
Taitao, Península de ✗¹ 102 46.30 S 74.25 W
T'aitung 82 22.44 N 121.09 E
Taiwan (T'aiwan) □¹ 80 23.30 N 121.00 E
Taiyuan 80 37.55 N 112.30 E
Taizhou 80 32.30 N 119.58 E
Ta'izz 86 13.38 N 44.04 E
Tajgonos, Poluostrov ✗¹ 78 61.20 N 161.00 E
Tajmura ≏ 78 63.46 N 98.01 E
Tajmyr, Ozero ⊜ 78 74.30 N 102.30 E
Tajmyr, Poluostrov ✗¹ 78 76.00 N 104.00 E
Tajo (Tejo) ≏ 78 55.57 N 98.00 E
Tajšet 78 55.57 N 98.00 E
Tajumulco, Volcán ⋀ 98 15.02 N 91.55 W
Takamatsu 80 34.20 N 134.03 E
Takaoka 80 36.45 N 137.01 E
Takapuna 93a 36.47 S 174.47 E
Takasaki 80 36.20 N 139.01 E
Takijq Lake ⊜ 94 66.15 N 113.05 W
Takla Lake ⊜ 94 55.25 N 125.53 W
Talara 100 4.34 S 81.17 W
Talas 76 42.32 N 72.14 E
Talaud, Kepulauan II 82 4.20 N 126.50 E
Talavera de la Reina 70 39.57 N 4.50 W
Talca 102 35.26 S 71.40 W
Talcahuano 102 36.43 S 73.07 W
Taldom 62 56.44 N 37.32 E
Taldy-Kurgan 76 45.00 N 78.23 E
Talgarreg 54 52.08 N 4.18 W
Talgarth 54 52.00 N 3.15 W
Taliabu, Pulau I 82 1.48 S 124.48 E
Talimpendi (Takla Makan) ←² 80 39.00 N 83.00 E
Talisker 58 57.17 N 6.27 W
Talladale 58 57.42 N 5.29 W
Tallaght 60 53.26 N 6.21 W
Tallahassee 96 30.25 N 84.16 W
Talla Reservoir ⊜¹ 58 55.29 N 3.24 W
Tallinn 62 59.25 N 24.45 E
Tallow 60 52.05 N 8.00 W
Talmine 58 58.31 N 4.26 W
Talsi 62 57.15 N 22.36 E
Taltal 102 25.24 S 70.29 W
Taltson ≏ 94 61.23 N 112.45 W
Talybont 54 52.29 N 3.59 W
Tamale 88 9.25 N 0.50 W
Tamanrasset 86 22.50 N 5.32 E
Tamar ≏ 54 50.22 N 4.10 W
Tamatave 90 18.10 S 49.23 E
Tambacounda 88 13.47 N 13.40 W
Tambov 62 52.43 N 41.25 E
Tamenglong 84 24.59 N 93.32 E
Tamerton Foliot 54 50.26 N 4.08 W
Tamiahua, Laguna de C 98 21.35 N 97.35 W
Tampa 96 27.57 N 82.27 W
Tampa Bay C 96 27.45 N 82.35 W
Tampere 62 61.30 N 23.45 E
Tampico 98 22.13 N 97.51 W
Tamworth, Austl. 92 31.05 S 150.55 E
Tamworth 54 52.39 N 1.41 W
Tana ≏, Kenya 90 2.32 S 40.31 E
Tana ≏, Nor. 62 70.30 N 28.23 E
Tana, Lake ⊜ 88 12.00 N 37.20 E
Tanahbala, Pulau I 82 0.25 S 98.25 E
Tanahmasa, Pulau I 82 0.12 S 98.27 E
Tanami Desert ←² 92 20.00 S 129.30 E
Tanat ≏ 54 52.46 N 3.07 W
Tanat 102 37.19 S 59.09 W
Tandil 72 37.35 N 6.04 E
Tanga 90 5.04 S 39.06 E
Tanganyika, Lake ⊜ 90 6.00 S 29.30 E
Tanger (Tangier) 86 35.48 N 5.45 W
Tangermünde 66 52.32 N 11.58 E
Tanggula Shan ⋀ 80 33.00 N 88.00 E
Tangshan 80 39.38 N 118.11 E
Tanimbar, Kepulauan II 82 7.30 S 131.30 E
Tanjungbalai 82 2.58 N 99.48 E
Tanjungpinang 82 2.45 S 107.39 E
Tannu-Ola, Chrebet ⋀ 80 51.00 N 94.00 E
Tannūrah, Ra's at- ➤ 86 26.40 N 50.30 E
Tanta 88 30.47 N 31.00 E
Tanworth 54 52.19 N 1.50 W
Tanworth-in-Arden 54 52.19 N 1.50 W
Tanzania □¹ 90 6.00 S 35.00 E
Taoerhe ≏ 80 45.42 N 124.05 E
Taormina 72 37.51 N 15.17 E
Taoudenni 88 22.45 N 3.59 W
Tapa 62 59.16 N 25.58 E
Tapachula 98 14.54 N 92.17 W
Tapajós ≏ 100 2.24 S 54.41 W
Tapanahoni ≏ 100 4.22 N 54.27 W
Tapiche ≏ 100 5.40 S 73.50 W
Taquari ≏ 102 19.15 S 57.17 W
Tarābulus (Tripoli), Lībiyā 88 32.54 N 13.11 E
Tarābulus (Tripoli) (Tripolitania) ⋀¹ 88 31.00 N 15.00 E
Tarancón 70 40.01 N 3.00 W
Taransay I 58 57.54 N 7.00 W
Taranto 72 40.28 N 17.15 E
Taranto, Golfo di C 72 40.10 N 17.20 E
Taraš 74 45.23 N 20.32 E
Tarauacá ≏ 100 6.42 S 69.48 W

---

Tarbat Ness ➤ 58 57.51 N 3.47 W
Tarbert, Eire 60 52.32 N 9.23 W
Tarbert, Scot., U.K. 58 57.54 N 6.49 W
Tarbert, Scot., U.K. 58 55.52 N 5.26 W
Tarbert, Loch C 58 55.57 N 6.00 W
Tarbes 68 43.14 N 0.05 E
Tarbolton 58 55.31 N 4.29 W
Tardoki-Jani, Gora ⋀ 78 48.55 N 138.04 E
Tarfside 58 56.54 N 2.50 W
Tarf Water ≏ 58 54.55 N 4.35 W
Tärgoviște 74 44.55 N 26.34 E
Tarija 100 21.31 S 64.45 W
Tarime 90 1.21 S 34.22 E
Tarland 58 57.08 N 2.52 W
Tarleton 54 53.41 N 2.50 W
Tarn ≏ 68 44.05 N 1.06 E
Tarnobrzeg 66 50.35 N 21.41 E
Tarnów 66 50.01 N 21.00 E
Tarnowskie Góry 66 50.27 N 18.52 E
Tarporley 54 53.09 N 2.40 W
Tarragona 70 41.07 N 1.15 E
Tarrant Hinton 54 50.53 N 2.05 W
Tarrasa 70 41.34 N 2.01 E
Tarsus 86 36.55 N 34.53 E
Tartagal 102 22.32 S 63.49 W
Tartu 62 58.23 N 26.43 E
Tarutung 82 2.01 N 98.58 E
Tarves 58 57.22 N 2.13 W
Tasauz 76 41.50 N 59.58 E
Tasejeva ≏ 78 58.06 N 94.01 E
Tashk, Daryācheh-ye ⊜ 86 29.20 N 54.05 E
Taškent 76 41.20 N 69.18 E
Tasman Sea ⩪² 93b 37.00 S 157.00 E
Tasmania I 92 42.00 S 147.00 E
Tastagol 78 52.47 N 87.53 E
Tata 72 47.34 N 18.18 E
Tatabánya 72 47.34 N 18.26 E
Tatarsk 78 55.13 N 75.58 E
Tatarskij Proliv U 78 50.00 N 141.15 E
Tathlina Lake ⊜ 94 60.32 N 117.32 W
Tatnam, Cape ➤ 94 57.16 N 91.00 W
Taujskaja Guba C 78 59.20 N 149.00 E
Taunton 54 51.01 N 3.06 W
Taunton, Vale of V 54 51.02 N 3.08 W
Tauragé 62 55.15 N 22.17 E
Tauranova 72 38.21 N 16.01 E
Tavda 78 58.03 N 65.15 E
Tavira 70 37.07 N 7.39 W
Tavistock 54 50.33 N 4.08 W
Tavoy 82 14.05 N 98.12 E
Tavşanlı 74 39.33 N 29.30 E
Tavy ≏ 54 50.16 N 4.10 W
Taw ≏ 54 51.04 N 4.11 W
Tawau 82 4.15 N 117.54 E
Tawitawi Island I 82 5.10 N 120.00 E
Tawkar 88 18.33 N 37.44 E
Taxco de Alarcón 98 18.33 N 99.36 W
Tay, Firth of C¹ 58 56.25 N 3.18 W
Tay, Loch ⊜ 58 56.30 N 4.10 W
Taylorville 96 39.32 N 89.17 W
Taymouth 58 56.35 N 3.04 W
Tayport 58 56.27 N 2.53 W
Tayside □⁴ 58 56.30 N 3.30 W
Taz ≏ 78 67.32 N 78.40 E
Tazin ≏ 94 59.48 N 109.55 W
Tazin Lake ⊜ 94 59.47 N 109.03 W
Tazovskaja Guba C 78 69.05 N 76.00 E
Tazovskij Poluostrov ✗¹ 78 68.35 N 76.00 E
Tbilisi 76 41.43 N 44.49 E
Tczew 66 54.06 N 18.47 E
Teague 54 52.08 N 4.18 W
Teano 72 41.15 N 14.04 E
Tebay 54 54.26 N 2.35 W
Tebessa 86 35.28 N 8.09 E
Tebingtinggi 82 0.54 N 102.45 E
Tebingtinggi, Pulau I 82 3.35 S 102.22 E
Tecuci 74 45.50 N 27.26 E
Tees ≏ 54 54.34 N 1.16 W
Tees Bay C 54 54.39 N 1.09 W
Teesdale V 54 54.37 N 2.10 W
Tefé ≏ 100 3.35 S 64.47 W
Tegal 82 6.52 S 109.08 E
Tegid, Llyn ⊜ 54 52.53 N 3.38 W
Tegucigalpa 98 14.06 N 87.13 W
Tehrān 86 35.40 N 51.26 E
Tehuacán 98 18.27 N 97.23 W
Tehuantepec, Golfo de C 98 16.00 N 94.50 W
Tehuantepec, Istmo de ✗³ 98 17.00 N 95.00 W
Teide, Pico de ⋀ 86 28.16 N 16.38 W
Teifi ≏ 54 52.07 N 4.42 W
Teifiside ←¹ 54 52.02 N 4.22 W
Teign ≏ 54 50.32 N 3.46 W
Teignmouth 54 50.33 N 3.30 W
Teith ≏ 58 56.08 N 3.59 W
Tejkovo 62 56.52 N 40.34 E
Tekeli 76 44.48 N 78.57 E
Tekirdağ 74 40.59 N 27.31 E
Telavi 76 41.55 N 45.28 E
Tel Aviv-Yafo 86 32.04 N 34.46 E
Telok Anson 82 4.01 N 101.01 E
Teltow 66 52.23 N 13.16 E
Telukbetung 82 5.27 S 105.16 E
Tema 88 5.37 N 0.01 E
Tembagapi, Lake ⊜ 94 46.58 N 80.02 W
Tembenči ≏ 78 64.36 N 99.58 E
Teme ≏ 54 52.09 N 2.18 W
Temirtau 78 50.05 N 72.56 E
Tempe 96 33.24 N 111.56 W
Temple 96 31.05 N 97.20 W
Temple Pausania 72 40.54 N 9.07 E
Templecombe 54 51.00 N 2.25 W
Temple Ewell 54 51.10 N 1.16 E
Templemore 60 52.48 N 7.50 W
Temple Sowerby 54 54.38 N 2.35 W
Temuco 102 38.44 S 72.36 W
Tenāli 84 16.14 N 80.40 E
Tenbury Wells 54 52.19 N 2.35 W
Tenby 54 51.41 N 4.43 W
Tenerife I 86 28.19 N 16.34 W
Tengiz, Ozero ⊜ 78 50.30 N 69.00 E
Tennessee □³ 96 35.50 N 85.30 W
Tennessee ≏ 96 37.04 N 88.33 W
Tenterden 54 51.05 N 0.42 E
Tenyes ⋀ 82 1.30 S 127.30 E
Teófilo Otoni 100 17.51 S 41.30 W
Tepic 98 21.30 N 104.54 W
Teplice 66 50.39 N 13.48 E
Tequedama, Salto de L 100 4.35 N 74.18 W
Ter ≏ 70 42.00 N 3.11 E
Teramo 72 42.39 N 13.42 E
Terceira I 86 38.43 N 27.13 W
Terek ≏ 76 43.44 N 46.33 E
Teresina 100 5.05 S 42.49 W
Terib'orka 76 69.08 N 35.06 E
Términos, Laguna de C 98 18.37 N 91.33 W
Termoli 72 41.59 N 14.59 E
Ternate 82 0.48 N 127.24 E
Terneuzen 66 51.20 N 3.50 E
Terni 72 42.34 N 12.37 E
Ternopol' 76 49.34 N 25.36 E
Terpenija, Mys ➤ 78 48.38 N 144.44 E

---

Tetbury 54 51.39 N 2.10 W
Tete 90 16.13 S 33.35 E
Teterow 66 53.46 N 12.34 E
Tétouan 86 35.34 N 5.23 W
Tetovo 74 42.01 N 20.58 E
Tettenhall 54 52.36 N 2.09 W
Tet'uche 78 44.35 N 135.35 E
Tet'uši 62 54.57 N 48.50 E
Teuco ≏ 102 25.38 S 60.12 W
Tevere ≏ 50 41.44 N 12.14 E
Teviot ≏ 54 55.36 N 2.50 W
Teviotdale V 58 55.23 N 2.55 W
Teviothead 58 55.20 N 2.56 W
Tewkesbury 54 51.59 N 2.09 W
Texarkana 96 33.26 N 94.03 W
Texas □³ 96 31.30 N 99.00 W
Texoma, Lake ⊜¹ 96 33.55 N 96.37 W
Teynham 54 51.20 N 0.50 E
Thabana Ntlenyana ⋀ 90 29.28 S 29.16 E
Thailand □¹ 82 15.00 N 100.00 E
Thailand, Gulf of C 82 11.00 N 101.00 E
Thai-nguyen 82 21.36 N 105.50 E
Thale 66 51.45 N 11.02 E
Thame 54 51.45 N 0.59 W
Thame ≏ 54 51.28 N 0.43 E
Thames ≏ 52 51.28 N 0.43 E
Thāna 84 19.12 N 72.59 E
Thanet, Isle of I 54 51.22 N 1.20 E
Thanh-hoa 82 19.48 N 105.46 E
Thanh-pho Ho Chi Minh (Sai-gon) 82 10.45 N 106.40 E
Thanjāvūr 84 10.48 N 79.09 E
Thar Desert (Great Indian Desert) ←² 84 27.00 N 71.00 E
Tharsunn, Beinn ⋀ 58 57.47 N 4.21 W
Thásos I 50 40.41 N 24.47 E
Thatcham 54 51.25 N 1.15 W
Thaxted 54 51.57 N 0.20 E
Theale 54 51.26 N 1.04 W
The Brothers I 86 12.08 N 53.12 E
The Cheviot ⋀ 52 55.28 N 2.09 W
The Deeps ⩪³ 58a 60.09 N 1.23 W
The Downs ⩪³ 54 51.13 N 1.27 E
The English Companys Islands II 92 11.50 S 136.32 E
The Everglades ≋ 96 26.00 N 80.40 W
The Fens ≙ 52 52.38 N 0.02 E
The Glenkens ←¹ 58 55.10 N 4.15 W
Thelon ≏ 94 64.16 N 96.05 W
The Long Mynd ⋀ 54 52.35 N 2.48 W
The Machars ✗¹ 58 54.50 N 4.30 W
The Machars □⁸ 54 54.50 N 4.33 W
The Minch U 58 58.10 N 5.50 W
The Moors ←¹ 54 51.34 N 4.00 W
The Mumbles 54 51.34 N 4.00 W
The Naze ➤ 52 51.53 N 1.16 E
The Needles ➤ 54 50.39 N 1.34 W
The Oa ⋀¹ 58 55.35 N 6.16 W
The Paps ⋀ 92 52.00 N 9.17 W
The Rhins ➤¹ 54 54.50 N 5.00 W
The Road ≡ 54a 49.56 N 6.20 W
Thesiger Bay C 94 71.30 N 124.05 W
The Solent U 54 50.46 N 1.20 W
Thessaloníki (Salonika) 74 40.38 N 22.56 E
The Storr ⋀ 58 57.31 N 6.12 W
The Swale ≡ 54 51.22 N 0.56 E
The Vale of V 54 52.25 N 3.22 W
Thetford 54 52.25 N 0.45 E
The Twelve Pins ⋀ 60 53.31 N 9.50 W
The Wash C 54 52.55 N 0.15 E
The Weald ✗¹ 54 51.05 N 0.05 E
The Wrekin ⋀² 54 52.40 N 2.33 W
Thiene 72 45.42 N 11.29 E
Thiers 68 45.51 N 3.33 E
Thies 88 14.48 N 16.56 W
Thika 90 1.03 S 37.05 E
Thimbu 84 27.28 N 89.39 E
Thionville 68 49.22 N 6.10 E
Thira I 74 36.24 N 25.29 E
Thirlmere ⊜ 54 54.33 N 3.04 W
Thirsk 54 54.26 N 2.35 W
Thivai (Thebes) 74 38.19 N 23.19 E
Thiviers 68 45.25 N 0.55 E
Thlewiaza ≏ 94 60.28 N 94.45 W
Thomastown 60 52.31 N 7.08 W
Thom Bay C 94 70.09 N 92.00 W
Thomsen ≏ 94 72.52 N 119.35 W
Thomson ≏ 92 25.11 S 142.53 E
Thonon-les-Bains 68 46.22 N 6.29 E
Thornaby 54 54.34 N 1.18 W
Thornbury 54 51.37 N 2.31 W
Thornbury 54 51.37 N 2.31 W
Thorndon 54 52.16 N 1.08 E
Thorney 54 52.37 N 0.06 W
Thornhill 58 55.15 N 3.46 W
Thornton 54 53.53 N 3.01 W
Thornton Dale 54 54.14 N 0.43 W
Thorpe-le-Soken 54 51.50 N 1.10 E
Thorpe Saint Andrew 54 52.38 N 1.22 E
Thouars 68 46.59 N 0.13 W
Thrace □⁹ 74 41.20 N 26.45 E
Thrapston 54 52.24 N 0.32 W
Three Bridges 54 51.07 N 0.09 W
Three Points, Cape ➤ 86 4.45 N 2.06 W
Threlkeld 54 54.37 N 3.03 W
Throckley 54 54.59 N 1.45 W
Thrushel ≏ 54 50.34 N 4.19 W
Thunder Bay 96 48.23 N 89.15 W
Thurles 60 52.41 N 7.49 W
Thurnscoe 56 53.31 N 1.19 W
Thursby 54 54.51 N 3.03 W
Thurso 58 58.35 N 3.32 W
Tianjin (Tientsin) 80 39.08 N 117.12 E
Tianmen 80 30.40 N 113.08 E
Tianshui 80 34.35 N 105.58 E
Tianshuihai 80 35.07 N 79.18 E
Tiaret 86 35.28 N 1.21 E
Tibasti, Sarīr ←² 88 22.50 N 18.50 E
Tibberton 54 52.41 N 2.25 W
Tibet ⋀¹ 80 32.00 N 90.00 E
Tiburón, Isla I 98 29.00 N 112.23 W
Ticehurst 54 51.03 N 0.25 E
Tichoreck 76 45.51 N 40.09 E
Tichvin 62 59.39 N 33.31 E
Tidra, Île I 88 19.44 N 16.24 W
Tiel 66 51.54 N 5.26 E
Tieling 80 42.18 N 123.49 E
Tielt 66 51.00 N 3.19 E
Tien Shan ⋀ 80 50.48 N 4.57 E
Tienen 80 50.48 N 4.57 E
Tierra del Fuego, Isla Grande de I 102 54.00 S 69.00 W
Tietê ≏ 102 20.40 S 51.35 W
Tighvein ⋀² 58 55.30 N 5.10 W
Tigris (Dicle) (Dijlah) ≏ 84 31.00 N 47.25 E
Tijuana 98 32.32 N 117.01 W
Tilburg 66 51.34 N 5.05 E
Tilbury 54 51.28 N 0.23 E
Till ≏, Eng., U.K. 54 55.41 N 2.12 W
Till ≏, Eng., U.K. 56 53.16 N 0.37 W
Tillicoultry 58 56.09 N 3.44 W
Tillyfourie 58 57.11 N 2.36 W
Tilmanstone 54 51.12 N 1.18 E
Tilt ≏ 58 56.46 N 3.50 W
Timaru 93a 44.23 S 171.15 E
Timiris, Cap ➤ 88 19.23 N 16.31 W
Timişoara 74 45.45 N 21.13 E
Timmins 94 48.28 N 81.20 W
Timoteo 74 45.45 N 27.49 E
Timor I 82 9.00 S 125.00 E
Timor Sea ⩪² 82 11.00 S 128.00 E
Timptom ≏ 78 58.43 N 127.12 E
Tinahely 60 52.47 N 6.28 W
Tinaquillo 98 9.55 N 68.18 W
Tindouf 86 27.42 N 8.10 W
Tinharé, Ilha de I 100 13.30 S 38.58 W
Tinian I 82 15.00 N 145.38 E
Tinogasta 102 28.04 S 67.34 W
Tínos I 74 37.38 N 25.10 E
Tinténiac 68 48.20 N 1.50 W
Tinthert, Plateau du ⋀¹ 86 29.00 N 9.00 E
Tintagel 54 50.40 N 4.45 W

| Name | Page | Lat ° ′ | Long ° ′ |
| --- | --- | --- | --- |
| Tintagel Head › | 54 | 50.41 N | 4.46 W |
| Tintern Parva | 54 | 51.42 N | 2.40 W |
| Tinto ∧ | 58 | 55.36 N | 3.39 W |
| Tioman, Pulau I | 82 | 2.48 N | 104.10 E |
| Tioro, Selat ⋓ | 82 | 4.40 S | 122.20 E |
| Tipperary | 60 | 52.29 N | 8.10 W |
| Tipperary □[6] | 52 | 52.40 N | 8.20 W |
| Tipton | 54 | 52.32 N | 2.05 W |
| Tip Top Mountain ∧ | 94 | 48.16 N | 85.59 W |
| Tiptree | 54 | 51.49 N | 0.45 E |
| Tiracambu, Serra do ⛰[1] | 100 | 3.15 S | 46.30 W |
| Tīrān, Jazīrat I | 88 | 27.56 N | 34.34 E |
| Tiranë | 74 | 41.20 N | 19.50 E |
| Tiraspol' | 76 | 46.51 N | 29.38 E |
| Tire | 74 | 38.04 N | 27.45 E |
| Tiree I | 52 | 56.31 N | 6.49 W |
| Tîrgovişte | 74 | 44.56 N | 25.27 E |
| Tîrgu-Jiu | 74 | 45.02 N | 23.17 E |
| Tîrgu Mureş | 74 | 46.33 N | 24.33 E |
| Tîrgu-Neamţ | 74 | 47.12 N | 26.22 E |
| Tîrgu-Ocna | 74 | 46.15 N | 26.37 E |
| Tirich Mīr ∧ | 84 | 36.15 N | 71.50 E |
| Tîrnăveni | 74 | 46.20 N | 24.17 E |
| Tírnavos | 74 | 39.45 N | 22.17 E |
| Tirry ≃ | 58 | 58.02 N | 4.26 W |
| Tiruchchirāppalli | 84 | 10.49 N | 78.41 E |
| Tirunelveli | 84 | 8.44 N | 77.41 E |
| Tiruppur | 84 | 11.06 N | 77.21 E |
| Tisbury | 54 | 51.04 N | 2.03 W |
| Tīsta ≃ | 84 | 25.23 N | 89.43 E |
| Tisza ≃ | 50 | 45.15 N | 20.17 E |
| Tiszavasvári | 74 | 47.58 N | 21.22 E |
| Titchfield | 54 | 50.51 N | 1.13 W |
| Titicaca, Lago ⊜ | 100 | 15.50 S | 69.20 W |
| Titograd | 74 | 42.26 N | 19.14 E |
| Titovo Užice | 74 | 43.51 N | 19.51 E |
| Titov Veles | 74 | 41.41 N | 21.48 E |
| Titterstone Clee Hill ∧[2] | 54 | 52.23 N | 2.35 W |
| Titusville | 96 | 28.37 N | 80.49 W |
| Tiumpan Head › | 58 | 58.16 N | 6.09 W |
| Tiverton | 54 | 50.55 N | 3.29 W |
| Tivoli | 72 | 41.58 N | 12.48 E |
| Tizimín | 98 | 21.10 N | 88.10 W |
| Tizi-Ouzou | 86 | 36.48 N | 4.02 E |
| Tlemcen | 86 | 34.52 N | 1.15 W |
| Toba, Danau ⊜ | 82 | 2.35 N | 98.50 E |
| Tobago I | 98 | 11.15 N | 60.40 W |
| Toba Kākar Range ⛰ | 84 | 31.15 N | 68.00 E |
| Tobercurry | 60 | 54.03 N | 8.43 W |
| Tobermory | 58 | 56.37 N | 6.05 W |
| Toberonochy | 58 | 56.13 N | 5.38 W |
| Tobi I | 82 | 3.00 N | 131.10 E |
| Tobol ≃ | 76 | 58.10 N | 68.12 E |
| Tobol'sk | 76 | 58.12 N | 68.16 E |
| Tocantins ≃ | 100 | 1.45 S | 49.10 W |
| Tocopilla | 102 | 22.05 S | 70.12 W |
| Toddington | 54 | 51.57 N | 0.32 W |
| Todmorden | 56 | 53.43 N | 2.05 W |
| Toe Head › | 58 | 57.50 N | 7.08 W |
| Togian, Kepulauan II | 82 | 0.20 S | 122.00 E |
| Togo □[1] | 86 | 8.00 N | 1.10 E |
| Tokat | 84 | 40.19 N | 36.34 E |
| Tokelau Islands II | 8 | 9.00 S | 171.45 W |
| Tokushima | 80 | 34.04 N | 134.34 E |
| Tōkyō | 80 | 35.42 N | 139.46 E |
| Tolbuhin | 74 | 43.34 N | 27.50 E |
| Toledo, Esp. | 70 | 39.52 N | 4.01 W |
| Toledo, Ohio, U.S. | 96 | 41.39 N | 83.32 W |
| Toledo Bend Reservoir ⊜[1] | 96 | 31.30 N | 93.45 W |
| Tolima, Nevado del ∧ | 100 | 4.40 N | 75.19 W |
| Toljatti | 62 | 53.31 N | 49.26 E |
| Tollesbury | 54 | 51.46 N | 0.50 E |
| Tolmezzo | 72 | 46.24 N | 13.01 E |
| Tolo, Teluk C | 82 | 2.00 S | 122.30 E |
| Tolob | 58a | 59.53 N | 1.19 W |
| Tolosa | 70 | 43.08 N | 2.04 W |
| Tolpuddle | 54 | 50.45 N | 2.18 W |
| Tolsta Head › | 58 | 58.20 N | 6.10 W |
| Tolstoj, Mys › | 78 | 59.10 N | 155.12 E |
| Toluca | 98 | 19.17 N | 99.40 W |
| Tom' ≃ | 78 | 56.50 N | 84.27 E |
| Tomakomai | 80 | 42.38 N | 141.36 E |
| Tomaszów Lubelski | 66 | 50.28 N | 23.25 E |
| Tomaszów Mazowiecki | 66 | 51.32 N | 20.01 E |
| Tomatin | 58 | 57.20 N | 3.59 W |
| Tombador, Serra do ⛰[1] | 100 | 12.00 S | 57.40 W |
| Tombigbee ≃ | 96 | 31.04 N | 87.58 W |
| Tombouctou (Timbuktu) | 86 | 16.46 N | 3.01 W |
| Tombstone Mountain ∧ | 94 | 64.25 N | 138.30 W |
| Tomdoun | 58 | 57.04 N | 5.03 W |
| Tomelloso | 70 | 39.10 N | 3.01 W |
| Tomich | 58 | 57.18 N | 4.48 W |
| Tomini, Teluk C | 82 | 0.20 S | 121.00 E |
| Tomintoul | 58 | 57.14 N | 3.22 W |
| Tomnavoulin | 58 | 57.18 N | 3.19 W |
| Tomo ≃ | 100 | 5.20 N | 67.48 W |
| Tomsk | 78 | 56.30 N | 84.58 E |
| Tonbridge | 54 | 51.12 N | 0.16 E |
| Tondano | 82 | 1.19 N | 124.54 E |
| Tonga Islands II | 8 | 20.00 S | 175.00 W |
| Tongchuan | 80 | 35.01 N | 109.01 E |
| Tongeren | 66 | 50.47 N | 5.28 E |
| Tonghua | 80 | 41.50 N | 125.55 E |
| Tongjosŏn-man C | 80 | 39.30 N | 128.00 E |
| Tongliao | 80 | 43.39 N | 122.14 E |
| Tongtianhe ≃ | 80 | 33.25 N | 96.32 E |
| Tongue | 58 | 58.28 N | 4.25 W |
| Tongue, Kyle of C | 58 | 58.30 N | 4.26 W |
| Tongxian | 80 | 39.55 N | 116.39 E |
| Tonkin, Gulf of C | 82 | 20.00 N | 108.00 E |
| Tønsberg | 64 | 59.17 N | 10.25 E |
| Tonyrefail | 54 | 51.36 N | 3.25 W |
| Toomebridge | 60 | 54.45 N | 6.27 W |
| Toomevara | 60 | 52.50 N | 8.02 W |
| Toormakeady | 60 | 53.39 N | 9.24 W |
| Toowoomba | 92 | 27.33 S | 151.57 E |
| Topeka | 96 | 39.03 N | 95.41 W |
| Topol'čany | 66 | 48.34 N | 18.10 E |
| Topsham | 54 | 50.41 N | 3.27 W |
| Torawitan, Tanjung › | 82 | 1.46 N | 124.58 E |
| Torbalı | 74 | 38.10 N | 27.21 E |
| Torbat-e Ḥeydarīyeh | 84 | 35.16 N | 59.13 E |
| Tor Bay C | 54 | 50.25 N | 3.30 W |
| Torez | 76 | 48.01 N | 38.37 E |
| Torgau | 66 | 51.34 N | 13.00 E |
| Torgelow | 66 | 53.37 N | 14.00 E |
| Torhout | 68 | 51.04 N | 3.06 E |
| Torino (Turin) | 72 | 45.03 N | 7.40 E |
| Torne ≃ | 56 | 53.36 N | 0.44 W |
| Torneälven ≃ | 50 | 65.48 N | 24.08 E |
| Torneträsk ⊜ | 50 | 68.20 N | 19.10 E |
| Torngat Mountains ⛰ | 94 | 59.00 N | 64.00 W |
| Toro | 70 | 41.31 N | 5.24 W |
| Toro, Cerro del ∧ | 102 | 29.08 S | 69.48 W |
| Törökszentmiklós | 74 | 47.11 N | 20.25 E |
| Toronto | 94 | 43.39 N | 79.23 W |
| Toropec | 62 | 56.30 N | 31.39 E |
| Toros Dağları ⛰ | 50 | 37.00 N | 33.00 E |
| Torphins | 58 | 57.06 N | 2.37 W |
| Torpoint | 54 | 50.22 N | 4.11 W |
| Torquay (Torbay) | 54 | 50.28 N | 3.30 W |
| Torre Annunziata | 72 | 40.45 N | 14.27 E |
| Torredonjimeno | 70 | 37.46 N | 3.57 W |
| Torrejón de Ardoz | 70 | 40.27 N | 3.29 W |
| Torrelavega | 70 | 43.21 N | 4.03 W |
| Torremaggiore | 72 | 41.41 N | 15.17 E |
| Torrens, Lake ⊜ | 92 | 31.00 S | 137.50 E |
| Torrente | 70 | 39.26 N | 0.28 W |
| Torreón | 98 | 25.33 N | 103.26 W |
| Torres Strait ⋓ | 92 | 10.25 S | 142.10 E |
| Torridge ≃ | 52 | 51.03 N | 4.11 W |
| Torridon | 58 | 57.33 N | 5.31 W |
| Torridon, Loch C | 58 | 57.35 N | 5.46 W |
| Torrin | 58 | 57.12 N | 6.02 W |
| Tórshavn | 50 | 62.01 N | 6.46 W |
| Torteval | 55b | 49.27 N | 2.38 W |
| Tortola I | 98 | 18.27 N | 64.36 W |
| Tortona | 72 | 44.54 N | 8.52 E |
| Tortosa | 70 | 40.48 N | 0.31 E |
| Tortue, Île de la I | 98 | 20.04 N | 72.49 W |
| Toruń | 66 | 53.02 N | 18.35 E |
| Tory Island I | 60 | 55.16 N | 8.14 W |
| Tory Sound ⋓ | 60 | 55.14 N | 8.14 W |
| Toržok | 62 | 57.03 N | 34.58 E |
| Toscaig | 58 | 57.24 N | 5.50 W |
| Tosno | 62 | 59.33 N | 30.53 E |
| Tot'ma | 62 | 59.57 N | 42.45 E |
| Totnes | 54 | 50.25 N | 3.41 W |
| Tottington | 56 | 53.37 N | 2.20 W |
| Totton | 54 | 50.56 N | 1.29 W |
| Tottori | 80 | 35.30 N | 134.14 E |
| Toubkal, Jbel ∧ | 86 | 31.05 N | 7.55 W |
| Touggourt | 86 | 33.10 N | 6.00 E |
| Toul | 68 | 48.41 N | 5.54 E |
| Toulon | 68 | 43.07 N | 5.56 E |
| Toulouse | 68 | 43.36 N | 1.26 E |
| Toungoo | 82 | 18.56 N | 96.26 E |
| Tourcoing | 68 | 50.43 N | 3.09 E |
| Tournai | 66 | 50.36 N | 3.23 E |
| Tours | 68 | 47.23 N | 0.41 E |
| Touside, Pic ∧ | 88 | 21.02 N | 16.25 E |
| Tove ≃ | 54 | 52.05 N | 0.38 W |
| Towan Head › | 54 | 50.25 N | 5.07 W |
| Towcester | 54 | 52.08 N | 1.00 W |
| Tower Hamlets ◆[8] | 54 | 51.32 N | 0.03 W |
| Tow Law | 56 | 54.44 N | 1.49 W |
| Townshend Island I | 92 | 22.15 S | 150.30 E |
| Townsville | 92 | 19.16 S | 146.48 E |
| Towuti, Danau ⊜ | 82 | 2.45 S | 121.32 E |
| Toyama | 80 | 36.41 N | 137.13 E |
| Toyohashi | 80 | 34.46 N | 137.23 E |
| Trabzon | 84 | 41.00 N | 39.43 E |
| Trakt | 62 | 62.44 N | 51.11 E |
| Tralee | 60 | 52.16 N | 9.42 W |
| Tralee Bay C | 52 | 52.15 N | 9.59 W |
| Tramore | 60 | 52.10 N | 7.10 W |
| Tranås | 64 | 58.03 N | 14.59 E |
| Tranent | 58 | 55.57 N | 2.58 W |
| Trang | 82 | 7.33 N | 99.36 E |
| Trangan, Pulau I | 82 | 6.35 S | 134.20 E |
| Trani | 72 | 41.17 N | 16.26 E |
| Trannon ≃ | 54 | 52.31 N | 3.25 W |
| Trapani | 72 | 38.01 N | 12.31 E |
| Traun | 66 | 48.13 N | 14.14 E |
| Traunstein | 66 | 47.52 N | 12.38 E |
| Traverse City | 96 | 44.46 N | 85.37 W |
| Travnik | 72 | 44.14 N | 17.40 E |
| Trawbreaga Bay C | 60 | 55.17 N | 7.18 W |
| Trawsfynydd | 54 | 52.54 N | 3.55 W |
| Trbovlje | 72 | 46.10 N | 15.03 E |
| Třebíč | 66 | 49.13 N | 15.53 E |
| Trebišov | 66 | 48.40 N | 21.47 E |
| Tredegar | 54 | 51.47 N | 3.16 W |
| Tregaron | 54 | 52.13 N | 3.55 W |
| Tregosse Islets II | 92 | 17.41 S | 150.43 E |
| Treharris | 54 | 51.41 N | 3.16 W |
| Treig, Loch ⊜[1] | 58 | 56.50 N | 4.44 W |
| Treinta y Tres | 102 | 33.14 S | 54.23 W |
| Trélazé | 68 | 47.27 N | 0.28 W |
| Trelew | 102 | 43.15 S | 65.18 W |
| Trelleborg | 64 | 55.22 N | 13.10 E |
| Tremadoc | 54 | 52.56 N | 4.09 W |
| Tremadoc Bay C | 56 | 52.52 N | 4.15 W |
| Tremblant, Mont ∧ | 94 | 46.16 N | 74.35 W |
| Trenčín | 66 | 48.54 N | 18.04 E |
| Trent ≃, Eng., U.K. | 52 | 53.42 N | 0.41 W |
| Trent ≃, Eng., U.K. | 54 | 53.12 N | 0.47 W |
| Trent, Vale of ∨ | 54 | 52.44 N | 1.50 W |
| Trento | 72 | 46.04 N | 11.08 E |
| Trenton | 96 | 40.13 N | 74.45 W |
| Tres Arroyos | 102 | 38.23 S | 60.17 W |
| Tresco I | 54a | 49.57 N | 6.19 W |
| Treshnish Isles II | 58 | 56.30 N | 6.24 W |
| Treshnish Point › | 58 | 56.33 N | 6.21 W |
| Três Lagoas | 100 | 20.48 S | 51.43 W |
| Tres Marías, Islas II | 98 | 21.25 N | 106.28 W |
| Três Marias, Reprêsa ⊜[1] | 100 | 18.12 S | 45.15 W |
| Tres Picos, Cerro ∧ | 102 | 38.09 S | 61.57 W |
| Tres Puntas, Cabo › | 102 | 47.06 S | 65.53 W |
| Tresta | 58 | 60.14 N | 1.21 W |
| Treviglio | 72 | 45.31 N | 9.35 E |
| Treviso | 72 | 45.40 N | 12.15 E |
| Trevose Head › | 52 | 50.33 N | 5.01 W |
| Trichūr | 84 | 10.31 N | 76.13 E |
| Trier | 66 | 49.45 N | 6.38 E |
| Trieste | 72 | 45.40 N | 13.46 E |
| Triglav ∧ | 50 | 46.23 N | 13.50 E |
| Tríkala | 74 | 39.34 N | 21.46 E |
| Trikora, Puncak ∧ | 82 | 4.15 S | 138.45 E |
| Trillick | 60 | 54.27 N | 7.30 W |
| Trim | 60 | 53.34 N | 6.47 W |
| Trincomalee | 84 | 8.34 N | 81.14 E |
| Třinec | 66 | 49.41 N | 18.40 E |
| Tring | 54 | 51.48 N | 0.40 W |
| Trinidad, Bol. | 100 | 14.47 S | 64.47 W |
| Trinidad, Cuba | 98 | 21.48 N | 79.59 W |
| Trinidad I | 98 | 10.30 N | 61.15 W |
| Trinidad and Tobago □[1] | 98 | 11.00 N | 61.00 W |
| Trinity ≃ | 96 | 29.47 N | 94.42 W |
| Trinity Bay C | 94 | 48.00 N | 53.40 W |
| Trípolis | 74 | 37.31 N | 22.21 E |
| Tristan da Cunha Group II | 8 | 37.15 S | 12.30 W |
| Triton Island I | 82 | 15.47 N | 111.12 E |
| Trivandrum | 84 | 8.28 N | 76.57 E |
| Trnava | 66 | 48.23 N | 17.35 E |
| Trobriand Islands II | 92 | 8.35 S | 151.05 E |
| Troick | 76 | 54.06 N | 61.35 E |
| Troina | 72 | 37.47 N | 14.37 E |
| Troisdorf | 66 | 50.49 N | 7.08 E |
| Trois-Rivières | 94 | 46.21 N | 72.33 W |
| Trojan | 74 | 42.51 N | 24.43 E |
| Trollhättan | 64 | 58.16 N | 12.18 E |
| Trombetas ≃ | 100 | 1.55 S | 55.35 W |
| Tromsø | 62 | 69.40 N | 18.58 E |
| Tronador, Monte ∧ | 102 | 41.10 S | 71.54 W |
| Trondheim | 64 | 63.25 N | 10.25 E |
| Troon | 58 | 55.32 N | 4.40 W |
| Trostan ∧ | 60 | 55.03 N | 6.10 W |
| Troup Head › | 58 | 57.41 N | 2.18 W |
| Trout ≃ | 94 | 61.19 N | 119.51 W |
| Trout Lake ⊜ | 94 | 60.35 N | 121.10 W |
| Trouville [-sur-Mer] | 68 | 49.22 N | 0.05 E |
| Trowbridge | 54 | 51.20 N | 2.13 W |
| Troy | 96 | 42.43 N | 73.40 W |
| Troyes | 68 | 48.18 N | 4.05 E |
| Truim ≃ | 58 | 57.02 N | 4.10 W |
| Trujillo, Esp. | 70 | 39.28 N | 5.53 W |
| Trujillo, Perú | 100 | 8.07 S | 79.02 W |
| Truro | 54 | 50.16 N | 5.03 W |
| Trutnov | 66 | 50.34 N | 15.55 E |
| Trwyn Cilan › | 54 | 52.46 N | 4.30 W |
| Tryweryn ≃ | 54 | 52.24 N | 3.35 W |
| Trzcianka | 66 | 53.03 N | 16.28 E |
| Trzebinia | 66 | 50.10 N | 19.18 E |
| Tsaratanana, Massif du ⛰ | 90 | 14.00 S | 49.00 E |
| Tshuapa ≃ | 90 | 0.14 S | 20.42 E |
| Tsiafajavona ∧ | 90 | 19.21 S | 47.15 E |
| Tsu | 80 | 34.43 N | 136.31 E |
| Tsugaru-kaikyō ⋓ | 80 | 41.35 N | 141.00 E |
| Tsumeb | 90 | 19.13 S | 17.42 E |
| Tsuruga | 80 | 35.39 N | 136.04 E |
| Tsuruoka | 80 | 38.44 N | 139.50 E |
| Tsushima II | 80 | 34.30 N | 129.22 E |
| Tual | 82 | 5.40 S | 132.45 E |
| Tuam | 60 | 53.31 N | 8.50 W |
| Tuamotu, Îles II | 8 | 19.00 S | 142.00 W |
| Tuapse | 76 | 44.07 N | 39.05 E |
| Tuath, Loch ⋓ | 58 | 56.30 N | 6.12 W |
| Tübingen | 66 | 48.31 N | 9.02 E |
| Ṭubruq | 88 | 32.05 N | 23.59 E |
| Tucson | 96 | 32.13 N | 110.58 W |
| Tud ≃ | 54 | 52.38 N | 1.15 E |
| Tudela | 70 | 42.05 N | 1.36 W |
| Tudweiliog | 54 | 52.54 N | 4.35 W |
| Tuguegarao | 82 | 17.37 N | 121.44 E |
| Tuirc, Beinn an ∧[2] | 58 | 55.34 N | 5.34 W |
| Tukangbesi, Kepulauan I | 82 | 5.40 S | 123.50 E |
| Tula | 62 | 54.12 N | 37.37 E |
| Tulancingo | 98 | 20.05 N | 98.22 W |
| Tulangbawang ≃ | 82 | 4.24 S | 105.52 E |
| Tulcán | 100 | 0.48 N | 77.43 W |
| Tulcea | 74 | 45.11 N | 28.48 E |
| Tuléar | 90 | 23.21 S | 43.40 E |
| Tulla | 60 | 52.52 N | 8.45 W |
| Tullamore | 60 | 53.16 N | 7.30 W |
| Tulle | 68 | 45.16 N | 1.46 E |
| Tullow | 60 | 52.48 N | 6.44 W |
| Tulsa | 96 | 36.09 N | 95.58 W |
| Tulsk | 60 | 53.47 N | 8.16 W |
| Tuluá | 100 | 4.06 N | 76.11 W |
| Tulun | 78 | 54.35 N | 100.33 E |
| Tumaco | 100 | 1.49 N | 78.46 W |
| Tuman-gang ≃ | 80 | 42.18 N | 130.41 E |
| Tumba | 64 | 59.12 N | 17.49 E |
| Tumbes | 100 | 3.34 S | 80.28 W |
| T'umen', S.S.S.R. | 76 | 57.09 N | 65.32 E |
| Tumen, Zhg. | 80 | 42.58 N | 129.49 E |
| Tumkūr | 84 | 13.21 N | 77.06 E |
| Tummel ≃ | 58 | 56.38 N | 3.40 W |
| Tumuc-Humac Mountains ⛰ | 100 | 2.20 N | 55.00 W |
| Tunbridge Wells | 54 | 51.08 N | 0.16 E |
| Tungabhadra ≃ | 84 | 15.57 N | 78.15 E |
| Tunis | 86 | 36.48 N | 10.11 E |
| Tunis, Golfe de C | 86 | 37.00 N | 10.30 E |
| Tunisia □[1] | 86 | 34.00 N | 9.00 E |
| Tunja | 100 | 5.31 N | 73.22 W |
| Tunstall | 54 | 53.05 N | 2.13 W |
| Tunuyán ≃ | 102 | 34.03 S | 66.45 W |
| Tunxi | 80 | 29.44 N | 118.18 E |
| Tuokusidawanling ∧ | 80 | 37.14 N | 85.47 E |
| Tupã | 100 | 21.56 S | 50.30 W |
| Tupungato, Cerro ∧ | 102 | 33.22 S | 69.47 W |
| Tura ≃ | 76 | 57.12 N | 66.56 E |
| Turda | 74 | 46.34 N | 23.47 E |
| Turek | 66 | 52.02 N | 18.30 E |
| Turgaj ≃ | 76 | 48.01 N | 62.45 E |
| Turgajskaja Dolina ∨ | 76 | 51.00 N | 64.30 E |
| Turgajskaja Stolovaja Strana ⛰[1] | 76 | 51.00 N | 64.00 E |
| Turgutlu | 74 | 38.30 N | 27.43 E |
| Turia ≃ | 50 | 39.27 N | 0.19 W |
| Turka | 66 | 49.10 N | 23.02 E |
| Turkestan | 76 | 43.18 N | 68.15 E |
| Túrkeve | 74 | 47.06 N | 20.45 E |
| Turkey □[1], As., Eur. | 50 | 39.00 N | 35.00 E |
| Turks and Caicos Islands □[2] | 98 | 21.45 N | 71.35 W |
| Turks Islands II | 98 | 21.24 N | 71.07 W |
| Turku (Åbo) | 64 | 60.27 N | 22.17 E |
| Turnagain ≃ | 94 | 59.06 N | 127.35 W |
| Turneffe Islands II | 98 | 17.22 N | 87.51 W |
| Turnhout | 66 | 51.19 N | 4.57 E |
| Turnov | 66 | 50.35 N | 15.10 E |
| Turnu-Măgurele | 74 | 43.45 N | 24.53 E |
| Turquino, Pico ∧ | 98 | 19.59 N | 76.50 W |
| Turriff | 58 | 57.32 N | 2.28 W |
| Turu ≃ | 78 | 64.38 N | 100.00 E |
| Turuchan ≃ | 78 | 65.56 N | 87.42 E |
| Tuscaloosa | 96 | 33.13 N | 87.33 W |
| Tusker Rock II[1] | 54 | 51.27 N | 3.40 W |
| Tutajev | 62 | 57.53 N | 39.32 E |
| Tuticorin | 84 | 8.50 N | 78.09 E |
| Tutrakan | 74 | 44.03 N | 26.37 E |
| Tutupaca, Volcán ∧[1] | 100 | 17.01 S | 70.22 W |
| T'uva-Guba | 62 | 69.08 N | 33.32 E |
| Tuvalu II | 8 | 8.00 S | 178.00 E |
| Ṭuwayq, Jabal ⛰ | 84 | 23.00 N | 46.00 E |
| Tuxpan | 98 | 21.57 N | 105.18 W |
| Tuxpan de Rodríguez Cano | 98 | 20.57 N | 97.24 W |
| Tuxtla Gutiérrez | 98 | 16.45 N | 93.07 W |
| Tuya ≃ | 94 | 58.05 N | 130.50 W |
| Tuz Gölü ⊜ | 50 | 38.45 N | 33.25 E |
| Tuzla | 74 | 44.32 N | 18.41 E |
| Tweed ≃ | 58 | 55.46 N | 2.00 W |
| Tweeddale ∨ | 58 | 55.37 N | 2.55 W |
| Tweedmouth | 56 | 55.45 N | 2.01 W |
| Twin Falls | 96 | 42.34 N | 114.28 W |
| Twitya ≃ | 94 | 64.10 N | 128.12 W |
| Twrch ≃ | 54 | 51.46 N | 3.46 W |
| Twyford, Eng., U.K. | 54 | 51.29 N | 0.53 W |
| Twyford, Eng., U.K. | 54 | 51.01 N | 1.19 W |
| Twymyn ≃ | 54 | 52.38 N | 3.44 W |
| Tychy | 66 | 50.09 N | 18.59 E |
| Tyldesley | 56 | 53.31 N | 2.28 W |
| Tyler | 96 | 32.21 N | 95.18 W |
| Tym ≃ | 78 | 59.25 N | 80.04 E |
| Tynagh | 60 | 53.09 N | 8.22 W |
| Tyndrum | 58 | 56.27 N | 4.44 W |
| Tyne ≃, Eng., U.K. | 52 | 55.01 N | 1.26 W |
| Tyne ≃, Scot., U.K. | 58 | 56.01 N | 2.37 W |
| Tyne and Wear □[6] | 56 | 54.55 N | 1.35 W |
| Tynemouth | 56 | 55.01 N | 1.24 W |
| Tyrrellspass | 60 | 53.23 N | 7.22 W |
| Tyrrhenian Sea ⊤[2] | 50 | 40.00 N | 12.00 E |
| Tywardreath | 54 | 50.22 N | 4.41 W |
| Tywi ≃ | 52 | 51.46 N | 4.22 W |
| Tywyn | 54 | 52.35 N | 4.05 W |
| **U** | | | |
| Uatumã ≃ | 100 | 2.26 S | 57.37 W |
| Ubangi (Oubangui) ≃ | 86 | 1.15 N | 17.50 E |
| Ụbe | 80 | 33.56 N | 131.15 E |
| Úbeda | 70 | 38.01 N | 3.22 W |
| Uberaba | 100 | 19.45 S | 47.55 W |
| Uberlândia | 100 | 18.56 S | 48.18 W |
| Ubon Ratchathani | 82 | 15.14 N | 104.54 E |
| Ubundi | 90 | 0.21 S | 25.29 E |
| Ucayali ≃ | 100 | 4.30 S | 73.27 W |
| Uchiura-wan C | 80 | 42.20 N | 140.40 E |
| Uchta | 62 | 63.33 N | 53.38 E |
| Uckfield | 54 | 50.58 N | 0.06 E |
| Učur ≃ | 78 | 58.48 N | 130.35 E |
| Uda ≃, S.S.S.R. | 78 | 56.05 N | 99.34 E |
| Uda ≃, S.S.S.R. | 78 | 51.47 N | 107.33 E |
| Uda ≃, S.S.S.R. | 78 | 54.42 N | 135.14 E |
| Udaipur | 84 | 24.35 N | 73.41 E |
| Uddevalla | 64 | 58.21 N | 11.55 E |
| Uddingston | 58 | 55.50 N | 4.06 W |
| Udine | 72 | 46.03 N | 13.14 E |
| Udon Thani | 82 | 17.26 N | 102.46 E |
| Udskaja Guba C | 78 | 54.50 N | 135.45 E |
| Ueckermünde | 66 | 53.44 N | 14.03 E |
| Uelzen | 66 | 52.58 N | 10.33 E |
| Uetersen | 66 | 53.41 N | 9.39 E |
| Ufa | 76 | 54.44 N | 55.56 E |
| Uffculme | 54 | 50.54 N | 3.20 W |
| Ugalla ≃ | 90 | 5.08 S | 30.42 E |
| Uganda □[1] | 90 | 1.00 N | 32.00 E |
| Ugie ≃ | 58 | 57.30 N | 1.47 W |
| Uglegorsk | 80 | 48.19 N | 38.17 E |
| Uglič | 62 | 57.32 N | 38.19 E |
| Ugoma ∧ | 90 | 4.00 S | 28.45 E |
| Uherské Hradiště | 66 | 49.05 N | 17.28 E |
| Uig, Scot., U.K. | 58 | 57.35 N | 6.22 W |
| Uig, Scot., U.K. | 58 | 58.12 N | 7.00 W |
| Uil ≃ | 76 | 48.36 N | 52.30 E |
| Uitenhage | 90 | 33.40 S | 25.28 E |
| Uj ≃ | 76 | 54.17 N | 64.58 E |
| Ụjandina ≃ | 78 | 68.23 N | 145.50 E |
| Újfehértó | 66 | 47.48 N | 21.40 E |
| Ujiji | 90 | 4.55 S | 29.41 E |
| Ujjain | 84 | 23.12 N | 75.46 E |
| Ujung Pandang (Makasar) | 82 | 5.07 S | 119.24 E |
| Ukerewe Island I | 90 | 2.03 S | 33.00 E |
| Ukmergė | 62 | 55.15 N | 24.45 E |
| Ulaanbaatar | 80 | 47.55 N | 106.53 E |
| Ulan-Ude | 78 | 51.50 N | 107.37 E |
| Ulcinj | 74 | 41.55 N | 19.11 E |
| Ulhāsnagar | 84 | 19.13 N | 73.07 E |
| Ulithi I[1] | 82 | 9.58 N | 139.40 E |
| Uljanovsk | 62 | 54.20 N | 48.24 E |
| Ullapool | 58 | 57.54 N | 5.10 W |
| Ullswater ⊜ | 56 | 54.34 N | 2.54 W |
| Ullŭng-do I | 80 | 37.29 N | 130.52 E |
| Ulm | 66 | 48.24 N | 10.00 E |
| Ulsan | 80 | 35.34 N | 129.19 E |
| Ulsta | 58 | 60.30 N | 1.09 W |
| Ulster □[9] | 52 | 54.35 N | 7.00 W |
| Ulster Canal ≊ | 56 | 54.27 N | 6.40 W |
| Uluguru Mountains ⛰ | 90 | 7.10 S | 37.40 E |
| Ulva I | 52 | 56.28 N | 6.12 W |
| Ulverston | 56 | 54.12 N | 3.06 W |
| Uman' | 76 | 48.44 N | 30.14 E |
| Umanak Fjord C[2] | 94 | 70.55 N | 53.00 W |
| Umba | 62 | 66.41 N | 34.15 E |
| Umeå | 64 | 63.50 N | 20.15 E |
| Umeälven ≃ | 50 | 63.47 N | 20.16 E |
| Umfuli ≃ | 90 | 17.30 S | 29.23 E |
| Umm Durmān (Omdurman) | 88 | 15.38 N | 32.30 E |
| 'Umrān | 84 | 15.50 N | 43.56 E |
| Umtali | 90 | 18.58 S | 32.40 E |
| Umtata | 90 | 31.35 S | 28.47 E |
| 'Unayzah | 84 | 26.06 N | 43.56 E |
| Uncompahgre Peak ∧ | 96 | 38.04 N | 107.28 W |
| Ungava, Péninsule d' ›[1] | 94 | 60.00 N | 74.00 W |
| Ungava Bay C | 94 | 59.30 N | 67.30 W |
| Uni | 62 | 57.46 N | 51.30 E |
| Unini ≃ | 100 | 1.41 S | 61.31 W |
| Union of Soviet Socialist Republics □[1], As., Eur. | 78 | 60.00 N | 80.00 E |
| Uniontown | 96 | 39.54 N | 79.44 W |
| United Arab Emirates □[1] | 84 | 24.00 N | 54.00 E |
| United Kingdom □[1] | 50 | 54.00 N | 2.00 W |
| United States □[1] | 96 | 38.00 N | 97.00 W |
| Unna | 66 | 51.32 N | 7.41 E |
| Unst I | 52 | 60.45 N | 0.55 W |
| Unža ≃ | 76 | 57.20 N | 43.08 E |
| Upavon | 54 | 51.18 N | 1.49 W |
| Upemba, Lac ⊜ | 90 | 8.36 S | 26.26 E |
| Up Holland | 56 | 53.33 N | 2.44 W |
| Upington | 90 | 28.25 S | 21.15 E |
| Upper Arrow Lake ⊜ | 94 | 50.30 N | 117.55 W |
| Upper Red Lake ⊜ | 96 | 48.10 N | 94.40 W |
| Upper Tean | 54 | 52.57 N | 1.58 W |
| Upper Volta □[1] | 86 | 13.00 N | 2.00 W |
| Uppingham | 54 | 52.35 N | 0.43 W |
| Uppsala | 64 | 59.52 N | 17.38 E |
| Upton | 56 | 53.13 N | 2.52 W |
| Upton upon Severn | 54 | 52.04 N | 2.13 W |
| Upwell | 54 | 52.36 N | 0.12 E |
| Ural ≃ | 76 | 47.00 N | 51.48 E |
| Ural'sk | 76 | 51.14 N | 51.22 E |
| Ural'skije Gory (Ural Mountains) ⛰ | 76 | 60.00 N | 60.00 E |
| Uraricoera ≃ | 100 | 3.02 N | 60.30 W |
| Ura-T'ube | 76 | 39.55 N | 68.59 E |
| Urbino | 72 | 43.43 N | 12.38 E |
| Urdoma | 62 | 61.47 N | 48.32 E |
| Ure ≃ | 52 | 54.01 N | 1.12 W |
| Urfa | 84 | 37.08 N | 38.46 E |
| Urgenč | 76 | 41.33 N | 60.38 E |
| Urie ≃ | 58 | 57.19 N | 2.30 W |
| Urla | 74 | 38.18 N | 26.46 E |
| Urlingford | 60 | 52.42 N | 7.35 W |
| Urmston | 56 | 53.27 N | 2.21 W |
| Urquhart, Glen ∨ | 58 | 57.20 N | 4.35 W |
| Urr Water ≃ | 56 | 54.53 N | 3.49 W |
| Ursus | 66 | 52.12 N | 20.53 E |
| Uruapan | 98 | 19.25 N | 102.04 W |
| Urubamba ≃ | 100 | 10.44 S | 73.45 W |
| Urubu ≃ | 100 | 2.55 S | 58.25 W |
| Uruçuí, Serra do ⛰[2] | 100 | 9.00 S | 44.45 W |
| Uruguay □[1] | 102 | 33.00 S | 56.00 W |
| Uruguay (Uruguai) ≃ | 102 | 34.12 S | 58.18 W |
| Urukthapel I | 82 | 7.15 N | 134.24 E |
| Urup, Ostrov I | 78 | 46.00 N | 150.00 E |
| Ur'upinsk | 76 | 50.47 N | 41.59 E |
| Uržum | 62 | 57.08 N | 50.00 E |
| Usa ≃ | 76 | 65.57 N | 56.55 E |
| Uşak | 74 | 38.41 N | 29.25 E |
| Usk | 54 | 51.43 N | 2.54 W |
| Usk ≃ | 52 | 51.36 N | 2.58 W |
| Üsküdar | 74 | 41.01 N | 29.01 E |
| Usolje | 62 | 59.25 N | 56.41 E |
| Usolje-Sibirskoje | 78 | 52.47 N | 103.38 E |
| Ussuri (Wusulijiang) ≃ | 78 | 48.27 N | 135.04 E |
| Ussurijsk | 78 | 43.48 N | 131.59 E |
| Ụster | 68 | 47.21 N | 8.43 E |
| Ụstí nad Labem | 66 | 50.40 N | 14.02 E |
| Ústí nad Orlicí | 66 | 49.58 N | 16.24 E |
| Ustka | 66 | 54.35 N | 16.50 E |
| Ust'-Kamenogorsk | 78 | 49.58 N | 82.38 E |
| Ust'-Kut | 78 | 56.46 N | 105.40 E |
| Uštobe | 76 | 45.16 N | 78.00 E |
| Ust'-Šonoša | 62 | 61.10 N | 41.18 E |
| Ust'urt, Plato ⛰[1] | 76 | 43.00 N | 56.00 E |
| Ust'užna | 62 | 58.51 N | 36.26 E |
| Usumacinta ≃ | 98 | 18.24 N | 92.38 W |
| Utah □[3] | 96 | 39.30 N | 111.30 W |
| Utah Lake ⊜ | 96 | 40.13 N | 111.49 W |
| Utembo ≃ | 90 | 17.06 S | 22.01 E |
| Utica | 96 | 43.05 N | 75.14 W |
| Utrecht | 66 | 52.05 N | 5.08 E |
| Utrera | 70 | 37.11 N | 5.47 W |
| Utsunomiya | 80 | 36.33 N | 139.52 E |
| Uttoxeter | 54 | 52.54 N | 1.51 W |
| Uvá ≃ | 100 | 3.41 N | 70.03 W |
| Uvs Nuur ⊜ | 78 | 50.20 N | 92.45 E |
| Uwajima | 80 | 33.13 N | 132.34 E |
| 'Uwaynāt, Jabal al- ∧ | 88 | 21.54 N | 24.58 E |
| Uyuni, Salar de ≚ | 100 | 20.20 S | 67.42 W |
| Užgorod | 66 | 48.37 N | 22.18 E |
| Uzunköprü | 74 | 41.16 N | 26.41 E |
| Užur | 78 | 55.20 N | 89.50 E |
| **V** | | | |
| Vaal ≃ | 90 | 29.04 S | 23.38 E |
| Vaasa (Vasa) | 64 | 63.06 N | 21.36 E |
| Vác | 74 | 47.47 N | 19.08 E |
| Vachš ≃ | 76 | 37.06 N | 68.18 E |
| Vadsø | 62 | 70.05 N | 29.46 E |
| Vaduz | 68 | 47.09 N | 9.31 E |
| Vaga ≃ | 76 | 62.48 N | 42.56 E |
| Váh ≃ | 50 | 47.55 N | 18.00 E |
| Vaich, Loch ⊜ | 58 | 57.43 N | 4.46 W |
| Vaila I | 58a | 60.12 N | 1.37 W |
| Vajgač, Ostrov I | 76 | 70.00 N | 59.30 E |
| Vākhān ◆[1] | 84 | 37.00 N | 73.00 E |
| Valašské Meziříčí | 66 | 49.28 N | 17.58 E |
| Valdagno | 72 | 45.39 N | 11.18 E |
| Valdaj | 62 | 57.59 N | 33.14 E |
| Valdajskaja Vozvyšennost' ⛰[2] | 76 | 57.00 N | 33.30 E |
| Valdepeñas | 70 | 38.46 N | 3.23 W |
| Valdés, Península ›[1] | 102 | 42.30 S | 64.00 W |
| Valdivia | 102 | 39.48 S | 73.14 W |
| Valdobbiadene | 72 | 45.54 N | 12.00 E |
| Valdosta | 96 | 30.50 N | 83.17 W |
| Vale | 55b | 49.29 N | 2.31 W |
| Valence | 68 | 44.56 N | 4.54 E |
| Valencia, Esp. | 70 | 39.28 N | 0.22 W |
| Valencia, Ven. | 100 | 10.11 N | 68.00 W |
| Valencia de Alcántata | 70 | 39.25 N | 7.14 W |
| Valencia Island I | 52 | 51.52 N | 10.20 W |
| Valenciennes | 68 | 50.21 N | 3.32 E |
| Valenza | 72 | 45.01 N | 8.38 E |
| Valera | 100 | 9.19 N | 70.37 W |
| Valjevo | 74 | 44.16 N | 19.53 E |
| Valka | 62 | 57.46 N | 26.00 E |
| Valkeakoski | 64 | 61.16 N | 24.02 E |
| Valkenswaard | 66 | 51.21 N | 5.28 E |
| Valladolid | 70 | 41.39 N | 4.43 W |
| Vall de Uxó | 70 | 39.49 N | 0.14 W |
| Valle de la Pascua | 100 | 9.13 N | 66.00 W |
| Valledupar | 100 | 10.29 N | 73.15 W |
| Vallenar | 102 | 28.35 S | 70.46 W |
| Valletta | 72 | 35.54 N | 14.31 E |
| Valls | 70 | 41.17 N | 1.15 E |
| Valmiera | 62 | 57.33 N | 25.24 E |
| Valparaíso | 102 | 33.02 S | 71.38 W |
| Vals, Tanjung › | 82 | 8.26 S | 137.38 E |
| Valsbaai C | 90 | 34.12 S | 18.40 E |
| Valverde del Camino | 70 | 37.34 N | 6.45 W |
| Van | 84 | 38.28 N | 43.20 E |
| Vancouver, B.C., Can. | 94 | 49.16 N | 123.07 W |
| Vancouver, Wash., U.S. | 96 | 45.39 N | 122.40 W |
| Vancouver, Cape › | 92 | 35.01 S | 118.12 E |
| Vancouver Island I | 94 | 49.45 N | 126.00 W |
| Vanderbijlpark | 90 | 26.42 S | 27.54 E |
| Vanderlin Island I | 92 | 15.44 S | 137.02 E |
| Van Diemen Gulf C | 92 | 11.50 S | 132.00 E |
| Vänern ⊜ | 50 | 58.55 N | 13.30 E |
| Vänersborg | 64 | 58.22 N | 12.19 E |
| Van Gölü ⊜ | 50 | 38.33 N | 42.46 E |
| Vangunu I | 92 | 8.38 S | 158.00 E |
| Vannes | 68 | 47.39 N | 2.46 W |
| Van Rees, Pegunungan ⛰ | 82 | 2.35 S | 138.15 E |
| Vārānasi (Benares) | 84 | 25.20 N | 83.00 E |
| Varaždin | 72 | 46.19 N | 16.20 E |
| Varazze | 72 | 44.22 N | 8.34 E |
| Varberg | 64 | 57.06 N | 12.15 E |
| Vardar (Axiós) ≃ | 50 | 40.35 N | 22.50 E |
| Vardø | 62 | 70.21 N | 31.02 E |
| Varel | 66 | 53.22 N | 8.10 E |
| Vareš | 74 | 44.09 N | 18.19 E |
| Varese | 72 | 45.48 N | 8.48 E |
| Varkaus | 64 | 62.19 N | 27.55 E |
| Varna | 74 | 43.13 N | 27.55 E |
| Värnamo | 64 | 57.11 N | 14.02 E |
| Varnsdorf | 66 | 50.52 N | 14.40 E |
| Várpalota | 74 | 47.12 N | 18.09 E |
| V'artsil'a | 62 | 62.11 N | 30.41 E |
| Vaslui | 74 | 46.38 N | 27.44 E |
| Västerås | 64 | 59.37 N | 16.33 E |
| Västervik | 64 | 57.45 N | 16.38 E |
| Vasto | 72 | 42.07 N | 14.42 E |
| Vas'ugan ≃ | 78 | 59.07 N | 80.46 E |
| Vas'uganje ≡ | 78 | 58.00 N | 77.00 E |
| Vaternish Point › | 58 | 57.36 N | 6.38 W |
| Vatersay I | 52 | 56.53 N | 7.28 W |
| Vathí | 74 | 37.45 N | 26.59 E |
| Vatican City □[1] | 72 | 41.54 N | 12.27 E |
| V'atka ≃ | 76 | 55.36 N | 51.30 E |
| Vatnajökull ⊡ | 50 | 64.25 N | 16.50 W |
| Vatra Dornei | 74 | 47.21 N | 25.21 E |
| V'atskije Pol'any | 62 | 56.14 N | 51.04 E |
| Vättern ⊜ | 50 | 58.24 N | 14.36 E |
| Vaupés (Uapés) ≃ | 100 | 0.02 S | 67.16 W |
| Växjö | 62 | 56.52 N | 14.49 E |
| V'az'ma | 62 | 55.13 N | 34.18 E |
| V'azniki | 62 | 56.15 N | 42.10 E |
| Vechta | 66 | 52.43 N | 8.16 E |
| Vecsés | 66 | 47.25 N | 19.16 E |
| Veendam | 66 | 53.06 N | 6.58 E |
| Veenendaal | 66 | 52.02 N | 5.34 E |
| Vega I | 50 | 65.39 N | 11.50 E |
| Veil, Loch ⊜ | 58 | 56.20 N | 4.25 W |
| Veisiejai | 66 | 54.06 N | 23.42 E |
| Vejer de la Frontera | 70 | 36.15 N | 5.58 W |
| Vejle | 64 | 55.42 N | 9.32 E |
| Velbert | 66 | 51.20 N | 7.02 E |
| Vélez-Málaga | 70 | 36.47 N | 4.06 W |
| Velhas, Rio das ≃ | 100 | 17.13 S | 44.49 W |
| Velikaja ≃, S.S.S.R. | 76 | 57.48 N | 28.20 E |
| Velikaja ≃, S.S.S.R. | 78 | 64.40 N | 176.20 E |
| Velikije Luki | 62 | 56.20 N | 30.32 E |
| Velikij-ust'ug | 62 | 60.48 N | 46.18 E |
| Veliko Târnovo | 74 | 43.04 N | 25.39 E |
| Veliž | 62 | 55.38 N | 31.12 E |
| Vella Lavella I | 92 | 7.45 S | 156.40 E |
| Velletri | 72 | 41.41 N | 12.47 E |
| Vellore | 84 | 12.56 N | 79.09 E |
| Vel'sk | 62 | 61.05 N | 42.05 E |
| Venachar, Loch ⊜ | 58 | 56.13 N | 4.19 W |
| Venado Tuerto | 102 | 33.45 S | 61.58 W |
| Vendôme | 68 | 47.48 N | 1.04 E |
| Venev | 62 | 54.21 N | 38.16 E |
| Venezia (Venice) | 72 | 45.27 N | 12.21 E |
| Venezuela □[1] | 100 | 8.00 N | 66.00 W |
| Venezuela, Golfo de C | 100 | 11.30 N | 71.00 W |
| Vénissieux | 68 | 45.41 N | 4.53 E |
| Venlo | 66 | 51.24 N | 6.10 E |
| Venosa | 72 | 40.57 N | 15.49 E |
| Ventimiglia | 72 | 43.47 N | 7.36 E |
| Ventnor | 54 | 50.36 N | 1.11 W |
| Ventry | 60 | 52.08 N | 10.22 W |
| Ventspils | 62 | 57.24 N | 21.36 E |
| Ventuari ≃ | 100 | 3.58 N | 67.02 W |
| Ventura | 96 | 34.17 N | 119.18 W |
| Ver ≃ | 54 | 51.42 N | 0.20 W |
| Veracruz | 98 | 19.12 N | 96.08 W |
| Verāval | 84 | 20.54 N | 70.20 E |
| Vercelli | 72 | 45.19 N | 8.25 E |
| Verchn'aja Salda | 76 | 58.02 N | 60.33 E |
| Verchn'aja Tajmyra ≃ | 78 | 74.15 N | 99.48 E |
| Verchnetulomskij | 62 | 68.38 N | 31.45 E |
| Verchnij Ufalej | 76 | 56.04 N | 60.14 E |
| Verchojansk | 78 | 67.35 N | 133.27 E |
| Verchojanskij Chrebet ⛰ | 78 | 67.00 N | 129.00 E |
| Verde ≃ | 100 | 21.12 S | 51.53 W |
| Verden | 66 | 52.55 N | 9.13 E |
| Verdun | 68 | 49.10 N | 5.23 E |
| Vereeniging | 90 | 26.38 S | 27.57 E |
| Vereja | 62 | 55.21 N | 36.11 E |
| Vereščagino | 62 | 58.05 N | 54.40 E |
| Vergara | 70 | 43.07 N | 2.25 W |
| Vermont □[3] | 96 | 43.50 N | 72.45 W |
| Vernon | 68 | 47.48 N | 1.38 E |
| Véroia | 74 | 40.31 N | 22.12 E |
| Verona | 72 | 45.27 N | 11.00 E |
| Versailles | 68 | 48.48 N | 2.08 E |
| Vert, Cap › | 86 | 14.43 N | 17.30 W |
| Vertou | 68 | 47.10 N | 1.29 W |
| Verviers | 66 | 50.35 N | 5.52 E |
| Verwood | 54 | 50.53 N | 1.52 W |
| Veryan | 54 | 50.13 N | 4.54 W |
| Vesjegonsk | 62 | 58.40 N | 37.16 E |
| Vesoul | 68 | 47.38 N | 6.10 E |
| Vesterålen II | 50 | 68.45 N | 15.00 E |
| Vestfjorden C[2] | 50 | 68.08 N | 15.00 E |
| Vestmannaeyjar | 62a | 63.26 N | 20.12 W |
| Veszprém | 74 | 47.06 N | 17.55 E |
| Vésztő | 66 | 46.55 N | 21.16 E |
| Vetlanda | 64 | 57.26 N | 15.04 E |
| Vetluga | 62 | 57.51 N | 45.47 E |
| Vevey | 68 | 46.28 N | 6.51 E |
| Viadana | 72 | 44.56 N | 10.31 E |
| Viana do Castelo | 70 | 41.42 N | 8.50 W |
| Viangchan (Vientiane) | 82 | 17.58 N | 102.36 E |
| Viareggio | 72 | 43.52 N | 10.14 E |
| Viborg | 64 | 56.26 N | 9.24 E |
| Vibo Valentia | 72 | 38.40 N | 16.06 E |
| Vicenza | 72 | 45.33 N | 11.33 E |
| Vich | 70 | 41.56 N | 2.15 E |
| Vichada ≃ | 100 | 4.55 N | 67.50 W |
| Vichy | 68 | 46.08 N | 3.26 E |
| Victoria, Cam. | 86 | 4.01 N | 9.12 E |
| Victoria, B.C., Can. | 94 | 48.25 N | 123.22 W |
| Victoria (Xianggang), H.K. | 80 | 22.17 N | 114.09 E |
| Victoria, Sey. | 90 | 4.38 S | 55.27 E |
| Victoria, Tex., U.S. | 96 | 28.48 N | 97.00 W |
| Victoria ≃ | 92 | 15.12 S | 129.43 E |
| Victoria, Lake ⊜ | 90 | 1.00 S | 33.00 E |
| Victoria, Mount ∧, Austl. | 92 | 8.55 S | 147.35 E |
| Victoria, Mount ∧, Mya. | 82 | 21.14 N | 93.55 E |
| Victoria, Mount ∧, Pap. N. Gui. | 92 | 8.55 S | 147.35 E |
| Victoria de las Tunas | 98 | 20.58 N | 76.57 W |
| Victoria Falls ↳ | 90 | 17.55 S | 25.51 E |
| Victoria Island I | 94 | 71.00 N | 114.00 W |
| Victoria Peak ∧ | 98 | 16.48 N | 88.37 W |
| Victoria Strait ⋓ | 94 | 69.15 N | 100.30 W |
| Vičuga | 62 | 57.13 N | 41.56 E |
| Vidin | 74 | 43.59 N | 22.52 E |
| Viedma, Lago ⊜ | 102 | 49.35 S | 72.35 W |
| Vienne | 68 | 45.31 N | 4.52 E |
| Vieques, Isla de I | 98 | 18.08 N | 65.25 W |
| Viersen | 66 | 51.15 N | 6.23 E |
| Vierzon | 68 | 47.13 N | 2.05 E |
| Vieste | 72 | 41.53 N | 16.10 E |
| Vietnam □[1] | 82 | 16.00 N | 108.00 E |
| Vigevano | 72 | 45.19 N | 8.51 E |
| Vignola | 72 | 44.29 N | 11.00 E |
| Vigo | 70 | 42.14 N | 8.43 W |
| Vijayawāda | 84 | 16.31 N | 80.37 E |
| Vikna I | 50 | 64.57 N | 10.58 E |
| Vila do Conde | 70 | 41.21 N | 8.45 W |
| Vilafranca del Panadés | 70 | 41.21 N | 1.42 E |
| Vila Franca de Xira | 70 | 38.57 N | 8.59 W |
| Vila Nova de Gaia | 70 | 41.08 N | 8.37 W |
| Vila Real | 70 | 41.18 N | 7.45 W |
| Vila Velha | 100 | 20.20 S | 40.17 W |
| Vilcabamba, Cordillera ⛰ | 100 | 13.00 S | 73.00 W |
| Viljandi | 62 | 58.22 N | 25.36 E |
| Vil'kickogo, Ostrov I | 78 | 73.29 N | 75.50 E |
| Vil'kickogo, Proliv ⋓ | 78 | 77.55 N | 103.00 E |
| Villacañas | 70 | 39.38 N | 3.20 W |
| Villacarrillo | 70 | 38.07 N | 3.05 W |
| Villach | 66 | 46.36 N | 13.50 E |
| Villacidro | 72 | 39.27 N | 8.44 E |
| Villafranca de los Barros | 70 | 38.34 N | 6.20 W |
| Villafranca di Verona | 72 | 45.21 N | 10.50 E |
| Villahermosa | 98 | 17.59 N | 92.55 W |
| Villa María | 102 | 32.25 S | 63.15 W |
| Villanueva de Córdoba | 70 | 38.20 N | 4.37 W |
| Villanueva de la Serena | 70 | 38.58 N | 5.48 W |
| Villanueva del Río y Minas | 70 | 37.39 N | 5.42 W |
| Villanueva y Geltrú | 70 | 41.14 N | 1.44 E |
| Villarrica | 102 | 25.45 S | 56.26 W |
| Villarrobledo | 70 | 39.16 N | 2.36 W |
| Villavicencio | 100 | 4.09 N | 73.37 W |
| Villefranche | 68 | 45.59 N | 4.43 E |
| Villefranche-de-Rouergue | 68 | 44.21 N | 2.02 E |
| Villena | 70 | 38.38 N | 0.51 W |
| Villeneuve-Saint-Georges | 68 | 48.44 N | 2.27 E |
| Villeneuve-sur-Lot | 68 | 44.25 N | 0.42 E |
| Villerupt | 68 | 49.28 N | 5.56 E |
| Villeurbanne | 68 | 45.46 N | 4.53 E |
| Villingen-Schwenningen | 66 | 48.04 N | 8.28 E |
| Vilnius | 62 | 54.41 N | 25.19 E |
| Vil'uj ≃ | 78 | 64.24 N | 126.26 E |
| Vilvoorde | 66 | 50.56 N | 4.26 E |
| Vina ≃ | 86 | 7.45 N | 15.36 E |
| Viña del Mar | 102 | 33.02 S | 71.34 W |
| Vinaroz | 70 | 40.28 N | 0.29 E |
| Vindhya Range ⛰ | 84 | 23.00 N | 77.00 E |
| Vineland | 96 | 39.29 N | 75.02 W |
| Vinh | 82 | 18.40 N | 105.40 E |
| Vinh-long | 82 | 10.15 N | 105.58 E |
| Vinkovci | 74 | 45.17 N | 18.49 E |
| Vinnica | 76 | 49.14 N | 28.29 E |
| Vinson Massif ∧ | 8 | 78.35 S | 85.25 W |
| Virbalis | 66 | 54.38 N | 22.49 E |
| Vire | 68 | 48.50 N | 0.53 W |
| Virginia, Eire | 60 | 53.49 N | 7.04 W |
| Virginia, S. Afr. | 90 | 28.12 S | 26.49 E |
| Virginia □[3] | 96 | 37.30 N | 78.45 W |
| Virginia Beach | 96 | 36.51 N | 75.58 W |
| Virginia Falls ↳ | 94 | 61.38 N | 125.42 W |
| Virgin Islands II | 98 | 18.00 N | 64.40 W |
| Virovitica | 72 | 45.50 N | 17.23 E |
| Vis, Otok I | 50 | 43.02 N | 16.11 E |
| Visayan Sea ⊤[2] | 82 | 11.35 N | 123.51 E |
| Visby | 64 | 57.38 N | 18.18 E |
| Viscount Melville Sound ⋓ | 94 | 74.10 N | 113.00 W |
| Viseu | 70 | 40.39 N | 7.55 W |
| Vishākhapatnam | 84 | 17.43 N | 83.19 E |
| Visoko | 74 | 43.59 N | 18.11 E |
| Vitarte | 100 | 12.02 S | 76.56 W |
| Vitebsk | 62 | 55.12 N | 30.11 E |
| Viterbo | 72 | 42.25 N | 12.06 E |
| Vitim ≃ | 78 | 59.26 N | 112.34 E |
| Vitória, Bra. | 100 | 20.19 S | 40.21 W |
| Vitoria, Esp. | 70 | 42.51 N | 2.40 W |
| Vitória da Conquista | 100 | 14.51 S | 40.51 W |
| Vitré | 68 | 48.08 N | 1.12 W |
| Vitry-le-François | 68 | 48.44 N | 4.35 E |
| Vittoria | 72 | 36.57 N | 14.32 E |
| Vittorio Veneto | 72 | 45.59 N | 12.18 E |
| Vivi ≃ | 78 | 63.52 N | 97.50 E |
| Vizcachas, Meseta de las ⛰[1] | 102 | 50.35 S | 71.55 W |
| Vize, Ostrov I | 78 | 79.30 N | 77.00 E |
| Vizianagaram | 84 | 18.07 N | 83.25 E |
| Vlaardingen | 66 | 51.54 N | 4.21 E |
| Vladimir | 62 | 56.10 N | 40.25 E |
| Vladivostok | 78 | 43.10 N | 131.56 E |
| Vlissingen (Flushing) | 66 | 51.26 N | 3.35 E |
| Vlorë | 74 | 40.27 N | 19.30 E |
| Voghera | 72 | 44.59 N | 9.01 E |
| Voiron | 68 | 45.22 N | 5.35 E |
| Voj-Vož | 62 | 62.56 N | 54.56 E |
| Volchov | 62 | 59.55 N | 32.20 E |
| Volchov ≃ | 76 | 60.08 N | 32.20 E |
| Volga ≃ | 76 | 45.55 N | 47.52 E |
| Volgograd (Stalingrad) | 76 | 48.44 N | 44.25 E |
| Volgogradskoje Vodochranilišče ⊜[1] | 76 | 49.20 N | 45.00 E |
| Völklingen | 66 | 49.15 N | 6.50 E |
| Vologda | 62 | 59.12 N | 39.55 E |
| Volokolamsk | 62 | 56.02 N | 35.57 E |
| Vólos | 74 | 39.21 N | 22.56 E |
| Vol'sk | 76 | 52.02 N | 47.23 E |
| Volta, Lake ⊜[1] | 86 | 7.30 N | 0.15 E |
| Volta Blanche (White Volta) ≃ | 86 | 9.10 N | 1.15 W |
| Volta Noire (Black Volta) ≃ | 86 | 8.41 N | 1.33 E |
| Volta Redonda | 100 | 22.32 S | 44.07 W |
| Volterra | 72 | 43.24 N | 10.51 E |
| Volžsk | 62 | 55.53 N | 48.21 E |
| Volžskij | 76 | 48.50 N | 44.44 E |
| Vordingborg | 64 | 55.01 N | 11.55 E |
| Vorίai Sporádhes II | 50 | 39.17 N | 23.23 E |
| Vorkuta | 62 | 67.27 N | 63.58 E |
| Vorlich, Ben ∧ | 58 | 56.20 N | 4.14 W |
| Voronež | 76 | 51.40 N | 39.10 E |
| Vorošilovgrad | 76 | 48.34 N | 39.20 E |
| Vorsma | 62 | 55.59 N | 43.16 E |
| Voskresensk | 62 | 55.19 N | 38.42 E |
| Vostočno-Sibirskoje More (East Siberian Sea) ⊤[2] | 78 | 74.00 N | 166.00 E |
| Vostočnyj Sajan ⛰ | 78 | 53.00 N | 97.00 E |
| Votkinsk | 62 | 57.03 N | 53.59 E |
| Vožega | 62 | 60.29 N | 40.12 E |
| Vraca | 74 | 43.12 N | 23.33 E |
| Vrangel'a, Ostrov I | 78 | 71.00 N | 179.30 W |
| Vranje | 74 | 42.33 N | 21.54 E |
| Vrbas | 74 | 45.35 N | 19.39 E |
| Vrchlabí | 66 | 50.38 N | 15.37 E |
| Vršac | 74 | 45.07 N | 21.18 E |
| Vryburg | 90 | 26.55 S | 24.45 E |
| Vsetín | 66 | 49.21 N | 17.59 E |
| Vught | 66 | 51.40 N | 5.17 E |
| Vukovar | 74 | 45.21 N | 19.00 E |
| Vulcan | 74 | 45.23 N | 23.17 E |
| Vuoksenniska | 64 | 61.13 N | 28.49 E |
| Vyborg | 62 | 60.42 N | 28.45 E |
| Vyčegda ≃ | 76 | 61.18 N | 46.36 E |
| Vygozero, Ozero ⊜ | 76 | 63.35 N | 34.42 E |
| Vyksa | 62 | 55.18 N | 42.11 E |
| Vyrnwy, Lake ⊜ | 54 | 52.47 N | 3.30 W |
| Vyškov | 66 | 49.16 N | 17.00 E |
| Vyšnij Voločok | 62 | 57.35 N | 34.34 E |
| Vysokoje | 66 | 52.22 N | 23.22 E |
| Vysokovsk | 62 | 56.19 N | 36.33 E |
| Vytegra | 62 | 61.00 N | 36.24 E |
| **W** | | | |
| Wa | 86 | 10.04 N | 2.29 W |
| Waalwijk | 66 | 51.42 N | 5.04 E |
| Wabasca ≃ | 94 | 58.22 N | 115.20 W |
| Wabash ≃ | 96 | 37.46 N | 88.02 W |
| Wąbrzeźno | 66 | 53.17 N | 18.57 E |
| Waco | 96 | 31.55 N | 97.08 W |
| Waddesdon | 54 | 51.51 N | 0.56 W |
| Waddingham | 56 | 53.27 N | 0.31 W |
| Waddington, Mount ∧ | 94 | 51.23 N | 125.15 W |


Symbols in the index entries are identified on page 111.

128 Wade—Zywi


| Name | Page | Lat° ′ | Long° ′ |
|---|---|---|---|
| Wadebridge | 54 | 50.32 N | 4.50 W |
| Wadhurst | 54 | 51.04 N | 0.21 E |
| Wādī Ḥalfā' | 88 | 21.56 N | 31.20 E |
| Wad Madanī | 88 | 13.25 N | 33.28 E |
| Wageningen | 66 | 51.58 N | 5.40 E |
| Wager Bay C | 94 | 65.26 N | 88.40 W |
| Wagga Wagga | 92 | 35.07 S | 147.22 E |
| Wągrowiec | 66 | 52.49 N | 17.11 E |
| Waiblingen | 66 | 48.50 N | 9.19 E |
| Waigeo, Pulau I | 82 | 0.14 S | 130.45 E |
| Wainfleet All Saints | 56 | 53.07 N | 0.14 E |
| Waingapu | 82 | 9.39 S | 120.16 E |
| Wakayama | 80 | 34.13 N | 135.11 E |
| Wakefield | 56 | 53.42 N | 1.29 W |
| Wakkanai | 80 | 45.25 N | 141.40 E |
| Walberswick | 54 | 52.19 N | 1.39 E |
| Wałbrzych (Waldenburg) | 66 | 50.46 N | 16.17 E |
| Walbury Hill ∧[2] | 54 | 51.21 N | 1.30 W |
| Wałcz | 66 | 53.17 N | 16.28 E |
| Waldbröl | 66 | 50.53 N | 7.37 E |
| Waldon ≃ | 54 | 50.22 N | 4.14 W |
| Wales □[8] | 52 | 52.30 N | 3.30 W |
| Wales Island I, N.W. Ter., Can. | 94 | 61.50 N | 72.05 W |
| Wales Island I, N.W. Ter., Can. | 94 | 68.00 N | 86.43 W |
| Walkden | 56 | 53.32 N | 2.24 W |
| Walker Lake ⊜ | 96 | 38.44 N | 118.43 W |
| Wallasey | 56 | 53.26 N | 3.03 W |
| Walla Walla | 96 | 46.08 N | 118.20 W |
| Wallingford | 54 | 51.37 N | 1.08 W |
| Walls | 58a | 60.14 N | 1.35 W |
| Wallsend | 56 | 55.00 N | 1.31 W |
| Walmer | 54 | 51.13 N | 1.24 E |
| Walney, Isle of I | 56 | 54.07 N | 3.15 W |
| Walpole Saint Peter | 54 | 52.42 N | 0.15 E |
| Walsall | 54 | 52.35 N | 1.58 W |
| Walsoken | 54 | 52.41 N | 0.12 E |
| Walsrode | 66 | 52.52 N | 9.35 E |
| Waltershausen | 66 | 50.53 N | 10.33 E |
| Waltham Abbey | 54 | 51.42 N | 0.01 E |
| Waltham Forest ◆[8] | 54 | 51.35 N | 0.01 W |
| Waltham on the Wolds | 54 | 52.49 N | 0.49 W |
| Walton, Eng., U.K. | 54 | 51.58 N | 1.21 E |
| Walton, Eng., U.K. | 54 | 51.24 N | 0.25 W |
| Walton-le-Dale | 56 | 53.45 N | 2.39 W |
| Walton-on-the-Naze | 54 | 51.51 N | 1.16 E |
| Walvisbaai (Walvis Bay) | 90 | 22.59 S | 14.31 E |
| Wamba ≃ | 90 | 3.56 S | 17.12 E |
| Wami ≃ | 90 | 6.08 S | 38.49 E |
| Wampool ≃ | 56 | 54.54 N | 3.14 W |
| Wanborough | 54 | 51.33 N | 1.42 W |
| Wandsworth ◆[8] | 54 | 51.27 N | 0.11 W |
| Wangen [im Allgäu] | 66 | 47.41 N | 9.50 E |
| Wangiwangi, Pulau I | 82 | 5.20 S | 123.35 E |
| Wankie | 90 | 18.22 S | 26.29 E |
| Wanne-Eickel | 66 | 51.32 N | 7.09 E |
| Wansbeck ≃ | 56 | 55.10 N | 1.34 W |
| Wantage | 54 | 51.36 N | 1.25 W |
| Wanxian | 80 | 30.52 N | 108.22 E |
| Wapiti ≃ | 94 | 55.08 N | 118.18 W |
| Warangal | 84 | 18.00 N | 79.35 E |
| Warburton Bay C | 94 | 63.50 N | 111.30 W |
| Warburton Creek ≃ | 92 | 27.55 S | 137.28 E |
| Wardha | 84 | 20.45 N | 78.36 E |
| Ward Hill ∧[2], Scot., U.K. | 52 | 58.54 N | 3.20 W |
| Ward Hill ∧[2], Scot., U.K. | 58 | 58.57 N | 3.09 W |
| Wardle | 56 | 53.39 N | 2.08 W |
| Wardour, Vale of ∨ | 54 | 51.05 N | 2.00 W |
| Ward's Stone ∧ | 56 | 54.02 N | 2.38 W |
| Ware | 54 | 51.49 N | 0.02 W |
| Wareham | 54 | 50.41 N | 2.07 W |
| Waren | 66 | 53.31 N | 12.40 E |
| Warendorf | 66 | 51.57 N | 7.59 E |
| Warks Burn ≃ | 56 | 55.03 N | 2.08 W |
| Warkworth | 56 | 55.21 N | 1.36 W |
| Warlingham | 54 | 51.19 N | 0.04 W |
| Warlington | 54 | 51.39 N | 1.01 W |
| Warmington | 54 | 52.08 N | 1.24 W |
| Warminster | 54 | 51.13 N | 2.12 W |
| Warrego ≃ | 92 | 30.24 S | 145.21 E |
| Warren | 96 | 42.28 N | 83.01 W |
| Warrenpoint | 60 | 54.06 N | 6.15 W |
| Warri | 86 | 5.31 N | 5.45 E |
| Warrington | 56 | 53.24 N | 2.37 W |
| Warrior Reefs ✢[2] | 92 | 9.35 S | 143.10 E |
| Warrnambool | 92 | 38.23 S | 142.29 E |
| Warsop | 56 | 53.13 N | 1.09 W |
| Warszawa (Warsaw) | 66 | 52.15 N | 21.00 E |
| Warta ≃ | 50 | 52.35 N | 14.39 E |
| Warton | 56 | 54.09 N | 2.47 W |
| Warwick | 54 | 52.17 N | 1.34 W |
| Warwick Channel U | 92 | 13.51 S | 136.16 E |
| Warwickshire □[6] | 52 | 52.13 N | 1.37 W |
| Wasbister | 58 | 59.10 N | 3.07 W |
| Washburn Lake ⊜ | 94 | 70.03 N | 106.50 W |
| Washington, Eng., U.K. | 56 | 54.55 N | 1.30 W |
| Washington, D.C., U.S. | 96 | 38.54 N | 77.01 W |
| Washington □[3] | 96 | 47.30 N | 120.30 W |
| Washington, Mount ∧ | 96 | 44.15 N | 71.15 W |
| Washurn ≃ | 56 | 53.54 N | 1.39 W |
| Wast Water ⊜ | 56 | 54.26 N | 3.18 W |
| Watampone | 82 | 4.32 S | 120.20 E |
| Watchet | 54 | 51.12 N | 3.20 W |
| Waterbeach | 54 | 52.16 N | 0.11 E |
| Waterbury | 96 | 41.33 N | 73.02 W |
| Waterford | 60 | 52.15 N | 7.06 W |
| Waterford □[6] | 52 | 52.10 N | 7.40 W |
| Waterford Harbour C | 52 | 52.10 N | 6.55 W |
| Watergate Bay C | 54 | 50.27 N | 5.05 W |
| Watergrasshill | 60 | 52.01 N | 8.21 W |
| Waterhen Lake ⊜ | 94 | 52.06 N | 99.34 W |
| Waterloo, Bel. | 66 | 50.43 N | 4.23 E |
| Waterloo, Eng., U.K. | 56 | 53.28 N | 3.02 W |
| Waterloo, Iowa, U.S. | 96 | 42.30 N | 92.20 W |
| Waterlooville | 54 | 50.53 N | 1.02 W |
| Waterside | 56 | 55.21 N | 4.28 W |
| Watertown | 96 | 43.59 N | 75.55 W |
| Waterville, Eire | 60 | 51.49 N | 10.13 W |
| Waterville, Maine, U.S. | 96 | 44.33 N | 69.38 W |
| Watford | 54 | 51.40 N | 0.25 W |
| Wathaman ≃ | 94 | 57.16 N | 102.52 W |
| Wath upon Dearne | 56 | 53.29 N | 1.20 W |
| Watlington | 54 | 51.37 N | 1.00 W |
| Watten, Loch ⊜ | 58 | 58.29 N | 3.19 W |
| Wattenscheid | 66 | 51.29 N | 7.08 E |
| Watton | 54 | 52.35 N | 0.48 E |
| Waukegan | 96 | 42.22 N | 87.50 W |
| Wausau | 96 | 44.59 N | 89.39 W |
| Waveney ≃ | 52 | 52.28 N | 1.45 E |
| Waver ≃ | 56 | 54.52 N | 3.17 W |
| We, Pulau I | 82 | 5.51 N | 95.18 E |
| Wear ≃ | 52 | 54.55 N | 1.22 W |
| Wearhead | 56 | 54.45 N | 2.13 W |
| Weaver ≃ | 56 | 53.19 N | 2.44 W |
| Weaverham | 56 | 53.16 N | 2.35 W |
| Weddell Sea ▾[2] | 8 | 72.00 S | 45.00 W |
| Wedel | 66 | 53.35 N | 9.41 E |
| Wedmore | 54 | 51.14 N | 2.49 W |
| Wednesbury | 54 | 52.34 N | 2.00 W |
| Wednesfield | 54 | 52.36 N | 2.04 W |
| Weedon Beck | 54 | 52.14 N | 1.05 W |
| Weert | 66 | 51.15 N | 5.43 E |
| Weiden in der Oberpfalz | 66 | 49.41 N | 12.10 E |
| Weifang | 80 | 36.42 N | 19.04 E |
| Weihai | 80 | 37.28 N | 122.07 E |
| Weihe ≃ | 80 | 34.30 N | 110.20 E |
| Weilheim | 66 | 47.50 N | 11.08 E |
| Weimar | 66 | 50.59 N | 11.19 E |
| Weinan | 80 | 34.29 N | 109.29 E |
| Weinheim | 66 | 49.33 N | 8.39 E |
| Weissenburg in Bayern | 66 | 49.01 N | 10.58 E |
| Weissenfels | 66 | 51.12 N | 11.58 E |
| Weisswasser | 66 | 51.30 N | 14.38 E |
| Weiz | 66 | 47.13 N | 15.37 E |
| Wejherowo | 66 | 54.37 N | 18.15 E |
| Welkom | 90 | 27.59 S | 26.45 E |
| Welland | 94 | 42.59 N | 79.15 W |
| Welland ≃ | 54 | 52.53 N | 0.02 E |
| Wellesbourne | 54 | 52.12 N | 1.35 W |
| Wellesley Islands II | 92 | 16.42 S | 139.30 E |
| Wellingborough | 54 | 52.19 N | 0.42 W |
| Wellington, N.Z. | 93a | 41.18 S | 174.47 E |
| Wellington, Eng., U.K. | 54 | 52.43 N | 2.31 W |
| Wellington, Eng., U.K. | 54 | 50.59 N | 3.14 W |
| Wellington, Isla I | 102 | 49.20 S | 74.40 W |
| Wellington Bay C | 94 | 69.30 N | 106.30 W |
| Wellington Channel U | 94 | 75.00 N | 93.00 W |
| Wells | 54 | 51.13 N | 2.39 W |
| Wells, Lake ⊜ | 92 | 26.43 S | 123.10 E |
| Wells-next-the-Sea | 54 | 52.58 N | 0.51 E |
| Welney | 54 | 52.31 N | 0.15 E |
| Wels | 66 | 48.10 N | 14.02 E |
| Welshpool | 54 | 52.40 N | 3.09 W |
| Welwyn Garden City | 54 | 51.50 N | 0.13 W |
| Wem | 54 | 52.51 N | 2.44 W |
| Wenatchee | 96 | 47.25 N | 120.19 W |
| Wendover | 54 | 51.46 N | 0.46 W |
| Wenlock ≃ | 92 | 12.02 S | 141.55 E |
| Wenlock Edge •[4] | 54 | 52.30 N | 2.40 W |
| Wenning ≃ | 56 | 54.07 N | 2.39 W |
| Wensleydale ∨ | 56 | 54.19 N | 2.00 W |
| Wensum ≃ | 54 | 52.37 N | 1.19 E |
| Went ≃ | 56 | 53.39 N | 0.59 W |
| Wenzhou | 80 | 28.01 N | 120.39 E |
| Weobley | 54 | 52.09 N | 2.51 W |
| Werdau | 66 | 50.44 N | 12.22 E |
| Werder | 66 | 52.23 N | 12.56 E |
| Werdohl | 66 | 51.16 N | 7.46 E |
| Werl | 66 | 51.33 N | 7.54 E |
| Werne [an der Lippe] | 66 | 51.40 N | 7.38 E |
| Wernigerode | 66 | 51.50 N | 10.47 E |
| Wesel | 66 | 51.40 N | 6.38 E |
| Wessel, Cape ≻ | 92 | 10.59 S | 136.46 E |
| Wessel Islands II | 92 | 11.30 S | 136.25 E |
| West Allen ≃ | 56 | 54.55 N | 2.19 W |
| West Auckland | 56 | 54.38 N | 1.43 W |
| West Bergholt | 54 | 51.55 N | 0.51 E |
| West Bridgford | 54 | 52.56 N | 1.08 W |
| West Bromwich | 54 | 52.31 N | 1.56 W |
| West Burra I | 58a | 60.05 N | 1.21 W |
| Westbury, Eng., U.K. | 54 | 51.16 N | 2.11 W |
| Westbury, Eng., U.K. | 54 | 52.41 N | 2.57 W |
| Westbury-on-Severn | 54 | 51.50 N | 2.24 W |
| West Calder | 58 | 55.52 N | 3.35 W |
| West Cape Howex ≻ | 92 | 35.08 S | 117.39 E |
| West Cleddau ≃ | 54 | 51.46 N | 4.54 W |
| Westerdale | 58 | 58.27 N | 3.30 W |
| Westerham | 54 | 51.16 N | 0.05 E |
| Western Ghāts ⋀ | 84 | 14.00 N | 75.00 E |
| Western Isles Islands □[4] | 52 | 57.40 N | 7.00 W |
| Western Sahara □[2] | 86 | 24.30 N | 13.00 W |
| Westerstede | 66 | 53.15 N | 7.55 E |
| West Falkland I | 102 | 51.50 S | 60.00 W |
| Westfield | 54 | 50.55 N | 0.35 E |
| Westgate-on-Sea | 54 | 51.23 N | 1.21 E |
| West Glamorgan □[6] | 52 | 51.35 N | 3.35 W |
| West Indies II | 98 | 19.00 N | 70.00 W |
| West Kilbride | 58 | 55.42 N | 4.51 W |
| West Kingsdown | 54 | 51.21 N | 0.17 E |
| West Kirby | 56 | 53.22 N | 3.10 W |
| West Linton | 58 | 55.46 N | 3.22 W |
| West Loch Roag C | 58 | 58.13 N | 6.53 W |
| West Loch Tarbert C, Scot., U.K. | 58 | 55.48 N | 5.32 W |
| West Loch Tarbert C, Scot., U.K. | 58 | 57.55 N | 6.54 W |
| West Looe | 54 | 50.21 N | 4.28 W |
| West Lulworth | 54 | 50.38 N | 2.15 W |
| West Malling | 54 | 51.18 N | 0.25 E |
| Westmeath □[6] | 52 | 53.30 N | 7.30 W |
| West Meon | 54 | 51.01 N | 1.05 W |
| West Mersea | 54 | 51.47 N | 0.55 E |
| West Midlands □[6] | 54 | 52.30 N | 2.00 W |
| West Moors | 54 | 50.49 N | 1.55 W |
| Weston-super-Mare | 54 | 51.21 N | 2.59 W |
| Weston upon Trent | 54 | 52.45 N | 2.02 W |
| West Palm Beach | 96 | 26.43 N | 80.04 W |
| Westport | 60 | 53.48 N | 9.32 W |
| Westray I | 52 | 59.18 N | 2.59 W |
| Westray Firth U | 58 | 59.12 N | 2.55 W |
| West Sussex □[6] | 52 | 50.55 N | 0.35 W |
| West Virginia □[3] | 96 | 38.45 N | 80.30 W |
| Westward Ho! | 54 | 51.02 N | 4.15 W |
| West Water ≃ | 58 | 56.47 N | 2.38 W |
| West Wellow | 54 | 50.58 N | 1.35 W |
| West Wycombe | 54 | 51.39 N | 0.49 W |
| West Yorkshire □[6] | 56 | 53.45 N | 1.40 W |
| Wetar, Pulau I | 82 | 7.48 S | 126.18 E |
| Wetherby | 56 | 53.56 N | 1.23 W |
| Wetwang | 56 | 54.01 N | 0.34 W |
| Wetzlar | 66 | 50.33 N | 8.29 E |
| Wexford | 60 | 52.20 N | 6.27 W |
| Wexford □[6] | 52 | 52.20 N | 6.40 W |
| Wexford Harbour C | 52 | 52.20 N | 6.55 W |
| Wey ≃ | 54 | 51.23 N | 0.28 W |
| Weybridge | 54 | 51.23 N | 0.28 W |
| Weymouth | 54 | 50.36 N | 2.28 W |
| Whaley Bridge | 56 | 53.20 N | 1.59 W |
| Whalley | 56 | 53.50 N | 2.24 W |
| Whalsay I | 52 | 60.22 N | 0.59 W |
| Whaplode | 54 | 52.48 N | 0.02 W |
| Wharfe ≃ | 56 | 53.51 N | 1.07 W |
| Wharfedale ∨ | 56 | 54.01 N | 1.56 W |
| Wharton Lake ⊜ | 94 | 64.00 N | 99.55 W |
| Whauphill | 56 | 54.49 N | 4.29 W |
| Wheathampstead | 54 | 51.49 N | 0.17 W |
| Wheatley Hill | 56 | 54.45 N | 1.23 W |
| Wheeler ≃ | 94 | 57.02 N | 67.13 W |
| Wheeler Peak ∧ | 96 | 36.34 N | 105.25 W |
| Wheeling | 96 | 40.05 N | 80.42 W |
| Wheelock ≃ | 56 | 53.12 N | 2.26 W |
| Whernside ∧ | 56 | 54.14 N | 2.23 W |
| Whidbey Islands II | 92 | 34.45 S | 135.04 E |
| Whiddon Down | 54 | 50.43 N | 3.51 W |
| Whiston | 56 | 53.25 N | 2.50 W |
| Whitburn | 58 | 55.52 N | 3.42 W |
| Whitby | 56 | 54.29 N | 0.37 W |
| Whitchurch, Eng., U.K. | 54 | 52.58 N | 2.41 W |
| Whitchurch, Eng., U.K. | 54 | 51.53 N | 0.51 W |
| Whitchurch, Eng., U.K. | 54 | 51.52 N | 2.39 W |
| Whitchurch, Eng., U.K. | 54 | 51.14 N | 1.20 W |
| Whitchurch, Wales, U.K. | 54 | 51.33 N | 3.14 W |
| White ≃, N.A. | 94 | 63.10 N | 139.36 W |
| White ≃, U.S. | 96 | 33.53 N | 91.03 W |
| White ≃, U.S. | 96 | 43.45 N | 99.30 W |
| White, Lake ⊜ | 92 | 21.05 S | 129.00 E |
| White Bay C | 94 | 50.00 N | 56.30 W |
| White Coomb ∧ | 56 | 55.26 N | 3.20 W |
| White Esk ≃ | 56 | 55.12 N | 3.10 W |
| Whitegate | 60 | 51.50 N | 8.14 W |
| Whitehall | 58 | 59.07 N | 2.37 W |
| Whitehaven | 56 | 54.33 N | 3.35 W |
| Whitehead | 60 | 54.46 N | 5.43 W |
| Whitehorse | 94 | 60.43 N | 135.03 W |
| White Horse, Vale of ∨ | 54 | 51.37 N | 1.37 W |
| Whitehorse Hill ∧[2] | 54 | 51.34 N | 1.34 W |
| Whitehouse | 58 | 57.13 N | 2.37 W |
| Whiten Head ≻ | 58 | 58.34 N | 4.36 W |
| White Nile (Al-Bahr al-Abyad) ≃ | 88 | 15.38 N | 32.31 E |
| White Volta (Volta Blanche) ≃ | 86 | 9.10 N | 1.15 W |
| Whitford Point ≻ | 54 | 51.38 N | 4.14 W |
| Whithorn | 56 | 54.44 N | 4.25 W |
| Whiting Bay | 56 | 55.29 N | 5.06 W |
| Whitland | 54 | 51.50 N | 4.37 W |
| Whitley Bay | 56 | 55.03 N | 1.25 W |
| Whitney, Mount ∧ | 96 | 36.35 N | 118.18 W |
| Whitstable | 54 | 51.22 N | 1.02 E |
| Whittingham | 56 | 55.24 N | 1.54 W |
| Whittington | 54 | 52.52 N | 3.00 W |
| Whittle, Cap ≻ | 94 | 50.11 N | 60.08 W |
| Whittlesey | 54 | 52.34 N | 0.08 W |
| Whitwick | 54 | 52.44 N | 1.21 W |
| Whitworth | 56 | 53.40 N | 2.10 W |
| Wholdaia Lake ⊜ | 94 | 60.43 N | 104.10 W |
| Wiay I | 58 | 57.23 N | 7.13 W |
| Wichita | 96 | 37.41 N | 97.20 W |
| Wichita Falls | 96 | 33.54 N | 98.30 W |
| Wick | 58 | 58.26 N | 3.06 W |
| Wick ≃ | 58 | 58.27 N | 3.05 W |
| Wickford | 54 | 51.38 N | 0.31 E |
| Wickham | 54 | 50.54 N | 1.10 W |
| Wickham Market | 54 | 52.09 N | 1.22 E |
| Wicklow | 60 | 52.59 N | 6.03 W |
| Wicklow □[6] | 52 | 53.00 N | 6.30 W |
| Wicklow Head ≻ | 52 | 52.58 N | 6.00 W |
| Wicklow Mountains ⋀ | 52 | 53.02 N | 6.24 W |
| Widecombe in the Moor | 54 | 50.35 N | 3.48 W |
| Widemouth Bay | 54 | 50.47 N | 4.32 W |
| Widnes | 56 | 53.22 N | 2.44 W |
| Wieliczka | 66 | 49.59 N | 20.04 E |
| Wieluń | 66 | 51.14 N | 18.34 E |
| Wien (Vienna) | 66 | 48.13 N | 16.20 E |
| Wiener Neustadt | 66 | 47.49 N | 16.15 E |
| Wiesbaden | 66 | 50.05 N | 8.14 E |
| Wigan | 56 | 53.33 N | 2.38 W |
| Wigglesworth | 56 | 54.01 N | 2.17 W |
| Wigmore | 54 | 52.19 N | 2.51 W |
| Wigston Magna | 54 | 52.36 N | 1.05 W |
| Wigton | 56 | 54.49 N | 3.09 W |
| Wigtown | 56 | 54.52 N | 4.26 W |
| Wigtown Bay C | 52 | 54.46 N | 4.15 W |
| Wilberforce Falls ↳ | 94 | 67.07 N | 108.47 W |
| Wilhelmina Gebergte ⋀ | 100 | 3.45 N | 56.30 W |
| Wilhelm-Pieck-Stadt Guben | 66 | 51.57 N | 14.43 E |
| Wilhelmshaven | 66 | 53.31 N | 8.08 E |
| Wilkes-Barre | 96 | 41.14 N | 75.53 W |
| Wilkhaven | 58 | 57.52 N | 3.45 W |
| Willemstad | 98 | 12.06 N | 68.56 W |
| Willenhall | 54 | 52.36 N | 2.02 W |
| Willerby | 56 | 53.46 N | 0.27 W |
| Williamsport | 96 | 41.14 N | 77.00 W |
| Willingdon | 54 | 50.47 N | 0.15 E |
| Willingham | 54 | 52.19 N | 0.04 E |
| Willington | 56 | 54.43 N | 1.41 W |
| Willis Group II | 92 | 16.18 S | 150.00 E |
| Williston Lake ⊜[1] | 94 | 55.40 N | 123.40 W |
| Williton | 54 | 51.10 N | 3.20 W |
| Willow Brook ≃ | 54 | 52.32 N | 0.24 W |
| Willow Lake ⊜ | 94 | 62.11 N | 119.10 W |
| Wills, Lake ⊜ | 92 | 21.25 S | 128.51 E |
| Wilmington, Del., U.S. | 96 | 39.44 N | 75.33 W |
| Wilmington, N.C., U.S. | 96 | 34.13 N | 77.55 W |
| Wilmslow | 56 | 53.20 N | 2.15 W |
| Wilshamstead | 54 | 52.05 N | 0.27 W |
| Wilson, Cape ≻ | 94 | 66.59 N | 81.28 W |
| Wilsons Promontory ≻ | 92 | 38.55 S | 146.20 E |
| Wilton | 54 | 51.05 N | 1.52 W |
| Wiltshire □[6] | 52 | 51.15 N | 1.50 W |
| Wimborne Minster | 54 | 50.48 N | 1.59 W |
| Wincanton | 54 | 51.04 N | 2.25 W |
| Winchcombe | 54 | 51.57 N | 1.58 W |
| Winchelsea | 54 | 50.55 N | 0.42 E |
| Winchester | 54 | 51.04 N | 1.19 W |
| Windermere | 56 | 54.23 N | 2.54 W |
| Windermere ⊜ | 56 | 54.22 N | 2.56 W |
| Windhoek | 90 | 22.34 S | 17.06 E |
| Windrush ≃ | 54 | 51.42 N | 1.25 W |
| Windsor, Ont., Can. | 94 | 42.18 N | 83.01 W |
| Windsor, Eng., U.K. | 54 | 51.29 N | 0.38 W |
| Windsor Forest ◆[3] | 54 | 51.27 N | 0.43 W |
| Windward Islands II | 98 | 13.00 N | 61.00 W |
| Windward Passage U | 98 | 20.00 N | 73.50 W |
| Wingham | 54 | 51.17 N | 1.13 E |
| Winisk Lake ⊜ | 94 | 52.55 N | 87.22 W |
| Winneba | 86 | 5.25 N | 0.36 W |
| Winnebago, Lake ⊜ | 96 | 44.00 N | 88.25 W |
| Winnipeg | 94 | 49.53 N | 97.09 W |
| Winnipeg ≃ | 94 | 50.38 N | 96.19 W |
| Winnipeg, Lake ⊜ | 94 | 52.00 N | 97.00 W |
| Winnipegosis, Lake ⊜ | 94 | 52.30 N | 100.00 W |
| Winona | 96 | 44.03 N | 91.39 W |
| Winschoten | 66 | 53.08 N | 7.02 E |
| Winsford, Eng., U.K. | 54 | 51.06 N | 3.33 W |
| Winsford, Eng., U.K. | 56 | 53.12 N | 2.32 W |
| Winshill | 54 | 52.48 N | 1.36 W |
| Winslow | 54 | 51.57 N | 0.54 W |
| Winston-Salem | 96 | 36.06 N | 80.15 W |
| Winterbourne Abbas | 54 | 50.43 N | 2.34 W |
| Winter Haven | 96 | 28.01 N | 81.44 W |
| Winterswijk | 66 | 51.58 N | 6.44 E |
| Winterthur | 68 | 47.30 N | 8.43 E |
| Winterton-on-Sea | 54 | 52.43 N | 1.42 E |
| Wipperfürth | 66 | 51.07 N | 7.23 E |
| Wirral ≻[1] | 52 | 53.20 N | 3.03 W |
| Wisbech | 54 | 52.40 N | 0.10 E |
| Wisconsin □[3] | 96 | 44.45 N | 89.30 W |
| Wisconsin ≃ | 96 | 43.00 N | 91.15 W |
| Wishaw | 58 | 55.47 N | 3.56 W |
| Wisła ≃ | 50 | 54.22 N | 18.55 E |
| Wismar | 66 | 53.53 N | 11.28 E |
| Wissey ≃ | 54 | 52.33 N | 0.21 E |
| Witbank | 90 | 25.56 S | 29.07 E |
| Witham | 54 | 51.48 N | 0.38 E |
| Witham ≃ | 56 | 53.06 N | 0.13 W |
| Witheridge | 54 | 50.55 N | 3.42 W |
| Withernsea | 56 | 53.44 N | 0.02 E |
| Witley | 54 | 51.09 N | 0.38 W |
| Witney | 54 | 51.48 N | 1.29 W |
| Witten | 66 | 51.26 N | 7.20 E |
| Wittenberg | 66 | 51.52 N | 12.39 E |
| Wittenberge | 66 | 53.00 N | 11.44 E |
| Wittstock | 66 | 53.10 N | 12.29 E |
| Witwatersrand ◆[1] | 90 | 26.00 S | 27.00 E |
| Wiveliscombe | 54 | 51.03 N | 3.19 W |
| Wivenhoe | 54 | 51.52 N | 0.58 E |
| Włocławek | 66 | 52.39 N | 19.02 E |
| Wnion ≃ | 54 | 52.45 N | 3.54 W |
| Woburn Sands | 54 | 52.01 N | 0.39 W |
| Wokam, Pulau I | 82 | 5.37 S | 134.30 E |
| Woking | 54 | 51.20 N | 0.34 W |
| Wokingham | 54 | 51.25 N | 0.51 W |
| Woleai I[1] | 82 | 7.21 N | 143.52 E |
| Wolfen | 66 | 51.40 N | 12.16 E |
| Wolfenbüttel | 66 | 52.10 N | 10.32 E |
| Wolf Rock I[2] | 52 | 49.57 N | 5.49 W |
| Wolfsberg | 66 | 46.51 N | 14.51 E |
| Wolfsburg | 66 | 52.25 N | 10.47 E |
| Wolf's Castle | 54 | 51.54 N | 4.58 W |
| Wolgast | 66 | 54.03 N | 13.46 E |
| Wollaston, Cape ≻ | 94 | 71.04 N | 118.07 W |
| Wollaston, Islas II | 102 | 55.40 S | 67.30 W |
| Wollaston Lake ⊜ | 94 | 58.15 N | 103.20 W |
| Wollaston Peninsula ≻[1] | 94 | 70.00 N | 115.00 W |
| Wollongong | 92 | 34.25 S | 150.54 E |
| Wołomin | 66 | 52.21 N | 21.14 E |
| Wolsingham | 56 | 54.44 N | 1.52 W |
| Wolverhampton | 54 | 52.36 N | 2.08 W |
| Wolverton | 54 | 52.04 N | 0.50 W |
| Wombwell | 56 | 53.31 N | 1.24 W |
| Wŏnju | 80 | 37.22 N | 127.58 E |
| Wŏnsan | 80 | 39.09 N | 127.25 E |
| Woodbridge | 54 | 52.06 N | 1.19 E |
| Woodbury | 54 | 50.41 N | 3.24 W |
| Woodchurch | 54 | 51.05 N | 0.46 E |
| Woodford | 60 | 53.03 N | 8.23 W |
| Woodford Halse | 54 | 52.10 N | 1.12 W |
| Woodlark Island I | 92 | 9.05 S | 152.50 E |
| Woodley | 54 | 51.28 N | 0.54 W |
| Woodmansey | 56 | 53.50 N | 0.29 W |
| Woodplumpton | 56 | 53.48 N | 2.47 W |
| Woodroffe, Mount ∧ | 92 | 26.20 S | 131.45 E |
| Woods, Lake ⊜ | 92 | 17.50 S | 133.30 E |
| Woods, Lake of the ⊜ | 94 | 49.15 N | 94.45 W |
| Woodstock, N.B., Can. | 94 | 46.09 N | 67.34 W |
| Woodstock, Eng., U.K. | 54 | 51.52 N | 1.21 W |
| Wool | 54 | 50.41 N | 2.14 W |
| Woolacombe | 54 | 51.10 N | 4.13 W |
| Wooler | 56 | 55.33 N | 2.01 W |
| Woolpit | 54 | 52.13 N | 0.54 E |
| Wooramel ≃ | 92 | 25.47 S | 114.10 E |
| Wootton Bassett | 54 | 51.33 N | 1.54 W |
| Wootton Wawen | 54 | 52.16 N | 1.47 W |
| Worcester, S. Afr. | 90 | 33.39 S | 19.27 E |
| Worcester, Eng., U.K. | 54 | 52.11 N | 2.13 W |
| Worcester, Mass., U.S. | 96 | 42.16 N | 71.48 W |
| Workington | 56 | 54.39 N | 3.35 W |
| Worksop | 56 | 53.18 N | 1.07 W |
| Wormit | 58 | 56.25 N | 2.59 W |
| Worms | 66 | 49.38 N | 8.22 E |
| Worms Head ≻ | 54 | 51.34 N | 4.20 W |
| Worthen | 54 | 52.38 N | 3.00 W |
| Worthing | 54 | 50.48 N | 0.23 W |
| Wotton-under-Edge | 54 | 51.39 N | 2.21 W |
| Wowoni, Pulau I | 82 | 4.08 S | 123.06 E |
| Wragby | 56 | 53.18 N | 0.19 W |
| Wrangell Mountains ⋀ | 94 | 62.00 N | 143.00 W |
| Wrath, Cape ≻ | 52 | 58.37 N | 5.01 W |
| Wreck Reef ✢[2] | 92 | 22.13 S | 155.17 E |
| Wrentham | 54 | 52.23 N | 1.40 E |
| Wrexham | 56 | 53.03 N | 3.00 W |
| Writtle | 54 | 51.44 N | 0.26 E |
| Wrocław (Breslau) | 66 | 51.06 N | 17.00 E |
| Wrotham | 54 | 51.19 N | 0.19 E |
| Wroughton | 54 | 51.31 N | 1.46 W |
| Wroxham | 54 | 52.42 N | 1.24 E |
| Września | 66 | 52.20 N | 17.34 E |
| Wuershunhe ≃ | 80 | 49.00 N | 117.41 E |
| Wugang | 80 | 26.40 N | 110.31 E |
| Wuhan | 80 | 30.36 N | 114.17 E |
| Wuhu | 80 | 31.21 N | 118.22 E |
| Wulanhaote | 80 | 46.05 N | 122.05 E |
| Wuliangshan ⋀ | 80 | 24.30 N | 100.45 E |
| Wuliaru, Pulau I | 82 | 7.27 S | 131.04 E |
| Wulumuqi (Urumchi) | 80 | 43.48 N | 87.35 E |
| Wunnummin Lake ⊜ | 94 | 52.55 N | 89.10 W |
| Wunstorf | 66 | 52.25 N | 9.26 E |
| Wuppertal | 66 | 51.16 N | 7.11 E |
| Würzburg | 66 | 49.48 N | 9.56 E |
| Wurzen | 66 | 51.22 N | 12.44 E |
| Wusulijiang (Ussuri) ≃ | 78 | 48.27 N | 135.04 E |
| Wutaishan ∧ | 80 | 39.04 N | 113.35 E |
| Wutongqiao | 80 | 29.26 N | 103.51 E |
| Wuvulu Island I | 82 | 1.45 S | 142.50 E |
| Wuxi | 80 | 31.35 N | 120.18 E |
| Wuzhishan ∧ | 80 | 18.57 N | 109.43 E |
| Wuzhong | 80 | 37.57 N | 106.10 E |
| Wuzhou | 80 | 23.30 N | 111.27 E |
| Wye | 54 | 51.11 N | 0.56 E |
| Wye ≃, U.K. | 54 | 51.37 N | 2.39 W |
| Wye ≃, Eng., U.K. | 54 | 51.37 N | 2.39 W |
| Wye ≃, Eng., U.K. | 56 | 53.12 N | 1.37 W |
| Wyke Regis | 54 | 50.36 N | 2.29 W |
| Wylye ≃ | 54 | 51.04 N | 1.52 W |
| Wymondham | 54 | 52.34 N | 1.07 E |
| Wynniatt Bay C | 94 | 72.55 N | 110.30 W |
| Wyoming □[3] | 96 | 43.00 N | 107.30 W |
| Wyre ≃ | 56 | 53.55 N | 3.00 W |
| Wyre Forest ◆[3] | 54 | 52.23 N | 2.23 W |
| Wyszków | 66 | 52.36 N | 21.28 E |
| Wyvis, Ben ∧ | 58 | 57.42 N | 4.35 W |
| **X** | | | |
| Xánthi | 74 | 41.08 N | 24.53 E |
| Xau, Lake ⊜ | 90 | 21.15 S | 24.38 E |
| Xiaguan | 80 | 33.37 N | 111.46 E |
| Xiahe | 80 | 35.06 N | 102.40 E |
| Xiamen (Amoy) | 80 | 24.28 N | 118.07 E |
| Xi'an (Sian) | 80 | 34.15 N | 108.52 E |
| Xiangfan | 80 | 32.03 N | 112.01 E |
| Xiangjiang ≃ | 80 | 29.00 N | 112.56 E |
| Xiangtan | 80 | 27.51 N | 112.54 E |
| Xianyang | 80 | 34.23 N | 108.40 E |
| Xianyou | 80 | 25.23 N | 118.40 E |
| Xiaogan | 80 | 30.55 N | 113.54 E |
| Xichang | 80 | 27.58 N | 102.13 E |
| Xijiang ≃ | 80 | 22.25 N | 113.23 E |
| Xinghua | 80 | 32.57 N | 119.50 E |
| Xingkathu (Ozero Chanka) ⊜ | 80 | 45.00 N | 132.24 E |
| Xingtai | 80 | 37.04 N | 114.29 E |
| Xingu ≃ | 100 | 1.30 S | 51.53 W |
| Xingyi | 80 | 25.06 N | 104.58 E |
| Xinhailian | 80 | 34.39 N | 119.16 E |
| Xining | 80 | 36.38 N | 101.55 E |
| Xinxiang | 80 | 35.20 N | 113.51 E |
| Xinyang | 80 | 32.19 N | 114.01 E |
| Xuancheng | 80 | 30.58 N | 118.45 E |
| Xuanhua | 80 | 40.37 N | 115.03 E |
| Xuchang | 80 | 34.03 N | 113.49 E |
| Xuyong | 80 | 28.10 N | 105.24 E |
| Xuzhou | 80 | 34.16 N | 117.11 E |
| **Y** | | | |
| Yaan | 80 | 30.03 N | 103.02 E |
| Yaheladazeshan ∧ | 80 | 35.12 N | 95.20 E |
| Yakima | 96 | 46.36 N | 120.31 W |
| Yalongjiang ≃ | 80 | 30.01 N | 101.07 E |
| Yalujiang (Amnok-kang) ≃ | 80 | 39.55 N | 124.22 E |
| Yamagata | 80 | 38.15 N | 140.15 E |
| Yamaguchi | 80 | 34.10 N | 131.29 E |
| Yamdena, Pulau I | 82 | 7.36 S | 131.25 E |
| Y'Ami Island I | 82 | 21.07 N | 121.57 E |
| Yamma Yamma, Lake ⊜ | 92 | 26.20 S | 141.25 E |
| Yamuna ≃ | 84 | 25.25 N | 81.50 E |
| Yanbu' | 84 | 24.05 N | 38.03 E |
| Yangjiang | 80 | 21.51 N | 111.56 E |
| Yangquan | 80 | 37.52 N | 113.36 E |
| Yangzhou | 80 | 32.24 N | 119.26 E |
| Yanji | 80 | 42.57 N | 129.32 E |
| Yanqi | 80 | 42.00 N | 86.15 E |
| Yantai (Chefoo) | 80 | 37.33 N | 121.20 E |
| Yaoundé | 86 | 3.52 N | 11.31 E |
| Yap I | 82 | 9.31 N | 138.06 E |
| Yapen, Pulau I | 82 | 1.45 S | 136.15 E |
| Yaqui ≃ | 98 | 27.37 N | 110.39 W |
| Yarcombe | 54 | 50.52 N | 3.05 W |
| Yare ≃ | 52 | 52.35 N | 1.44 E |
| Yarí ≃ | 100 | 0.23 S | 72.16 W |
| Yarīm | 84 | 14.29 N | 44.21 E |
| Yarmouth | 54 | 50.42 N | 1.29 W |
| Yarrow | 58 | 55.32 N | 3.01 W |
| Yarrow Water ≃ | 56 | 55.34 N | 2.51 W |
| Yarty ≃ | 54 | 50.47 N | 3.01 W |
| Yata ≃ | 100 | 10.29 S | 65.26 W |
| Yate | 54 | 51.32 N | 2.25 W |
| Yathkyed Lake ⊜ | 94 | 62.41 N | 98.00 W |
| Yatsushiro | 80 | 32.30 N | 130.36 E |
| Yatta Plateau ⋀[1] | 90 | 2.00 S | 38.00 E |
| Yatton | 54 | 51.24 N | 2.49 W |
| Yavarí (Javari) ≃ | 100 | 4.21 S | 70.02 W |
| Yaví, Cerro ∧ | 100 | 5.32 N | 65.59 W |
| Yaxley | 54 | 52.31 N | 0.16 W |
| Yazd | 84 | 31.53 N | 54.25 E |
| Yazoo ≃ | 96 | 32.22 N | 91.00 W |
| Yeadon | 56 | 53.52 N | 1.41 W |
| Yealm ≃ | 54 | 50.18 N | 4.03 W |
| Yealmpton | 54 | 50.21 N | 3.59 W |
| Yecla | 70 | 38.37 N | 1.07 W |
| Yeerqianghe (Yarkand) ≃ | 80 | 40.28 N | 80.52 E |
| Yell I | 52 | 60.35 N | 1.05 W |
| Yellowhead Pass )( | 94 | 52.53 N | 118.28 W |
| Yellowknife | 94 | 62.27 N | 114.21 W |
| Yellowknife ≃ | 94 | 62.31 N | 114.19 W |
| Yellow Sea ▾[2] | 80 | 36.00 N | 123.00 E |
| Yellowstone ≃ | 96 | 47.58 N | 103.59 W |
| Yellowstone Lake ⊜ | 96 | 44.25 N | 110.22 W |
| Yell Sound U | 52 | 60.33 N | 1.15 W |
| Yelverton | 54 | 50.30 N | 4.05 W |
| Yemen □[1] | 84 | 15.00 N | 44.00 E |
| Yemen, People's Democratic Republic of □[1] | 84 | 15.00 N | 48.00 E |
| Yenangyaung | 82 | 20.28 N | 94.52 E |
| Yendi | 86 | 9.26 N | 0.01 W |
| Yenişehir | 74 | 40.16 N | 29.39 E |
| Yeo ≃ | 54 | 51.02 N | 2.49 W |
| Yeo Lake ⊜ | 92 | 28.04 S | 124.23 E |
| Yeovil | 54 | 50.57 N | 2.39 W |
| Yerupajá, Nevado ∧ | 100 | 10.16 S | 76.54 W |
| Yerushalayim (Jerusalem) | 84 | 31.46 N | 35.13 E |
| Yes Tor ∧ | 54 | 50.42 N | 4.00 W |
| Yetminster | 54 | 50.53 N | 2.33 W |
| Yiannitsá | 74 | 40.48 N | 22.25 E |
| Yibin | 80 | 28.47 N | 104.38 E |
| Yichang | 80 | 30.42 N | 111.11 E |
| Yichun, Zhg. | 80 | 27.50 N | 114.23 E |
| Yichun, Zhg. | 80 | 47.42 N | 128.55 E |
| Yilan | 80 | 46.19 N | 129.34 E |
| Yiliang | 80 | 24.58 N | 103.07 E |
| Yinchuan | 80 | 38.30 N | 106.18 E |
| Yinghe ≃ | 80 | 32.30 N | 116.32 E |
| Yingkou | 80 | 40.40 N | 122.14 E |
| Yining (Kuldja) | 80 | 43.55 N | 81.14 E |
| Yiyang | 80 | 28.36 N | 112.20 E |
| Yogyakarta | 82 | 7.48 S | 110.22 E |
| Yokkaichi | 80 | 34.58 N | 136.37 E |
| Yokohama | 80 | 35.27 N | 139.39 E |
| Yokosuka | 80 | 35.18 N | 139.40 E |
| Yom ≃ | 82 | 15.52 N | 100.16 E |
| Yonago | 80 | 35.26 N | 133.20 E |
| Yonezawa | 80 | 37.55 N | 140.07 E |
| Yongdinghe ≃ | 80 | 39.39 N | 116.13 E |
| York, Eng., U.K. | 56 | 53.58 N | 1.05 W |
| York, Pa., U.S. | 96 | 39.58 N | 76.44 W |
| York, Cape ≻ | 92 | 10.42 S | 142.31 E |
| York, Vale of ∨ | 56 | 54.10 N | 1.20 W |
| Yorke Peninsula ≻[1] | 92 | 35.00 S | 137.30 E |
| Yorkshire Wolds ⋀[2] | 56 | 54.00 N | 0.40 W |
| York Sound U | 92 | 14.50 S | 125.05 E |
| Yos Sudarsa, Pulau I | 82 | 7.50 S | 138.30 E |
| Yŏsu | 80 | 34.46 N | 127.44 E |
| Youghal | 60 | 51.51 N | 7.50 W |
| Youghal Bay C | 52 | 51.52 N | 7.50 W |
| Youjiang ≃ | 80 | 22.50 N | 108.06 E |
| Youngstown | 96 | 41.06 N | 80.39 W |
| Ysbyty Ystwyth | 54 | 52.20 N | 3.48 W |
| Yscir ≃ | 54 | 51.57 N | 3.27 W |
| Ystad | 64 | 55.25 N | 13.49 E |
| Ystalyfera | 54 | 51.47 N | 3.47 W |
| Ystrad ≃ | 56 | 53.13 N | 3.20 W |
| Ystrad Aeron | 54 | 52.11 N | 4.11 W |
| Ystradfellte | 54 | 51.48 N | 3.34 W |
| Ystradgynlais | 54 | 51.47 N | 3.45 W |
| Ystwyth ≃ | 52 | 52.24 N | 4.05 W |
| Ythan ≃ | 58 | 57.18 N | 2.00 W |
| Yuanling | 80 | 28.20 N | 110.16 E |
| Yūbari | 80 | 43.04 N | 141.59 E |
| Yucatan Channel U | 98 | 21.45 N | 85.45 W |
| Yucatan Peninsula ≻[1] | 98 | 19.30 N | 89.00 W |
| Yuci | 80 | 37.45 N | 112.41 E |
| Yueyang | 80 | 29.23 N | 113.06 E |
| Yugoslavia □[1] | 50 | 44.00 N | 19.00 E |
| Yujiang ≃ | 80 | 23.24 N | 110.16 E |
| Yukon □[4] | 94 | 64.00 N | 135.00 W |
| Yukon ≃ | 94 | 65.00 N | 154.00 W |
| Yulin, Zhg. | 80 | 22.36 N | 110.07 E |
| Yulin, Zhg. | 80 | 38.20 N | 109.29 E |
| Yuma | 96 | 32.43 N | 114.37 W |
| Yumen | 80 | 39.56 N | 97.51 E |
| Yuncheng | 80 | 35.00 N | 110.59 E |
| Yunhe (Grand Canal) Ξ | 80 | 32.12 N | 119.31 E |
| Yupanyang C | 80 | 30.30 N | 121.46 E |
| Yurimaguas | 100 | 5.54 S | 76.05 W |
| Yushu | 80 | 33.28 N | 96.18 E |
| Yutian | 80 | 36.51 N | 81.40 E |
| Yverdon | 68 | 46.47 N | 6.39 E |
| **Z** | | | |
| Zaandam | 66 | 52.26 N | 4.49 E |
| Zabarjad, Jazīrat I | 88 | 23.37 N | 36.12 E |
| Ząbkowice Śląskie | 66 | 50.36 N | 16.53 E |
| Zabrze | 66 | 50.18 N | 18.46 E |
| Zacatecas | 98 | 22.47 N | 102.35 W |
| Zadar | 72 | 44.07 N | 15.14 E |
| Zadetkyi Kyun I | 82 | 9.58 N | 98.13 E |
| Zafra | 70 | 38.25 N | 6.25 W |
| Żagań | 66 | 51.37 N | 15.19 E |
| Zagorsk | 62 | 56.18 N | 38.08 E |
| Zagreb | 72 | 45.48 N | 15.58 E |
| Zāgros, Kūhhā-ye ⋀ | 84 | 33.40 N | 47.00 E |
| Zāhedān | 84 | 29.30 N | 60.52 E |
| Zaḥlah | 84 | 33.51 N | 35.53 E |
| Zaire □[1] | 90 | 4.00 S | 25.00 E |
| Zaječar | 74 | 43.54 N | 22.17 E |
| Zajsan, Ozero ⊜ | 78 | 48.00 N | 84.00 E |
| Zákinthos | 74 | 37.47 N | 20.53 E |
| Zákinthos I | 50 | 37.52 N | 20.44 E |
| Zakopane | 66 | 49.19 N | 19.57 E |
| Zalaegerszeg | 66 | 46.51 N | 16.51 E |
| Zalău | 74 | 47.11 N | 23.03 E |
| Zambezi (Zambeze) ≃ | 90 | 18.55 S | 36.04 E |
| Zambia □[1] | 90 | 15.00 S | 30.00 E |
| Zamboanga | 82 | 6.54 N | 122.04 E |
| Zambrów | 66 | 53.00 N | 22.15 E |
| Zamora | 70 | 41.30 N | 5.45 W |
| Zamora de Hidalgo | 98 | 19.59 N | 102.16 W |
| Zamość | 66 | 50.44 N | 23.15 E |
| Zandvoort | 66 | 52.22 N | 4.32 E |
| Zanesville | 96 | 39.56 N | 82.01 W |
| Zanjān | 84 | 36.40 N | 48.29 E |
| Zanjón ≃ | 102 | 31.16 S | 67.41 W |
| Zanzibar | 90 | 6.10 S | 39.11 E |
| Zanzibar Island I | 90 | 6.10 S | 39.20 E |
| Zaoz'ornyj | 78 | 55.58 N | 94.42 E |
| Zapadnaja Dvina | 62 | 56.16 N | 32.04 E |
| Zapadnaja Dvina (Daugava) ≃ | 76 | 57.04 N | 24.03 E |
| Zapadno-Sibirskaja Nizmennost' ≚ | 78 | 60.00 N | 75.00 E |
| Zapadnyj Sajan ⋀ | 78 | 53.00 N | 94.00 E |
| Zapol'arnyj, S.S.S.R. | 62 | 69.26 N | 30.48 E |
| Zapol'arnyj, S.S.S.R. | 62 | 67.30 N | 63.42 E |
| Zaporožje | 76 | 47.50 N | 35.10 E |
| Zaragoza | 70 | 41.38 N | 0.53 W |
| Zarajsk | 62 | 54.46 N | 38.53 E |
| Zárate | 102 | 34.06 S | 59.02 W |
| Zard Kūh ∧ | 84 | 32.22 N | 50.04 E |
| Zarečensk | 62 | 66.41 N | 33.18 E |
| Zaria | 86 | 11.07 N | 7.44 E |
| Żary (Sorau) | 66 | 51.38 N | 15.09 E |
| Zāskār Mountains ⋀ | 84 | 33.00 N | 78.00 E |
| Zastavna | 74 | 48.31 N | 25.50 E |
| Žatec | 66 | 50.18 N | 13.32 E |
| Zavolžsk | 62 | 57.30 N | 42.10 E |
| Zawiercie | 66 | 50.30 N | 19.25 E |
| Zāwiyat al-Bayḍā' | 88 | 32.46 N | 21.43 E |
| Ždanov | 76 | 47.06 N | 37.33 E |
| Zduńska Wola | 66 | 51.36 N | 18.57 E |
| Zehdenick | 66 | 52.59 N | 13.20 E |
| Zeil, Mount ∧ | 92 | 23.24 S | 132.23 E |
| Zeist | 66 | 52.05 N | 5.15 E |
| Zeitz | 66 | 51.03 N | 12.08 E |
| Zeja ≃ | 78 | 50.13 N | 127.35 E |
| Zele | 66 | 51.04 N | 4.02 E |
| Zelenogorsk | 62 | 60.12 N | 29.42 E |
| Zelenogradsk [Cranz] | 66 | 54.58 N | 20.29 E |
| Železnodorožnyj, S.S.S.R. | 62 | 62.37 N | 50.55 E |
| Železnodorožnyj, S.S.S.R. | 66 | 54.22 N | 21.19 E |
| Železnogorsk-Ilimskij | 78 | 56.37 N | 104.08 E |
| Zella-Mehlis | 66 | 50.39 N | 10.39 E |
| Zel'onodol'sk | 62 | 55.51 N | 48.33 E |
| Zeml'a Franca-Iosifa II | 8 | 81.00 N | 55.00 E |
| Zenica | 74 | 44.12 N | 17.55 E |
| Zeravšan ≃ | 76 | 39.22 N | 63.45 E |
| Zerbst | 66 | 51.58 N | 12.04 E |
| Zereh, Gowd-e ⊜ | 84 | 29.45 N | 61.50 E |
| Zeulenroda | 66 | 50.39 N | 11.58 E |
| Zevenaar | 66 | 51.56 N | 6.05 E |
| Zgierz | 66 | 51.52 N | 19.25 E |
| Zhalinghu ⊜ | 80 | 34.53 N | 97.58 E |
| Zhalinhu ⊜ | 80 | 31.10 N | 88.15 E |
| Zhangguangcailing ⋀ | 80 | 45.25 N | 129.20 E |
| Zhangjiakou (Kalgan) | 80 | 40.50 N | 114.53 E |
| Zhangye | 80 | 38.57 N | 100.37 E |
| Zhangzhou | 80 | 24.33 N | 117.39 E |
| Zhanjiang | 80 | 21.16 N | 110.28 E |
| Zhaoan | 80 | 23.44 N | 116.11 E |
| Zhaotong | 80 | 27.19 N | 103.48 E |
| Zhengzhou | 80 | 34.48 N | 113.39 E |
| Zhenjiang | 80 | 32.13 N | 119.26 E |
| Zhenyuan | 80 | 26.53 N | 108.19 E |
| Zhob ≃ | 84 | 32.04 N | 69.50 E |
| Zhongshan | 80 | 22.31 N | 113.22 E |
| Zhoucun | 80 | 36.47 N | 117.48 E |
| Zhuangaerpendi ≚[1] | 80 | 45.00 N | 88.00 E |
| Zhujiangkou C | 80 | 23.36 N | 113.44 E |
| Zhuoxian | 80 | 39.30 N | 115.58 E |
| Zhuzhou | 80 | 27.50 N | 113.09 E |
| Žiar nad Hronom | 66 | 48.36 N | 18.52 E |
| Zibo | 80 | 36.47 N | 118.01 E |
| Zielona Góra (Grünberg) | 66 | 51.56 N | 15.31 E |
| Zigana Dağları ⋀ | 84 | 40.37 N | 39.30 E |
| Zigong | 80 | 29.24 N | 104.47 E |
| Ziguinchor | 86 | 12.35 N | 16.16 W |
| Žigulevsk | 62 | 53.25 N | 49.27 E |
| Žilina | 66 | 49.14 N | 18.46 E |
| Zima | 78 | 53.55 N | 102.04 E |
| Zimnicea | 74 | 43.39 N | 25.21 E |
| Zinder | 86 | 13.48 N | 8.59 E |
| Zishui ≃ | 80 | 28.45 N | 112.25 E |
| Žitomir | 76 | 50.16 N | 28.40 E |
| Zittau | 66 | 50.54 N | 14.47 E |
| Ziway, Lake ⊜ | 88 | 8.00 N | 38.50 E |
| Zizhong | 80 | 29.48 N | 104.50 E |
| Zlatoust | 76 | 55.10 N | 59.40 E |
| Złotoryja | 66 | 51.08 N | 15.55 E |
| Złotów | 66 | 53.22 N | 17.02 E |
| Znamensk | 66 | 54.37 N | 21.13 E |
| Znojmo | 66 | 48.52 N | 16.02 E |
| Zomba | 90 | 15.23 S | 35.18 E |
| Zone Point ≻ | 54 | 50.08 N | 5.00 W |
| Zrenjanin | 74 | 45.23 N | 20.24 E |
| Zubcov | 62 | 56.10 N | 34.34 E |
| Zug | 68 | 47.10 N | 8.31 E |
| Zugdidi | 76 | 42.30 N | 41.53 E |
| Zugspitze ∧ | 50 | 47.25 N | 10.59 E |
| Zujevka | 62 | 58.25 N | 51.10 E |
| Zunyi | 80 | 27.39 N | 106.57 E |
| Zuqar, Jazīrat I | 84 | 14.00 N | 42.45 E |
| Zürich | 68 | 47.23 N | 8.32 E |
| Zutphen | 66 | 52.08 N | 6.12 E |
| Zvolen | 66 | 48.35 N | 19.08 E |
| Zweibrücken | 66 | 49.15 N | 7.21 E |
| Zwickau | 66 | 50.44 N | 12.29 E |
| Zwischenahn | 66 | 53.11 N | 8.00 E |
| Zwolle | 66 | 52.30 N | 6.05 E |
| Zyr'anovsk | 78 | 49.43 N | 84.20 E |
| Żyrardów | 66 | 52.04 N | 20.25 E |
| Żywiec | 66 | 49.41 N | 19.12 E |


**Symbols in the index entries are identified on page 111.**